2020-2021
SEPTEMBER–AUGUST
KJV

KING JAMES VERSION

EDITORIAL TEAM

RONALD L. NICKELSON
Senior Editor

JANE ANN KENNEY
Commentary Editor

MARGARET K. WILLIAMS
Activity Page Editor

Volume 68

In This Volume

Fall Quarter 2020 (page 1)
Love for One Another

Lesson Development.................... Douglas Redford (1–4), Lee M. Fields (5), Christopher Cotten (6), Andrew Sloan (7), Tom Thatcher (8), Mark S. Krause (9–13)
Verbal Illustrations................. Charles R. Boatman (1–4), Petra L. Miller (5), Andrew Sloan (6, 9, 13), Jim Eichenberger (7–8), Lee Hall-Perkins (10–11), Mark A. Taylor (12)
Involvement Learning.......................... Lorraine Wadman (1), Judith Odor (2), David Mehrle (3), Jerry Bowling (4, 7), Cheryl Frey (5), Kyle Taft (6), Katrina Bass (8–9), Jonathan Feathers (10), Jim Eichenberger (11–13)
What Do You Think?... Ronald L. Nickelson (1–13)

Winter Quarter 2020–2021 (page 113)
Call in the New Testament

Lesson Development.....................Christian Wilder (1), Tom Thatcher (2–4, 8), Jeffrey L. Cockrell (5), Andrew Sloan (6–7), Mark S. Krause (9–13)
Verbal Illustrations ....Lyndsey Gambrell (1), David Graves (2, 4), Laura McKillip Wood (3), David Faust (5, 8), Andrew Sloan (6, 9), Charles R. Boatman (7, 10–11), Candace M. Wood (12), Chuck Terrill (13)
Involvement Learning...................Lu Ann J. Nickelson (1–4), Mark A. Taylor (5–8, 10), Jeff Gerke (9), Douglas C. Schmidt (11), David Mehrle (12–13)
What Do You Think?... Ronald L. Nickelson (1–13)

Spring Quarter 2021 (page 225)
Prophets Faithful to God's Covenant

Lesson Development.................. Douglas Redford (1, 2, 4–5, 7), Mark Hahlen (3), Patrick Mitchell (6), Jane Ann Kenney (8), Larry Shallenberger (9–10, 12–13), Steve Cook (11)
Verbal Illustrations .... Charles R. Boatman (1–7), David Faust (8), Lyndsey Gambrell (9), Chuck Terrill (10–12), Laura McKillip Wood (13)
Involvement Learning...............................Stacey Davis (1–3, 8), Mark A. Taylor (4–7, 9–13)
What Do You Think?... Samantha Hee (1–13)

Summer Quarter 2021 (page 337)
Confident Hope

Lesson Development.............. Jon Weatherly (1–4), Mark S. Krause (5–9, 13), Christopher Cotten (10–11), Jeffrey L. Cockrell (12)
Verbal Illustrations ....David Faust (1, 4), David Graves (2), Laura McKillip Wood (3), April Bumgardner (5), Lee Hall-Perkins (6, 8), Petra L. Miller (7, 9), Charles R. Boatman (10–13)
Involvement Learning....................................Mark A. Taylor (1–12), Kaitlyn Depoister (13)
What Do You Think?............................. Ronald L. Nickelson (1–9), Kaitlyn Depoister (10–13)

INDEX OF PRINTED TEXTS

The printed texts for 2020–2021 are arranged here in the order in which they appear in the Bible.

Cumulative Index

A cumulative index for Scripture passages used in the Standard Lesson Commentary *for September 2016–August 2020 (of the 2016–2022 cycle) is provided below.*

Standard Lesson Resources

Whether you use Standard Lesson Commentary® or Standard Lesson Quarterly®, you'll find a wealth of additional helps in the Standard Lesson Resources® line. These printed and digital products provide the most comprehensive resources for teaching the *ISSL/Uniform Series* available anywhere!

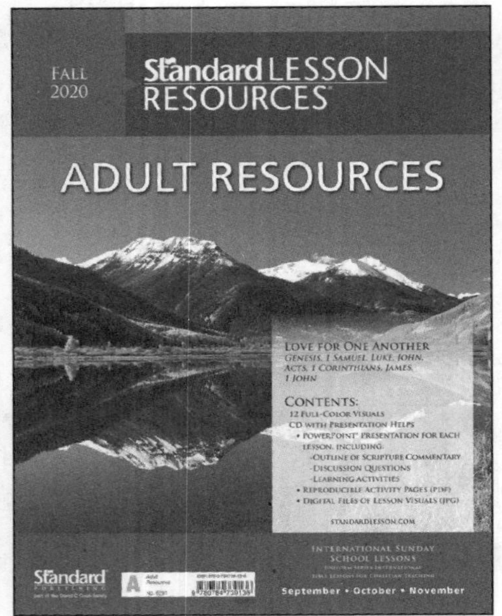

Adult Resources

This pack provides 12 full-color visuals to illustrate the lesson each week. Also included is a Presentation Tools CD that includes digital images of all the visuals and a PowerPoint® presentation for each lesson.

In the World

This online feature draws from a current event—something your students are probably talking about that very week—and helps you use it to illustrate the lesson theme.

Devotions®

Reflect on each Sunday's lesson outside of the classroom. Devotions® supplements the daily Bible readings recommended in Standard Lesson to challenge you to experience personal growth in Christ.

Explore these resources and more at:
https://www.standardlesson.com/standard-lesson-resources/

LOVE FOR ONE ANOTHER

Special Features

Lessons

Unit 1: Struggles with Love

Unit 2: Inclusive Love

Unit 3: Godly Love Among Believers

QUARTERLY QUIZ

Use these questions as a pretest or as a review. The answers are on page iv of This Quarter in the Word.

Lesson 1

1. Joseph's brothers felt deep affection for him. T/F. *Genesis 37:4*

2. Joseph's brothers sold him to Midianite ________. *Genesis 37:28*

Lesson 2

1. Pharaoh's dream meant that Egypt would experience seven years of ________, followed by seven years of ________. *Genesis 41:28-30*

2. Joseph was unsure about the meaning of Pharaoh's dream. T/F. *Genesis 41:32*

Lesson 3

1. When Joseph's brothers came to Egypt, they did not recognize him. T/F. *Genesis 42:8*

2. Joseph retained ________ as a hostage. *Genesis 42:24*

Lesson 4

1. After revealing himself to his brothers, Joseph wanted to know about whom? (Rachel, Benjamin, Jacob) *Genesis 45:3*

2. Joseph arranged for his brothers and their families to live in ________. *Genesis 45:10*

Lesson 5

1. In what way did Jonathan speak of David? (ill, well, disrespectfully) *1 Samuel 19:4-5*

2. Saul took an oath not to seek David's life. T/F. *1 Samuel 19:6*

Lesson 6

1. Jesus instructed us to express what to our enemies? (indifference, love, spite) *Luke 6:27*

2. We are to be ________, just as our heavenly Father is ________. *Luke 6:36*

Lesson 7

1. In the parable of the merciful Samaritan, the religious leaders acted nobly. T/F. *Luke 10:30-32*

2. How was the Samaritan described by the lawyer? (as the one who showed mercy, as an outlaw, as a true believer) *Luke 10:37*

Lesson 8

1. The exercise of spiritual gifts without love is futile. T/F. *1 Corinthians 13:1-3*

2. Among faith, hope, and charity (love), the greatest is ______. *1 Corinthians 13:13*

Lesson 9

1. Jesus washed the disciples' what? (clothes, hands, feet) *John 13:5*

2. Jesus wants His followers to be known for their _______ for one another. *John 13:35*

Lesson 10

1. Jesus described himself as the vine, and His followers as the ________. *John 15:5a*

2. According to Jesus, His followers can do nothing apart from Him. T/F. *John 15:5c*

Lesson 11

1. Followers of Jesus should be surprised if the world hates them. T/F. *1 John 3:13*

2. According to John, we are not to love with word or tongue but in deed and in __________. *1 John 3:18*

Lesson 12

1. The first Christians shared everything with one another. T/F. *Acts 4:32-35*

2. Ananias and Sapphira were struck dead for not giving everything they had received for the sale of their property. T/F. *Acts 5:4*

Lesson 13

1. Believers are to avoid favoritism of the rich over the poor. T/F. *James 2:1-4*

2. According to James, mercy rejoices against ______. *James 2:13*

QUARTER AT A GLANCE

by Jim Eichenberger

RADICAL ACTIVIST Jerry Rubin made a profound observation about the English language. In response to a commercial that ran in the late 1960s claiming that "Cars *love* Shell [gasoline]," Rubin complained that the word *love* had lost its meaning. How can a word used to describe how cars "feel" about gasoline also be applied to a husband and wife, a parent and child, or a glutton and cupcakes?

Love can be either good or bad, depending on one's motive and the object of the love (contrast the love in John 3:16 with that noted in 2 Timothy 4:10 and 1 John 2:15). A survey of key Old and New Testament passages directs us properly.

Love and Families

It has been said, "You can choose your friends; family you're stuck with!" There is a lot of truth in this modern proverb. Some of the most difficult people to love are those we know best.

Our first unit illustrates how love can overcome the most difficult challenges in family life. Joseph was an insufferable little brother who received special treatment from his dad. After his brothers faked his death and sold him into slavery, Joseph could have let any love for his family die. Yet a love that kept him faithful to God did more than allow him to survive. In Joseph we see a persevering love. This love that began with dedication to God kept on loving those who betrayed him.

Love Beyond Allies

Over the last decade (at least), American politics has become increasingly more partisan, emphasizing divisions rather than points of agreement. We have seen the effects of raw tribalism. Is love reserved for those who agree with us? We wring our hands, looking for a better way.

Our second unit examines the better way. We see those who practiced a risky love, a love that reached beyond one's faction. Jonathan, son of King Saul, was heir to the throne. David was a populist hero whom Saul saw as a threat to his dynasty. Yet Jonathan and David became fast friends and refused to let political differences sully their relationship. Jesus taught that people could love those who occupied their nation and accept those of a despised ethnic group as neighbors. Finally, Paul poetically described what love *could* do and what real love should *never* do.

Love as Selflessness

Robert Ringer, a businessman and motivational speaker in the 1970s, directed those looking to succeed in life to the path of *Winning Through Intimidation* and *Looking Out for #1*. His books claimed that the only way to thrive in a hostile world was to practice a selfish love that kept one from being manipulated by others.

Our third unit demonstrates how the first-century church was characterized by those who put others before themselves. Jesus set the example as He shared a Passover meal with His disciples. Instead of being a domineering boss, Jesus took the role of a servant. He encouraged His disciples to abide in His love, following that example in daily life. The apostle John counseled believers to practice Jesus' love confidently. The earliest Christians selflessly gave to fellow believers—to the point where no one lacked what was needed. Finally, James warned fellow believers to show love without partiality.

> ***Is love reserved for those who agree with us?***

The world may say that cars love gasoline, that opponents of any kind do not deserve love, or that true love is looking out only for ourselves. But we know that *love* has a very real meaning. We love because we are recipients of divine love!

Get the Setting

by Jim Eichenberger†

Many of us remember those pencil marks on an interior doorway in a family home. Mom and Dad would have each of their children stand in that doorway, then mark each child's height. Over the years, it was easy for a child to observe, by comparing pencil marks, how much growth he or she had achieved.

If the family of God had a measuring wall, what would it show? Perhaps the most dramatic growth would be how people of faith matured in their understanding and practice of love for one another.

Love and Power

The human family has always been a place of love and nurture (ideally, at least). Nevertheless, the lust for power in the ancient world could invade the safety and sanctity of the home. The most jarring example is the practice of child sacrifice, especially in fertility religions. The book of Leviticus warned the Israelites not to engage in the behavior common in ancient Canaan (Leviticus 18:21). Yet this command was violated. Practice of child sacrifice was given as one of the reasons for the fall of the northern kingdom of Israel (2 Kings 17:7-8, 17). To the south, the most notorious kings of Judah, namely Ahaz and Manasseh, also sacrificed their sons (16:1, 3; 21:1, 6).

Parents could also be slain in order to make way for their children to come to power. For instance, King Sennacherib of Assyria threatened to conquer Judah, but he was betrayed by his own family. Two of his sons assassinated him, resulting in another son taking the throne (2 Kings 19:36-37).

Even among worshippers of the one true God, family units were not devoid of destructive conflict. From Cain and Abel, Jacob and Esau, and the murderous intrigue within the royal household of David, families often came up short when measured by their love. Love needed both a strong definition and a definitive example.

New Family, New Standard

Jesus declared that He was doing more than offering prophetic instruction. He was creating a new family made up of all those intent on doing the will of His Father in Heaven (Matthew 12:47-50). That new family was to be marked by love for and unity with one another (John 13:35; 17:20-23). The way Jesus modeled love's ideal caused a noticeable growth spurt on the "measuring wall" of God's children.

The church of the first three centuries took this new standard to heart. The great North African theologian Tertullian (about AD 160–220) taught that the Christian life practiced in the church was so morally superior to pagan culture that it should be obvious to all. He desired that pagans look at Christians, even while persecuting them, and say, "Look how they love one another!"

Justin Martyr (about AD 100–165), another early church father, spoke often of love as the mark of the Christian. In a world in which it was common to refuse to associate with those of another race or nation, he pointed to the practice of living cross-culturally and even loving enemies.

Love for enemies was no more obvious than during a pandemic that afflicted the Roman Empire about AD 249–262. Cyprian of Carthage (AD 200–258) witnessed and described the plague. Those afflicted often blamed Christians. But while pagans were throwing infected members of their own families into the streets even before they died, Christians cared for the sick at the risk of contracting the plague themselves.

The ancient world spoke of love, but far too often selfishness overruled the best impulses of people. Then into the world came the very definition of *love* (1 John 4:10). In providing forgiveness of sins and reconciliation with God, Jesus called into being His church to demonstrate such love continually. The church became for the world the new measuring wall of love.

†See note on bottom of next page.

Mon, Nov. 16	**Preparing to Become a Deacon**	1 Timothy 3:8-13
Tue, Nov. 17	**Healing Ministry Grows the Church**	Acts 5:12-16
Wed, Nov. 18	**Church Sharing Plan Enlarged**	Acts 6:1-7
Thu, Nov. 19	**Stephen's Ministry Opposed**	Acts 6:8-15
Fri, Nov. 20	**Sharing All of Life Together**	Acts 2:42-47
Sat, Nov. 21	**Prayer for Boldness and Signs**	Acts 4:23-31
Sun, Nov. 22	**Challenged to Share**	Acts 4:32–5:11

Mon, Nov. 23	**Mercy over Sacrifice**	Matthew 12:1-8
Tue, Nov. 24	**Love One Another from the Heart**	1 Peter 1:17-23
Wed, Nov. 25	**Gentiles Share the Faith**	Galatians 3:6-9, 13-14
Thu, Nov. 26	**Faith of Levite Mother Saves Moses**	Exodus 2:1-10
Fri, Nov. 27	**Unexpressed Faith Has No Value**	James 2:14-17
Sat, Nov. 28	**Complementary Faith and Works**	James 2:18-26
Sun, Nov. 29	**Disdain the Practice of Partiality**	James 2:1-13

Answers to the Quarterly Quiz on page 2

Lesson 1—1. false. 2. merchantmen. **Lesson 2**—1. plenty, famine. 2. false. **Lesson 3**—1. true. 2. Simeon. **Lesson 4**—1. Jacob. 2. Goshen. **Lesson 5**—1. well. 2. true. **Lesson 6**—1. love. 2. merciful, merciful. **Lesson 7**—1. false. 2. as the one who showed mercy. **Lesson 8**—1. true. 2. charity/love. **Lesson 9**—1. feet. 2. love. **Lesson 10**—1. branches. 2. true. **Lesson 11**—1. false. 2. truth. **Lesson 12**—1. true. 2. false. **Lesson 13**—1. true. 2. judgment.

This Quarter in the Word

Mon, Aug. 31	**Rachel, Mother of Two**	Genesis 30:22-24; 35:16-20
Tue, Sep. 1	**Joseph and His Brothers**	Genesis 37:12-17
Wed, Sep. 2	**Jacob Convinced of Joseph's Death**	Genesis 37:29-36
Thu, Sep. 3	**From Slave to Ruler**	Psalm 106:1-6, 16-22
Fri, Sep. 4	**God Was with Joseph**	Acts 7:9-15a
Sat, Sep. 5	**Disputes May Lead to Violence**	James 4:1-7
Sun, Sep. 6	**Jealousy Divides Families**	Genesis 37:2-11, 23-24a, 28

Mon, Sep. 7	**Paul and Barnabas Appointed**	Acts 13:1-5
Tue, Sep. 8	**Joseph, Interpreter of Dreams**	Genesis 41:9-13
Wed, Sep. 9	**Dreams Explained**	Genesis 41:14-24
Thu, Sep. 10	**Preparing for Famine**	Genesis 41:34-36
Fri, Sep. 11	**Storing Grain for the Future**	Genesis 41:41-49
Sat, Sep. 12	**Egypt Feeds the Middle East**	Genesis 41:53-57
Sun, Sep. 13	**Leadership During Crisis**	Genesis 41:25-33, 37-40, 50-52

Mon, Sep. 14	**Have Mercy on Me, a Sinner**	Psalm 51:1-12
Tue, Sep. 15	**Pilate's Judgment of Jesus**	Luke 23:9-15
Wed, Sep. 16	**Brothers Sent to Egypt**	Genesis 42:1-5
Thu, Sep. 17	**Joseph Returns Money**	Genesis 42:26-28
Fri, Sep. 18	**Joseph Questions Brothers**	Genesis 42:29-34
Sat, Sep. 19	**Jacob Vows Not to Send Benjamin**	Genesis 42:35-38
Sun, Sep. 20	**Joseph Confronts Brothers**	Genesis 42:6-25

†Jim Eichenberger, a former senior editor of this commentary, passed into eternity on March 6, 2019, at age 66.

Mon, Sep. 21	**During Trouble, Maintain Hope in God**	Psalm 43
Tue, Sep. 22	**Benjamin Sent to Joseph with Gifts**	Genesis 43:1-15
Wed, Sep. 23	**Stolen Cup Found**	Genesis 44:1-13
Thu, Sep. 24	**Brothers Offer to Become Slaves**	Genesis 44:14-17
Fri, Sep. 25	**Judah Pleads with Joseph**	Genesis 44:18-26
Sat, Sep. 26	**Will Jacob Die?**	Genesis 44:27-34
Sun, Sep. 27	**Joseph and Brothers Reconcile**	Genesis 45:1-8, 10-15
Mon, Sep. 28	**Brother and Coworker**	1 Thessalonians 3:1-6
Tue, Sep. 29	**David Slays Philistine**	1 Samuel 17:41-51
Wed, Sep. 30	**Bonded in Love**	1 Samuel 18:1-5
Thu, Oct. 1	**Saul Fears David**	1 Samuel 18:12-18
Fri, Oct. 2	**Jonathan Honors David**	1 Samuel 23:14-18
Sat, Oct. 3	**David Provides for Jonathan's Son**	2 Samuel 9:1-10a
Sun, Oct. 4	**Saul's Promise**	1 Samuel 19:1-7
Mon, Oct. 5	**The Lord Is Merciful and Gracious**	Psalm 103:1-14
Tue, Oct. 6	**Responding to Demands**	Matthew 5:38-42
Wed, Oct. 7	**Handling Family Difficulties**	Leviticus 25:35-39
Thu, Oct. 8	**Home Life of the Faithful**	Psalm 128
Fri, Oct. 9	**Forgiving the Ignorant**	Luke 23:32-36
Sat, Oct. 10	**Blessed and Rewarded**	Matthew 5:1-12
Sun, Oct. 11	**Love and Forgive Your Enemies**	Luke 6:27-36
Mon, Oct. 12	**Help Your Neighbor in Need**	Deuteronomy 15:7-11
Tue, Oct. 13	**Love God and Brothers and Sisters**	1 John 4:16b-21
Wed, Oct. 14	**Adopt the First Commandments**	Mark 12:28-34
Thu, Oct. 15	**Healed Samaritan Thanks Jesus**	Luke 17:11-19
Fri, Oct. 16	**Village Refuses to Welcome Jesus**	Luke 9:51-56
Sat, Oct. 17	**Jesus' Offer to a Samaritan Woman**	John 4:1-15
Sun, Oct. 18	**Follow the Samaritan's Example**	Luke 10:25-37

Mon, Oct. 19	**Share Victories**	1 Samuel 30:21-25
Tue, Oct. 20	**The New Life in Christ**	Romans 12:1-8
Wed, Oct. 21	**Live by the Mind of Christ**	Philippians 2:1-11
Thu, Oct. 22	**Faith, Hope, and Love in Action**	Colossians 1:3-8
Fri, Oct. 23	**Gifts for the Good of All**	1 Corinthians 12:4-11
Sat, Oct. 24	**Pray with Mind and Spirit**	1 Corinthians 14:13-19
Sun, Oct. 25	**The Life of Love**	1 Corinthians 13
Mon, Oct. 26	**Rebekah Found**	Genesis 24:24-33
Tue, Oct. 27	**Brothers Provided Water**	Genesis 43:20-25
Wed, Oct. 28	**Servants and Masters**	Ephesians 4:6-9
Thu, Oct. 29	**Peter Denies Jesus**	John 13:36-38; 18:15-18, 25-27
Fri, Oct. 30	**Jesus Betrayed**	Psalm 41:8-10; John 13:21-30
Sat, Oct. 31	**Mary Anoints Jesus' Feet**	John 12:1-7
Sun, Nov. 1	**Jesus Washes Disciples' Feet**	John 13:1-15, 34-35
Mon, Nov. 2	**God Is Disappointed with Israel**	Isaiah 5:1-7
Tue, Nov. 3	**God Will Redeem Israel**	Isaiah 27:2-6
Wed, Nov. 4	**Believers Continue God's Work**	John 14:8-14
Thu, Nov. 5	**Jesus Freely Lays Down His Life**	John 10:11-18
Fri, Nov. 6	**Facing the World as Jesus Did**	John 15:18-25
Sat, Nov. 7	**Jesus Tends to His Vineyard**	John 15:1-3
Sun, Nov. 8	**Always Love One Another**	John 15:4-17
Mon, Nov. 9	**Faith and Obedience**	1 Thessalonians 2:1-10
Tue, Nov. 10	**Then Darkness, Now Light**	Ephesians 5:8-16
Wed, Nov. 11	**Live by the Light**	John 3:16-21
Thu, Nov. 12	**God's Children Love**	1 John 2:28–3:10
Fri, Nov. 13	**Walking Faithfully in the Truth**	3 John 1-4
Sat, Nov. 14	**Imitate What Is Good**	3 John 9-12
Sun, Nov. 15	**Love One Another**	1 John 3:11-24

LESSON CYCLE CHART

International Sunday School Lesson Cycle, September 2016–August 2022

Year	Fall Quarter (Sep, Oct, Nov)	Winter Quarter (Dec, Jan, Feb)	Spring Quarter (Mar, Apr, May)	Summer Quarter (Jun, Jul, Aug)
2016–2017	**The Sovereignty of God** (Isaiah, Matthew, Hebrews, Revelation)	**Creation: A Divine Cycle** (Psalms, Luke, Galatians)	**God Loves Us** (Psalms, Joel, Jonah, John, Romans, Ephesians, 1 Peter, 1 John)	**God's Urgent Call** (Exodus, Judges, Prophets, Acts)
2017–2018	**Covenant with God** (Pentateuch, 1 & 2 Samuel, Nehemiah, Jeremiah, Ezekiel, 1 Corinthians, Hebrews)	**Faith in Action** (Daniel, Matthew, Acts, Ephesians, 1 Timothy, James)	**Acknowledging God** (Pentateuch, 2 Chronicles, Psalms, Luke, John, 2 Corinthians, Hebrews, Revelation)	**Justice in the New Testament** (Matthew, Luke, Romans, 2 Corinthians, Colossians)
2018–2019	**God's World and God's People** (Genesis)	**Our Love for God** (Deuteronomy, Joshua, Psalms, Matthew, Luke, Epistles)	**Discipleship and Mission** (Matthew, Mark, Luke, Acts, Romans)	**Covenant in God** (Ruth, 1 Samuel, Matthew, Mark, Ephesians, Colossians, Hebrews)
2019–2020	**Responding to God's Grace** (Pentateuch, 1 Samuel, 1 Kings, Luke, Epistles)	**Honoring God** (1 Kings, 1 Chronicles, Matthew, Luke)	**Justice and the Prophets** (Esther, Prophets, 1 Corinthians)	**Many Faces of Wisdom** (Proverbs, Ecclesiastes, Gospels, James)
2020–2021	**Love for One Another** (Genesis, 1 Samuel, Luke, John, Acts, Epistles)	**Call in the New Testament** (Gospels, Acts, Romans, 1 Corinthians, Hebrews)	**Prophets Faithful to God's Covenant** (Deuteronomy, Joshua, 1 & 2 Kings, Ezra, Nehemiah, Lamentations, Prophets)	**Confident Hope** (Leviticus, Matthew, Luke, Romans, 2 Corinthians, Hebrews, 1 John)
2021–2022	**Celebrating God** (Exodus, 2 Samuel, Psalms, Mark, Acts, Revelation)	**Justice, Law, History** (Pentateuch, 2 Samuel, Ezra, Job, Isaiah, Nahum)	**God Frees and Redeems** (Deuteronomy, Ezra, Matthew, John, Romans, Galatians)	**Partners in a New Creation** (Isaiah, John, Revelation)

EMPOWER CO-LEARNING

Teacher Tips by Jerry Bowling

Facilitating discussions in Bible study can anticipate, invite, and empower meaningful co-learning. Discussion as a learning tool can draw all students in a class into participation such that they feel they share a vital role in the lesson. As they discuss a Bible passage together, learners help others who are present grasp God's truth and integrate it into life. That's co-learning.

Preparing for Discussion

Teachers can empower co-learning when they prepare for it. Advance preparation for co-learning discussion comes in various forms: previewing resources such as blogs, Bible dictionaries, or videos; inviting students to bring their own questions; anticipating counterarguments; reflecting on the sets of questions in this teacher guide; etc. Successful discussion begins with good preparation!

To foster meaningful discussion in upcoming class sessions, teachers can communicate details about lessons through e-mail, social media, or web links. All this advance preparation will serve to engage the prior knowledge that students bring to the classroom, inspire deeper faith integration, and foster further reflection. The result will be enhanced discipleship.

Importance of Ground Rules

Ground rules are a simple set of agreed upon assumptions that clarify and guide the use of discussion. Having explicit ground rules is a fundamental prerequisite for Bible class discussions. Teachers can, of course, elect to introduce their own ground rules. But a even greater sense of ownership is created when teacher and students work together in developing them. Either way, it is imperative for class members to understand these guidelines before discussion begins.

An indispensable component of ground rules is that you, the teacher, models their use as you facilitate the lesson presentation and accompanying discussion. This creates student confidence and increases the likelihood that learners will honor the ground rules themselves in holistic collaboration.

A sample set of ground rules might include some of the following:

- *Open-minded and nonjudgmental dialogue.*
- *Confidential and respectful discussion.*
- *No interruptions, demeaning comments, or other disruptive behavior.*
- *Active attention when a classmate is talking.*
- *Using "I language" (rather than "you language") to challenge ideas.*

Results of a Co-Learning Culture

Having ground rules to frame Bible class discussions serves to create an inclusive learning environment as it welcomes diverse viewpoints. Establishing trust is the key for doing so. When that trust is established, the result will be a classroom setting that is open to insights—insights that empower growth in faith and service. Discussions in a co-learning classroom environment create the dynamic of shifting learning expectations toward students' participation. Discussions can underscore previously overlooked values that come to light in the hearing of others' views.

The ultimate perspective the students must hear is, of course, that of the author's original intent in writing the Scripture text. This is where you, the teacher, walk a tightrope. Invalid perspectives do exist (compare Galatians 2:11-21). But when you, the teacher, challenge wrong ideas within the framework of the ground rules, the co-learning culture is maintained as a learner comes to the conclusion *on his or her own* that the voiced perspective is in need of serious rethinking.

Biased Love

Devotional Reading: Psalm 105:1-6, 16-22
Background Scripture: Genesis 25:28; 35:23-26

Genesis 37:2-11, 23-24a, 28

2 These are the generations of Jacob. Joseph, being seventeen years old, was feeding the flock with his brethren; and the lad was with the sons of Bilhah, and with the sons of Zilpah, his father's wives: and Joseph brought unto his father their evil report.

3 Now Israel loved Joseph more than all his children, because he was the son of his old age: and he made him a coat of many colours.

4 And when his brethren saw that their father loved him more than all his brethren, they hated him, and could not speak peaceably unto him.

5 And Joseph dreamed a dream, and he told it his brethren: and they hated him yet the more.

6 And he said unto them, Hear, I pray you, this dream which I have dreamed:

7 For, behold, we were binding sheaves in the field, and, lo, my sheaf arose, and also stood upright; and, behold, your sheaves stood round about, and made obeisance to my sheaf.

8 And his brethren said to him, Shalt thou indeed reign over us? or shalt thou indeed have dominion over us? And they hated him yet the more for his dreams, and for his words.

9 And he dreamed yet another dream, and told it his brethren, and said, Behold, I have dreamed a dream more; and, behold, the sun and the moon and the eleven stars made obeisance to me.

10 And he told it to his father, and to his brethren: and his father rebuked him, and said unto him, What is this dream that thou hast dreamed? Shall I and thy mother and thy brethren indeed come to bow down ourselves to thee to the earth?

11 And his brethren envied him; but his father observed the saying.

. . . .

23 And it came to pass, when Joseph was come unto his brethren, that they stript Joseph out of his coat, his coat of many colours that was on him;

24a And they took him, and cast him into a pit.

. . . .

28 Then there passed by Midianites merchantmen; and they drew and lifted up Joseph out of the pit, and sold Joseph to the Ishmeelites for twenty pieces of silver: and they brought Joseph into Egypt.

Key Verse

His brethren envied him; but his father observed the saying. **—Genesis 37:11**

LOVE FOR ONE ANOTHER

Unit 1: Struggles with Love

LESSONS 1–4

LESSON AIMS

After participating in this lesson, each learner will be able to:

1. Identify the cause and effects of Jacob's favoritism.

2. Explain how Joseph contributed to the effects of the problem.

3. Repent of having demonstrated biased love and seek to make amends for having done so.

LESSON OUTLINE

Introduction
- A. House vs. Home
- B. Lesson Context

I. A Family's Discord (Genesis 37:2-4)
- A. Friction (v. 2)
- B. Favoritism (v. 3)
- C. Fury (v. 4)

II. A Brother's Dreams (Genesis 37:5-11)
- A. In the Fields (vv. 5-8)
- B. In the Sky (vv. 9-11)
  - *Dreaming of Grandeur*

III. Brothers' Disdain (Genesis 37:23-24a, 28)
- A. Shaming Joseph (vv. 23-24a)
- B. Selling Joseph (v. 28)
  - *Who Suffers from Favoritism?*

Conclusion
- A. Imperfect Family, Perfect God
- B. Prayer
- C. Thought to Remember

Introduction

A. House vs. Home

Why don't we use the expression "house, sweet house"? A house is just a structure or place of residence. Without a family within, the building can never be a home. *Home* has much more sentiment attached to its meaning, evoking different emotions based on the family life within the house. A home consists of all that goes on within that structure. It is the place where memories are made.

When we consider the family life of the patriarch Jacob in the Old Testament, "home, sweet home" is not the first phrase to cross our minds. "Family feud" seems more appropriate! The strife and hard feelings within that family are seen in today's lesson text.

B. Lesson Context

Joseph was born around the year 1916 BC. In world historical context, this would be near the middle of the Bronze Age, which began around 3000 BC. Other technological and societal advancements made this a time of important, though comparatively slow, change.

The struggles with love involving Joseph go back years before Joseph to his father Jacob (about 2007–1860 BC). Jacob was raised in a home where favoritism appears to have been the primary parenting skill of his father and mother, Isaac and Rebekah. Genesis 25:28 tells us all we need to know: "Isaac loved Esau, because he did eat of his venison: but Rebekah loved Jacob."

Such a scenario was bound to produce family conflict. This infighting came to a head when Rebekah learned of Isaac's desire to bless his favorite son, Esau (the older of the two). This would solidify Esau's privileged position, with promises of abundance for the future. She disguised Jacob so that he would feel hairy like Esau in the presence of blind Isaac. The ruse worked, and the blessing intended for Esau was pronounced on Jacob (Genesis 27:1-41).

To escape Esau's vengeance, Jacob traveled to Haran, where Rebekah's brother Laban lived (Genesis 27:42-43). There Jacob married the two daughters of Laban, namely Leah and Rachel, and became the father of one daughter and 11 of his eventual 12 sons (29:15–30:24). Joseph was the last son born to Jacob in Haran (30:22-24). On the way back to Canaan, after residing in Haran for 20 years (31:38), Benjamin was born. He and Joseph were the only two sons of Rachel. Tragically, Rachel died while giving birth to Benjamin (35:16-20).

Eventually, Jacob settled with his family in Canaan near Bethel (Genesis 35:1), a journey hundreds of miles from Haran. Perhaps he believed that he would enjoy his last years in relative calm, as opposed to all the strife he had experienced thus far. However, some of Jacob's most heartbreaking trials were yet to come, sown from seeds in his own past.

I. A Family's Discord

(Genesis 37:2-4)

A. Friction (v. 2)

2a. These are the generations of Jacob.

The book of Genesis is organized partially by the use of the Hebrew phrase translated *these are the generations of*, used for the last time here. The phrase first appears in Genesis 2:4: "These are the generations of the heavens and of the earth when they were created" (see also Genesis 5:1; 6:9; 10:1; 11:10, 27; 25:12, 19; 36:1, 9). Each instance emphasizes the continuation of life and introduces stories concerned with those lives in some way. Importantly, *Jacob* was the grandson of Abraham (Matthew 1:2), who was given great covenant promises by God (Genesis 12:1-3; 17:1-16).

2b. Joseph, being seventeen years old, was feeding the flock with his brethren.

Joseph's birth is recorded in Genesis 30:22-24. Genesis 33:1-2 mentions how Jacob placed Rachel and Joseph in the rear of the entourage as Jacob prepared to meet Esau. This preferential treatment foreshadowed the family dynamics that would contribute to the drama present in today's text. Since Rachel was Jacob's preferred wife and Joseph was her only son so far, Jacob wanted to reduce the risk of their being harmed should Esau come seeking revenge for Jacob's previous deceitful actions (see Lesson Context).

Jacob was a very successful shepherd (Genesis 30:25-43), and apparently he intended for *Joseph* to follow in his footsteps. To that end, we see Joseph learning the family operation. In this relatively dry region, it was necessary to move the flocks and herds around to provide them with daily food. Sometimes herdsmen would have to go long distances to find that food.

2c. And the lad was with the sons of Bilhah, and with the sons of Zilpah, his father's wives.

Bilhah and *Zilpah* are called Jacob's *wives,* though the actual status of each was that of a handmaid. Zilpah was given to Leah when she married Jacob (Genesis 29:23-24); Bilhah was given to Rachel at the same time (29:29). According to the custom of the time, children born to a wife's handmaidens by her husband were counted as the wife's own children (examples: 30:1-8). Bilhah's *sons* were Dan and Naphtali (35:25); Zilpah's were Gad and Asher (35:26).

2d. And Joseph brought unto his father their evil report.

The content of Joseph's *report* about these brothers is unknown. The Hebrew word translated *evil* does not necessarily imply something cruel or morally wrong, though it certainly can. In this case, it may mean that Joseph's brothers have done something disrespectful or mean to their younger brother. It could also be that Joseph brought word of a poor work ethic or other misbehavior.

What Do You Think?

How do we teach children the difference between bringing to an adult a needed report of behavior versus merely being a tattletale?

Digging Deeper

How do Genesis 27:5-10; 1 Samuel 22:9-19; Esther 2:21-23; and/or Acts 23:16-22 inform your response? Why?

B. Favoritism (v. 3)

3. Now Israel loved Joseph more than all his children, because he was the son of his old age: and he made him a coat of many colours.

Here we see Jacob's name *Israel,* given to him after his wrestling match in Genesis 32:22-30.

Its use reminds the reader that God blessed Israel when He changed the patriarch's name (compare 17:1-8).

While Joseph's tattling didn't cultivate good brotherly feelings, Israel's favoritism likely caused even more tension. The favor that was revealed at the meeting with Esau (see commentary on Genesis 37:2b, above) became even more pronounced once Jacob's family had settled in the land. Jacob made no secret of the greater love he had for *Joseph.* Not only was Joseph one of Rachel's two sons, but he was also born late in Jacob's life—Jacob was about 90, based on Joseph's age relative to Jacob's when the whole family arrived in Egypt (comparing 41:46-47; 45:6; and 47:9).

There were likely many ways in which Jacob demonstrated his fondness for Joseph. One concrete way Jacob expressed this love was by making *a coat of many colours* only for Joseph. The coat resembled a robe more than a jacket or winter coat. It stood out against any garment the brothers had been given.

What Do You Think?

In what ways would you change, were you to accept the challenge to "not be like Jacob"?

Digging Deeper

What other Bible character's example will help you most in this regard? Why?

C. Fury (v. 4)

4. And when his brethren saw that their father loved him more than all his brethren, they hated him, and could not speak peaceably unto him.

Something as conspicuous as a multicolored robe is impossible not to notice. This article of clothing became a physical, tangible reminder not only to Joseph but also to his brothers that Jacob played favorites. Simply by looking at Joseph in the coat, the *brethren* could see *that their father loved* Joseph *more than* any of the rest of them. Events from their family history foreshadow what may happen to Joseph as a result of the hatred his brothers feel (compare Genesis 27:41; see Lesson Context).

What Do You Think?

Without giving directive advice, how would you counsel someone who is in the less-loved position as were Joseph's brothers?

Digging Deeper

Assume that changing the attitude of the one exhibiting favoritism is not viable.

II. A Brother's Dreams

(Genesis 37:5-11)

A. In the Fields (vv. 5-8)

5. And Joseph dreamed a dream, and he told it his brethren: and they hated him yet the more.

Now comes another reason for Joseph's brothers to have *hated him*: his dreams. Dreams of revelation are found primarily in Genesis and Daniel in the Old Testament (examples: Genesis 20:3; Daniel 2:28). *Joseph* was one of the few to whom God spoke in this manner. Equally important is the fact that Joseph later demonstrated the God-given ability to interpret the dreams of others (example: Genesis 41:25-32; see lesson 2). This ability opened doors for Jacob's family to come to Egypt.

6-7. And he said unto them, Hear, I pray you, this dream which I have dreamed: for behold, we were binding sheaves in the field, and, lo, my sheaf arose, and also stood upright; and, behold, your sheaves stood round about, and made obeisance to my sheaf.

This dream uses images from a grain harvest. Men and women would go out with hand sickles and cut the grain. As they did, they gathered the cut stalks into *sheaves.* The sheaves were stacked *in the field* to await transport to the place of threshing (compare Ruth 2:7).

To make *obeisance* means to bow down in an act of great respect or worship. Here it signifies that someone else has (or will have) power over those who are doing the bowing. Why would Joseph think it prudent to tell his brothers about a dream in which they were under his power? Being a very young man, around age 17, Joseph simply may not have developed a sense of tact or appropriateness. Or perhaps he sensed already that his dream had come from God and was a word his brothers needed to hear. The Bible is silent concerning Joseph's motivations.

8. And his brethren said to him, Shalt thou indeed reign over us? or shalt thou indeed have dominion over us? And they hated him yet the more for his dreams, and for his words.

The symbolism of the dream did not confuse Joseph's brothers: Joseph saw himself as one who would *reign over* the brothers. They immediately grasped its meaning and *hated him yet the more* because of it! Whether they took the dream seriously or considered it an attempt at self-promotion, the brothers recognized that, once again, their younger brother was placed above them.

Though the Bible is silent on this matter, it is possible that the brothers have already discussed killing Joseph (compare Esau's idea in Genesis 27:41). Joseph's brothers, of course, did not know how important the fulfillment of Joseph's dreams would be for the men's own lives (42:6-9; 43:26, 28; 44:14; 50:18; see lesson 3).

> *What Do You Think?*
> What do Joseph's announcement and his brothers' reaction teach you about discretion?
> *Digging Deeper*
> How do passages such as Proverbs 2:11 and Daniel 7:28 help inform your answer?

B. In the Sky (vv. 9-11)

9. And he dreamed yet another dream, and told it his brethren, and said, Behold I have dreamed a dream more; and, behold, the sun and the moon and the eleven stars made obeisance to me.

For Joseph, the second *dream* likely provided verification that the message of the first was true since the two dreams concern the same subject. We may compare this with Pharaoh's two dreams in the same night; those dreams had different images but the same meaning (Genesis 41:25).

Joseph's second dream has implications as serious as the first. Not only would *the eleven stars,* representing his 11 brothers, offer *obeisance* to him, so would Jacob and Leah (who still lived and represented her sister, Joseph's mother, now deceased per Genesis 35:19). The number 11 leaves no doubt about whom these images signify!

10. And he told it to his father, and to his brethren: and his father rebuked him, and said unto him, What is this dream that thou hast dreamed? Shall I and thy mother and thy brethren indeed come to bow down ourselves to thee to the earth?

Jacob responded first to Joseph's second *dream.* Even though Joseph was his favorite son, Jacob was bothered by the dream and *rebuked* Joseph for sharing it. In a patriarchal society where the father held the primary authority and where birth order determined standing within a family, it was hard to believe that the next-to-youngest son, Joseph, would be the one to whom Jacob, Leah, and the 11 brothers would *bow down*—no matter how much Jacob loved the boy.

> *What Do You Think?*
> In what instances does indiscreet speech call for rebuke rather than no response?
> *Digging Deeper*
> What Scripture passages help you most to be discerning in this regard?

Jacob, of course, was no stranger to dreams. He had dreamed as he departed from Canaan and traveled toward Haran (Genesis 28:10-16). In Haran he told Rachel and Leah of another dream, one in which God told him to return to Canaan (31:10-13). Even so, he did not seem to grasp that these dreams were more than fanciful nocturnal fabrications on Joseph's part.

Dreaming of Grandeur

In a dream I had recently, several of us Christian bikers were at a gas station, my friends on Japanese motorcycles and I on my German BMW. I mention the origins of our bikes because a group of Harley riders arrived next. Harley riders tend to look down on Japanese bikes in particular, though they generally admire the German Beemer.

This real-life disdain resulted in the dream

bullies stopping to harass us, looking to make trouble. My friends backed away, and there I was by my Beemer. I courageously told the Harley riders to leave my friends alone and go away peacefully.

Maybe my dream tells the future; more likely, it expresses some anxiety I have or my desire to be a hero. Unlike me, Joseph had no doubt about the meaning and importance of his dreams. He knew they revealed something about God's plan in Joseph's life. Do our aspirational dreams align with God's plan as Joseph's nocturnal ones did?

—C. R. B.

11a. And his brethren envied him.

Here the brothers' reaction to Joseph's second dream differs from the hatred that has defined them heretofore. Perhaps they were beginning to wonder whether Joseph's dreams have some real meaning to them, or possibly they wished *they* could be the ones having such dreams.

The emotion of envy suggests a stronger and more significant passion than even hatred. The emotion magnifies the possibility that their feelings would spill over into violence (see commentary on Genesis 37:8).

11b. But his father observed the saying.

Observed the saying means that Jacob will watch for one or more events through which Joseph's dream will be fulfilled. This is similar to Mary's own watchfulness in Luke 2:19.

III. Brothers' Disdain

(Genesis 37:23-24a, 28)

A. Shaming Joseph (vv. 23-24a)

23-24a. And it came to pass, when Joseph was come unto his brethren, that they stript Joseph out of his coat, his coat of many colours that was on him; and they took him, and cast him into a pit.

As the story picks up at this point, Jacob had sent *Joseph* to his brothers who were tending the herds. Joseph found them in Dothan, close to one of the major trade routes to Egypt. When the brothers saw Joseph approaching, they decided it was a good time to kill him. His brother Reuben, however, suggested instead that Joseph be thrown *into a pit* (see Genesis 37:12-22, not in our printed text).

The act of stripping Joseph *out of his coat* symbolically stripped him of his status as Jacob's favorite. It likely represents more than anything the brothers' resentment of the favoritism that Joseph received from their father. When they decided to pretend he had died, the coat became evidence in support of their story (Genesis 37:31-33). Their revenge continued when they threw Joseph into a pit, which is probably a dry cistern (compare Isaiah 36:16, same Hebrew word). It was impossible for him to climb out of it.

B. Selling Joseph (v. 28)

28. Then there passed by Midianites merchantmen; and they drew and lifted up Joseph out of the pit, and sold Joseph to the Ishmeelites for twenty pieces of silver: and they brought Joseph into Egypt.

Are the *Midianites* and *Ishmeelites* (also spelled *Ishmaelites*; see below) two names for the same group of people? On the one hand, Genesis 37:36 says that the Midianites sold Joseph to Potiphar, while Genesis 39:1 says it was the Ishmaelites; this suggests they were the same people by two names. Similarly, we later find Gideon fighting against "the Midianites" (Judges 7:24-25; 8:1), who wore "golden earrings, because they were Ishmaelites" (8:24).

On the other hand, some scholars suggest that the Midianite *merchantmen* acted as middlemen

HOW TO SAY IT

Bethel	*Beth*-ul.
Bilhah	*Bill*-ha.
Canaan	*Kay*-nun.
Dothan	*Doe*-thun (*th* as in *thin*).
Esau	*Ee*-saw.
Haran	*Hair*-un.
Ishmeelites	*Ish*-may-el-ites.
Israel	*Iz*-ray-el.
Laban	*Lay*-bun.
Midianites	*Mid*-ee-un-ites.
obeisance	oh-*bee*-sense.
Zilpah	*Zil*-pa.

for the Ishmaelites and were not actually part of the same people. At the very least, the two groups shared Abraham as a common ancestor (see Genesis 16:15; 25:1-2).

The relative value of *twenty pieces of silver* is uncertain. Such an amount seems to be the going price for slaves in the time of Joseph. His sale brought monetary profit to the brothers as well as providing them a way of enacting their revenge without actually killing him. The brothers then slaughtered a goat, smeared its blood on the coat they tore up, and presented the coat to their father as evidence that the favorite son was dead, killed by a wild animal (Genesis 37:31-35). Meanwhile, Joseph was taken *into Egypt*, presumably never to be heard from again.

Who Suffers from Favoritism?

I knew a businessman who pressured all his children to follow in his footsteps. All but one of them entered a father-approved career field. These were blessed with his favor, but the one who chose a different way suffered many consequences.

When the father died, his estate was divided equally among his children. However, in a final act of favoritism, those who had done what the father said received their shares immediately. The other son found that his inheritance was placed in an investment account from which he received only the yearly dividends. He would never receive the full amount of his share as his siblings did.

In Jacob's family, only Joseph was favored. In both families, everyone eventually suffered because of favoritism, whether it benefited them initially or not. And so it still is. —C. R. B.

Conclusion

A. Imperfect Family, Perfect God

Today's tragic episode impresses on us what favoritism can do and has done in families. Jacob's showing favoritism to Joseph created hatred in his older sons that festered and was mixed with envy, finally erupting in violence. Biased love toward one son resulted in the others starving for their father's favor and taking out their neglect on the object of his affection.

Visual for Lesson 1. *Point to this visual as you discuss the nature of Joseph's family. Ask for "lessons learned" for today.*

Still, God's sovereign plan and purpose moved forward under His guiding hand. God had told Joseph's great-grandfather Abraham that his family would sojourn in Egypt for 400 years (Genesis 15:13). Joseph was being sent ahead as a kind of point man for his family. Though Joseph saw only slavery ahead of him, God saw the fulfillment of Joseph's dreams and the blessing he would be to his brothers (45:4-11; see lesson 4).

In God's providential work through Joseph, we are reminded that God is never thwarted by the evil intentions of human beings. Though we struggle to see God at work in our trials today, He remains the unseen mover in our lives just as He was in Joseph's life.

B. Prayer

Dear Father, help us to love as You do, without neglecting some and favoring others. In Jesus' name we pray. Amen.

C. Thought to Remember

God's love favors *all* His children.

INVOLVEMENT LEARNING

Enhance your lesson with KJV Bible Student *(from your curriculum supplier) and the reproducible activity page (at www.standardlesson.com or in the back of the* KJV Standard Lesson Commentary Deluxe Edition*).*

Into the Lesson

Option. Before class members arrive, place in chairs copies of the "Yep—That's Family!" exercise from the activity page, which you can download. Your early arrivers can work on this as indicated.

Write the following on the board:

What is the difference between a house and a home?

As volunteers share their responses, jot their ideas on the board. Then ask how a house becomes a home. After several responses, flip it around and ask what actions and attitudes could cause a home to devolve into being merely a house?

After learners offer responses regarding family strife, make a transition by saying, "Family strife is nothing new—it goes clear back to Genesis 4. Let's examine a case of reconciliation to see what it can teach us today."

Into the Word

Ask learners what they know about Esau and Jacob, the sons of Isaac and Rebekah. (*Expected responses:* they were twins; Isaac favored Esau; Rebekah favored Jacob; etc.) If no one does so, summarize Jacob's "like father, like son" favoritism. Ask students to share how the parents' favoritism caused calamity in the family. (*Expected responses are per* Genesis 25:27-34; 27:1-45.)

Distribute handouts (you prepare) titled "Family Conflict" that feature four columns headed *Lesson Text / Jacob's Actions / Joseph's Actions / Brothers' Actions.* Under the far left column (*Lesson Text*), have printed the following as labels to rows: A–verse 2; B–verses 3-4; C–verses 5-11; D–verses 23-24a; E–verse 28. Include these instructions: "Read through each section of the lesson text of Genesis 37:2-11, 23-24a, 28. As you do, fill in the chart as the headers imply concerning actions that contributed to family conflict. Not every box will require a response."

Have learners discuss and complete the chart in small groups, then reconvene for whole-class discussion. Using the rows to go verse by verse through the lesson text, ask "What's so?" as you pause at each intersection of row and header. After appropriate responses (which should be obvious from the text), ask "So what?" to dig below a mere recitation of historical facts. Probe for different conclusions. Encourage learners not to allow personal experiences of family conflict to read into the text something that is not there. (*Option.* Distribute copies of the "Exegesis, Not Eisegesis" activity from the activity page for learners to complete as indicated.)

Into Life

Form learners into study pairs and give each a handout (you prepare) on which are printed the following questions:

1–In what ways does favoritism damage family relationships today?
2–When have you seen accusations of favoritism where none existed?
3–How can you make amends for your own errors regarding questions 1 and 2?
4–What are some ways you can minister to those who bear the scars of favoritism, either as victim or perpetrator?
5–What are some practices church staff members can adopt to avoid perceptions of favoritism?

Case study. An elder in a church has two grandsons: one is a grandson of natural descent; the other became a grandson when the man's daughter married a man who had a son. The grandfather set up a snack vending service at his workplace, with proceeds going to a college fund for the grandson of natural descent only. This is causing friction with the son-in-law, who is the natural father of both boys. The grandfather defends his favoritism by saying, "Blood is thicker than water." How would you counsel this man?

Obedient Love

Devotional Reading: 1 Peter 5:5b-11
Background Scripture: Genesis 41:14-57

Genesis 41:25-33, 37-40, 50-52

25 And Joseph said unto Pharaoh, The dream of Pharaoh is one: God hath shewed Pharaoh what he is about to do.

26 The seven good kine are seven years; and the seven good ears are seven years: the dream is one.

27 And the seven thin and ill favoured kine that came up after them are seven years; and the seven empty ears blasted with the east wind shall be seven years of famine.

28 This is the thing which I have spoken unto Pharaoh: What God is about to do he sheweth unto Pharaoh.

29 Behold, there come seven years of great plenty throughout all the land of Egypt:

30 And there shall arise after them seven years of famine; and all the plenty shall be forgotten in the land of Egypt; and the famine shall consume the land;

31 And the plenty shall not be known in the land by reason of that famine following; for it shall be very grievous.

32 And for that the dream was doubled unto Pharaoh twice; it is because the thing is established by God, and God will shortly bring it to pass.

33 Now therefore let Pharaoh look out a man discreet and wise, and set him over the land of Egypt.

. . . .

37 And the thing was good in the eyes of Pharaoh, and in the eyes of all his servants.

38 And Pharaoh said unto his servants, Can we find such a one as this is, a man in whom the Spirit of God is?

39 And Pharaoh said unto Joseph, Forasmuch as God hath shewed thee all this, there is none so discreet and wise as thou art:

40 Thou shalt be over my house, and according unto thy word shall all my people be ruled: only in the throne will I be greater than thou.

. . . .

50 And unto Joseph were born two sons before the years of famine came, which Asenath the daughter of Potipherah priest of On bare unto him.

51 And Joseph called the name of the firstborn Manasseh: For God, said he, hath made me forget all my toil, and all my father's house.

52 And the name of the second called he Ephraim: For God hath caused me to be fruitful in the land of my affliction.

Key Verses

Pharaoh said unto Joseph, Forasmuch as God hath shewed thee all this, there is none so discreet and wise as thou art: thou shalt be over my house, and according unto thy word shall all my people be ruled: only in the throne will I be greater than thou. —**Genesis 41:39-40**

LOVE FOR ONE ANOTHER

Unit 1: Struggles with Love

LESSONS 1–4

LESSON AIMS

After participating in this lesson, each learner will be able to:

1. Describe how God blessed Joseph in his difficult circumstances.
2. Identify other situations in which God made himself known through the faithfulness of His people in their tribulations.
3. Write a prayer thanking God for His care during an especially trying time.

LESSON OUTLINE

Introduction

A. New Life, New God?

Immigrants face a host of difficulties when settling into new countries. Cultural differences can be the biggest hurdles to being accepted in a community, a neighborhood, or by coworkers.

Some immigrants do not invest the time or resources necessary to adopt the cultural mores of their new country. Sometimes it's not about lack of time or resources but about lack of desire; fitting in with cultural expectations of the new country may threaten the identity that a person has come to cherish. Fear of losing that identity can be isolating.

One way self-identity is threatened is by rejecting the religion of the immigrant's country of origin. When a particular religion or faith expression has been integral to personal identity for decades, then challenges to that religion or expression may result in an identity crisis.

Today's lesson features a man who faced a similar challenge: Joseph, sold into slavery in Egypt, adopted various facets of Egyptian culture as his own while being most resistant to changing his "one God" worldview, known as monotheism. Joseph looked, acted, and spoke like an Egyptian most of the time. But he did not lose his sense of dependence on God in a pagan culture. Whether in prison or in power, Joseph remained God's man—obedient, faithful, and willing to give God the credit.

B. Lesson Context

Following the events of last week's lesson, Joseph was sold to an Egyptian official named Potiphar (Genesis 37:36). Joseph quickly found favor in Potiphar's eyes and was promoted to a position of great responsibility within Potiphar's household.

Potiphar's wife, however, constantly pressured Joseph to sleep with her. Joseph refused every time (Genesis 39:9-10). When on one occasion Joseph ran from Potiphar's wife, his cloak was torn from him and left behind; she used it to accuse Joseph falsely of attempted rape. As a result, Potiphar had Joseph thrown in prison (39:11-20).

Here too Joseph proved himself worthy of responsibility (Genesis 39:20-23). Dreams once again enter Joseph's story (compare 37:5-11; see lesson 1) through two fellow prisoners. Joseph's experience had taught him that only God can reveal the true meaning of dreams (40:8; 41:16). The divinely inspired interpretations Joseph provided for each man's dream came true: one man was put to death, and the other man was restored to his position. Joseph requested of the latter that after regaining his position, he would mention Joseph to the Pharaoh. The man, however, forgot about Joseph for two years (40:1–41:1).

Pharaoh had his own incomprehensible dreams. Though the content was easily conveyed, neither Pharaoh nor any of his magicians or wise men understood them (Genesis 41:1-8). In the first dream, seven healthy cows had come forth from the Nile River. They were followed by seven cows "ill favoured and leanfleshed" (41:3); Pharaoh described them as "such as I never saw in all the land of Egypt for badness" (41:19). Amazingly, the ugly cows devoured the healthy ones.

Much the same occurred in Pharaoh's second dream, though the details differed. Seven ears of corn appeared on a single stalk. Then there appeared seven withered ears that had been scorched by a hot east wind. The withered ears proceeded to eat up the fully grown ears.

When Pharaoh spoke of this conundrum, the forgetful former prisoner remembered Joseph and told Pharaoh of Joseph's ability to interpret dreams accurately. Joseph was quickly taken from the prison, made presentable, and brought before Pharaoh (Genesis 41:9-14).

I. Disturbing Dreams

(Genesis 41:25-33)

A. Interpretation (vv. 25-32)

25. And Joseph said unto Pharaoh, The dream of Pharaoh is one: God hath shewed Pharaoh what he is about to do.

Though *Pharaoh* had dreamed two dreams (Genesis 41:5; see Lesson Context), they carried *one* and the same message. After Pharaoh recounted his dreams, the first words Joseph spoke tell us something of the heart of this faithful servant of the Lord: "It is not in me: God shall give Pharaoh an answer of peace" (41:16). God, not Joseph, would set Pharaoh's anxious mind at ease (see Lesson Context; compare Daniel 2:45).

26. The seven good kine are seven years; and the seven good ears are seven years: the dream is one.

The number *seven* in both dreams represents a number of *years*. Joseph's reassurance that *the dream is one* clarifies that the *good kine* (another word for cows; see translation of the same word in Isaiah 11:7). The *good ears* represent the same 7 years, not 14.

27. And the seven thin and ill favoured kine that came up after them are seven years; and the seven empty ears blasted with the east wind shall be seven years of famine.

Similarly, *the seven* ugly cows and *the seven empty ears* represent a new set of *seven years*. These 7 years will be defined by *famine.*

28. This is the thing which I have spoken unto Pharaoh: What God is about to do he sheweth unto Pharaoh.

Again Joseph emphasized that he himself was not the source of the interpretation (compare Genesis 40:8; 41:25). The significance of insisting on honoring *God* is partially found in ancient beliefs about the way gods ruled. Most people took for granted that multiple gods existed and governed the world. These gods were often associated with a group of people in a specific locale. Whenever a person moved to another nation or people group, it was believed that he or she had left that deity's jurisdiction and come under the reign of another (compare 1 Kings 20:28; 2 Kings 17:26).

Joseph, however, held to a very different view of God, one consistent with what the Bible teaches (Genesis 1; Psalm 47:7; 97:9; etc.). This knowledge about God's character and dominion left Joseph with no doubt that God (1) had sent the dreams, (2) provided the interpretation, and (3) would follow through on what the dreams had revealed. Joseph's God was not a fictitious Egyptian deity; the Lord would show himself able to carry out His will in any country, not just among the people who knew Him.

> *What Do You Think?*
> When discussing spiritual matters with unbelievers, under what circumstances, if any, is it better to refer to God rather than to Jesus in particular? Why?
> *Digging Deeper*
> How do Paul's various experiences in Acts 17 influence your conclusions?

29-30. Behold, there come seven years of great plenty throughout all the land of Egypt: And there shall arise after them seven years of famine; and all the plenty shall be forgotten in the land of Egypt; and the famine shall consume the land.

For the first time, Joseph revealed specifically what the healthy cows and the healthy grain represented (see commentary on Genesis 41:26, above).

31. And the plenty shall not be known in the land by reason of that famine following; for it shall be very grievous.

The Hebrew word translated *grievous* describes something too oppressive or "heavy" to bear (example: Numbers 11:14). The phrases are piled up, repeating in stark language that the good years will be forgotten as the *famine* would end up being a nationally devastating event.

32. And for that the dream was doubled unto Pharaoh twice; it is because the thing is established by God, and God will shortly bring it to pass.

Once again repetition serves to emphasize. This time the emphasis is by *the dream* having come *unto Pharaoh* in two forms. God was firmly committed to the years of plenty and of famine that the dreams predicted (compare Isaiah 46:11). As Joseph spoke to Pharaoh, he might have remembered his own *doubled* dreams that his family would bow to him (Genesis 37:5-10). Though Joseph didn't know when, he could be confident that God would bring these things *to pass* (example: 42:6; see lesson 3).

The twofold format also suggested urgency in heeding the dreams: God would soon fulfill what He had revealed. We do not know exactly how long after these dreams the seven years of plenty began. But the implication of the twice-dreamed dream was clear: Pharaoh had no time to waste in preparing for what lay ahead for his people.

Once more Joseph emphasized God's work in granting Pharaoh the dreams and giving Joseph their interpretation (see on Genesis 41:28, above). Instead of taking credit for his own wisdom and insight, thus promoting his own interests, Joseph continued to point to God's work through him.

> *What Do You Think?*
> What guardrails can we erect against the dangers of dream interpretation today?
> *Digging Deeper*
> How do Job 33:13-17; Ecclesiastes 5:3, 7; Jeremiah 23:27-28, 32; Acts 2:17; Hebrews 1:1-2; and Jude 8 help frame your answer?

God may have seemed absent to Joseph, especially when a fellow prisoner forgot him for two years (Genesis 41:1). But God's continued favor in giving Joseph interpretations undoubtedly reassured the man that the Lord was present with him, even in (or especially in) prison. The Lord had not forgotten His faithful servant. At the beginning of Joseph's time both in Potiphar's house and in prison, we are reminded that the Lord was "with Joseph" (39:2, 23). Whether Joseph was aware of it yet or not, God never left his side.

Feast or Famine

The phrase "feast or famine" describes situations of extremes with no middle-ground result. Farmers may use the phrase to describe a year's rainfall when early spring drenching makes fields too wet to plant, but then summer drought keeps the harvest from growing and maturing. Those who work on commission may experience feast or famine times on a regular basis!

The *feast or famine* aspects of Pharaoh's dreams were to be fulfilled literally. But a spiritual aspect is also present: Pharaoh's wise men were in a *famine* state when it came to interpreting their leader's dreams. However, Pharaoh was blessed that God had given Joseph a *feast* of discernment with which to interpret the dreams. That fact leads to a natural question: How does the Christian move from spiritual famine to spiritual feast? It all begins with knowing God's will—not as He has revealed it in dreams, but as He has revealed it in Scripture (Psalm 119:11; 2 Timothy 2:15; etc.). Where does your feast/famine meter read in that regard? —C. R. B.

B. Advice (v. 33)

33. Now therefore let Pharaoh look out a man discreet and wise, and set him over the land of Egypt.

Knowing what the dreams meant was of vital importance. However, that knowledge was worthless without a plan to use the information appropriately. Thus Joseph took the initiative in making the suggestion we see here. Joseph further suggested a plan for the appointed man to put into action (Genesis 41:34-36, not in today's text).

II. Pharaoh's Favor

(Genesis 41:37-40)

A. Praising Joseph (vv. 37-38)

37. And the thing was good in the eyes of Pharaoh, and in the eyes of all his servants.

The phrase *all his servants* likely refers to various officials in Pharaoh's government, including the magicians and wise men who had been unable to interpret Pharaoh's dream (Genesis 41:8). Their unanimous approval may indicate God's having blessed not only Joseph with understanding but also the bestowal of wisdom on the Egyptians gathered.

38. And Pharaoh said unto his servants, Can we find such a one as this is, a man in whom the Spirit of God is?

Pharaoh's words here do not necessarily reflect faith in God (compare acknowledgement of "the spirit of the holy gods" in Daniel 4:18; 5:11-14). There is no indication that he renounced other gods or came to believe in the one true God. He simply acknowledged that a deity (or deities, since the Hebrew can be translated plural) who sent the dream also sent the interpretation to the man of His choosing. In the same way, Pharaoh would likely expect that if an Egyptian god sent a dream, then that same deity would be the one who gave

Visual for Lesson 2. *Use this visual to begin a discussion about the dangers of sharing either wisdom or love without the other.*

or withheld interpretation (compare Daniel 2:11; 4:8-9).

In any case, the phrasing acknowledged divine favor on Joseph. Though Joseph was a foreigner, a slave, and a prisoner in Egypt, Pharaoh didn't mention any of this. Of greatest significance to him was that Joseph showed himself to be the man Egypt needed. Perhaps to discourage any questions about Joseph's loyalty or skill, Pharaoh gave him an Egyptian name, Zaphnathpaaneah, which may mean something like "revealer of secrets" (Genesis 41:45).

B. Promoting Joseph (vv. 39-40)

39. And Pharaoh said unto Joseph, Forasmuch as God hath shewed thee all this, there is none so discreet and wise as thou art.

No one else had Joseph's divinely given insight. The *God* who had sent the dreams had also provided a particular man to interpret them. *Pharaoh* agreed with *Joseph* completely in that the dreams and their interpretation were not of human origin.

HOW TO SAY IT

Asenath	*As*-e-nath.
Ephraim	*Ee*-fray-im.
Manasseh	Muh-*nass*-uh.
Potiphar	*Pot*-ih-far.
Potipherah	*Pot*-i-***fee***-ruh.
Zaphnathpaaneah	***Zaf***-nath-*pay*-uh-nee-uh.

Since the man Joseph obviously had been given a divine stamp of approval, Pharaoh followed suit.

40. Thou shalt be over my house, and according unto thy word shall all my people be ruled: only in the throne will I be greater than thou.

To Pharaoh it seemed only right that someone with the insight and intelligence that Joseph clearly possessed should be the one to administer the plan he suggested. Joseph's responsibilities were very similar to what they had been in Potiphar's house (Genesis 39:4-6) and the prison (39:20-23). The key difference was that the only person in a higher position was Pharaoh himself (see Psalm 105:16-22; Acts 7:10).

Hindsight tells us that God had been preparing Joseph for this position ever since he arrived in Egypt. What an amazing change of status for someone who, just 24 hours earlier, had been a forgotten prisoner! Joseph went from pit to power.

What Do You Think?

To whose preparation do you most relate: that of Moses (whose life in a palace prepared him to lead in a wilderness) or Joseph (whose life in a wilderness prepared him to lead in a palace)? Why?

Digging Deeper

In what ways has that preparation surprised you?

Genesis 41:41-45 (not in our printed text) records the actions taken by Pharaoh to confirm Joseph's new position in Egypt. Joseph diligently carried out the task of amassing grain in preparation for the coming famine (41:48-49).

III. Foreign Family

(Genesis 41:50-52)

A. Sons Born (v. 50)

50a. And unto Joseph were born two sons before the years of famine came.

Though this is a normal relational progression (marriage, then children), this note also shows the depth of Joseph's trust in God. *Joseph* was preparing for the *famine* that he firmly believed was coming. Yet he was so confident that God had provided for those lean *years* that he was not hesitant about introducing new mouths to Egypt. This may foreshadow his care for other nations and especially his estranged family (Genesis 45:10-11; see lesson 4).

50b. Which Asenath the daughter of Potipherah priest of On bare unto him.

On was a city in Egypt, located just northeast of modern Cairo. On was the location of a temple devoted to the worship of the Egyptian sun god Ra (the Greeks later called the city Heliopolis, meaning "city of the sun"). The name *Potipherah* (not to be confused with Potiphar) means "he whom Ra has given."

Joseph's marriage to *Asenath the daughter of* a pagan *priest* raises eyebrows. After all, her family was devoted to idolatry, and pagan wives had a way of introducing compromise into a husband's devotion to the Lord (example: 1 Kings 11:1-6). Yet there is no suggestion here or elsewhere that Asenath ever influenced Joseph toward idolatry. Even in marriage to an Egyptian bride, Joseph relied on the one true God only.

B. Sons Named (vv. 51-52)

51. And Joseph called the name of the firstborn Manasseh: For God, said he, hath made me forget all my toil, and all my father's house.

Manasseh sounds like the Hebrew word meaning "forget" (example: Isaiah 44:21). *God* caused Joseph to forget the hard times that had characterized his life for the previous 13 years (compare Joseph's age in Genesis 37:2 with that recorded in 41:46). In relation to his *father's house*, this probably means that Joseph no longer held any grudges or ill will toward his brothers since he could begin to see those circumstances in a new light (see 45:4-8).

At the same time, it is clear that Joseph had not forgotten God, nor had God forgotten him. Though the name of his firstborn emphasizes forgetting, the name would also remind Joseph of what had been "forgotten" and ensure that it was not *really* lost to his memory.

52. And the name of the second called he Ephraim: For God hath caused me to be fruitful in the land of my affliction.

Ephraim sounds like a Hebrew word meaning

"twice fruitful" (compare Genesis 17:6). It probably reflects the fact that God had given Joseph two sons. The name likely praised God for the blessing that Joseph was experiencing in Egypt. Furthermore, the name may have celebrated the abundance of a land about to be hit by famine. This suggests once again that Joseph confidently trusted in God's provision during the lean times. Just as God has brought Joseph through *affliction* before, Joseph came to anticipate that God would bring him, his family, and all Egypt through a great famine.

The name Ephraim also seems to foreshadow the story of Jacob's family in Egypt for generations to come (see Genesis 47:27; Exodus 1:8-11; 3:7-10). God would not forget Jacob (Israel), just as God had not forgotten Joseph.

What Do You Think?

Do you agree with the statement that "the value of service someone renders to God is not just measured by how remarkable the end result is"? Why, or why not?

Digging Deeper

How should your response influence your service to Christ in the week ahead?

Joseph himself was given a new Egyptian name (Genesis 41:45; see commentary on 41:38) and, by implication, an Egyptian identity (compare Daniel 1:1-16). But he gave both of his sons Hebrew names (Genesis 41:51-52). Doing so acknowledged the presence and provision of the God of his (Hebrew) family in his life. It also emphasized that Joseph still thought about the family of his youth, apparently fondly enough to choose names in his native tongue.

From "Why?" to "What's Next?"

Ice-skater Nancy Kerrigan was set to compete in the 1994 U.S. Women's Championship. After a practice session, an assailant struck her knee with a police baton. Kerrigan was videotaped clutching her knee in pain and crying, "Why, why, why, why me?"

The events that placed Joseph in Egypt and the evils done to him as an innocent person gave him plenty of reasons to ask a bitter "Why?" He may have done so, but none is recorded. Instead, he seems to have replaced any *Why?* lament with a *What's next?* The result was to remain faithful to God.

Joseph's afflictions are a vital part of his story of triumph. So also are Kerrigan's, albeit on a much smaller scale. What about yours? When tragedy strikes, the natural tendency is to cry out "Why, why, why?" There's nothing wrong with that—for a time. But to get out of a holding pattern of despair, the *Why?* must eventually be replaced with *What's next?* In what regard is God calling you to do just that right now? —C. R. B.

Conclusion

A. Firm Faith on Strange Soil

The God whom Joseph served and honored is the God we serve and honor today. No matter the circumstance, He does not change (Malachi 3:6). He remains in control. Whether we find ourselves in a pit or a palace, He is there.

Joseph demonstrated radical faith in his God. Even though God might have seemed far away during the 13 years of slavery, God continued to give Joseph evidence that He had not forgotten the imprisoned man. How does your life witness to the same truth?

What Do You Think?

How useful is it for the Christian to attempt to determine what God "caused" versus what He "allowed" in the story of Joseph?

Digging Deeper

Which other Bible texts help you answer this question? Why?

B. Prayer

Father, help us be mindful that as You were with Joseph, so You are with us! Strengthen us to greater faithfulness. In Jesus' name. Amen.

C. Thought to Remember

Change is constant, but so is God's faithfulness.

Involvement Learning

Enhance your lesson with KJV Bible Student *(from your curriculum supplier) and the reproducible activity page (at www.standardlesson.com or in the back of the* KJV Standard Lesson Commentary Deluxe Edition*).*

Into the Lesson

Give each learner a large index card. Ask them to draw a graph of their lives, tracing major ups and downs. Allow one minute to complete the task, then form small groups of four or five for sharing their graphs, summarizing the ups and downs of their life experiences.

Alternative. Distribute copies of the "Storytelling" exercise from the activity page, which you can download. Have learners pair off and share their stories. Ask for volunteers to tell briefly their stories of someone whose faith helped them through a difficult time.

After either activity say, "Everyone's life has its ups and downs. This was especially true of Joseph. Let's see part of the result of his faithfulness."

Into the Word

Read aloud the lesson text of Genesis 41:25-33, 37-40, and 50-52. Focus on the last word of verse 52 as you ask, "What afflictions did Joseph endure while he was in Egypt?" (*Expected responses* include being enslaved, being falsely accused of attempted rape by Potiphar's wife and thrown into prison, and being forgotten by a fellow inmate whom he had helped.)

Continue to set the context by asking, "How did God make Joseph fruitful in the midst of his troubles? (*Expected responses include* being put in charge of Potiphar's household, being put in charge of the prison, and receiving revelations from God that resulted in release from prison.)

Invite learners to consider how Joseph's faithfulness shaped his character as Genesis 41:25-33, 37-40, and 50-52 is read aloud again, this time by three volunteers. Then divide the class into three groups. Assign each group one of the verse segments: 25-33, 37-40, and 50-52. Ask groups to identify fruit or character traits of Joseph in their assigned segment. After a few minutes reconvene for whole-class discussion.

Next, read John 15:4-8 (which is part of the text for lesson 10). Ask learners to consider what the fruits they have listed suggest about Joseph's relationship with God and what Joseph believed about Him. Explore the relationship between *the fruits* and *the roots* of Joseph's life in either whole-class or small-group discussion. Be prepared to offer your own conclusions in that regard.

Option. Ask, "Who are some other people in the Bible who went through hard times but came through it stronger because of their faith and faithfulness?" As learners mention names such as Job, Abraham, Jacob, Moses, Hannah, Elijah, Jeremiah, etc., jot those names on the board and ask for details.

Into Life

Distribute handouts (you prepare) that list helpful practices that learners may use in the week ahead to remind them of specific attributes of God. Also include a listing of such attributes. (*Examples:* God is good, trustworthy, patient, just, all-powerful, all-knowing, holy.) Further include at least one Scripture text with each attribute, along with these instructions: "Create a key phrase for each characteristic of God listed. Then incorporate those summaries into your devotional time this week."

Form small groups to discuss those key phrases. Have groups share those phrases in the ensuing whole-class discussion. Challenge learners each to (1) choose for prayer focus one key phrase that resonates with them and (2) will remind them daily in the week ahead of who God truly is and how they are to live. Remind learners that the goal is to grow deep roots in God as Joseph did. Discuss the relationship between deep and shallow roots as related to bearing fruit.

Option. Distribute copies of the "Your Life Tree" exercise from the activity page to complete as indicated. This can be a take-home activity.

September 20
Lesson 3 (KJV)

Victorious Love

Devotional Reading: Psalm 51
Background Scripture: Genesis 42

Genesis 42:6-25

6 And Joseph was the governor over the land, and he it was that sold to all the people of the land: and Joseph's brethren came, and bowed down themselves before him with their faces to the earth.

7 And Joseph saw his brethren, and he knew them, but made himself strange unto them, and spake roughly unto them; and he said unto them, Whence come ye? And they said, From the land of Canaan to buy food.

8 And Joseph knew his brethren, but they knew not him.

9 And Joseph remembered the dreams which he dreamed of them, and said unto them, Ye are spies; to see the nakedness of the land ye are come.

10 And they said unto him, Nay, my lord, but to buy food are thy servants come.

11 We are all one man's sons; we are true men, thy servants are no spies.

12 And he said unto them, Nay, but to see the nakedness of the land ye are come.

13 And they said, Thy servants are twelve brethren, the sons of one man in the land of Canaan; and, behold, the youngest is this day with our father, and one is not.

14 And Joseph said unto them, That is it that I spake unto you, saying, Ye are spies:

15 Hereby ye shall be proved: By the life of Pharaoh ye shall not go forth hence, except your youngest brother come hither.

16 Send one of you, and let him fetch your brother, and ye shall be kept in prison, that your words may be proved, whether there be any truth in you: or else by the life of Pharaoh surely ye are spies.

17 And he put them all together into ward three days.

18 And Joseph said unto them the third day, This do, and live; for I fear God:

19 If ye be true men, let one of your brethren be bound in the house of your prison: go ye, carry corn for the famine of your houses:

20 But bring your youngest brother unto me; so shall your words be verified, and ye shall not die. And they did so.

21 And they said one to another, We are verily guilty concerning our brother, in that we saw the anguish of his soul, when he besought us, and we would not hear; therefore is this distress come upon us.

22 And Reuben answered them, saying, Spake I not unto you, saying, Do not sin against the child; and ye would not hear? therefore, behold, also his blood is required.

23 And they knew not that Joseph understood them; for he spake unto them by an interpreter.

24 And he turned himself about from them, and wept; and returned to them again, and communed with them, and took from them Simeon, and bound him before their eyes.

25 Then Joseph commanded to fill their sacks with corn, and to restore every man's money into his sack, and to give them provision for the way: and thus did he unto them.

Key Verse

Reuben answered them, saying, Spake I not unto you, saying, Do not sin against the child; and ye would not hear? therefore, behold, also his blood is required. —**Genesis 42:22**

Love for One Another

Unit 1: Struggles with Love

Lessons 1–4

Lesson Aims

After participating in this lesson, each learner will be able to:

1. Outline the events that occurred when Joseph's brothers went to Egypt to buy grain.
2. Explain the possible motivations behind Joseph's treatment of his brothers.
3. Resolve an estrangement gracefully.

Lesson Outline

Introduction

A. Surprise Encounters

What's the best surprise you ever experienced? The announcement of a forthcoming grandchild? The renewed health of a loved one? A broken relationship repaired? For some, the answer will be an unexpected family reunion. Those who have been deployed for service overseas seem very happy to surprise their loved ones with an early return after a lengthy absence. Sometimes arrangements are made for the returnee to show up unexpectedly at a ball game or other public event where the person's family is in attendance.

The looks of astonishment and then unbridled joy are very touching. Though families expect that their loved ones will return eventually, their reactions reveal that the emotions of an anticipated reunion are magnified when that reunion happens without warning. Part of the joy in watching such a reunion is in seeing what happens when there hasn't been time to prepare psychologically for the reunion. And so it was with Joseph.

B. Lesson Context

When the Egyptians began to feel the effects of the predicted famine (see lesson 2), they cried out to Pharaoh for relief. Pharaoh sent them to Joseph (Genesis 41:55), whom he had appointed to prepare Egypt for the years of famine. The famine, however, affected lands other than Egypt as well. As a result, "all countries" came to Egypt to buy food (41:57). Joseph's homeland was among those, and Jacob urged his sons to travel to Egypt and purchase food (42:1-2). Exactly how much of the seven-year famine had occurred before the brothers went to Egypt is not clear. Later, when Joseph revealed his identity (see lesson 4), he told them that only two of seven total years had passed (45:6).

For the first journey to Egypt, Jacob did not permit Benjamin—one of two sons of Jacob's beloved wife Rachel, the other son being Joseph (Genesis 35:24)—to go. Jacob had already lost his favorite son, Joseph; Jacob did not want to risk losing his second favorite, Benjamin (42:3-4). Thus 10 brothers traveled to Egypt without him.

I. Doubt

(Genesis 42:6-17)

A. Brothers' Arrival (vv. 6-8)

6a. And Joseph was the governor over the land, and he it was that sold to all the people of the land.

Joseph had been appointed as *governor* and second in command to Pharaoh after his proposal for how to prepare Egypt for the coming years of famine (Genesis 41:33-43; see lesson 2). His tasks of preparation for the famine were complete; now the tasks of distributing aid were his primary responsibility. At this point, *the people* still had enough money to purchase the food that they needed (contrast 47:13-26).

6b. And Joseph's brethren came, and bowed down themselves before him with their faces to the earth.

Showing respect for a foreign dignitary, the brothers *bowed* appropriately *before* Joseph. This almost fulfills Joseph's dream of some two decades earlier recorded in Genesis 37:9. We say *almost* because only 10 of the 11 "stars" (brothers) were doing the bowing at this point.

7-8. And Joseph saw his brethren, and he knew them, but made himself strange unto them, and spake roughly unto them; and he said unto them, Whence come ye? And they said, From the land of Canaan to buy food. And Joseph knew his brethren, but they knew not him.

Joseph recognized his brothers immediately, even though about 20 years had passed since he last saw them (compare Genesis 37:2 and 41:46; see lesson 2). One can only imagine the look on Joseph's face at this surprise encounter! Perhaps he had thought he would never see them again. But there they were! How should he treat them? What should he say? The recognition is not two-way, however, as indicated by the phrase *but they knew him not*. Contributing factors are Joseph's Egyptian clothing and a closely trimmed beard in keeping with Egyptian custom (compare 41:14). Above all, none of the brothers expected to encounter Joseph *anywhere,* let alone in the position of governor of Egypt!

Joseph had probably pondered on many a day how he would respond to his brothers if he ever saw them again. As he spoke *roughly*, or with a tone of harshness and severity, Joseph may have been buying time to ponder his forthcoming "big reveal" in more depth.

B. Joseph's Accusation (vv. 9-14)

9a. And Joseph remembered the dreams which he dreamed of them.

Seeing his brothers bow to him brought back to Joseph's memory his *dreams* of authority in his family (Genesis 37:5-10; see lesson 1). He surely must also have remembered how much his brothers despised him on account of those dreams (37:8, 11). Ironically, their actions to prevent any ascent to power on Joseph's part had done the opposite in contributing directly to his current status. Human nature suggests that there may have been some sense of satisfaction on Joseph's part when he *remembered* his dreams while his brothers bowed before him.

9b. And said unto them, Ye are spies; to see the nakedness of the land ye are come.

Why the memory of his dreams caused Joseph to accuse his brothers of something he knew was false is unclear, but there are some theories. One suggestion is that even though we wouldn't call this revenge, Joseph can't resist making his brothers squirm a bit. Another theory is that Joseph uses the line of interrogation we see here to test his brothers' character. Have they improved any in the two decades since selling him into slavery?

The accusation has a ring of believability. Coming to spy under the guise of buying food is quite plausible: buying food would take resources from the nation while also providing a cover story as the brothers scout out Egypt's *nakedness*—places vulnerable to attack by an enemy. Though a payback

HOW TO SAY IT

Canaan	*Kay*-nun.
Pharaoh	*Fair*-o or *Fay*-roe.
Reuben	*Roo*-ben.
Simeon	*Sim*-ee-un.
Zaphnathpaaneah	***Zaf***-nath-*pay*-uh-nee-uh.

or revenge motive seems reasonable from a purely human standpoint, Joseph's true motivation seems to have been more noble than that. The longer he could hide his identity behind a mask of harshness, the more likely it was to elicit truthful statements from his brothers.

> *What Do You Think?*
>
> When someone claims to be honest (Genesis 42:11) but we know of previous dishonesty (37:31-32), what kinds of tests, if any, are legitimate to evaluate reform?
>
> *Digging Deeper*
>
> How do passages such as 2 Corinthians 8:8; Galatians 6:4-5; and 1 Thessalonians 5:20-22 influence your conclusions?

Joseph surely noticed that Benjamin, his younger brother and the other son of their mother, Rachel, was absent from the group of brothers. He must have wondered if Benjamin was dead. And what about their father, Jacob? It is also possible that Joseph desired to find out more about his brothers. Did they still despise him after all these years? Had they repented of their treatment of him?

10. And they said unto him, Nay, my lord, but to buy food are thy servants come.

Modern interrogation practice is to interview suspects separately to see if their stories match. But Joseph knows most of the important parts of the story already! His accusation seems to have been intended to put his brothers on the defensive. If so, the desired effect is achieved.

11. We are all one man's sons; we are true men, thy servants are no spies.

Joseph may well have found dark humor in the claim of his brothers to be *true men,* even though he doesn't yet know that they lied to his father regarding Joseph's fate (Genesis 37:31-34).

12. And he said unto them, Nay, but to see the nakedness of the land ye are come.

Joseph continued in accusation mode. People under stress may make unguarded comments. We may speculate that Joseph hoped that his brothers would do just that, revealing in the process important family information.

13. And they said, Thy servants are twelve brethren, the sons of one man in the land of Canaan; and, behold, the youngest is this day with our father, and one is not.

In their hasty denials, the brothers reveal several pieces of information that Joseph could immediately verify as true. Therefore he had no reason to doubt the parts he could not verify: both his *father,* Jacob, and his *youngest* brother, Benjamin, were still alive.

14. And Joseph said unto them, That is it that I spake unto you, saying, Ye are spies.

Still *Joseph* challenged the men's truthfulness with a terrifying accusation of spying. How could they prove their innocence if this powerful man was convinced of their guilt?

Trust, but Verify

The Cold War was a worldwide concern in the 1980s. The importance of having nuclear arms agreements could not be overstated. As US President Reagan was preparing to meet with U.S.S.R. General Secretary Gorbachev, an adviser informed Reagan of Russians' love of proverbs. Perhaps learning a few would help aid the negotiations.

Doveryai, no proveryai—"trust, but verify"—caught Reagan's fancy. It expressed the tension of believing in good faith what one was told while also doing the research to corroborate statements. To Reagan, it expressed well the American attitude toward Soviet assurances.

Before Joseph could trust his brothers, he needed to verify their character. How well does Joseph's "trust, but verify" method work as a Christian principle? —C. R. B.

C. Joseph's Alternative (vv. 15-17)

15-16. Hereby ye shall be proved: By the life of Pharaoh ye shall not go forth hence, except your youngest brother come hither. Send one of you, and let him fetch your brother, and ye shall be kept in prison, that your words may be proved, whether there be any truth in you: or else by the life of Pharaoh surely ye are spies.

Joseph gave the men what seemed to them to be a chance to prove that they were who they claimed. But Joseph already knew they were telling the *truth*. His agenda was therefore different from what it seemed to be to the brothers, an agenda that becomes clearer as the story unfolds.

Perhaps to emphasize how serious he was, Joseph swore twice *by the life of Pharaoh*. The ruse of pretending to be thoroughly Egyptian continued.

17. And he put them all together into ward three days.

Why this three-day "time out"? It may have been a tactic to emphasize Joseph's power to impose his will. Alternatively, it could have been that Joseph needed more time to consider how best to convince his brothers it was necessary to bring Benjamin to him.

II. Decision

(Genesis 42:18-25)

A. Joseph's Requirement (vv. 18-20)

18. And Joseph said unto them the third day, This do, and live; for I fear God.

On *the third day*, apparently after more thought, Joseph was ready to dictate a different set of conditions. Before revealing his new plan, however, Joseph gave the rationale for his decision: his *fear* of *God*.

From our viewpoint, Joseph clearly referred to his fear of the God of Abraham, Isaac, and Jacob (Genesis 32:9; 50:24; see also Exodus 3:6). Such a statement might have tipped his brothers off that something was different about this Egyptian governor. However, his brothers should be excused for not understanding what Joseph was asserting. For one thing, the name used to refer to God is a plural word that often refers to the true God (over 1,000 times in the Old Testament) but can also refer generically to supernatural beings who may be mistaken for gods (example: Psalm 82:1).

Though God could be differentiated from false gods easily by identifying Him as the Creator and the God of Abraham, Isaac, and Jacob, He has not yet revealed His name (Exodus 3:14-15). So context could cause the brothers to think that Joseph feared *some* god, but which *one* remained a mystery.

To further muddle the situation, Joseph looked

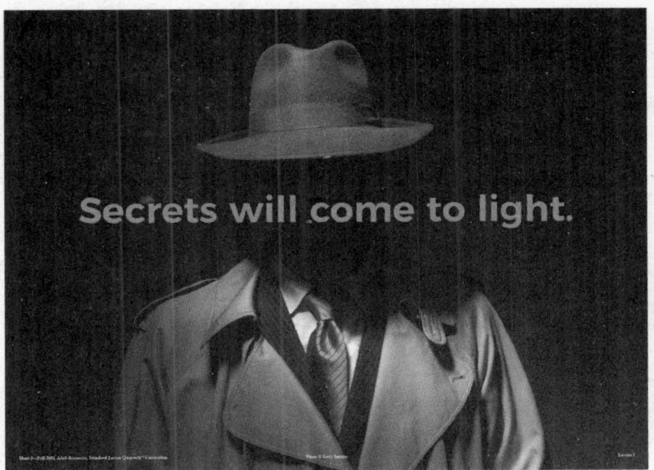

Visual for Lesson 3. *Ask the class if the text of this visual is more reassuring or unnerving. Offer a short prayer for patience and repentance as needed.*

Egyptian, had an Egyptian name (Zaphnath-paaneah; Genesis 41:45), and was married to the daughter of the priest of Ra (41:50; see lesson 2). Joseph's brothers probably assumed Zaphnath-paaneah worshipped Ra and other Egyptian gods.

19. If ye be true men, let one of your brethren be bound in the house of your prison: go ye, carry corn for the famine of your houses.

Only *one* brother rather than nine would be required to stay in Egypt as a ransom; the others would *carry corn* (and Joseph's orders) back to Canaan. The Hebrew word translated *corn* is a general term for grain since maize as we know it probably doesn't exist in the Egypt of Joseph's day.

20a. But bring your youngest brother unto me; so shall your words be verified, and ye shall not die.

Joseph did not tell them when to come back, only that they must bring the *youngest brother* with them. Judging from Joseph's words, the punishment for espionage was death.

20b. And they did so.

The following verse continues as though this sentence never happened. This represents a significant jump in the narrative (see Genesis 43:1-16).

B. Brothers' Remorse (vv. 21-23)

21a. And they said one to another, We are verily guilty concerning our brother, in that we saw the anguish of his soul, when he besought us, and we would not hear.

Though the biblical account does not mention Joseph's *anguish* at the time (Genesis 37:26-28), we are unsurprised to learn that Joseph's suffering was evident to his brothers. So intense was their hatred and contempt that Joseph's cries for mercy went willfully unheard.

Yet, those cries echoed back to them in this moment, confirming their *guilt* and heralding that punishment was finally at hand for their crime (or so they believed). It is striking that these 10 men were blaming themselves for the death of the man who was standing before them!

What Do You Think?

Without giving directive advice, how would you counsel someone who seems to be mentally enslaved by guilt of a past misdeed?

Digging Deeper

How would your counseling differ between a believer and an unbeliever? Why?

21b. Therefore is this distress come upon us.

The brothers believed that when one encountered *distress* or troubles, it was a punishment for some previous wrongdoing. That thinking is reflected throughout the Bible (examples: Job 11:13-18; John 9:1-2). We may still feel that our struggles are God's judgment on us for our past sins. But, like the brothers, we see only part of each story and should be wary of interpreting too confidently God's intentions in any situation.

Ironically, this trouble *has* visited them because of Joseph—not as punishment but because God has worked through their sin to save them (Genesis 45:5, 7-8; see lesson 4). Though the brothers believe God is punishing them, in fact He is about to deliver their whole family from famine.

What Do You Think?

In what ways do you see God advancing his plan in spite of the character flaws of those who carry out that plan?

Digging Deeper

Who can you choose as an accountability partner to help you identify and overcome your own character flaws?

22. And Reuben answered them, saying, Spake I not unto you, saying, Do not sin against the child; and ye would not hear? therefore, behold, also his blood is required.

Reuben is Jacob's firstborn (Genesis 49:3). Before this moment, Joseph knew nothing of what Reuben had said in his defense (37:21-23). Reuben's statement that Joseph's *blood is required* confirmed that he believed Joseph had died and that he considered all of the brothers present to be guilty of that death.

What Do You Think?

Under what kinds of modern circumstances, if any, is "I told you so" adequate to let someone off the hook for failing to oppose a wrong more strongly? Why?

Digging Deeper

Discuss the concept of "the lesser of two evils" in light of this question.

23. And they knew not that Joseph understood them; for he spake unto them by an interpreter.

Because of Joseph's cunning use of *an interpreter*, the brothers have been speaking frankly before him without realizing he could understand their "private" conversation. For long years, he must have wondered whether they felt any guilt or remorse for their actions against him. Though he had clearly found great purpose in his Egyptian life, part of Joseph wanted to know if his brothers had ever overcome their hatred of him.

C. Joseph's Reaction (vv. 24-25a)

24a. And he turned himself about from them, and wept,

Joseph was not prepared for what he heard. The brothers' words of remorse, coupled with Reuben's personal expression of regret, proved more than Joseph could handle.

Big Boys Don't Cry

It is sometimes said that "big boys don't cry." To whatever extent this is true, it is (excuse the pun) a crying shame. Tears help express and even expel strong emotions, especially painful ones.

For me, losing my first wife has been the cause of many tears. Pat, my wife of 58 years, succumbed to cancer more than 6 years ago.

Even now, there are still occasions when a tender memory catches me off guard, and I find myself choking up, unable to express my feelings except through tears. Unexpectedly hearing a song we shared, or finding an object that belonged to her, makes me cry.

For Joseph, the strong leader of Egypt, hearing remorse was a crying moment. Can character be evaluated by what brings a person to tears and what doesn't? —C. R. B.

24b. And returned to them again, and communed with them, and took from them Simeon, and bound him before their eyes.

After composing himself, Joseph probably voiced again the terms necessary for safe return to Egypt (Genesis 42:19-20). Joseph imprisoned *Simeon* as a surety until the brothers returned with the youngest one.

Joseph probably had meant to detain the oldest son, Reuben, due to his status as firstborn son, but changed his mind after hearing Reuben's confession. *Simeon* is the second oldest of Jacob's sons (Genesis 29:32-33).

25. Then Joseph commanded to fill their sacks with corn, and to restore every man's money into his sack, and to give them provision for the way: and thus did he unto them.

Before sending his brothers back to Canaan, Joseph took certain calculated steps. Because it was within his authority to set prices for *corn*, Joseph decided to send the food back with his brothers at no charge. But he refunded their *money* without telling them.

This strategy served Joseph in at least two ways. First, he blessed his brothers by not accepting their payment, thus allowing that money to be used for other purposes as necessary.

Second, by not telling them what he would do, Joseph's actions made them fear God (Genesis 42:28). Would the governor see them as thieves as well as spies? Was this finally God's plan to punish them for Joseph's death? How much worse could things get?

Conclusion

A. The Importance of Tears

Joseph had settled into life in Egypt, secure in his powerful position. He had married and started a family. He had taken over the responsibility of providing grain for those who had traveled from near and far to Egypt because of the severe famine that had ravaged many countries. It was business as usual for Joseph until he looked up and saw a group of 10 men dressed like he used to be when he lived in Canaan. And then he realized—these were his brothers! They too had come to Egypt to buy grain.

That Joseph's motives for acting as he did toward his brothers were not rooted in selfishness or vindictiveness is seen most of all in his tears. He could not control his emotions when he learned that Reuben had actually intended to spare his life. Though the brothers did not know it, the governor of Egypt was already planning how to see his father again and keep his whole family safe.

What Do You Think?

What guardrails can we erect to keep from crossing the line between legitimate testing (evaluation) and desire for revenge?

Digging Deeper

Where in Scripture, if anywhere, do you see that line being crossed?

While Joseph was hiding his true identity from his brothers, his declaration that "I fear God" was the truth. The brothers did not realize what a comfort that declaration should have been to them. Joseph's tears revealed his heart for all time.

B. Prayer

Our Father, thank You that You use even our most desperate circumstances to serve Your loving purposes. Let our fear of You guide us as Joseph's fear guided him. We pray in Jesus' name, amen.

C. Thought to Remember

Fear of God
must guide our decisions.

Involvement Learning

Enhance your lesson with KJV Bible Student *(from your curriculum supplier) and the reproducible activity page (at www.standardlesson.com or in the back of the* KJV Standard Lesson Commentary Deluxe Edition*).*

Into the Lesson

As learners arrive, have this question written on the board:

What are some of the tensions regarding revenge that you have seen in movies?

Encourage learners to share examples; allow time for open discussion.

Alternative. Distribute copies of the "Movie Plot: Revenge Is Mine!" exercise from the activity page, which you can download. Divide the class into groups to complete as indicated. After 10 minutes or so, have groups share results.

After either activity, share a story of a time when you entertained thoughts of revenge against a family member. Say, "I am sure many if not all of us have our own revenge stories, whether of revenge merely pondered or actually carried out. Let's see how one servant of God dealt with this same temptation."

Into the Word

Give each learner a handout (you prepare) on which is printed a variety of emoji. As a minimum, have emoji depicting anger, surprise, horror, laughter, skepticism, embarrassment, disbelief, guilt, deviousness, cluelessness, and boredom. (*Option.* Depending on the nature of your class, the handout may or may not feature definitions alongside the emoji.) Have these instructions printed at the top of the handout: "As you hear Genesis 42:6-25 read, match emoji with verses. Each emoji can be used once, more than once, or not at all. And each verse can take more than one emoji."

Before the reading, pause to evaluate the class for comprehension. If learners seem to need further explanation, suggest one or more of the following matches: regarding verse 6: cluelessness emoji for the brothers; regarding verse 7: surprise emoji for Joseph.

Have learners make their emoji matches while you read Genesis 42:6-25 slowly. After you have finished, lead a discussion that compares and contrasts learners' results. (*Option.* Have learners do this in pairs or triads.)

Wrap up the discussion by asking, "In what ways can decisions about taking revenge poison one's future?" Encourage open discussion.

Option. Split the class in half and give each group copies of the "Be It Resolved . . ." exercise from the activity page. Conduct the indicated debate after groups develop their arguments. (*Alternative.* Use an informal point/counterpoint format instead.)

Make a transition by focusing on Genesis 42:24-25 as you ask how strong emotions can influence one's decision to take or not take revenge.

Into Life

Lead a discussion on how past misdeeds (both as perpetrator and victim) can be emotionally and relationally poisonous. Ask for examples without names; jot responses on the board as they are mentioned. Focus on one as you distribute to study pairs handouts (you prepare) on which are printed the following statements:

1–If acting in revenge, the following could happen: ________________.

2–If we were to act in love, the following could happen: ________________.

After a few minutes, reconvene for the whole class to compare and contrast the responses.

Write the text of Romans 12:19 on the board. Have learners read it aloud in unison. Distribute index cards on which learners can copy this text. Challenge them to post it in a place where they will see it several times daily in the week ahead. State that the first thing the class will do when reconvening next week is recalling the text aloud in unison as learners have memorized it.

September 27
Lesson 4 (KJV)

Revealed Love

Devotional Reading: John 14:1-14
Background Scripture: Genesis 43; 45:1-15

Genesis 45:1-8, 10-15

1 Then Joseph could not refrain himself before all them that stood by him; and he cried, Cause every man to go out from me. And there stood no man with him, while Joseph made himself known unto his brethren.

2 And he wept aloud: and the Egyptians and the house of Pharaoh heard.

3 And Joseph said unto his brethren, I am Joseph; doth my father yet live? And his brethren could not answer him; for they were troubled at his presence.

4 And Joseph said unto his brethren, Come near to me, I pray you. And they came near. And he said, I am Joseph your brother, whom ye sold into Egypt.

5 Now therefore be not grieved, nor angry with yourselves, that ye sold me hither: for God did send me before you to preserve life.

6 For these two years hath the famine been in the land: and yet there are five years, in the which there shall neither be earing nor harvest.

7 And God sent me before you to preserve you a posterity in the earth, and to save your lives by a great deliverance.

8 So now it was not you that sent me hither, but God: and he hath made me a father to Pharaoh, and lord of all his house, and a ruler throughout all the land of Egypt.

. . . .

10 And thou shalt dwell in the land of Goshen, and thou shalt be near unto me, thou, and thy children, and thy children's children, and thy flocks, and thy herds, and all that thou hast:

11 And there will I nourish thee; for yet there are five years of famine; lest thou, and thy household, and all that thou hast, come to poverty.

12 And, behold, your eyes see, and the eyes of my brother Benjamin, that it is my mouth that speaketh unto you.

13 And ye shall tell my father of all my glory in Egypt, and of all that ye have seen; and ye shall haste and bring down my father hither.

14 And he fell upon his brother Benjamin's neck, and wept; and Benjamin wept upon his neck.

15 Moreover he kissed all his brethren, and wept upon them: and after that his brethren talked with him.

Key Verse

Be not grieved, nor angry with yourselves, that ye sold me hither: for God did send me before you to preserve life. —**Genesis 45:5**

LOVE FOR ONE ANOTHER

Unit 1: Struggles with Love

LESSONS 1–4

LESSON AIMS

After participating in this lesson, each learner will be able to:

1. Recount the occasion on which Joseph revealed his identity to his brothers.

2. Explain the importance of Joseph's understanding of God's plan when seeking to reassure his brothers.

3. Plan and implement best steps and actions in modeling love and forgiveness.

LESSON OUTLINE

Introduction
- A. "[Luke,] I am your . . ."
- B. Lesson Context

I. Revealing Identity (Genesis 45:1-8)
- A. Privacy Demanded (vv. 1-2)
- B. Truth Acknowledged (v. 3)
- C. Brothers Assured (vv. 4-8)
  - *Dealing with a Guilty Conscience*

II. Relaying Instructions (Genesis 45:10-13)
- A. To Come to Egypt (vv. 10-11)
- B. To Confirm His Identity (v. 12)
- C. To Convince His Father (v. 13)
  - *"A Picture Is Worth..."*

III. Reaching Out in Love (Genesis 45:14-15)
- A. To Benjamin (v. 14)
- B. To His Brothers (v. 15)

Conclusion
- A. "Don't Be Angry with Yourselves"
- B. Prayer
- C. Thought to Remember

Introduction

A. "[Luke,] I am your . . ."

How does that sentence end? In the Western world, even people who haven't seen any of the *Star Wars* movies probably know to fill in "father." Yet Darth Vader shows Luke Skywalker no love; he shows his son no mercy. They are mortal enemies, and it becomes clear that one of them must die. This fact becomes all the more tragic because Luke didn't know the truth about his parentage until Episode V (the second movie of the original trilogy). Darth Vader's also being Dad did nothing to weaken the enmity with Luke. It only complicated it, made it all the sadder because of the truth it reveals: our families are sometimes the origin of our greatest enemies.

Joseph had experienced just that. At the root of all his struggles in Egypt were those who had sent him to that place to begin with: his brothers. So like Darth Vader (in this one respect), Joseph hid his identity. Yet the revelation of Joseph's true identity had quite a different outcome from that of Darth Vader's revelation.

B. Lesson Context

Lesson 3 covered the first trip that Joseph's brothers made to Egypt without Benjamin (Genesis 42:6-25). Though they returned with food, it inevitably ran out, and the brothers were faced with traveling to Egypt again. But they knew they could not return without Benjamin. Jacob, however, was still very reluctant to allow Benjamin to go. Finally, after Judah guaranteed Benjamin's safety and offered to bear the blame should Benjamin not return, Jacob relented (43:1-14).

When the brothers arrived in Egypt, they first spoke to Joseph's steward about the silver they had found in their sacks. He assured them all was well (Genesis 43:19-23a). Later, after Joseph released Simeon (43:23b) and fed the brothers a meal (43:31-34), he sent them back to Canaan with more supplies. But he also instructed his steward to place each man's silver in his sack and, in addition, to put Joseph's special silver cup in Benjamin's sack (44:1-2).

Following the brothers' departure, Joseph sent

his steward to catch up with the men and accuse them of taking Joseph's cup. When the cup was discovered in Benjamin's sack of grain, the brothers tore their clothing in despair and returned to Egypt to face Joseph (Genesis 44:3-13).

After Joseph told his brothers that Benjamin would have to remain in Egypt, Judah stepped forward and voiced an impassioned plea not to keep Benjamin in Egypt. Such an action would break his father Jacob's heart to the point of hastening his death. Judah offered himself in place of Benjamin (Genesis 44:17-34). This act represented a drastic departure from the way Judah had treated Joseph those many years before (37:26-27).

I. Revealing Identity

(Genesis 45:1-8)

A. Privacy Demanded (vv. 1-2)

1. Then Joseph could not refrain himself before all them that stood by him; and he cried, Cause every man to go out from me. And there stood no man with him, while Joseph made himself known unto his brethren.

At this point, it appears that *Joseph* had finally gathered enough evidence to be confident his brothers were not the scoundrels they once were (see lesson 3). Listening to Judah's heartfelt plea not to keep Benjamin in Egypt and his offer to take Benjamin's place was more than Joseph could take (see Lesson Context).

Joseph demanded that all his servants and attendants leave the room. Perhaps this was because the reunion was so emotional for Joseph that he didn't want anyone other than his brothers to witness his breakdown. Or maybe he wanted to be able to speak openly without letting his Egyptian household know immediately everything that would be told.

HOW TO SAY IT

Canaan	*Kay*-nun.
Egyptians	Ee-*jip*-shuns.
Goshen	*Go*-shen.
Pentecost	*Pent*-ih-kost.
Pharaoh	*Fair*-o or *Fay*-roe.

What Do You Think?

Under what circumstances, if any, could a masquerade like Joseph's be justified today, given God's hatred of lying (Exodus 20:16; Proverbs 6:16-17)?

Digging Deeper

How do the deceptions of Joshua 2:1-7; 8:3-14; Judges 7:15-21; and/or 1 Samuel 21:10-15 help frame your conclusions?

2. And he wept aloud: and the Egyptians and the house of Pharaoh heard.

Joseph had been moved to tears on two occasions prior to this one (Genesis 42:24; 43:30), but at this moment his emotions were fully released. *The house of Pharaoh* must have wondered why they *heard* such intense weeping.

B. Truth Acknowledged (v. 3)

3a. And Joseph said unto his brethren, I am Joseph.

We easily imagine the emotional shock wave that rippled through the room as the brothers heard this high Egyptian official claim, in their native tongue, to be their long-absent brother. Up to this point, Joseph had been conversing through an interpreter (Genesis 42:23). The brothers must have found the statement incredible, even unbelievable. Yet who other than *Joseph* himself would say such a thing to them—and in Hebrew no less?

3b. Doth my father yet live?

The brothers had no time to digest the shocking news before Joseph inquired as to the welfare of his *father*. Not long before this, the brothers had reported that Jacob was "in good health" (Genesis 43:28). Perhaps Joseph thought the brothers were simply being polite, not wanting to tell a powerful governor the truth of any family difficulties.

3c. And his brethren could not answer him; for they were troubled at his presence.

The brothers had been stunned into silence. They seem to have assumed Joseph to be dead, given their statements in Genesis 42:13, 32. When we do the math from the time references in Genesis 37:2; 41:29-30, 46, 53-54; and 45:6 (below), we conclude that what Joseph revealed had been some 22 years in the making. That's how long it had been since the brothers sold him into slavery at age 17. So Joseph was now about age 39.

Furthermore, the brother they had mistreated was now in a position of enormous power. He could throw them all into prison (which he seemed quite willing to do; Genesis 42:16). Or he could starve them by withholding aid. Would Joseph take revenge for mistreating him?

C. Brothers Assured (vv. 4-8)

4. And Joseph said unto his brethren, Come near to me, I pray you. And they came near. And he said, I am Joseph your brother, whom ye sold into Egypt.

The brothers were probably standing at a respectful distance from the governor of Egypt before *Joseph* called them forward. They may have even stepped backward in fear on hearing this man's incredible claim. Joseph's reference to their cruel deed bolstered his claim further.

5. Now therefore be not grieved, nor angry with yourselves, that ye sold me hither: for God did send me before you to preserve life.

Joseph had heard his brothers' remorse over what they did to him (Genesis 42:21-22; 44:18-34). But they didn't need to harbor negative feelings or bear a burden of guilt any longer. What had happened to Joseph was being used of *God . . .to preserve* the lives of untold numbers of people via Joseph's preparation for the famine that was underway. Like Esther in Persia hundreds of years later, Joseph had come to his position in Egypt "for such a time as this" (Esther 4:14).

The verse before us offers the first of three declarations by Joseph that God's sovereign hand had been carefully guiding all that had happened to him (see Genesis 45:7-8 and commentary below). God's work redeemed Joseph's sale into slavery and his experiences in Egypt. The brothers were indeed culpable for Joseph's servitude in Egypt, and the Ishmeelites really had brought him there. But Joseph had come to understand that God had used these circumstances for His own good purposes. In that way, it was as though God himself, not the jealous brothers, *did send* Joseph.

Joseph's conclusions were undergirded by his experience with divinely given dreams and the ability to interpret them (lessons 1–3). In one sense, Joseph is simply stating Romans 8:28 in his own way: "We know that all things work together for good to them that love God, to them who are the called according to his purpose."

Joseph's words to his brothers can be applied to our understanding and acceptance of the forgiveness Jesus offers. So often the issue with which we wrestle is not that of accepting Jesus' forgiveness; rather, it's in accepting that we have been forgiven. We continue to beat ourselves up over the sins we've committed and the mistakes we've made. Such an attitude smothers any sense of joy or peace in having been forgiven—blessings that are among the many promised to followers of Jesus.

Dealing with a Guilty Conscience

Most of us can speak from experience about the pain of a loved one's hurtful, impulsive actions or even a cruel pattern of behavior. Perhaps we are even willing to admit the times we have been the ones who hurt others.

It's important for transgressors to confess and repent of what they have done. It's also important for the repentant to realize and accept the fact that they have been forgiven. Looking ahead to Genesis 50:15 gives us a glimpse of how heavily the troubled consciences of Joseph's brothers continued to weigh on them after Joseph's kind words in our text.

Yet this reconciliation story doesn't focus on the sins of Joseph's brothers or even their remorse. Instead, the story highlights Joseph's response. That response suggests that God may be as interested in the conscience of the victim as He is in the conscience of the perpetrator. What's your conscience saying to you right now? —C. R. B.

6. For these two years hath the famine been in the land: and yet there are five years, in the which there shall neither be earing nor harvest.

Joseph continued by placing events on a time line of sorts. The bottom line was that things would get worse before they got better. Over the coming *five years*, agricultural activity would remain at a standstill. The desperation of famine would continue to be the case in many places, including Canaan. *Earing* means "to plow" (compare Exodus 34:21)

7. And God sent me before you to preserve you a posterity in the earth, and to save your lives by a great deliverance.

For the second time, Joseph stated his conviction that *God sent* him to Egypt (see commentary on Genesis 45:5, above). Despite the brothers' intent to do away with Joseph and his dreams, God's sovereign plan was being fulfilled. God's purpose in protecting Jacob's family is in keeping with His promises to Abraham (Genesis 12:1-3; 17:1-8). Joseph's declaration indicated that there would be difficult times ahead but not total destruction.

> *What Do You Think?*
> What are some ways, if any, to distinguish between what God "allows" versus what He "causes" today?
>
> *Digging Deeper*
> What dangers attend to claiming to be able to make that distinction? Why?

The manner in which Joseph treated his brothers is similar to how Jesus treats us by way of His death on the cross for our sins. We need not be troubled at His presence (see commentary on Genesis 45:3c, above) even though He has every right to condemn us. He is willing to forgive. This was the attitude of Joseph, both at this occasion and later following the death of Jacob (50:15-21).

8. So now it was not you that sent me hither, but God: and he hath made me a father to Pharaoh, and lord of all his house, and a ruler throughout all the land of Egypt.

For a third time Joseph emphasized that the brothers were not the ones who ultimately put him in Egypt (see Genesis 45:5, 7, above). *God* had *sent* him there. Joseph had entered the land as a slave to end up in a position of great authority within Pharaoh's household and *throughout all the land of Egypt*. God is able to work through wrong attitudes and actions, and this is one example of that fact.

That Joseph referred to himself as *a father to Pharaoh* is in keeping with usage of the word *father* in ancient times to describe someone who served as an adviser to another (perhaps in giving what would be considered "fatherly advice"; compare Job 29:16). The image may also reflect Joseph's role as a fatherly provider for Egypt during a time of great need.

> *What Do You Think?*
> How can we ensure that God has sanctioned someone as a leader today? Or is that even possible? Why do you say that?
>
> *Digging Deeper*
> How do passages such as Romans 14:16-18; 1 Corinthians 11:17-19; Galatians 1:10; 1 Thessalonians 2:4; and 2 Timothy 2:15 influence your answer?

II. Relaying Instructions
(Genesis 45:10-13)

A. To Come to Egypt (vv. 10-11)

10. And thou shalt dwell in the land of Goshen, and thou shalt be near unto me, thou, and thy children, and thy children's children, and thy flocks, and thy herds, and all that thou hast.

Verse 9, not in our printed text, records Joseph's plea to the brothers to return quickly to Canaan and convey a message to his father, Jacob. Joseph's message began with the statement that God had made him "lord of all Egypt" (Genesis 45:9) to urge Jacob to come at once to Egypt. In this way, Joseph provided an enduring example by giving credit to God for the things that have happened. Joseph might have been good-looking (39:6), intelligent, capable, and powerful, but he knew that it is God who deserved the glory.

It would not be easy for Jacob to leave the land of Canaan, since his grandfather Abraham migrated there over 200 years prior. Joseph made the new situation more attractive by telling them that they were to settle in *Goshen.* This is the first mention of Goshen in the Bible. It was located in the northeastern section of the Nile River's delta, which is a series of tributaries resembling a fan as they appear on a map. Goshen was a very fertile region, excellent for grazing and for growing crops. It would be more than adequate for the numbers of *flocks* and *herds* that Jacob and his family possessed. The entire family would have plenty of room to reside.

Joseph had been separated from his beloved father, Jacob, for more than 20 years (see commentary on verse 3c, above). He eagerly anticipated Jacob's being *near* him after such a long time. Joseph's hopes ended up being fulfilled (see Genesis 45:25–46:30).

What Do You Think?

Under what circumstances, if any, should Christians sequester themselves and live apart from the larger unbelieving society? Why?

Digging Deeper

How do passages such as Matthew 28:19-20; 1 Corinthians 5:9-10; 10:27; and 1 John 2:15 help frame your conclusions?

11. And there will I nourish thee; for yet there are five years of famine; lest thou, and thy household, and all that thou hast, come to poverty.

Joseph promised to take care of both Jacob and his *household* through the duration of the coming *five years of famine*. This would save them the trips back and forth for the remainder of the famine and deliver Jacob from living his final years in *poverty* and perhaps dying as a result.

B. To Confirm His Identity (v. 12)

12. And, behold, your eyes see, and the eyes of my brother Benjamin, that it is my mouth that speaketh unto you.

Joseph resumed addressing his brothers directly. In a manner similar to how the risen Christ would reassure His disciples that He really was standing before them (Luke 24:39), Joseph told his brothers to believe what they were seeing.

If they could not believe their *eyes*, they should believe their ears. Joseph had spoken to his brothers in their native Hebrew tongue, without need for his interpreter (Genesis 42:23). The specific mention of *Benjamin*—who was Joseph's only full *brother* of the 11, by Jacob's wife Rachel (46:19)—reveals the closeness that Joseph still felt toward him (see commentary on 45:14, below).

C. To Convince His Father (v. 13)

13. And ye shall tell my father of all my glory in Egypt, and of all that ye have seen; and ye shall haste and bring down my father hither.

Joseph wanted Jacob to know that, far from being "rent in pieces" (Genesis 37:33), Joseph had risen in *glory*, or to an esteemed position, *in Egypt*. The brothers were to report *all that* they had *seen* in order to verify that what they said of Joseph was true. Joseph again urged them to *bring* Jacob to Egypt as quickly as possible (45:9). There was no time to waste!

The "great deliverance" (Genesis 45:7, above) that was being accomplished by God would foreshadow the greater deliverance that He later brought about under Moses (Exodus 12:31-36). Ironically, the migration of Joseph's extended family to Egypt was to set the stage for that event (1:1-14; 2:23-25).

"A Picture Is Worth . . ."

I have a picture taken more than 30 years ago at a family reunion. On that occasion my grandmother was celebrating her 96th birthday. That picture shows Grandma, my father, me, my daughter, and her first child—all five generations of us in one photo!

I could tell so many stories about the occasion and of each person in the photograph. For those of us pictured, the photo triggers memories of the occasion that make words unnecessary. As we say, "A picture is worth a thousand words."

How much would Joseph have loved to have had a picture of his father, taken just before the brothers' second journey began! And how his father would have loved to have received a picture of Joseph! But everything had to rely on the testimony of his brothers. The saying "A picture is worth a thousand words" therefore not applying, Joseph had to anticipate a face-to-face meeting with his father. What parallel does this have for us? (Hint: see 1 John 3:2.) —C. R. B.

III. Reaching Out in Love

(Genesis 45:14-15)

A. To Benjamin (v. 14)

14. And he fell upon his brother Benjamin's neck, and wept; and Benjamin wept upon his neck.

Joseph's emotions once again came to the forefront as he embraced *Benjamin*. The feeling was mutual, for Benjamin *wept upon his neck*.

B. To His Brothers (v. 15)

15. Moreover he kissed all his brethren, and wept upon them: and after that his brethren talked with him.

Joseph then showed deep affection for *all his* brothers. This is quite a contrast to the first time he saw *them* in Egypt, when he "spake roughly" to them (Genesis 42:7; see lesson 3). One can only surmise what was spoken when Joseph's brothers *talked with him*. Joseph's forgiveness made reconciliation possible.

What Do You Think?

Under what circumstances, if any, are emotions best kept private? Why?

Digging Deeper

Which Scripture passages support your conclusions?

These exchanges were followed by extensive preparations for the trip to Canaan and back (Genesis 45:16-23). Joseph's final directive before the brothers leave is rather humorous: "See that ye fall not out by the way" (45:24)—meaning, "Don't argue on the way back!"

Conclusion

A. "Don't Be Angry with Yourselves"

Imagine yourself standing before Jesus, who has asked you to draw near, as Joseph told his brothers to draw near to him (Genesis 45:4). Jesus speaks and says, "I am Jesus, whom you crucified.

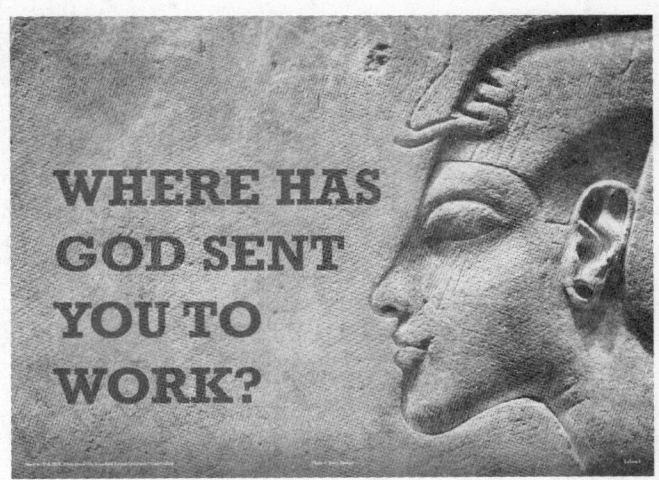
WHERE HAS
GOD SENT
YOU TO
WORK?

Visual for Lesson 4. *Use the visual as a jumping off point to discuss circumstances in which God is currently using each student for His purposes.*

Your sins are the reason I gave my life as a sacrifice on the cross. But don't be angry with yourself. I want to forgive you, not condemn you." Jesus does indeed say this—and He means it.

Joseph's words about God's higher purpose being carried out can also be applied to Jesus. Men killed Him because they wanted to reverse His influence, dishearten His followers, and destroy the movement He had begun. But God accomplished a great deliverance through the cross and the empty tomb. As Peter told the crowd gathered on the Day of Pentecost, "[Jesus], being delivered by the determinate counsel and foreknowledge of God, ye have taken, and by wicked hands have crucified and slain: whom God hath raised up" (Acts 2:23-24).

Salvation is truly a gift of God's grace (Ephesians 2:8-9). It must be received as such, without our placing conditions on it that God himself has never placed. Don't be angry with yourself. Like Joseph's brothers, you need to accept forgiveness.

B. Prayer

Father, thank You for revealing Your loving forgiveness to us through Jesus' death and resurrection! Help us to forgive others as we have been forgiven. In Jesus' name. Amen.

C. Thought to Remember

God has revealed His love to us.
Are we revealing it to others?

Involvement Learning

Enhance your lesson with KJV Bible Student *(from your curriculum supplier) and the reproducible activity page (at www.standardlesson.com or in the back of the* KJV Standard Lesson Commentary Deluxe Edition*).*

Into the Lesson

Solicit volunteers to share (briefly) details of a time when they remained hopeful while facing a negative life change. After a few such stories, ask the class to identify common threads of perseverance in the accounts.

Make a transition by saying, "Of all the hurts we suffer, betrayal is likely the most painful. Let's see how a Bible hero dealt with this problem."

Into the Word

Write *Reasons for Weeping* at the top of the board. Underneath, write *Sadness* and *Joy* as headers for two columns. Ask the class to voice specific types of sadness and joy for a person who might shed tears; jot responses in the respective columns. (*Possible responses for tears of sadness:* death of a loved one, estrangement, guilt over wrongdoing, etc.; *for tears of joy:* a significant material gain, reconciliation, reversal of a loss, etc.)

Divide the class into four groups, designating them **Joseph's Tears, Benjamin's Tears, Egyptians' Interpretation,** and **Brothers' Interpretation.** Distribute handouts (you prepare) with these instructions: "Read today's text of Genesis 45:1-8, 10-15. If your group is named after a person, determine why that person wept. If your group name designates a collective, state how those people probably interpreted the tears and wailing."

After several minutes, reconvene for whole-class discussion. Allow each group in turn to share conclusions; encourage the non-presenting groups to question and challenge those conclusions.

At appropriate points, ask the presenting group how God might be seen at work in the strong emotions present in the text. Allow time for thorough discussion. Expect "me too" stories to be voiced; don't discourage these, but don't let them drag out either.

Lead a discussion of the text by posing the following questions for whole-class discussion. Be sure to pause between questions to allow learners time to respond.

1–From a Hollywood movie standpoint, what did Joseph's brothers deserve to receive from him?
2–What made it possible for Joseph to overcome his desire for revenge?
3–Was Joseph's reaction the same as forgiveness? Why, or why not?
4–What was the bigger picture that Joseph realized?
5–Do you agree that Genesis 45:5 is the key verse of today's text? Why, or why not?

Option. For lively discussion, have a volunteer secretly prepared to disagree with either a yes or no answer on questions 3 and/or 5, giving reasons why.

Option. Distribute copies of the "Joseph's Actions and Mine" exercise from the activity page, which you can download, for learners to discuss and complete in study pairs.

Into Life

Distribute handouts (you create) titled "My Prayer and Discipleship Time," featuring these two challenges:

My best steps in modeling love are

____

My best actions in modeling forgiveness are

____

Have learners make commitments to study partners to use the two fill-in statements as daily prayer focus in the coming week.

Option. Distribute copies of the "Grateful for God's Blessings" exercise from the activity page for learners to complete as indicated in study pairs. Allow time for whole-class sharing.

Option. To see the spiritual values of Joseph's family members in the larger context of Genesis, distribute copies of the "Values Matrix" exercise from the activity page; use as a small-group exercise as time permits.

October 4
Lesson 5 (KJV)

Love That Intercedes

Devotional Reading: Matthew 5:43-48
Background Scripture: 1 Samuel 19:1-7; 23:1-18; 2 Samuel 9

1 Samuel 19:1-7

1 And Saul spake to Jonathan his son, and to all his servants, that they should kill David.

2 But Jonathan Saul's son delighted much in David: and Jonathan told David, saying, Saul my father seeketh to kill thee: now therefore, I pray thee, take heed to thyself until the morning, and abide in a secret place, and hide thyself:

3 And I will go out and stand beside my father in the field where thou art, and I will commune with my father of thee; and what I see, that I will tell thee.

4 And Jonathan spake good of David unto Saul his father, and said unto him, Let not the king sin against his servant, against David; because he hath not sinned against thee, and because his works have been to thee-ward very good:

5 For he did put his life in his hand, and slew the Philistine, and the Lord wrought a great salvation for all Israel: thou sawest it, and didst rejoice: wherefore then wilt thou sin against innocent blood, to slay David without a cause?

6 And Saul hearkened unto the voice of Jonathan: and Saul sware, As the Lord liveth, he shall not be slain.

7 And Jonathan called David, and Jonathan shewed him all those things. And Jonathan brought David to Saul, and he was in his presence, as in times past.

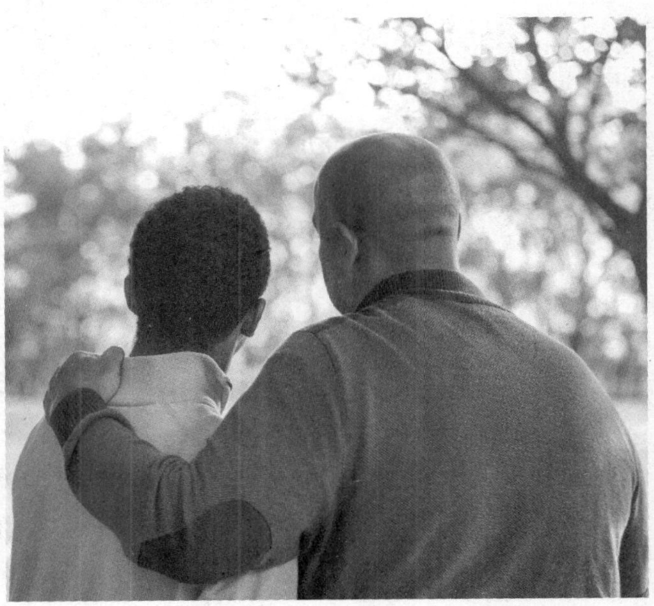

Key Verse

Jonathan spake good of David unto Saul his father, and said unto him, Let not the king sin against his servant, against David; because he hath not sinned against thee, and because his works have been to thee-ward very good. —**1 Samuel 19:4**

Photo: digitalskillet / iStock / Thinkstock

Love for One Another

Unit 2: Inclusive Love

Lessons 5–8

Lesson Aims

After participating in this lesson, each learner will be able to:

1. Summarize Jonathan's defense of David and Saul's reaction.

2. Explain the risks Jonathan faced in the reconciliation process.

3. Identify opportunities to counsel reconciliation and do so.

Lesson Outline

Introduction
- A. Targeting Peacemakers
- B. Lesson Context

I. The Plot (1 Samuel 19:1-3)
- A. Execution Order (vv. 1-2)
- B. Clemency Plan (v. 3)

II. The Intercession (1 Samuel 19:4-5)
- A. Exemplary Record (vv. 4-5b)
- B. Rhetorical Question (v. 5c)
  Unlikely Friendship

III. The Aftermath (1 Samuel 19:6-7)
- A. Vow (v. 6)
  The Unbreakable Vow
- B. Reconciliation (v. 7)

Conclusion
- A. Roles People Play
- B. Prayer
- C. Thought to Remember

Introduction

A. Targeting Peacemakers

What risks do peacemakers face in areas of conflict? A study, begun in 2010 by the Uppsala Conflict Data Program, seeks to answer that question. The fact that such a study exists confirms the sad truth that we all know: peacemakers sometimes come to very violent ends.

A government that doesn't want outside influence can forcefully remove peaceful humanitarian efforts. One side or another of a military conflict might attack the peacemakers, hoping that the aid they would have given to their opponents will result in victory. Or one individual who stands opposed to a specific peacemaker can kill that one, hoping the movement will end with his or her death. We need only recall conflicts in Syria or Sudan, or assassinations like those of Martin Luther King Jr. or Oscar Romero, to realize that peacemaking can be a very dangerous business.

There is no guarantee that efforts for reconciliation will work. But Jonathan, son of King Saul, believed the risk was worth taking. His actions are an example to all of us about the potential power of peacemaking.

B. Lesson Context

Two of the Old Testament's books of history are 1 and 2 Samuel. They take their name from Samuel, the last judge of Israel. He was instrumental in the transition from the period of the judges to the time of kings. As such, the two books record the transition from the theocracy (when the Lord reigned as sole king of Israel, with human leaders in the roles of judges) to the monarchy of human kings.

This transition began about the year 1050 BC. It began with the Israelites' demand that Samuel give them an earthly king "like all the nations" (1 Samuel 8:5). This demand was not primarily a rejection of Samuel or his sons but of the Lord as their king (8:7). God had called Israel to be His special nation (Exodus 19:5-6), and their desire for a king expressed a wish to be not quite *so* special. Samuel proclaimed the Lord's warning of the negative consequences of a human king (1 Samuel

8:11-18). But the people persisted, and the Lord granted their request (8:19-22).

The Lord selected Saul as the first king of Israel (1 Samuel 9:17; 10:17-24). Saul started well, but when he failed to carry out faithfully the Lord's commands, the Lord selected a different king (15:16-26). Samuel informed Saul of his being rejected by God, and Samuel anointed David as the next king (16:1-13). That signified that Saul's royal line would end when David took the throne.

When the Philistines challenged Israel, it was young David who slew Goliath, which in turn led to a routing of the Philistines (1 Samuel 17:1-54). After this great victory, David became a member of Saul's royal household in two important ways. First, David and Jonathan, Saul's son and heir to the throne, became fast friends (18:3). Second, David married Michal, daughter of Saul (18:27).

When military victories were celebrated, however, people esteemed David's accomplishments more highly than Saul's (1 Samuel 18:6-8). This made Saul angry, jealous, and suspicious of David to the point that Saul attempted to kill him (18:10-11; 19:9-10).

I. The Plot

(1 Samuel 19:1-3)

A. Execution Order (vv. 1-2)

1. And Saul spake to Jonathan his son, and to all his servants, that they should kill David.

This verse continues the story of 1 Samuel 18, giving the consequences of Saul's jealous rage. We may wonder why *Saul* would charge *his servants* to implement the deadly deed of killing *David*. The word translated *servants* occurs about 800 times in the Old Testament, with a broad range of applications. It applies to various levels of service to the king, not just what we might term butlers and maids. Faithful subjects of a king were considered to be servants (1 Kings 12:7).

Notice the progression: Saul had tried to *kill* David by his own hand (see Lesson Context), then by stealth by putting David in peril (1 Samuel 18:17, 25). The text before us represents a new attempt. It involved not Saul himself or the Philistines but instead his son and his court.

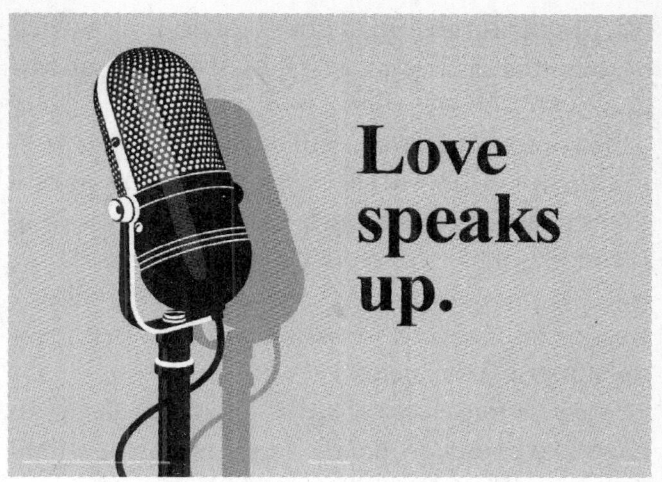

Visual for Lesson 5. *Use the visual as a backdrop to a discussion on how love speaks up. Use 1 Corinthians 13 as a reference, as well as the lesson text.*

2a. But Jonathan Saul's son delighted much in David.

The author interjects this important detail to remind us of Jonathan's potentially split allegiance. Emphasizing Jonathan's relationship to his father, Saul, ratchets up the tension. Would Jonathan's loyalty to his father (and potentially his own future place on the throne) determine his path? Or would his delight *in David* decide Jonathan's course of action?

The situation was made more problematic by the covenant between Jonathan and David (1 Samuel 18:3-4). It should prevent Jonathan from obeying his father's orders to kill David. In order to save his friend and honor their covenant, Jonathan would have to disobey his father. And the king could certainly punish his son any way he saw fit for such an act of rebellion.

2b. And Jonathan told David, saying, Saul my father seeketh to kill thee.

The reader doesn't wait long in suspense. *Jonathan* clearly chose his love for *David* over his devotion to his *father*, the king. The role of a son was to honor his father (Exodus 20:12), which included obeying him (Proverbs 23:22; compare Ephesians 6:1-3). Jonathan's informing David of Saul's pronouncement undermined his father's will.

Since the Lord had rejected Saul in favor of David (1 Samuel 15:28), the contrast highlights for the reader Saul's opposition to the will of God. It may also show Jonathan's acceptance of David's place as the future king rather than himself (which becomes clearer later; see 23:16-17) and thus as a man who followed God's will.

No doubt there was a full conversation between Jonathan and David, but only Jonathan's revelation of Saul's plot is reported. Jonathan's warning consisted of (1) the report, (2) three commands (see commentary on 1 Samuel 19:2c-d, below), and (3) four actions Jonathan will take (see commentary on 19:3, below).

Seeketh emphasizes Saul's very active desire to have David put to death. He was not just daydreaming. The king was coming up with plans *to kill* David.

> *What Do You Think?*
> Under what circumstances should a Christian violate confidential communication to prevent a wrong?
> *Digging Deeper*
> How does Proverbs 11:13 speak to this issue, if at all?

2c. Now therefore, I pray thee.

Grammatically, a request and a command appear the same. Determining whether Jonathan commanded David (so that David needed to obey him) or requested of David (so that David could make up his own mind) is a matter of context. Considering each man's status relative to the other's leads to an impasse. At the moment, Jonathan is of higher status because he is the king's son and heir apparent to the throne. However, he and David both knew that David had been chosen by God to be the next king (compare 1 Samuel 16:1-13; 20:31).

Furthermore, a warning, though it comes as a command, can be softened by the concern of the one who issues it. One can imagine that Jonathan, though apparently ordering David to do what he said, would have been open to other suggestions as long as they were intended to keep David safe from harm.

2d. Take heed to thyself until the morning.

The fact that the warning *take heed* is followed by *until the morning* indicated that the threat was an immediate danger. This was not the kind of general "take care" advisory with which we end casual conversations today!

2e. And abide in a secret place, and hide thyself.

These two imperatives reveal Jonathan's intention to give David an active-yet-passive part in the plan. The active part was for David to *hide* himself; the passive part is to *abide* (meaning "wait") after he did so. Jonathan did not know if his attempt to convince his father not to kill David would succeed; thus this precautionary measure.

B. Clemency Plan (v. 3)

3a. And I will go out and stand beside my father in the field where thou art.

And I points out a shift of focus from David's tasks to Jonathan's. The first pair, seen here, describes where Jonathan would be: standing with David's sworn enemy in the same field near David. Apparently the secret place where David was to hide (see 1 Samuel 19:2e, above) would be secret only from Saul, not from Jonathan. Therefore David would be completely vulnerable in trusting Jonathan not to betray him.

3b. And I will commune with my father of thee; and what I see, that I will tell thee.

Jonathan's second pair of actions describes what he planned to say, first to Saul, then to David. Once again, David would have to trust that Jonathan planned to *tell* him everything that he needed to know to survive.

> *What Do You Think?*
> Were you to attempt to mediate a reconciliation, what tactics would you consider to be off-limits? Why?
> *Digging Deeper*
> What Scripture passages can you cite to support your answer?

II. The Intercession

(1 Samuel 19:4-5)

A. Exemplary Record (vv. 4-5b)

4a. And Jonathan spake good of David unto Saul his father, and said unto him, Let not the king sin against his servant, against David.

Jonathan's intercession with *Saul* leaves the reader to assume that *David* had already done what *Jonathan* required. Once again, Saul's position as Jonathan's *father* is emphasized. This brings to mind the complicated responsibilities Jonathan had toward him. The expression *let not the king*, in third person, is more polite than a bald command, "Do not!" Jonathan's address of his father as king may be designed to calm Saul's insecurity over his kingship.

We also recall that resisting kings was dangerous. In the Law of Moses, before the existence of kings in Israel, disobeying priests and judges was punishable by death (Deuteronomy 17:12-13). This practice extended to kings in Israel in that they had power over life and death of their subjects (example: 1 Kings 2:23-25), as did kings in the surrounding nations (Daniel 3:13-15).

However, Jonathan's address also reminded the king that he had a duty to God not to *sin* against others. Although "might makes right" seems to have been the rule throughout history, God's people are to be different. We live by standards given by the Lord, not rules determined by people. For this reason, Saul did not have the moral authority to have David killed. That would go against God's injunctions about killing innocent people, which even the king is meant to obey and uphold.

David is identified as Saul's *servant.* By the use of this term, Jonathan describes David as a faithful member of Saul's court just like the servants of verse 1.

> *What Do You Think?*
>
> Under what circumstances should one wait to be asked to mediate a reconciliation rather than taking personal initiative in doing so?
>
> *Digging Deeper*
>
> How does God's taking the initiative to reconcile us to himself (described in 2 Corinthians 5:18-20) help shape your answer?

4b. Because he hath not sinned against thee, and because his works have been to thee-ward very good.

Again, *not sinned* means David had done nothing to bring harm to Saul. In fact, David was committed to supporting the king as the anointed of the Lord, even though Saul was seeking David's life (compare 1 Samuel 26:9-11; 2 Samuel 1:14). *Thee-ward* means "towards you" or "for your benefit." The *works* that had been *very good* refer to all the noble acts David had done in service to King Saul. These included not just military service (see commentary on 1 Samuel 19:5a, next) but also playing the harp to soothe Saul in his times of distress (16:16-23).

5a. For he did put his life in his hand, and slew the Philistine, and the LORD wrought a great salvation for all Israel.

David had risked his own life for Saul in slaying *the Philistine* Goliath (1 Samuel 17). Though everyone else in the army had been too afraid to confront the giant, David had trusted in the Lord's protection and His intention to defeat the Philistines. Because of his faith in God, David was able to brave Goliath's threats and use the skills learned as a shepherd to defeat and kill Israel's fearsome enemy.

The result *the Lord* had granted *Israel* through David was nothing less than *a great salvation* from an oppressive foe, the Philistines (1 Samuel 17:52-53). Jonathan mentioned only the military deeds of David. Those and other victories were the cause of David's popularity (18:5-7), which in turn was the cause of Saul's deadly jealousy and plan to execute David. For that reason, reminding Saul that David's popularity was a result of his service to the king could soothe the king's feeling that he had been usurped.

5b. Thou sawest it, and didst rejoice.

Then Jonathan pointed out Saul's eyewitness status and reaction at the defeat of Goliath. Saul had appreciated David's service not only at that time (1 Samuel 17:50-58), but also when David played the harp to comfort him in his affliction (16:14-23).

B. Rhetorical Question (v. 5c)

5c. Wherefore then wilt thou sin against innocent blood, to slay David without a cause?

Jonathan concluded his argument by returning to his beginning exhortation (1 Samuel 19:4a, above), couching it as a rhetorical question. Such a question is designed to make a point, rather than seek information. The answer here was obvious to the king: he should not *slay David* because then the king himself would become guilty and deserving of death (Deuteronomy 19:10-13).

Blood refers to the life force (compare Genesis 9:4 for "life" and 42:22 for "death"). Thus *innocent blood* refers specifically to David's manner of living: David had acted faithfully as a servant in the court of Saul. David had never given Saul *a cause* for Saul's anger and retribution.

Unlikely Friendship

My youngest son always struggled with his need to be popular, often getting in trouble at school for related issues. One day when he was in eighth grade, he came home from school with a note. This time he had been suspended for fighting. I felt deflated. We had just moved to a new town, and I was really hoping for a fresh start.

However, when he told me more, a glimmer of parental pride crept in. He had come across a crowd of people surrounding two students who were fighting, and the one who was substantially bigger had the other in a headlock. As the bigger boy pummeled the smaller one, my son had jumped in and (admittedly roughly) pulled the bigger kid off the smaller one.

Despite the suspension, I was proud of my son. Months later, he came home with an invitation to the rescued student's birthday party. To this day, they are fast friends. That is something of a reverse, mirror-image of 1 Samuel 19. There the friendship came first and the rescue followed. God rescued us while we were His enemies (Romans 5:10). Realizing that, under what conditions would you be willing to stand up for Him at the risk of losing relationships, job, or even life?

—P. L. M.

III. The Aftermath

(1 Samuel 19:6-7)

A. Vow (v. 6)

6. And Saul hearkened unto the voice of Jonathan: and Saul sware, As the Lord liveth, he shall not be slain.

Jonathan's argument had the desired effect. *Hearkened unto* means to heed; that is, both to hear and to act in accordance with what was said (example: Genesis 21:12). Similarly, the exodus from Egypt was initiated because God not only heard but acted on the groaning of the children of Israel (Exodus 2:24-25).

Jonathan's intervention thus culminated in Saul's making a vow that David would not be put to death. Making a vow or taking an oath is equivalent to making a covenant (Deuteronomy 4:31). It is quite to Saul's credit that he relented from his own call for David's execution. Although Saul had a history of rebellion against the Lord (example: 1 Samuel 15:17-23), in this case he honored God by heeding wise counsel and choosing not to sin against David.

The Lord expected the king to keep his vow (Numbers 30:2; see also Matthew 5:33-37). Deuteronomy 23:21-23 declares that vows must be kept, while Ecclesiastes 5:4-6 reminds the reader that breaking a vow angers the Lord. By swearing that David will live, Saul bound himself to do all in his power to protect David.

What Do You Think?

In what situations should one discontinue mediation attempts should those attempts be met with hostility and rejection?

Digging Deeper

How do 1 Samuel 20:18-33 and Acts 7:23-29 help frame your response?

The Unbreakable Vow

I had a friend who had been married a long time. Her husband was a God-loving man who took care of her and their family. But for various reasons my friend had spent years building up resentment against him.

One day she said she intended to leave him. How could I tell her I wouldn't support this decision because it was *wrong*? I prayed silently as she poured out her heart. And then I blurted out, "What if it were cancer?"

She looked at me blankly. I asked, "Would you leave him then?" Of course she wouldn't, she said.

"Why not?" I pressed her. She broke down as it dawned on her: she had vowed to be with him not just in sickness and health but in bad times as well as good. Breaking this vow would mean sinning against her husband *and* God.

Jonathan cautioned the same to Saul. Thankfully, just like my friend, Saul saw reason and realized his mistake. The choice is for us too: Will we honor our vows to honor God? —P. L. M.

B. Reconciliation (v. 7)

7. And Jonathan called David, and Jonathan shewed him all those things. And Jonathan brought David to Saul, and he was in his presence, as in times past.

David emerged from his prearranged hiding place after hearing Jonathan's call. As promised (see 1 Samuel 19:3), *Jonathan* reported to David everything that had happened. This would have included especially Saul's change of heart and his vow not to put David to death.

For David to return to Saul's *presence* indicates that David believed Jonathan completely and no longer had any fear that Saul would try to kill him. The result of all of Jonathan's efforts was that David resumed his place in Saul's court *as in times past.* This phrase calls back to mind how well David and Saul had worked together initially. The reader is left to wonder, in view of Saul's past behavior toward David, how long this peace will be observed.

> *What Do You Think?*
> In what situations should estranged parties be left to work out reconciliation on their own rather than be encouraged to use a mediator?
> *Digging Deeper*
> How is Christ's service as a mediator (Hebrews 8:6; etc.) helpful in answering this question, if at all? Why?

Conclusion

A. Roles People Play

The three characters in this story illustrate positions people find themselves in today. Saul was a person in power who was abusing his position in doing wrong toward another. David, of lower status, was the innocent victim of that wrath. Jonathan was the one who risked sharing that wrath by standing up for the victim. He cared for both the wrongdoer and the wronged as he sought to end the conflict by reconciling them.

Doing wrong and suffering wrong can lead to conflict. Hurt feelings can break relationships and end communication. Differences in status, such as employer-employee or parent-child, can make restoring relationships difficult. The one in power finds it difficult to admit wrong. The one of lower status does not feel safe to confront the enraged offender. At these times, restoration is practically impossible without an intermediary.

At various times of conflict, we may find ourselves in any of the three roles. The boss who is rankled by the exceptional skill of an employee may feel threatened, becoming bitterly jealous in the process. Perhaps such a boss will belittle the employee or make sure that promotions or raises are not offered. The boss's subordinate might be puzzled and feel wronged for trying to give the best effort. Someone who genuinely cares for both the boss and employee, and whom both parties trust, may be in a position to reconcile those in conflict.

Finally, it must be emphasized that Jonathan, the peacemaker, was not the offender's peer; Jonathan was subordinate to Saul both as a son and as a subject of the king. Jonathan's brave and respectful challenge of his own father and king serves as a model for us in handling conflict.

B. Prayer

Heavenly Father, show us opportunities to reconcile strife. Grant us courage to act and wisdom in speech. In Jesus' name we pray. Amen.

C. Thought to Remember

Peacemakers seek to turn others away from sinning.

HOW TO SAY IT

Goliath Go-*lye*-uth.
Philistine Fuh-*liss*-teen or *Fill*-us-teen.

Involvement Learning

Enhance your lesson with KJV Bible Student *(from your curriculum supplier) and the reproducible activity page (at www.standardlesson.com or in the back of the* KJV Standard Lesson Commentary Deluxe Edition*).*

Into the Lesson

Have the following quote, from an internet blog, written on the board as learners arrive:

> One of the most profound lessons I learned long ago was the difference between a peace-lover and a peace-maker. . . . Peace-lovers stand idly by while evil is doing its perfect work. . . . [They} want everything to just be OK without their input.

Pose the following questions for discussion: 1–Why is it harder to be a peacemaker than a peace lover? 2–What risks do peacemakers take?

Alternative. Distribute to pairs of learners handouts (you prepare) on which are written the following: "Discuss the circumstances of a time you tried to help resolve a serious conflict between two people (no names!) and how it turned out."

After several minutes ask who has a story that ended well. After one or two such stories, call for stories that did not end well.

After either activity say, "Being able to mediate a dispute successfully is something we can all learn. Let's see how."

Into the Word

Ask for three volunteers to share in reading 1 Samuel 19:1-7 aloud. One person will be the narrator, another will read all words spoken by Jonathan, and the third will read the one line spoken by Saul.

Next, divide the class into three groups. Give each group a handout (you prepare) on which is listed the group's name and task as follows. Advise your learners that most questions will require their "sanctified imaginations" to answer, using the text as a foundation, rather than finding the answer directly in the text.

Better-Action Group: 1–What would have been a more fitting action on the part of Saul toward David instead of plotting to kill him? Why? 2–If Saul had followed through and killed David, in what ways would it have damaged his own reputation and moral authority to be king?

Worse-Action Group: 1–In what ways (note the plural) might Jonathan have benefited from David's death? 2–What risks (again, note the plural) did Jonathan take by interceding on David's behalf?

God-Pleasing Action Group: In what ways (note the plural) are Jonathan's actions similar to those in Acts 4:18-20 and 5:29?

Allow time for groups to share their conclusions in whole-class discussion. As each group does so, encourage the other two groups to challenge and improve on the conclusions being presented.

Alternative. Distribute to small groups copies of the "What Could Go Wrong?" exercise from the activity page, which you can download, for learners to complete as indicated. This poses similar questions to the above, but with all groups having identical assignments.

Into Life

Distribute on handouts (you prepare) the following scenarios to the groups formed above. Include these instructions: "Select one scenario and propose either a way to mediate or why not to get involved, considering Proverbs 26:17."

A–Two of your siblings are angry with each other and haven't spoken in years. You want to invite both to your daughter's wedding.

B–Two coworkers have expressed different ideas for the future of your department, becoming antagonists in the process. You are friends with both, but you think one proposal is better.

C–Your child has had a falling out with a friend. You consider approaching the other child's parents about the situation.

Alternative. Distribute copies of the "Loyalty and Intercession" exercise from the activity page for learners to complete individually as indicated. Since this will take more than a minute, it is best used as a take-home activity.

Love for Enemies

Devotional Reading: Isaiah 1:12-17
Background Scripture: Luke 6:27-36

Luke 6:27-36

27 But I say unto you which hear, Love your enemies, do good to them which hate you,

28 Bless them that curse you, and pray for them which despitefully use you.

29 And unto him that smiteth thee on the one cheek offer also the other; and him that taketh away thy cloke forbid not to take thy coat also.

30 Give to every man that asketh of thee; and of him that taketh away thy goods ask them not again.

31 And as ye would that men should do to you, do ye also to them likewise.

32 For if ye love them which love you, what thank have ye? for sinners also love those that love them.

33 And if ye do good to them which do good to you, what thank have ye? for sinners also do even the same.

34 And if ye lend to them of whom ye hope to receive, what thank have ye? for sinners also lend to sinners, to receive as much again.

35 But love ye your enemies, and do good, and lend, hoping for nothing again; and your reward shall be great, and ye shall be the children of the Highest: for he is kind unto the unthankful and to the evil.

36 Be ye therefore merciful, as your Father also is merciful.

Key Verses

I say unto you which hear, Love your enemies, do good to them which hate you, bless them that curse you, and pray for them which despitefully use you. —**Luke 6:27-28**

Photo: majivecka / iStock / Thinkstock

Love for One Another

Unit 2: Inclusive Love

Lessons 5–8

Lesson Aims

After participating in this lesson, each learner will be able to:

1. Restate Jesus' teaching about loving one's enemies.

2. Contrast Jesus' teachings with commonly held ideas about how to navigate adversarial relationships.

3. Express ways to grow in mercy toward all people, especially one's enemies.

Lesson Outline

Introduction
- A. "We Must Not Think Evil of This Man"
- B. Lesson Context

I. Love for Enemies (Luke 6:27-30)
- A. In Return for Hatred (v. 27)
- B. Bless and Pray (v. 28)
  - *Check Your Prayer List*
- C. Be Forgiving and Generous (vv. 29-30)

II. Love for All (Luke 6:31-36)
- A. Above Average Standards (vv. 31-34)
- B. Acting Like God's Children (vv. 35-36)
  - *Doing Good on Thin Ice*

Conclusion
- A. The Challenge of Discipleship
- B. Prayer
- C. Thought to Remember

Introduction

A. "We Must Not Think Evil of This Man"

At 10:25 a.m. on October 2, 2006, Carl Roberts entered the West Nickel Mines School, an Amish one-room schoolhouse in Bart Township, Pennsylvania. After ordering the two teachers and all the male students to leave, Roberts tied up 10 female students and settled in for a siege. Within half an hour, with Pennsylvania state police surrounding the building, Roberts had shot all 10 girls, killing 5 of them, before killing himself.

In the face of so much devastation to a tiny, rural community, what kind of reaction might we expect? On the day of the shootings, reporters overheard the grandfather of one of the victims say, "We must not think evil of this man." In the wake of funerals where they had buried their own children, grieving Amish families accounted for half of the people who attended the killer's burial. Roberts's widow was deeply moved by their presence. The imperative to forgiveness went beyond even this: the Amish community also generously supported a fund for the shooter's family.

The desire for revenge is one of the deepest of human impulses. Sadness, rage, powerlessness, and a host of other emotions drive us to this. Jesus calls us to something very different, a new way of living in the world. We see this new way embodied in the reaction of that Amish community to an act of unspeakable brutality. Today's lesson, drawn from Jesus' Sermon on the Plain, further depicts the nature of this new way of life.

B. Lesson Context

Luke 6 contains an account of what has traditionally been called the Sermon on the Plain. Much attention has been given over the years to the relationship between the Sermon on the Plain and Matthew's account of the Sermon on the Mount. Some commentators have seen them as different versions of the same event. Others (perhaps most) have understood them to be independent of each other. This seems to be the best line of interpretation, and it is the one we will follow here.

The differences between the two sermons are readily apparent. One was delivered on a mountain (Matthew 5:1), the other on a plain (Luke 6:17). The Sermon on the Plain is about one-quarter the length of the Sermon on the Mount. The Beatitudes, which open the Sermon on the Mount (Matthew 5:3-11), contain blessings only; the Sermon on the Plain opens with (fewer) blessings that are followed by a set of corresponding woes (Luke 6:20-26).

A cursory comparison of Luke 6:20-49 with Matthew 5–7 also shows how much these sermons have in common. Both sermons show great concern for the poor and socially outcast (examples: Matthew 5:5, 10; Luke 6:20-22), teaching love for enemies (example: Matthew 5:43-48), the centrality of mercy in the nature of the kingdom (example: 5:7), opposition to hypocrisy (examples: 6:2, 5, 16; Luke 6:42), and so forth. That both of these sermons deal with these themes indicates just how commonly they appeared in Jesus' preaching and ministry.

In Luke 6, the sermon comes on the heels of a controversy with the Pharisees (Luke 6:1-11), after which Jesus left to pray on a mountain (6:12). As on other occasions, deep prayer precedes a significant moment in Jesus' ministry (example: 3:21-22). On this occasion, prayer preceded Jesus' choosing of the Twelve (6:13-16). After that, He came down to the plain (6:17).

When Jesus opened His mouth to speak, "he lifted up his eyes on his disciples" (Luke 6:20). In other words, it was the disciples—those who were already committed in word and deed to follow the Lord—who were the primary audience for what He had to say. Others were present ("the people," 6:19), but they were overhearing a message directed at Jesus' followers, not primarily at them. This is an important point to bear in mind as we undertake our study. Jesus was describing the nature of the kingdom in these verses. He painted a picture of the community that He was forming around him, of its way of life. These still are not words directed at outsiders or at the world at large.

The Sermon on the Plain opens with a series of blessings and woes (Luke 6:20-26; see above). They undercut the conventional view of the world that justified the way in which most of Jesus' hearers lived out their daily lives. Most people, both then and now, would point to the rich and powerful, the popular and elite, as successful and honored in this life. Jesus says this is not so. Rather, it is the poor and hungry, the bereft and the persecuted, who are truly blessed. They can look forward to unimaginable blessings on the last day.

I. Love for Enemies

(Luke 6:27-30)

A. In Return for Hatred (v. 27)

27a. But I say unto you which hear.

But I say sets up the audience (whether hearing or reading) to discover a contrast. *Unto you which hear* seems to be equivalent in meaning to that familiar phrase from the Gospels, "he that hath ears to hear, let him hear" (Matthew 11:15; Mark 4:9; etc.). The one who hears is not merely capable of making out audible sounds or speech. Rather, hearing requires understanding and—more critically—obedience to what is heard (Luke 11:28; James 1:22). It is about receptivity to the message, a willingness to transform one's life in accordance with the demands of the message.

27b. Love your enemies, do good to them which hate you.

The command that came out of Jesus' mouth was, and still is, counterintuitive. There is nothing else like it in all the texts that have come down to us from the ancient world. For instance, the poet Hesiod gives the typical understanding of one's obligations to his enemies: "Love those who love you, and help those who help you. / Give to those who give to you, never to those who do not" (*Works and Days*, lines 353–354). It is not a part of unsanctified human nature to *love . . . enemies.*

HOW TO SAY IT

Beatitudes	Bee-*a*-tuh-toods (*a* as in *mat*).
Hesiod	*Hee*-see-uhd.
Iscariot	Iss-*care*-ee-ut.
Judea	Joo-*dee*-uh.
Maccabean	Mack-uh-*be*-un.
Pharisees	*Fair*-ih-seez.
Philo	*Fie*-low.
Zealot	*Zel*-ut.

The demand that Jesus makes in this verse is one that most of us will resist almost instinctively. It is a high standard, and not natural for us, but it is surely attainable. The key lies in the perfection that Jesus calls for elsewhere (example: Matthew 19:21). Perfection (except in reference to God) connotes not absolute, unblemished sinlessness. Rather, perfection assumes a process of continual, steady growth toward maturity (example: 2 Corinthians 7:1; contrast Hebrews 10:14; 11:40). The believer who is growing becomes increasingly able to extend love to enemies. Love is defined by action (*do good*), not sentiment or feeling. Love costs something; it does not come cheap.

What Do You Think?

What is the single most needed act of love you can express to an enemy in the week ahead?

Digging Deeper

What enemies do Christians face that are most like those of Acts 18:17; 21:32; and 23:2?

B. Bless and Pray (v. 28)

28. Bless them that curse you, and pray for them which despitefully use you.

This verse deals with love demonstrated in speech. These are examples that most likely would have come from the daily experiences of Jesus' hearers. Many of them were socially marginal or poor, thus already not commanding the respect of their peers.

We can add to this picture the social pressures (from family, friends, neighbors, and religious leaders) that would have resulted from the decision to follow Jesus.

It would have been easy—and perfectly natural—for the believers to return curses for curses or to otherwise retaliate for the abuse they suffered. Instead of this, Jesus called them (and us) to do the opposite, to *bless* those who *curse* them and to offer up prayers for those who took advantage of them (example: Acts 7:59-60).

Check Your Prayer List

I feel blessed to have lived 63 years without encountering many enemies. My most painful experiences have come in the employment arena. On three different occasions, I have lost jobs. In each instance, I felt some degree of being ill-used.

Looking back, I'm not proud of my responses. Although I didn't lash out, neither did I put those who initiated these painful scenarios on my prayer list! I'm sure I spent much more time feeling sorry for myself than praying for them.

Jesus didn't say we have to enjoy being treated poorly. But regardless of our feelings, we can honor Jesus' command to pray for anyone who has caused us pain. Often people mean us no harm, so we're actually praying mostly for our own attitude. If they really *are* out to get us, we can forgive them in prayer and ask God to work in their hearts.

Is there someone you need to add to your prayer list?

—A. S.

C. Be Forgiving and Generous (vv. 29-30)

29a. And unto him that smiteth thee on the one cheek offer also the other.

Love is demonstrated in specific actions. Indeed, the love Jesus calls for is demonstrated by going beyond: the disciple of Jesus should offer *also the other* after being struck *on the one cheek.*

Again, it is not at all in our nature to take this kind of treatment. The desire for retaliation is exceedingly strong in these kinds of situations. Jesus' standards are not based on what people do naturally. Instead they are based on God's own character and conduct. Jesus would demonstrate this truth in His last days. We need only consider His suffering and how easily He could have put an end to it to realize that Jesus modeled exactly what He preached (Matthew 26:36–27:50).

29b-30. And him that taketh away thy cloke forbid not to take thy coat also. Give to every man that asketh of thee; and of him that taketh away thy goods ask them not again.

Enemy love extends to our attitude toward our possessions as well. If the *cloke* is required of a man, he should offer also his *coat.* This goes well beyond the law, which would not allow the coat to be taken as surety for debt owed. Followers of Christ are not to be stingy with our things, because they are not ours to begin with (example: 2 Corinthians 9:6-11). Moreover, we should trust

God's provision enough to not expect to be repaid for what we give, much as Israel was called to trust Him when they sacrificed the best of their flocks and fields (Leviticus 22:21; etc.).

> *What Do You Think?*
> What are some ways to give generously without violating 2 Thessalonians 3:10?
> *Digging Deeper*
> How do Deuteronomy 15:7-8; Psalm 37:21, 26; and/or Proverbs 19:17; 21:26b help you answer this question, if at all?

Jews in Jesus' time looked forward to the day of deliverance that would come at the hands of a strong Messiah, who would drive the Romans out of Judea. Indeed, the coming Messiah was frequently envisioned as a military leader. This desire can be seen in events like the Maccabean Revolt (167–160 BC) when a leader, a hoped-for messiah, would rebel against Rome and their chosen Jewish leaders in an attempt to free Judeans from their oppressors.

In light of this, we can imagine that commands such as these would have rubbed many in the multitude the wrong way. (Indeed, some of Jesus' closest followers, Simon the Zealot and Judas Iscariot for example, may have been disturbed by these words.) We see that more clearly in other places in the Gospels, where Jesus' messianic self-understanding did not match up with the expectations that the crowds had for who the Messiah would be (see John 6:14-15).

II. Love for All
(Luke 6:31-36)

A. Above Average Standards (vv. 31-34)

31. And as ye would that men should do to you, do ye also to them likewise.

Jesus turned to a new line of discussion. Whereas Luke 6:27-30 describes specific behaviors that characterize the kingdom Jesus had come to establish, verses 31-36 speak to the motives for those behaviors. It is noteworthy here that we are no longer strictly focused on treatment of one's enemies but on people in general. The focus of

Visual for Lessons 6 & 7. *Point to this visual as you pose for discussion the questions associated with verse 27b.*

Jesus' words had broadened to include everyone with whom the believer interacted.

This verse is Jesus' statement of what we commonly call the Golden Rule. The Golden Rule is an expansion of Leviticus 19:18: "Thou shalt not avenge, nor bear any grudge against the children of thy people, but thou shalt love thy neighbour as thyself: I am the Lord" (compare Matthew 7:12).

Several versions of this principle can be found in ancient literature. Philo of Alexandria (20 BC–AD 50), a Greek-speaking Jewish philosopher, said, "No one shall do to his neighbor what he would be unwilling to have done to himself" (*Hypothetica*). Seneca the Younger (4 BC–AD 65), a Roman philosopher, similarly wrote, "Let us give in the manner that would have been acceptable if we were receiving" (*De Beneficiis*). These examples from both Jewish and Roman backgrounds show that at least some philosophers assumed a stance of reciprocal good that is expanded on in Jesus' teaching in the Sermon on the Plain.

32. For if ye love them which love you, what thank have ye? for sinners also love those that love them.

Sinners here simply refers to all those who operate on "normal" human terms with regard to personal relationships, exchange, and so forth. Everyone who does not conform their lives to the standards of the new kingdom that Jesus proclaimed lives this way. They *love those that love them*, no more and no less.

Jesus called on His disciples to go beyond this limited (and limiting) standard. They were to give and to do good without expectation of return or reward of any kind. This is the higher standard, "exceed[ing] the righteousness of the scribes and Pharisees" (Matthew 5:20), that Jesus explicitly called for.

33. And if ye do good to them which do good to you, what thank have ye? for sinners also do even the same.

This verse presents the same question as Luke 6:32 with slightly different phrasing. Jesus envisioned the end of merely repaying *good* for *good.* Our behavior, in this new reality that Jesus preached, is not to be predetermined by our sense of what we are owed or what we owe. Good should be shown to others for its own sake, not for the sake of anything that we might receive in return.

34. And if ye lend to them of whom ye hope to receive, what thank have ye? for sinners also lend to sinners, to receive as much again.

The observant reader will have noticed that Luke 6:32-34 constitutes a three-part question. All three make the same basic point: The way of life expounded by Jesus makes demands on those who would follow Him—demands that fall outside the boundaries of "normal" human relationships and cultural expectations. Roman society was based on the fulfillment of obligations between patrons and clients, between the elites and the masses. Jesus' words in the Sermon on the Plain cut to the heart of that arrangement and undermine it. The kingdom of God is marked by a new approach to human relationships that explodes our ideas about status, possessions, what we believe we are entitled to, and many other subjects.

What is our attitude toward lending our possessions or resources? This is arguably one of the touchiest aspects of interpersonal relationships. How many friendships have ended over the loaning of money or other possessions? This is to say nothing of relationships that are not nearly as close to begin with.

B. Acting Like God's Children (vv. 35-36)

35a. But love ye your enemies, and do good, and lend, hoping for nothing again.

Verse 35 is a kind of a summary statement for this entire passage, a concise repetition of its main themes. Again the emphasis is on action.

It is tempting for us to agree with Jesus that genuine Christian love does not seek any benefit beyond the opportunity to act in love. We could nod our heads in affirmation and then turn to the next verse. But if we stop and think about how Jesus repeated this idea, and if we reflect also on the fact that love is the dominant ethic in the New Testament, then perhaps we ought to pause to investigate our own intentions carefully.

In all honesty, are we able to act in a way that is self-sacrificing? Can we act in the interests of others with *no* expectation of anything in return? Can we act with no expectation of thank-you cards or pats on the back?

> *What Do You Think?*
> In what contexts today is the giving commanded in Luke 6:35 to be limited by the prohibition of 2 John 9-11?
> *Digging Deeper*
> Should the answer to that question be the same for all Christians? Why, or why not?

35b. And your reward shall be great, and ye shall be the children of the Highest.

As John the Baptist implies in Luke 3:8-9, to be the child of someone or something is to share in the character of that person or object. To be *children of the Most High,* Jesus' hearers (and we) are called to do the same things that God does, especially loving our enemies (Romans 5:10-11).

These motives also become benefits to us when we demonstrate the kind of love that Jesus had in mind. Jesus was clearly stressing that the ability to love others in a self-sacrificial manner is an important component of our eternal *reward.* This kind of love is a vital part of our identity as the children of the Most High.

Thus Jesus' sermon presents the idea that the motivation for living a certain kind of life is not based on "what we can get out of it" in the here and now. Even so, isn't the motivation of an eternal reward at least somewhat selfish in and of itself?

> *What Do You Think?*
> What guardrails can we erect to keep our motives pure regarding expectation of reward?
> *Digging Deeper*
> Which Scriptures help you most in this area?

35c. For he is kind unto the unthankful and to the evil.

God's character is to be *kind*, even to people who are *ungrateful* and *wicked* (example: Matthew 5:45). His character is our ultimate example. Our desire to please Him is our ultimate motivation.

Jesus introduced this point so that we can understand that the way we're being called to live is not arbitrary. Rather, it is a life that imitates our heavenly Father. So here we have the motivation for achieving the objectives Jesus laid out for us throughout this sermon.

Doing Good on Thin Ice

In 1569 in the Netherlands, Dirk Willems was arrested for being a member of a group of Christians who rejected certain doctrines. He escaped from a prison window and was chased by a guard. Coming to an icy pond, Dirk safely made his way across. But the ice broke under his pursuer.

Hearing the guard's cry, Dirk ran back and pulled the man out of the frigid water. The guard then seized Dirk and led him back to the prison. Soon afterward he was burned at the stake.

Dirk took the teachings of Jesus seriously. He dared to love his enemy and "do good" to him (Luke 6:27). Chances are you'll never have to make the kind of decision Dirk Willems faced. But you'll still have plenty of opportunities to apply Jesus' challenging words. The next time you feel pursued by an enemy, turn around and do good to that person. —A. S.

36. Be ye therefore merciful, as your Father also is merciful.

A way of summarizing Jesus' point in verse 35 is to say that God *is merciful*. His actions toward us are gracious and ultimately intended for our redemption (2 Peter 3:9). The primacy of mercy in the character of God likewise points us to a new way of life—*be merciful*—in which the critical value is not reciprocity but behavior imitative of our merciful Father (see Luke 11:4).

Conclusion

A. The Challenge of Discipleship

What is said in today's text actually requires very little in the way of commentary. There are no textual issues or obscure cultural references that need to be explained in order for the reader to comprehend this passage. This is not a difficult passage to understand.

It is, however, an exceedingly difficult passage to put into practice. As we suggested at the outset, this is because the way of life that Jesus described here runs counter to the fundamentals of human nature: the deep-seated desire for revenge, for redress of injustice, for the respect of others. In light of this, it is common to view the teachings of Jesus in the Sermon on the Plain as impractical or unrealistic—even among Christians—and to seek ways to get around the implications of Jesus' words. The truest and best application we may make of Jesus' words is simply to reject this way of thinking, thus clearing the way for His words about love of enemies to reshape our hearts and our lives.

> *What Do You Think?*
> What part of today's text do you find most difficult to apply personally? Why?
> *Digging Deeper*
> Who can you confide in to help you overcome this difficulty?

B. Prayer

Heavenly Father, grant us the courage to pattern our lives after the teachings of Jesus rather than after what is acceptable according to our culture. In Jesus' name we pray. Amen.

C. Thought to Remember

Jesus calls us to a new way of life.

Involvement Learning

Enhance your lesson with KJV Bible Student *(from your curriculum supplier) and the reproducible activity page (at www.standardlesson.com or in the back of the* KJV Standard Lesson Commentary Deluxe Edition*).*

Into the Lesson

Distribute blank index cards and tell students they have one minute to create an "enemies list." Say, "Include the names or initials of those who have treated you as an enemy in the past." Assure learners that you will not collect the lists. After you call time, have students pair up to discuss their lists. As they do, write the following headers of five columns on the board: *Family / Personal / Professional / Religious / Other.*

During the ensuing whole-class discussion, call for shows of hands regarding enemies in these categories, tallying results for each (no names should be mentioned).

Ask, "Who were the enemies of first-century Jews?" (*expected responses include* tax collectors and the Romans) Ask, "What about enemies of Jesus himself?" (*expected responses include* the Jewish authorities, the Romans, and/or Judas Iscariot) Make a transition by saying, "Let's find out how we should treat enemies."

Into the Word

Read aloud Luke 6:27-36. Then say, "I'm going to give you a list of five statements that each have one word wrong. You have one minute to find the one wrong word in each and replace it with the right one. Closed Bibles!"

Then distribute the following statements on handouts (you prepare). The correct words are given in parentheses and are not to be included.

1–Love your friends.
2–Do similar to those who hate you.
3–Bless those who love you.
4–If hit on one cheek, protect the other.
5–Your reward will be proportional.

After you call time, have learners score their own results. (*Answers:* 1–~~friends~~ enemies; 2–~~similar~~ good; 3–~~love~~ curse; 4–~~protect~~ offer; 5–~~proportional~~ great)

Alternative. For a more comprehensive exercise, reproduce copies of the entire lesson text (which exceeds 200 words) with one word in each verse turned into a blank line for a total of 10 blanks. Have the 10 missing words printed off to the side as the choices for the blanks. Allow one minute, closed Bibles.

Option. If you choose to spend more time working through the text in depth, distribute copies of the "Natural or Godly" note-taker from the activity page, which you can download.

Into Life

Pose one or more of the following scenarios for whole-class or small-group discussion.

1–You are talking with someone who says, "I just can't let people walk all over me. It's not good for their character." How do you respond? What Scriptures in addition to today's text are relevant?

2–You become aware that a certain person is always talking about you behind your back. What do you do? What Scriptures in addition to today's text are relevant?

3–Another driver makes an obscene gesture at you in traffic for a perceived discourtesy on your part. How do you react, if at all? What Scriptures in addition to today's text are relevant?

4–A friend complains that his brother-in-law never repays borrowed money. How do you respond? What Scriptures in addition to today's text are relevant?

Have students form prayer-pairs. Ask pairs to read Luke 6:28, then take time to pray for specific enemies, without mentioning names. Remind students that what is said during this time should remain confidential.

Option. Distribute copies of the "Now It's Personal" lesson reminder from the activity page as a take-home. Encourage learners to use it daily as indicated. To encourage its use, promise to ask for results at the beginning of next week's class.

Love for Neighbors

Devotional Reading: John 5:1-15
Background Scripture: Leviticus 19:18, 34; Luke 10:25-37

Luke 10:25-37

25 And, behold, a certain lawyer stood up, and tempted him, saying, Master, what shall I do to inherit eternal life?

26 He said unto him, What is written in the law? how readest thou?

27 And he answering said, Thou shalt love the Lord thy God with all thy heart, and with all thy soul, and with all thy strength, and with all thy mind; and thy neighbour as thyself.

28 And he said unto him, Thou hast answered right: this do, and thou shalt live.

29 But he, willing to justify himself, said unto Jesus, And who is my neighbour?

30 And Jesus answering said, A certain man went down from Jerusalem to Jericho, and fell among thieves, which stripped him of his raiment, and wounded him, and departed, leaving him half dead.

31 And by chance there came down a certain priest that way: and when he saw him, he passed by on the other side.

32 And likewise a Levite, when he was at the place, came and looked on him, and passed by on the other side.

33 But a certain Samaritan, as he journeyed, came where he was: and when he saw him, he had compassion on him,

34 And went to him, and bound up his wounds, pouring in oil and wine, and set him on his own beast, and brought him to an inn, and took care of him.

35 And on the morrow when he departed, he took out two pence, and gave them to the host, and said unto him, Take care of him; and whatsoever thou spendest more, when I come again, I will repay thee.

36 Which now of these three, thinkest thou, was neighbour unto him that fell among the thieves?

37 And he said, He that shewed mercy on him. Then said Jesus unto him, Go, and do thou likewise.

Key Verses

Which now of these three, thinkest thou, was neighbour unto him that fell among the thieves? And he said, He that shewed mercy on him. Then said Jesus unto him, Go, and do thou likewise. —**Luke 10:36-37**

Photo: zimmytws / iStock / Thinkstock

LOVE FOR ONE ANOTHER

Unit 2: Inclusive Love

LESSONS 5–8

LESSON AIMS

After participating in this lesson, each learner will be able to:

1. Define *neighbor* as Jesus does and provide current examples.

2. Explain the importance of how Jesus shifts the focus from legalism to true obedience.

3. Make a plan to proactively love a neighbor he or she has historically preferred to avoid.

LESSON OUTLINE

Introduction
- A. Good Samaritans at Altitude
- B. Lesson Context

I. Questioning (Luke 10:25-29)
- A. Regarding Eternal Life (vv. 25-28)
- B. Regarding Neighbors (v. 29)
  - *Won't You Be a Neighbor?*

II. Storytelling (Luke 10:30-37)
- A. The Victim (v. 30)
- B. Two Potential Heroes (vv. 31-32)
- C. One Actual Hero (vv. 33-35)
  - *How Unexpected!*

III. Directing (Luke 10:36-37)
- A. Short Review (vv. 36-37a)
- B. Lifetime Call (v. 37b)

Conclusion
- A. Looking for a Loophole
- B. Prayer
- C. Thought to Remember

Introduction

A. Good Samaritans at Altitude

Late in September 2018, Joshua Mason and his girlfriend, Katie Davis, flew from Texas to Colorado. The next day Joshua took Katie on a hike in the mountains northwest of Denver. After hiking about eight miles, they reached the nearly 13,000-foot summit of Jasper Peak. Joshua was hoping to find an isolated and beautiful spot to "pop the question." Jasper Peak provided such a location, and Katie said yes to the surprise proposal.

But then things took a turn. Because they didn't leave the trailhead till about noon and the trail to Jasper Peak isn't clearly marked, the newly engaged couple became lost and disoriented when it started to get dark. Far from cellphone service, they weren't equipped or dressed to camp overnight in the cold of the high country, and they only had a little water. Coming to a cliff and unable to go any further, they began yelling for help.

About midnight, a camper who was hiking in the area heard their screams. When he discovered Joshua and Katie, they were showing signs of altitude sickness and severe dehydration. He led them to a group of his friends who were camping at a nearby lake. The campers provided the couple with water, food, and shelter in their tent, trying to help them get warm. But recognizing the seriousness of the situation, one of the campers hiked down to her vehicle and drove to where she could call 911.

Rescue crews reached Joshua and Katie about 4:30 a.m. Determining that they needed to move to a lower altitude immediately, the rescuers escorted them down to the trailhead.

This story includes several Good Samaritans who went out of their way to help Joshua and Katie. Today we will consider the Scripture passage that prompted that now-common term.

B. Lesson Context

In his Gospel, Luke recounts Jesus' ministry in three major sections: (1) events in and around Galilee (Luke 4:14–9:50); (2) Jesus on His way to Jerusalem (9:51–19:44); and (3) the events of Jesus' final week in Jerusalem (19:45–24:53). Luke's Gospel is unique in its central section, which begins shortly before our lesson text. The majority of the parables found in Luke are located in this section, the first being the parable in our text.

A primary theme of Jesus' ministry in Judea was God's love for the lost and lowly: sinners (example: Luke 15), outcasts (example: 14:15-24), Samaritans, and the poor (example: 16:19-31). Jesus' countercultural teaching in last week's lesson text, Luke 6:27-36, challenged us to demonstrate inclusive love even toward our enemies. Today's text calls us once again to practice inclusive love. In the passage just prior to our text (10:1-24), Jesus sent out 70 of His followers in pairs to proclaim, through word and deed, that "the kingdom of God is come nigh unto you" (10:9). Both Jesus and His 70 emissaries rejoiced at God's power working through them (10:17-21).

Immediately preceding our lesson passage, Jesus spoke with His 70 followers at the conclusion of their fruitful mission (Luke 10:17-20). Although some commentators view Jesus' interaction with this "lawyer" (10:25) as an interruption of His debriefing discussion with the disciples, the exact time and place of this scene is unspecified.

This parable is unique to Luke, but its subject matter and setting are similar to texts found in Matthew and Mark. Matthew 22:34-40 and Mark 12:28-34 are clearly parallel to one another, but the connection to Luke is less certain (compare Luke 10:27, below). The Lucan event appears to be a separate incident covering the same theme.

I. Questioning

(Luke 10:25-29)

A. Regarding Eternal Life (vv. 25-28)

25a. And, behold, a certain lawyer stood up, and tempted him.

This man wasn't a *lawyer* in the sense familiar to us, but rather was a scholar educated in the Old Testament law and the Jewish traditions surrounding it. The fact that the lawyer *stood up* indicates that Jesus was speaking and His listeners were sitting. This was a typical, respectful pose when listening to a rabbi teach.

The idea of tempting is the same as in Jesus' temptation (Luke 4:1-13), which can be appropriately also considered a test. Evidently the lawyer wasn't sincerely seeking to be taught by Jesus as much as he was interested in how Jesus would answer. We have to wonder if the lawyer was hoping to show up Jesus.

25b. Saying, Master, what shall I do to inherit eternal life?

By calling Jesus *Master*, the lawyer at least wanted to give the impression that he respected Jesus. His question conveyed a perspective of salvation by works. Yet his response to Jesus' own question showed that the lawyer knew that mere works without faith are dead (compare James 2:14-26; see commentary on Luke 10:27, below).

The lawyer's question likely has its basis in the connection between obedience to the law and gifts of inheritance and life (see Deuteronomy 6:16-25). In the Old Testament, obedience to God is often associated with His blessings while rebellion against Him is similarly associated with curses (example: Deuteronomy 28). The lawyer may have wanted to be able to identify Jesus with either the Sadducees, who denied any resurrection of the dead (Matthew 22:23), or the Pharisees, whose emphasis on keeping the law frequently resulted in outward actions that did not reflect a heart yielded to God (example: 23:13-36). The lawyer would be well acquainted with both groups and likely had some level of affiliation with one or the other.

26. He said unto him, What is written in the law? how readest thou?

Instead of answering immediately, Jesus asked His own questions. Given the fact that the questioner is a Jewish scholar, it is fitting that Jesus asked him *how* he read and interpreted *the law.*

27. And he answering said, Thou shalt love the Lord thy God with all thy heart, and with all thy soul, and with all thy strength, and with all thy mind; and thy neighbour as thyself.

The lawyer's reply alludes to the great Shema of Deuteronomy 6:5, which Jews recited daily: "Thou shalt love the Lord thy God with all thine heart, and with all thy soul, and with all thy might."

To that the lawyer adds the law of neighbor love found in Leviticus 19:18: "Thou shalt love thy neighbour as thyself." These answers showed that the lawyer knew mere rule-keeping was not the path to life. Instead, love of God expressed as love for neighbor leads to life. This combination of loving the Lord your God and loving your neighbor as yourself has become known as the "great commandment."

28. And he said unto him, Thou hast answered right: this do, and thou shalt live.

Jesus' seemingly final word to the lawyer was this commendation of the man's *right* answer.

B. Regarding Neighbors (v. 29)

29. But he, willing to justify himself, said unto Jesus, And who is my neighbour?

The lawyer found himself challenged (see commentary on Luke 10:25a, above) and so looked to *justify himself*. Although the lawyer acknowledged previously that Leviticus 19:18—"Thou shalt love thy neighbour as thyself"—is a summary statement of the law (see Luke 10:27), he took advantage of the ambiguity of the word *neighbour*. In the original context of Leviticus 19:18, love for neighbors is love for fellow Israelites, although that love was to be extended to "strangers" who came to Israel from another land and lived among them (see Leviticus 19:33-34). The land of Israel in Jesus' day under Roman occupation was comprised of many who were not Israelites.

With his question, the lawyer clearly seemed to be trying to create a distinction, making the point that some people are neighbors (and thus required to be loved) and some people are not. The notion that some people are *not* neighbors is what Jesus addressed in His parable.

What Do You Think?

Under what circumstances, if any, should Christians ask questions regarding who should be helped and who should not?

Digging Deeper

How do Matthew 5:45; 10:16; 2 Thessalonians 3:10; 1 Timothy 5:3-12; 2 John 9-11; and 3 John 5-8 help frame your answer?

Won't You Be a Neighbor?

Mister Rogers' Neighborhood began airing in 1968 and ran for 895 episodes. Dressed in his signature cardigan sweater, Mr. Rogers invited children to visit his neighborhood with his theme song, "Won't You Be My Neighbor?"

Fred Rogers trained to be a Presbyterian minister but decided to go into television because he hated the medium of TV! While children's programming typically featured animation and frantic action, Rogers labeled those features as "bombardment." He did not play a character as did his contemporaries like Captain Kangaroo and Soupy Sales. Rogers believed that being one's honest self was one of the greatest gifts one person could give to another.

Fred Rogers was not afraid to expand his neighborhood. During a time of racial segregation, Mr. Rogers was shown cooling his feet in a pool on a hot day with Officer Clemmons, an African-American policeman. In addition, Rogers championed children with disabilities on the show, including having a young quadriplegic boy demonstrate how a wheelchair worked. Rogers did not ask, "Who is my neighbor?" He knew! —J. E.

II. Storytelling

(Luke 10:30-37)

A. The Victim (v. 30)

30. And Jesus answering said, A certain man went down from Jerusalem to Jericho, and fell among thieves, which stripped him of his raiment, and wounded him, and departed, leaving him half dead.

Rather than answering the lawyer's question directly, Jesus told a story. Like other Jewish teachers in His time, Jesus used a parable to explain a Scripture text—in this case, Leviticus 19:18. Since the details of parables were true to life, we can increase our understanding of the parable by exploring the historical and cultural contexts supporting it.

Although Jesus' audience likely assumed the opening character to have been a Jew, Jesus never specified his identity. The man remains anonymous throughout the story.

Since *Jerusalem* is about 2,500 feet above sea level and *Jericho* is about 800 feet below sea level, a traveler setting out from Jerusalem certainly would have gone *down* in order to reach Jericho. Winding its way through rocky desert, this 17-mile road was infamous for its danger. The caves along the way presented *thieves* with numerous opportunities to ambush travelers.

Jesus focused on the violent mistreatment the man received at the hands of the thieves. They were not content to simply take *his raiment*, or garments; the thieves left him for *dead*. One would hope that these evildoers were the only characters in the parable to show such callous disdain for human life.

B. Two Potential Heroes (vv. 31-32)

31-32. And by chance there came down a certain priest that way: and when he saw him, he passed by on the other side. And likewise a Levite, when he was at the place, came and looked on him, and passed by on the other side.

Priests, who were descendants of Levi and Aaron, served as God's representatives to the people; Levites served as assistants to priests (2 Chronicles 13:10). So, why didn't these servants of God serve the wounded man? Some speculate that they feared that whoever attacked the man was lurking nearby and might attack them as well. Or perhaps they feared becoming ritually unclean, and thus unable to fulfill their religious duties, by touching what appeared to be a dead body (see Leviticus 21:1-4; Numbers 5:2; etc.).

The latter argument has been countered by geography: to go *down* from Jerusalem indicated that they had completed their temple responsibilities and were heading home. In addition, the Jewish practice was to bury a dead person on the same day. This should have compelled both priest and Levite to investigate the victim's status with regard to that requirement.

But before getting too deep into the weeds of speculative mind-reading, we remind ourselves that this is a fictional story—a parable to make a point. Since no motive is stated by Jesus, there is no motive to be discerned. The characters of negligent priest and Levite serve as the stark backdrop to what comes next.

C. One Actual Hero (vv. 33-35)

33. But a certain Samaritan, as he journeyed, came where he was: and when he saw him, he had compassion on him.

When the northern kingdom of Israel was exiled to Assyria centuries earlier, some Israelites were left behind. The intermarriage of some of these Israelites with the Gentiles who were brought into the land (see 2 Kings 17:24) resulted in the population known as Samaritans. The Samaritans accepted only the Pentateuch (Genesis through Deuteronomy) and asserted that God must be worshipped on Mount Gerizim rather than Jerusalem (consider the question in John 4:20). The Jews in Jesus' day despised the Samaritans and refused to associate with them (4:9). And of course the feelings were mutual. Needless to say, a Samaritan would be the last person a Jew would expect to show *compassion* to another Jew.

> *What Do You Think?*
>
> What has experience taught you about compassion that is *reactive* (sees a problem happen, then helps) versus *proactive* (anticipates a problem, then helps before it happens)?
>
> *Digging Deeper*
>
> In which type of compassion can you help your church improve most?

34. And went to him, and bound up his wounds, pouring in oil and wine, and set him on his own beast, and brought him to an inn, and took care of him.

In stark contrast to the inactivity of the priest and the Levite, the Samaritan actively ministered to the needy man. Both Jews and Greeks appear to have used *wine* and *oil* widely for medicinal purposes. Wine would have been used to clean the man's wounds, the alcohol having an antiseptic effect. Olive oil would ease the man's pain. The Samaritan then *set him on his own beast*, likely

HOW TO SAY IT

Lucan	Lu-*kehn*.
picaro	pee-*kah*-ro.
Samaritans	Suh-*mare*-uh-tunz.

a donkey, which means he himself now had to walk. Inns were places of potential danger, not just for theft but also potentially murder. But from beginning to end, the Samaritan considered the *care* of the injured man of greater value than the risk involved.

> *What Do You Think?*
> If you saw a car broken down on the side of the road, would using a cell phone to call for assistance be the same as stopping to offer help personally? Why, or why not?
> *Digging Deeper*
> If stopping to help personally meant risking your own safety in the process, would you do it?

35. And on the morrow when he departed, he took out two pence, and gave them to the host, and said unto him, Take care of him; and whatsoever thou spendest more, when I come again, I will repay thee.

Some scholars estimate that *two pence* would have been sufficient for two months of room and board in an inn. By entering into such an open-ended arrangement with the innkeeper, the Samaritan was running the risk of being a victim himself—of extortion. As Jonathan interceded with his father, King Saul, on David's behalf (1 Samuel 19:1-7; see lesson 5), here the Samaritan interceded on the wounded man's behalf. Both Jonathan and the Samaritan demonstrated faithful love—Jonathan in the context of an existing covenant and the Samaritan in his obvious regard for human life.

How Unexpected!

The English language doesn't have a word that completely captures the idea of an "unexpected hero," such as we see in the case of the Good Samaritan. Various words have been proposed—words such as *antihero* and *picaro*—to only partial success. The problem is that those words and others bring with them nuances that may not apply to the unexpected hero who is under consideration. A picaro, for example, is a societal outcast, but that status is due to his or her own roguish behavior. The Good Samaritan was a societal outcast as well, but that status was due to no behavior of his own! Rather, it was an issue of bloodline.

Jesus used unexpected heroes in parables to challenge contemporary thinking. In addition to that of today's text, we are drawn to the parables of the prodigal son (Luke 15:11-32), the shrewd manager (16:1-12), and a penitent tax collector (18:9-14). We have a choice when we read these: the unexpected hero in each can be a model for us or we can be the contrast to the unexpected hero in each. It's our choice. —J. E.

> *What Do You Think?*
> Under what circumstances is it better to help others through efforts of group ministries rather than personally?
> *Digging Deeper*
> How do the changing procedures of Acts 2:45; 4:32-35; 6:1-6; 1 Timothy 5:3-11 inform your response?

III. Directing
(Luke 10:36-37)

A. Short Review (vv. 36-37a)

36. Which now of these three, thinkest thou, was neighbour unto him that fell among the thieves?

Having finished His parable, Jesus countered the lawyer's question with one of His own. The lawyer had asked "Who is my neighbour?" (Luke 10:29). Jesus changed the question and shifted the focus to, "Who acted like a neighbor?" In Jesus' view, trying to identify whom one is called to love is an obvious attempt to relinquish responsibility. To do so is to reveal one's motivation of trying to find ways to avoid obeying God rather than embracing the call to love as God loves.

37a. And he said, He that shewed mercy on him.

The lawyer cannot bring himself to say the word *Samaritan*! As a Jew, he couldn't fathom the notion of a good Samaritan. But at least the lawyer grasped the point of Jesus' parable, recognizing the mercy and action that set the Samaritan apart from the priest and the Levite. Just as the lawyer "answered right" in the first exchange

(Luke 10:27-28), so he answered correctly here. However, his avoidance of saying the word *Samaritan* likely revealed that the lawyer still considered some people neighbors and others unworthy of that designation.

B. Lifetime Call (v. 37b)

37b. Then said Jesus unto him, Go, and do thou likewise.

Here is Jesus' final word (compare Luke 10:28). The lawyer appeared to be hoping that he could limit his responsibility by being a neighbor to only a select few. With this profound parable, Jesus conveyed that rather than calculating who is a neighbor and who is not, the lawyer should heed Jesus' call to *be* a neighbor to whoever crosses his path.

This is the only reference to this lawyer in the Bible. We don't know how he responded to Jesus and the gospel later on. He heard Jesus' message. Did he embrace it and act on it? Did he remember it whenever a foul joke was told about Samaritans or he encountered one on the road to Jericho?

Conclusion

A. Looking for a Loophole

By asking the question "Who is my neighbor?" the lawyer in our lesson text was looking for a loophole—a loophole of being able to choose whom he was responsible to care about and care for. Surely God didn't intend for him to love *all* people. Surely some people did not merit his time and resources.

> *What Do You Think?*
>
> Case study: Your next-door neighbor, who is a single mother, calls you from jail asking you to post her $5,000 bond. You have the money, but discover that that's only the 10 percent cash portion required. The other 90 percent must come from the court's putting a lien on your house. What do you do?

Like the lawyer, we can be guilty of looking for a loophole. When we hear the Bible's teaching about loving our neighbors as ourselves, we can grasp the meaning in principle that we are to love and serve people everywhere in need. But it's tempting to embrace that as a theoretical concept in a way that leads to no tangible action. Or we can be tempted to care for those neighbors who look like us, speak like us, or share our social status, and we fail to care for those who are different. How could Jesus possibly mean that *every single person* is someone we should strive to love?

Visual for Lessons 6 & 7. *Use this visual to discuss the overlap between enemies and neighbors. Ask the class if there is any overlap with friends as well.*

Jesus' parable of today's lesson leaves no room for self-justification. If we are looking for a way out of loving that person who is too difficult, or in too much trouble, or frankly probably wouldn't help us if the tables were turned, then we betray our hearts that do not love as God loves. Instead of looking for loopholes, let us search for opportunities to use what God has given us to bless *all* our neighbors.

B. Prayer

Thank You, Lord, for giving us the great commandment for Your glory and our fulfillment. We want to love You with all that is within us. And we want to love our neighbors—whomever You place before us—in the same way we love ourselves. In Jesus' name we pray. Amen.

C. Thought to Remember

Good Samaritans ask,
"How can I *be* a neighbor?"

INVOLVEMENT LEARNING

Enhance your lesson with KJV Bible Student *(from your curriculum supplier) and the reproducible activity page (at www.standardlesson.com or in the back of the* KJV Standard Lesson Commentary Deluxe Edition*).*

Into the Lesson

Write this question on the board:

On a scale from 1 (very easy) to 10 (almost impossible), how difficult is it for two people from very different socioeconomic and cultural backgrounds to develop a neighborly relationship? Why?

Have learners work in groups of three to wrestle with this question. After a few minutes, reconvene for whole-class discussion of results. Explore issues of differences in wealth, race, age, gender, religion, etc., that can interfere with a neighborly relationship.

Begin a transition by asking two questions (if participants have not already done so):

1–What definition of *neighborly* did the groups work from to reach their conclusions?

2–At what point does wrestling with the definition cross the line from being useful to being hairsplitting and legalistic?

Use learner responses to the second question to complete the transition to the next segment. (Allow responses to the first question before posing the second—don't ask both in the same breath.)

Into the Word

Have four volunteers read the text of Luke 10:25-37 aloud: one each as narrator, Jesus, the lawyer, and the Samaritan. After the reading, ask participants to close their Bibles as you distribute 15 index cards you have prepared in advance, each card having one of the following 15 statements:

1–I tested Jesus with a question;
2–I attacked people;
3–I knew the law of God;
4–I said to love God with one's entire being;
5–I told him do similar;
6–I was not willing to become unclean;
7–I selflessly served a stranger;
8–I robbed him of everything valuable;
9–I thought no one was going to help me;
10–I saw an injured man, but I passed on by;
11–I knew I needed to bandage his wounds;
12–I wanted to know the definition of *neighbor*;
13–I put the injured man on my donkey;
14–I tossed the lawyer's question back to him;
15–I was left half dead.

After distributing the cards as evenly as possible, write these possible answers on the board:

Lawyer / Victim / Robber / Priest / Levite / Jesus / The Samaritan

Going in numerical or randomized order (your option), have the learner with the card in question read aloud what is on it, followed by the question "Who am I?" Repeat for all cards, pausing each time to allow a different participant to answer. Before beginning, however, offer these two ground rules: (1) some cards can take more than one answer and (2) no one is allowed to give a second answer until everyone has given a first answer. Finish by leading the class in a discussion of insights gained.

Into Life

Ask students to identify patterns of values that can make it challenging to overcome biased thinking in terms of whom we will help and whom we won't. (*Option.* Precede this discussion by distributing copies of the exercise "Your Actions: A Case Study" from the activity page, which you can download. Have class members work in groups of three to process the variables as indicated.)

Close with a minute of silence during which time learners write to themselves the challenge of one change they are willing to make in order to serve others as Christ would have them. (*Option.* Enhance this segment by distributing copies of the exercise "More Compassion, Less Rationalizing" from the activity page. Have learners complete it during the closing minute of silence, then take it home for further reflection.)

Love Never Fails

Devotional Reading: Romans 12:9-21
Background Scripture: 1 Corinthians 12:27–14:1

1 Corinthians 13:1-13

1 Though I speak with the tongues of men and of angels, and have not charity, I am become as sounding brass, or a tinkling cymbal.

2 And though I have the gift of prophecy, and understand all mysteries, and all knowledge; and though I have all faith, so that I could remove mountains, and have not charity, I am nothing.

3 And though I bestow all my goods to feed the poor, and though I give my body to be burned, and have not charity, it profiteth me nothing.

4 Charity suffereth long, and is kind; charity envieth not; charity vaunteth not itself, is not puffed up,

5 Doth not behave itself unseemly, seeketh not her own, is not easily provoked, thinketh no evil;

6 Rejoiceth not in iniquity, but rejoiceth in the truth;

7 Beareth all things, believeth all things, hopeth all things, endureth all things.

8 Charity never faileth: but whether there be prophecies, they shall fail; whether there be tongues, they shall cease; whether there be knowledge, it shall vanish away.

9 For we know in part, and we prophesy in part.

10 But when that which is perfect is come, then that which is in part shall be done away.

11 When I was a child, I spake as a child, I understood as a child, I thought as a child: but when I became a man, I put away childish things.

12 For now we see through a glass, darkly; but then face to face: now I know in part; but then shall I know even as also I am known.

13 And now abideth faith, hope, charity, these three; but the greatest of these is charity.

Key Verse

Now abideth faith, hope, charity, these three; but the greatest of these is charity. **—1 Corinthians 13:13**

Photo: LuckyTD / iStock / Thinkstock

LOVE FOR ONE ANOTHER

Unit 2: Inclusive Love

LESSONS 5–8

LESSON AIMS

After participating in this lesson, each learner will be able to:

1. Recite the characteristics of charity (love) as Paul listed them.

2. Explain why love is essential to the proper use of spiritual gifts.

3. Identify one way that he or she can express love to others by use of personal spiritual gifts.

LESSON OUTLINE

Introduction
- A. Global Success, Personal Failure
- B. Lesson Context

I. Love Matters (1 Corinthians 13:1-3)
- A. When Using Gifts (vv. 1-2)
  - *Removing Mountains*
- B. When Sacrificing (v. 3)

II. Love Acts (1 Corinthians 13:4-7)
- A. What It Does (v. 4a)
- B. What It Does Not (vv. 4b-6)
- C. Without Exception (v. 7)
  - *Sing It Out*

III. Love Lasts (1 Corinthians 13:8-13)
- A. When the Gifts Run Out (v. 8)
- B. When We Fully Know God (vv. 9-13)

Conclusion
- A. Not Optional
- B. Prayer
- C. Thought to Remember

Introduction

A. Global Success, Personal Failure

At the time of his death at age 56 in 2011, Steve Jobs's net worth exceeded $10 billion. He was widely recognized not only as a leader in the technology industry but as a significant shaper of global culture. As the founder of Apple and then Pixar Animation, Jobs set new standards for innovation in consumer technology and corporate culture. Apple effectively created both the home computer and the desktop publishing industry, as well as *Toy Story*—the first fully computer-animated feature film. Jobs was also a major force in the development of streaming music and movies and touch-screen personal devices. Famous for bypassing market research, Jobs had an uncanny ability to intuitively sense what consumers would want, even before they realized they wanted it.

While Steve Jobs was a uniquely gifted individual who has left an indelible mark on many aspects of global culture, his personal life was less successful. Jobs fathered a child at age 23 and spent the first seven years of her life denying paternity. Although he eventually accepted her into his family, she revealed in a 2018 memoir that Jobs was a difficult and demanding person to live with. Her testimony is consistent with numerous reports of Jobs's erratic behavior in the workplace. He fired people without notice or severance numerous times, famously asked inappropriate personal questions to prospective employees, and humiliated staff members by criticizing or even firing them publicly at meetings.

Steve Jobs was a profoundly gifted person who left a huge mark on the world while damaging many people around him because he didn't act in love. Our lesson today reminds us that love is the essential ingredient to all kinds of success—most importantly, for living as godly people.

B. Lesson Context

Corinth was a major city in ancient Greece. Paul spent 18 months in the city on his second missionary journey, despite much opposition there (Acts 18:1-17). Writing 1 Corinthians from Ephesus in about AD 56 while on his third missionary journey, Paul addressed a variety of issues and problems that had arisen in the Corinthian church in his absence.

That church's many problems seemed to have been rooted in pride, which went hand in hand with airs of spiritual superiority. Some thought themselves to be superior because they identified with a particular leader (1 Corinthians 1–4). Some thought themselves to be exempt from moral expectations (chapters 5–7). Some thought themselves to be superior because of the foods they ate or refused to eat (chapters 8–10). Some thought that they were so superior to other Christians that they could neglect the needs of others (chapter 11). The issue of spiritual gifts was also a problem at Corinth in this context.

Many individuals in the first-century church were empowered by the Spirit to accomplish important tasks, including miraculous manifestations such as prophecy (example: Acts 21:8-9) and speaking in tongues (example: 10:44-46). First Corinthians 12 begins a long section on the pride and arrogance that had entered the church through, ironically, the use of spiritual gifts. That discussion continues in chapter 14, but in the midst of it Paul pauses to offer a single, simple, concise answer to all the Corinthians' questions: love each other.

Love, properly understood, will put everything else into perspective, unifying the church and empowering believers to glorify Christ together.

I. Love Matters

(1 Corinthians 13:1-3)

A. When Using Gifts (vv. 1-2)

1. Though I speak with the tongues of men and of angels, and have not charity, I am become as sounding brass, or a tinkling cymbal.

Paul began with the example of an impressive gift, speaking in *tongues.* This gift of the Spirit was publicly displayed in the proclamation of the gospel at the church's inauguration at Pentecost (Acts 2:1-11). In that context, the disciples' ability to speak a number of foreign languages symbolized the universal nature of the gospel: through Christ, people of different nations and cultures would come together as God's people. This in turn confirmed God's love for each person in all nations (Matthew 28:18-20; John 3:16). Ironically, the Corinthians had turned this power into a source of division, requiring Paul to discuss the proper use of tongues in detail in 1 Corinthians 14.

The ability to speak languages by the Spirit's power is a marvelous thing. But how much more impressive to speak the very language used by the *angels* in Heaven! This would surely represent the highest form of the gift. Yet if a person were to speak that angelic language from selfish motives—to draw attention to oneself or prove his or her superiority—it would be of no use to anyone. As far as God is concerned, without *charity* even the most elegant speech is just the noise of a *brass* instrument or a *cymbal.*

Many of us are familiar with the Greek word *agape* from its inclusion in the names of parachurch organizations and Sunday school classes. This word appears more than 100 times in the New Testament, and the *King James Version* translates it as *love* in the majority of cases (examples: 1 Corinthians 4:21; 16:24). In a minority of cases, it is translated *charity,* as we see here. This use of the word *charity* should not be confused with the narrow idea of provision for the relief of the needy, as the word *charity* is commonly used today.

2. And though I have the gift of prophecy, and understand all mysteries, and all knowledge; and though I have all faith, so that I could remove mountains, and have not charity, I am nothing.

Paul turned to a second gift that is typically expressed in highly public settings, *prophecy.* While prophecy sometimes refers broadly to an ability to speak God's word to a particular situation (similar to modern preaching), Paul seemed to be thinking of the more obviously miraculous gift of knowing future events (see Acts 21:10-11). Suppose that someone was so gifted that he or she possessed *all knowledge* of future events, and even of divine *mysteries* of Heaven?

While we might regard the information such a person could share as priceless, it would be worthless, Paul said, if not exercised in charity. Faith

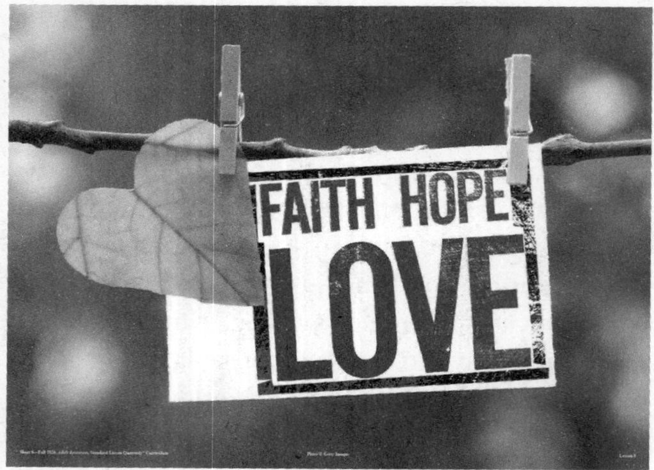

Visual for Lesson 8. *While discussing verse 13, point to the visual and ask how faith and hope help us to love others as God calls us to do.*

here refers to supernatural trust in God that would apparently express itself through great power in prayer (see 1 Corinthians 12:9). Jesus gave the example of people whose faith is so great that their prayers could move a mountain into the sea (Matthew 17:20). Such faith would indeed be impressive to others, but Paul said that God will be impressed only if the prayer is offered in love.

Removing Mountains

The Gotthard Pass in Switzerland has been an important trade route from northern to southern Europe since the thirteenth century. This pass was slowly traversed on foot and later with horses, stagecoaches, and automobiles. In 1992, a majority of Swiss voters agreed on an ambitious solution to speed travel in the pass. They would remove parts of the mountain range to construct the world's longest and deepest railway traffic tunnel—the first flat, low-level route through the Swiss Alps.

The 35-mile Gotthard Base Tunnel took 17 years and $12.5 billion to complete. About 31 million tons of material was removed. Tragically, nine workers died due to accidents during construction. In the end, however, mountains were literally moved, making it possible for up to 15,000 shipping containers to pass through the Alps each day.

The image of moving a mountain is used in Scripture to describe an act of great power (Job 9:5) and faith (Matthew 17:20). But even (re)moving mountains means nothing if it is done without love.

—J. E.

B. When Sacrificing (v. 3)

3. And though I bestow all my goods to feed the poor, and though I give my body to be burned, and have not charity, it profiteth me nothing.

Generosity is not listed as a manifestation of the Spirit in 1 Corinthians 12, but Paul does include it in his list of gifts in Romans 12:6-8. All people are obligated to give of their means, but some people are specially gifted with the ability to freely give to those in need.

Paul's *give my body to be burned* may be referring to surrendering faithfully to death in martyrdom. Any acts of service and sacrifice—even martyrdom—can be twisted into something self-serving. Even acts that mimic God's self-sacrificial gift in Jesus are invalidated when we do them to exalt ourselves rather than to bless others. Paul is one who dedicates himself completely to the Lord's service, suffering great physical distress in the process (2 Corinthians 11:23-27).

Paul is referring to the ultimate in self-sacrifice. But even the most extreme act of sacrifice is worth nothing if we do it so we can boast about our own spirituality. Nothing we do is worth anything if our actions are not guided by genuine love for other people.

What Do You Think?

How have you found growth in Christ to be related to growth in love?

Digging Deeper

How would you teach this connection to a new Christian?

II. Love Acts

(1 Corinthians 13:4-7)

A. What It Does (v. 4a)

4a. Charity suffereth long, and is kind.

Paul defined love in terms of what love does and doesn't do. Love is not an emotion but rather a lifestyle, a set of behaviors that reveal a spirit driven by true Christian *charity*.

Suffereth long does not mean that loving always brings pain, but rather emphasizes that love does not express itself through vengeance, retaliation, or by giving up on people quickly.

B. What It Does Not (vv. 4b-6)

4b. Charity envieth not.

Though we use the two words very similarly, jealousy and envy have distinct meanings throughout the Bible. Jealousy is often a strong desire to protect a faithful, committed relationship. The Bible sometimes refers to God as jealous in His love for His people because He desires them to be faithful to Him (example: Zechariah 1:14). Envy is a desire to obtain what other people have, often accompanied by feelings of bitterness or hatred. Envy and covetousness are never motivated by genuine love.

4c. Charity vaunteth not itself, is not puffed up.

At the same time, a person who loves does not try to make other people envious by bragging about the things that he or she has. Loving people are not prideful and do not seek to draw attention to what God has given them. Paul was thinking here especially of the pride that people might take in their spiritual gifts. Since all gifts are given by the same Spirit and all are of equal importance to the church (1 Corinthians 12:4-7), it is senseless to boast about them or to envy what someone else has received.

5a. Doth not behave itself unseemly.

Paul emphasized four things that people driven by love will *not* do. The Greek word translated *behave* is used one other time in the New Testament; in the other instance Paul advised unmarried men not to act "uncomely" by failing to honor a commitment to marry (1 Corinthians 7:36). Love does not lead us to do anything that we would be ashamed of later. Following from verse 4, Paul was probably thinking of envious or prideful things we might say.

5b. Seeketh not her own.

Pride and envy are categorically eliminated by the fact that love is not selfish, but instead is always acting in the best interests of others.

5c. Is not easily provoked, thinketh no evil.

Love is not expressed in a hot temper. Of course, we may be angry at the sins that people commit and may be frustrated by their poor choices, but these feelings should be motivated by genuine concern that the person is doing something harmful to himself, others, or the cause of Christ.

For this reason, love is quick to forgive. *Thinketh no evil* here means that we should not continue to harbor ill feelings toward those who make us angry. Instead, we should forgive what needs forgiving and forget the small stuff.

> *What Do You Think?*
> What are some circumstances in which you should take care that your loving actions not be misinterpreted as unloving?
> *Digging Deeper*
> How are Paul's declarations in 1 Corinthians 5; 2 Thessalonians 3:10; and 1 Timothy 1:20; 5:9-10 appropriate actions for loving people?

6. Rejoiceth not in iniquity, but rejoiceth in the truth.

Many of the Corinthian Christians seem to have been arrogant about their spiritual gifts. We can easily become envious of, and resentful toward, arrogant people, and we may feel gratified to see them do something wrong because this justifies our judgmental attitude. Real love, however, always wants to see other people succeed and do the right thing.

> *What Do You Think?*
> What are some spiritual disciplines you can use to ensure that your acts of love remain closely connected with truth?
> *Digging Deeper*
> In addition to Ephesians 4:15 and 1 Peter 1:22, what texts help you most in this regard?

C. Without Exception (v. 7)

7. Beareth all things, believeth all things, hopeth all things, endureth all things.

This verse highlights four ways that a loving person treats others, with the repetition of *all things* stressing that we are to act this way no matter what other people do. Love does not break under pressure but instead always bears up. *Believeth* and *hopeth* do not mean that loving people are naïve, but rather that love always remains positive. This attitude is tempered by the fact that love also *endureth*. Far from wearing rose-colored glasses, loving people see the reality of situations and choose to love anyway.

Earlier in this letter, Paul drew a parallel between the Christian life and the athletic contests of running and boxing (1 Corinthians 9:24-27; compare Galatians 5:7; 2 Timothy 4:7). Though in the middle of enduring we may think other people are enemies, our opponent is actually Satan and his influences. Instead of competing against others, we extend loving hands of patience, kindness, humility, etc., to help others cross the finish line with us.

Sing It Out

Many song titles begin with the words "Love Is." but fail to offer accurate or complete definitions. Consider the following: one title declares that "Love Is Blind." Another opines that "Love Is Blue." A third proposes that "Love Is a Battlefield." Yet another contends that "Love Is a Losing Game" to express the singer's regret at ever having given her heart to another.

None of these songs express the biblical truth about love. Their focus on romantic love is one-side. Paul's clear explanation of what love is and what love is not often contradicts contemporary thinking on the subject. What steps can you take to resist secular definition of love? —J. E.

III. Love Lasts

(1 Corinthians 13:8-13)

A. When the Gifts Run Out (v. 8)

8. Charity never faileth: but whether there be prophecies, they shall fail; whether there be tongues, they shall cease; whether there be knowledge, it shall vanish away.

This verse establishes a contrast between love and spiritual gifts. Paul selected three gifts from the list in 1 Corinthians 12:8-10 that all reveal information about God and His will. The time will come when we will not need such revelations, but we will always need love. That is true in this life and in the next.

What Do You Think?

In what modern contexts might the exercise of a spiritual gift be unloving?

Digging Deeper

How do Romans 12 and 1 Corinthians 12 help frame your answer?

B. When We Fully Know God (vv. 9-13)

9. For we know in part, and we prophesy in part.

At present, our knowledge of God is limited. God is so great, so far beyond human comprehension, that it would be impossible for any human being to know all that there is to know about Him. Indeed, human language could not express all that He is, and our finite minds could never fully grasp His perfection and holiness. As such, even prophecy can provide only a partial knowledge of God. Any person who takes pride in knowledge should realize that he or she doesn't know everything.

10. But when that which is perfect is come, then that which is in part shall be done away.

This verse reads like a proverb, a general statement about how things work in this world. *Perfect* here has a sense of maturity, lacking nothing. As a rule, things that are lacking become obsolete as soon as the full package becomes available. In this regard, one proposal is that the perfect thing being referred to is the completion of the New Testament. When that happens, *that which is in part,* referring to the previous verse, is obsolete. Regarding another theory, see verse 12, below.

11. When I was a child, I spake as a child, I understood as a child, I thought as a child: but when I became a man, I put away childish things.

This verse serves as an example of the principle in 1 Corinthians 13:10. *A child* thinks and talks according to his or her limited physical and mental capacity. But as we grow older, these simple ways of thinking are replaced by a more informed perspective, one based on a better understanding of the world around us.

12. For now we see through a glass, darkly; but then face to face: now I know in part; but then shall I know even as also I am known.

As noted in 1 Corinthians 13:9, the revelatory gifts of knowledge, prophecy, and others like them grant believers partial knowledge. Paul therefore compared the knowledge of God we gain through these gifts to a reflection in a looking *glass.* Ancient mirrors were made of polished metal rather than glass and therefore could not provide a sharp image. Similarly, spiritual gifts give us an incomplete knowledge of God.

But Paul anticipated a time of seeing *face to face.* Scholars have various theories regarding what Paul was referring to. One theory is given with verse 10, above. Another theory is that Paul was thinking of the second coming (1 John 3:2; Revelation 15:3-4). Yet another proposes that Paul was referring more generally to life in Heaven, where we will dwell in God's presence and behold His perfect glory. While some Bible students support their case by holding that *face to face* must be understood in its most literal sense of "in person" (2 John 12; etc.), others point to a figurative meaning of "clear communication" (see Exodus 33:11, 20).

13. And now abideth faith, hope, charity, these three; but the greatest of these is charity.

The word *now* focuses the reader on present, earthly experience. At present, we must exhibit *faith,* trusting that He knows best.

Hope is not wishful thinking but rather is confident expectation. Hope will be out of place when we reach Heaven because, as Paul asked rhetorically, "hope that is seen is not hope: for what a man seeth, why doth he yet hope for?' (Romans 8:24).

But love will never be obsolete: it will continue to characterize our relationship with God and other redeemed saints forever. Love is therefore *the greatest* because it never ends. As such, when we exercise our gifts in a spirit of love, we are acting with eternity in view.

HOW TO SAY IT

agape *(Greek)*	Uh-*gah*-pay.
Corinth	*Kor*-inth.
Corinthians	Ko-*rin*-thee-unz (*th* as in *thin*).

Conclusion

A. Not Optional

From the perspective of the world, love is not an essential ingredient in the use of gifts. A large financial donation still helps the needy even if the donor gives the money simply to save on income taxes. A gifted teacher can lead a powerful lesson that changes lives, even if the teacher only wishes to draw attention to himself or herself.

But from God's perspective, these efforts are of no value to the individual who exercises the gift because their exercise is not done with the right motive. Central to the Christian understanding of God is that He is a loving God. This becomes "real" for us when we have a personal relationship with Him.

God is not a dispassionate Creator. The Lord God as revealed by Jesus is one who loves us in a personal way. God's love is not based on our loveliness or deservedness. Love is the guiding force in everything that God does and must be the guiding force in the life of anyone who wishes truly to serve Him. It's not optional.

What Do You Think?

As your actions are motivated by love this week, how will you ensure that you honor the context of 1 Corinthians 13?

Digging Deeper

How do Galatians 5:6, 14, and 22-23 help clarify the context Paul intends?

B. Prayer

Father, help us to be truly loving and forgiving people. Give us the wisdom to use the gifts You have given us in humility and for Your glory and honor. In Jesus' name we pray. Amen.

C. Thought to Remember

Love never fails.

INVOLVEMENT LEARNING

Enhance your lesson with KJV Bible Student *(from your curriculum supplier) and the reproducible activity page (at www.standardlesson.com or in the back of the* KJV Standard Lesson Commentary Deluxe Edition*).*

Into the Lesson

Give each learner a handout (you prepare) featuring 12 horizontal lines for writing. Ask learners to take no more than a minute to write on the lines the names of up to six people they love and up to six things and/or activities they love. As they finish, write on the board these definitions of the verbs *love* and *like*:

Love (verb)*: to hold dear, cherish*

Like (verb): *to feel attraction toward*

In light of these definitions, challenge learners to cross through things and/or activities they merely like rather than love. Explore with learners what things and activities survived the cut and why.

Alternative. Distribute copies of the "Healthy or Unhealthy Love?" exercise from the activity page, which you can download. Have learners work in pairs to complete as indicated.

After either activity say, "Brace yourselves: today we are going to examine the most famous passage in the Bible on the topic of love."

Into the Word

Divide the class into three groups. Give each group a handout (you prepare) on which is printed one of the following assignments.

Love Matters Group—Read 1 Corinthians 13:1-3. How are our spiritual gifts and acts of charity affected by whether or not we have love?

Love Materializes Group—Read 1 Corinthians 13:4-7. How can you tell if it's really love?

Love Matures Group—Read 1 Corinthians 13:8-13. In what ways does our understanding of love mature?

After groups have had time to formulate answers to their questions, reconvene for whole-class discussion and sharing of conclusions. Possible conclusions include the following: *Love Matters*—Paul shares his experiences as they relate to all the gifts, goods, and possessions he holds that do not matter if they are not done, used, or given in love. *Love Materializes*—Paul describes the essence of love and the actions of love. He also names other actions that are not connected with love. *Love Matures*—Paul concludes that his ideas about love have developed, changed, and matured over time. Yet one truth remains unchanged: the greatest quality is love.

Option. Instruct each group to use Paul's words to create a public service announcement (PSA) that answers the group's assigned question about love. Remind the groups that most people's attention span is very short, therefore their PSA should be brief—even as short as 10 seconds. Allow eight minutes to develop and practice a script; then reconvene for presentation of PSAs.

Into Life

Make a transition by noting that it's no accident that the Scripture for today is preceded by descriptions of spiritual gifts. Ask learners to form groups of three as you give them these identical instructions on handouts (you prepare):

1–Turn back one chapter to 1 Corinthians 12 and review the list of spiritual gifts.

2–Identify your strongest gift and make a note of it at the bottom of this handout.

3–Determine how love connects with spiritual gifts.

4–*Optional.* As time allows, review Romans 12 for further insight on how spiritual gifts are to connect with the imperative of love.

During the ensuing whole-class discussion, expect learners to identify love as the motive behind the use of spiritual gifts. *Option.* To extend the application, distribute copies of the "Using Our Gifts in Love" exercise from the activity page as a take-home to complete as indicated. To encourage its use, promise to begin next week's class with a discussion of results.

Serving Love

Devotional Reading: John 15:18–16:4a
Background Scripture: John 13:1-35

John 13:1-15, 34-35

1 Now before the feast of the passover, when
Jesus knew that his hour was come that he
should depart out of this world unto the Father,
having loved his own which were in the world,
he loved them unto the end.
2 And supper being ended, the devil having now put into the heart of Judas Iscariot,
Simon's son, to betray him;
3 Jesus knowing that the Father had given
all things into his hands, and that he was come
from God, and went to God;
4 He riseth from supper, and laid aside his
garments; and took a towel, and girded himself.
5 After that he poureth water into a bason,
and began to wash the disciples' feet, and to
wipe them with the towel wherewith he was
girded.
6 Then cometh he to Simon Peter: and Peter
saith unto him, Lord, dost thou wash my feet?
7 Jesus answered and said unto him, What I
do thou knowest not now; but thou shalt know
hereafter.
8 Peter saith unto him, Thou shalt never
wash my feet. Jesus answered him, If I wash
thee not, thou hast no part with me.
9 Simon Peter saith unto him, Lord, not my
feet only, but also my hands and my head.
10 Jesus saith to him, He that is washed
needeth not save to wash his feet, but is clean
every whit: and ye are clean, but not all.
11 For he knew who should betray him;
therefore said he, Ye are not all clean.
12 So after he had washed their feet, and had
taken his garments, and was set down again,
he said unto them, Know ye what I have done
to you?
13 Ye call me Master and Lord: and ye say
well; for so I am.
14 If I then, your Lord and Master, have
washed your feet; ye also ought to wash one
another's feet.
15 For I have given you an example, that ye
should do as I have done to you.

. . . .

34 A new commandment I give unto you,
That ye love one another; as I have loved you,
that ye also love one another.
35 By this shall all men know that ye are my
disciples, if ye have love one to another.

Key Verse

I have given you an example, that ye should do as I have done to you. —**John 13:15**

Love for One Another

Unit 3: Godly Love Among Believers

Lessons 9–13

Lesson Aims

After participating in this lesson, each learner will be able to:

1. List the ways that Jesus showed His love for the disciples at the last supper.
2. Explain the connection between loving others and serving others.
3. Volunteer with a ministry that serves humbly in the church or community.

Lesson Outline

Introduction
- A. Dirty Jobs
- B. Lesson Context

I. Clean Feet (John 13:1-11)
- A. Enduring (v. 1)
- B. Betraying (v. 2)
- C. Washing (vv. 3-11)

II. Clean Lives (John 13:12-15, 34-35)
- A. Serving (vv. 12-15)
  - *Literal Foot Washing*
- B. Loving (vv. 34-35)
  - *Service to the Bride*

Conclusion
- A. A Matter of Heart
- B. Prayer
- C. Thought to Remember

Introduction

A. Dirty Jobs

A popular cable television show with a different twist is *Dirty Jobs* (and its later version, *Somebody's Gotta Do It*). In each episode of this show, the host finds himself embedded in a job circumstance that includes disgusting or dangerous elements. Situations have included sewer inspector, pig farmer, hot-tar roofer, bat guano collector, roadkill cleaner, and sausage maker.

There are many dirty jobs in our world. The circumstances of these jobs make a difference in our willingness to tackle them. But when we consider a job to be below us, are we really honoring Jesus?

B. Lesson Context

The apostle John was one of Jesus' closest associates. Jesus trusted him enough to task him with the care of Jesus' own mother, Mary, at the cross (John 19:26-27). Church tradition says that John later moved to the great city of Ephesus, taking Mary with him. There he ministered for many years, dying sometime between AD 95 and 100. His exile to Patmos is also well known (Revelation 1:9).

There are five books in the Bible written by John: the Gospel, 1–3 John, and Revelation. The other three Gospels are called the Synoptic Gospels because they share much of the same perspective (as shown in the amount of shared material). John's stands alone, with much unique content. It was written after the other three, likely between AD 90 and 94, though dates both earlier and later have been suggested.

All four Gospels include a retelling of the last supper, but the earliest surviving account is from Paul. He shared a description of the supper, material he learned from the Lord (1 Corinthians 11:23a), about 25 years after the actual event. While the accounts from Matthew 26:17-30; Mark 14:12-26; Luke 22:7-39; and 1 Corinthians 11:23b-26 are similar, the way John records the story is quite different. The focus of the other accounts (the bread and cup) are in the background of John's last supper. Rather than the institution of the elements of the Lord's Supper, John includes two things the other accounts leave out. The first is the content of our lesson today. The second is nearly five chapters of Jesus' oral teaching and a lengthy prayer (John 13–17), mostly unique material found nowhere else in the New Testament.

I. Clean Feet

(John 13:1-11)

A. Enduring (v. 1)

1a. Now before the feast of the passover.

The Jewish people of Jesus' day saw *the Passover* as one of the most important annual feasts. It commemorated the exodus events, when the Lord "passed over" (Exodus 12:27) the homes of the people of Israel that were obediently marked with blood on the doorposts and lintels of their homes (12:7, 23). The unmarked Egyptian homes suffered the final of 10 plagues, death of the firstborn (12:29-30). This led Pharaoh to relent and allow the people of Israel to leave Egypt and its oppression (12:31-32).

Passover, then, had both spiritual and physical themes for Jewish people like Jesus and His disciples, which likely resonated harshly because of the oppression of the Romans in Jerusalem and all of Judea. In Jesus' day, celebration of the Passover was already more than 1,000 years old. The feast was (and remains) a pilgrimage festival. In Jesus' time, this meant that Jewish believers from all over Judea and further abroad attempted to be in Jerusalem itself for the weeklong celebration. This was partly so the Passover lamb could be slaughtered in the temple precincts by a priest. Jesus and His disciples were Galileans, from an area about 100 miles north of Jerusalem. Passover was their reason for being in the city.

1b. When Jesus knew that his hour was come that he should depart out of this world unto the Father, having loved his own which were in the world, he loved them unto the end.

Several times in the Gospel of John, it is said that Jesus' time was not complete (see John 7:6, 8, 30; 8:20), meaning He was not finished with His earthly work. This verse represents a turning point. Jesus' *hour was come* because all that

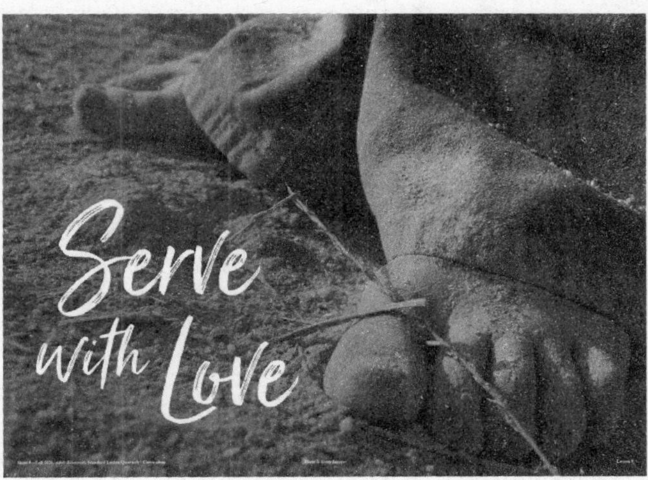

Visual for Lesson 9. *Use this visual to discuss opportunities for loving service that includes neighbors, enemies, and fellow Christians.*

remained were the events leading up to and including His crucifixion (John 18–19), resurrection (20:1-10), and appearances thereafter (20:11–21:23). After completing His mission, Jesus would return to His *Father* in Heaven. His death was imminent, but He did not leave work early. Rather than just saying goodbyes, Jesus used this occasion to show His love for His disciples.

B. Betraying (v. 2)

2. And supper being ended, the devil having now put into the heart of Judas Iscariot, Simon's son, to betray him.

Luke and John both stated that the prompting of *the devil* motivated *Judas* (see Luke 22:3, which says Satan "entered" Judas). Matthew indicates that Judas betrayed Jesus because of Judas's love of money (Matthew 26:15; see John 12:6). These two causes, Satan and money-loving, are not incompatible. Satan may tempt us at our weakest point, just as his first temptation for Jesus was to use Jesus' power to create bread for himself when He was extremely hungry (Luke 4:2-3). Further, the love of money pits a person against the Lord (Matthew 6:24; Luke 16:13).

Betrayal is working against someone who trusts you. Jesus' long-running controversy with the Jewish leaders in Jerusalem had escalated to the point where they sought to kill Him (John 11:53). This required some plotting, however, for these leaders feared Jesus' popularity with the common people. They needed an isolated place and time to seize Him, an opportunity best identified by one of Jesus' closest followers. Judas's betrayal of Jesus would provide this opportunity for Jesus' enemies.

John gives us a glimpse into the spiritual battle being waged that evening. Satan seemed to think Jesus' death would be a victory (consider the victory of the disciples' falling away; Matthew 26:31-35). Satan did not understand how Jesus' sacrificial death would serve the Father's purposes (John 1:29, 36). Jesus' subsequent resurrection from the dead thwarted all of Satan's plans. As Paul proclaimed, "O grave, where is thy victory?" (1 Corinthians 15:55). Judas's act of betrayal surely pleased Satan, but God used that evil to further His own plan.

C. Washing (vv. 3-11)

3. Jesus knowing that the Father had given all things into his hands, and that he was come from God, and went to God.

John gives three insights into the state of mind of Jesus at this critical time. First, *Jesus* was fully aware of His power and authority. He was in control of *all things*, including what would happen to Him next. Nothing compelled Him to act as a servant but His own decision and desire.

Second, Jesus was aware of His origin in *God*. John often presents Jesus this way, as one on a mission from God (example: John 5:30). Third, Jesus was aware that He would return to the Father when all things were accomplished. He was ready and prepared for what lay ahead.

4-5. He riseth from supper, and laid aside his garments; and took a towel, and girded himself. After that he poureth water into a bason, and began to wash the disciples' feet, and to wipe them with the towel wherewith he was girded.

Without a word, Jesus rose from the table, surely causing every disciple present to wonder what He was doing. The participants at the meal would have been on couches in a semi-reclining position. Jesus removed His outer clothing (both for more mobility and to keep His robe clean), for what He was about to do was grimy work.

The necessities for washing *feet* were present. The *towel* was a substantial piece of cloth, long enough for Jesus to wrap it around His waist and have a yard or so hanging out to use for washing *the disciples'* feet. The *bason* was a large bowl, big enough to submerge feet in *water*.

Foot washing was a filthy job. Jerusalem was a hot and dusty city. People either wore sandal-type shoes that allowed dirt in easily or walked barefoot without any protection. Because they walked almost everywhere, people frequently stepped in mud and other undesirable flotsam on the streets and pathways. A good host would provide guests with a servant to wash their feet. This foot-washer was the lowest of the household servants who likely took no pleasure in such a demeaning task. It was this dirty job that our Lord Jesus chose to illustrate what it meant to be a servant in His service.

What Do You Think?

In what ways have you discovered that shared meals offer witnessing or service opportunities today not available at other times?

Digging Deeper

Going the other way, what witnessing or service opportunities are best not initiated at mealtimes? Why?

6. Then cometh he to Simon Peter: and Peter saith unto him, Lord, dost thou wash my feet?

The washing proceeded one at a time, perhaps in silent embarrassment from the disciples. Jesus was their esteemed *Lord*, their master and teacher (see John 13:13, below), and such an honored person should never be expected to wash feet!

Simon Peter may have been last in line (and certainly wasn't first). If it took a couple of minutes to do each pair of feet, we can imagine that over 20 minutes passed, probably with little conversation and all eyes fixed on Jesus. Peter broke the silence to protest. It was not that Peter's feet didn't need washing, but that it was demeaning for Jesus to do so, and Peter did not intend to allow it.

7. Jesus answered and said unto him, What I do thou knowest not now; but thou shalt know hereafter.

Jesus' response to Peter's refusal was somewhat

cryptic, implying that there was more to the situation than Peter understood. He would understand in the future, but Jesus wasn't concerned about clearing up the matter all at once. The *hereafter* is more than just the finishing of foot washing. It points to the horrible night of agony, betrayal, arrest, and crucifixion, but also to the coming triumph of the empty tomb and the resurrection.

8a. Peter saith unto him, Thou shalt never wash my feet.

Peter was emboldened by this answer and underlined his refusal, maybe raising his voice as he did so.

8b. Jesus answered him, If I wash thee not, thou hast no part with me.

This response seems as cryptic as Jesus' first. His warning that Peter's refusal would mean the disciple had *no part with* Him does not mean that Jesus would disown him. Instead, Peter would cut himself off from Jesus and His blessings. Jesus connected the meaning of this foot washing to His mission of cleansing souls.

Generations before, David asked the Lord to create in him a clean heart (Psalm 51:10). He had committed grievous sins: adultery and murder. He had covered them up, and the result was that he knew his heart was dirty with hidden, spiritual filth. David begged the Lord not to take the Holy Spirit from him (51:11), for he understood that cleansing came from God's presence. David knew he must offer God a "broken spirit" and a "contrite heart" (51:17) to be forgiven, to be clean. We can pray David's words, asking Jesus to wash us so that we will not be separated from Him.

What Do You Think?

In what ways have you seen people argue with Jesus today?

Digging Deeper

How do you know when to counter those arguments as you think Jesus would versus simply remaining silent?

9. Simon Peter saith unto him, Lord, not my feet only, but also my hands and my head.

In an instant, *Peter* shifted from outright refusal to a desire for both *hands* and *head*—his entire being—to be made clean. Peter glimpsed that Jesus the servant is also Jesus the Lamb, who cleanses us of sin (Revelation 7:14). Jesus' great intersection of humility, service to others, and the cleaning away of dirt points us directly to the coming cross.

10. Jesus saith to him, He that is washed needeth not save to wash his feet, but is clean every whit: and ye are clean, but not all.

Jesus corrected Peter's zeal by saying that one who is fully *washed* does not need to take a second bath, only *to wash his feet*. This seems to be saying that one who comes to faith and is covered by the cleansing blood of Jesus is spiritually clean, counted innocent in the eyes of God. This is the essence of the atonement, the satisfaction of the penalty for our sins through the sacrifice of Jesus. But as the Jewish visitors to the temple knew, even after they took a purification bath before entering, their feet became dirty from walking. Symbolically, we are saved from our sins (the bath) but still commit sins (dirty feet). We all need a repeated washing of our spiritual feet. This process is often referred to as sanctification, the ongoing process of learning through the Holy Spirit and growing in our relationship with Christ.

What Do You Think?

Which of these "wash" texts influences you most to live as one who models Christ: Acts 22:16; 1 Corinthians 6:9-11; 1 Timothy 5:9-10; Titus 3:3-7; Hebrews 10:20-24? Why?

Digging Deeper

What seems to tempt Christians to forget their state of having been washed? Why?

11. For he knew who should betray him; therefore said he, Ye are not all clean.

Jesus *knew*, however, that not everyone in the room would have the spiritual bath. One in their midst was not *clean*. Judas might have sat quietly while the Master washed the filth from his feet, but his heart was set on doing Satan's will, giving himself no hope of spiritual cleansing (see John 6:70-71; 18:2-3). He was a betrayer. Peter, when he understood, had allowed Jesus to wash his feet.

II. Clean Lives

(John 13:12-15, 34-35)

A. Serving (vv. 12-15)

12. So after he had washed their feet, and had taken his garments, and was set down again, he said unto them, Know ye what I have done to you?

Jesus, ever the teacher, calmly put His dinner clothes back on and resumed His spot at the table. The question is rhetorical, shown by the fact that Jesus went straight into explanation without waiting for answers.

13. Ye call me Master and Lord: and ye say well; for so I am.

Jesus asserted His rightful position among them. *Master* indicates that Jesus was the one to whom they listened and from whom they learned (see John 13:6, above, regarding *Lord*). His service to them did not change His authority over them.

14. If I then, your Lord and Master, have washed your feet; ye also ought to wash one another's feet.

When we celebrate the Lord's Supper with others in our churches, we partially reenact the final meal Jesus shared with His disciples. Our practices center around eating a piece of bread and tasting the fruit of the vine. Some churches go further by including foot-washing as part of their annual events, often on Maundy Thursday (the Thursday before Easter Sunday).

Some might ask why all churches don't reenact the foot washing every time we take the Lord's Supper. The answer is addressed by the next verse.

> *What Do You Think?*
>
> Comparing the lesson text with Luke 7:44 and 1 Timothy 5:9-10, what would be some modern equivalents to the foot-washing practice of the first century AD?
>
> *Digging Deeper*
>
> What would have to happen for you to begin demonstrating love to others in one such way?

15. For I have given you an example, that ye should do as I have done to you.

While there would be nothing wrong with foot washing in and of itself, history tells us it was not practiced in the first-century church as witnessed by the book of Acts and other early Christian sources. The reason is that Jesus lifted up His action as *an example* of humble service. He was not introducing a new custom among the people of Israel. Rather, the command is for all disciples of Jesus to be servants of one another (Mark 10:42-45). This is the very essence of following Jesus. We honor His words in seeing the bread as a symbol of His body and the fruit of the vine as a symbol of His blood (Mark 14:22-24). Therein, our celebration of the Lord's Supper is a remembrance of Christ's sacrificial and atoning death for our sins on the cross. But an example of service is just that.

Jesus' conclusion is remarkable when we consider the setting of the last supper. Jesus knew that torture and death loomed shortly. He knew His disciples were going to be scattered, confused, and discouraged. But the example He gave sums up His entire ministry. They needed to do more than remember His words. They were called to servanthood as He had modeled it for them. To the very end of the book and even now, Jesus calls for us to follow (see John 21:22).

Literal Foot Washing

For several years I was part of a group that practiced literal foot washing. In the early days of the Protestant Reformation, members of this tradition first experienced foot washing in homes and later included it in observances of the Lord's Supper. The churches I was part of practiced foot washing on a day leading up to Easter.

Since I hadn't grown up with foot washing, I initially recoiled at the practice. I could *definitely* relate to Peter's reluctance to allow Jesus to wash his feet. But as I experienced foot washing firsthand ("firstfoot"), I was impressed and inspired by its significance. It was more than a mere symbol; I appreciated the bond of unity and mutual humility that foot washing fostered.

It's been many years now since I've participated in a foot washing ritual. So I ask myself: *What are other tangible ways that I am submitting to Jesus' example of being a servant?* How about you?

—A. S.

> *What Do You Think?*
> What visual aspects of today's text are practical to work into your church's communion service?
> *Digging Deeper*
> What would be the benefit in doing so?

B. Loving (vv. 34-35)

34. A new commandment I give unto you, That ye love one another; as I have loved you, that ye also love one another.

A few verses later, Jesus framed the foot-washing lesson in a different way: He gave the command for His disciples to *love,* a *commandment* with important qualifications. First, this love is to be mutual. His disciples should be a community where every member is loved by every other member without exception. Second, Jesus pointed to His own example of service as the best way to understand this love. Mutual love might involve some short-term tasks such as cleaning feet, but for Jesus it extended to giving up His life for those He *loved* (see John 15:12-13).

35. By this shall all men know that ye are my disciples, if ye have love one to another.

This loving community will be noticed by others. The old chorus stated, "They will know we are Christians by our love." Such a loving community is unlike anything naturally occurring in the world. For *all men* to see the difference in Jesus' *disciples,* our *love* must not look like worldly love (example: Luke 6:27-36; see lesson 6). The church is intentional and empowered by the presence of the Holy Spirit to love as Jesus loves. A local church might be known for many things: its building, its summer VBS, its worship music, its preaching, its mission trips, etc. It should always be known for its love.

Service to the Bride

Little did I know when Ardith and I got married 40 years ago that my vow "to have and to hold" her "in sickness" would be seriously tested. Just a few years later, she developed chronic headaches that became much more than an interruption in routine—and that have gotten progressively worse. This reality has left me with what, from the outside, might look like an unfair share of responsibility for shopping and cleaning.

Our service is still very much mutual. I am exempted from cooking and laundry duty. And Ardith's companionship and encouragement constitute an invaluable pillar of support and strength in my life. We delight in serving each other—and in thanking and affirming each other for doing so.

My wife and I both have the calling and privilege to serve—and be served by—one another. What acts of service delight you to offer to Christ's bride, the church? —A. S.

Conclusion

A. A Matter of Heart

Are you "clean every whit" but still have dirty feet from pride and lack of love? Is your heart, your inner being, truly clean? Washing your feet or your hands will not clean your heart. No doctor prescribes handwashing for heart disease. Jesus does not seek people with hard, dirty spirits who have immaculate personal hygiene. He wants those with "clean hands, and a pure heart" (Psalm 24:4; contrast Matthew 23:25-26).

Jesus bids us to take action. As we serve others, we follow Jesus. When we humble ourselves, our hearts are changed. Loving service will help our hearts stay clean. Can you think of someone you can serve this week? Remember, they will not know you by your love if you do not show your love in service.

B. Prayer

Father, You sent Your Son to die for us because of Your great love. Cleanse our hearts that we may model that love! In Jesus' name we pray. Amen.

C. Thought to Remember

Show your love!

HOW TO SAY IT

Iscariot	Iss-*care*-ee-ut.
Judas	*Joo*-dus.

INVOLVEMENT LEARNING

Enhance your lesson with KJV Bible Student *(from your curriculum supplier) and the reproducible activity page (at www.standardlesson.com or in the back of the* KJV Standard Lesson Commentary Deluxe Edition*).*

Into the Lesson

Read aloud the following job description:

Roadkill Collector: Must be able to work long hours braving oncoming traffic while picking up creatures of various sizes and breeds in various states of decay. Benefits include working outdoors. Strong stomach a plus.

Call for a show of hands of those who would be willing to take this job. Ask if anyone has held a "dirtier" job than this.

Lead into the Bible study by saying, "John's Gospel tells the story of Jesus' willingness to take on a dirty job in order to teach an important lesson to His disciples. Let's see what it was."

Into the Word

Ask a participant to read aloud the lesson text of John 13:1-15, 34-35. Then divide the class into four groups, and distribute assignments on handouts (you prepare) to groups as follows.

Background Group: Summarize John 13:1-3 in terms of setting the backdrop against which the story that follows is cast.

Process Group: Explain why John 13:4-5 is such a shock, even today, when seen against the backdrop of 13:1-3.

Dialogue Group: Condense the conversation between Peter and Jesus in John 13:6-11 to half as many words each. Since the text has Peter speaking 24 words and Jesus speaking 45, your condensed summary will have no more than 12 words for Peter and 22 for Jesus.

Lesson Group: Explain the connection between John 13:12-15 and John 13:34-35. Determine how the word *example* functions in helping do this.

After an appropriate amount of time, reconvene for whole-class presentation of each group's results in turn. Use the commentary to clarify and to correct misconceptions. Conclude each of the four presentations and discussions by asking learners what they found surprising and why.

Option 1. To help learners see broader connections with other parts of Jesus' earthly ministry, form learners into study pairs as you give them handouts (you create) titled "The Big Picture." Under that title have the following questions listed:

1–What connection(s) do you see between John 13:1 and Luke 2:41; John 5:1; 6:4; 11:55?
2–What connection(s) do you see between John 13:4-5 and Mark 10:45; Luke 22:27 and Philippians 2:7?
3–How is the "new commandment" of John 13:34 related to the "old commandment" of 1 John 2:7-8, if at all?

Be prepared to offer your own conclusions to these questions.

Option 2. If your learners need help grasping the difference between literal and figurative language, distribute copies of the "What Does the Context Imply?" exercise from the activity page, which you can download. Have learners work in groups of three to reach understanding.

Into Life

Ask class members to name jobs that some people might consider "beneath" them; jot responses on the board. Remind the class that Jesus' action to wash feet was considered a menial job fit only for servants to perform.

Take an opinion poll vote regarding which job listed on the board the class members consider to be least desirable. Follow by brainstorming how to turn that task into a class service project; make a definite plan to do so.

Option. Conclude the class with a few minutes of silent reflection by distributing copies of the "My (Un)Willingness" exercise from the activity page. Ask learners to complete this individually. Assure them that their written responses are theirs alone to keep—you will not collect them.

Abiding Love

Devotional Reading: Psalm 80:7-19
Background Scripture: John 15:4-17

John 15:4-17

4 Abide in me, and I in you. As the branch cannot bear fruit of itself, except it abide in the vine; no more can ye, except ye abide in me.

5 I am the vine, ye are the branches: He that abideth in me, and I in him, the same bringeth forth much fruit: for without me ye can do nothing.

6 If a man abide not in me, he is cast forth as a branch, and is withered; and men gather them, and cast them into the fire, and they are burned.

7 If ye abide in me, and my words abide in you, ye shall ask what ye will, and it shall be done unto you.

8 Herein is my Father glorified, that ye bear much fruit; so shall ye be my disciples.

9 As the Father hath loved me, so have I loved you: continue ye in my love.

10 If ye keep my commandments, ye shall abide in my love; even as I have kept my Father's commandments, and abide in his love.

11 These things have I spoken unto you, that my joy might remain in you, and that your joy might be full.

12 This is my commandment, That ye love one another, as I have loved you.

13 Greater love hath no man than this, that a man lay down his life for his friends.

14 Ye are my friends, if ye do whatsoever I command you.

15 Henceforth I call you not servants; for the servant knoweth not what his lord doeth: but I have called you friends; for all things that I have heard of my Father I have made known unto you.

16 Ye have not chosen me, but I have chosen you, and ordained you, that ye should go and bring forth fruit, and that your fruit should remain: that whatsoever ye shall ask of the Father in my name, he may give it you.

17 These things I command you, that ye love one another.

Key Verse

I am the vine, ye are the branches: He that abideth in me, and I in him, the same bringeth forth much fruit: for without me ye can do nothing. —**John 15:5**

Photo: CattleyaArt / iStock / Thinkstock

Love for One Another

Unit 3: Godly Love Among Believers

Lessons 9–13

Lesson Aims

After participating in this lesson, each learner will be able to:

1. Define how the vine/branches metaphor describes our relationship to Christ.
2. Connect love and obedience as complementary elements in the Christian life.
3. Identify ways to abide in Christ more faithfully.

Lesson Outline

Introduction

A. Wired for Relationship

Most of us in the West are highly connected to others. We check our phones constantly for new texts, new posts, and new updates. Our thumbs are flying in response. We have internet news outlets that we check daily, not satisfied to wait for the evening news or the morning newspaper. Though family or friends live far away, their faces come to us instantly in video calls. We live online in many ways.

But these connections can be fragile or even illusory. Think of the lonely woman who connects with a man who lives 500 miles away, only to discover that the "man" is actually a bunch of "borrowed" pictures being used for a teenager's entertainment. Or consider how easily an online connection can be severed, with just the click of a button. Though we are wired for relationships, we may find that those relationships are not always what we think and definitely not what we need.

Our lesson today speaks of a different type of connectedness, the one between Jesus and His followers. How does this work though? How can we be connected to Him?

B. Lesson Context

John 15 is at the center of the Farewell Discourse (John 13–17), a series of speeches and a prayer given by Jesus during the last supper. Generally, this section has material unique to John among the Gospels (see lesson 9 Lesson Context). The content makes up about 17 percent of the total text of John.

Jesus builds His case for mutual love by using common observations from the vineyard. The vineyard was a staple of agriculture in the ancient world. In the Bible, Noah is the first recorded grape grower (Genesis 9:20), and human society has prized the fruit of the vine ever since. The fruit thereby produced became a source of sustenance year-round, with many of the harvested grapes being converted into raisins and wine for later consumption (see 2 Samuel 16:1). One of the enticing descriptions of the promised land was its productive vineyards (Deuteronomy 6:10-

11; 8:7-10). Indeed, a physical sign brought back by the ill-fated spying expedition into the promised land was a massive cluster of grapes (Numbers 13:23).

Vineyards were a common sight throughout Galilee, Samaria, and Judea in Jesus' day. Besides today's text, He also used vineyard imagery in His parables of the workers in the vineyard (Matthew 20:1-16), the two sons (21:28-32), the wicked husbandmen (21:33-39), and the barren fig tree (Luke 13:6-9). Common experiences regarding vineyards are also assumed in 1 Corinthians 9:7.

Grapevines would be pruned severely at a certain time of the year, leaving little more than a leafless, branchless stump that would be propped up with a rock or two. All the old branches would be cut off and carried away, providing valuable fuel for home fires.

After new branches had grown, a second pruning would occur to remove the smaller branches. This allowed the larger branches to produce bigger clusters of larger grapes. Such pruning was part of the process known as dressing the vines (Deuteronomy 28:39).

I. The Vine and the Branches

(John 15:4-8)

A. Connected and Fruitful (vv. 4-5)

4. Abide in me, and I in you. As the branch cannot bear fruit of itself, except it abide in the vine; no more can ye, except ye abide in me.

The same Greek word translated *abide* is translated many ways depending on context, including forms of *remain* (example: John 1:33), *continue* (example: 11:54), and *dwell* (example: 14:10). The same word appears in John 8:31 where Jesus proclaimed, "If ye continue in my word, then are ye my disciples indeed." The word's wide semantic range suggests many ways of staying connected. We cannot abide in the physical body of Jesus. We abide in Jesus when we follow His word, His teachings, as a result of our relationship with Him (6:56).

John's first readers were little different from us when it comes to connecting with Jesus. They believed He rose from the dead and ascended to Heaven, as we do. But that happened 50 or 60 years earlier for John's readers (see lesson 9 Lesson Context), making remembered face-to-face contact with their Lord unlikely. Yet John insisted that the command to abide in Christ was also for them. The vineyard metaphor reassures readers even today that we will see the *fruit* of our relationship with Jesus when we remain faithful to Him (see commentary on John 15:8, below).

What Do You Think?

What one extra practice can you adopt to strengthen your connection to the vine?

Digging Deeper

How would you answer this question in terms of "philosophy and vain deceit" (Colossians 2:8) you should confront?

5. I am the vine, ye are the branches: He that abideth in me, and I in him, the same bringeth forth much fruit: for without me ye can do nothing.

The *vine* is the main, above-ground stalk of the plant. Each grape plant will have one vine, but many *branches* splitting off it. The vine is the source of water and nutrients that come from the roots to nourish the branches and *fruit*. The branches need to stay connected to the vine if they are to live.

In the same way, disciples will be intimately connected to Jesus for life-giving spiritual nourishment and leadership. If this relationship is strong, the natural result will be the production of fruit.

Grounded in Prayer

I recently took a tough job as the head of an organization that had faced many challenges in the previous year: a decrease in revenue, infighting among staff, and low productivity. I knew it would take time to learn about the people, the culture, and the backstory of the current challenge. I also knew that I would have to keep myself grounded in prayer in order to lead well.

As I researched records and met with stakeholders, I discovered that the problems were worse than I had been told. Some days were grueling as

I searched through many documents. I was frustrated by the issues I was tasked with fixing. By the end of each work week, I felt exhausted. However, I noticed that the weeks that I experienced the most fatigue were those in which I sacrificed my time with God to keep working.

Jesus said, "Without me ye can do nothing" (John 15:5). Jesus is the very source of our life. Staying connected to Him is not an option; it's a necessity. —L. H.-P.

B. Severed or Withered (vv. 6-8)

6. If a man abide not in me, he is cast forth as a branch, and is withered; and men gather them, and cast them into the fire, and they are burned.

Not all branches coming out of the vine are productive or even survive. Some branches are visibly damaged in various ways or even dead. Others simply have no fruit well into the growing season, thus becoming like parasites that suck life-giving water and nutrients from the vine and its roots. Such branches are removed from the vine to allow the remaining branches more room to flourish.

Fuel for fires was always in demand, but these branches seem to be a bonfire just to dispose of trash. This is an image of judgment (compare Luke 3:9). To be thrown into the fire is a negative judgment on the faithless and disobedient (see Ezekiel 19:12; Matthew 13:42; Revelation 20:15).

> *What Do You Think?*
> What false vine have you seen as most dangerous in drawing people away from Christ?
> *Digging Deeper*
> Which false vine seen in Matthew 7:15; 2 Corinthians 11:12-14, 26; Galatians 2:4; 2 Peter 2:1-3; and 1 John 4:1-3 most threatens to sever you from the true vine? How will you resist?

7. If ye abide in me, and my words abide in you, ye shall ask what ye will, and it shall be done unto you.

Jesus began a more direct description of what it means to *abide in* Him, tying it to having His *words abide in* a person. This means to have our ways of thinking and ways of acting guided by the teachings of Jesus. To live in Christ is to live with His commands and teachings as our chief influence (see Colossians 3:16).

Understanding this helps us know what Jesus meant when He promised that we can *ask* whatever we *will* and expect it will *be done,* a reference to prayer. This is not some sort of magical formula though. Praying to find a chest of pirate treasure so we can be rich would not be within the scope of Jesus' promise. Even asking for good things may go against God's will and thus not be given (example: Mark 14:35-36). In all cases, such asking and promised answering is only for those who are deep in the mind-set of Jesus (John 14:14). If we are abiding as He asks, we will not ask something that is clearly contrary to the will of our Lord (16:23-24).

8. Herein is my Father glorified, that ye bear much fruit; so shall ye be my disciples.

Jesus summed this up in three ways. First, this faithful abiding and resulting obedience bring glory to the *Father.* Our actions reflect on our Lord. Faithful, gracious actions bring God glory. Second, faithful abiding will *bear much fruit.* This might be evidence of a godly life, what Paul described as the "fruit of the Spirit" (Galatians 5:22-23). It is also the reproduction of one's life in the creation of new disciples.

This leads to the third item in Jesus' summary: doing this is the core of being a disciple of Christ. *Disciple,* though now a churchly word, is similar to the English word *student.* Jesus is the teacher from whom we learn. He is the teacher we never outgrow. We are Jesus' disciples for life.

> *What Do You Think?*
> In which area of discipleship are Christians weaker: their way of thinking or their way of living? Why?
> *Digging Deeper*
> Considering passages such as Titus 2:11 and Jude 3, what guardrails can Christians erect to avoid rationalizing in either area?

II. The Lord and His Friends

(John 15:9-17)

A. Loving, Joyful Obedience (vv. 9-11)

9. As the Father hath loved me, so have I loved you: continue ye in my love.

Jesus moved beyond the vine analogy to speak more directly about the relationship between His disciples and himself, and among the disciples themselves. He began with the most fundamental dynamic in the universe: God's love. Jesus testified to the Father's love for Him throughout the book of John. This love is demonstrated by the authority the *Father* gave the Son (John 3:35) and the Father's revealing His plans to the Son (5:20). The Father also loves the Son for His willingness to give His life for sinners (10:17).

The love of the Father for the Son has no starting date (John 17:24). This relationship of love for the Son by the Father is eternal. It is therefore an unchanging quality that we can depend on. God's love never changes and never fails. All these things that describe the Father's incredible love for Jesus describe, in turn, Jesus' incredible *love* for His disciples. Yet experiencing that love fully requires believers to *continue in* Jesus' love.

10. If ye keep my commandments, ye shall abide in my love; even as I have kept my Father's commandments, and abide in his love.

Jesus pushed the connection between command-keeping and love-abiding beyond His relationship with His disciples to the ultimate paradigm: His relationship with His Father. Jesus asked them to consider that He always kept His Father's commands and never departed from His deep, abiding relationship with His Father.

We should remember that in our relationship with God, there is not a progression from command-keeping to being loved. We are not loved because we are obedient; we are loved because we are God's creatures. We cannot earn God's love. The relationship begins with the eternal love of the Father for us, just as the Father's love for the Son has no beginning or end. We are obedient because we are loved and return that love through keeping the Father's commandments. That is how we *abide in* the Father's *love.*

> *What Do You Think?*
>
> What guardrails or spiritual disciplines can you put in place to ensure that your keeping of Jesus' commandments does not result in pride or a sense of entitlement?
>
> *Digging Deeper*
>
> Going the other way, what kinds of guardrails probably won't work? Why?

11. These things have I spoken unto you, that my joy might remain in you, and that your joy might be full.

Loving God (and therefore being obedient to Him) is not drudgery. It brings *joy*, a full lifetime of joy. It may seem bizarre for Jesus to speak of great joy on the night of the last supper because of what lay ahead: agony in prayer (Luke 22:42-44), betrayal (22:48), a sense of abandonment (Matthew 26:56; 27:46; compare Psalm 22), unjust trials (Matthew 26:57-68; Luke 22:66–23:25), brutal beating (Matthew 27:26), and death by crucifixion (27:27-50). He would truly be the "man of sorrows" in the hours ahead (Isaiah 53:3). Sorrows are temporary, though, and the reward for endurance is eternal (2 Corinthians 4:16-18). A little later, Jesus promised His disciples that their great sorrow and emotional pain would turn into joy (John 16:20-22), a situation aided by the coming of the Holy Spirit (16:12-15).

B. Great, Sacrificial Love (vv. 12-14)

12. This is my commandment, That ye love one another, as I have loved you.

This command is found in many places in the New Testament. In John's Gospel, it is first introduced in 13:34. Paul also taught this command for believers (Romans 12:10; 13:8; 1 Thessalonians 4:9), as did Peter (1 Peter 1:22). Neither of these apostles learned this new commandment by reading John. Instead, the command was learned from Jesus himself, just as John records.

Therefore, this command is one of the core elements of being a Christian. A non-Christian may indeed be a loving person, but it is difficult to understand how a Christian could be an unloving person. There are many deep and complex

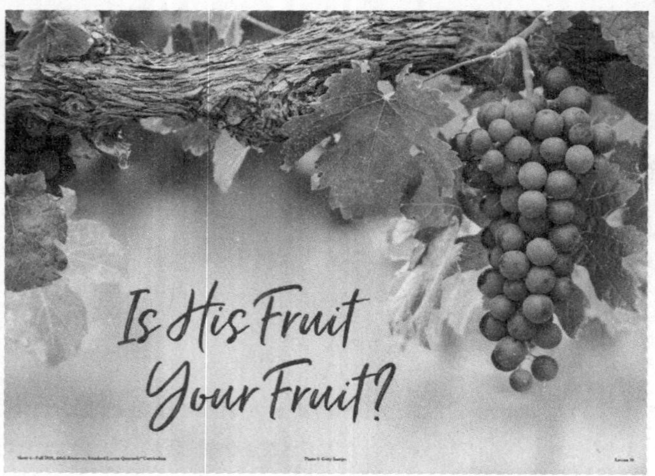

Visual for Lesson 10. *While discussing verse 8, ask this question of the class. Ask how they have grown in Jesus and how they hope to grow in the future.*

issues to the Christian faith, but this is not one of them. When asked whom we must love, Jesus told a story of actively loving one's enemies (Luke 10:25-37; see lesson 7). If we love our enemies, who are we entitled *not* to love?

13. Greater love hath no man than this, that a man lay down his life for his friends.

Earlier, Jesus taught that this was to be the ultimate sign of discipleship, a demonstration that would mark Christians as different to those outside the fellowship (John 13:35). Now He clarified that this love has no limitations. We should love one another even to the point of dying for one another. This is a tall order indeed!

There is a sense of poignancy here when we consider that John, the author of this book, would be the only disciple present to die of natural causes. According to church history and tradition, all the others in the room would give their lives for Jesus and the church. John remembered that Jesus loved His disciples to the end (John 13:1), but they would love Him to their ends too. There is no *greater love* than this.

14. Ye are my friends, if ye do whatsoever I command you.

Again, Jesus circled back to the expression of our love for Him: doing His commands. When we accept that the Father has great love for us, we will love Him in return. We will express our love for Him by obedience, not rebellion or apathy (compare 1 John 4:19-21). As this love-and-obey pattern gains strength in our lives, we will find joy that comes from God. This puts us in a new category. We are Jesus' *friends*, motivated out of love to do what God requires of us.

C. Chosen Messengers (vv. 15-17)

15. Henceforth I call you not servants; for the servant knoweth not what his lord doeth: but I have called you friends; for all things that I have heard of my Father I have made known unto you.

A *servant* ultimately obeys out of fear. A servant could be harshly punished with near impunity for the owner in the legal system of Jesus' day. Servants were not confidantes of their masters. Their job was to obey without knowledge or comment.

Such blind obedience is not what Jesus expects. His disciples are not servants but *friends.* These are not acquaintances or business associates; a friend is one for whom a person feels deep affection and demonstrates loyalty. Few servants would ever be considered beloved friends of their masters. Jesus disclosed that friendship is the relationship He has been working toward throughout His three-year ministry with the disciples. Their knowledge has grown because of Jesus' many revelations of the nature of the Father and of the plans He and the Father have for the future. The disciples are "insiders," friends considered worthy of receiving *all things* Jesus has *heard* from His *Father.*

What Do You Think?

What would have to change, if anything, for you to be convinced that Jesus considers you a "friend" instead of a "servant"?

Digging Deeper

How do Exodus 33:11; Isaiah 41:8; John 11:11; and James 2:23 help you answer this?

Jesus Is a True Friend

During my college years, a popular Christian song referred to God as a friend. A classmate protested anytime he heard it. He thought it was blasphemy to refer to God—the holy Creator of the universe—as a friend. He observed people falling in and out of relationship with God just as they did with their other friends. He saw Christians not honoring God with their actions, in the same way they disrespected their friends. He pushed the idea that people need to respect God as God and not treat Him as they treated their friends.

My colleague was partially right, but he missed what Jesus said. Jesus was willing to sacrifice His own life for His friends—friends who would not be as loyal and deeply invested. Jesus, God in the flesh, exemplified what a true friend is. If Christ was willing to lay down His life for the world, then we all owe Him our lives too. —L. H.-P.

16. Ye have not chosen me, but I have chosen you, and ordained you, that ye should go and bring forth fruit, and that your fruit should remain: that whatsoever ye shall ask of the Father in my name, he may give it you.

Jesus also revealed that His relationship with His disciples was all part of His plan. To be *ordained* in this sense does not refer to a ceremony, but to having been chosen for a position of responsibility. They were Jesus' friends-with-purpose, and that purpose is to produce *fruit.* This is to be *fruit* that will *remain,* a reference not to grapes but to new disciples, new friends-with-purpose. This is why they were chosen: Jesus' multigenerational plan for expanding the number and maturity of His followers.

The disciples were reminded that God will give them resources in this work. After Jesus had gone, *the Father* would continue to be with them, giving what they asked for. These plans and promises are for us also, still the disciples of Jesus two millennia later. We are expected to *bring forth fruit.* The vine of Jesus continues to produce the fruit of new disciples and spiritual growth even today and will do so in the future.

HOW TO SAY IT

Galilee	*Gal*-uh-lee.
Judas	*Joo*-dus.
Judea	Joo-*dee*-uh.
Samaria	Suh-*mare*-ee-uh.

17. These things I command you, that ye love one another.

Jesus ended this section by restating the great *command.* Within a few hours, the disciples would witness the greatest act of love in history: Jesus' willing, sacrificial death for the sin of the world (John 19:16-30). There is no greater love.

There is no expiration date on this directive. It overrides all things that confront us in the Christian life. Jesus' disciples will have disagreements. Conflicts will be inevitable. But there is never an excuse for not loving our brothers and sisters in the Lord (1 John 4:7-12).

Conclusion

A. Unselfish Love

Abiding, obeying, and loving—these are the central elements of discipleship. The love of Jesus exemplifies all of these. He abides with the Father in a relationship so intimate, it is beyond our understanding. He always obeys the Father. And His great love for the Father overflows to His chosen disciples.

In this we understand what biblical love is all about. It is conditioned by a lasting, faithful relationship and expressed by obedience. It is unselfish love, given without condition or expectation of return. In the Gospel of John, the last supper finds Jesus teaching about these things. The arrest, trials, and crucifixion find Him acting out these things. The resurrection shows the Father approving of these things for Jesus: His teachings and His actions. Thereby the disciples of Jesus have been motivated ever since to follow Him unselfishly with the purposes of being obedient disciples themselves and of producing new disciples in every generation.

B. Prayer

Father, may we show our love for You by obeying Your commands. Nurture us so we bear the fruit You want to see in our lives. In Jesus' name we pray. Amen.

C. Thought to Remember

When we love, we obey.

INVOLVEMENT LEARNING

Enhance your lesson with KJV Bible Student *(from your curriculum supplier) and the reproducible activity page (at www.standardlesson.com or in the back of the* KJV Standard Lesson Commentary Deluxe Edition*).*

Into the Lesson

Divide the class into groups of three. Instruct groups to take one minute to list on a sheet of paper the ways people connect with others. After calling time, reconvene for whole-class sharing of lists. (*Possible responses:* face-to-face conversations, e-mail, text messaging, phone calls, social media, etc.) Jot responses on the board.

Take a show-of-hands survey of class members who use each method. Then pose the following questions, but not all at once; allow time for discussion before moving to the next question.

1–What has been the most significant change in communication for you in the last decade?

2–How about the decade before that?

3–How about the decade before even that?

Alternative. If you wish to focus exclusively on social media, distribute copies of the "Connecting" activity from the activity page, which you can download. Have learners work together in groups of three to complete as indicated.

After either exercise above, make a transition by saying, "Let's see what today's lesson tells us about the best way to connect with Jesus."

Into the Word

Write the following words on the board as headers to columns, one word per column:

Abide / Branch(es) / Vine

Have learners form study pairs (or triads). Then distribute handouts (you prepare) on which you have reproduced the entirety of the lesson text of John 15:4-17. If your learners have the student book, they can use the Scripture page there for this activity instead of a handout.

Point to the board and ask pairs to count how many times each word occurs in the text. This will go faster if learners have pencils or highlighters of different colors with which to mark findings. The second-best procedure is to mark findings with different geometric shapes: a square around instances of *abide,* a triangle around instances of *vine,* etc. After pairs finish, call for findings and correct oversights, noting that *abide, branch(es),* and *vine* occur nine, three, and two times, respectively. Put those tallies on the board under the headers.

Repeat all the above with the words *fruit, if,* and *I have.* After recording tallies of five, four, and six (or eight counting the two instances of "have I") respectively, ask pairs to decide the two most important connections they see among those words. As pairs offer their conclusions in whole-class discussion, be prepared to state two of your own. Work toward consensus.

Into Life

Pose one or more of the following scenarios for whole-class discussion. (*Option.* Reproduce one or more of them on handouts for either whole-class or small-group consideration.)

Scenario 1–You inform your boss that the restructuring your company requires would result in layoffs.

Scenario 2–You discover that your teenager has been sneaking out after bedtime.

Scenario 3–An acquaintance who is known to have sociopathic tendencies has been saying untrue things about you behind your back.

Pose this question for learners' responses to any or all of the scenarios: "How should today's lesson text have a bearing on framing your thoughts and actions regarding this situation?"

Option. Distribute copies of the "Obeying" exercise from the activity page for learners to complete individually as indicated. When the time limit of one minute expires, ask for volunteers to share responses; don't put anyone on the spot. Close with prayer for mentioned and unmentioned challenges.

Confident Love

Devotional Reading: Hebrews 13:1-8
Background Scripture: 1 John 3:11-24; 2 John 4-11; 3 John 5-8

1 John 3:11-24

11 For this is the message that ye heard from the beginning, that we should love one another.

12 Not as Cain, who was of that wicked one, and slew his brother. And wherefore slew he him? Because his own works were evil, and his brother's righteous.

13 Marvel not, my brethren, if the world hate you.

14 We know that we have passed from death unto life, because we love the brethren. He that loveth not his brother abideth in death.

15 Whosoever hateth his brother is a murderer: and ye know that no murderer hath eternal life abiding in him.

16 Hereby perceive we the love of God, because he laid down his life for us: and we ought to lay down our lives for the brethren.

17 But whoso hath this world's good, and seeth his brother have need, and shutteth up his bowels of compassion from him, how dwelleth the love of God in him?

18 My little children, let us not love in word, neither in tongue; but in deed and in truth.

19 And hereby we know that we are of the truth, and shall assure our hearts before him.

20 For if our heart condemn us, God is greater than our heart, and knoweth all things.

21 Beloved, if our heart condemn us not, then have we confidence toward God.

22 And whatsoever we ask, we receive of him, because we keep his commandments, and do those things that are pleasing in his sight.

23 And this is his commandment, That we should believe on the name of his Son Jesus Christ, and love one another, as he gave us commandment.

24 And he that keepeth his commandments dwelleth in him, and he in him. And hereby we know that he abideth in us, by the Spirit which he hath given us.

Key Verse

He that keepeth his commandments dwelleth in him, and he in him. And hereby we know that he abideth in us, by the Spirit which he hath given us. —**1 John 3:24**

Photo: cihanterlan / iStock / Thinkstock

Love for One Another

Unit 3: Godly Love Among Believers

Lessons 9–13

Lesson Aims

After participating in this lesson, each learner will be able to:

1. List several ways Jesus called His disciples to show love for fellow believers.

2. Explain what Jesus meant when He promised that the world will hate Christians.

3. Recruit an accountability partner to help him or her grow in keeping God's command to love.

Lesson Outline

Introduction
- A. Hated by the World
- B. Lesson Context

I. Cain's Example (1 John 3:11-15)
- A. Loving from the Beginning (v. 11)
  - *A Gentle Reminder*
- B. Lifeless like Murderers (vv. 12-15)
  - *The End of Hate Is Death*

II. Christ's Sacrifice (1 John 3:16-18)
- A. Imitate Jesus (v. 16)
- B. Demonstrate Love (vv. 17-18)

III. Faith's Test (1 John 3:19-24)
- A. Of the Heart (vv. 19-22)
- B. Of Actions (vv. 23-24)

Conclusion
- A. Evidence Required
- B. Prayer
- C. Thought to Remember

Introduction

A. Hated by the World

Blogger Carey Nieuwhof has written that non-Christians hate Christians because they think they are judgmental, hypocritical, and insincere friends. But history tells the stories of many Christians who were none of these things. We can find many examples in our churches today of Christians who refuse to be judgmental, whose lives are not hypocritical, and whose friendships are sincere both with believers and nonbelievers. Still, some of these exemplary folks suffer persecution, even death. There must be a deeper dynamic here.

Most Christians have plenty of room to be more Christlike in our relationships with non-Christians. But nothing we do will earn the world's love. This was also true for John's readers. What is to be done in a seemingly no-win situation?

B. Lesson Context

The three letters of John were likely written about the same time as the Gospel of John, in the AD 80s or 90s. The letters reflect a personal relationship with the readers, like a pastor writing to his flock. Indeed, early Christian sources indicate that the apostle John left Jerusalem and his home region of Galilee to settle in the city of Ephesus. Paul had founded the church of Ephesus in the mid-50s on his third missionary journey (Acts 19:1-22). The city had become a center of Christian activity, and this was strengthened by the arrival of John 15 to 20 years after Paul. At the time of the writing of 1 John, the apostle had served as a pastor for the Ephesians for more than a decade.

John wrote as the senior statesman of the church, likely the last living of the 12 original apostles. First John contains a wide range of topics that summarize the aged apostle's teachings and advice for his beloved "children," the Christians of Ephesus. The letters of John deal with factions within and outside the church of Ephesus, which had begun to teach many false things (examples: 1 John 2:18, 22; 4:3). Included in this list were things like the denial of the true humanity of Christ (and therefore His atoning death), of the reality of sin in the lives of the teachers, and of the assurance of salvation for believers as taught by Jesus.

John wrote this epistle against a background of false teachers who came to be known as gnostics. Among other things, gnostics taught that it did not really matter if a person had morality or love—as long as he or she had "secret knowledge." To combat this false teaching, John emphasized the interconnection of right belief, right actions, and right love. To put it another way, it is the right involvement of head, hands, and heart. The child of God must believe the truth, obey the commands, and love brothers and sisters in Christ.

John showed that such threats to the faith must be dealt with firmly and without compromise, yet with a spirit of love. Christians cannot return hate and abuse with more hate and abuse. Even in the most contentious relationships, love must prevail. Surely this applied to John himself, whose teachings were under attack by these heretics. His original readers may have witnessed firsthand his response to his antagonists, and if this had been anything but love, the message of 1 John would have a hollow ring.

John demonstrated that if we are in the right and "walkest in the truth" (3 John 3), we can bring great confidence to our relationship with anyone. This is not arrogance or elitism, but inner strength that does not depend on the approval of others for personal well-being.

I. Cain's Example

(1 John 3:11-15)

A. Loving from the Beginning (v. 11)

11. For this is the message that ye heard from the beginning, that we should love one another.

The *beginning* for John refers to his original teachings among his readers. His *message* has not evolved or changed, and the basic message is still that *we should love one another.* Furthermore, this key concept can be found in the teachings of Jesus (see John 13:34-35). These words of his master made a strong impression on the young John 50 years earlier, and he never forgot them. He does not want his readers to forget or neglect them either.

A Gentle Reminder

When the new preacher arrived at our church, the members were glad that he was young. They thought he would bring new energy to the congregation, which he did. For a month and a half, this minister led the congregation through the basic principles of the Christian faith and life.

By the fifth week, one of the older members told the young man that they already knew what he was teaching. The preacher smiled and told her, "I said I would not be sharing anything you didn't already know. This series on discipleship is only a reminder of how we are supposed to live as Christians in the world."

John was doing the same thing that this young preacher was doing. Sometimes we all need a gentle reminder of the central message of the Christian faith—not because we don't already know it, but to make sure we're living it out in the world.

—L. H.-P.

B. Lifeless like Murderers (vv. 12-15)

12. Not as Cain, who was of that wicked one, and slew his brother. And wherefore slew he him? Because his own works were evil, and his brother's righteous.

While we usually see hate as the opposite of love, John gives a biblical example that shows the complexity of our relationships. Why would we hate another person? In the story of *Cain* and *his brother,* Abel, there was an underlying dynamic of jealousy. God judged Cain's offering of agricultural products to be *evil,* while Abel's offering of choice portions from the animals of his flock were deemed *righteous* (Genesis 4:1-5).

What Do You Think?

Which kind of Bible character inspires you more to act in love: positive examples of those who did or negative examples of those who didn't?

Digging Deeper

What biblical characters, other than Jesus or Cain, can you name as examples?

We know from the later laws of Israel that a "meat [grain] offering" was not repugnant to the Lord (see Leviticus 6:14; Numbers 4:16), so the fault of Cain was in the unrighteous condition of his heart. John's point is that Cain's actions confirmed his evil heart. His jealousy grew to hatred and resulted in murder.

13. Marvel not, my brethren, if the world hate you.

When John wrote of *the world*, he meant something more specific (and sinister) than the general populace. The world represents those who are in rebellion against God, defiantly sinning against God's commands. They have rejected God's rules for living and resent any restrictions on their freedom to sin.

The world's hatred for the church flows out of its hatred for God himself. The people of God will never be accepted by those who reject God. Such hatred of the righteous by the unrighteous has changed little in the thousands of years since Cain and Abel. This ancient dynamic persists in the way the world views the church.

14a. We know that we have passed from death unto life, because we love the brethren.

While the world is dead in its wickedness and hatred, believers have moved from *death unto life*. This fact calls and then empowers Christians to *love* each other, a sign of genuine life in Christ. Our assurance of salvation is based on more than our love for Jesus. We cannot claim to love the Lord while hating others. This reinforces what John has already taught about the world. The world hates Christians because it hates Jesus.

Hate, of course, may seem strong to describe the world's reaction to Christ. Some people genuinely seem to respect Jesus as a philosopher or even prophet who had important things to say. However, by rejecting His claim that He is the Son of God who redeems people from their sins, they fail to love Him as they ought. For this reason, the world dwells in death when it could pass into life, if only it would love Jesus and accept His lordship.

The hatred of Cain is an old story, and the hatred of the world is probably not surprising.

HOW TO SAY IT

Ephesus *Ef*-uh-sus.
Galilee *Gal*-uh-lee.

But what about hatred within the family of God? It is inconceivable! If a believer doesn't love other members of Christ's body, it signifies that such a person either has never come all the way into life or has gone back and now abides in death.

14b. He that loveth not his brother abideth in death.

This verse represents an absolute truth for Christians: if you hate your brothers and sisters in the faith, you abide *in death*, spiritual separation from God. Such people have not experienced the eternal life promised to those who put their faith in Jesus (see John 5:24). They are still under condemnation because of sin (3:18).

15. Whosoever hateth his brother is a murderer: and ye know that no murderer hath eternal life abiding in him.

Jesus taught that anger and disrespectful behavior are comparable to murder (Matthew 5:21-22). Anger and hate feed one another. Human anger does not produce God's righteousness (James 1:20). Unchecked and unresolved anger may indeed lead to violence and even murder, things that should have no place in the church.

Though murder can be coldly calculated (and thus reveal a horrifying depth of hatred), more often it is a crime of passion committed in a fit of anger and hate. This was the case with Cain, who seethed with anger against God and his brother (Genesis 4:5-6). The Lord described this deadly mix of animosity as "sin . . . at the door" (4:7).

What Do You Think?

What do you need to do to reject the kind of hatred described in 1 John 2:9, 11; 3:15; and 4:20 while embracing the kind of hatred Jesus describes in Luke 14:26?

Digging Deeper

Which of those two tasks will be harder for you? Why?

The End of Hate Is Death

One of my favorite television shows depicted a long-held feud between two brothers. Since childhood, their father favored the older son because he always showed interest in the family business.

When the father died, he left the business to both sons. The younger brother despised the father's sticking him with a business he didn't want and a partner he resented.

Then the older brother had an accident on the job, which sent him to the hospital. Doctors discovered he needed a liver transplant immediately. His brother was a match, but would not help unless his older brother sold the business. The brother refused; they exchanged hateful words. These two brothers were so concerned with their personal vendettas that one of them almost died.

Hate and jealousy can become fatal. The death-dealing nature of hate is literal but also subtle. These brothers missed out on the loving, life-giving relationship that they could have had. The energy to exert hate is not worth the costs. Christians are called to choose love and life over hate and death. —L. H.-P.

II. Christ's Sacrifice

(1 John 3:16-18)

A. Imitate Jesus (v. 16)

16. Hereby perceive we the love of God, because he laid down his life for us: and we ought to lay down our lives for the brethren.

Jesus' Jewish opponents hounded and threatened Him throughout His ministry (example: John 11:8). If Jesus had decided to let His emotions turn to murderous hate, He had far greater resources than whatever murder weapon Cain used. Jesus could have summoned thousands of warrior angels to exact His vengeance (Matthew 26:53). But he didn't. Instead, He willingly died for the sake of all people, including His killers (Luke 23:34), John's first-century readers, and even us. Jesus acted out His love with willing purpose, the polar opposite of the angry hate of a murderer.

Thus the first measure of *love* is a practical test. When God loved the world, He sent Heaven's greatest gift. Jesus came and *laid down His life for us*—unrepentant enemies of God (see John 3:16; Romans 5:8, 10; Colossians 1:21-22). Love like God's love could give nothing less. God's children should resemble their Father in this kind of love. We should be willing to do just about anything for our *brethren.*

> *What Do You Think?*
> How would you explain to someone that 1 John 3:16 is just as important to memorize as John 3:16?
>
> *Digging Deeper*
> How would your explanation to a fellow believer differ from your explanation to an unbeliever, if at all? Why?

B. Demonstrate Love (vv. 17-18)

17. But whoso hath this world's good, and seeth his brother have need, and shutteth up his bowels of compassion from him, how dwelleth the love of God in him?

Today we might talk about hardening one's heart instead of shutting up one's *bowels* (compare Exodus 8:15; 9:34; 2 Corinthians 6:11). Jesus' death for His brothers and sisters serves as the ultimate act of love, in contrast to Cain's act of hate.

John pushed this to a smaller scale, something within his readers' daily experience. Most of us will not literally die for others (compare Matthew 16:24-27), yet we have opportunities daily to give of our livelihoods, our personal resources (*this world's good*), to help those in *need*. Love, like faith, requires evidence in our actions (James 2:15-17). When we accept *the love of God*, we also take the responsibility to prove that love in our relationships with others.

18. My little children, let us not love in word, neither in tongue; but in deed and in truth.

Any claim for loving God should result in observable deeds of compassion for others. Lack of concern for the needy brings the entire status of a Christian into question. John used *truth* here in the sense of veracity, of verifiable actions. He also taught that love for God and hate for others cannot coexist (1 John 4:20).

John knows that these stern words might convict some of their unfaithful deeds, so he spoke with urgency to his *little children*, his beloved flock. Although false teachers seemed unworried about physical actions as evidence of faith, John

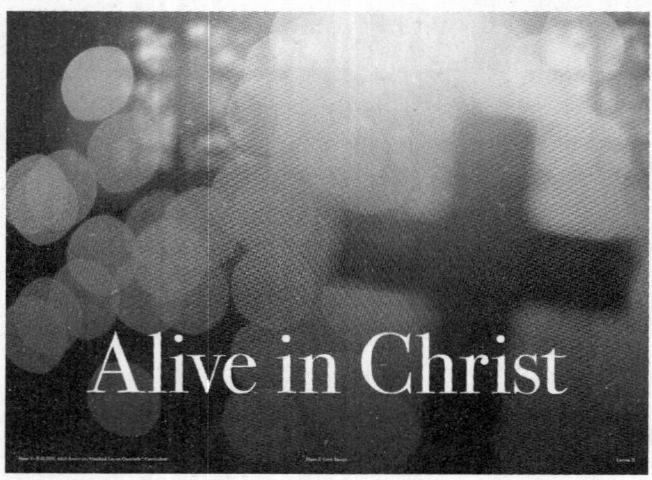

Visual for Lesson 11. *While discussing verse 24, use the visual to ask the class how the Spirit's work in their lives has confirmed that they live in Christ.*

insisted that loving behavior is the only way to really demonstrate love in one's heart.

> *What Do You Think?*
>
> What are some situations in today's churches in which John's stress on the importance of truth (a word occurring dozens of times in his Gospel and letters) requires the greatest measure of tact in light of the need for grace (compare John 1:14-17; 2 John 3)?
>
> *Digging Deeper*
>
> What have you learned from such situations that were handled wrongly in that regard?

III. Faith's Test

(1 John 3:19-24)

A. Of the Heart (vv. 19-22)

19. And hereby we know that we are of the truth, and shall assure our hearts before him.

John offers a test to determine whether *we are of the truth* (see 1 John 3:20 commentary, below). To be *of the truth* is John's way of saying our actions prove we are not acting with guile or deceit, but with godly sincerity and honesty.

We should pay attention to *our hearts*, but not as an infallible guide. The heart in biblical thought is not simply the center of emotions. The heart is the source of our deepest impulses, our motivations, our freewill decisions. It is where we make choices.

20. For if our heart condemn us, God is greater than our heart, and knoweth all things.

Here, a *heart* that condemns may be rightly convicting us of sin that has not been rooted out. This seems especially to be what John had in mind; if our hearts condemn us, then *God* has even more reason to condemn us because He sees our hearts even more clearly than we do!

Yet John's encouragement is that God *is greater than our heart*. Our inner voice can be misleading, an embodiment of our self-centered tendencies or shameful previous behavior. God sees not only what our hearts tell us, but also what He knows about us. His great love does not *condemn us* when we are in Christ.

21. Beloved, if our heart condemn us not, then have we confidence toward God.

If the *heart* does not *condemn us*—does not resist helping the needy with acts of love—we should feel *confidence* in our relationship with *God*. We have tamed the heart of stony selfishness and allowed it to be a soft heart of obedience and kindness. The hard heart is liable for the judgmental wrath of God (see Romans 2:5). When we act in kindness for others, we show that we have a new heart, the heart recreated by God's grace (see Psalm 51:10; Ezekiel 11:19).

22. And whatsoever we ask, we receive of him, because we keep his commandments, and do those things that are pleasing in his sight.

The path forward for the believer is to *ask* the right *things* of God and to *do* the right things for God (see John 15:7; lesson 10). We are self-testing when we look at these things critically. When we pray, do we pray for things necessary to do God's will? When we act, do our actions please God rather than disappoint Him?

B. Of Actions (vv. 23-24)

23a. And this is his commandment.

The *commandment* that John stated here did not come from the apostle but from God.

23b. That we should believe on the name of his Son Jesus Christ, and love one another, as he gave us commandment.

To *believe on the name of his Son Jesus Christ* (compare John 6:29) and to *love one another* cannot be disconnected from each other. True believers in Jesus Christ will practice mutual love always. Jesus mentioned this repeatedly on the final night He spent with His disciples in the upper room (see John 13:34; 15:12, 17). Many decades later, John showed us that he had not forgotten his master's words of that night. Despite the many problems and challenges of the church(es) John addressed, this controlling ethic never lost its power or authority.

Although there are many layers to John's teachings, he often simplified his discussions to essential basics at appropriate places. Pleasing God requires a clean heart that acts with love for others. This is the act of surrender, of putting full trust in Jesus with a heart that is willing to follow His teachings. John only taught his "little children" (1 John 3:18; see commentary above) what Jesus taught him.

24. And he that keepeth his commandments dwelleth in him, and he in him. And hereby we know that he abideth in us, by the Spirit which he hath given us.

We *know* we are in fellowship with God if we keep *his commandments.* We see evidence of our obedience when our lives show that we are loving one another faithfully. *The Spirit* abides in us, changing our hearts so that we keep the commands from pure motives, not just fear of punishment.

A loving church that serves the needy of its community gives witness to the Spirit of God in its midst. We please the Father when we follow the teachings of His Son and allow His Spirit to guide our acts of love for others.

Conclusion

A. Evidence Required

A few years ago, my wife had knee-replacement surgery. I chose not to witness the procedure. When she came back to her room, I could see incisions and stitches, but I could not see an artificial appliance made of metal and plastic under her skin. A small, paranoid part of me wondered briefly if it was all fake. Maybe the surgeon and hospital conspired to make a few cuts to give the appearance of surgery, charged thousands of dollars, and left her old, worn-out knee intact.

It takes time to recover from this operation. At first, the pain of healing outweighed the previous pain of a crippled knee. Gradually, though, her knee got better. Now, after complete recovery, she has much better mobility and much less pain than before. Even though I did not see it placed there and cannot see it now, I know there is a new knee in my wife's right leg. I witness the evidence every day.

John asks if we love God. He insists we cannot make a credible claim to loving God if we hate other people. Furthermore, we cannot claim to love other people without evidence. Does the love of God in our hearts result in acts of kindness toward others?

Cain's heart of hate and anger resulted in murder, a heinous but accurate reflection of his inner thoughts. Jesus Christ's heart of love resulted in the willing sacrifice of His life as the Lamb of God to take away the sin of the world (John 1:29), the same world that John warns will hate Jesus' followers (1 John 3:13). The paradox is profound, but the evidence is there with Jesus. While we were His enemies, He died for us (Romans 5:8-10).

What does the evidence of our lives reveal about the secrets of our hearts?

> *What Do You Think?*
>
> What are the one or two most important things you learn about pastoral care from today's text?
>
> *Digging Deeper*
>
> What is the most important thing you can do this week to initiate such care directly or to support someone who already does so?

B. Prayer

Loving Father, when the world hates us, comfort us with Your love. Give us the presence of Your Holy Spirit and new hearts that love one another and show our love in our actions. In Jesus' name we pray. Amen.

C. Thought to Remember

Loving God is shown by loving people.

INVOLVEMENT LEARNING

Enhance your lesson with KJV Bible Student *(from your curriculum supplier) and the reproducible activity page (at www.standardlesson.com or in the back of the* KJV Standard Lesson Commentary Deluxe Edition*).*

Into the Lesson

Option. Before class begins, place in chairs copies of the "Simon Says" exercise on the activity page, which you can download, for learners to complete as they arrive.

As class begins, have the following written on the board:

How can I be confident that . . .
my car will make the trip?
I am dressed appropriately for the weather?
I have enough food for company?
what I am baking will turn out right?
I will have enough money to retire?
I am on time for my appointment?
I am eating food that is good for me?
my children are behaving?
I will wake up on time?
I am doing a good job at work?

Working down the list line by line, call for a show of hands on each entry as you ask, "Who has ever had a lack of confidence in this area?" Move quickly, and do not get bogged down by discussing any single response.

Make a transition to Bible study saying, "We have been taught by authority or experience what works and what doesn't! Let's find out what the ultimate authority has to say about the number one principle that is to frame our actions."

Into the Word

Divide the class into three groups. Assign designations and passages to study as follows: **Cherish Group:** 1 John 3:11-15; **Sacrifice Group:** 1 John 3:16-18; and **Confidence Group:** 1 John 3:19-24. Challenge all groups to use their assigned passages to answer this question: "How do we know we are acting in love as God desires?" Challenge groups to summarize their conclusions in 140 characters or less, which is the traditional limit for tweets. You should decide in advance whether spaces count in those 140 characters. By comparison, the first paragraph on this page has 140 characters, not counting the 27 spaces. (*Option.* Allow summaries of up to 280 characters, which is the revised limit for tweets.)

Allow groups at least 10 minutes. Move among the groups to offer hints as needed; a first hint is to be found in the name of each group. After calling time, have groups share their summaries and explain their reasoning. Expect responses such as the following (others are possible): **Cherish Group:** 1 John 3:11-15—Godly love treats others as family members to be cherished, not as rivals to be conquered. **Sacrifice Group:** 1 John 3:16-18—Godly love sacrifices for the good of others, never using others for personal benefit. **Confidence Group:** 1 John 3:19-24—Godly love makes us increasingly confident of God's care.

Option. Begin the above activity with a mini lecture on the context. Focus on the contrast between the way people of worldly and Christian outlooks interact both with those of their kind and with those of the opposite viewpoint in terms of love (or lack thereof). Distribute copies of the "God's Outlook vs. World's Outlook" exercise from the activity page for learners to complete as indicated. You can use it as a framework for the mini lecture.

Into Life

Have learners form pairs of accountability partners. Include yourself in the pairings if you have an odd number of class members. In the coming week, accountability partners should contact each other once or twice to ask the following questions (create and distribute these on handouts):

1–What positive characteristic of a non–family member did you appreciate better so far this week?

2–In what way have you made a purposeful sacrifice for the good of someone so far this week?

3–In what way have you experienced more closeness with God by modeling His kind of love?

Responsive Love

Devotional Reading: 2 Corinthians 6:1-10
Background Scripture: Acts 4:32–5:11

Acts 4:32-37

**32 And the multitude of them that believed
were of one heart and of one soul: neither said
any of them that ought of the things which he
possessed was his own; but they had all things
common.
33 And with great power gave the apostles
witness of the resurrection of the Lord Jesus:
and great grace was upon them all.
34 Neither was there any among them that
lacked: for as many as were possessors of lands
or houses sold them, and brought the prices of
the things that were sold,
35 And laid them down at the apostles' feet:
and distribution was made unto every man
according as he had need.
36 And Joses, who by the apostles was surnamed Barnabas, (which is, being interpreted,
The son of consolation,) a Levite, and of the
country of Cyprus,
37 Having land, sold it, and brought the
money, and laid it at the apostles' feet.**

Acts 5:1-11

**1 But a certain man named Ananias, with
Sapphira his wife, sold a possession,
2 And kept back part of the price, his wife
also being privy to it, and brought a certain
part, and laid it at the apostles' feet.
3 But Peter said, Ananias, why hath Satan
filled thine heart to lie to the Holy Ghost, and
to keep back part of the price of the land?
4 Whiles it remained, was it not thine own?
and after it was sold, was it not in thine own
power? why hast thou conceived this thing in
thine heart? thou hast not lied unto men, but
unto God.
5 And Ananias hearing these words fell
down, and gave up the ghost: and great fear
came on all them that heard these things.
6 And the young men arose, wound him up,
and carried him out, and buried him.
7 And it was about the space of three hours
after, when his wife, not knowing what was
done, came in.
8 And Peter answered unto her, Tell me
whether ye sold the land for so much? And she
said, Yea, for so much.
9 Then Peter said unto her, How is it that
ye have agreed together to tempt the Spirit of
the Lord? behold, the feet of them which have
buried thy husband are at the door, and shall
carry thee out.
10 Then fell she down straightway at his feet,
and yielded up the ghost: and the young men
came in, and found her dead, and, carrying her
forth, buried her by her husband.
11 And great fear came upon all the church,
and upon as many as heard these things.**

Key Verse

The multitude of them that believed were of one heart and of one soul: neither said any of them that ought of the things which he possessed was his own; but they had all things common. —**Acts 4:32**

LOVE FOR ONE ANOTHER

Unit 3: Godly Love Among Believers

LESSONS 9–13

LESSON AIMS

After participating in this lesson, each learner will be able to:

1. List faithful practices of the first-century church.
2. Contrast the actions of the first-century church in general with the actions of Ananias and Sapphira specifically.
3. Examine personal giving practices and create a plan to correct any selfish or dishonest habits that have been formed.

LESSON OUTLINE

Introduction
- A. Never a Discouraging Word
- B. Lesson Context

I. Generosity Exercised (Acts 4:32-37)
- A. Unity in Purpose (vv. 32-35)
- B. Example of Giving (vv. 36-37)
  - *More Than Words*

II. Deception Exposed (Acts 5:1-11)
- A. A Couple's Plan (vv. 1-2)
- B. Satan and Ananias (vv. 3-6)
- C. The Spirit and Sapphira (vv. 7-11)
  - *Fraud Reports*

Conclusion
- A. An Encouraging Word
- B. Prayer
- C. Thought to Remember

Introduction

A. Never a Discouraging Word

Today's country music reflects many influences. One of these from the past century was the singing cowboy. Cowboy music was not about cheatin' husbands and loyal wives standin' by their men. It was about "The Red River Valley" or the "Streets of Laredo." They sang, "Yippee-kai-yai-ay, get along, little dogies." It might seem strange now, but many cowboy singers included yodeling in their repertoire.

One classic cowboy song induced nostalgia for when American culture was not urbanized. Written in 1872 by Brewster Higley, "Home on the Range" includes this chorus:

Home, home on the range,
Where the deer and the antelope play;
Where seldom is heard a discouraging word
And the skies are not cloudy all day.

Such a romantic picture of the past! Is there a place now "where seldom is heard a discouraging word"? Who wouldn't want to live there?

Discouragement thrives among us today, but we are not unusual. The history of the Wild West, where the cowboys sang, was full of reasons for discouragement, not the least of which was the violence against the native peoples. The early church also had its share of discouragement. Then, like now, encouragers were needed to be examples.

B. Lesson Context

Luke and Acts comprise a two-volume work written by a single author, assumed to be Luke, the physician and companion of Paul (Colossians 4:14). The first volume, the Gospel of Luke, tells the story of Jesus: His birth, ministry, crucifixion, and resurrection. The second volume, the Acts of the Apostles, tells the story of the first-century church, beginning in Jerusalem and ending with Paul's arrival in the imperial capital city, Rome.

We look to the book of Acts to understand the nature of the church in its infancy. By so doing, we hope to understand better Christ's intention for His church, as enacted through His trusted apostles, and thereby understand what the church should be today. From Acts we realize the church's primary mission: to share the gospel "unto the uttermost part of the earth" (Acts 1:8). We learn that this imperative to preach the good news about Jesus must withstand ridicule (example: 2:13), doubters (example: 3:11-12), and even coordinated persecution (example: 4:1-3).

Yet the first-century church in Jerusalem had its share of problems. It faced leadership succession issues (Acts 1:15-26). It had organizational challenges (6:1-6). The beloved fellowship even suffered from dishonesty concerning financial disclosure (Acts 5:1-11; see commentary below).

I. Generosity Exercised

(Acts 4:32-37)

A. Unity in Purpose (vv. 32-35)

32. And the multitude of them that believed were of one heart and of one soul: neither said any of them that ought of the things which he possessed was his own; but they had all things common.

The multitude here does not refer to crowd size but to those *that believed.* This is a unanimous majority, for they are *of one heart and of one soul. Heart* signifies the determined will of these people —they had common desires and plans. *Soul* represents the inner self, the life force. The Old Testament uses this combination of terms, "heart and soul," as Luke does here, to indicate the entire person (examples: Deuteronomy 13:3; Joshua 22:5). In these examples, the people are called to love God with all of their being; they were to leave no part separate to adore any other god.

Just as the church was united in devotion to the Lord, so they were united in showing that love through service to one another. Their purpose was to share wealth so that no one suffered poverty's devastations (Acts 2:44-45). They held *all things common.* This does not mean they surrendered *all* their money, possessions, and property to the church leaders and lived a fully communal life. Instead, everyone gave generously to provide for those in need. This fulfilled the intent of the law to ensure there were "no poor among you" (Deuteronomy 15:4), a longtime goal for the people of God.

33-34a. And with great power gave the apostles witness of the resurrection of the Lord Jesus: and great grace was upon them all. Neither was there any among them that lacked.

This loving, unified community allowed *the apostles* to continue their powerful preaching without undue distractions. With the crucifixion still fresh in the minds of Jerusalem's residents, the apostles proclaimed *the resurrection of . . . Jesus.* Nonbelievers witnessed a community bound by love for one another and heard a life-changing message from their leaders.

Grace is a sign of God's favor (examples: Luke 2:40; Acts 11:23). Although we primarily think of grace as a factor in forgiveness, it is not exclusively linked to forgiveness. It is a gift given by God to strengthen His people. God worked through their willingness to serve and blessed them as they loved one another.

34b-35. For as many as were possessors of lands or houses sold them, and brought the prices of the things that were sold, and laid them down at the apostles' feet: and distribution was made unto every man according as he had need.

Pentecost saw 3,000 men respond to Peter's preaching (Acts 2:41), a number that grew to 5,000 (4:4). Perhaps not all of these were active in the fellowship, for some had likely been short-term pilgrims to Jerusalem (2:5). Even so, many hundreds (at least) were involved on a weekly, even daily, basis. This large group would have naturally included some wealthy folks and some struggling to put food on their tables.

In this situation, God chose to provide for needs not through miraculous multiplication of loaves and fish (Luke 9:16-17) or through manna from Heaven (Psalm 78:24). Instead, the Spirit moved

HOW TO SAY IT

Ananias	An-uh-*nye*-us.
Barnabas	*Bar*-nuh-bus.
Cyprus	*Sigh*-prus.
Joses	*Jo*-sez.
Salamis	*Sal*-uh-mis.
Sapphira	Suh-*fye*-ruh.

the hearts of the wealthy to sell *houses* and *lands* and release the proceeds to the apostles. This was done by bringing the money from such sales and laying the coins *at the apostles' feet*, thus giving it to the church's leaders to be used appropriately.

At least one way the *distribution was made* was in food for the hungry (see Acts 6:1). The church leaders may also have distributed money to the believers (consider 2 Corinthians 8:19-20), trusting that any funds requested were needed and trusting the Spirit to guide their giving aid. This resulted in a community where needs were met.

> *What Do You Think?*
> How do you see the progressive modifications to meeting needs from Acts 2:44-45 to 4:32-35 to 6:1-6 to 1 Timothy 5:3-16 applying to your church?
> *Digging Deeper*
> How should your own role change in that regard?

B. Example of Giving (vv. 36-37)

36. And Joses, who by the apostles was surnamed Barnabas, (which is, being interpreted, The son of consolation,) a Levite, and of the country of Cyprus.

Joses (a form of the name Joseph) has a nickname, given to him *by the apostles,* that reflects his character. He has earned the designation *the son of consolation* by his talk and actions. This is the only verse in the book of Acts that refers to him as Joses; elsewhere (more than two dozen times) he is always *Barnabas*.

> *What Do You Think?*
> What positive and descriptive nickname would you like to have with regard to your service for Christ?
> *Digging Deeper*
> What do you need to do to move toward such a bestowal or recognition?

Barnabas was from the tribe of Levi, which was the priestly tribe (Deuteronomy 18:1-8). We don't know whether he lived in Jerusalem or was only visiting there from *Cyprus*, the third largest island in Mediterranean. That island hosted a considerable Jewish population, as suggested by the multiple synagogues in the city of Salamis (Acts 13:5). It is possible that Barnabas had some duties to attend to that took him to the temple.

Later, Barnabas is reintroduced as an emissary from the Jerusalem church to the congregation in Antioch of Syria (Acts 11:22). Here, Barnabas is described as a "good man" who was "full of the Holy Ghost and of faith" (11:24a). In Antioch, Barnabas lived up to his name, with the result that many were added to the church (11:24b). Barnabas was the first in Jerusalem to put aside suspicion and welcome Paul as a brother in Christ (9:27). The two were missionaries together (Acts 13–14) and close companions (examples: 1 Corinthians 9:6; Galatians 2:1, 9, 13).

37. Having land, sold it, and brought the money, and laid it at the apostles' feet.

Barnabas serves as the example of those who owned *land* and *sold it* to raise *money* for the care of the needy in the congregation. He acted in a straightforward manner, already outlined (see commentary on Acts 4:34b-35, above). He gave with no expectation of receiving anything in return (see Luke 6:34).

More Than Words

"Discouragement is not the absence of adequacy but the absence of courage" (Neal A. Maxwell). People all around us have the ability, but not the courage, to accomplish their full potential. When we encourage them, we are not building them up with platitudes or falsehoods. Instead, we're helping them see the truth about themselves and the situation they're facing.

Sometimes our encouragement offers more than words. When we help a struggling college student with his tuition, when we buy a bag of groceries for an underpaid single mother, or when we send a Christmas gift to a missionary far from home, we're doing more than *telling* them better days are ahead. We're actually relieving pressure that is preventing them from doing their best.

Study the life of Barnabas and you'll see that he always did more than talk. He gave. He helped.

He accompanied. Which of those last three is your weakest area? —M. T.

II. Deception Exposed
(Acts 5:1-11)

A. A Couple's Plan (vv. 1-2)

1-2. But a certain man named Ananias, with Sapphira his wife, sold a possession, and kept back part of the price, his wife also being privy to it, and brought a certain part, and laid it at the apostles' feet.

Ananias and *Sapphira* serve as the negative counterpoint to Barnabas. Our initial impression may be that the negative part is that in selling *a piece of property* and, unlike Barnabas, giving less than 100 percent of the proceeds is the problem. But that will prove to be the wrong conclusion as the rest of the story unfolds.

B. Satan and Ananias (vv. 3-6)

3-4. But Peter said, Ananias, why hath Satan filled thine heart to lie to the Holy Ghost, and to keep back part of the price of the land? Whiles it remained, was it not thine own? and after it was sold, was it not in thine own power? why hast thou conceived this thing in thine heart? thou hast not lied unto men, but unto God.

The decision by *Ananias* and Sapphira to sell property was not wrong. Giving less than 100 percent of the proceeds for distribution among the needy was not wrong. What *was* wrong was the deliberate misrepresentation (lying). The plot to deceive the apostles, by the two making themselves appear to be more generous than they actually were, tainted what otherwise could have been an act that modeled generosity. To lie to *unto men* is bad enough; *to lie to the Holy Ghost* is much worse! Ananias knew that the money he had placed at Peter's feet was only part of the sale price, and, to his surprise, Peter knew it too.

An honest accounting of the sale would have been something like, "We sold land, but because of our financial situation, we can give only half the money." This could have served as a giving-stimulus to others who felt it necessary to keep part of what was received in a sale of property. But by misrepresenting the proceeds as the *whole* instead of only the *part* that it actually was, Ananias committed moral fraud.

Peter's accusation *thou hast not lied unto men, but unto God* repeats and emphasizes the accusation of sinning against the deity. This also betrays Ananias's lack of belief in the ability of God to be aware of such an attempt. The masquerade further betrays that Ananias's lack of belief in the Holy Spirit's power to work His will in the church.

Thus we are struck by the absurdity of attempting to lie to God. God always knows the truth and will never be fooled by human deception. Yet Ananias carried out a plan that depended on God's not knowing and/or not caring! Peter's condemnation came in stark terms—and Peter himself knew what it was like to be accused of being under the influence of Satan (see Matthew 4:10; compare Luke 22:3).

What Do You Think?

How does this lesson cause you to rethink your own giving pattern?

Digging Deeper

How important are the additional considerations of Luke 3:11; 18:22 to your answer?

5a. And Ananias hearing these words fell down, and gave up the ghost.

Neither God nor Peter gave *Ananias* a chance to mount a defense. The time for lying was over. The man's instant death was clear evidence to those watching that God knew Ananias's heart and was angered by what He saw.

5b. And great fear came on all them that heard these things.

Fear is sometimes an unfaithful reaction, as when it causes a person to act without faith in God. But in this case, the fear seems to be of the type that causes greater respect for God. Though this reaction may have been limited to believers, likely others living in Jerusalem also *heard* the tale and were afraid. There is no record of anyone having cried "Injustice!" when they heard. That is perhaps a testimony to the reputation of Ananias. The reaction was fear of God's wrath rather than indignation on behalf of the dead man.

> *What Do You Think?*
> What deeper role should accountability play in your service to Christ's church?
> *Digging Deeper*
> How do texts such as Ezra 8:33-34; Nehemiah 13:13; Daniel 6:1-4; and/or Hebrews 13:17 help shape your conclusion?

6. And the young men arose, wound him up, and carried him out, and buried him.

The burial was hasty and unceremonious. Any funeral was no more than what was minimally necessary (compare and contrast John 19:40).

C. The Spirit and Sapphira (vv. 7-11)

7. And it was about the space of three hours after, when his wife, not knowing what was done, came in.

News of the death spread quickly, but no one told Ananias's *wife*, Sapphira. This emphasizes how quickly events were moving along: she was not even present when they buried her husband. She entered the room assuming that Ananias had delivered his gift and received praise and honor. She likely expected the same thing.

8. And Peter answered unto her, Tell me whether ye sold the land for so much? And she said, Yea, for so much.

Peter confronted Sapphira immediately, asking only if the price quoted by Ananias was true. This gave her a chance to be honest where her husband had been deceitful. Sadly, her story matched Ananias's, confirming that her husband had acted with her full knowledge and approval.

Acts does not reveal what motivated Ananias and Sapphira to perpetrate this fraud. But we can easily imagine it was tied to esteem in the church. After seeing Barnabas's standing improve following his generous gifts, this couple was probably envious and wanted to garner such positive recognition too.

9a. Then Peter said unto her, How is it that ye have agreed together to tempt the Spirit of the Lord?

Peter wasted no time and minced no words telling Sapphira where she had gone wrong. She had tempted *the Spirit of the Lord.* We can never *tempt* God with evil and expect Him to fail (see James 1:13). We can, however, try the patience of God with a test. Those who test the patience of God play a dangerous game, a fool's game (see Deuteronomy 6:16). The sense of testing here is very similar to Jesus' temptation (Luke 4:1-13). Satan there intended to make Jesus act contrary to His identity as the Son of God; here Ananias and Sapphira unwittingly tested the Spirit, only to learn that He is also powerful in the church to guide it in holiness. Jesus did not fail in the wilderness; the Spirit did not fail in Jerusalem.

> *What Do You Think?*
> If a similar situation regarding intentional deception in your church came to your attention, what would you do?
> *Digging Deeper*
> Is there a single, step-by-step way to handle such a situation? Why, or why not?

Fraud Reports

Forbes magazine quoted the study *Status of Global Mission 2013* that reported a staggering amount of embezzlement fraud among churchgoers. One line item, "Ecclesiastical Crime," projected losses of $37 billion worldwide. Another $8 billion was lost due to mismanagement of funds. The study contrasts these amounts with the $32 billion it says was given to mission work the same year.

Ananias and Sapphira may have been the first believers to commit financial fraud in the church, but clearly they were not the last. These reports do not document the effect on the individuals who commit these crimes. Their dishonesty or desperation has damaged their souls, and that fact leads us to look at our own attitudes toward the money we give to the church.

Are we giving only because others are giving? Are we pretending that we're giving a sacrificial gift, while actually contributing from our overflow? Although our names may never make it into a fraud report, the "fraud" label might nevertheless apply.

—M. T.

9b-10. Behold, the feet of them which have buried thy husband are at the door, and shall carry thee out. Then fell she down straightway at his feet, and yielded up the ghost: and the young men came in, and found her dead, and, carrying her forth, buried her by her husband.

As with *her husband*, Sapphira had no further opportunity to defend herself. Barely three hours after Ananias was struck dead, *the young men* finished interring him only to return to more work. Without resting, they *buried* Sapphira *by her husband*. The haste suggests that neither the Spirit nor the church would waste any time before rooting out wickedness in the midst of the body of Christ.

This story may trouble some of us. A primary problem is that the penalty of death may seem too severe. These two did something good (gave money for the poor), although in a selfish manner. Didn't they deserve some credit?

Furthermore, the story puts Peter in an uncomfortable role as the stern judge who does not hesitate to pronounce the fate that befell Sapphira. Couldn't he at least have given Sapphira a warning when asking about the details? "Don't lie to me, sister, I'm warning you!"

Both of these objections again find their best answer in the Spirit's interest in keeping the church holy. Though the world may claim that the ends justify the means, Christian ethics requires the ends and the means to work together virtuously.

When Paul wrote later about spiritual gifts, he made a similar point. No gift on its own is worth anything; only the correct motivation, coming from the heart, can give those gifts any value (1 Corinthians 13; see lesson 8).

11. And great fear came upon all the church, and upon as many as heard these things.

The community *fear* caused by Ananias and Sapphira's deaths intensified. Surely the people wondered what was going on in this fellowship! No one seemed to question that God had acted in a powerful, judicious way. Barnabas encouraged all who aspired to be generous; Ananias and Sapphira terrified all who believed they could fool God and the church with false piety and lies.

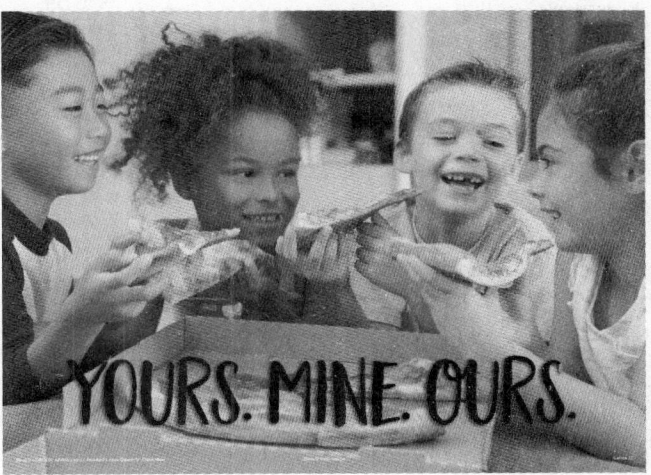

Visual for Lesson 12. *While discussing Acts 4:32, use the visual to ask the class how they see the church holding resources in common today.*

Conclusion

A. An Encouraging Word

While we may not understand exactly how the Spirit works in the church or what He is up to all the time, church business is serious business. Faith and fraud cannot coexist. For this reason, when we allow the Spirit to lead us, we will be genuine givers like Barnabas, not sly and deceitful like Ananias and Sapphira.

Dishonesty within the church can destroy it entirely and must be dealt with severely. The very thought of doing a good deed to receive kudos and honors violates the spirit of charity. As Jesus taught, when we give for relief of the poor, it should be so private that our left hand doesn't know about the money our right hand put in the offering basket (Matthew 6:3). This requires a delicate balance of being a witness at the same time (5:16). But when we yield our hearts to the Spirit, we know that he sees our deeds and blesses them (6:4).

B. Prayer

Lord God, forgive us when we attempt to deceive You and Christ's body. Help us to genuinely seek to encourage. In Jesus' name we pray. Amen.

C. Thought to Remember

The Spirit works powerfully in the church.

Involvement Learning

Enhance your lesson with KJV Bible Student *(from your curriculum supplier) and the reproducible activity page (at www.standardlesson.com or in the back of the* KJV Standard Lesson Commentary Deluxe Edition*).*

Into the Lesson

Write these two propositions on the board:

Overall, we live in a generous culture.
Overall, we live in a selfish culture.

Divide the class in half, assigning one proposition to each. Direct each group to take about five minutes to list reasons that support its assigned proposition.

After calling time, have groups share their lists in whole-class discussion. Possible responses to expect in support of "generous culture" are accounts of volunteering to clean up after natural disasters and donations to charitable organizations. Responses in support of "selfish culture" may include examples of insider-trading scandals in the stock market and frauds perpetrated on the elderly.

Alternative. Distribute copies of the "Truth from an Atheist?" exercise from the activity page, which you can download. Have learners form study pairs to complete it as indicated.

After either activity ask, "As we consider our own needs and wants, how do we know when we've crossed the line into selfishness? And how do we ensure that our generosity isn't really a form of selfishness? Let's consider how today's text can answer such questions."

Into the Word

Divide the class in half. One half will take the role of Barnabas and the other the role of Ananias and Sapphira in answering the following interview questions. Provide groups with these questions on handouts (you prepare):

1–How does the Jerusalem church respond to the needs of its members?
2–What have you seen this initiative accomplish?
3–Why should people see this work as an act of God rather than simply as good people doing good things?
4–How do you personally feel about parting with your possessions?
5–We understand that you made a substantial contribution. How would you like people to react to your generosity?

Allow groups about 15 minutes to read the text of Acts 4:32–5:11 and prepare responses in the character of either Barnabas or Ananias and Sapphira, as assigned. As groups work, move among them to help as needed. Encourage use of the text to inform learners' "sanctified imaginations" to depict the motivation of their assigned character(s). Act as interviewer in posing the above questions after group preparations are complete.

Into Life

Write on the board the following habits of generous people:

Generous people budget their money and time.

Generous people build relationships that make them available to help others.

Generous people avoid the spotlight.

In whole-class discussion, invite learners to respond to this list in explaining the value of each. Expect responses such as these: *Having budgets* helps avoid wasting resources by considering how they will be spent; we cannot know what we can give if we do not know what we have. *Building relationships* recognizes that we accomplish more together; being an active part of a serving group increases our outreach. *Avoiding the spotlight* honors Jesus' instruction in Matthew 6:1-4, as balanced by Matthew 5:14-16.

Option. Distribute copies of the "My Response to Need" exercise from the activity page for learners to complete the first part as indicated, time limit of one minute. This can also be a take-home exercise. If the latter, increase the likelihood of completion by announcing that you will begin the next class by asking volunteers to share results.

Impartial Love

Devotional Reading: Matthew 12:1-8
Background Scripture: James 2

James 2:1-13

1 My brethren, have not the faith of our Lord Jesus Christ, the Lord of glory, with respect of persons.

2 For if there come unto your assembly a man with a gold ring, in goodly apparel, and there come in also a poor man in vile raiment;

3 And ye have respect to him that weareth the gay clothing, and say unto him, Sit thou here in a good place; and say to the poor, Stand thou there, or sit here under my footstool:

4 Are ye not then partial in yourselves, and are become judges of evil thoughts?

5 Hearken, my beloved brethren, Hath not God chosen the poor of this world rich in faith, and heirs of the kingdom which he hath promised to them that love him?

6 But ye have despised the poor. Do not rich men oppress you, and draw you before the judgment seats?

7 Do not they blaspheme that worthy name by the which ye are called?

8 If ye fulfil the royal law according to the scripture, Thou shalt love thy neighbour as thyself, ye do well:

9 But if ye have respect to persons, ye commit sin, and are convinced of the law as transgressors.

10 For whosoever shall keep the whole law, and yet offend in one point, he is guilty of all.

11 For he that said, Do not commit adultery, said also, Do not kill. Now if thou commit no adultery, yet if thou kill, thou art become a transgressor of the law.

12 So speak ye, and so do, as they that shall be judged by the law of liberty.

13 For he shall have judgment without mercy, that hath shewed no mercy; and mercy rejoiceth against judgment.

Key Verse

Hearken, my beloved brethren, Hath not God chosen the poor of this world rich in faith, and heirs of the kingdom which he hath promised to them that love him? **—James 2:5**

Photo: Skathi / iStock / Thinkstock

Love for One Another

Unit 3: Godly Love Among Believers

Lessons 9–13

Lesson Aims

After participating in this lesson, each learner will be able to:

1. Identify specific behaviors that demonstrated the church's underlying partiality.
2. Explain how following Jesus' command to love should have prevented Christians from showing favoritism.
3. Discuss practices of his or her church that may discriminate against certain types of individuals and develop a plan to correct those actions.

Lesson Outline

Introduction

A. Discrimination

A long-standing view among many people of various faiths holds that wealth is a sign of God's blessing. We reason (even if subconsciously) that if God is showing favor to this person, we should honor that person also. On the other hand, poverty is a sign of God's withholding His favor, perhaps even of God's curse. We reason that if people are suffering from poverty, their relationship with God must be negative, and we should not accommodate them.

Nowhere is this erroneous belief seen more clearly than in prosperity gospel preaching and teaching. Simply put, ministers of this false doctrine teach that healing and wealth can both be yours . . . if you have enough faith, which is shown through how much money you give to the church. This often results in the ministers themselves becoming wealthy while their congregants wait for miracles of health and wealth that never seem to show up. The ministers are afforded great honor and position while many people suffer. But *should* wealthy members receive more attention and have more influence than members with little money? Are the wealthy *really* more beloved by God?

B. Lesson Context

James described himself as a "servant of . . . the Lord Jesus Christ" (James 1:1). This author could have made a bolder claim, however, for he was the half brother of Jesus. Everyone in their hometown of Nazareth assumed they were natural brothers, two out of five: Jesus, James, Joses, Juda, and Simon (Mark 6:3). The order the brothers are listed in implies that James was the second oldest of the brothers and would have become the family head after the death, resurrection, and ascension of Jesus. The boys grew up together in a faithful Jewish household in rural Galilee. They both learned the carpenter's trade in their father's workshop and studied and worshipped in the village synagogue.

Although James did not believe in Jesus as the Messiah during Jesus' ministry (John 7:5), a dramatic change occurred after the resurrection, following an encounter with the risen Christ (1 Corinthians 15:7). Acts tells us that the brothers of Jesus (including James) were part of the earliest fellowship in Jerusalem that became the church (Acts 1:14). James became a leader in the Jerusalem church (15:13).

It is not surprising, therefore, to find that James was very familiar with Jesus' teachings. He echoes the oral instruction of Jesus with confidence that his own teaching is true to Jesus' original intent.

The epistle of James reflects a very early stage in the development of the church, when it was composed primarily of Jewish Christians. The congregation he is addressing in the letter seems to be made up entirely of Jewish believers in Christ. So, for example, James could easily reference Jewish customs or laws without needing to explain himself to his audience (see James 2:8-11, below). His audience would have been familiar with the value of the Jewish law for ethical guidance, while understanding its inadequacy for salvation by faith in Christ.

I. Favoring the Wealthy

(James 2:1-4)

A. Attitude of Jesus (v. 1)

1. My brethren, have not the faith of our Lord Jesus Christ, the Lord of glory, with respect of persons.

Following the assertion that religion God desires from His people requires caring for the afflicted and pursuing holiness (James 1:27), James transitioned to a discussion about *respect of persons.* This biased treatment can be seen in favoritism, where we treat one person better than others. It can also be seen in prejudice, in which we treat a person worse than others. Note that James does not seem concerned about whether a person deserves better or worse treatment.

The grammar of this verse may be difficult, but James was not saying that Jesus discriminated against people. Far from it! James exhorted his audience to be faithful in following the example *of our Lord Jesus Christ* in the ways they interact with others. Doing so requires knowing how Jesus interacted with others. Because Jesus is God, Christians can look at God's own attributes and know what Jesus is like, and vice versa. So if God is not a respecter of persons (Romans 2:11; Ephesians 6:9; Colossians 3:25), we know that Jesus is also no respecter of persons.

Paul also used the idea of impartiality toward others in several ways. It served as an assumption for his famous speech in Athens, where he claimed that all human beings are the offspring of one man and one God (Acts 17:24-28). Peter, too, with an initial animosity toward Gentiles, also came to understand that God wants to welcome all people into His family (10:34-35; see 15:7), allowing Peter to evangelize and baptize Cornelius and his household (10:44-48).

A Special Football Camp

In 2010, Ed McCaffrey, a former wide receiver for the Denver Broncos, recruited former and current Broncos players to serve as coaches at a new football camp. High school players attended, but as mentors and friends, not campers. The campers were about 40 players with Down syndrome, from age 7 to adults.

To this day at the Dare to Play Football Camp, each camper is paired with a buddy from a high school football team. The camp fills a need often lacking for people who have Down syndrome—the opportunity to play a team sport. The experience not only teaches football skills but also nurtures friendships for children and adults who are frequently left out of group activities.

Sadly, it's not just secular society that pushes certain people to the sidelines. Churches often struggle to be communities where children and adults with special needs are genuinely integral to the faith family. What can you and your church do to team up with people who usually don't get to participate?

—A. S.

B. Case Study (vv. 2-4)

2-3. For if there come unto your assembly a man with a gold ring, in goodly apparel, and there come in also a poor man in vile raiment; and ye have respect to him that weareth the gay clothing, and say unto him, Sit thou here in

a good place; and say to the poor, Stand thou there, or sit here under my footstool.

James offered a hypothetical situation to illustrate why having *respect* for one person over another is unfitting for Christians. What if during your weekly *assembly* as a church, two visitors appeared? One wears expensive, sparkling-clean clothes and flaunts his wealth by wearing an expensive *gold ring*. The other one wears dirty, ragged clothes and has no jewelry.

James suggested the man with the appearance of wealth would be escorted to a comfortable seat where he could hear and see everything in the service. The man who seems poor would be told to *sit* on the floor or *stand* in the back. These behaviors would seem natural in a boardroom or restaurant perhaps, but in the church, this hypothetical situation should make us feel very uneasy.

What Do You Think?

How do the implications of verses 2-3 for you change, if at all, as you realize that those working at minimum wage in America are in the top 10 percent standard of living in the world?

Digging Deeper

In what ways are "the poor" of today wealthier than "the rich" of the first century AD? Why is this question important?

4. Are ye not then partial in yourselves, and are become judges of evil thoughts?

Because this scenario would not be surprising in many settings, it is not hard to imagine that such a thing could happen in a church assembly. James's two-part rhetorical question leaves no wiggle room to justify the behavior he described. Such actions reveal partiality in the fellowship. Anyone who participated in that partiality is a judge whose *evil thoughts* run counter to what God desires.

The Greek word translated *thoughts* here has a deeper sense than ideas that simply drift through our brains, quickly dismissed or discarded. It implies a pattern of thinking, a reasoning process (compare Matthew 15:19). Such corrupt reasoning makes it easy to justify one's reasons for sinning against others. In this case, the ungodly thing is to show partiality by discrimination for the wealthy and against the poor.

What Do You Think?

In what way could you turn sympathy into action were you to see the issue of James 2:2-3 actually occur in your church?

Digging Deeper

Should your action focus on correcting the perpetrator or on comforting the victim? Why?

II. Favoring the Poor

(James 2:5-7)

A. In Faith (v. 5)

5. Hearken, my beloved brethren, Hath not God chosen the poor of this world rich in faith, and heirs of the kingdom which he hath promised to them that love him?

Throughout the Old Testament, *God* expressed in various ways that He has *chosen the poor* (examples: Leviticus 23:22; Zechariah 7:10). Though this may imply that God does not care for the wealthy, that is clearly untrue. We all "live, and move, and have our being" (Acts 17:28) in God, no matter our socioeconomic status (compare Exodus 23:3). Instead, God's choosing the poor acknowledges that they require His help in unique ways because their low status disadvantages them. Even today, we see the wealthy often having better access to education, job opportunities, legal representation, etc. The Lord does not shun or neglect the poor as society often does, but cares for them and expects His people to do the same (examples: Deuteronomy 15:11; Psalm 72:4; Isaiah 25:4).

Because the poor do not possess wealth, James suggested that it is easier for them to be *rich in faith* and trust in God, not worldly riches (contrast 1 Timothy 6:10). As Jesus taught, the poor are *heirs of the kingdom* (Luke 6:20; compare Matthew 5:3). They must inherit this kingdom, because they would never have the wealth to purchase it. They would never seize it, because it has been *promised to them* if they truly *love* the Lord. All worldly goods may be stripped away, but no one can prevent anyone from loving God or prevent God from loving that person.

My good friend Kathy, a recently retired nurse, has participated in three short-term missions to Niger. She was overwhelmed during her first trip by all the poverty she saw: the makeshift homes, the unsanitary conditions, the suffocating smoke from kerosene cooking fires. It wasn't until the second mission trip that she could actually see the people. That trip enabled Kathy to answer the question "Hasn't God chosen the world's poor to be rich in faith?" with a resounding *yes!*

Kathy's team serves a group of about 40 widows, teaching nutrition and conducting medical clinics for them and their children. Following the team's work, these first-generation Christians (formerly Muslims) always lead the team in worship. Kathy has been profoundly touched by these women, who have little materially but sing and dance and preach with great passion and joy because of Jesus.

Joy without material possessions? Faith without economic security? In Christ, these things are the rule, not the exception! How does this challenge your own ideas about faith? —A. S.

B. Against Oppression (vv. 6-7)

6. But ye have despised the poor. Do not rich men oppress you, and draw you before the judgment seats?

The charge of despising *the poor* implies that the church really was honoring the rich. Remember, these were visitors to the assembly, not rich members whose deeds (whether good or bad) were known to the church in general. The only reason they were treated with esteem was a preference for and deference to *rich* people.

The prophets of the Old Testament frequently summarized the corruption of Israelite society by pointing out how its rulers and rich landowners oppressed others (see Ezekiel 18:12; Zechariah 7:10). This offended the Lord, becoming a primary cause of His judgment (Malachi 3:5). This resulted in the Babylonian conquest of Jerusalem, destruction of the temple, and deportation of many of the people of Judah to Babylon in 586 BC (2 Chronicles 36:15-21).

The wealthy in James's society notoriously oppressed the poor and used the corrupt courts to their advantage. Their wealth and their influence made them invincible in controversies with the poor (contrast Luke 18:1-5). Honoring those who so treated others put the church in danger of honoring people just like those God had judged in the exile.

What Do You Think?

What discrimination and/or favoritism challenges do Christians face regarding someone considered "poor" by US standards but "rich" by third-world standards?

Digging Deeper

How does that question speak to you personally?

7. Do not they blaspheme that worthy name by the which ye are called?

The word translated *blaspheme* is elsewhere translated "reviled" (Matthew 27:39) and "defamed" (1 Corinthians 4:13). Though it does not always have religious overtones, the Greek word always identifies deep disrespect and contempt. The dishonoring tactics of the rich are an insult to *that worthy name*, Jesus Christ (Philippians 2:9-11). Attacking and exploiting poor people, those God has chosen for an extra measure of love and grace, is a grave insult to God himself.

No person should be denied access to the fellowship of believers based on economic status, whether rich, poor, or somewhere in between. At the same time, any societal power structure that facilitates preference for the rich and disrespect of the poor should not be tolerated within the church. We *are called* to teach and act as Jesus did when it comes to "respect of persons" (James 2:1).

What Do You Think?

When finding yourself a victim of discrimination, in what contexts is it best to push back verbally versus merely walking away? Why?

Digging Deeper

Considering the reverse, how should you react in cases where others behave in a patronizing or overly deferential way toward you? Why?

III. Favoring the Neighbor

(James 2:8-13)

A. Royal Law (vv. 8-11)

8. If ye fulfil the royal law according to the scripture, Thou shalt love thy neighbour as thyself, ye do well.

The designation *royal law* works on two levels. First, this is the "king of laws," the one that controls and orders all things we should do. Second, this is the "law of the King." No law that contradicts this one will come from Jesus, and no law will replace it.

This magnificent meta-command comes from *the scripture* as originally delivered by Moses, *Thou shalt love thy neighbour as thyself* (Leviticus 19:18). This command served as the backdrop for Jesus' teaching on who one was obliged to love as a neighbor (Luke 10:36-37). This law is also found in Paul's letters (examples: Romans 13:9; Galatians 5:14). Only in keeping this law can it be said that *ye do well.*

The royal law is the overriding ethic applicable in any situation. We should always act with love for others. When we have an opportunity to show God's love to others, we must do so.

If we violate this law, we are certainly guilty of violating others. If we keep the law of love, however, we cover a multitude of other sins (see 1 Peter 4:8).

9. But if ye have respect to persons, ye commit sin, and are convinced of the law as transgressors.

Acting with *respect to persons* (see commentary on James 2:1, above) violates the intent of the royal *law* and is therefore sinful. Showing preference for the rich and dishonoring the poor reveals us as *transgressors.*

10-11. For whosoever shall keep the whole law, and yet offend in one point, he is guilty of all. For he that said, Do not commit adultery, said also, Do not kill. Now if thou commit no adultery, yet if thou kill, thou art become a transgressor of the law.

The *law* was a package, not a pick-and-choose buffet of options. To be in compliance meant 100 percent blamelessness. One violation made a person a breaker of *the whole law.* The standard is not comparative ("I keep the law better than my brother"), but absolute ("I keep the law perfectly"). A murderer who avoids committing *adultery* still violates the entire law.

James was not interested in every obscure commandment in the law of Moses or trying to bind such things upon Jewish Christian believers. Perfect adherence to the Jewish laws was not a means of salvation apart from faith in Christ. Jesus both taught and lived the ethic that we should love our neighbors, regardless of economic standing. James's point to any self-satisfied readers was for them to correct their neglect of the direct teachings of Jesus. They could not reflexively disregard the poor and honor the rich and claim to keep Jesus' own law.

B. Law of Liberty (vv. 12-13)

12. So speak ye, and so do, as they that shall be judged by the law of liberty.

The law of liberty is the other foundational ethic that runs throughout this chapter: love frees us to keep God's commands rather than constraining us with the commands. In other words, instead of trying to prevent us from destructive actions, it encourages us to act in life-affirming ways, ultimately beneficial for us and for other involved parties. It is freeing to have relationships within the church not based on social status. It is liberating not to focus on ourselves and instead care for the poor, the elderly, the ill, and the mistreated of our society. Our faith in Jesus makes us "free indeed" (John 8:36).

This law frees us from the discrimination our society encourages but that God does not tolerate. Freedom for our souls comes when we stop judging others on the basis of wealth, education, social status, family connections, race, or age. The true

HOW TO SAY IT

Galilee	*Gal*-uh-lee.
Jerusalem	Juh-*roo*-suh-lem.
Leviticus	Leh-*vit*-ih-kus.
Messiah	Meh-sigh-uh.
Nazareth	*Naz*-uh-reth.

seeker of Jesus should find a welcoming fellowship in the church, no matter what.

13. For he shall have judgment without mercy, that hath shewed no mercy; and mercy rejoiceth against judgment.

Jesus, in teaching the Lord's Prayer, warned that if we withhold forgiveness, we should not expect God's forgiveness (Matthew 6:14-15). This is not some bargain we make with God, as though God will be nice to us if we are nice to others. It is a test of one's heart. In the same way, if we fail to show *mercy*, we await *judgment without mercy*.

Discrimination, prejudice, and partiality are all types of judging others. When we favor a rich person because of her wealth and disfavor a poor person because of his poverty, we make moral judgments without mercy. James wants mercy to win this battle. He wants mercy to win out in our lives and to be shown in the way we treat others. In this way, mercy will overrule judgment.

Conclusion

A. Two Laws

Over 1,900 years ago, James gave definitive answers for how the church should live and behave. James offered these two ethical foundations—the royal law and the law of liberty—to guide the church. Both of these were learned from his half brother, Jesus.

These two laws go together. If we see others as our neighbors in need—whether they are beloved friends or reviled enemies—we must show mercy, not discrimination. If we set aside our natural impulse to favor certain visitors, we will find unexpected opportunities to share the love that wells up in our hearts. We should lead with love, never doubting God's willingness to show kindness to us.

Churches should practice self-examination using these complementary laws. What things do we do that favor certain people over others? Do our church leaders represent the diversity of our church body, or are they predominately well-off financially, well-educated, and of a certain ethnicity that does not represent the whole? Is our con-

Visual for Lesson 13. *Use this visual to discuss with the class the importance of seeing people in order to be able to follow the royal law of verse 8.*

gregation known as a loving place or a judgmental place? Our answers to these questions will help us see as a congregation how we measure up to the standard of the two laws.

Jesus did not treat people according to divisions of wealth or poverty, or perceived blessings or curses. James, his brother, did not either. Instead, James and Jesus show that God loves the poor, and we should too. This issue has not gone away in the nearly 2,000 years since James wrote, and we do well to listen to him today.

> *What Do You Think?*
> What more can you do to stay alert to unbiblical cultural trends that creep into the church?
> *Digging Deeper*
> Do we eliminate favoritism within the church by refusing to recognize social classes, or does such refusal invite other problems? Why?

B. Prayer

Father God, You created all people. You did not create us to discriminate and hate, but to love and accept others. You have loved us without partiality. May we love You in return and show this as we love others who cross our paths. In Jesus' name we pray. Amen.

C. Thought to Remember

Begin with love.

Involvement Learning

Enhance your lesson with KJV Bible Student *(from your curriculum supplier) and the reproducible activity page (at www.standardlesson.com or in the back of the* KJV Standard Lesson Commentary Deluxe Edition*).*

Into the Lesson

Begin class by telling this true story.

> John Barrier walked into Old National Bank after parking his pickup truck in a nearby lot. His job involved refurbishing old buildings, so he was wearing his tattered work clothes when he went to a teller to cash a check.
>
> After doing so, Barrier asked the teller to validate his parking voucher. The teller refused, telling him that the bank only validated parking when a customer made a transaction and that cashing a check wasn't a transaction.
>
> Because of the way he was dressed, the teller assumed that Barrier was a person of no significance. She was wrong. Barrier was a millionaire who had his money at that bank! He promptly closed his account and opened a seven-figure account at the bank down the street.

Alternative. Distribute copies of the matching exercise "He'll Never Amount to Anything" from the activity page, which you can download, for learners to work on for no more than one minute.

After either activity, ask the class about times they reacted to someone inappropriately based on the person's appearance, vocational failure, or other external factor. Make a transition to Bible study by noting that the Bible has much to teach us in this regard.

Into the Word

Divide the class into three groups, with the following designations: **Clothing Group, Networking Group,** and **Discrimination Group.** Distribute handouts (you prepare) on which are printed the following:

Clothing Group: Mark Twain said, "Clothes make a man," reflecting a thought that can be traced as far back as the Greek poet Homer, who lived many centuries before Christ. What does James 2:1-4 have to say regarding that thought? What other Scripture passages speak to this issue?

Networking Group: The popular declaration "It's not what you know that counts so much, as who you know" has been traced to a 1914 magazine article—to be repeated often since then. What does James 2:5-7 have to say regarding this dictum? What other Scripture passages speak to this issue?

Discrimination Group: Oliver Wendell Holmes Jr. said, "I have no respect for the passion of equality, which seems to me merely idealizing envy." What does James 2:8-11 have to say regarding that outlook? What other Scripture passages speak to this issue?

Allow about 15 minutes for group work before calling for conclusions in whole-class discussion. Refer to the commentary to correct and clarify conclusions. In particular, be prepared to offer your own research on the question "What other Scripture passages speak to this issue?" in each case. The verses Leviticus 19:15; Deuteronomy 1:17; 16:19; 2 Chronicles 19:7; Proverbs 24:23; 28:21; Acts 10:34-35; Romans 2:11; Ephesians 6:9; and Colossians 3:25 apply in various ways to each group's questions, but there are others as well.

Into Life

Play a video (from a video-sharing site) featuring the lyrics of Steve Taylor's satirical song "I Want to Be a Clone." Introduce the video by explaining that the song pokes fun at unwritten church rules that seem to promote conformity rather than individuality. After playing the video, discuss church practices that run the danger of displacing biblical values with conformities traceable to questionable cultural values. (If the style of music would be distracting to your group, turn off the sound and display the lyrics alone.)

Alternative: Distribute copies of the exercise "A Place for Everyone?" from the activity page. Allow no more than one minute for learners working individually to complete Part 1; call for a show of hands to tally results on the board. Engage learners in whole-class discussion to complete Part 2.

CALL IN THE NEW TESTAMENT

Special Features

Lessons

Unit 1: The Beginning of a Call

Unit 2: Jesus and Calls in His Ministry

Unit 3: The Call of Women

QUARTERLY QUIZ

Use these questions as a pretest or as a review. The answers are on page iv of This Quarter in the Word.

Lesson 1

1. What non-Israelite was grandmother of King David? (Rahab, Orpah, Ruth) *Matthew 1:5-6*

2. Hebrews says in these last days, God has spoken to us by His _______. *Hebrews 1:1-2*

Lesson 2

1. When Mary became pregnant, Joseph admitted that he was the father. T/F. *Matthew 1:18-19*

2. Who encouraged Joseph to take Mary as his wife? (an angel, his father, a priest) *Matthew 1:20*

Lesson 3

1. When the wise men came to Jerusalem, whom did they visit first? (Herod, Joseph, Mary) *Matthew 2:7*

2. The gifts of the wise men for Jesus included gold, _______, and myrrh. *Matthew 2:11*

Lesson 4

1. John the Baptist wore clothes made of what? (linen, camel's hair, wool) *Matthew 3:4*

2. John baptized people in which river? (Nile, Euphrates, Jordan) *Matthew 3:6*

Lesson 5

1. Jesus avoided teaching in synagogues. T/F. *Luke 4:15*

2. The town where Jesus had been brought up was what? (Nazareth, Bethlehem, Rome) *Luke 4:16*

Lesson 6

1. When Simon Peter admitted to being sinful, he fell down at Jesus' knees. T/F. *Luke 5:5-8*

2. Simon Peter was a rival of James and John in the fishing business. T/F. *Luke 5:10*

Lesson 7

1. Friends of a man who was disabled brought him to Jesus by lowering him through the roof. T/F. *Mark 2:4*

2. Religious experts who heard Jesus forgive sins thought Jesus guilty of _______. *Mark 2:6-7*

Lesson 8

1. At the last supper, Jesus prayed for God to remove His disciples from the world. T/F. *John 17:15*

2. In that same prayer, Jesus asked that His disciples be sanctified through God's what? (truth, miracles, Spirit) *John 17:17*

Lesson 9

1. Which prophet did Peter quote on the Day of Pentecost to explain the outpouring of God's Spirit? (Isaiah, Joel, Jonah) *Acts 2:16-17*

2. Philip the evangelist was "one of the five" T/F. *Acts 21:8 [compare Acts 6:1-5]*

Lesson 10

1. The words *Christ* and *Messiah* refer to the same person. T/F. *John 4:25*

2. The Samaritans who heard the woman's testimony about Jesus scoffed at her. T/F. *John 4:39*

Lesson 11

1. Jesus had delivered Mary Magdalene from seven devils. T/F. *Luke 8:2*

2. At first, Mary mistook the risen Jesus for whom? (gardener, guard, angel) *John 20:15*

Lesson 12

1. Paul first met Aquila and Priscilla in the city of _______. *Acts 18:1-2*

2. Priscilla and Aquila taught a Jew named ____ "the way of God more perfectly." *Acts 18:24-26*

Lesson 13

1. Lydia and other women met Paul while praying in a synagogue. T/F. *Acts 16:13-14*

2. Lydia ran a business that sold green-colored pottery. T/F. *Acts 16:14*

Quarter at a Glance

by Mark S. Krause

The lessons for this quarter focus on God's calling individuals to specific ministries according to His plans. Those called included John the Baptist, the wise men, Jesus' parents, and (most of all) Jesus himself. The final unit focuses on women in the New Testament who were called to vocations of service to God's people. The New Testament sees a broad calling of all people to salvation and a narrower calling of certain individuals to specific ministries in the church.

Calls Then

The lessons of this quarter begin by examining the ancestry of Jesus, which leads us to consider God's calls in the Old Testament era. Eighteen hundred years before Jesus' birth, Abraham was called by the Lord and told that all the peoples of the earth would be blessed through him (Genesis 12:3); this prophecy was fulfilled in his descendant Jesus. Nine hundred years before Jesus, David was called to be king and promised that his throne would be eternal (2 Samuel 7:16)—an heir of David would always reign as God's king. This prophecy also was fulfilled in Jesus (Hebrews 1:3, 8). The calling of Jesus to save us from sin has the background of these ancestors and the effect of fulfilling their calls.

A very different calling of God came to the wise men of Matthew 2 (lesson 3) as God called them through a sign regarding a coming king. Their calling eventually led them to Bethlehem, where they lavished gifts on the young child and worshipped Him. The story illustrates God's call on non-Jews to recognize Jesus as king—a call the wise men obediently answered.

Another surprising call came to a Samaritan woman who encountered Jesus at Jacob's well (John 4; lesson 10). Her call came when she realized that Jesus was no ordinary man; she knew she needed to testify to her fellow Samaritans of the marvelous conversation she had just had.

Jesus' own call and sense of purpose comes out clearly in our lesson regarding His visit to the synagogue in His hometown, Nazareth. He expressed His call by reading a passage from Isaiah 61. Jesus embodied three things from this text: that God's Spirit was upon Him, that He had therefore been anointed by God, and that He had been appointed to preach good news (Luke 4:18). Jesus acknowledged this prophesied role as His calling by announcing that that Scripture was fulfilled in their hearing that very day (4:21). In all these lessons and others of this quarter, we find examples of people who accepted the challenges and privileges of their calls.

Calls Now

As we ponder how God calls people to ministries today, we can note means and methods in both Old and New Testaments. Some calls were startlingly direct (examples: Exodus 3:10; Acts 9:1-6). Other calls were via specifically directed actions of intermediaries (examples: 1 Samuel 9:15-17; 16:1-13; Acts 10:34-43). That leads to the question of how to recognize calls of God today, realizing that these examples involve *very* few individuals in the history of God's people.

> ***The calls were for people to join God's plan, . . . not for God to join theirs.***

As a result, various "tests of calling" have been proposed. One source proposes that divine calls have three characteristics, nine attributes, and five aspects to recognize.

That's all rather complicated! But one overarching feature of the calls in this quarter's lessons should be kept in mind for application today: the calls were for people to join God's plan; the calls were not for God to join theirs. And so it still must be.

GET THE SETTING

by Mark S. Krause

WHAT IS your vocation? Many will hesitate before answering, then respond with their current employment. "I drive a bus." "I'm a farmer." "I'm a surgical nurse." "I teach kindergarten." This reflects the common sense of the word *vocation* as referring to one's job. Some might even respond to the question by saying, "I'm retired"—an ironic way of tying vocation to lack of employment!

English and Latin

The English language inherited its word *vocation* from the Latin word *vocare*, meaning "to call, to summon." This idea assumes a person's using his or her voice to give audible direction to another. This sense is still present in our words *vocal* and *vocalize*. A vocation, then, was a calling. This sense became more pronounced in the medieval church, where vocation indicated a religious calling—a personal orientation to join a monastic community, etc.

While some religious communities still retain this usage today, the meaning of *vocation* has broadened to signify any career one might choose. The choice of career is seen as all ours, not a call from someone else. We have little sense of being called into a career by anything other than our personal desires and preferences.

Pagans and Destiny

In the ancient world of paganism, there are examples of eminent teachers personally calling people to be their students. Socrates (about 470–399 BC) is recorded as confronting young Xenophon (430–354 BC) with questions and, finding his answers lacking, saying, "Follow me . . . and learn." In another case, a bookseller pointed an inquiring young man to a famous philosopher, saying, "Follow him." Both examples are somewhat like Elijah's calling of Elisha to be his successor as the primary prophet of Israel (1 Kings 19:16, 19-21).

The ancient pagans did not normally expect to receive a divine calling for a specific task, however. More common were prophecies concerning destinies. For example, a mythical king of Thebes and his wife sought a word from the oracle of Delphi concerning their infant son, Oedipus. The prophecy was that Oedipus was fated to kill his father and marry his mother. Despite the father's having knowledge of this prediction, he was indeed killed by the adult Oedipus, who then received his own mother as his wife—thereby fulfilling his destiny.

The oracle of Delphi (about 100 miles northwest of Athens, Greece), was a world-renowned shrine. There a prophetess answered questions posed to her. Alexander the Great (356–323 BC) consulted the oracle before he began his campaign of conquest. The prophetess pronounced Alexander to be "the unconquerable one," giving him a sign of his destiny he followed until death.

Emperor Nero (AD 37–68) often consulted those who claimed ability to divine the future. In his last years, he was told that his destiny was to be "deserted by all the world." Nero traveled to Greece to seek a second opinion from the oracle of Delphi. He was told to beware of the 73rd year. Thinking this meant he would live to be 73, the 30-something Nero relaxed, only to die a few years later at the hands of a 73-year-old Roman general.*

Fated Life vs. Called Life

For the pagans, fate was unalterable. Even if a mortal might be given a task by a god, the outcome was predetermined. A divine "call" was also a sentence to a fated life. The Bible's sense of calling shows God's entrusting people with missions vital to His plan. Our callings by the Lord are conditioned by our faithful response. This quarter's lessons give us great examples of just that fact.

---

* This is not to praise the accuracy of the oracle at Delphi. Its power (if any) was likely demonic in nature (compare Acts 16:16-18; 19:11-20).

Mon, Feb. 15	**Paul Reflects on His Ministry**	2 Timothy 4:9-18
Tue, Feb. 16	**Greetings to Saints in Jesus Christ**	Colossians 4:7-15
Wed, Feb. 17	**The Holy Kiss**	2 Corinthians 13:11-13; 1 Thessalonians 5:23-28
Thu, Feb. 18	**Ministry Shifts from Jews to Gentiles**	Acts 18:4-11
Fri, Feb. 19	**Proconsul Refuses to Settle Dispute**	Acts 18:12-17
Sat, Feb. 20	**Greetings to Fellow Workers**	Romans 16:1-2, 6-7, 12-13, 16
Sun, Feb. 21	**Key Outreach Minister**	Acts 18:1-3, 18-21, 24-26; Romans 16:3-4

Mon, Feb. 22	**Serve One Another**	1 Peter 4:7-11
Tue, Feb. 23	**Everyday Hospitality**	Romans 12:9-19
Wed, Feb. 24	**Hospitality, Part 1**	Acts 16:35-40
Thu, Feb. 25	**Hospitality, Part 2**	1 Timothy 5:9-10; 3:2
Fri, Feb. 26	**God's Power and Wisdom**	1 Corinthians 1:18-25
Sat, Feb. 27	**Know the Crucified Lord**	1 Corinthians 2:1-5
Sun, Feb. 28	**Model of Hospitality**	Acts 16:11-15, 40; 1 Corinthians 1:26-30

Answers to the Quarterly Quiz on page 114

Lesson 1—1. Ruth. 2. Son. **Lesson 2**—1. false. 2. an angel. **Lesson 3**—1. Herod. 2. frankincense. **Lesson 4**—1. camel's hair. 2. Jordan. **Lesson 5**—1. false. 2. Nazareth. **Lesson 6**—1. true. 2. false. **Lesson 7**—1. true. 2. blasphemy. **Lesson 8**—1. false. 2. truth. **Lesson 9**—1. Joel. 2. false. **Lesson 10**—1. true. 2. false. **Lesson 11**—1. true. 2. gardener. **Lesson 12**—1. Corinth. 2. Apollos. **Lesson 13**—1. false. 2. false.

This Quarter in the Word

Mon, Nov. 30	**God's Anointed Ruler of All Nations**	Psalm 2
Tue, Dec. 1	**Blessed and Chosen in Christ**	Ephesians 1:1-14
Wed, Dec. 2	**Christ, Head over All**	Ephesians 1:15-23
Thu, Dec. 3	**In the Family Line of David**	Matthew 1:6b-15
Fri, Dec. 4	**God Anoints Jesus King**	Hebrews 1:6-9
Sat, Dec. 5	**Jesus, Creator and Eternal Ruler**	Hebrews 1:10-14
Sun, Dec. 6	**Expectations of Jesus Before Birth**	Hebrews 1:1-5; Matthew 1:1-6, 16-17

Mon, Dec. 7	**Sign of God's Presence**	Isaiah 7:10-15
Tue, Dec. 8	**Called as Light to the Nations**	Isaiah 42:1-9
Wed, Dec. 9	**Called to Mission Before Birth**	Isaiah 49:1-7
Thu, Dec. 10	**Birth of Jesus Foretold to Mary**	Luke 1:26-38
Fri, Dec. 11	**Simeon Foretells Jesus' Ministry**	Luke 2:34-38
Sat, Dec. 12	**Mary, in the Lineage of Ruth**	Ruth 4:9-17
Sun, Dec. 13	**Miracle of the Holy Spirit Conception**	Matthew 1:18-25

Mon, Dec. 14	**Midwives Ignore Pharaoh's Decree**	Exodus 1:15-22
Tue, Dec. 15	**God Answers Solomon's Dream**	1 Kings 3:5-14
Wed, Dec. 16	**Insight into the Meaning of Dreams**	Daniel 1:8-17
Thu, Dec. 17	**In Christ No Divisions Allowed**	Galatians 3:25-29
Fri, Dec. 18	**Gracious Ruler from Bethlehem**	Micah 5:1-5
Sat, Dec. 19	**Successful Return from Egypt**	Matthew 2:19-23
Sun, Dec. 20	**Safe in the Midst of Danger**	Matthew 2:7-15

Mon, Dec. 21	**A Voice Cries, "Comfort My People"**	Isaiah 40:1-5
Tue, Dec. 22	**John the Baptist Is the Greatest**	Matthew 11:2-15
Wed, Dec. 23	**The Baptist's Testimony of Faith**	John 1:19-34
Thu, Dec. 24	**Jesus, the Father's Beloved Son**	Matthew 17:1-8
Fri, Dec. 25	**In John, Elijah Has Come**	Matthew 17:9-13; Malachi 4:4-5
Sat, Dec. 26	**John Baptizes Jesus in the Jordan**	Matthew 3:13-17
Sun, Dec. 27	**John Prepares the Way for Jesus**	Matthew 3:1-12
Mon, Dec. 28	**Live by God's Word**	Deuteronomy 8:1-11
Tue, Dec. 29	**Jubilee, Year of God's Favor**	Leviticus 25:8-17
Wed, Dec. 30	**Miracle of the Meal and Oil**	1 Kings 17:8-16
Thu, Dec. 31	**Naaman's Leprosy Healed**	2 Kings 5:1-14
Fri, Jan. 1	**Jesus Overcomes Temptation**	Luke 4:1-13
Sat, Jan. 2	**Jesus Driven out of Nazareth**	Luke 4:23-30
Sun, Jan. 3	**Jesus' Mandate for Ministry**	Luke 4:14-22a
Mon, Jan. 4	**Called to Lead Israelites from Egypt**	Exodus 3:1-12
Tue, Jan. 5	**Called to Save Israel from Midianites**	Judges 6:11-16
Wed, Jan. 6	**Called and Cleansed for Ministry**	Isaiah 6:1-8
Thu, Jan. 7	**Single Mindedness to Follow Jesus**	Luke 9:57-62
Fri, Jan. 8	**Repentance, Goal of God's Kindness**	Romans 2:1-11
Sat, Jan. 9	**Jesus Calls Peter to Ministry**	John 21:15-19
Sun, Jan. 10	**Don't Be Afraid to Catch People**	Luke 5:1-11
Mon, Jan. 11	**Peace and Healing Will Come**	Isaiah 57:14-21
Tue, Jan. 12	**Healed by Christ's Wounds**	1 Peter 2:18-25
Wed, Jan. 13	**Daughter Healed by Mother's Faith**	Matthew 15:21-28
Thu, Jan. 14	**Anoint Sick with Oil and Prayer**	James 5:13-16
Fri, Jan. 15	**Woman Healed by Her Faith**	Mark 5:21-34
Sat, Jan. 16	**The Sick Need a Physician**	Mark 2:13-17
Sun, Jan. 17	**Jesus Heals and Forgives the Paralytic**	Mark 2:1-12

Mon, Jan. 18	**Prayer for Peter in Prison**	Acts 12:5-11
Tue, Jan. 19	**Pray for a Successful Ministry**	Romans 15:22-33
Wed, Jan. 20	**Pray for Inner Strength and Power**	Ephesians 3:14-21
Thu, Jan. 21	**Pray the Prayer of Our Lord**	Matthew 6:7-13
Fri, Jan. 22	**Pray for Your Abusers**	Luke 6:22-33
Sat, Jan. 23	**Pray to Avoid Trials**	Luke 22:39-46
Sun, Jan. 24	**Jesus Prays for His Disciples**	John 17:14-24
Mon, Jan. 25	**Jesus Supports Mary's Choice**	Luke 10:38-42
Tue, Jan. 26	**Jesus Responds to Sisters' Call**	John 11:1-11
Wed, Jan. 27	**Jesus Raises Lazarus; Mary Believes**	John 11:38-45
Thu, Jan. 28	**Women Carry Resurrection Message**	Luke 24:5-10
Fri, Jan. 29	**Jesus' Final Words and Ascension**	Luke 24:44-53
Sat, Jan. 30	**Simeon Sees Impact of Jesus' Ministry**	Luke 2:28-35
Sun, Jan. 31	**The Spirit Empowers**	Luke 2:36-38; Acts 2:16-21; 21:8-9
Mon, Feb. 1	**Receive the Water of Life**	Revelation 21:1-7
Tue, Feb. 2	**Jesus Declares, "I Am from Above"**	John 8:21-30
Wed, Feb. 3	**God's Children Led by the Spirit**	Romans 8:12-17
Thu, Feb. 4	**Simon and Andrew First Disciples**	John 1:37-42
Fri, Feb. 5	**Philip and Nathanael Become Disciples**	John 1:43-51
Sat, Feb. 6	**Jesus Heals Son of Galilean Official**	John 4:43-54
Sun, Feb. 7	**Samaritans Come to Jesus**	John 4:25-42
Mon, Feb. 8	**Jesus Appears to Paul**	1 Corinthians 15:1-11
Tue, Feb. 9	**Present with Jesus at the Cross**	John 19:25b-30
Wed, Feb. 10	**Spices Prepared to Anoint Jesus' Body**	Mark 16:1-8
Thu, Feb. 11	**Mary Magdalene Finds Tomb Empty**	John 20:1-9
Fri, Feb. 12	**Angel Confirms Jesus' Resurrection**	Matthew 28:1-10
Sat, Feb. 13	**Jesus Commissions His Disciples**	John 20:19-23
Sun, Feb. 14	**Mary Magdalene, Faithful Disciple**	Luke 8:1-3; Mark 15:40; John 20:10-18

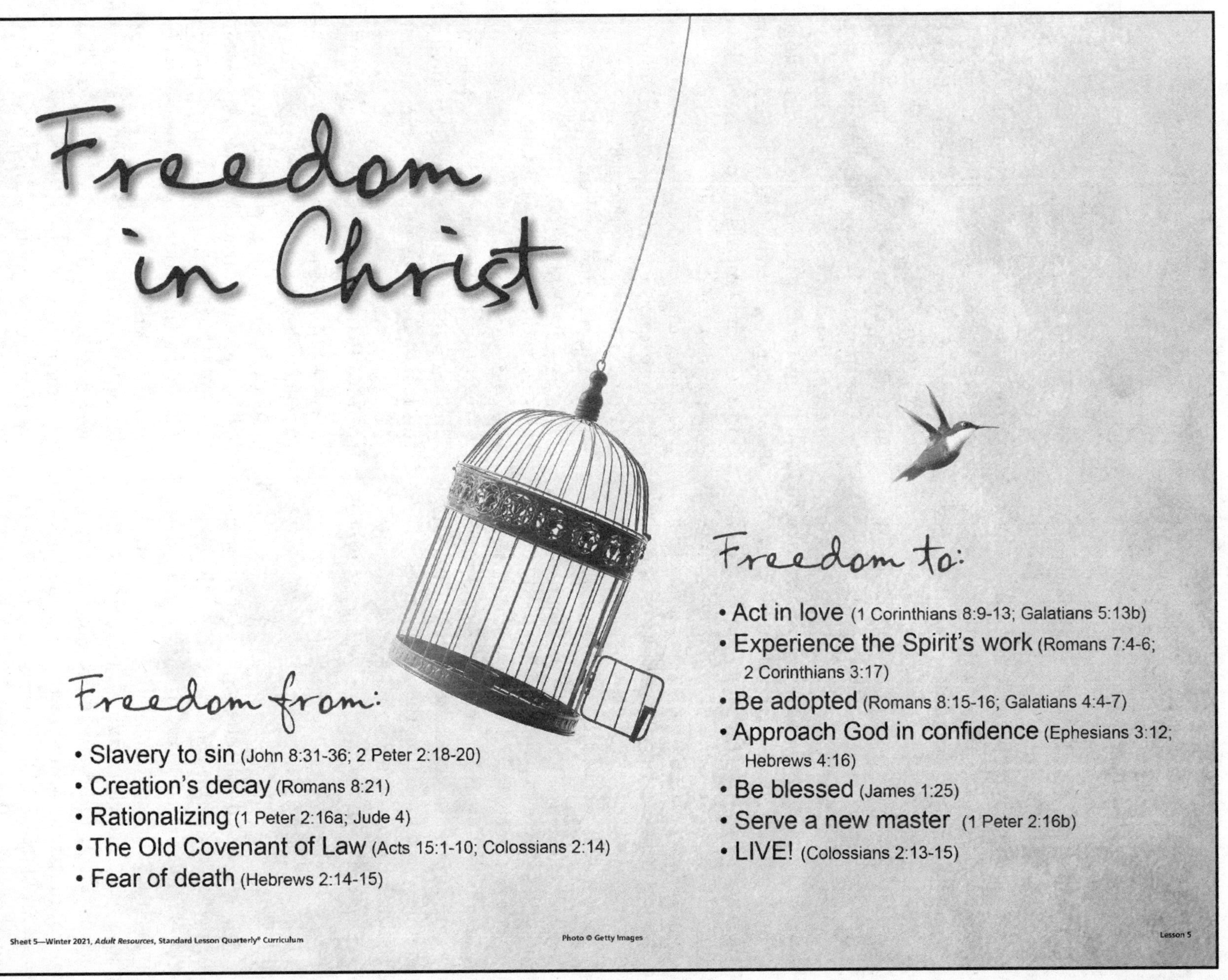
Freedom in Christ
Freedom from:
• Slavery to sin (John 8:31-36; 2 Peter 2:18-20)
• Creation's decay (Romans 8:21)
• Rationalizing (1 Peter 2:16a; Jude 4)
• The Old Covenant of Law (Acts 15:1-10; Colossians 2:14)
• Fear of death (Hebrews 2:14-15)
Freedom to:
• Act in love (1 Corinthians 8:9-13; Galatians 5:13b)
• Experience the Spirit's work (Romans 7:4-6; 2 Corinthians 3:17)
• Be adopted (Romans 8:15-16; Galatians 4:4-7)
• Approach God in confidence (Ephesians 3:12; Hebrews 4:16)
• Be blessed (James 1:25)
• Serve a new master (1 Peter 2:16b)
• LIVE! (Colossians 2:13-15)
Sheet 5—Winter 2021, Adult Resources, Standard Lesson Quarterly® Curriculum
Photo © Getty Images
Lesson 5

TEACHING BY DISCUSSION

Teacher Tips by Jerry Bowling

DISCUSSION-BASED teaching methods can be a vital tool in the Bible teacher's repertoire—but only if the teacher knows the *why* and *how* of their use. When unskilled, undirected discussion takes place in the Bible classroom, the result is often merely a common pooling of ignorance and/or a "what it means to me" approach to Scripture that bypasses the original intent of the author. But that need not happen!

The Why

Bible-class leaders who are skillful at using discussion methods cultivate openness and vulnerability in ways that lecture methods simply cannot. As the teacher figuratively steps down from a lecture-based position of authority, the vulnerability he or she reveals in discussion-based classes encourages openness and vulnerability on the part of learners as well.

Lecture-based methods focus almost exclusively on the transmission of facts. Discussion-based methods take this a step further by exploring how those scriptural facts and truth can and do interact with "real life." Discussion methods help learners process their experiences as they explore successes and failures in connecting their inner lives with the Bible. In short, discussion-based teaching supports internalization of spiritual values as those values drive behavior.

The How

Discussion-based teaching requires that teachers be prepared to focus Bible lessons on the context of life today, particularly the "gray areas." For example, the scriptural prohibitions against stealing and lying are clear enough (Exodus 20:15; Leviticus 19:11; Ephesians 4:25, 28; etc.). But what counts as "stealing" in the everyday gray areas of life? For example, if I make a one-minute personal phone call while at work, have I stolen from my employer? Or if I exaggerate or slightly misrepresent facts in a conversation to spare the feeling of a friend, have I sinned? As gray-area issues are wrestled with, learners realize they are not alone in such struggles.

One way the teacher encourages such discussion is by creating space where students can feel safe talking about their inner values that drive their outward behavior. No one is pressured to do so, of course. But the teacher who does so personally sets the example for learners to do so as well.

Confronting fear about changing methods is perhaps the hardest step for a teacher to take in making a successful transition into using discussion methods. Teachers need to address any resistance or reluctance they may have about their willingness to do so. Bible teachers do well to remember that learning entails change and that the prospect of such change is particularly intimidating for some to undertake.

Praying for God's wisdom (James 1:5) is the best place to begin stretching beyond the comfortable and familiar. And God may be calling you to do just that!

The limited space here does not allow fullest discussion of how-tos. Many additional ideas in this regard are easily found on the internet.

Reflecting on Your Role as Teacher

Adopting a discussion method will require you to reflect on your role as teacher. A critical competency for teaching via discussion is that you will be assisting learners to take responsibility and become self-directing in maturing spiritually as you model that yourself. You will model not only expertise in Bible content, but also an interpersonal "fellow struggler" rapport with your learners.

Called to Be Heir

Devotional Reading: Psalm 102:12-22
Background Scripture: Matthew 1:1-17; Hebrews 1

Matthew 1:1-6, 16-17

1 The book of the generation of Jesus Christ, the son of David, the son of Abraham.

2 Abraham begat Isaac; and Isaac begat Jacob; and Jacob begat Judas and his brethren;

3 And Judas begat Phares and Zara of Thamar; and Phares begat Esrom; and Esrom begat Aram;

4 And Aram begat Aminadab; and Aminadab begat Naasson; and Naasson begat Salmon;

5 And Salmon begat Booz of Rachab; and Booz begat Obed of Ruth; and Obed begat Jesse;

6 And Jesse begat David the king; and David the king begat Solomon of her that had been the wife of Urias.

. . . .

16 And Jacob begat Joseph the husband of Mary, of whom was born Jesus, who is called Christ.

17 So all the generations from Abraham to David are fourteen generations; and from David until the carrying away into Babylon are fourteen generations; and from the carrying away into Babylon unto Christ are fourteen generations.

Hebrews 1:1-5

1 God, who at sundry times and in divers manners spake in time past unto the fathers by the prophets,

2 Hath in these last days spoken unto us by his Son, whom he hath appointed heir of all things, by whom also he made the worlds;

3 Who being the brightness of his glory, and the express image of his person, and upholding all things by the word of his power, when he had by himself purged our sins, sat down on the right hand of the Majesty on high;

4 Being made so much better than the angels, as he hath by inheritance obtained a more excellent name than they.

5 For unto which of the angels said he at any time, Thou art my Son, this day have I begotten thee? And again, I will be to him a Father, and he shall be to me a Son?

Key Verse

[God] hath in these last days spoken unto us by his Son, whom he hath appointed heir of all things, by whom also he made the worlds. —**Hebrews 1:2**

Call in the New Testament

Unit 1: The Beginning of a Call

Lessons 1–4

Lesson Aims

After participating in this lesson, each learner will be able to:

1. Recall key names in the lineage of Jesus.
2. Explain why Jesus' heritage was central to His mission on earth.
3. State a way to improve acknowledgement of his or her spiritual heritage in Jesus.

Lesson Outline

Introduction
- A. Who Am I?
- B. Lesson Context: Matthew's Gospel
- C. Lesson Context: The Book of Hebrews

I. Wanderers to Kings (Matthew 1:1-6)
- A. Abraham to Jesse (vv. 1-5)
  - *The More You Know*
- B. Jesse to Solomon (v. 6)

II. Captives to the King (Matthew 1:16-17)
- A. Jacob to Jesus (v. 16)
- B. The Generations (v. 17)

III. The King as the Son (Hebrews 1:1-5)
- A. Greater than Prophets (vv. 1-2)
- B. Seated in Heaven (v. 3)
  - *Image*
- C. Over the Angels (vv. 4-5)

Conclusion
- A. Heritage of the King
- B. Prayer
- C. Thought to Remember

Introduction

A. Who Am I?

Heritage connects people to the past and provides roots for understanding themselves in the larger world. In my case, my "Italianness" was always an important part of my self-identity. Growing up, it helped me understand that I shared a history with millions of other people, a history that began long before I was born. I felt this connection despite being adopted by a non-Italian family with no discernible Italian influences.

Both Matthew and the writer of Hebrews concerned themselves with Jesus' heritage. In that regard, the focus remained on God's work in a specific family to bring about His purposes. Also, Jesus' divine superiority to every created being was of utmost importance to emphasize. These two writers remind us that Jesus' beginnings are both humble and unimaginably glorious.

B. Lesson Context: Matthew's Gospel

From the exile in Babylon of 586 BC onward, Judea was rarely free of foreign powers that imposed their will on the nation. After Babylon came Persia, then Greece, and finally Rome. In about 38 BC, Rome declared Herod to be king of Judea.

Herod imposed Greek and Roman culture onto the Jews, even erecting a temple to the goddess Roma in Caesarea Maritima. The Jews despised Herod not only for these acts but also because he wasn't Jewish by heritage and thus not a rightful king. Matthew wrote against this background, which makes his genealogy more than a list of names. It is a link to a time when David's line held the throne, saying something important about Jesus' birthright.

C. Lesson Context: The Book of Hebrews

Hebrews is a bit unusual. It ends with greetings like an epistle (Hebrews 13:20-25), yet the beginning is unlike that of a normal letter (contrast its opening verses with those of Colossians, etc.). Its original readers were likely Christians of Jewish background who had been undergoing some persecution, which tempted them to give up on Christianity for old ways that had been superseded

(10:32-39; etc.). We can almost hear the original readers' questions that prompt our author to write chapter 1: "We know about angels; is Jesus as strong as they?" "He died; is He powerful enough to save?" The author of Hebrews has clear answers.

I. Wanderers to Kings

(Matthew 1:1-6)

A. Abraham to Jesse (vv. 1-5)

1. The book of the generation of Jesus Christ, the son of David, the son of Abraham.

The names *Jesus Christ, David*, and *Abraham* all represent turning points in Israel's history. Only by looking at the covenants associated with David and Abraham can a person properly understand Jesus' importance as the fulfillment of those promises. Connecting Jesus to David foreshadows the rest of Matthew's Gospel, where we learn that Jesus fulfilled the promises to David (examples: Matthew 2:20-21; 21:5; see commentary on 1:6, below).

> *What Do You Think?*
> What guardrails can we erect to ensure that we do not misuse biblical genealogies?
> *Digging Deeper*
> How do Matthew 3:9; 1 Timothy 1:4; and Titus 3:9 help you answer this question?

The More You Know

Several years ago, my father was shaken when he found out that the man he believed to be his biological father wasn't. Sadly, the answers to his questions were buried with the few people who could have answered them. He believed he would never have a clear picture of his heritage.

Today, with the help of DNA testing and hours and hours of research, my father has identified his biological family *and* traced his lineage back nearly 1,000 years, to William the Conqueror. He even established his legitimate claim to gain admittance into his Scottish clan.

Matthew's genealogy establishes Jesus as the fulfillment of both the Abrahamic and Davidic covenants. Jesus' lineage proves His earthly identity and supports His rightful place as heir to the throne of David and, therefore, the means by which the whole world can be blessed. How can you ensure that you won't miss out? —L. G.

2a. Abraham begat Isaac.

Abraham received the covenant that ultimately established the people of Israel. The story of Abraham is one of faithfulness—from both the patriarch and God (Genesis 12:1-7; 15; 17).

Despite Isaac's being the only son of promise (Genesis 17:19-21), Abraham was faithful in preparing to sacrifice him on Mount Moriah (22:1-10). God showed His faithfulness to Abraham again by sending a ram to replace Isaac on the altar and then renewing the covenant (22:11-18).

2b. And Isaac begat Jacob.

After Abraham's death, the covenant promise passed to *Isaac*. Little is said about Isaac, but his and Rebekah's parenting style of playing favorites (Genesis 25:28) blighted his sons (27:19-41).

2c. And Jacob begat Judas and his brethren.

God met *Jacob* at Bethel and promised him land and children (Genesis 28:13-15), echoing promises made to Abraham (see Matthew 1:2a, above). Of Jacob's 12 sons, *Judas* (spelled Judah in Genesis 49:8-10) unexpectedly inherited the promise of a royal line (see Matthew 1:6, below); he wasn't the first-, second-, or even third-born son (Genesis 29:32-35). Further, he was born to Leah, who was "hated" by her husband (29:31).

HOW TO SAY IT

Aminadab	Uh-*min*-uh-dab.
Bathsheba	Bath-*she*-buh.
Caesarea Maritima	Sess-uh-*ree*-uh Mar-uh-*tee*-muh.
Judas	*Joo*-dus.
Moriah	Mo-*rye*-uh.
Obed	*O*-bed.
patriarch	pay-tree-ark.
Phares (Pharez)	*Fair*-ezz.
Rachab	*Ray*-hab.
Salmon	*Sal*-mun.
Thamar	*Thay*-mer.
Urias	Yu-*rye*-uhs.
Zara (Zarah)	*Zair*-uh.

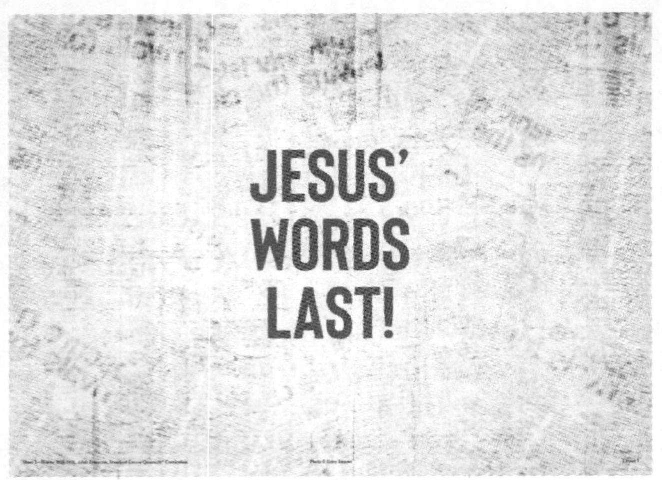

Visual for Lesson 1. *Use this visual to begin a discussion about how students can further Jesus' lasting impact.*

3a. And Judas begat Phares and Zara of Thamar.

The rarity of women in this genealogy should draw attention to all five who *are* mentioned, as each was uniquely notable. *Thamar* (spelled Tamar in Genesis 38:6) is the first woman listed. She was widowed before bearing children for her husband, so *Judas* (Judah), her father-in-law, told her to wait until that man's brother was old enough to become wed to her. But detecting deception on the part of Judas, she tricked him into impregnating her (38:13-25). On learning the truth, he declared, "She hath been more righteous than I" (38:26).

Phares and Zara (spelled Pharez and Zarah in Genesis 38:29-30) were twins. During their births, Zara put out his hand first and thus had a scarlet thread tied to him to mark him as firstborn. But Phares (meaning "he who bursts forth") was actually born first, thus his inclusion in the next verse.

3b. And Phares begat Esrom.

Little is known of *Phares* outside of his birth story other than the fact that his house maintained a good reputation (Ruth 4:12). *Esrom* (spelled Hezron in Genesis 46:12) was born in Canaan and journeyed to Egypt with Jacob and the rest of the family (46:7-9). His name establishes a link between the beginnings of the 12 tribes in Genesis and their fertility and subsequent struggle in described in Exodus (compare Numbers 26:21).

3d. And Esrom begat Aram.

Aram (spelled Ram in Ruth 4:19) was one of the children born in Egypt, part of the evidence of Israel's fruitfulness in that land (Exodus 1:7).

4-5a. And Aram begat Aminadab; and Aminadab begat Naasson; and Naasson begat Salmon. And Salmon begat Booz of Rachab.

The male names in this segment match those in 1 Chronicles 2:10-11. These loosely represent the period of the judges (about 1380–1050 BC), and therein lies a bit of a problem: there are not enough names in either record to cover that 330-year period of time. Instead, the names represent all that time. This drives the narrative represented by the genealogy closer to David (see also on Matthew 1:6, 17, below).

Not mentioned in the genealogy in 1 Chronicles 2 is *Rachab* (spelled Rahab in Joshua 6:17), second of four women mentioned in Matthew's genealogy. She hid the Israelite spies in Jericho, thereby saving their lives (Joshua 2:3-16; Hebrews 11:31). Her inclusion here points not only to the importance of women in Jesus' lineage but also to God's love for non-Israelites (compare Matthew 12:20-21). The way she honored God in speech and deed transcended both her deception and occupation (Joshua 2:1-21). For this reason, she was welcomed without question into Israel despite being born in an unfaithful nation (Joshua 6:25; James 2:25).

Like his father *Salmon*, *Booz* (spelled Boaz in Ruth 4:21) is often overshadowed by the remarkable woman he married (see Matthew 1:5b, next).

5b. And Booz begat Obed of Ruth; and Obed begat Jesse.

Ruth is the third woman listed in the lineage. She was from Moab, a nation that Israel was to avoid or else risk being led astray (example: Numbers 25). Ruth represents an exception based on faithfulness: she took her mother-in-law Naomi's God and family as her own (Ruth 1:16). Ruth met and later married *Booz* (Boaz; Ruth 2:1; 4:13). Their son *Obed* became the father of *Jesse*, grandfather of David (see Matthew 1:6, next).

B. Jesse to Solomon (v. 6)

6. And Jesse begat David the king; and David the king begat Solomon of her that had been the wife of Urias.

This verse marks a transition from the period of the judges to the time of the united monarchy (about 1050–930 BC). *David the king* comes with many stories of faithfulness to God (example: 1 Samuel 17). However, the story line Matthew reminds his readers about was ultimately one of God's faithfulness in the midst of human sin: God kept His promise even after David's sin against *Urias* (spelled Uriah in 2 Samuel 11) and Bathsheba. She is the fourth woman listed, but referred to only as *the wife of Urias*. The full account and its consequences are recorded in 2 Samuel 11–12.

Bathsheba's second son was *Solomon*. As a result of intrigue and violence in the royal family, this son inherited the throne (1 Kings 1:1-35). He was a wise man (example: 10:1-5) who nevertheless stumbled into faithlessness (11:1-13).

II. Captives to the King

(Matthew 1:16-17)

A. Jacob to Jesus (v. 16)

16. And Jacob begat Joseph the husband of Mary, of whom was born Jesus, who is called Christ.

The final three names in the genealogy seem like history repeating itself as they remind us of others who bore the names before (see Genesis 37:3; 45:8-11; 47:13-26). *Jesus* is the Greek form of the Hebrew name Joshua. *Mary,* the fifth woman in this list, is a Greek form of the Hebrew name Miriam (Exodus 15:20).

B. The Generations (v. 17)

17. So all the generations from Abraham to David are fourteen generations; and from David until the carrying away into Babylon are fourteen generations; and from the carrying away into Babylon unto Christ are fourteen generations.

This verse highlights a pattern that Matthew wants the genealogy to portray, as the names are broken into three sections of *fourteen* names each. This may be a simple memory device since the three consonants of the name David occupy the fourth, sixth, and fourth places in the Hebrew alphabet, respectively—adding up to 14. If so, there's no mystical numerology involved, just a simple and useful memory device. This possibility gains strength when we realize that Matthew chose not to include certain names in Matthew 1:8, 11 that are included in 1 Chronicles 3:10-16. The result is that each of Matthew's three sections adds to 14.

> *What Do You Think?*
> What Scripture memorization techniques do you find most helpful personally?
> *Digging Deeper*
> How do passages such as Psalm 119:105 and Matthew 4:4 speak to this topic?

The phrase *from the carrying away into Babylon unto Christ are fourteen generations* summarizes the story of God's leading His people home again. That began with the return from exile in about 538 BC.

III. The King as the Son

(Hebrews 1:1-5)

A. Greater than Prophets (vv. 1-2)

1-2a. God, who at sundry times and in divers manners spake in time past unto the fathers by the prophets, hath in these last days spoken unto us by his Son.

In the past, God primarily communicated indirectly. Considering that the Old Testament is God's revelation through many writers over the course of many centuries, we understand what the author means by the phrase *at sundry times in divers manners*. Those diverse ways included a burning bush (Exodus 3), dreams (1 Kings 3), and visions (Ezekiel 1).

The phrase *unto the fathers* refers to Jewish ancestors, the recipients of God's communication that resulted in Scripture. The instrument God used to communicate was *the prophets*. Unlike those prophets, however, Jesus is God's own *Son*. This equates Jesus with God (John 1:1; 5:18). Attention is now to turn away from the prophets to Jesus and His message. The phrase *these last days* refers to the time that began with Christ's first coming and continues through our own days (see 1 John 2:18).

What Do You Think?

How would you respond to a fellow Christian who believes that Hebrews 1:1-2, along with passages such as Colossians 2:14, implies that the Old Testament can be disregarded?

Digging Deeper

In what circumstances would it be useful to introduce Romans 15:4; 1 Corinthians 10:1-13; and/or 2 Timothy 3:16 into the dialogue?

2b. Whom he hath appointed heir of all things, by whom also he made the worlds.

Jesus, the *heir of all things*, has divine authority and ownership, far more than any created being since *all things* means everything that exists. It is He who fulfills the promises of the Old Testament covenants (see Hebrew 1:5, below). These certainly include God's promise to Abraham to bless all the nations (Genesis 12:3). Jesus declares in Matthew 28:18 that His authority is absolute.

Jesus in the one who brought *the worlds* into existence (John 1:1-4). The Greek word translated *worlds* often refers to eternity in this epistle (Hebrews 1:8; 5:6; 6:20; 7:17, 21, 24, 28; 13:8, 21), but here the word *worlds* fits better (as it also does in 11:3). Think about how foolish it is not to trust Jesus to bring God's message into the existence that Jesus himself created!

B. Seated in Heaven (v. 3)

3a. Who being the brightness of his glory, and the express image of his person.

The Father has *glory* of His own, of course. At the same time, the Son also has actual light—*brightness* or radiance. Thus the Son is not reflected light, as we see coming from the moon, but has light himself, as we see from the sun.

Moreover, the Son bears the image of God in ways we do not (Genesis 1:26-27). The term for *express image* is used of the imprint stamped on coins. *Person* refers to God's real essence or actual being. These two terms make clear that the Son, though distinct as a person from the Father, is of the same divine nature as the Father. Whatever the "stuff" is that makes the Father to be God also makes the Son to be God. The relationship between the Father and Son is best summarized by Jesus: "He that hath seen me hath seen the Father" (John 14:9).

Image

As a child, I was the spitting image of my father, and I had precious little resemblance to my mother. Whenever the two of us went to the store, strangers would proclaim how wonderful it was that my mother chose to adopt. Although she agrees that adoption is a praiseworthy choice, she was disappointed that I was not recognizable as her flesh and blood.

I am no longer the spitting image of my father. I have grown to look more and more like my mother. Today it would be impossible not to see how I am related to both of them.

In a similar vein, I am not an exact reflection of the image of God. His image in me is marred by sin. However, as I continue to grow into maturity, I can catch more and more glimpses of God in my reflection. I will never be the express image of God. Only Jesus is and can be. Praise God that by His grace you and I both can have enough resemblance to be identified as family! —L. G.

3b. And upholding all things by the word of his power.

The Son sustains *all things*. Deuteronomy 33:27 speaks of God's everlasting arms being Israel's refuge. Isaiah 46:4 says God will carry His people and deliver them. The Son uses *the word of his power* to do this; this recall the power of God's word revealed at the beginning in Genesis 1. The Son's role as sustainer is that which only the divine one can fill.

3c. When he had by himself purged our sins, sat down on the right hand of the Majesty on high.

The Son brought about the purging, or cleansing, from *sins* when He died on the cross. Jesus' ability to purge sins reinforces His deity, as only God can forgive sins (Mark 2:7).

To be seated at *the right hand* is a position of honor (1 Kings 2:19; Luke 20:42) given for the Son's completed work on earth. This is a repeated theme in this epistle (Hebrews 8:1; 10:12; 12:2).

C. Over the Angels (vv. 4-5)

4. Being made so much better than the angels, as he hath by inheritance obtained a more excellent name than they.

Jews of the first century AD had a pervasive fascination with *angels*. We see evidence of this in some of the nonbiblical writings that came into being in the time between the Old and New Testaments (the intertestamental writings). In all the ways already mentioned so far, the Son is as superior to the angels as His *name* is to theirs. What names? *Son* versus *angel*. Whereas an angel is a created messenger, the Son is the divine, uncreated Creator. The difference is infinite.

> *What Do You Think?*
> How can this text help you guard yourself against mistaken beliefs about angels?
> *Digging Deeper*
> What vital dimensions do 2 Corinthians 11:14 and Colossians 2:18 add to that question?

5a. For unto which of the angels said he at any time, Thou art my Son, this day have I begotten thee?

The word *he* refers to God. The phrase *Thou art my Son, this day have I begotten thee* is from Psalm 2:7. It is used here to make a vital point: no angel is called *my Son*. That is a title reserved for the unique Son of God, as described in Hebrews 1:1-4, above. Though the promises made by the Lord in Psalm 2:8-9 apply in part to David, they can apply fully only to Jesus.

5b. And again, I will be to him a Father, and he shall be to me a Son?

This quotation is from 2 Samuel 7:14. It comes from the passage that established the Davidic covenant. David wished to build a temple for the Lord. Through Nathan the prophet, the Lord explained that He did not need a special house. Instead, the Lord would establish a house for David.

In 2 Samuel 7:12-16, the Lord said He would raise up David's "seed" and establish his kingdom. It was that seed who would build His house; the seed, ultimately, is the Lord's Son. His house, unlike Solomon's temple, endures eternally. Solomon governed a nation in a golden age, but that kingdom did not endure. The Son's kingdom, by contrast, will never end (Isaiah 9:7; Luke 1:33).

> *What Do You Think?*
> How will Jesus' absolute authority affect your service to Him in the week ahead?
> *Digging Deeper*
> Which area of thoughts, actions, and speech need the most improvement in this regard?

Conclusion

A. Heritage of the King

Matthew told his readers about Jesus' human heritage: Jesus is the king promised to bless all nations. The major theme is God's faithfulness, which situates Jesus as the final step in God's fulfillment of His old and new covenant promises. The theme of covenant promises prepares us for the message and mission.

The author of Hebrews, by comparison, focused on Jesus' divine heritage. When Jesus finished His earthly ministry, He was honored by the Father, further indicating the importance of accepting His message.

Through these texts, the Holy Spirit directs us to pay attention to Jesus' message. He is God's Son, greater than any angel or prophet. But He is also God himself.

B. Prayer

Father, thank You for sending Your Son to fulfill Your promises! Help us to live each day remembering that our future is in Him. In Jesus' name we pray. Amen.

C. Thought to Remember

Our future is in Jesus Christ, the Son of God.

Involvement Learning

Enhance your lesson with KJV Bible Student *(from your curriculum supplier) and the reproducible activity page (at www.standardlesson.com or in the back of the* KJV Standard Lesson Commentary Deluxe Edition*).*

Into the Lesson

Have this statement displayed on the board as learners arrive:

Share with someone how far back you can trace your ancestry.

Give each student an index card. Ask students to record on it a few known facts about one of their ancestors (no names, and not Adam!). Collect the cards after a minute, shuffle them, then give each student one. Have the cards read aloud; allow class members to guess who they believe wrote the card. (For larger classes, have this done within groups of five or more to save time.)

Lead into Bible study by saying, "While knowing facts of one's ancestors can be interesting, Jesus' ancestry is more than that. Let's see why."

Into the Word

Announce a pretest as you distribute the following list of names on identical handouts (you create): Abraham / Ai / Aminadab / Aram / Booz / David / Esau / Esrom / Gideon / Isaac / Ishmael / Jacob / Jesse / Joseph / Judas / Naasson / Obed / Phares / Rachab / Ruth / Salmon / Solomon.

Tell learners they have one minute, working individually with Bibles closed, to strike out the four names that are not in Matthew 1:1-6, 16-17. Have learners check their results according to those verses. (*Alternatives.* Use this exercise at the end of the Into the Word segment instead, as a posttest; or create enough copies to do both.)

Follow by having a learner read aloud Hebrews 1:1-5; then divide the class into three groups. Give each group a designation and handouts (you prepare) as follows.

Faithfulness Group: Create a poster based on Matthew 1:1-6, 16-17 to answer these questions: 1–What were some prominent ways God showed faithfulness to certain of these people? 2–In what ways do we see God's faithfulness today?

Female Gentiles Group: Create a poster based on Matthew 1:1-6, 16-17 to answer these questions: 1–Which names are those of female Gentiles and which are female Israelites? 2–Why would Matthew have chosen to list Gentiles?

Jesus as Heir Group: Create a poster based on Hebrews 1:1-5 to answer these question: 1–What preceded Jesus' having the inheritance listed? 2–Why is that question important?

After no more than 15 minutes, allow groups to share their posters with the class. Encourage whole-class discussion. Bring discussion to a climax by asking why it's important to know about both Jesus' human and divine heritages.

Option. Distribute copies of the "Jesus' Heritage" exercise from the activity page, which you can download. Have students work in pairs or small groups to complete as indicated. After no more than 15 minutes, have students share their conclusions. Use the commentary to fill in any gaps.

Make a transition to Into Life by saying, "While we *don't* have any control over our human heritage, we *do* have control over our spiritual heritage."

Into Life

Give each learner an index card. Say, "On a scale from 1 (rarely) to 10 (daily), write how often you acknowledge your spiritual heritage in Jesus." [Pause as they do so.] Continue: "Now jot some ideas on ways to improve that score in the week ahead."

Call time after one minute. Ask for volunteers to share responses, but don't put anyone on the spot.

Option. Close by distributing copies of the "Jesus, My Savior, Is All Things to Me" from the activity page. As someone reads aloud the words to the hymn, encourage students to remember and acknowledge that their spiritual heritage is in Jesus—and what a wonderful heritage it is!

Called to Be Emmanuel

Devotional Reading: Isaiah 42:1-9
Background Scripture: Matthew 1:18-25

Matthew 1:18-25

18 Now the birth of Jesus Christ was on this wise: When as his mother Mary was espoused to Joseph, before they came together, she was found with child of the Holy Ghost.

19 Then Joseph her husband, being a just man, and not willing to make her a publick example, was minded to put her away privily.

20 But while he thought on these things, behold, the angel of the Lord appeared unto him in a dream, saying, Joseph, thou son of David, fear not to take unto thee Mary thy wife: for that which is conceived in her is of the Holy Ghost.

21 And she shall bring forth a son, and thou shalt call his name Jesus: for he shall save his people from their sins.

22 Now all this was done, that it might be fulfilled which was spoken of the Lord by the prophet, saying,

23 Behold, a virgin shall be with child, and shall bring forth a son, and they shall call his name Emmanuel, which being interpreted is, God with us.

24 Then Joseph being raised from sleep did as the angel of the Lord had bidden him, and took unto him his wife:

25 And knew her not till she had brought forth her firstborn son: and he called his name Jesus.

Key Verses

Joseph, thou son of David, fear not to take unto thee Mary thy wife: for that which is conceived in her is of the Holy Ghost. And she shall bring forth a son, and thou shalt call his name Jesus: for he shall save his people from their sins. —**Matthew 1:20b-21**

Call in the New Testament

Unit 1: The Beginning of a Call

Lessons 1–4

Lesson Aims

After participating in this lesson, each learner will be able to:

1. List the choices Joseph faced in his dilemma.
2. Explain the meaning and significance of the name Emmanuel.
3. Write a prayer of thanksgiving for the gift of Jesus.

Lesson Outline

Introduction

A. Not What Some People Would Think

Several years ago, the president of a small chain of savings and loans received a polite but firm letter from an account holder. The letter stated his desire to withdraw all funds immediately. A quick review of accounts revealed that this would be a significant loss: the investor in question had more than $5 million in assets. Alarmed, the president called the disgruntled man to see what was wrong.

The customer was an older gentleman who had retired as a multimillionaire by age 60, but very few people were aware of his true net worth. This was partly because the man continued to take care of his own farm, drove an older pickup truck, and preferred boots and work overalls as clothing.

On a recent occasion, he had gone into a branch of the bank in another town to cash a check. Not knowing him and seeing his rough appearance and dirty hands, the tellers had treated him with disregard. He left feeling that he did not like the way that bank's employees treated "average working people," hence the reason for the letter's stated intent to close out his accounts.

"I guess," he said as he hung up the phone, "I'm just not what some people would think."

It's easy to conclude that someone who dresses or talks a certain way, works at a certain kind of job, or drives a certain type of vehicle must necessarily be a certain kind of person. Judging the Joseph of today's text based on appearance might have led his contemporaries to conclude that he had no special place in God's plans. How could he be the type of person who would be called to raise the promised Messiah?

B. Lesson Context

Today's lesson focuses on the unlikely hero Joseph of Nazareth. Joseph's background was unremarkable in a number of ways. First, his place of residence, Nazareth (Luke 2:4; 4:16, 22), was a tiny village well off the beaten path. In Joseph's day the town was so insignificant that it is not mentioned in contemporary sources outside the

Bible. Even the first-century Jewish historian Josephus didn't include Nazareth in his list of Galilean villages subdued by the Romans during the great Jewish revolt of AD 66–72. The majority of the inhabitants of Nazareth would have worked as subsistence farmers or day laborers, living the peasant lifestyle typical of Rome's occupied provinces (compare John 1:46).

Second, even within Nazareth, Joseph's social standing would have been nothing special. In Matthew 13:55, its residents were dismissive of the adult Jesus, calling Him "the carpenter's son"—a reference that reveals Joseph's trade. The Greek word often translated "carpenter" could refer to a skilled woodworker, boutique craftsman, or construction worker.

In the first century AD, Galilean laborers like Joseph were employed on major construction projects funded by the Roman client-king Herod Antipas, where they worked with stone, wood, and other materials to build roads and public buildings. Joseph may have spent most of his life working on the new and elegant Roman colony at Sepphoris, a three-mile walk north from Nazareth.

Life was hard for poor laborers in that era, a fact that may explain why Joseph apparently did not live to see Jesus' ministry. While he is mentioned as the father of the adult Jesus in John 6:42, he last appears in the Gospels in Luke 2:41-50, a story that took place when Jesus was 12 years old.

In ancient times, tradespeople like Joseph were not protected by labor laws or collective-bargaining contracts. As a result, they were subject to long workdays, dangerous conditions, and the typically high levels of taxation that Rome levied on its subjects. It is highly unlikely that Joseph had received any kind of formal education, and almost certain that he could not read or write with any level of proficiency. Were it not for his association with Jesus, Joseph would have been lost to the pages of history.

But despite his humble origins, Joseph stood out among his peers in at least two respects. First, Joseph was a descendant of King David (see Matthew 1:1-16; lesson 1), and thus a member of Israel's royal line. This fact explains why Joseph took his pregnant wife from Galilee to Bethlehem (a Judean village about six miles from Jerusalem) to register for the Roman tax census (Matthew 2:1; Luke 2:1-4). Bethlehem was David's hometown (1 Samuel 16:1). David was widely understood to be the ancestor of the coming Messiah, who would rule Israel on David's restored throne (2 Samuel 7; Jeremiah 23:5-6).

The second way Joseph stood out among his peers is part of today's lesson.

I. Facing the News

(Matthew 1:18-19)

A. Unexpected Pregnancy (v. 18)

18. Now the birth of Jesus Christ was on this wise: When as his mother Mary was espoused to Joseph, before they came together, she was found with child of the Holy Ghost.

This verse summarizes a great deal of information that is discussed in detail in Luke 1:26-38. Following the Jewish custom of that day, *Joseph* was probably considerably older than his bride-to-be, perhaps in his mid to late 20s while she was in her mid to late teens. Before their wedding, *Mary* was told by the angel Gabriel that she would soon bear a child—a human impossibility in view of the fact that she was still a virgin (Luke 1:34).

Matthew 1:18 picks up Mary's story after her return to Nazareth from a three-month visit with Elisabeth (Luke 1:39-40, 56). One can only imagine how Joseph felt upon discovering that his fiancée was *with child*. Any explanation from her that this was the result not of unfaithfulness but of the power of *the Holy Ghost* must have been mind-boggling, to say the least.

What Do You Think?

How can you help your church do a better job of extending grace to those experiencing out-of-wedlock pregnancies?

Digging Deeper

What guardrails would need to be put in place to prevent the appearance of condoning pre-marital sex?

B. Private Planning (v. 19)

19. Then Joseph her husband, being a just man, and not willing to make her a publick example, was minded to put her away privily.

Mary and *Joseph her husband* were not yet married, in the sense that they were not living together in the same household. But ancient Jewish custom considered betrothed couples to be legally bound to one another once their engagement had been announced and the dowry paid.

Joseph's presumed anger over the situation could have inclined him to demand the justice that the Law of Moses clearly prescribes. Leviticus 20:10 and Deuteronomy 22:22 both state that those convicted of adultery are to be executed (see also John 8:5). At the very least, Joseph could have publicly terminated the engagement and kept the dowry. That also would have brought disgrace to Mary and her family. Such a move would have been completely justified, given what Joseph knew at this point.

> *What Do You Think?*
>
> Under what circumstances, if any, would you support the public shaming of someone? Why?
>
> *Digging Deeper*
>
> What passages in addition to Matthew 18:15-17; 1 Corinthians 4:14; 6:5; and 15:34 inform your answer?

Yet in this case, compassion won the day. Realizing that the child was not his, Joseph decided to call off the engagement quietly. His attitude was reflected in the description of Joseph as *a just man.* His faithfulness to the law was appropriately matched by his desire to be merciful.

> *What Do You Think?*
>
> How can you help your church do a better job of ministering to those who are divorced or are going through a divorce?
>
> *Digging Deeper*
>
> What difference, if any, should the distinction between a scriptural and an unscriptural divorce play in the ministry effort (Matthew 5:31-32; 1 Corinthians 7:10-15)?

Though many men would have qualified to be Jesus' adoptive father based on being part of David's lineage, Joseph's faith was of utmost importance for raising the Son of God. Joseph was clearly a man of remarkable faith and compassion. These traits come to the forefront of today's passage and are critical to Matthew's larger account of the circumstances of Jesus' birth and early childhood.

II. Seeing the Big Picture

(Matthew 1:20-23)

A. Through Dreams (vv. 20-21)

20a. But while he thought on these things, behold, the angel of the Lord appeared unto him in a dream.

Matthew's account of the events leading to Jesus' birth is filled with dreams. No fewer than five times, characters received divine revelation through dreams that significantly impacted the course of events. One of these dreams was given to the wise men to warn them not to return to the treacherous King Herod (Matthew 2:12), advice that may have saved the wise men from imprisonment or death at the tyrant's hands. The other four dreams were all communications to Joseph, calculated to empower him to protect Mary and Jesus from harm (2:13, 19-20, 22).

While anyone would be awed by even one such experience, Joseph in particular must have been surprised by these revelatory dreams. In the Old Testament, very few people learned about God's plans in dreams; they include Abraham (Genesis 15:12-16), Jacob (28:10-15), Joseph (37:5-9), Solomon (1 Kings 3:5), and Daniel (Daniel 7:1-27). Undoubtedly, there had been nothing in Joseph's life to this point to suggest that he would be numbered with this select group.

20b. Saying, Joseph, thou son of David, fear not to take unto thee Mary thy wife: for that which is conceived in her is of the Holy Ghost.

What Joseph shared with most others who experienced revelatory dreams in the Bible was faithfulness to God. And what he learned from his first dream was more significant than anything God had ever revealed to anyone before.

Mary's pregnancy was supernatural in origin, not the result of sin. Joseph was called to partner with God in caring for both her and her baby in order for God's eternal purposes to be fulfilled.

The phrase *of the Holy Ghost* parallels the angel Gabriel's announcement to Mary in Luke 1:35. Luke underscores the implication of the virgin birth by noting that Jesus, having no biological father, would be "Son of the Highest" (Luke 1:32). This title has less to do with the manner of His conception and more to do with Christ's rights and authorities as the sole heir of everything that belongs to His divine Father (see John 1:14-18).

> *What Do You Think?*
> What procedure should Christians use to determine the Lord's will when faced with a decision having lifelong impact?
> *Digging Deeper*
> Which Bible texts help you most in this regard?

21. And she shall bring forth a son, and thou shalt call his name JESUS: for he shall save his people from their sins.

Ancient names were often symbolic, associating a person with an event or identifying an important attribute (examples: Genesis 17:5, 15-16; John 1:42). Following a similar pattern, *Jesus* is the Greek version of the common Hebrew name Joshua, which means "God saves."

Joseph perhaps thought of the biblical hero Joshua, whom God used to lead Israel into the promised land. Joseph's adopted son, Jesus, would not *save . . . his people* from political oppression (as many Jews in that time expected of the Messiah), but instead would save them *from their sins*. In His death, Jesus saved the world from sin by becoming the ultimate sacrifice (Romans 5:8-11). But in order for Jesus to save people later, Joseph needed to protect Jesus right then by caring for Mary.

B. Through Scripture (vv. 22-23)

22. Now all this was done, that it might be fulfilled which was spoken of the Lord by the prophet, saying.

Matthew pauses the story to remind his readers of a second way in which the significance of Christ's birth and mission was revealed to the world: the ancient and public testimony of the Hebrew Scriptures. *The prophet* in view here is Isaiah (see Matthew 1:23 below).

Matthew quotes or makes reference to prophetic texts several other times in his account of Jesus' birth (Matthew 1:23; 2:6, 15, 18, 23). These citations, combined with Jesus' genealogy (1:1-17; see lesson 1), work together to demonstrate that the circumstances of the Messiah's birth, although not what most Jews anticipated, were nevertheless consistent with what God had promised. Put another way, while many Jews and pagan religious experts like the wise men (2:1-2) would have expected the king of the Jews to be born in a royal palace, Matthew shows from Scripture that Jesus' humble origins are actually proofs of His messianic identity.

23. Behold, a virgin shall be with child, and shall bring forth a son, and they shall call his name Emmanuel, which being interpreted is, God with us.

This prophecy from Isaiah 7:14 was delivered during a particularly dark period in Israel's history. Isaiah lived in the eighth century BC, about 200 years after the split between the northern and southern tribes following the death of Solomon (1 Kings 11:41–12:24). Sometime in the 740s BC, the northern kingdom, Israel, allied with Syria and invaded the southern kingdom, Judah (2 Kings 16:5). During the ensuing siege of Jerusalem, Isaiah met with the Judean King Ahaz to encourage him, promising that God would overthrow his enemies. Isaiah even invited him to ask for a divine sign that victory would come (Isaiah 7:1-11).

Feigning piety, King Ahaz refused, saying that he did not want to test God (Isaiah 7:12). In fact, he had already decided to seek protection from an earthly ally: he had sent ambassadors to negotiate with the Assyria's King Tiglathpileser, padding the offer with a large quantity of gold and silver taken from the Jerusalem temple. Assyria responded by attacking and subjugating Israel. As a gesture of thanks, the king of Judah built an altar in the temple, patterned after one he had seen in the Assyrian capital, Damascus (2 Kings 16:10-18).

While these actions seemed politically expedient at the time, Isaiah recognized the faithlessness of this strategy. He responded by offering the king of Judah a sign quite different from one the wicked king might have requested: as evidence that God himself would deliver Judah from its enemies, a child named "Immanuel" (Isaiah 7:14) was to be born. Before a certain child reached age 12 or 13 (Isaiah 10:16), the nations of which the king was so terrified would cease to exist. After the Assyrian defeated those nations, they would "get theirs" at the hands of the Babylonians, who destroyed tiny Judah in 586 BC.

It's unclear whether Isaiah himself saw this prophecy about "Immanuel" partially fulfilled through the birth of his own son the following year (Isaiah 8:1-10). Matthew definitely saw the fullest significance of Isaiah's words in the birth of Jesus. But in the long term, this sign referred to the coming of the Christ, the ultimate "Emmanuel . . . God with us" (Matthew 1:23). The Bible emphasizes the importance of God being "with" his people (examples: Genesis 26:3; 31:3; Exodus 3:12; Isaiah 43:2; John 14:3; Revelation 3:20). This is more than a figure of speech. In Jesus it has become a fact: "the Word was made flesh, and dwelt among us" (John 1:14).

Isaiah's more detailed promises in Isaiah 9 were also fulfilled—see Matthew 4:12-16. Through

HOW TO SAY IT

Ahaz	*Ay*-haz.
Assyria	Uh-*sear*-ee uh.
Assyrians	Uh-*sear*-ee unz.
Babylonians	Bab-ih-*low*-nee-unz.
Emmanuel	E-*man*-you-el.
Galilee	*Gal*-uh-lee.
Herod	*Hair*-ud.
Isaiah	Eye-*zay*-uh.
Josephus	Jo-*see*-fus.
Judean	Joo-*dee*-un.
Nazareth	*Naz*-uh-reth
Sepphoris	*Sef*-uh-ris.
Tiglathpileser	*Tig*-lath-pih-*lee*-zer.

Jesus' ministry, God would indeed be with His people in an unprecedented way.

Following "God with Us"

"You're bringing a baby here?!" The aid worker's eyes were wide with disbelief. We were about to land in an African refugee camp in a politically and militarily volatile region. Malaria, typhoid, and yellow fever were active in the area. Far away from any urban amenities, we would start by building a mud hut to live in. What in the world were we thinking, going there with a child?

We were trying to follow Jesus' example. He was Emmanuel, God with us. The Word became flesh. He talked face-to-face with people from all kinds of backgrounds, and He loved them.

Our son took his first steps in that camp. He played with children while we visited with their parents. We lived our lives side by side with the refugees, whose language had never been written down and most of whom did not know Christ. How can you follow the one who is "God with us" in your circumstances? —D. G.

III. Accepting the Call
(Matthew 1:24-25)

A. A Marriage (v. 24)

24. Then Joseph being raised from sleep did as the angel of the Lord had bidden him, and took unto him his wife.

Any doubts Joseph may have had were settled by his remarkable dream. Consistent with his faithful character, he did not question what God showed him or hesitate to act (contrast Luke 1:18). Instead, he immediately proceeded with the marriage. It's not difficult to imagine that Joseph moved the date of the wedding to ensure that Mary would be cared for during her pregnancy.

I Could Never Do That!

As a college student, I was painfully shy. I dreaded walking between classes, not knowing how to interact with people I passed. I sat alone in the cafeteria. On Sunday morning, I would leave the service the moment it ended. Sometimes I'd even start trembling if a lot of people were around.

Yet, I felt called to ministry. I talked to my professors about my dilemma. I continued studying. While pursuing a graduate degree, I heard about Bible translation. That sounded like a perfect mission for an introvert!

With every hesitant step I took, God went before me. An internship led to a career. I experienced community, met my future wife, and worked side by side with national translators as they brought God's Word into their own languages.

Alone I could never have the ministry God wanted for me. Listen to His call, step out in faith, and prepare to be amazed at what He will do.

—D. G.

What Do You Think?

How does Joseph's obedience serve as an example and challenge to you?

Digging Deeper

How do texts such as Exodus 4:13 and Isaiah 6:8 influence your answer?

B. A Birth (v. 25)

25. And knew her not till she had brought forth her firstborn son: and he called his name Jesus.

Joseph not only obeyed God's instruction to take Mary as his wife, but also went a step further by not consummating the marriage until Jesus had been born. God had not told him to do this, and the Law of Moses did not forbid sex during pregnancy. So Joseph's choice of abstinence most likely reflected his own sense of the gravity of the situation. This point is stressed to ensure that there can be no confusion about Jesus' paternity: Mary had not been sexually active *at any point* before or during her miraculous pregnancy.

Following the birth of Jesus, the couple clearly had a normal married life. This is evident from the fact that Jesus had at least four brothers and three sisters (see Matthew 13:55-56; Mark 6:3). Two of His half brothers eventually became leaders in the church. They wrote the two epistles in our New Testament that bear their names: James and Jude.

Visual for Lesson 2. *Use the visual to start a discussion about how students can best celebrate "God with us" during the Christmas season.*

Conclusion

A. "Yes, You"

Matthew's account of Jesus' birth is a classic "Yes, you" story. Throughout the Bible, we see people who were surprised when God called them to do something, and who responded to the call with a "Who, me?" Consider Abraham and Sarah (Genesis 17:17; 18:12), Moses (Exodus 4:13), Isaiah (Isaiah 6:5), Jeremiah (Jeremiah 1:6), and Peter (Luke 5:1-10). All these people went on to play key roles in the story of salvation. But first they had to get over the "Who, me?" barrier.

Joseph and Mary lived out the classic "Who me?/Yes, you" storyline in a unique way. Neither was particularly outstanding as the world judges such things. But when called, they did what they were asked.

How tragic when God has a task but finds no one to respond (example: Ezekiel 22:30)! When we say "Who, me?" God typically responds, "Yes, you."

B. Prayer

Father, help us remember what it means that Jesus was born "God with us." Let Your presence give us the confidence to be obedient whenever You call. In Jesus' name we pray. Amen.

C. Thought to Remember

Faithful people trust God, especially in extraordinary situations.

INVOLVEMENT LEARNING

Enhance your lesson with KJV Bible Student *(from your curriculum supplier) and the reproducible activity page (at www.standardlesson.com or in the back of the* KJV Standard Lesson Commentary Deluxe Edition*).*

Into the Lesson

Have this quote written on the board as learners arrive:

> *Life is a matter of choices, and every choice you make makes you.* —John C. Maxwell

After a time of agree/disagree discussion, read aloud each of the following pairs of choices, and ask learners to indicate their choices by raising hands:

1–Eat vanilla ice cream or chocolate ice cream.
2–Watch TV or listen to music.
3–Shop in a store or shop online.
4–Eat at a restaurant or eat at home.
5–Drink coffee or drink tea.
6–Dress up or dress casually.

Alternative. Distribute handouts (you prepare) with the choices listed above. Ask students to circle their choices, time limit of one minute.

After either alternative, lead into Bible study by saying, "The choices Joseph faced were far more important than any of these! Let's see what his decisions can teach us."

Into the Word

Recruit a student in advance to be interviewed as Joseph. Ask him to be ready to talk about the difficult choices he faced regarding the facts that (1) Mary was expecting a baby, but he was not the father and (2) an angel appeared to him with information and instructions.

Have students take turns reading Matthew 1:18-25 aloud; then conduct the interview. Possible interview questions are as follows; modify these and ask follow-up questions of your own devising as appropriate. Help "Joseph" with advance preparation by furnishing interview questions to him ahead of time.

1–When you found out that Mary was pregnant, what thoughts other than those recorded in Matthew 1 crossed your mind? 2–When the angel appeared to you in a dream, how did you know the dream was not merely an ordinary one? 3–What was the deciding factor that caused you to honor the angel's instructions?

Be sure to fill in any gaps with information from the lesson commentary; encourage "Joseph" in advance to use his "sanctified imagination" to give reasonable answers when answers are not found in the text. After the interview, thank your "Joseph" and encourage reactions during whole-class discussion. (*Option 1:* Have "Joseph" wear Bible-times clothing. *Option 2:* Distribute copies of the "Joseph's Options" exercise from the activity page, which you can download. Have learners work in small groups to complete as indicated.)

Ask a learner to read verses 22 and 23 again. Write "Emmanuel" on the board. Give each student a sticky note as you say, "In no more than one minute, write on your sticky note why the name Emmanuel is an appropriate name for Jesus." Encourage thoughts deeper than the obvious meaning "God with us" from the text. Have learners affix their notes on the board. Read some or all of them aloud for whole-class discussion.

Into Life

Divide learners into small groups. Encourage each group to work together to write a prayer of thanks for the gift of Jesus. After a few minutes, ask each group to pray together the prayer they have written.

Option. To extend this activity, distribute copies of "Step Up Your Thanks!" from the activity page as a take-home exercise. You have two options regarding words to be found: either include a list of the 13 to be found or don't. The latter option will make the puzzle harder to solve and is recommended. To encourage completion, promise to call for results at the beginning of next week's class.

December 20
Lesson 3 (KJV)

Called to Worship

Devotional Reading: Exodus 1:8-22
Background Scripture: Matthew 2:7-15

Matthew 2:1-2, 7-15

1 Now when Jesus was born in Bethlehem of Judaea in the days of Herod the king, behold, there came wise men from the east to Jerusalem,

2 Saying, Where is he that is born King of the Jews? for we have seen his star in the east, and are come to worship him.

. . . .

7 Then Herod, when he had privily called the wise men, enquired of them diligently what time the star appeared.

8 And he sent them to Bethlehem, and said, Go and search diligently for the young child; and when ye have found him, bring me word again, that I may come and worship him also.

9 When they had heard the king, they departed; and, lo, the star, which they saw in the east, went before them, till it came and stood over where the young child was.

10 When they saw the star, they rejoiced with exceeding great joy.

11 And when they were come into the house, they saw the young child with Mary his mother, and fell down, and worshipped him: and when they had opened their treasures, they presented unto him gifts; gold, and frankincense, and myrrh.

12 And being warned of God in a dream that they should not return to Herod, they departed into their own country another way.

13 And when they were departed, behold, the angel of the Lord appeareth to Joseph in a dream, saying, Arise, and take the young child and his mother, and flee into Egypt, and be thou there until I bring thee word: for Herod will seek the young child to destroy him.

14 When he arose, he took the young child and his mother by night, and departed into Egypt:

15 And was there until the death of Herod: that it might be fulfilled which was spoken of the Lord by the prophet, saying, Out of Egypt have I called my son.

Key Verse

When they were come into the house, they saw the young child with Mary his mother, and fell down, and worshipped him: and when they had opened their treasures, they presented unto him gifts; gold, and frankincense, and myrrh. —**Matthew 2:11**

Call in the New Testament

Unit 1: The Beginning of a Call

Lessons 1–4

Lesson Aims

After participating in this lesson, each learner will be able to:

1. Identify the Old Testament sources used within the lesson text.
2. Compare and contrast the motives behind the two expressed desires to worship Jesus.
3. Worship the Lord in the reverent and sacrificial spirit of the wise men.

Lesson Outline

Introduction
- A. Mirror, Mirror
- B. Lesson Context

I. Going West (Matthew 2:1-2)
- A. The Journey (v. 1)
- B. The Star (v. 2)

II. Seeking the King (Matthew 2:7-12)
- A. Led by Men (vv. 7-8)
- B. Led by God (vv. 9-10)
- C. The Joy of Discovery (vv. 11)
- D. The Return Home (v. 12)
  A Dream Come True

III. Fleeing to a Strange Land (Matthew 2:13-15)
- A. The Warning (v. 13)
- B. The Flight to Egypt (vv. 14-15)
  Sacrificial Faith

Conclusion
- A. Expect the Unexpected
- B. Prayer
- C. Thought to Remember

Introduction

A. Mirror, Mirror

The 1937 Disney film *Snow White* has given us many lasting catchphrases, including the famous (misquoted) rhyme, "Mirror, Mirror on the wall, who's the fairest of them all?" In the movie, these words are spoken each day by the beautiful-but-evil queen to her magic mirror, which has knowledge of all things. The vain queen's sense of prestige and self-worth are tied to the mirror's daily affirmation that she herself is, in fact, "the fairest in the land." So fragile is her ego that she becomes enraged beyond reason when the mirror finally says one day that a lowly peasant girl is now "the fairest in the land." The powerful queen promptly disguised herself as a witch so she could destroy Snow White.

Our passage today describes a similar scenario that also bore tragic and deadly fruit.

B. Lesson Context

Matthew and Luke provide unique details on the story of Jesus' birth. Both contain genealogies that trace Jesus' human heritage (see lesson 1). Both mention that angels announced Mary would conceive. Luke describes the message delivered to Mary before her pregnancy (Luke 1:26-38), while Matthew describes how Joseph learned of its origins after she was found to be with child (Matthew 1:18-25; see lesson 2).

Luke then offers a detailed description of the events leading up to the night of Jesus' birth, including Joseph and Mary's journey from Nazareth to Bethlehem for the Roman tax census, the fact that the newborn child was laid in a manger, and the visit of the shepherds (Luke 2:1-20). Matthew skips the actual birth story to describe the strange appearance of wealthy and mysterious Gentiles to honor the baby Jesus (Matthew 2:1-18; see lesson text).

The two accounts broaden our awareness of the events surrounding Jesus' birth and also offer complementary perspectives on the implications of Christ's coming. Luke's focus on the manger and the shepherds anticipates Jesus' later emphasis on the poor and outcast (example: Luke 6:20-

21). Matthew's story of the wise men shows how Christ's life and death would reach far beyond the borders of Israel to bring salvation to people of many races and nationalities (example: Matthew 28:18-20). Taken together, the two Gospels underscore a key feature of Christ's ministry: reaching across barriers to bring salvation to all (John 3:16-18).

I. Going West

(Matthew 2:1-2)

A. The Journey (v. 1)

1a. Now when Jesus was born in Bethlehem of Judaea.

Bethlehem (about six miles south of Jerusalem) was the site of many important events that Jewish audiences likely remembered. While Bethlehem was a small village in Jesus' time, it was the place where Jacob's wife Rachel—mother of 2 of the 12 patriarchs whose offspring became the 12 tribes of Israel (Genesis 35:24; 49:1-28)—died in childbirth and was buried (35:19).

The events of the book of Ruth are set in Bethlehem (Ruth 1:19). Ruth's great-grandson, King David, was raised there (Ruth 4:21-22; 1 Samuel 16:4-13). Because God had promised David that one of his descendants would rule over God's people forever (2 Samuel 7:8-16), it was widely understood that the Messiah—a descendant of David—would also be associated with Bethlehem (see Micah 5:2, 4; quoted in Matthew 2:6, not in today's lesson text). The word *Bethlehem* means "house of bread."

1b. In the days of Herod the king.

Herod was installed as *king* of Judea by Rome in about 38 BC. He reigned until his death in 4 BC. While powerful, Herod was never popular with traditional Jews, who questioned his lineage. (Herod was ethnically Idumean, native of what was called Edom in the Old Testament.) They resented his pro-Roman policies. Upon his death, widespread revolt erupted across Judea.

1c. Behold, there came wise men from the east to Jerusalem.

While the precise origin of the *wise men* is unknown, they are clearly portrayed as Gentiles (non-Jews). In ancient paganism, wise men were considered experts in discerning the will of the gods and divining the future. This was accomplished through observation of various elements of nature, such as stars, weather patterns, and the behavior of animals. Wise men commonly served as counselors at the courts of royalty, giving advice on the basis of their supposed supernatural insight (compare Genesis 41:8; Daniel 2:2-11).

The citizens of many nations were prophesied to come to Israel to worship when the Messiah appeared. This would usher in a new era of peace and prosperity as all joined as one people under God (compare Micah 4:1-5). The appearance of the Gentile wise men is the first indication of God's intention to fulfill this prophecy through Jesus' life, death, and resurrection and the church's proclamation of those facts.

The east may refer to Babylon or Persia, which had been home to large numbers of Jews since the Babylonian exile. That was during the time of Jeremiah, Ezekiel, and Daniel in the sixth century BC. Some scholars, noting that Herod attempted to kill Jesus by ordering the execution of all boys age 2 and under (Matthew 2:16-18), propose that the events of Luke 2 occurred around 6 BC.

One would think that Jesus could not have been born in any year BC, just by definition. The blame lies with a well-intentioned monk of the sixth century AD who made a mistake in computation. The wise men may have arrived as much as two years later, during the last year of Herod's reign (see commentary on Matthew 2:11, below).

HOW TO SAY IT

Batanea	*Bah*-tuh-***nee***-uh.
Bethlehem	*Beth*-lih-hem.
frankincense	*frank*-in-sense.
Galilee	*Gal*-uh-lee.
Herod	*Hair*-ud.
Hosea	Ho-*zay*-uh.
Idumean	Id-*you*-me-un.
Judaea (Judea)	Joo-*dee*-uh.
myrrh	mur.
Perea	Peh-*ree*-uh.
Samaria	Suh-*mare*-ee-uh.

Visual for Lessons 3 & 9. *Use the visual to start a discussion about how your learners can be alert to calls from God.*

B. The Star (v. 2)

2a. Saying, Where is he that is born King of the Jews?

This is the first time in Matthew's Gospel that Jesus is referred to as *King of the Jews*. This title is a glimpse of Jesus' trial before Pilate, torture, and execution (Matthew 27:11, 29, 37).

2b. For we have seen his star in the east.

The wise men witnessed an unusual astronomical phenomenon. It was widely believed in antiquity that stars, eclipses, comets, and other astral events heralded significant events. Attempts to explain away the star's value by identifying it with datable astronomical events have often been little more that attempts to deny the miracle of the wise men's travel.

The Law of Moses clearly forbids the occult practices in which the wise men were experts (Deuteronomy 4:19; 18:9-14). Still, God communicated with these pagan astrologers in terms they could understand. Since the wise men sought wisdom in the stars, God chose to speak to them through that medium, calling them to leave their home country in search of a newborn king. If it seems strange for God to speak through a forbidden practice, consider also that God forbade witchcraft (Deuteronomy 18:10) but chose to communicate with King Saul in such a setting (1 Samuel 28). His ways are not our ways. Clearly, God ensured that Gentiles were included on the momentous occasion of today's text.

2c. And are come to worship him.

The wise men seemed aware of Scriptures that spoke of a coming King. They may have been sent by their own king to *worship* and pay the respects typical of royal births. Because this was a royal event, they went first to Jerusalem, the political and religious center of Judea.

Verse 3 (not included in the lesson text) indicates that Herod was deeply suspicious of the wise men. Herod had spent almost four decades establishing himself as king of the Jews, and in the process had undertaken a series of brutal military actions and massive civil works projects to convert Judea, Samaria, Galilee, Perea (east of the Jordan), and Batanea (east of the Sea of Galilee) into productive areas. Since Herod had no newborn children at this time, the notion that a royal messianic figure might be coming could only spell rebellion. He may have suspected that the wise men were impostors, involved in a plot to create dissent.

II. Seeking the King

(Matthew 2:7-12)

A. Led by Men (vv. 7-8)

7. Then Herod, when he had privily called the wise men, enquired of them diligently what time the star appeared.

In Matthew 2:4-6 (not in our lesson text), Herod's own religious experts advised him from Micah 5:2-4 that the Messiah would be born in Bethlehem, about six miles south of Jerusalem. Herod's inquiry into the timing of the star's appearance foreshadowed his intention to quell this threat (see Matthew 2:14, below; also 2:16).

8. And he sent them to Bethlehem, and said, Go and search diligently for the young child; and when ye have found him, bring me word again, that I may come and worship him also.

Based on the information his own experts had provided, Herod *sent* the wise men *to Bethlehem* in hopes that they would locate a potential political rival. The wise men, interpreting the situation in religious rather than political terms, appeared to be oblivious to his scheme. Herod spoke deceitfully when he claimed that he too wanted to *worship* this *young child* (Matthew 2:13).

B. Led by God (vv. 9-10)

9. When they had heard the king, they departed; and, lo, the star, which they saw in the east, went before them, till it came and stood over where the young child was.

The reference to *the star* going *before* the wise men has generated considerable discussion. Because Bethlehem was essentially a suburb of Jerusalem, it would seem unnecessary for the star to guide them there. Yet the wise men were clearly not from the area and would need guidance to find *the young child,* especially at night.

The star here functions in a way similar to the manger in Luke's account. The shepherds were told to go into Bethlehem and look for a newborn child, not knowing the specific place. For the shepherds, the sign that they had found the right person took the form of a manger (Luke 2:8-16). The image of the star remaining over the place there Jesus was recalls the pillars of cloud and fire that guided the Israelites (Exodus 13:21).

10. When they saw the star, they rejoiced with exceeding great joy.

The wise men doubtless *rejoiced* because their confusion had been resolved. While their initial observations simply led them to Jerusalem, they certainly would have been surprised and confused to learn that there had been no royal births in Herod's household. Some students propose that the travelers had not seen *the star* for some time; now its reappearance, framed by references to the prophecies of the sacred Scriptures, was clearly a direct sign from God. The long journey was reaching its goal.

> *What Do You Think?*
>
> With whom will you share the joy of the wise men this Christmas?
>
> *Digging Deeper*
>
> What can you do to create (not just expect) opportunities to do so?

C. The Joy of Discovery (v. 11)

11a. And when they were come into the house, they saw the young child with Mary his mother, and fell down, and worshipped him.

Mary and Joseph, who were from Nazareth, were still in Bethlehem. The wise men first saw Jesus at a certain *house* rather than in the manger where the shepherds met the family (Luke 2:16). It is possible that the wise men saw the star and began their journey some months before Jesus was born; in that case, what they described in Matthew 2:2 would have occurred sometime before 2:1. The result would be to see Jesus days or weeks after His birth. Matthew 2:16 may indicate an even longer period of time (see on 2:1c, above).

The worship offered by the wise men does not mean they fully understood Jesus' identity. In fact, almost no one seemed to grasp Jesus' identity fully until after His resurrection (examples: Matthew 16:13-23; Acts 2:14-39). More likely their reverence reflects the typical gestures of obeisance that would be offered to any ancient king.

> *What Do You Think?*
>
> How do we convince others that a "mere human" is worthy of being worshipped?
>
> *Digging Deeper*
>
> Before engaging in such a conversation, how do we ensure that everyone in the discussion shares the same definition of *worship*?

11b. And when they had opened their treasures, they presented unto him gifts; gold, and frankincense, and myrrh.

The *gifts* offered were consistent with the mission of the wise men to honor a newborn king. *Gold,* of course, was precious. *Frankincense* and *myrrh* were rare and expensive items, imported from southern Arabia and what today is known as Somaliland. Matthew surely sees the actions of the wise men as a fulfillment of prophecies such as Isaiah 60:1-9.

The number of visitors is unknown. The common view is that there were three, which corresponds to the number of gifts. Even if only three dignitaries came to see Jesus, they certainly would have traveled with a large retinue of servants and security officers. Oddly, none of the Jewish advisers to Herod seemed to have been interested in this new king, since there is no record of their joining the foreign men in seeking Him.

What Do You Think?

What can we do to connect better our Christmas gift-giving with that of the wise men's gifts to baby Jesus?

Digging Deeper

How will you deal with the tension between Matthew 5:16 and 6:1 in this regard?

D. The Return Home (v. 12)

12. And being warned of God in a dream that they should not return to Herod, they departed into their own country another way.

God continued to communicate with the wise men in a way familiar to them. As a result, they *departed* the country secretly rather than reporting Jesus' identity and location to Herod.

Herod was likely made aware that Micah 5 predicted that the Messiah from Bethlehem would destroy oppressors and their pagan religious customs. To Herod, this could only mean a challenge to his own pro-Roman policies. Periodic insurrections were not unknown in this time and place (compare Acts 5:36-37), and Herod was infamous for eliminating opposition.

What Do You Think?

How will you know when you should avoid someone rather than trying to confront or witness to him or her?

Digging Deeper

Which among 1 Corinthians 15:33; Galatians 2:11-21; 2 Thessalonians 3:6; Titus 3:10; and 3 John 9-10 is most compelling to you in this regard? Why?

A Dream Come True

A Muslim friend of mine who was just beginning his walk with Jesus struggled with taking the final step because his mother did not approve of his affiliation with Christians. Once while he was contemplating Christianity, his mother traveled to a faraway city.

One night in that strange place, she got lost. Confused and afraid, she sat down on the corner and began to cry. She prayed that if the Jesus her son spoke about were real, He would help her get home. She then felt hands on her back, pushing her gently in one direction, all the way to her friend's house. She never saw anyone behind her.

This woman returned to her son full of excitement and sure that Jesus himself had guided her. He had answered her prayer. She joined her son in his new faith.

God uses different methods to reach different people. Even so, His communication to the wise men through the star and then a dream was only a start. They needed more information later (see Romans 10:17; Hebrews 1:1-2). Where are you along this path? Where *should* you be?

—L. M. W.

III. Fleeing to a Strange Land

(Matthew 2:13-15)

A. The Warning (v. 13)

13a. And when they were departed, behold, the angel of the Lord appeareth to Joseph in a dream, saying, Arise, and take the young child and his mother, and flee into Egypt, and be thou there until I bring thee word: for Herod will seek the young child to destroy him.

The angel of the Lord had earlier appeared to Joseph in a dream to inform him that Mary's pregnancy was indeed miraculous (Matthew 1:20-24; see lesson 2). This time the angel warned *Joseph* of the looming consequences of the wise men's informing *Herod* about a new king.

The Roman province of *Egypt* was to be the place of refuge. It was home to a large and influential Jewish community at that time. Traffic between Israel and Egypt was common, and Joseph could easily find work and support there without drawing too much attention. The wise men's gifts, especially the gold, would be a huge help to the family during the sojourn.

Herod is often portrayed as attempting to fight against God himself. How could any human being hope to thwart the divine plan by killing the Christ, whom God had sent? Nothing in Matthew's account, however, suggests that Herod believed God was behind the appearance of the wise men. In his view, they were either crackpot pagans or, more likely and more seriously, foreign agents involved in an elaborate hoax to generate unrest among the Jewish people. His failure to see the hand of God in the situation stands as a timeless lesson on the need to be mindful of God's movement at all times.

B. The Flight to Egypt (vv. 14-15)

14-15. When he arose, he took the young child and his mother by night, and departed into Egypt: and was there until the death of Herod: that it might be fulfilled which was spoken of the Lord by the prophet, saying, Out of Egypt have I called my son.

Prophecies are often explicitly cited in Matthew's Gospel. For instance, Matthew 1:23 connects the angel's announcement to Joseph with Isaiah 7:14 (compare Matthew 2:6). The verses before us quote Hosea 11:1 to explain why Jesus had to be taken to Egypt. Matthew 2:18 connects the massacre of the infants to Jeremiah 31:15, and an otherwise unknown prophecy explains why Jesus grew up in Nazareth (Matthew 2:21-23). These references to Scripture, combined with the various dreams (1:20; 2:12-13, 19) and unusual star, work together to stress the unique role of Jesus in God's total plan of salvation.

What Do You Think?

Which do you have the most problem with: jumping the gun and starting too soon or procrastinating and starting too late?

Digging Deeper

How can you solve this problem?

Sacrificial Faith

When the Bible college where I work relocated from a small town to a larger city a couple of hours away, the faculty and staff faced a huge decision. Would they also move?

Many had children in schools in the area. The cost of living was higher in the city, and a booming housing market meant they'd get less house for more money. They believed that the move would be good for the college and its students. But did they believe it enough to make changes in their personal lives?

Most of the faculty and staff did decide to go. They stepped out in faith. They acted in the assurance that God would work through the move and would provide for their families in the city. They believed in the mission of the school enough to sacrifice for it.

It is easy to sit back and say we'd give up everything for Jesus. But when we have the opportunity to sacrifice, do we take it? —L. M. W.

Conclusion

A. Expect the Unexpected

Matthew's account foreshadows a deep tragedy of Christ's ministry: those who should have been most prepared to accept Him did not (John 1:11). Instead, pagan astrologers welcomed Him with worship and expensive gifts!

This story is filled with the unexpected. No one expected pagan wise men to appear at Herod's palace with congratulations on the birth of a royal child, especially since no such child had been born in Jerusalem! The wise men certainly did not expect to find the king of the Jews in a peasant's house outside the capital. Jews did not expect the Christ to be born into danger so that His parents would need to flee to Egypt to protect Him. Most significantly, one would assume that the chief priests and appointed king of Judea would welcome the newborn Messiah.

Matthew's account thus demonstrates the need to remain open to the unexpected. It encourages us to watch for God in action, even when (or especially when) He acts through people we might not anticipate. We still need eyes to see and ears to hear (Matthew 13:16-17).

B. Prayer

Father, help us to interpret Your Word correctly and to listen carefully for Your voice. Give us the strength to follow Your call whenever and however it comes. In Jesus' name we pray. Amen.

C. Thought to Remember

Those who faithfully seek Jesus find Him.

Involvement Learning

Enhance your lesson with KJV Bible Student *(from your curriculum supplier) and the reproducible activity page (at www.standardlesson.com or in the back of the* KJV Standard Lesson Commentary Deluxe Edition*).*

Into the Lesson

Option. Before learners arrive, place in chairs copies of the "Worship Around the World" exercise from the activity page, which you can download. Discuss results to begin class.

Challenge students to think of synonyms for the word *venerate*; write ideas on the board as they are voiced. Be sure to add *adore, revere,* and *ascribe worth* if no one mentions them. Then divide the class into small groups and ask groups to create lists of things that are venerated in today's culture. After a few minutes, have groups compare lists in whole-class discussion.

Lead into the Bible study by saying, "I think we can agree that some people are confused about who they should worship. But some of those we will study about today got it right. Let's see why."

Into the Word

Have students take turns reading Matthew 2:1-2, 7-15 aloud. Say, "There are many Old Testament prophecies about Jesus' birth. Let's see if we can match some of those prophecies to events surrounding Jesus' birth."

Ask a learner to read Jeremiah 23:5 aloud and another learner to read Numbers 24:17 aloud. Ask, "What verse from today's Scripture do these two prophecies match up with?" (*Answer:* Matthew 2:2). Follow the same process for Isaiah 60:3, 9 and Psalm 72:10 (*Answer:* Matthew 2:11) and Hosea 11:1 (*Answer:* Matthew 2:15).

Option. For deeper study of Old Testament predictions of the Messiah, distribute copies of the "Old Testament Prophecies" exercise from the activity page. Have learners work in study pairs or triads to complete as indicated. After an appropriate amount of time, reconvene for whole-class comparisons of conclusions.

Next, divide the class in half. Designate one of the halves to be **Wise Men's Group** and the other half to be **Herod's Group**. If the halves are too large for the exercise to follow, form smaller groups with identical names.

Distribute handouts (you prepare) of the following questions to the **Wise Men's Group**: 1–What kind of "GPS" did the wise men rely on? 2–What was their physical posture in worship? 3–What gifts accompanied their worship? (*Answers* are in Matthew 2:9, 11a, and 11b, respectively.) Concurrently, distribute handouts (you prepare) of the following questions to **Herod's Group**: 1–What instructions did Herod give the wise men? 2–What was Herod's stated motive in giving those instructions? 3–What was his real motive? (*Answers* are in Matthew 2:8a, 8b, and 13, respectively.)

When groups finish, check for accuracy during whole-class discussion. Use the commentary to correct misconceptions and fill in gaps. Ask students to summarize the similarities and differences among the motives of the wise men and King Herod.

Make a transition to Into Life by saying, "Let's see what the wise men can teach us regarding the connection between *who* to worship and the *why* and *how* of that worship."

Into Life

Write these two phrases on the board as column headers:

What's So / So What?

In whole-class discussion, ask, "What are the stated facts regarding the wise men's worship of Jesus?" Jot responses under the *What's so* column. After there are no more responses, continue by pointing to each of those responses in turn as you ask, "How might this be one model for our worship?" Jot replies under the *So what?* header. Make sure that the concepts of joy, humility, and sacrifice are addressed in both columns. Close by singing "We Three Kings"; distribute handouts of lyrics so class members can sing all five stanzas.

Called to Prepare

Devotional Reading: John 1:19-34
Background Scripture: Matthew 3

Matthew 3:1-12

1 In those days came John the Baptist,
preaching in the wilderness of Judaea,
2 And saying, Repent ye: for the kingdom of
heaven is at hand.
3 For this is he that was spoken of by the
prophet Esaias, saying, The voice of one crying in the wilderness, Prepare ye the way of the
Lord, make his paths straight.
4 And the same John had his raiment of
camel's hair, and a leathern girdle about his
loins; and his meat was locusts and wild honey.
5 Then went out to him Jerusalem, and all
Judaea, and all the region round about Jordan,
6 And were baptized of him in Jordan, confessing their sins.
7 But when he saw many of the Pharisees
and Sadducees come to his baptism, he said
unto them, O generation of vipers, who hath
warned you to flee from the wrath to come?
8 Bring forth therefore fruits meet for
repentance:
9 And think not to say within yourselves, We
have Abraham to our father: for I say unto you,
that God is able of these stones to raise up children unto Abraham.
10 And now also the axe is laid unto the root
of the trees: therefore every tree which bringeth not forth good fruit is hewn down, and
cast into the fire.
11 I indeed baptize you with water unto
repentance: but he that cometh after me is
mightier than I, whose shoes I am not worthy to bear: he shall baptize you with the Holy
Ghost, and with fire:
12 Whose fan is in his hand, and he will
throughly purge his floor, and gather his wheat
into the garner; but he will burn up the chaff
with unquenchable fire.

Key Verse

This is he that was spoken of by the prophet Esaias, saying, The voice of one crying in the wilderness, Prepare ye the way of the Lord, make his paths straight. **—Matthew 3:3**

Call in the New Testament

Unit 1: The Beginning of a Call

Lessons 1–4

Lesson Aims

After participating in this lesson, each learner will be able to:

1. List salient points of John the Baptist's ministry and message.
2. Compare and contrast the two baptisms of which John spoke.
3. Correct one attitude that puts him or her in danger of being viper-like.

Lesson Outline

Introduction
- A. The Voice
- B. Lesson Context

I. Called to Testify (Matthew 3:1-4)
- A. Setting (v. 1)
- B. Message (vv. 2-3)
  - *Voice in the Wilderness*
- C. Messenger (v. 4)

II. Called to Repent (Matthew 3:5-10)
- A. Receptive Audience (vv. 5-6)
- B. Unrepentant Adversaries (vv. 7-10)
  - *Fruits of Repentance*

III. Called to Prepare (Matthew 3:11-12)
- A. John's Work (v. 11a)
- B. Prophesied Work (vv. 11b-12)

Conclusion
- A. Voices in the Wilderness
- B. Prayer
- C. Thought to Remember

Introduction

A. The Voice

In 2010, the reality television show *The Voice* premiered in Holland before arriving in the United States, becoming an international sensation. Similar to the long-running *X Factor* and *American Idol* franchises, contestants compete in weekly singing competitions in hopes of earning a cash prize and a recording contract.

Perhaps the most well-known element of the show is its distinctive selection process. At the beginning of each season, hopeful amateurs perform for a panel of celebrity recording artists. From the pool, each celebrity chooses a "team" of would-be entertainers to coach through the remainder of the season.

To ensure that the panelist-coaches make their initial selections on the basis of vocal talent rather than appearance, the celebrities sit in chairs facing the audience rather than the stage during initial performances. The judges must, in other words, choose prospects solely on the basis of "the voice." Each season's winner is appropriately dubbed "The Voice" to emphasize that person's outstanding singing abilities.

Our passage for today describes the work of a biblical figure who was known in his own time as "the voice," John the Baptist. But would John be acknowledged as a truly great voice with a great message?

B. Lesson Context

In Jesus' day as before, mainstream Jewish religion centered primarily on the Jerusalem temple (which was controlled by wealthy pro-Roman Sadducees) and secondarily on local synagogues (which often were led by Pharisees and scribal experts in the Jewish Scriptures). As Jesus himself pointed out, both had become oppressive, actually hindering people in their relationships to God (example: Matthew 23:13-39). The religious authorities placed heavy burdens on the average worshipper (23:4). This implied that God was not readily accessible to common people. Those authorities had developed a complex system of rules and regulations that people could not keep.

Aside from the fact that these approaches made God largely inaccessible, they also were closely tied to the efforts of the Jewish elite to maintain peace with the Roman Empire (John 11:48). Reacting to this situation, some Jews turned to monastic movements. Others adopted an ascetic lifestyle and sought God through seasons of meditation in the wilderness. Still others were drawn into fringe prophetic movements that promised deliverance from Roman oppression; these sometimes led to rebellion (example: Acts 5:34-37).

John the Baptist's work was familiar within this religious landscape. But it was unique in two significant ways that made him a popular figure. The first of those distinctives is evident from the epithet we still use for him today: he was "the Baptist" (Matthew 3:1, today's text) or "the Baptizer." While Jews regularly washed their hands, feet, and household items for purposes of religious purification—including full-body washings on many occasions—they washed only themselves, never other people.

Such washing was viewed as a way of removing sin and impurity (compare Ezekiel 36:25). In standard Jewish thinking it was not possible for one person to remove another person's impurities. No priest or rabbi would wash someone else, not least because doing so would make the one giving the bath unclean as well! John, however, was different. His hands-on baptism served as a powerful symbol of the content of his message.

That message was the second distinctive of John's ministry. He did not tell people to withdraw into the wilderness, nor did he promise freedom from Roman rule. Rather, John the Baptist told them to repent in preparation for a great work of God that was looming on the horizon.

John's focus on second chances and emphasis on the reality of God's presence made him a popular figure with Jews from a wide range of backgrounds. Both the New Testament and the ancient Jewish historian Josephus (about AD 37–100) attest to John's popularity (*Antiquities of the Jews* 18.5.2). His refusal to compromise and his commitment to speaking the truth ultimately led to his death at the hands of Herod Antipas, Rome's client-king (Matthew 14:1-12).

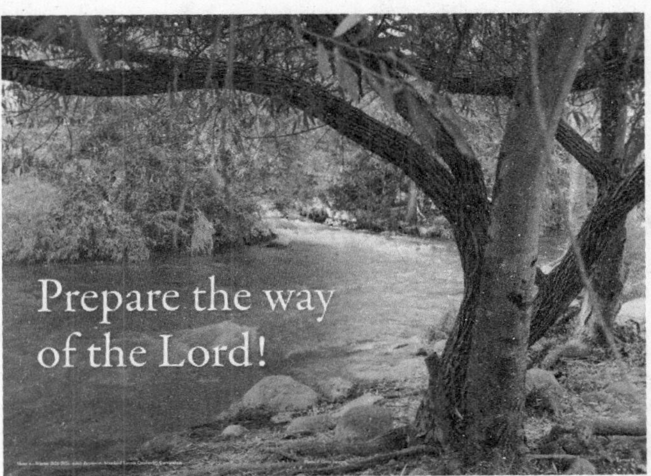
Prepare the way
of the Lord!

Visual for Lesson 4. *Use this image to start a discussion about how students can prepare someone's heart for God.*

I. Called to Testify

(Matthew 3:1-4)

A. Setting (v. 1)

1. In those days came John the Baptist, preaching in the wilderness of Judaea.

The phrase *those days* moves Matthew's story from the events of Jesus' birth and early childhood to a period some two decades later. During this time, Jesus' cousin *John*, the son of a priest from the Judean hill country (Luke 1:5, 39-40, 57-66), came to adulthood with a distinct sense of mission and calling of his own.

At some point, probably during his teenage years, John adopted an ascetic lifestyle and began to live alone *in the wilderness of Judaea* (see also Luke 1:80; compare Numbers 6:1-21). That location, the large desert area east of Jerusalem around the Jordan River valley, was popular with those who wished to focus on prayer and meditation.

B. Message (vv. 2-3)

2. And saying, Repent ye: for the kingdom of heaven is at hand.

John's message can be summarized in a single word: *Repent*. The person who repents becomes truly sorry for past misdeeds, changes the way that he or she thinks and, as a result, starts behaving differently. Exactly how John thought people's minds should change is not specified here (see on Matthew 3:6, below).

The immediate need for this change of mind was indicated by the fact that *the kingdom of heaven* was *at hand*. Jews would have understood that phrase both temporally (as already present or coming soon) and geographically (as coming to Israel). As sovereign Creator of the universe, God is always king over everything. But His reign was about to become evident in a unique way. Repentance would make the people ready to stand in the king's presence when He arrived.

The Jewish people had not had their own, sovereign nation since the exile of 586 BC, except for brief times of rebellions. The people were looking for God to expel the foreign rulers in preparation to reestablish the throne of David (compare Acts 1:6). What God had in mind required different preparation than ridding the nation of outsiders, however. His spiritual kingdom required not a change of personnel, but a change of heart.

Here as elsewhere, Matthew uses the phrase *kingdom of heaven* (32 times in his Gospel) while Mark and Luke prefer "kingdom of God" (Matthew, 5 times; Mark, 15 times; Luke, 32 times). *Heaven* in this context is most likely a gesture of respect to avoid saying God's name. Matthew's preference for this terminology has led to the conclusion that he was writing to an audience that was primarily of Jewish background. They would appreciate this gesture of respect. The phrase also recalls Daniel's prophecies of "one like the Son of man" who is to come "with the clouds of heaven" (Daniel 7:13).

3. For this is he that was spoken of by the prophet Esaias, saying, The voice of one crying in the wilderness, Prepare ye the way of the Lord, make his paths straight.

John earned the title *the voice of one crying in the wilderness* from prophecy spoken by *Esaias*, more commonly known to us as Isaiah (see Isaiah 40:3). In its original context, the prophecy envisions God as a great king on a journey, with messengers and servants preceding Him to make people ready for His arrival. John the Baptist considered himself one of these messengers (John 1:23), announcing that the great king, *the Lord*, would soon appear. Repentance would *make* things *straight* in preparing the people for the king's arrival.

What Do You Think?

Under what circumstances will your witness for Christ be better served by dressing in a way that is distinctively different from that of culture customs? How might that hinder?

Digging Deeper

How do passages such as Leviticus 19:19, 27; 1 Corinthians 9:19-23; 11:3-16; 1 Timothy 2:9-10; and 1 Peter 3:3 inform your decision?

Voice in the Wilderness

Fred knows all about being a "voice in the wilderness." He learned the language of an unreached people group in West Africa and lived with them as he labored to bring them God's Word in their own language. After two decades, however, not a single person had been baptized.

Fred's son grew up in that village, speaking the local language. After completing college in the United States, he returned with his wife and children to the same people group his father had served. The son discovered that the seeds his father had sown were finally beginning to sprout! A key leader had expressed his faith in Christ. The once-barren fields appeared ripe for harvest.

Do you feel like a "voice in the wilderness" to your family or neighbors? Don't give up! Keep spreading the word and trust the Lord to change hearts and minds at just the right time. —D. G.

C. Messenger (v. 4)

4a. And the same John had his raiment of camel's hair, and a leathern girdle about his loins.

John's attire of rough clothing and sparse diet (see Matthew 3:4b, below) reflected his ascetic lifestyle. More significantly, John's choice of clothing recalls that of the great prophet Elijah (see 2 Kings 1:8). According to Malachi 4:5-6, Elijah would return one day to call the Jews to repentance before the day of judgment. John fulfilled that task in unexpected fashion (Matthew 17:11-13).

4b. And his meat was locusts and wild honey.

Locusts were clean foods according Leviticus 11:22, readily found in the wilderness. *Honey* was a key descriptor regarding the abundance of the promised land (example: Exodus 3:8). John lived off the land, sustained by the two foods God provided.

II. Called to Repent
(Matthew 3:5-10)

A. Receptive Audience (vv. 5-6)

5. Then went out to him Jerusalem, and all Judaea, and all the region round about Jordan.

Judaea was the Roman province in which the city of *Jerusalem* was located; *the region round about* the *Jordan* River extended northward into Galilee, Jesus' home territory. Since John performed no miracles (John 10:41), his fame as a prophet must have been based on the integrity of his lifestyle and the nature of his message.

6a. And were baptized of him in Jordan.

Jews were aware of the symbolism of the *Jordan* River. Generations before, Joshua had led the Israelites across the Jordan to claim the promised land (Joshua 3–4). Now John was symbolically preparing Israel for the kingdom of Heaven, whose leader was much greater than any who had come before.

6b. Confessing their sins.

The types of *sins* that concerned John are hinted at in Luke 3:10-14. The very notion of the kingdom of Heaven assumes that God is a sovereign ruler who must be obeyed. *Confessing* that one's life was not completely submitted to God (see Matthew 3:2, above) was essential to the repentance that John called for in preparation.

B. Unrepentant Adversaries (vv. 7-10)

7. But when he saw many of the Pharisees and Sadducees come to his baptism, he said unto them, O generation of vipers, who hath warned you to flee from the wrath to come?

Some religious leaders of the day doubtless accepted John's message. But appearances of *Pharisees and Sadducees* rarely led to positive encounters with either Jesus or John. Because Jewish thought viewed washing purification as something that happened through rituals of personal cleansing, the leading priests and rabbis challenged John's authority to baptize. He replied with a challenge of his own, publicly identifying them as *vipers.* Like poisonous snakes, they hid their intentions from the masses so they could harm them (compare Matthew 12:34; 23:33). Their status as the religious elite would not exempt them from judgment, God's *wrath to come.*

What Do You Think?

Under what circumstances, if any, are Christians justified in speaking harshly to others as John did? Why do you say that?

Digging Deeper

In addition to Acts 8:20; 18:6; Titus 1:13; and 1 Peter 3:15-16, what passages help frame your answer?

8. Bring forth therefore fruits meet for repentance.

John uses the common New Testament metaphor of *fruits* to describe behavior based on belief (examples: John 15:16; Romans 7:4-5). Exactly what such fruit would look like is not specified here. By comparison with a similar account in Luke 3, fruit should take the form of visible changes in behavior. In particular, actions should show that the baptized individual is obedient to divine standards of justice—helping those in need and refusing to take advantage (Luke 3:10-14).

The characteristic behavior of the religious elite—ignoring John's message and instead challenging his authority to preach and baptize—demonstrated that they themselves were as much in need of *repentance* as the masses they instructed. Rather than being arrogant, the Pharisees needed to humbly examine themselves to determine whether they were indeed prepared for the coming of God's kingdom.

What Do You Think?

As new Christians begin to produce the fruit of the Spirit (Galatians 5:22-23), which of the rotten fruits (5:19-21) should be first to go? Why?

Digging Deeper

Which of the lists in Romans 1:29-31; 2 Corinthians 12:20; Ephesians 4:25-32; 5:3-5; Philippians 4:8-9; and Colossians 3:5, 8, 12 convict you most in this regard? Why?

❧ *Fruits of Repentance* ❧

I had never seen anyone stop for the one traffic light in this East African city. I didn't stop either—until two policeman carrying large rifles waved me down, and one climbed into my back seat to escort me to the police station. When I asked how much my fine would be, he said, "200,000." In local currency, that was 10 times the rate of a normal traffic violation. Unsurprisingly, I was being extorted.

Another time, a non-Christian traffic policeman had commandeered a ride. My friend was sharing the gospel with him. The policeman, revealing knowledge of John's words in Luke 3:14, said, "I could never become a Christian. Then I'd have to stop taking bribes."

Even the corrupt policeman knew that repentance requires a change in behavior! What about you? —D. G.

9. And think not to say within yourselves, We have Abraham to our father: for I say unto you, that God is able of these stones to raise up children unto Abraham.

Many Jews of John's day believed they would receive the promises made to *Abraham* their *father* simply by virtue of being part of the family (Genesis 12:1-3). Although following the law became very important after the exile of 586 BC, the emphasis remained on being born into God's covenant people.

John challenged this line of thinking at a foundational level. Being descended from Abraham was not proof of being in a right relationship with God. One had to seek God earnestly. John's message anticipates the later New Testament teaching that salvation is based on faith that results in obedience, never on a supposed birthright.

10. And now also the axe is laid unto the root of the trees: therefore every tree which bringeth not forth good fruit is hewn down, and cast into the fire.

John used a dramatic analogy to drive his point home: the barren *trees* that should be bearing *good fruit* have been marked for destruction. Without a change of heart, these barren trees would become firewood. God is patient, but His patience has limits (compare Luke 13:6-9). Those who accepted John's message would be prepared for what (and who) was coming. Those who did not would not participate in God's kingdom, regardless of their lineage or religious standing.

It is important to recall the nature of John's audience: with the possible exception of those mentioned in Luke 3:14, he was not preaching to pagans. Rather, he was preaching to Jews who already believed in God and were attempting, at some level, to live by the Law of Moses. John's audience included religious leaders who were experts in the Scriptures; they too needed to prepare.

HOW TO SAY IT

Esaias	E-*zay*-us.
Herod Antipas	*Hair*-ud *An*-tih-pus.
Isaiah	Eye-*zay*-uh.
Josephus	Jo-*see*-fus.
Judean	Joo-*dee*-un.
Malachi	*Mal*-uh-kye.
Messiah	Meh-*sigh*-uh.
Pentecost	*Pent*-ih-kost.
Pharisees	*Fair*-ih-seez.
Sadducees	*Sad*-you-seez.
synagogue	*sin*-uh-gog

III. Called to Prepare

(Matthew 3:11-12)

A. John's Work (v. 11a)

11a. I indeed baptize you with water unto repentance.

John viewed the act of submitting to *water* baptism as evidence of *repentance* (compare Acts 19:4). Those undergoing this baptism were admitting that they needed to change. They needed to be cleansed of sinfulness. They needed to begin producing the kind of fruit that John called for.

B. Prophesied Work (vv. 11b-12)

11b. But he that cometh after me is mightier than I, whose shoes I am not worthy to bear: he shall baptize you with the Holy Ghost, and with fire.

John's baptism was not an end in and of itself;

rather, it looked to the future. John was the Messiah's forerunner. Greater things were coming. John's baptism would give way to the baptism Jesus would bring (that is, Christian baptism).

Two (and possibly three) actions by God lay ahead. One was the blessing that came on the Day of Pentecost when Peter preached the first post-resurrection gospel sermon. That message included the directive to "repent, and be baptized every one of you in the name of Jesus Christ for the remission of sins, and ye shall receive the gift of *the Holy Ghost*" (Acts 2:38; compare 10:44-48).

> *What Do You Think?*
> What can you do to recognize and appreciate more fully the work of the Holy Spirit in your life?
> *Digging Deeper*
> Does your thinking trend more toward things you need to start doing or things you need to stop doing? Why is that?

Second, John predicted a *fire* to come. Some Bible students see this as judgment on the disobedient (compare Jude 7). Others, however, see it as a purifying fire for the repentant (compare 1 Peter 4:12). It could be both, for a total of three things John predicted.

The one to bring about such things is the Messiah. John, as a lowly servant, felt unworthy even *to bear* Jesus' *shoes* (compare Matthew 3:13-15; John 1:29-30). Jesus' ministry would be greater than John's. We today can testify to that fact since we are on this side of the cross and the empty tomb.

12. Whose fan is in his hand, and he will throughly purge his floor, and gather his wheat into the garner; but he will burn up the chaff with unquenchable fire.

Chaff is the outer husk that surrounds seeds of *wheat*. In antiquity, the husk was separated from the grain by tossing the wheat into the air; the chaff would drift to the side while the heavier seed fell in a pile on the threshing floor. The worthless chaff was then burned. God's *unquenchable fire* would be even more thorough in removing those who refused to repent (compare Matthew 13:40-43).

John had begun the work of separation by calling people to repent in preparation for the Lord's coming. Even today, those who repent and follow the biblical plan of salvation will be gathered up like the good grain. But those who do not will, like the useless chaff, be discarded and destroyed. The message is clear: choose your fate and act accordingly before it is too late.

> *What Do You Think?*
> What plan can you make to get rid of the chaff in your life?
> *Digging Deeper*
> What would be the advantages and disadvantages of recruiting an accountability partner for this task?

Conclusion

A. Voices in the Wilderness

Whenever a person emerges as the lone advocate for an important cause and is later proven to be right, we may refer to that individual as "a voice in the wilderness." Such people often feel that way themselves, alone in their cries for change and often criticized for their views. They call others to prepare for a future that is obscure to most but that they themselves foresee (or think they foresee) clearly. Like John the Baptist, these individuals are often attacked rather than appreciated.

Today's lesson reminds us of the need to prepare for Christ's coming—in our case, His second coming. Part of our preparation involves serving as voices in the wilderness as we speak out against the evil we see both in the world and among God's people.

B. Prayer

Father, help us to know our own hearts so that we can be ready for Your Son's return. Help us bear the fruit You have called us to bear and to be strong in telling others that Your kingdom is near. In Jesus' name we pray. Amen.

C. Thought to Remember

The time to repent is now.

Involvement Learning

Enhance your lesson with KJV Bible Student *(from your curriculum supplier) and the reproducible activity page (at www.standardlesson.com or in the back of the* KJV Standard Lesson Commentary Deluxe Edition*).*

Into the Lesson

Have this question written on the board as learners arrive:

Are you a person who likes to be prepared, or more of a person who likes to take things as they come?

After a few minutes of discussion, divide your class into pairs (or triads), giving each group an index card. Ask learners to work in their pairs to create a list of preparations for a job interview. After a few minutes, reconvene for whole-class comparisons of lists.

Alternative. Distribute copies of the "How Would You Prepare?" exercise from the activity page, which you can download. Have learners work in pairs to complete as indicated.

After either activity, lead into Bible study by saying, "Today's lesson has something important to teach us about preparation. Let's see what it is."

Into the Word

Have students take turns reading Matthew 3:1-12 aloud. Then divide the class into three groups, giving each group one of the handouts below (you create). Have Bible dictionaries and other resources available for groups that need them.

Who He Was Group: Who was John the Baptist, and what do we know about him?

What He Said Group: What significant things did John the Baptist say?

What He Did Group: What significant things did John the Baptist do?

After no more than 15 minutes, allow groups to share findings. Use the lesson commentary to fill in gaps. (*Some responses to anticipate:* **Who He Was Group**—the son of elderly parents, John was prophesied to be the one to prepare the way for the Messiah. **What He Said Group**—preached repentance and the nearness of the kingdom of Heaven. **What He Did Group**—baptized and called out those guilty of hypocrisy)

Then write on the board the phrases *Baptism by John* and *Baptism from Jesus* as the headers to two columns. Follow by writing *Who it's for /What it does / When it happens* as the titles of three rows down the left-hand side of the board. Read verses 11 and 12 again, and ask learners to help you make the proper entries at the intersections of the rows and columns. (*Expected responses* are per the Scripture text for the lesson. Use the commentary to fill in gaps and correct misconceptions.)

Option. For an extended study on baptism, distribute copies of the "Baptism in the New Testament" exercise from the activity page for learners to complete in small groups as indicated. If time is short, this can be a take-home.

Make a transition to the Into Life segment by saying, "While John the Baptist had the task of preparing for Jesus' first coming, we have the important task of preparing for His second coming."

Into Life

Write on the board the following:

hypocrisy / cunning / wicked ways /
attention to outward appearances

Say, "By calling the Pharisees and Sadducees 'vipers,' John may have been referring to these attributes." Give each student a slip of paper. Ask students to think of an attitude they may hold that falls into one or more of the categories listed that puts them in danger of being viper-like. Suggest that students write that attitude on their papers—an attitude that works against preparing for Jesus' return.

Offer a chance for volunteers to voice what they have written. Encourage them each to put their paper in a place where it will remind them daily to ask God for His help in correcting that attitude. Close by urging students to continue preparing well for Jesus' second coming.

Called to Proclaim

Devotional Reading: Deuteronomy 8:1-11
Background Scripture: Luke 4

Luke 4:14-22a

**14 And Jesus returned in the power of the
Spirit into Galilee: and there went out a fame of
him through all the region round about.
15 And he taught in their synagogues, being
glorified of all.
16 And he came to Nazareth, where he had
been brought up: and, as his custom was, he
went into the synagogue on the sabbath day,
and stood up for to read.
17 And there was delivered unto him the
book of the prophet Esaias. And when he had
opened the book, he found the place where it
was written,
18 The Spirit of the Lord is upon me, because
he hath anointed me to preach the gospel to
the poor; he hath sent me to heal the brokenhearted, to preach deliverance to the captives,
and recovering of sight to the blind, to set at
liberty them that are bruised,
19 To preach the acceptable year of the Lord.
20 And he closed the book, and he gave it
again to the minister, and sat down. And the
eyes of all them that were in the synagogue
were fastened on him.
21 And he began to say unto them, This day
is this scripture fulfilled in your ears.
22a And all bare him witness, and wondered
at the gracious words which proceeded out of
his mouth.**

רוח אדני יהוה עלי
יען משח יהוה אתי
לבשר ענוים שלחני לחבש
לנשברי־לב
לקרא לשבוים דרור
ולאסורים פקח־קוח
לקרא שנת־רצון

Key Verses

The Spirit of the Lord is upon me, because he hath anointed me to preach the gospel to the poor; he hath sent me to heal the brokenhearted, to preach deliverance to the captives, and recovering of sight to the blind, to set at liberty them that are bruised, to preach the acceptable year of the Lord. —**Luke 4:18-19**

CALL IN THE NEW TESTAMENT

Unit 2: Jesus and Calls in His Ministry

LESSONS 5–8

LESSON AIMS

After participating in this lesson, each learner will be able to:

1. Identify the passage of Scripture Jesus read in the synagogue of Nazareth.
2. Explain the meaning and significance of Jesus' declaration regarding that passage.
3. Make a list of ways he or she can continue to fulfill the tasks in the mission of Jesus.

LESSON OUTLINE

Introduction
- A. Going Home
- B. Lesson Context

I. Power (Luke 4:14-15)
- A. Spirit-Filled Ministry (v. 14a)
- B. Successful Ministry (vv. 14b-15)

II. Preaching (Luke 4:16-17)
- A. In Nazareth (v. 16)
- B. From Isaiah (v. 17)

III. The Point (Luke 4:18-22a)
- A. Jesus' Call (vv. 18-19)
  - *Blindsided*
- B. Jesus' Mission (vv. 20-22a)
  - *Today Is the Day*

Conclusion
- A. Come Home
- B. Prayer
- C. Thought to Remember

Introduction

A. Going Home

A memorable line from the classic film *The Wizard of Oz* is Dorothy's declaration, "There's no place like home." Returning home can have different meanings for many people. For some, home can be a good place to get away from the busyness of life and relax. Others, however, can become anxious after a few days of vacation away from home—eager to return to comfortable routines and familiar surroundings.

College is a great way to begin an independent life. But it's nice to return home to experience again the loving support of one's parents and to connect with old friends. Even so, it eventually dawns on every college student that once he or she leaves for that first class of the freshman year, there's a figurative sense of never returning home. Things are different when coming back on spring break. Family dynamics have changed permanently. The sense of a permanent break is heightened as the years go by, when people "back home" remember you only as you were, not acknowledging who you've turned out to be. Something similar was the case with Jesus.

B. Lesson Context

The Gospel of Luke, source of today's study, is one of the three so-called synoptic Gospels, the other two being Matthew and Mark. The word *synoptic* means "presenting or taking the same or common view," and that's what these three Gospels generally do. The operative word here is *generally* since there are exceptions.

Today's text is one of those exceptions. All three synoptic Gospels document Jesus' baptism (Matthew 3:13-17; Mark 1:9-11; and Luke 3:21-22) and His testing in the wilderness, where the tempter's proposed solutions to hunger, greed, and insecurity failed (Matthew 4:1-11; Mark 1:12-13; Luke 4:1-13). And all three make note of Jesus' subsequent beginning of ministry in Galilee (Matthew 4:12; Mark 1:14; Luke 4:14). But we should note a gap of time between Luke 4:13 and our text for today, which begins at 4:14. That gap of several months includes the events recorded in John 1:19–4:42.

I. Power

(Luke 4:14-15)

A. Spirit-Filled Ministry (v. 14a)

14a. And Jesus returned in the power of the Spirit into Galilee.

The record of the presence of *the Spirit* in Jesus' life in the early chapters of Luke is noteworthy: the Spirit had descended on Jesus at His baptism (Luke 3:22), had led Him into the wilderness for 40 days of preparation (4:1), and had contributed to His *power* as He began ministering in *Galilee.* Jesus undoubtedly walked along one or all of the three main roads that connect Galilee to the rest of the world: a road south to Jerusalem, a road east to Arabia, and a road connecting Egypt to Damascus.

Later in the book of Acts, the author Luke recorded something similar from Peter's sermon on the Day of Pentecost, when Peter spoke of "how God anointed Jesus of Nazareth with the Holy Ghost and with power" (Acts 10:38).

Luke emphasizes the presence and power of the Spirit in the lives of others as well. These include John the Baptist (Luke 1:15-17), Mary (1:35), Elisabeth (1:41), Zacharias (1:67), and Simeon (2:25). In Acts, the presence and power of the Spirit was evident in the lives of Peter (Acts 4:8; 11:12); the seven men chosen to oversee an important benevolence program (namely, Stephen, Philip, Prochorus, Nicanor, Timon, Parmenas, and Nicolas per 6:3-5; 7:55; 8:29, 39); Barnabas (11:22-24); Agabus (11:28); and Paul (13:9).

B. Successful Ministry (vv. 14b-15)

14b-15. And there went out a fame of him through all the region round about. And he taught in their synagogues, being glorified of all.

Jesus' three-and-a-half-year ministry is often described today in terms of the rough time segments in the outline at the bottom of page 158. The depiction also offers some insight into the time gap discussed in the Lesson Context. Therefore, Jesus' *fame* that the verse before us notes has been building over several months by this point.

The region of Galilee was an area administratively distinct from Judea to the south. At this time, Galilee was ruled by Herod Antipas (see Matthew 14:1-12).

While in this area, Jesus was given opportunities to speak *in their synagogues*, and He was successful in so doing. Everyone was talking about Jesus (Luke 4:15, 37)! Ideally, the place to worship was the temple in Jerusalem. But wherever a certain number of Jewish families lived, there could be a synagogue. That Greek word means "place of gathering," and these became centers of communal religious life. The concept developed when worship in the temple became impossible after its destruction in 586 BC or soon after the Jews' returned to Judea from captivity.

Luke does not give the substance of Jesus' teaching at this time. Later, when Jesus was in Capernaum, Luke noted that the people were "astonished at his doctrine: for his word was with power" (Luke 4:31-32). The Gospel of John adds that Galileans welcomed Jesus because they had seen what He had done while He was in Jerusalem (John 4:45); many believed in Him when they saw the miracles He performed (2:23).

HOW TO SAY IT

Agabus	*Ag*-uh-bus.
Arabia	Uh-*ray*-bee-uh.
Corinthians	Ko-*rin*-thee-unz (*th* as in *thin*).
Barnabas	*Bar*-nuh-bus.
Capernaum	Kuh-*per*-nay-um.
Damascus	Duh-*mass*-kus.
Esaias	E-*zay*-us.
Galilee	*Gal*-uh-lee.
Isaiah	Eye-*zay*-uh.
Judea	Joo-*dee*-uh.
Messiah	Meh-*sigh*-uh.
Nazareth	*Naz*-uh-reth.
Nicanor	Nye-*cay*-nor.
Parmenas	*Par*-meh-nas.
Pentateuch	*Pen*-ta-teuk.
Pentecost	*Pent*-ih-kost.
Prochorus	*Prock*-uh-rus.
synagogue	*sin*-uh-gog.
Timon	*Ty*-mon.
Zacharias	Zack-uh-*rye*-us.

II. Preaching

(Luke 4:16-17)

A. In Nazareth (v. 16)

16a. And he came to Nazareth, where he had been brought up.

Part of Jesus' teaching and preaching tour of Galilee involved a stop in His boyhood home of *Nazareth.* The Gospel writer spoke briefly in Luke 2 of Jesus' upbringing there, indicating that Jesus grew up in a typical Jewish family. He was circumcised in accordance with the Law of Moses and attended the yearly Passover celebration with His parents—standard things for Jewish boys at the time. Nazareth itself was a village on the lower slopes of Galilee. A topographical feature was that of "the brow of the hill whereon their city was built" (Luke 4:29).

16b. And, as his custom was, he went into the synagogue on the sabbath day, and stood up for to read.

The phrase *as his custom was* indicates a regular practice of teaching and/or preaching in synagogues (compare similar practice of Paul in Acts 17:1-2). This hints at a habit of faithful Sabbath Day attendance developed during boyhood days. There were many practices and attitudes of synagogue leadership that Jesus found lacking (Luke 13:14-16; etc.), but such people did not dissuade Him from His own faithful attendance.

> *What Do You Think?*
>
> How does Jesus' regular attendance ("as his custom was") at weekly worship challenge your own practice in that regard?
>
> *Digging Deeper*
>
> What does Hebrews 10:25 add to that challenge?

Mention of *the sabbath day* is a reminder of God's creative work. The word *Sabbath,* meaning "rest, cessation from labor," first appears in Exodus 16:23-30. That text served to remind the covenant people of the requirement for a day of rest, echoing God's own rest after six days of creating (Exodus 20:8-11; compare Genesis 2:2-3). Sabbath observance is a sign of faithfulness to the covenant between God and Israel. "Verily my sabbaths ye shall keep: for it is a sign between me and you throughout your generations; that ye may know that I am the Lord that doth sanctify you" (Exodus 31:13).

After Jesus' death and resurrection, there is a transition from Saturday (the seventh day of the week) to Sunday (the first day of the week). Nine of the Ten Commandments are based on the nature of God; and since His nature never changes, neither does the application of those nine. The one commandment that is based on God's work rather than His nature is the one on keeping the Sabbath. After Jesus' resurrection, a shift occurs away from focus on the old creation to focus on the new creation available in Christ. The result is corporate worship on the first day of the week in light of His resurrection on that day (Luke 24:1-7; compare Acts 20:7; 1 Corinthians 16:2; Revelation 1:10).

B. From Isaiah (v. 17)

17. And there was delivered unto him the book of the prophet Esaias. And when he had opened the book, he found the place where it was written.

The ruler of the synagogue supervised the service to see that it was carried out in accordance with tradition (compare Luke 8:41; Acts 13:15; 18:8). There are distinct parts to Sabbath services: prayers, reading from the five books of Moses (the Pentateuch), reading from the Prophets, and a sermon or lesson.

The Scripture readings followed a definite cycle. In some synagogues, the entire Pentateuch was covered in one year, with each reading supplemented by a reading from the Prophets. If a distinguished visitor was present, he was asked to give the teaching. This procedure is seen in Acts 13:13-47, where Paul delivered the message after the readings from the Law and the Prophets.

In the Nazareth synagogue, Jesus was given *the book of the prophet Esaias* (Isaiah) to read. This was not a book as we normally think of one today. It was actually a scroll (sometimes called roll; example: Jeremiah 36:2). Scrolls for use in copying Scripture could be made from paper made from the papyrus plant, which grew along the

Nile River in Egypt (compare the various translations "bulrushes" and "rush[s]" in Exodus 2:3; Job 8:11; Isaiah 18:2; 35:7). The scroll handed to Jesus, however, was more likely made from animal skin, which was more durable (contrast the ease with which a papyrus scroll was destroyed in Jeremiah 36:23).

The Great Isaiah Scroll, one of the Dead Sea Scrolls discovered in 1947, is 24 feet long and about 10 inches high. The scroll handed to Jesus may have been similar.

> *What Do You Think?*
>
> What percentage of your Bible study time should you devote to reading the Old Testament? Why?
>
> *Digging Deeper*
>
> How do Romans 15:4 and 1 Corinthians 10:1-11 guide your decision?

III. The Point

(Luke 4:18-22a)

A. Jesus' Call (vv. 18-19)

18a. The Spirit of the Lord is upon me, because he hath anointed me to preach the gospel to the poor.

The place from which Jesus reads is Isaiah 61:1-2, which speaks of God's servant being *anointed* with *the Spirit* and given several responsibilities. The servant's work will be for the good of people, cities, and nations. God will use the servant to bring salvation and fulfill His covenant. The servant is to proclaim good news by saying that the situation will change. The words of Isaiah describe the current situation in Jesus' ministry.

To be anointed refers to the act of pouring oil on someone's head to symbolize being set apart to a special office, such as priest or king (example: 1 Samuel 16:13). Anointing also symbolized the endowment of the Holy Spirit on someone's life. Together, these ideas indicate the consecration of Jesus to His messianic role and task.

To preach the gospel to the poor is exactly what Jesus was tasked to do—and did (Luke 6:20; 7:22; etc.). In Isaiah 66:2 God says, "To this man will I look, even to him that is poor and of a contrite spirit, and trembleth at my word." Those who are poor have nothing to offer God, but therein lies the opportunity to realize one's need.

> *What Do You Think?*
>
> What guardrails can your church erect to ensure it maintains evangelistic focus on those who are poor in spirit while not neglecting to help those who are economically destitute?
>
> *Digging Deeper*
>
> How do texts such as Matthew 5:3; Romans 15:26; Galatians 2:10; James 2:1-7; and Revelation 3:17 help frame the task?

18b. He hath sent me to heal the brokenhearted, to preach deliverance to the captives.

The first phrase here does not appear in certain ancient manuscripts of the New Testament, although it does appear in Isaiah 61:1.

The word *captives* often refers to prisoners of war who are dragged into an exile of servitude by their conquerors (example: Isaiah 5:13); it is also used in contexts of those captives' *deliverance* (52:2). Spiritually, the devil holds people captive with no hope of escape on their own (2 Timothy 2:26). Jesus came to set everyone free.

> *What Do You Think?*
>
> How do you resist those things that put you at greatest risk of reentering the captivity of sin?
>
> *Digging Deeper*
>
> Which is most helpful to you in that regard: remembering consequences of your past captivity "to the law of sin" (Romans 7:23) or focusing on the positive captivity of your obedience to Christ (2 Corinthians 10:5)? Why?

18c. And recovering of sight to the blind, to set at liberty them that are bruised.

Jesus' subsequent ministry resulted in several recorded instances of healings from physical blindness (Luke 7:22; etc.). Healing spiritual blindness proved to be more difficult because of unbelief (8:10). The original word behind the translation *bruised* carries the idea of "oppressed," as it is translated in the old Greek version of Isaiah 58:6.

Blindsided

When I was 8 years old, I attended a basketball game with my parents. Throughout the evening, I frequently asked them to tell me the score. They repeatedly said, "The scoreboard is right there. Just look for yourself." Finally, my parents realized that my vision was blurry since I couldn't see the scoreboard. A few days later, they took me to the optometrist to buy my first pair of glasses. My vision needed correction.

Spiritual vision can also require correction. Reading the Bible like a rule book, hating yourself or others, or seeking fulfillment outside of your marriage can all indicate spiritual visual impairment.

Isaiah prophesied that the Messiah would restore sight to the blind, and on several occasions Jesus did so literally (example: John 9:1-7). He can fix your blind spots too. Will you invite the Lord to open your eyes and wipe away anything that blurs your spiritual vision? —D. F.

> *What Do You Think?*
> How do Matthew 7:1-5; 23:13-36; John 8:7; 1 Timothy 4:6; 2 Timothy 2:25; and Titus 2 interact to prohibit you from pointing out someone else's spiritual blind spots? How do those text require you to do so?
>
> *Digging Deeper*
> Under what circumstances, if any, would you encourage other Christians to point out to you your own spiritual blind spots?

19. To preach the acceptable year of the Lord.

This refers to the Year of Jubilee, described in Leviticus 25. God instructed the nation of Israel that every seventh year the land was to rest (have a Sabbath). Then after seven such rests (49 years) was to be the year of jubilee. During this 50th year, slaves were to be set free, debts cancelled, etc. It was to be a time of great rejoicing.

B. Jesus' Mission (vv. 20-22a)

20. And he closed the book, and he gave it again to the minister, and sat down. And the eyes of all them that were in the synagogue were fastened on him.

Each synagogue had a *minister* (an assistant) who took care of the building and called the people to the service. He was also responsible to hand the speaker the scroll and to return it to its proper place. Handing back the scroll and sitting down marked a transition to the next phase of the service. The fact that *the eyes of all them that were in the synagogue were fastened on* Jesus implies a great sense of expectation. Today we might say, "You could hear a pin drop!"

21. And he began to say unto them, This day is this scripture fulfilled in your ears.

This announcement means that the spiritual year of jubilee has come. Luke connects the *ears* with eyes (Luke 4:20, above). Jesus was and is the Messiah proclaimed by the prophet Isaiah.

As we see Luke connecting eyes with ears in these two verses, we note a sad contrast of the same connection in Acts 28:27: "Their ears are dull of hearing, and their eyes have they closed; lest they should see with their eyes, and hear with their ears, . . . and should be converted."

Today Is the Day

At 112 years old, Richard Overton was likely the oldest man in the United States when he died in December 2018. A military veteran, Richard had served his country during World War II. On Veterans Day in 2013, President Obama honored him in a ceremony. All that was well and good, but here's the best part of the story: Mr. Overton

Ministry Years of Jesus
(Not Including His Final Week)

	Matthew	Mark	Luke	John
Ministry Begins →	3:13–4:22	1:9-34	3:19-23; 4:14–5:11	1:19–4:54
Popularity Rises →	4:23–9:34; 11:2–13:58	1:35–6:6	5:12–8:56	5:1-47
Opposition Increases →	9:35–11:1; 14:1–20:34	6:7–10:52	9:1–19:27	6:1–11:54

accepted Christ and was baptized at age 107. He said "it was about time"!

Jesus told the crowd in His hometown synagogue that He was fulfilling Isaiah's messianic prophecy that very day. Hundreds of years had passed since Isaiah predicted that the Messiah would come to bring the good news and deliverance. After centuries of waiting, God's plan was being fulfilled through Jesus right then and there.

Today is the day of salvation (2 Corinthians 6:2). What will you do to continue bringing the message of the gospel? Don't put it off. Very few, if any, of the people you might speak to today will live to be 112. —D. F.

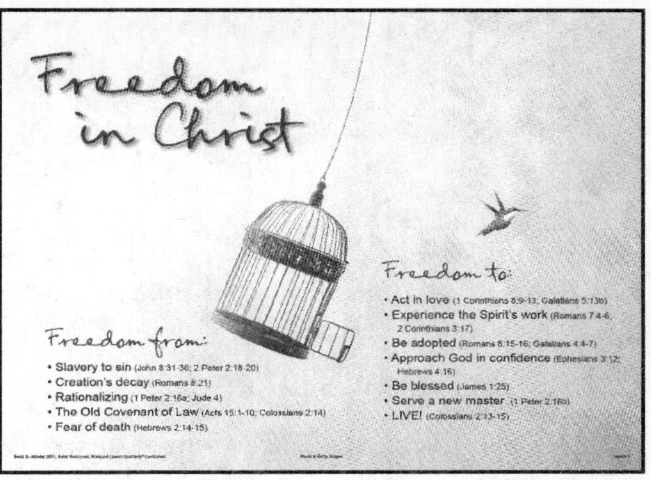

Visual for Lesson 5. *Start a discussion by pointing to this visual and asking your learners what they would add to each list.*

22a. And all bare him witness, and wondered at the gracious words which proceeded out of his mouth.

Jesus' *gracious words* reflects the fact that "the grace of God was upon him" (Luke 2:40). Indeed, the gospel itself is "the gospel of the grace of God" (Acts 20:24; compare 20:32).

Given that the townspeople's next words and actions were much less gracious, even deadly (Luke 4:22b-29; compare John 6:42), we wonder why the difference! Jesus gave a reason in Luke 4:24: "No prophet is accepted in his own country." Jesus' ministry was characterized not only by grace but also by truth (John 1:14, 17). The "hometown boy syndrome" had blinded them to reality.

Conclusion

A. Come Home

Messiah has come to set us free from the bondage of sin and death (Galatians 5:1). The whole purpose of Christ's coming was to rescue us. To do so, He had to die that He "might destroy him that had the power of death, that is, the devil" (Hebrews 2:14; compare 1 John 3:8).

Whoever we are, wherever we are physically or spiritually, God's message is clear: He wants all to be rescued. He wants us to come home. The acronym COME reminds us of this fact. He wants ***c***hildren, ***o***ld people, ***m***iddle-aged, and ***e***veryone else to come back to Him. Jesus wrapped a robe of flesh around himself and came to die to pay sin's price to make that possible. And He departed this world on the promise that He would prepare a place in Heaven for His disciples (John 14:1-3).

There is a star in the northern sky that never sets. The Phoenicians, Vikings, and sailors long ago used this star to get their bearings and to help them reach their destination. For thousands of years it has been a reliable guide for travelers. It is called the North Star. You can find it rather easily by using the stars in the handle of the Big Dipper (Ursa Major) as an imaginary line to point to it. As travelers can use that star yet today to guide them, how much more is Jesus still the only reliable light for our path to Heaven!

We can find our way home only by following Jesus and by following Jesus only. He is the light of the world to lead us all from the path of darkness into the light of the Father. Like Jesus did for His audience at Nazareth, Jesus calls us to Him.

B. Prayer

Father, we thank You for sending Jesus to die for our sin. May our eyes and ears be ever fixed on Him as we continue His mission. We pray this in Jesus' name. Amen.

C. Thought to Remember

Jesus, the Messiah,
has come to set us free.

INVOLVEMENT LEARNING

Enhance your lesson with KJV Bible Student *(from your curriculum supplier) and the reproducible activity page (at www.standardlesson.com or in the back of the* KJV Standard Lesson Commentary Deluxe Edition*).*

Into the Lesson

Have these scrambled words displayed on the board as class members arrive:

EMOOWNTH ROEH

As learners arrive, challenge them to unscramble the phrase silently—in their heads or on a slip of paper. Call the class to order and ask how many came up with "hometown hero" as the correct answer.

Then ask for a show of hands of those who received a hero's welcome on their most recent return to their hometown. Ask someone with a smartphone to look up the phrase *hometown hero* and share the result with the class. (*Option:* Offer this additional sarcastic definition: "A person who achieves local fame for accomplishments in high school, then fades into obscurity.") Ask why it can be difficult for an adult to gain respect from those among whom he or she grew up.

Alternative. Distribute copies of the "Minute Match" exercise from the activity page, which you can download. Allow no more than one minute for the matching part; how much time to allow for the compare part is at your discretion.

After either activity, write this multiple choice question on the board:

Where was Jesus from?
A. Bethlehem B. Nazareth C. Heaven

After discussion, explain that each answer is correct in a different sense, but the sense at issue in today's lesson is B.

Into the Word

Before class, recruit a volunteer to prepare and present a two-minute explanation of the context of today's lesson. Ask another volunteer to read the printed text while class members listen for answers to the following questions, which you distribute on handouts that you prepare: 1–What did Jesus do, and why? 2–What was Jesus' mission? 3–What did Jesus claim?

In the ensuing whole-class discussion of results, expect the following answers: 1–Jesus went to the synagogue in His hometown of Nazareth and read from the prophet Isaiah. 2–Mission statement and tasks per Luke 4:18-19. 3–Jesus claimed to be the fulfillment of this prophecy; in so doing, His claim was messianic.

Divide the class into groups of no more than four; assign each group of them one of the six items of Jesus' mission as listed in Luke 4:18-19. Allow about five minutes for groups to think of examples showing how Jesus actually accomplished this mission in His ministry. Stress the importance of spiritual fulfillment over physical fulfillment (compare John 9:39-41).

Into Life

Ask each of the above groups to make a list of ways Christians today continue to fulfill the six tasks in the mission of Jesus. After a few minutes, reconvene for whole-class discussion. Write these two words on the board as column headers:

Physical / Spiritual

Work down through the six tasks by calling for actions under each of the two headers. Be prepared to add your own ideas, particularly in "thin" areas. Introduce a minute of silent commitment as you challenge learners to choose one of the tasks of Luke 4:18-19 and decide how to live it out as a calling. Stress again that although the physical aspects of the tasks are important, the spiritual aspects are even more so. After that minute of silent commitment, ask volunteers to share their decisions, but don't put anyone on the spot.

Option. Extend the above activity by distributing copies of the "My Mission" prayer-writing exercise on the activity page. Use this to close the class or as a take-home.

Called to Follow

Devotional Reading: Luke 9:57-62
Background Scripture: Luke 5:1-11

Luke 5:1-11

1 And it came to pass, that, as the people pressed upon him to hear the word of God, he stood by the lake of Gennesaret,

2 And saw two ships standing by the lake: but the fishermen were gone out of them, and were washing their nets.

3 And he entered into one of the ships, which was Simon's, and prayed him that he would thrust out a little from the land. And he sat down, and taught the people out of the ship.

4 Now when he had left speaking, he said unto Simon, Launch out into the deep, and let down your nets for a draught.

5 And Simon answering said unto him, Master, we have toiled all the night, and have taken nothing: nevertheless at thy word I will let down the net.

6 And when they had this done, they inclosed a great multitude of fishes: and their net brake.

7 And they beckoned unto their partners, which were in the other ship, that they should come and help them. And they came, and filled both the ships, so that they began to sink.

8 When Simon Peter saw it, he fell down at Jesus' knees, saying, Depart from me; for I am a sinful man, O Lord.

9 For he was astonished, and all that were with him, at the draught of the fishes which they had taken:

10 And so was also James, and John, the sons of Zebedee, which were partners with Simon. And Jesus said unto Simon, Fear not; from henceforth thou shalt catch men.

11 And when they had brought their ships to land, they forsook all, and followed him.

Key Verse

Jesus said unto Simon, Fear not; from henceforth thou shalt catch men. **—Luke 5:10b**

Call in the New Testament

Unit 2: Jesus and Calls in His Ministry

Lessons 5–8

Lesson Aims

After participating in this lesson, each learner will be able to:

1. Recite the plot twists in Luke 5:1-11.
2. Explain the nature of Jesus' calling of the fishermen.
3. Write a statement that rephrases his or her job in terms of Jesus' call to evangelism.

Lesson Outline

Introduction
- A. The Power of Children's Songs
- B. Lesson Context

I. Shallow-Water Teaching (Luke 5:1-3)
- A. Press of the Crowd (v. 1)
- B. Solution of the Ship (vv. 2-3)

II. Deep-Water Miracle (Luke 5:4-7)
- A. The Reluctant Expert (vv. 4-5)
- B. Bursting Net (v. 6)
  Obedience Before Knowledge
- C. Sinking Ships (v. 7)

III. Simon's Epiphany (Luke 5:8-10a)
- A. A Sinner's Confession (v. 8)
- B. The Fishermen's Astonishment (vv. 9-10a)

IV. Jesus' Call (Luke 5:10b-11)
- A. Fear Not (v. 10b)
- B. Fish for Men (v. 10c)
- C. Forsake All and Follow (v. 11)
  The Sacrifice of Goers . . . and Senders

Conclusion
- A. What's My Line?
- B. Prayer
- C. Thought to Remember

Introduction

A. The Power of Children's Songs

I don't think there is any doubt that putting words to music (or even just to rhythm) helps people learn and memorize. For instance, one of the first songs I remember learning in Sunday school was "I Will Make You Fishers of Men." Even though I don't think I've heard or sung the song in years, both the lyrics and the accompanying motions are still rooted in my memory.

Two generations later, my grandchildren participate in a curriculum group that includes learning facts and concepts via memorized songs. Thanks to one of these songs, my 3-year-old granddaughter was able to keep up with her two older brothers in memorizing all 45 US presidents!

I'm sure my understanding of becoming a fisher of men was quite limited when I memorized the song. But I believe the lyrics made a positive and permanent impression on my developing heart and mind. Looking back, I feel certain that I realized Jesus was extending to me a personal invitation to *follow* Him. And I grasped that He was offering me an opportunity for fulfilling service: He would make me a fisher of men.

Today we study one of the passages in which Jesus called men to follow Him when they didn't know exactly what that meant. Allow it to renew and re-inspire your sense that Jesus Christ has called you to something eternally significant.

B. Lesson Context

Luke 5:1-11 is part of the third of six major sections of Luke's Gospel. These sections present themselves as follows:

I: Jesus' human relationships (1:5–2:52)
II: Jesus' baptism and testing (3:1–4:13)
III: Jesus' ministry in Galilee (4:14–9:50)
IV: Jesus' journey to Jerusalem (9:51–19:44)
V: Jesus' rejection and sacrifice (19:45–23:46)
VI: Jesus' resurrection and ascension (24:1-53)

The third section covers Jesus' time and energy spent teaching, preaching, and performing miracles. All activities served as demonstrations of the good news, all were essential to Jesus' mission, and all called for response. That is certainly the case in

Luke 5:1-11, today's text. (Matthew 4:18-22 and Mark 1:16-20 are parallel accounts.)

I. Shallow-Water Teaching

(Luke 5:1-3)

A. Press of the Crowd (v. 1)

1. And it came to pass, that, as the people pressed upon him to hear the word of God, he stood by the lake of Gennesaret.

In Luke 4 we see Jesus teaching and preaching in synagogues; now we see Him ministering out in the open for the first time in this Gospel. *The lake of Gennesaret* was named for the fertile region on the northwest side of the lake (compare Matthew 14:34; Mark 6:53); the word *Gennesaret* means "garden of riches." The authors of the other Gospels refer to this freshwater body as "the sea of Galilee" (Matthew 4:18; Mark 1:16; John 6:1), and John also calls it "the sea of Tiberias" (John 6:1; 21:1). In the Old Testament it is known as "the sea of Chinneroth" (Joshua 12:3). At 13 miles long and 7 miles wide, this picturesque lake served as the backdrop for much of Jesus' ministry.

Jesus had just healed many people at Capernaum (Luke 4:31-41), located on the northwest shore of the lake. Reports about Jesus and His amazing deeds "went out into every place of the country round about" (4:37). The result was that *the people pressed upon him to hear the word of God* (compare 4:42). The phrase *the word of God* could mean either the word that comes *from* God or the word that tells *of* God. Either way, this marked Jesus' ministry as prophetic for Jews steeped in the Old Testament, (compare 1 Kings 12:22; 1 Chronicles 17:3; etc.).

> *What Do You Think?*
>
> What plan can you create to identify and eliminate distractions that work against your hearing the Word of God?
>
> *Digging Deeper*
>
> Would it help to categorize the distractions in terms of "from the world" (example: 1 John 2:15-17) and "from within oneself" (example: James 1:14)?

B. Solution of the Ship (vv. 2-3)

2. And saw two ships standing by the lake: but the fishermen were gone out of them, and were washing their nets.

The 1986 discovery of "the Kinneret boat," dated to the first or second century AD, offers insight into what these *two ships* may have looked like. Constructed mostly of cedar and oak, the boat measures about 27 feet long, 7 feet wide, and 4 feet deep. It could have supported about a ton of weight—either about 15 passengers or 5 crew members and their catch of fish. (Luke 8:22 may indicate at least 13 people in a boat.)

Fishermen of the era often used a large dragnet, which required two or more men to deploy, or else a smaller and circular casting net. After returning from fishing, they needed to wash and stretch *their nets* to prepare them for the next outing.

3a. And he entered into one of the ships, which was Simon's, and prayed him that he would thrust out a little from the land.

This was not the first time Simon and Jesus had met (see Luke 4:31-38a). At Simon's home, Jesus had healed Simon's mother-in-law from a "great fever" (4:38b-39), and many others were brought there with illnesses and demonization (4:40-41). See also the description of a previous meeting with Simon in John 1:40-42.

3b. And he sat down, and taught the people out of the ship.

Boarding *the ship* solved the problem of the crowd's pressing on Jesus, allowing Him to still be seen and heard. Jesus then *sat down*, the normal position for teaching (example: Luke 4:20-21). This was not be the only time that Jesus taught from a boat (see Mark 3:9; 4:1).

II. Deep-Water Miracle

(Luke 5:4-7)

A. The Reluctant Expert (vv. 4-5)

4-5. Now when he had left speaking, he said unto Simon, Launch out into the deep, and let down your nets for a draught. And Simon answering said unto him, Master, we have toiled all the night, and have taken nothing: nevertheless at thy word I will let down the net.

Although Jesus addressed *Simon* in the first of these two verses, the instructions Jesus gave included Simon's partners; the word translated *let down* is plural in the original language. Jesus' directions would have seemed absurd to a professional fisherman. Simon and his partners had *toiled all the night* without catching anything!

But Simon had already witnessed the power of Jesus in miracles and teaching (see observations on Luke 4:38-41 in 5:3a, above). Those undoubtedly stood behind Simon's addressing Jesus as *Master*, an acknowledgment of His authority to direct Simon (compare 8:45; 9:33). And so the expert fisherman yielded to the *word* of the carpenter. This is foundational to Simon's future faithfulness in leadership (examples: Acts 2:14-40; 10:23b-48; 15:7-11, where he is known as Peter—see commentary on Luke 5:8, below).

B. Bursting Net (v. 6)

6. And when they had this done, they inclosed a great multitude of fishes: and their net brake.

Despite the apparent foolishness of casting nets after having "toiled all the night" and catching nothing (previous verse), *a great multitude of fishes* was caught! If Simon and his fellow fishermen had followed conventional wisdom instead of Jesus, they would not have experienced this miraculous catch. Jesus did not tell the men to cast their net in order to catch a paltry or even ordinary haul of fish: the abundance was such that *their net brake.* This is also the case in the lives of believers today. Though the blessings we will experience because of our faithfulness are not always obvious or even what we desired at a given time, our God is a God who delights in giving generously to His people.

His giving is not only in terms of quantity but also of quality (Matthew 7:7-11; John 2:10; 10:10b; James 1:17-18). The haul of fish in our text won't be the last one that obedience resulted in (see discussion of John 21:1-11 in commentary on Luke 5:11, below).

Obedience Before Knowledge

About 10 years ago, our church outgrew its facilities and moved to a new building. For the next several years, our expenses exceeded our income. Then a few years ago, we sensed the Lord calling us to partner with an evangelist to build a Christian school for orphaned children in Gojo, Ethiopia.

It made about as much sense to build a school on the other side of the globe as it did for Simon to let down a net in the middle of the day after catching nothing all night. But the results have been similarly amazing. The year after donating $120,000 to Gojo, we made budget for the first time in our new building. A Christian school that was renting our facilities spent $2.1 million to build an education wing—which we now own and the school uses rent free! Even better, many orphans in Gojo are receiving a quality education and responding to the good news about Jesus.

Follow Simon's example: you can act for God on His timing *before* you know completely what He is doing. —A. S.

C. Sinking Ships (v. 7)

7. And they beckoned unto their partners, which were in the other ship, that they should come and help them. And they came, and filled both the ships, so that they began to sink.

Simon's *partners . . . in the other ship* were James and John (see Luke 5:10a, below). The blessing of the fish was so overwhelming that *both the ships* together were barely able to handle the catch! This further emphasizes the nature of the miracle that Luke 5:6 describes.

> *What Do You Think?*
> In what ways can you help your church see evangelism as best achieved through partnerships rather than by lone rangers?
> *Digging Deeper*
> What cultural lone-ranger mores might you have to overcome personally in the process?

III. Simon's Epiphany

(Luke 5:8-10a)

A. A Sinner's Confession (v. 8)

8a. When Simon Peter saw it.

All four Gospels mention that Jesus gave *Simon* the name *Peter* (Matthew 16:18; Mark 3:16; Luke

6:14; and John 1:42, which adds "Cephas"). The Gospel writers refer to him as Simon Peter a total of 17 times, but 15 of these are in the Gospel of John. The text before us is the only such occurrence in Luke's writings of the books of Luke and Acts). This is important in studies of the Gospels because this man goes by the names Simon, Peter, and Simon Peter; the reference is to one and the same person (compare 2 Peter 1:1).

8b. He fell down at Jesus' knees, saying, Depart from me; for I am a sinful man, O Lord.

Following the miraculous catch of fish, and the breaking nets and sinking boats that result, we come to the third focus of Luke's narrative. Simon Peter's response, in word and behavior, was rightly characterized by awe and respect.

Luke uses the word translated *sinful man* more than the other three Gospel writers combined. Luke's strong tendency is to use this word in a compassionate way in referring to the targets of God's grace (compare Luke 5:32; 7:36-48). Realizing himself to be in the presence of a man of God led Simon to the confession we see here.

What Do You Think?

What kind of crisis would have to happen for you to react to Jesus as Simon Peter did?

Digging Deeper

Did you answer that question more in terms of a crisis of unexpected blessing (Peter's situation) or in terms of an unexpected loss or potential loss (example: Matthew 9:18)? Why might this distinction be important?

This scene reminds us of similar ones in the Old Testament. The call of the prophet Isaiah provides one example (Isaiah 6:5; compare Genesis 18:27; Exodus 3:4-6). We should point out that Simon Peter's recognition of Jesus as a man of God isn't necessarily bound up in his address of Jesus as *Lord* at this point. The word being translated that way is often just a polite term of respect, sometimes translated as "sir" (examples: John 4:19; 20:15).

Perhaps a more fitting comparison (given Simon Peter's limited awareness of Jesus' full identity at the time) are the actions of Joseph's brothers when they met him in Egypt. They bowed before Joseph, knowing that he had the power to approve or deny their aid request (Genesis 42:3, 6), but they did not know his true identity (42:7-8). Even so, that did not prevent them from recognizing his authority.

B. The Fishermen's Astonishment (vv. 9-10a)

9-10a. For he was astonished, and all that were with him, at the draught of the fishes which they had taken: and so was also James, and John, the sons of Zebedee, which were partners with Simon.

James and *John, the sons of Zebedee,* Simon's business *partners,* are mentioned by name for the first time in Luke's Gospel. Jesus would soon choose all three men to be counted among the "twelve . . . apostles" (Luke 6:12-16; see 9:28-36). But for now the focus is on Simon Peter as these others are mentioned only in passing.

IV. Jesus' Call

(Luke 5:10b-11)

A. Fear Not (v. 10b)

10b. And Jesus said unto Simon, Fear not.

Though *Jesus* addressed *Simon* directly, it seems safe to assume that James and John could hear the comforting *fear not.* This phrase previously was spoken in Luke's Gospel in contexts of angelic visitations to Zacharias, Mary, and the shepherds (Luke 1:13, 30; 2:10, respectively). This suggests that Jesus' presence was similarly disturbing, perhaps even terrifying.

HOW TO SAY IT

Capernaum	Kuh-*per*-nay-um.
Cephas	*See*-fus.
Chinneroth	*Kin*-eh-ruth or *Chin*-neh-ruth.
Galilee	*Gal*-uh-lee.
Gennesaret	Geh-*ness*-uh-ret (*G* as in *get*).
Nazareth	*Naz*-uh-reth.
synagogue	*sin*-uh-gog.
Tiberias	Tie-*beer*-ee-us.
Zacharias	Zack-uh-*rye*-us.
Zebedee	*Zeb*-eh-dee.

B. Fish for Men (v. 10c)

10c. From henceforth thou shalt catch men.

Jesus' words *from henceforth* reveal that this moment was a turning point (compare Luke 1:48; Acts 18:6). A dramatic break with the past is at hand, and Jesus' announcement of Simon's career shift was a masterful play on words and concepts. Unlike fish, which are killed when caught, the individuals Simon Peter would *catch* would be brought from death to life (Ephesians 2:1-6). Jesus turned a normally deadly activity into an analogy of something precious and life-giving. He was doing nothing less than calling Simon to participate in Jesus' mission of gathering people into the kingdom of God. Rather than using tools like boats and nets, the fishermen would be empowered by the Spirit (Acts 1:8; 2:1-4; etc.).

> *What Do You Think?*
> What can you do to help your church evaluate and improve the effectiveness of its evangelistic methods?
> *Digging Deeper*
> How would you word a prayer for the Lord's help in this regard?

C. Forsake All and Follow (v. 11)

11. And when they had brought their ships to land, they forsook all, and followed him.

When comparing Simon's call in the four Gospels, various details make it a challenge to piece together exactly when and how Jesus called him. Matthew 4:18-22 and Mark 1:16-20 record Simon's calling; these accounts are briefer and include the call of Andrew, who was Simon Peter's brother. John 1:40-42 records Simon's calling *as a result of* Andrew's meeting Jesus before Simon Peter did. So the call and response may have involved multiple steps, with Luke recording the culminating event: Simon and others leaving their fishing vocation to follow Jesus permanently.

The word *they* indicates that James and John took Jesus' words of calling Simon to include them as well. So the three men left *their ships*, the nets, and the equipment—as well as the greatest catch of fish they had seen in all their lives—to follow Jesus. With one minor exception (Matthew 17:27), this was the last day for three years that Simon, James, and John would spend as fishermen (Mark 10:28; compare John 21:1-14, see below).

In addition to the obvious economic ramifications, forsaking everything brought fundamental social consequences to the men. Their daily routine and their sense of identity would be forever changed. The three had entered into relationship with Jesus, thereby becoming key figures in the community beginning to form around Him.

> *What Do You Think?*
> What life changes have you made and will you make to "forsake all" in following Jesus?
> *Digging Deeper*
> Categorize your response in terms of thoughts, behaviors, and speech patterns.

It is interesting to fast-forward the story by about three years, to the days following Jesus' resurrection. Having three times denied knowing Jesus during Jesus' trial (Luke 22:54-62), Simon Peter's calling as a servant-leader needed to be restored. Once again Simon and his companions fished all night without catching a single fish (John 21:3). Once again Jesus gave instructions to cast their net (21:6a). And once again they immediately caught an incredible number of fish (21:6b, 11). Then three times Jesus told Simon Peter to feed Jesus' sheep, culminating with the simple command, "Follow me" (21:15-19).

An essential purpose of today's lesson passage is to convey to Luke's audience the proper response to Jesus and His calls to ministry. Simon Peter's confession of his sinfulness (Luke 5:8, above), followed by the three fishermen's forsaking all to follow Jesus, stands in sharp contrast to what we see in the surrounding narratives. The people of Nazareth rejected Jesus, even trying to throw Him off a cliff (4:29)! Amazed by Jesus' authority to teach and perform miracles, the people of Capernaum demonstrated the opposite extreme, begging Jesus not to leave them (Luke 4:42; but see a contrast in Matthew 11:23).

In Luke 5 we continue to see both extremes. The common people swarm on Jesus in order to be healed of their afflictions (5:15), but the religious elite who came brought skepticism and opposition (5:21, 30).

The Sacrifice of Goers . . . and Senders

Shortly after I committed to Jesus, I felt strongly that the Lord was calling me to ministry. I wasn't sure what that meant. But I responded by leaving Colorado to go to a Christian college and major in biblical studies. I met my Missourian wife there. After graduate school, we were glad to both be hired by a church just an hour from her family.

Two years later we accepted a call to minister in a small church in Pennsylvania. We ended up living there 12 years. Though it was a sacrifice to be far from both our families, I didn't struggle much with self-pity. But now that our son is grown with a wife and children, I have a keen appreciation for the sacrifice that our parents felt—and that they rarely complained about it.

Forsaking all, as the fishermen did, can take many forms today. What would be a prayer you could pray to invite God to test your willingness in this regard? —A. S.

Conclusion

A. What's My Line?

When I was a child, I enjoyed a game show called *What's My Line?* Each week a panel of celebrities tried to guess the contestants' line of work by asking only yes or no to questions. Any Christian who appeared on the show really should have been regarded as a trick contestant. Regardless of that person's workaday occupation, he or she also had work to do for Jesus.

Do you realize that *you also* have another line of work? Everyone who responds to Jesus' call to follow Him shares a common job title and description (see Matthew 28:19-20). The way in which we live out that calling varies greatly. But the key component is that we further God's plan of extending His kingdom, which is based and built on the good news of His Son, Jesus.

Simon Peter, James, and John did indeed pull up stakes to travel with Jesus. That fact may serve as an example-call to follow today as Christians relocate to the other side of the globe as missionaries. But strong argument can be made that although Luke 5:1-11 depicts the fishermen's call to full-time, vocational ministry, that text does not thereby serve as a directive that all followers of Jesus must do exactly likewise. Think of the man who wanted to go with Jesus after Jesus delivered him from demonization: Jesus told him to return home and share with the people there what God had done for him (Luke 8:26-39).

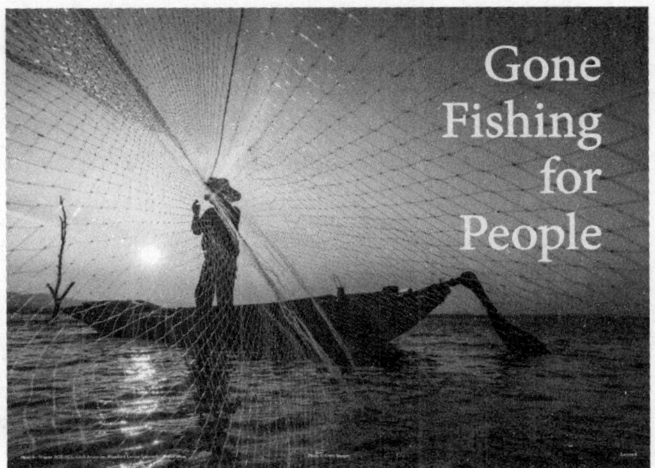

Visual for Lesson 6. *Have this visual on display as a backdrop when you pose the discussion question associated with Luke 5:10c.*

Jesus used the disciples' occupation as fishermen as an analogy of what He was calling them to do in ministry for Him. How could you do likewise regarding your job? For example, if you are a farmer, what would it look like for you to be a "farmer of people"? Whether your calling is to full-time vocational ministry or to Christian witness in the secular workplace or to serve your family as a homemaker, how can you state your calling as a purpose statement for your life in Christ's kingdom?

B. Prayer

Thank You, Father, for the privilege of responding to Your Son's call! Help us fulfill our calls to fish for people. In the Son's name we pray. Amen.

C. Thought to Remember

Followers of Jesus fish for people.
Start fishing!

Involvement Learning

Enhance your lesson with KJV Bible Student *(from your curriculum supplier) and the reproducible activity page (at www.standardlesson.com or in the back of the* KJV Standard Lesson Commentary Deluxe Edition*).*

Into the Lesson

Distribute slips of paper on which you ask learners to complete this sentence:

When I was a child, here's what I said I wanted to be when I grew up: ________

Ask class members *not* to sign their slips of paper as they fold them in half and give them to you. Redistribute them so that everyone has a slip that is not their own.

Ask class members to guess who wrote the answer on the slip they've been given. Allow time for persons named to confirm or deny the correctness of the guesses.

Say, "Today we're going to talk about vocation; that is, what we're doing now that we're grown up—and what the Lord may be calling us to do."

Into the Word

Designate two halves of the class for a responsive reading of today's printed text as follows:

Group A	Group B
verse 1	verses 2-3
verse 4	verse 5
verses 6-7	verses 8-10a
verse 10b	verse 11

Form small groups and distribute identical handouts (you prepare) with these challenges:

Explain the nature of Jesus' calling of the fishermen—both in terms of the calling itself in verse 10b and what Simon and the others gave up in the process in verse 11—

1–as the fishermen may have understood the calling and the sacrifice at the time

2–as we understand the calling and the sacrifice for those fishermen now.

Inform your groups that they are allowed to use their sanctified imaginations on the first challenge and should provide scriptural justification for the answers to the second (expect as a minimum the mention of Matthew 28:19-20).

Option. Dig deeper into the first challenge by distributing to small groups the "What Were They Thinking?" exercise from the activity page, which you can download. After several minutes, reconvene for whole-class discussion.

Into Life

Divide the class into groups of four to six. Make sure at least one member of each group has a smartphone with internet access. Distribute handouts (you prepare) on which are printed these instructions: 1–Search the internet for lists of professions or occupations. 2–Choose several of those (possibly at random) and ask, for each, "How could God use a Christian in this profession or occupation to serve Him in a unique way?"

Alternative. If an internet search isn't possible or practical, introduce the above activity as a brainstorming exercise. Give the class two minutes to voice as many professions as they can while you write their answers on your board rapidly. Then proceed with item 2 of the small-group activity above.

After several minutes, reconvene for whole-class discussion of conclusions. Finish by adding this challenge: "Take no more than one minute to write your response to this addition to our 'Explain the nature of Jesus' calling' exercise of earlier: How do you understand verses 10b-11 in terms of your own calling today?" Allow volunteers to reveal what they have written, but don't put anyone on the spot.

Option. Distribute copies of the "All to Jesus I Surrender" exercise from the activity page. Give students a minute to jot thoughts in this chart, and then invite them to share those thoughts with a study partner. End the class session by leading the class in singing "All to Jesus I Surrender." Provide copies of additional stanzas as appropriate.

Called in Authority

Devotional Reading: Psalm 103:1-14
Background Scripture: Mark 2:1-12

Mark 2:1-12

1 And again he entered into Capernaum after some days; and it was noised that he was in the house.

2 And straightway many were gathered together, insomuch that there was no room to receive them, no, not so much as about the door: and he preached the word unto them.

3 And they come unto him, bringing one sick of the palsy, which was borne of four.

4 And when they could not come nigh unto him for the press, they uncovered the roof where he was: and when they had broken it up, they let down the bed wherein the sick of the palsy lay.

5 When Jesus saw their faith, he said unto the sick of the palsy, Son, thy sins be forgiven thee.

6 But there were certain of the scribes sitting there, and reasoning in their hearts,

7 Why doth this man thus speak blasphemies? who can forgive sins but God only?

8 And immediately when Jesus perceived in his spirit that they so reasoned within themselves, he said unto them, Why reason ye these things in your hearts?

9 Whether is it easier to say to the sick of the palsy, Thy sins be forgiven thee; or to say, Arise, and take up thy bed, and walk?

10 But that ye may know that the Son of man hath power on earth to forgive sins, (he saith to the sick of the palsy,)

11 I say unto thee, Arise, and take up thy bed, and go thy way into thine house.

12 And immediately he arose, took up the bed, and went forth before them all; insomuch that they were all amazed, and glorified God, saying, We never saw it on this fashion.

Key Verse

Whether is it easier to say to the sick of the palsy, Thy sins be forgiven thee; or to say, Arise, and take up thy bed, and walk? **—Mark 2:9**

CALL IN THE
NEW TESTAMENT

Unit 2: Jesus and Calls in His Ministry

LESSONS 5–8

LESSON AIMS

After participating in this lesson, each learner will be able to:

1. Summarize the account of the paralyzed man who was made whole in body and spirit.
2. Compare and contrast the differing perspectives of those present.
3. Write a prayer of thanksgiving for the assurance of Jesus' forgiveness.

LESSON OUTLINE

Introduction
- A. No Room in the "Farm"
- B. Lesson Context

I. A Packed House (Mark 2:1-2)
- A. Coming to Capernaum (v. 1)
- B. Capacity Crowd (v. 2)
  - *Standing Room Only?*

II. A Paralyzed Man (Mark 2:3-5)
- A. Extraordinary Entrance (vv. 3-4)
- B. Surprising Statement (v. 5)

III. Cynical Bystanders (Mark 2:6-9)
- A. Silent Skepticism (vv. 6-7)
  - *A Reformed Cynic*
- B. Perceptive Judgment (vv. 8-9)

IV. An Amazing Miracle (Mark 2:10-12)
- A. Absolute Authority (vv. 10-12a)
- B. Glorifying God (v. 12b)

Conclusion
- A. A Different Diagnosis
- B. Prayer
- C. Thought to Remember

Introduction

A. No Room in the "Farm"

In October 2018, the owners of a popular Denver restaurant announced it would be closing at the end of the year. White Fence Farm had served family-style fried chicken dinners for 45 years. The gift shop, the "barn" with live music, a children's slide, and the petting zoo (in addition to the good food) had made White Fence Farm more than a restaurant. It was a place to create wonderful memories.

My siblings and I have a tradition of taking each other out to eat for our birthdays. As soon as I heard the news, I announced that I wanted to go to White Fence Farm since my birthday was approaching. Although the restaurant had stopped taking reservations, we were told that since we were coming on a Thursday, we should be OK as long as we got there at 5:30. Well, when we arrived, we discovered a two-and-a-half-hour wait! So we decided to go elsewhere.

The following Thursday my brother-in-law called and asked if I was game to try again. This time we got there just before the restaurant opened at 4:30. I groaned—the line leading to the door was about 50 yards long!

When we got inside, we were told the wait might be two hours. Not wanting to leave with an empty stomach again, I persuaded the others to stay. Thanks to the hostess's cautious estimate and two sweet ladies who were happy to include us in their party, it wasn't long before I was savoring all the chicken, sides, and fritters I could eat!

Today's lesson considers an occasion when a crowd of people wanted to get into a house where Jesus was. The venue was so popular that one couldn't even get near the door. For those who faithfully persisted, the reward was *much better* than a fried chicken dinner.

B. Lesson Context

The Gospel of Mark is a book of action. After an introduction of only three verses, the record begins with "John did baptize . . . and preach" (Mark 1:4). Jesus continued to be on the move (1:9, 12, 14). While the other three Gospels often slow down the action, Mark moves right along with his condensed style.

Mark 2:1-12, today's text, is parallel to quite similar accounts in Matthew 9:1-8 and Luke 5:17-26. Although the chronological order of events varies in the three synoptic Gospels (see Lesson Context for lesson 5), all three locate this scene in Capernaum during Jesus' initial ministry in Galilee.

According to the passage just prior, a man with leprosy had come to Jesus and pled with Him to be made "clean" (Mark 1:40-45; also Luke 5:12-15). Jesus healed the man but told him not to tell others about it. Jesus may not have wanted to ignite the popular but erroneous hope that a miracle-working Messiah had come to deliver the Jews from Roman oppression. But the man "began to publish it much . . . insomuch that Jesus could no more openly enter into the city, . . . and they came to him from every quarter" (Mark 1:45). That shock wave continued into today's passage.

I. A Packed House

(Mark 2:1-2)

A. Coming to Capernaum (v. 1)

1. And again he entered into Capernaum after some days; and it was noised that he was in the house.

Although Jesus grew up in the small town of Nazareth in Galilee (Matthew 2:21-23), He had made *Capernaum* His base of operations when He began His public ministry in that region (4:12-16). Capernaum was a town on the northwest shore of the Sea of Galilee. Jesus had frequent interactions there (Matthew 4:12-13; 9:1-9; Luke 7:1-5; etc.).

As news spread of Jesus' presence in Capernaum, He was likely at *the house* of Simon and his brother Andrew (Mark 1:21, 29). Simon's mother-in-law had been healed there and showed herself happy to offer Jesus hospitality (1:30-31). Many female disciples supported Jesus in His ministry through funds and hospitality (example: Matthew 27:55-56); Simon's mother-in-law was probably one of these women. Although there is no indication that she left Capernaum, her daughter—Simon Peter's wife—did (see 1 Corinthians 9:5).

B. Capacity Crowd (v. 2)

2. And straightway many were gathered together, insomuch that there was no room to receive them, no, not so much as about the door: and he preached the word unto them.

Partially as a consequence of a healed man's spreading the news about Jesus (see Lesson Context), *there was no room* in or even near the house where Jesus was. The house was probably a rectangular, one-story building surrounded by a large, walled courtyard.

The site where archaeologists believe Peter's house had been is about 28 feet long. Evidently the door was left open so that others could at least cram close to it and hear what was being said. Those who could do so listened to Jesus' preach *the word*—that is, the good news regarding the impending kingdom of God and the necessity of repentance and faith (see Mark 1:14-15).

Standing Room Only?

Many years ago, a young congregation was looking for ways to raise community awareness of their small church. One of the elders, a strong-willed man, was convinced that a certain tent-revival preacher could achieve this. So that man was called to do an evangelistic crusade.

The evangelist was known for the somewhat circus-like atmosphere that pervaded the services held inside his "big tent." The meeting got off to a small start, with about 90 percent of the seats empty. Undeterred, the revivalist went on local media the following day to report "capacity crowds."

Even though the meeting continued for two weeks, there were never any "standing room only"

HOW TO SAY IT

Capernaum	Kuh-*per*-nay-um.
Corinthians	Ko-*rin*-thee-unz (*th* as in *thin*).
Galatians	Guh-*lay*-shunz.
Galilee	*Gal*-uh-lee.
Isaiah	Eye-*zay*-uh.
Leviticus	Leh-*vit*-ih-kus.
Messiah	Meh-*sigh*-uh.
Nazareth	*Naz*-uh-reth.

crowds. It took the church several years to recover from the embarrassment.

There was no need for false reports to get a crowd around Jesus. What happened when Jesus came to town was more spectacular than anyone imagined. But do we still tend to look to gimmicks to bring people to Christ? —C. R. B.

II. A Paralyzed Man

(Mark 2:3-5)

A. Extraordinary Entrance (vv. 3-4)

3. And they come unto him, bringing one sick of the palsy, which was borne of four.

Meanwhile, *four* men carrying a fifth man approached the packed house. The only thing we know for sure about this man who was *sick of the palsy* is that he was unable to walk. He may not even have had use of his arms.

His condition could have been from birth (compare Acts 3:2; 14:8) or as the result of an accident, a stroke, etc. The determination of the man's friends to bring him to Jesus suggests that he was in dire straits, and those four believed Jesus could help.

> *What Do You Think?*
> What could you do to help your church start or expand a ministry of driving people to medical appointments when they are unable to do so themselves?
> *Digging Deeper*
> What role should 1 Timothy 5:3-16 play in limiting or focusing such a ministry, if any?

4. And when they could not come nigh unto him for the press, they uncovered the roof where he was: and when they had broken it up, they let down the bed wherein the sick of the palsy lay.

The action of breaking a hole in *the roof* isn't as destructive as it seems. Houses in Israel in Jesus' day generally had a flat roof that was accessible by a ladder or stairway. The wooden crossbeams were overlaid with reeds, branches, and baked mud or clay. This thatched material had to be repacked with a stone roller every fall before the winter rains. It wouldn't have been difficult for the four men to dig through the thatch, and their deconstruction could be repaired with relative ease.

Even so, imagine the drama of the scene: people in the house below are being sprinkled with debris; they are startled and confused. Then light begins to filter in as the hole becomes bigger. Then the light is blotted out by something being lowered through the hole. Not just something—a man on a bed! Where there was no room before, certainly the crowd jostles and divides to make room for this newcomer. Likely a few step forward to help with the lowering once they realize what is happening.

> *What Do You Think?*
> If you were attending a modern-day ministry event that was as crowded as the one in the text, under what conditions would you give up your seat or ticket to someone else? Why?
> *Digging Deeper*
> Were those gathered around Jesus selfish for not making way for the disabled man and his friends in the first place? Why, or why not?

B. Surprising Statement (v. 5)

5a. When Jesus saw their faith.

The reason given for what Jesus said in response is *their faith*. The plural *their* is important since it includes the faith of the friends rather than just that of the afflicted man. Seeing the great lengths these men went to, Jesus realized that they believed He had the power to heal their friend (compare: Matthew 9:2; Luke 5:20).

> *What Do You Think?*
> How can you do better at developing the kind of faith that others can see?
> *Digging Deeper*
> How do you balance Matthew 5:14-16 with 6:1-4 in this regard?

5b. He said unto the sick of the palsy, Son, thy sins be forgiven thee.

What Jesus had to say in reaction to this extraordinary entrance surprises us! Wouldn't we have expected Jesus to say something like, "Son, be healed"?

Instead, what Jesus said got at the heart of most people's assumptions about illness. The Old Testament frequently assumes a direct connection between sin and sickness. God's forgiveness is often required for physical healing, and healing is often the evidence of forgiveness (examples: Exodus 15:26; 2 Chronicles 7:14; Psalm 41:3-4; Isaiah 19:22). This belief persisted into Jesus' own day; it's what led the disciples to ask regarding a blind man, "Who did sin, this man, or his parents, that he was born blind?" (John 9:2).

Back to our text at hand, the sequence of events suggests that Jesus treated the paralysis as being the result of a spiritual malady. Every issue of humanity's physical frailty can be traced in a general sense to the sin of Adam and Eve (Genesis 2:16-17; 3:1-19). But that doesn't mean every specific illness is traceable to a specific sin of a person (see John 9:3). Regardless of why the man was paralyzed (a discussion Jesus did not engage in with this crowd), Jesus recognized that the man's greater need was to be *forgiven* for his *sins*.

III. Cynical Bystanders

(Mark 2:6-9)

A. Silent Skepticism (vv. 6-7)

6a. But there were certain of the scribes sitting there.

The scribes were educated both in God's written law and its oral interpretation. By proportion, Mark mentions them the most frequently of the four Gospels. But only one time is one of them depicted in other than a negative light (see Mark 12:28-34). *Sitting* was often a posture of teaching, which suggests that these scribes were anticipating more of a debate with Jesus than being taught by Jesus (also Luke 5:17).

6b-7. And reasoning in their hearts, Why doth this man thus speak blasphemies? who can forgive sins but God only?

Mark does not describe the reaction of the paralyzed man, his friends, or the larger crowd to Jesus' surprising statement, but only the unspoken skepticism of the scribes. Priests could offer sacrifices for forgiveness on behalf of those who took the proper steps of repentance (example: Leviticus 5:5-6). The scribes were well aware that the Old Testament taught that no one *can forgive sins but God only* (Exodus 34:6-9; Psalm 130:2-4; Isaiah 43:25).

But Jesus spoke as though He had the same power to forgive sins as God. If the scholars even considered whether Jesus could be God, they would have rejected the idea out of hand. There was no precedent for God becoming man.

The scribes were therefore left to conclude that Jesus was speaking *blasphemies*. They viewed Jesus' presumption to forgive sins as an arrogant offense to the authority and majesty of God. The Law of Moses pronounced the penalty for blasphemy to be death by stoning (Leviticus 24:10-16; Numbers 15:30-31). That will indeed be attempted later (John 10:31-33), but not on this occasion.

What Do You Think?

What are some ways to guard against jealousy when someone else's ministry results in attention and honor that you do not share?

Digging Deeper

In addition to Philippians 1:15-18, what passages help you most to answer this?

A Reformed Cynic

Every Bible professor has to deal with the occasional student who "knows it all." One such student—let's call him Jim—started the semester with a perpetual smirk on his face. His body language let his classmates know that whatever I said was already old stuff to him. If Jim disagreed with me, he would look around with that smirk.

I don't know what eventually shattered his sense of pride, but Jim changed during that semester. By the end of the school year, he had accepted a ministry position in a community where many citizens were cynical about the Christian faith. Jim seemed to know what drove their cynicism. He was able to counter that attitude, and the church began to grow.

The cynics in Jesus' audience were know-it-alls. Unlike Jim, they persisted in refusing to learn,

even when the Messiah was their teacher. Who are you more like: the skeptics in the text, who never learned, or Jim, who grew in humility?
—C. R. B.

B. Perceptive Judgment (vv. 8-9)

8a. And immediately when Jesus perceived in his spirit that they so reasoned within themselves.

We can be confident that Jesus' judgment here went beyond merely reading the body language of the skeptics. Scripture clearly affirms God's ability to know people's hearts (Jeremiah 17:10; Acts 1:24; 15:8; etc.).

8b-9. He said unto them, Why reason ye these things in your hearts? Whether is it easier to say to the sick of the palsy, Thy sins be forgiven thee; or to say, Arise, and take up thy bed, and walk?

Jesus met the scribes' unspoken disapproval with questions of His own. The use of counterquestions was common in rabbinic debate and employed frequently by Jesus (example: Mark 11:27-33). Here Jesus' counterquestion challenged the skeptics' belief that Jesus had offered the man something that wasn't in His power to give. And it paved the way for Jesus' upcoming declaration of physical healing.

It is *easier* to declare forgiveness than to tell a paralyzed man to *walk,* since the former can't be objectively verified and the latter has physical proof. But the declaration of forgiveness is more essential—and difficult. Most likely, Jesus was emphasizing that both declarations are impossible for human beings and easy for God.

IV. An Amazing Miracle
(Mark 2:10-12)

A. Absolute Authority (vv. 10-12a)

10-11. But that ye may know that the Son of man hath power on earth to forgive sins, (he saith to the sick of the palsy,) I say unto thee, Arise, and take up thy bed, and go thy way into thine house.

In this climactic pronouncement, Jesus refers to himself as *the Son of man.* This rather mysterious title seems to have its origin in Daniel 7:13-14, which states that God would bestow on this heavenly figure dominion and glory in the end times. "Son of man" was a favorite self-designation Jesus used. The phrase occurs some 80 times in the Gospels—and only on one occasion on the lips of anyone other than Jesus (see John 12:34).

The ambiguity of the title spared it from preconceived ideas in Jesus' day. Therefore, He was able to infuse it with His own definition. In the Gospels, this messianic title is connected with the nature of Jesus' person and work—who He is and what He does. In addition to having authority *to forgive sins,* the Son of man is Lord of the Sabbath (Mark 2:28), who came to give His life as a ransom (10:45) and rise from the dead (8:31; 10:33-34). He is the one who will one day come "in the clouds with great power and glory" (13:26; see also 14:62).

Jesus was able and willing to show the scribes —and everyone else—that He had *power on earth to forgive sins.* Although there is a technical distinction between power ("the ability to do something") and authority ("the right to do something"; see Luke 4:36; 9:1; etc.), Mark doesn't make a sharp distinction. Jesus has both! And that is the crux of this story. His ability to heal physically was tangible proof of ability to heal spiritually by forgiving sins.

After Jesus addressed the scribes in particular (and perhaps the crowd in general), He shifted focus to the paralyzed man. If the man could obey Jesus' command to *arise,* it would be evidence that Jesus was capable of miraculous healing. The man's obedience would also imply that Jesus' earlier pronouncement of forgiveness was as effective as His pronouncement of healing.

12a. And immediately he arose, took up the bed, and went forth before them all.

To put it simply, the man believed and obeyed. As there could be no evidence of the man's forgiveness without the healing, there could be no evidence of his faith without his obedience. *The bed* was likely rolled and carried.

B. Glorifying God (v. 12b)

12b. Insomuch that they were all amazed, and glorified God, saying, We never saw it on this fashion.

Mark speaks of people's being *amazed* several times in his Gospel to describe reaction to what Jesus said with authority and/or did as miraculous. The evidence Jesus offered affirmed that His declaration of forgiveness was legitimate. This event was startling evidence that the kingdom of God was indeed at hand (Mark 1:15).

We might think Mark's statement that *all . . . glorified God* is overstated. Surely the scribes weren't included! But they too had to acknowledge the miracle, whether or not they believed that forgiveness had also been granted. For them to glorify God wouldn't necessarily mean that they thanked God for sending Jesus. The scribes, along with everyone else, simply had *never* seen events after *this fashion*.

What Do You Think?

What can your church do to help people have a sense of awe in worship? What will be your part in this effort?

Digging Deeper

What is your reaction to this statement: "Worship will be only as meaningful as we have prepared ourselves to make it"?

Conclusion

A. A Different Diagnosis

Today's lesson reminds us of the spiritual components involved in genuine and integrated health and healing. Whether Jesus diagnosed this man's paralysis as being a result of sin, the man certainly couldn't be made whole without spiritual healing.

No significant and permanent healing can occur apart from reconciliation with God. As we have seen, God alone forgives sins. And God alone is the source of healing. Jesus still has the power and authority to provide healing by bringing release from the crippling burden of sin. As God in the flesh, Jesus Christ was the incarnation of the profound statement recorded in Exodus 15:26: "I am the Lord that healeth thee."

This is not always seen in physical healing of maladies in this current life on earth; but it will absolutely be seen in the resurrection bodies that

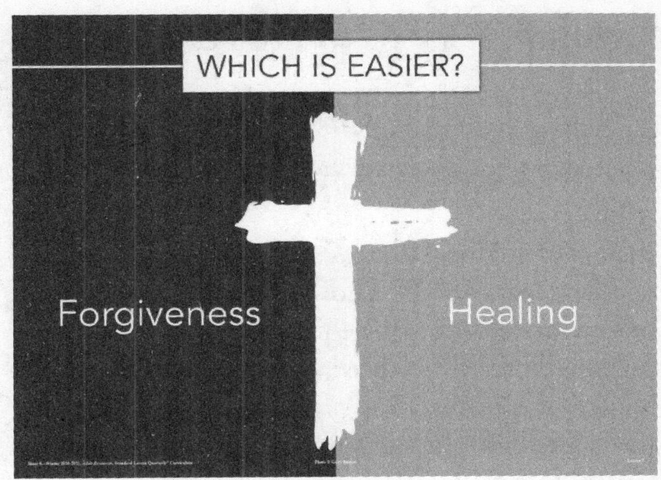

Visual for Lesson 7. *Use this visual as a backdrop for a mock debate: have half the class argue for forgiveness being easier and the other half for healing.*

grow from the seed of our present bodies (1 Corinthians 15:42-54).

This story also reminds us of how much we need our fellow brothers and sisters in the body of Christ. Although we probably won't need them to carry us on a stretcher to church or a prayer meeting, we do need to "bear . . . one another's burdens" (Galatians 6:2). And there are times when we need to heed and practice the instruction of James 5:16: "Confess your faults one to another, and pray one for another, that ye may be healed."

As you reflect on Mark 2:1-12 and consider how it applies to your life, write a prayer that brings before the Lord your various needs. Lay out your physical, spiritual, emotional, relational, and material needs—and your questions about them. Call on the absolute authority of Jesus Christ to make you whole so that you can better glorify, honor, and serve Him.

B. Prayer

Heavenly Father, we recognize that You have power and authority both to forgive sins and to heal sickness. We present to You every aspect of our lives; may we love You with all our hearts, souls, minds, and strength. In Jesus' name we pray. Amen.

C. Thought to Remember

Jesus still has absolute authority and power to both forgive and heal.

Involvement Learning

Enhance your lesson with KJV Bible Student *(from your curriculum supplier) and the reproducible activity page (at www.standardlesson.com or in the back of the* KJV Standard Lesson Commentary Deluxe Edition*).*

Into the Lesson

Place magazines and newspapers on chairs before learners arrive. Begin your session by forming small groups of three or four. Have all groups look in the publications for examples of our culture's search for physical and spiritual health. After several minutes, ask groups to share what they've found. Pose questions such as these:

1–Which search was easier?

2–Which kind of health concerns people more these days?

3–Which of the two kinds of health issues are more likely to drive people to seek unproven or unscriptural methods of cure?

Option. Ask class members to use their own memories and/or smartphones instead of surveying printed publications.

Lead into Bible study by noting that search for cures isn't new, and that an ancient account points us in the right direction in that regard.

Into the Word

Ask a volunteer to read aloud Mark 2:1-12. Challenge class members to listen for key issues regarding Jesus and attitudes toward Him. Call for responses at the end of the reading; jot those responses on the board.

Introduce the next activity by saying, "Each of the characters would tell the story differently, mentioning details they most noticed and including their own opinions or biases. Reflect these in your brief retelling; feel free to use your 'sanctified imagination' to make reasonable inferences."

Divide the class into five groups or study pairs for this activity; assign each group one of the following from the story: (1) Jesus, (2) the gathered crowd, (3) the man on the mat, (4) the four men carrying the mat, and (5) the scribes. Assign group names according to the designated character(s), and ask each group to write a brief retelling of the story from the point of view of their character(s).

Allow groups six to eight minutes to create their retellings. If they don't have time to write smooth narratives, they may simply list some things their assigned character(s) might have said or done. As each group reports in the ensuing whole-class discussion, ask those not in that group to comment on the unique spin each character or set of characters puts on the story as seen by the reporting group's conclusions. Encourage discussion by asking what might be added and why.

Option. Distribute copies of the "Be Healed!" exercise on the activity page, which you can download. Assign each Scripture there to a different class member or study pair to paraphrase and then share results with the whole class.

Into Life

Tell the following true story:

> A man in an adult Bible-study class decided to record and categorize the prayer requests he heard expressed over a 10-week period in the class. He himself made no prayer requests in order not to bias the outcome. When the 10-week period was over, he discovered that the prayer requests could be categorized and tallied this way:
>
> Prayers for physical healing: 97 requests
> Prayers for situations (job loss, etc.): 26 requests
> Prayers for spiritual healing: 3 requests

Follow the story by asking, "What's wrong with this picture?" *Teacher Tip:* Be absolutely silent after asking the question! If class members are themselves silent, resist the temptation to "say something" yourself. Let the discomfort of the silence continue for 15 seconds or so before you add thoughts of your own. Discuss as appropriate.

Wrap up by asking learners to share thoughts they'd include in a prayer of thanksgiving for God's healing forgiveness. *Option.* Distribute copies of the "Finding Forgiveness" exercise on the activity page. Have learners work in study pairs to complete it. Allow time for whole-class sharing.

Called for the World's Belief

Devotional Reading: 1 Timothy 2:1-7a
Background Scripture: John 17:14-24

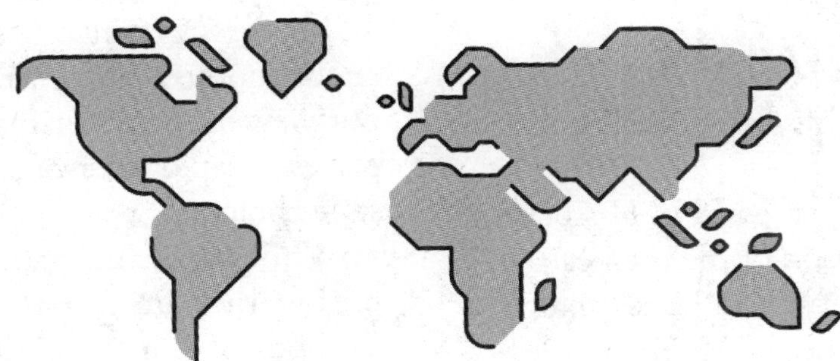

John 17:14-24

14 I have given them thy word; and the world hath hated them, because they are not of the world, even as I am not of the world.

15 I pray not that thou shouldest take them out of the world, but that thou shouldest keep them from the evil.

16 They are not of the world, even as I am not of the world.

17 Sanctify them through thy truth: thy word is truth.

18 As thou hast sent me into the world, even so have I also sent them into the world.

19 And for their sakes I sanctify myself, that they also might be sanctified through the truth.

20 Neither pray I for these alone, but for them also which shall believe on me through their word;

21 That they all may be one; as thou, Father, art in me, and I in thee, that they also may be one in us: that the world may believe that thou hast sent me.

22 And the glory which thou gavest me I have given them; that they may be one, even as we are one:

23 I in them, and thou in me, that they may be made perfect in one; and that the world may know that thou hast sent me, and hast loved them, as thou hast loved me.

24 Father, I will that they also, whom thou hast given me, be with me where I am; that they may behold my glory, which thou hast given me: for thou lovedst me before the foundation of the world.

Key Verse

Neither pray I for these alone, but for them also which shall believe on me through their word.

—John 17:20

Call in the New Testament

Unit 2: Jesus and Calls in His Ministry

Lessons 5–8

Lesson Aims

After participating in this lesson, each learner will be able to:

1. List Jesus' desires as expressed in His prayer.
2. Explain the intersection of the themes of suffering, unity, and witness in Jesus' final prayer.
3. Commit to adopting Jesus' prayer priorities as his or her own.

Lesson Outline

Introduction
- A. Why Don't They Come?
- B. Lesson Context

I. Different like Jesus (John 17:14-19)
- A. Kept from Evil (vv. 14-16)
  - *Stay in the Game*
- B. Sent to the World (vv. 17-19)

II. United as One (John 17:20-24)
- A. With One Another (vv. 20-23)
  - *Unify to Multiply*
- B. With Christ (v. 24)

Conclusion
- A. The Streisand Effect
- B. Prayer
- C. Thought to Remember

Introduction

A. Why Don't They Come?

In August 2018, the Pew Research Center published results of a survey on religious behaviors. The study had polled more than 1,300 individuals who identified their religious preference as "nothing in particular." Fifty-one percent of respondents explained their preference by saying, "I question a lot of religious teachings." In two separate questions, 47 percent said they were not involved because "I don't like the positions churches take on social/political issues," and 34 percent said, "I don't like religious organizations."

The survey results suggest that individuals who choose not to affiliate with any religious group do not view such gatherings as safe and welcoming places to explore personal religious beliefs and lifestyle choices.

While the results of this survey may not be surprising, they are nevertheless tragic. The church is the body of Christ and the vehicle through which God is working to reach a lost world. It can be discouraging to realize that many choose to avoid the church because they view it as irrelevant, or even as hostile, to their well-being. Yet this is not what Christ intended the church to be. Today's lesson explains why.

B. Lesson Context

Matthew 26:36-44; Mark 14:32-40; and Luke 22:39-46 give brief accounts of Jesus' prayer in the Garden of Gethsemane. Their focus is on His agonized petition that He might be spared the crucifixion. John's Gospel, by contrast, doesn't include that prayer. Instead, it features Jesus' lengthy and detailed prayer for His disciples.

That prayer comes at the end of a lengthy section known as the Farewell Address (John 13–17), the longest recorded speech by Jesus. After washing the disciples' feet and dismissing Judas into the night (13:1-30), Jesus told His confused followers that He would not be with them much longer (13:33). He gave them a "new commandment" to be followed after His departure from the world: "As I have loved you, . . . also love one another" (13:34).

The remainder of Jesus' goodbye speech builds on this theme by explaining how God would express His love for the disciples (examples: John 14:8-21; 15:26-27; 16:5-15), why "the world" would hate them (example: 15:18-25), what it means for Christians to love one another, and why it was essential to do so (17:20-24; see commentary below).

In the opening section of the prayer (John 17:1-13), Jesus reflected on His pending death and reminded the Father that the Son's mission would continue through the disciples. Therefore Jesus asked His heavenly Father to equip the disciples in certain ways so they could continue His work. The form and content of that equipping is the subject of today's text.

I. Different like Jesus

(John 17:14-19)

A. Kept from Evil (vv. 14-16)

14a. I have given them thy word.

This phrase summarizes Jesus' ministry to this point. God's *word* is the truth that Jesus has been teaching. In John's Gospel, this message focused particularly on God's revelation in Christ (John 1:14). He is superior to any other revelation, including the teachings of Moses (example: 1:17-18) and John the Baptist (example: 3:27-30).

14b. And the world hath hated them.

God loves *the world*—so much so that He gave His only Son so that believers could receive eternal life (John 3:15-16). Yet this love was and is largely unrequited, as the majority of people *hated* Jesus and those who believe in Him (3:17-21). All people are called to make a decision about Christ. Those who do not accept Him place themselves in the same category as the Pharisees, chief priests, and others who actively persecuted Jesus. There is no middle ground.

Knowing the truth about God is a great blessing, but it comes with a cost. Although the disciples had not been persecuted directly thus far, they were with Jesus on several occasions when His life was in peril (see John 7:1, 30; 8:58-59; 11:45-54). The story of the man born blind reveals that at least some people who associated with Jesus were threatened with, or may have actually experienced, excommunication from the synagogue (9:1-41). As the church was established (Acts 2) and Christianity began to spread throughout the Roman world, persecution became a universal experience (Acts 8:1; etc.).

> *What Do You Think?*
>
> In what ways can you prepare yourself for times of discrimination against Christians?
>
> *Digging Deeper*
>
> What situations call for passive acceptance (example: Matthew 27:14)? for self-defense or explanation (example: Acts 25:8)? for pushing back (example: Acts 16:37)? Explain.

14c. Because they are not of the world, even as I am not of the world.

The cause of the world's hatred for Jesus and His followers is stated in terms of group membership or identification: it is *because they are not of this world.* Their whole set of values was different (Ephesians 2:1-10).

Jesus had come down from the Father (John 3:13, 31-36) and was about to return to Heaven (13:33; 16:28). Unlike Christ, the disciples were natural human beings, made up of both human flesh and human spirit as all of this world are. But the disciples had been "born again" (3:3). Therefore, they were no longer recognized as family by the disbelieving world. The disciples had made themselves outsiders, citizens of Heaven who temporarily resided in a foreign land as unwelcome noncitizens (1 Peter 2:11).

15. I pray not that thou shouldest take them out of the world, but that thou shouldest keep them from the evil.

The disciples wanted to be wherever Jesus was (John 14). But they could not accompany Jesus in leaving *the world*, no matter how bad things

HOW TO SAY IT

Gethsemane	Geth-*sem*-uh-nee (*G* as in *get*).
Pharisees	*Fair*-ih-seez.
sanctification	*sank*-tuh-fuh-***kay***-shun.
Tertullian	Tur-*tull*-yun.

became. They needed to remain because they would be the vehicle through which others could hear the good news and receive salvation (15:26; 17:18, 20).

Jesus did ask, however, that they be kept *from the evil*—that is, the devil. He works through worldly people to intensify persecution and suffering in an effort to silence godly witnesses (John 15:20; 16:1-4; 1 John 3:8; Revelation 2:9-10; etc.). This divine protection did indeed come, but not in the form of stopping the sources of pain. Rather, it came by the strength of the Holy Spirit to endure (John 14:16, 25-27).

Stay in the Game

As a young man, I joined a recreational basketball league. One night, only five players showed up—the minimum needed to play. Near the end of the first half, I leaped for a rebound, got tangled with another player, and landed hard on the back of my head.

Today we understand the dangers of concussions, and we pull players off the court for their own safety. But every successful athlete understands that there are times to stay in the game when injured. I was groggy, but I didn't want to let my teammates down. I played the entire second half, and my team won a narrow victory.

Jesus knew His disciples would face hatred and pain, but it wasn't time to remove them from the world. They needed to keep serving Him and helping others. Do you ever feel like imploring the Lord to let you "sit this one out"? Are you willing to "stay in the game" anyway? See 1 Corinthians 4:11-13; 2 Corinthians 1:8-10. —D. F.

16. They are not of the world, even as I am not of the world.

The language of John 17:14c (above) is repeated for emphasis. Taken as something of a unit, 17:14-16 explains why Christians suffer, sometimes even to the point of death. In the early centuries of the church, passages such as this were used to support the argument that people who experience martyrdom receive special eternal blessings.

Today, these verses are sometimes cited as evidence that believers who are not experiencing suffering must be deficient in their faith in light of Jesus' comment that the world loves its own (15:19). The logic is that if you experience love from worldly people, then you must be one of them.

Jesus' statements should be taken not as abstract principles but rather as prophecies of realities. The original readers of this Gospel came to know persecution firsthand. Many believers today live in cultures where their faith is not legally protected; they experience persecution as a result. But we should not conclude from these verses either that (1) true believers will *only* experience persecution or that (2) *only* true believers will experience persecution. Jesus' larger point is that we should be prepared to continue to witness, no matter what. And the key to being able to do so is to focus on the fact that we *are not of the world.*

> *What Do You Think?*
>
> What personal deficiencies will you address to be better equipped to be *in* the world but not *of* the world?
>
> *Digging Deeper*
>
> Which of John 1:10; 15:19; 1 Corinthians 1:12; 5:9-11; 2 Corinthians 10:3-4; James 4:4; 2 Peter 1:4; 2:20; and 1 John 2:15-16 speak to you most clearly in this regard? Why?

B. Sent to the World (vv. 17-19)

17. Sanctify them through thy truth: thy word is truth.

The Greek verb translated *sanctify* means "to make holy or set apart." Things in the ancient world that were set apart were often found in temples or other sacred places. Jesus, however, asked God to sanctify the disciples themselves (compare 1 Corinthians 6:19-20). It was through their knowledge of *truth* that this sanctification would come. Such knowledge concerned faith in Jesus—faith that is based on evidence (John 14:11; 1 John 1:1-2; etc.). Jesus himself was and is both the *truth* (John 14:6) and the one who proclaimed the *word* of truth about God to the world (8:31-32). Jesus' life and words revealed God perfectly (14:9). Those who abandon falsehood to accept Christ and His words are set apart by their faith.

We can note in passing that sanctification has two aspects or phases. The first is the onetime event when an unbeliever joins the ranks of the saved (see 1 Corinthians 6:11); this may be called *initial sanctification.* The second phase can be termed *progressive sanctification* since it is a continuing transformation (2 Peter 3:18; 1 John 3:3; etc.).

> *What Do You Think?*
> How can you better demonstrate that God's truth has set you apart while avoiding giving an off-putting "holier than thou" impression in the process?
>
> *Digging Deeper*
> How do John 13:15; 1 Corinthians 11:1; Ephesians 5:1; Philippians 2:1-11; 3:17; Titus 2:6-8; and 1 Peter 2:21; 3:15 help you frame your answer?

18. As thou hast sent me into the world, even so have I also sent them into the world.

These words, spoken before the Great Commission (Matthew 28:18-20), shed further light on the mission of the disciples and the church. Jesus had been *sent* from Heaven to testify about God to a hostile *world* (John 1:10-11; 5:23-24, 36-38; 8:42-47; etc.). Jesus handed this mission on to His apostles, who were then *sent* in turn *into the world* to testify. The fact that the apostles were sent by Jesus provided them with a unique authority. For this reason, rejecting what the apostles say about God is equivalent to rejecting what Jesus says (compare Luke 9:1-6; 2 Corinthians 1:1; 5:20; Ephesians 1:1; 6:20; etc.).

19. And for their sakes I sanctify myself, that they also might be sanctified through the truth.

This verse reemphasizes John 17:17, above. Because Christ is God incarnate, in one sense He is sanctified just by definition. Jesus, however, was likely referring to the example of holy living that He set before the disciples throughout His ministry. Jesus is consistently portrayed as consumed by a desire to do anything and everything that God has called Him to do (2:17; etc.). Indeed, Jesus' very sustenance was "to do the will of him that sent me, and to finish his work" (4:34).

II. United as One

(John 17:20-24)

A. With One Another (vv. 20-23)

20. Neither pray I for these alone, but for them also which shall believe on me through their word.

This verse extends the scope of Jesus' commission to include all believers in all times and places.

21a. That they all may be one; as thou, Father, art in me, and I in thee, that they also may be one in us.

Unity is essential to Jesus' vision for the church (compare 1 Corinthians 12:12-13; Galatians 3:28; Ephesians 4:11-13; etc.). His prayer for future followers is tied to a statement about His own identity: Christ and the *Father* are *one,* and therefore believers should be united as *one.*

The focus here is less on Christ's identity with the Father as members of the Trinity and more on the notion that Jesus always acts in a way that shows that He is united with God in essence and purpose. Seeing Jesus is equivalent to seeing the Father (John 14:9-12).

Unify to Multiply

It was a beautiful day, and I wanted to be outdoors, not painting the basement. My wife and I had moved into the house a few weeks before. Now that the boxes were unloaded, this job remained.

I had figured it would take several days to paint the ceiling, walls, and trim. We had bought the paint, readied our drop cloths and paintbrushes, and prepared to tackle the task ourselves.

Then our friends showed up. Not just a few friends—nine of them, including people we had never met. These unified coworkers dove enthusiastically into the work, all of us talking and laughing as we went. By late afternoon, the entire basement was painted, and the supplies were cleaned up. My wife and I had time to enjoy a walk.

What happens when Jesus' disciples serve in unity? Work gets done. Friendships are forged. God is honored. Blessings are multiplied. Do your relationships with others demonstrate God's call to multiply, not divide?

—D. F.

What Do You Think?

What three specific things can you begin doing to foster the kind of unity among believers that Christ desires?

Digging Deeper

Frame your three responses in terms of what you can do locally within your church and how you can contribute nationally and internationally, one each.

21b. That the world may believe that thou hast sent me.

The goal of the disciples' unity is effective witness, the result of which will be others drawn to Christ. Christ intends that the disciples obey His command to set themselves apart from the world in their unity in this regard.

22a. And the glory which thou gavest me I have given them.

Glory here refers to God's divine nature and attributes. Christ and the Father are one by their very nature (Hebrews 1:3). The human Jesus has illustrated this by doing and saying exactly what God the Father desired. Now He passes that glory along to all present and future disciples (*them*).

The glory that Jesus passes along does not, of course, include what are called God's incommunicable attributes—things of His nature that belong to Him and Him alone (example: self-existence, John 8:58).

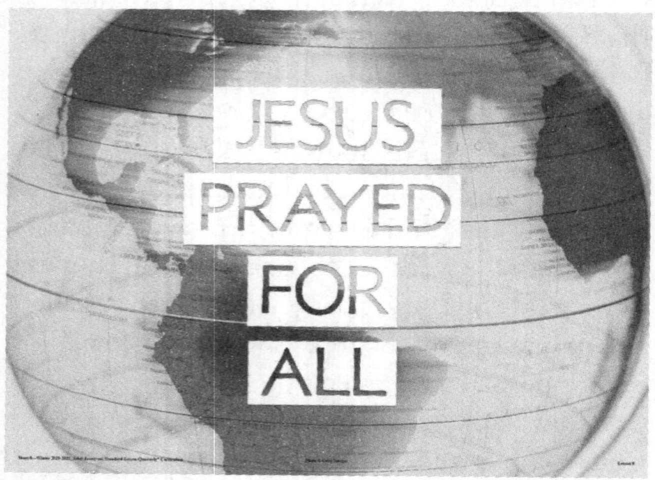

Visual for Lesson 8. *Ask learners to hold up smartphones as you point to this visual and ask, "Should I just pray for everyone in your contact lists?"*

22b. That they may be one, even as we are one.

Unity is described here as a result of the gift of John 17:21a, above. Elsewhere, unity is a command (example: Ephesians 4:3). The Farewell Address began with Jesus' washing the disciples' feet and telling them to follow His example in serving one another (John 13:2-17). Jesus also commanded three times that believers love one another as Jesus himself loved them (13:14; 15:12, 17). The love command is so significant that people can recognize us as disciples by observing whether we show love for other believers (13:35).

In Jesus' view, even the most hostile opponents of the faith should be struck by the love and unity that prevails among His followers. The love of the disciples is to continue as a sign to an unbelieving world about the good news of Jesus Christ.

23. I in them, and thou in me, that they may be made perfect in one; and that the world may know that thou hast sent me, and hast loved them, as thou hast loved me.

The church's unity must be *perfect* in the sense that it lacks nothing. But we know that unbreakable unity is not typically experienced anywhere. Yet this is the very reason why it can serve as supernatural evidence of the nature of Jesus.

Unity can only attract *the world* if it is more than superficial. It must go beyond the camaraderie that worldly people experience. It must rise to the level of an unwavering commitment to God and His church. When broken people are redeemed, brought together by God, and united in a common purpose, unbelievers must conclude that something special is happening!

B. With Christ (v. 24)

24. Father, I will that they also, whom thou hast given me, be with me where I am; that they may behold my glory, which thou hast given me: for thou lovedst me before the foundation of the world.

Jesus has already told His disciples that He was returning to Heaven and that He would prepare a place for them there (John 14:1-3). He wanted them to leave the fallen world eventually in order to be in that place of peace with Him. Once we arrive there, we will *behold* Christ's *glory* in the sense that we ourselves will witness what Jesus has been claiming to be true about His relationship with the Father (compare 1 John 3:2). The full extent the Father's love for the Son will then be clearest.

Conclusion

A. The Streisand Effect

Marketing companies are becoming increasingly interested in a phenomenon known as the Streisand Effect. This term is based on the name of singer/actress Barbra Streisand, and it refers to an episode in which she was involved in 2003.

A photographer was contracted to take a series of photographs that would document patterns of coastline erosion throughout the state. When Streisand learned that these included one picture of her seaside Malibu mansion, she sued the photographer to have its posting removed. Before the lawsuit was filed, the photo in question had been downloaded only six times, including two downloads by Streisand's own attorneys; but when the story hit the media, the picture was viewed by 420,000 curious web surfers within 30 days! This incident is now cited as a classic illustration of the principle of "psychological reactance," which means that an attempt to suppress information tends to increase people's desire to access and share it.

While the internet is a relatively new phenomenon on the time line of history, the Streisand Effect is not—people have always been curious to learn new information, especially when it seems to be available only to a small number of people.

The Christian apologist Tertullian (AD 160–220) realized something of a parallel to this principle in his famous observation that "the blood of the martyrs is [the] seed [of the church]" (*Apology* 50). Tertullian observed that public persecutions against the church by the Roman government had led even more people to become curious about the faith. Rome actually made the world aware of Christianity and thereby encouraged people to explore this new and emerging religion. Those who looked into the church's beliefs and practices were impressed by the conviction and unity demonstrated by believers. The result was that the church grew during periods of persecution.

Against this backdrop, Jesus' prayer raises important questions for the church today: In a world where many people do not participate in church because they think there is nothing of value there, what would happen if they actually "looked under the hood"? Would they discover that, contrary to what they have been told, the church is a place of remarkable unity and love? Would they be forced to abandon their beliefs that Christians are legalistic and thereby be drawn to the spirit of love that exists among us? Or would encounters with Christians reinforce their belief that the church is not a safe place?

Our passage for today highlights several key themes that run through John's Gospel, two of which are particularly significant. First, Jesus stresses His own oneness with the Father. Christ demonstrated this unity through absolute obedience to God the Father in His resolve to fulfill the Father's mission of offering salvation. Second, Jesus presented His relationship with the Father as a model for the way His disciples should relate to one another. Christians are to be completely united with both Christ and one another so that Christ's mission can continue through the work of the church. It can't happen any other way.

What Do You Think?

What's the first thing you should do were you to find yourself in a situation where Christians are disunited, at odds with one another?

Digging Deeper

How should your reaction differ in situations that involve doctrinal essentials versus those that don't? Why?

B. Prayer

Father, help us to love one another the way You love us so that the world can see You at work through us. In Jesus' name we pray. Amen.

C. Thought to Remember

Christians are one in Christ Jesus.

Involvement Learning

Enhance your lesson with KJV Bible Student *(from your curriculum supplier) and the reproducible activity page (at www.standardlesson.com or in the back of the* KJV Standard Lesson Commentary Deluxe Edition*).*

Into the Lesson

Place four chairs in the front of the classroom, facing the front of the room, and ask a volunteer to come sit in each one. Attach one each of the following labels to the backs of the chairs so that the class can see them but the volunteers can't:

Attorney / Elected Official / Union Negotiator / Real Estate Agent

Have the four volunteers take turns asking questions of the class in order to determine what their labels say.

After several minutes, reveal answers to the volunteers and ask the class what these professions have in common. If no one gets the answer, say, "Although they are much different from one another, each of these acts on behalf of someone else to achieve something for them—an intercessor. Today we're going to look at the greatest intercessor of all."

Alternative. Distribute copies of the "What I Pray for Most" exercise on the activity page, which can be downloaded. Allow one minute to complete; then call for volunteers to share the entries on their lists. Make a transition by saying, "Today as we look at a prayer priority of Jesus, it will be interesting to compare and contrast it with our typical prayers."

Into the Word

Distribute handouts (you prepare) featuring five blank rows intersected by two blank columns, one column headed *Verse Reference* and the other headed *What Jesus Prayed For.* Ask a volunteer to read the lesson text out loud slowly while class members listen for answers to the blanks on their charts. Divide the class into groups to compare and complete their charts as necessary.

Verse references (which you may decide to include on the chart) and answers (which you will not include) are as follows:

- Verse 15: Protect my disciples from the evil one.
- Verse 17: Sanctify them (set them apart) by the knowledge of Your truth.
- Verses 20-23: Create unity among my believers so that the world will know I was sent by You, Father.
- Verse 21: May my believers be unified with You and me, Father, as well as with each other.
- Verse 24: I want my believers to join us someday for eternity.

Ask the groups to report what they've written, making sure all the blanks are completed correctly. Then point to a list of adjectives you've written on the board while groups worked:

surprising / inspiring / comforting / challenging / unattainable / difficult

Ask which of these adjectives the class members would choose to describe the prayer of Jesus and what adjectives might they add.

Option 1. If you used the "What I Pray for Most" exercise on the activity page, distribute copies of the "The Prayer Requests of Jesus" exercise from that same page for learners to complete as indicated in study pairs. After three minutes, compare and contrast the results of the two exercises.

Option 2. Form study pairs to look at Jesus' prayer another way by completing the "Three Important Themes" exercise on the activity page. Correct omissions in the ensuing whole-class discussion.

Into Life

Ask, "What can we include in our prayers to make them more like today's prayer of Jesus?" Write answers on the board as learners suggest them. Then send members back to their original groups. Ask each group to compose a prayer that includes some of these elements. Close with a prayer time in which a representative from each group prays the prayer their group has written.

Called to Prophesy

Devotional Reading: Joel 2:28-32
Background Scripture: Luke 2:36-38; Acts 1:12-14; 2:16-21; 21:8-9

Luke 2:36-38

**36 And there was one Anna, a prophetess,
the daughter of Phanuel, of the tribe of Aser:
she was of a great age, and had lived with an
husband seven years from her virginity;
37 And she was a widow of about fourscore and four years, which departed not from
the temple, but served God with fastings and
prayers night and day.
38 And she coming in that instant gave
thanks likewise unto the Lord, and spake of
him to all them that looked for redemption in
Jerusalem.**

Acts 2:16-21

**16 But this is that which was spoken by the
prophet Joel;
17 And it shall come to pass in the last days,
saith God, I will pour out of my Spirit upon
all flesh: and your sons and your daughters
shall prophesy, and your young men shall see
visions, and your old men shall dream dreams:
18 And on my servants and on my handmaidens I will pour out in those days of my
Spirit; and they shall prophesy:
19 And I will shew wonders in heaven above,
and signs in the earth beneath; blood, and fire,
and vapour of smoke:
20 The sun shall be turned into darkness,
and the moon into blood, before that great and
notable day of the Lord come:
21 And it shall come to pass, that whosoever shall call on the name of the Lord shall
be saved.**

Acts 21:8-9

**8 And the next day we that were of Paul's
company departed, and came unto Caesarea:
and we entered into the house of Philip the
evangelist, which was one of the seven; and
abode with him.
9 And the same man had four daughters, virgins, which did prophesy.**

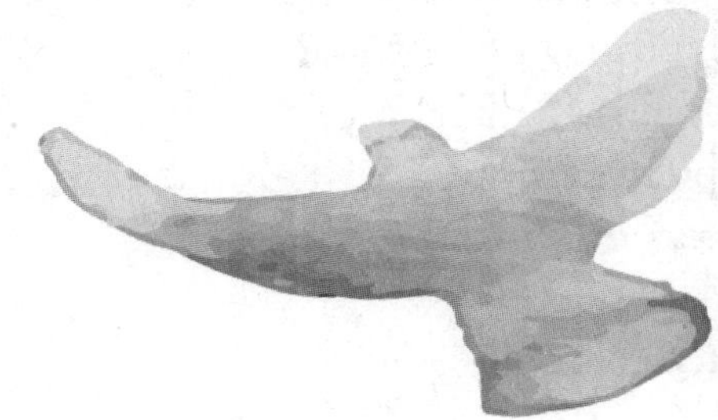

Key Verse

It shall come to pass in the last days, saith God, I will pour out of my Spirit upon all flesh: and your sons and your daughters shall prophesy, and your young men shall see visions, and your old men shall dream dreams. —**Acts 2:17**

Call in the New Testament

Unit 3: The Call of Women

Lessons 9–13

Lesson Aims

After participating in this lesson, each learner will be able to:

1. Summarize the text quoted from Joel.
2. Explain the significance of fulfillment of Joel's prophecy.
3. Repent of valuing the Spirit's influence in some people more than in others.

Lesson Outline

Introduction
- A. Willing to Tell Others
- B. Lesson Context: Judaism
- C. Lesson Context: Paganism

I. In the Temple (Luke 2:36-38)
- A. Faithful Widow (vv. 36-37)
  - *My Praying Mother*
- B. Expressive Witness (v. 38)

II. In Jerusalem (Acts 2:16-21)
- A. Unbiased Spirit (vv. 16-18)
- B. Wonders and Signs (vv. 19-21)

III. In Caesarea (Acts 21:8-9)
- A. Evangelist Father (v. 8)
- B. Prophetesses (v. 9)
  - *Prayerful Impressions*

Conclusion
- A. Gifted Women
- B. Prayer
- C. Thought to Remember

Introduction

A. Willing to Tell Others

Consider the following actual and planned ministries. (Some of those mentioned work in dangerous settings, so no names are used.)

- Woman A planned to go to a country so remote and so expensive to get to that no missionary organization would sponsor the idea. She went anyway.
- Woman B, a missionary in the Far East, is age 91—and still working.
- Woman C, a tiny but bold person, rescues children in danger of sex trafficking.
- Woman D, against the advice of others in a certain foreign country, visited Buddhist temples and spent time talking about Jesus with the monks there.
- Woman E deliberately hires non-Christians to work for her Christian ministry in order to influence and help them.
- Woman F has plans to minister to shrine and temple prostitutes. (Yes, there's still such a thing.)
- Woman G would sing in bars—free of charge—if management would let her include a Christian song with each set.

We might wonder at the apparent lack of preparation of some of the above. But God isn't interested in perfection—He's interested in willingness. Where are you in your preparation for ministry? Are you waiting until you're perfect? If so, you will never answer God's call when it comes! Few of us will preach to massive crowds or build a megachurch. But through His Spirit, God recruits people for amazing assignments nonetheless. This lesson touches on just a few examples.

B. Lesson Context: Judaism

The five lessons of this quarter's final unit look at examples of faithful women in the first-century church. All three of today's lesson texts come from the author Luke. Analysis of his two books (Luke and Acts) shows that he had special regard for women (Luke 7:11-14; 10:38-42; 13:11-13; Acts 1:14; 16:13; etc.). These texts and others affords an opportunity to celebrate stories that are sometimes overlooked. These women, named or not, played important roles in the ministry of Jesus that continued in the church.

The Jews of Luke's day lived not only in Palestine but also in enclaves of Greek and Roman cities throughout the empire (examples: Acts 2:5; 6:9; 14:1). Jews maintained their own practices regarding women's roles, as directed by their understanding of Scripture and of family structure from ancient times. In general, a Jewish female was attached to a man who served as her provider, protector, and authority. Normally, a father held this role for a daughter and a husband for a wife.

Devout Jews honored God's concern for widows (see Deuteronomy 27:19). These often were older women who had no opportunities to remarry or be employed. For them, the likelihood of having a male provider was limited, necessitating help from the community (compare Acts 6:1-7; James 1:27).

Women were allowed to attend synagogue gatherings, but only as observers. They were usually seated in a balcony or in some other section apart from men. The temple in Jerusalem that was rebuilt after the exile had a courtyard for women, beyond which women were not allowed.

C. Lesson Context: Paganism

Jewish communities experienced varying degrees of influence from Greek and Roman cultures. As the Roman Empire expanded, Romans brought their traditions to their conquered peoples. Roman society was dominated by men at all levels: business, politics, government, and military. But some women gained influence by their association with powerful men. In particular, some wives of the emperors achieved notoriety and celebrity. Sometimes mothers, wives, or sisters would even appear on the coinage of an emperor.

Women also played an important role in the civic religion of Rome, with the revered Vestal Virgins recognized as maintaining the ancient traditions of the city. However, the primary sphere of influence for Roman women was within the home, where they managed the household and saw to the proper raising of children. The Romans idealized the "matron," the upper-class woman who managed her home well and remained chaste, modest, and loyal to her husband (in many cases, in spite of his own lack of sexual fidelity).

Although the Greeks had been conquered by the Romans, Greek culture survived and remained influential in reshaping Roman society. Greek culture, like that of the Romans, was male-dominated; the home was considered to be the proper realm of women. The Greeks, however, were not as uniformly tradition-bound as the Romans in this regard. Some Greek women were people of business, and their wealth gave them influence in their communities (compare Acts 17:12).

Even so, relationships within families varied in pagan cultures. Some husbands loved and respected their wives and saw them as equal partners in life. Other men had little affection for their wives and might abuse or ignore them, with few consequences from society outside the home. Wives often tolerated sexual infidelity by men, but women who were unfaithful were liable to divorce, disgrace, or even death. No one considered this to be a double standard, but simply the proper state of things in society. The prominence of even a few women in the New Testament accounts is therefore both surprising and instructive.

I. In the Temple

(Luke 2:36-38)

When Jesus was eight days old, Joseph and Mary took Him to the Jerusalem temple to

HOW TO SAY IT

Aser	*A*-ser.
Assyrians	Uh-*sear*-e-unz.
Caesarea Maritima	Sess-uh-*ree*-uh Mar-uh-*tee*-muh.
Ethiopian	E-thee-*o*-pee-un (*th* as in *thin*).
eunuch	*you*-nick.
Huldah	*Hull*-duh.
Isaiah	Eye-*zay*-uh.
Messiah	Meh-*sigh*-uh.
Pentecost	*Pent*-ih-kost.
Phanuel	Fuh-*nyoo*-el.
Samaritans	Suh-*mare*-uh-tunz.

consecrate Him as required by Scripture (Exodus 13:2; see Luke 2:21-24). In the temple courts, the little family encountered two people who were waiting for the Messiah (Luke 2:25, 36). One was a widow named Anna, considered next.

A. Faithful Widow (vv. 36-37)

36a. And there was one Anna, a prophetess, the daughter of Phanuel, of the tribe of Aser.

Anna is a Greek form of the name Hannah, the mother of the prophet Samuel (1 Samuel 1:20). Hannah's prayer of thanksgiving for Samuel (2:1-10) echoes throughout Mary's song of praise (Luke 1:46-55). Luke likely appreciated this further connection to that time past when a longed-for baby boy was born.

A prophet or a *prophetess* is someone chosen by God to speak for Him as He brings something to mind. In the Old Testament, four women are designated as being prophetesses: Miriam (Exodus 15:20), Deborah (Judges 4:4), Huldah (2 Kings 22:14), and the unnamed wife of Isaiah (Isaiah 8:3). Though their words are not recorded at length like those of Moses or Jeremiah, these women served in the same ways by communicating what God revealed to them for the people to hear.

The mention of Anna's father, *Phanuel,* suggests that he was a well-remembered resident of Jerusalem as Luke wrote this account. His name means "face of God," or "presence of God." This implies his religious dedication, a faithfulness that was passed down to his daughter. Fittingly, his daughter would see God face-to-face when she met the baby Jesus.

The tribe of Aser (Asher; see Exodus 1:1-4) was one of the 10 northern tribes destroyed by the Assyrians in 722 BC. Though many were taken into captivity at that time, others were left behind. Some became the people known as Samaritans through intermarriage with non-Israelites. Anna's family apparently was left in the land but did not intermarry with other peoples, thus remaining recognizably as being from a tribe.

36b-37a. She was of a great age, and had lived with an husband seven years from her virginity. And she was a widow of about fourscore and four years.

Fourscore and four years can refer either to Anna's age (84 years old) or to the approximate amount of time she had been widowed. Either possibility means that she was old enough to remember when the Romans conquered the Jewish homeland in 63 BC.

37b. Which departed not from the temple, but served God with fastings and prayers night and day.

Rather than find a new spouse, Anna devoted herself to spiritual service within the temple. She fasted (probably weekly) and prayed (surely daily). Though she literally may not ever have left *the temple,* more likely the language is meant to emphasize her continual devotion to serving *God.*

> *What Do You Think?*
> What role should fasting play in your own devotional life? Why do you say that?
> *Digging Deeper*
> How do the precedents in Esther 4:15-16; Acts 13:2-3; 14:23 help frame your answer?

My Praying Mother

My mother, Helen, was only 46 when my dad died. At the time, she was a nominal Christian. But a few years later, she experienced transformative renewal in Christ.

One demonstrable change was my mother's commitment to prayer. She made two lifestyle changes regarding prayer. The first was to pray for an hour a day. The second was to establish a literal prayer closet in an old storage space. Mom cleared stuff out to make room for a small table and a lamp. A little door ensured privacy. And a kneeling posture was required—there wasn't room to stand! As long as she lived in that house, Mom faithfully sought the Lord and made daily intercession for others in her prayer closet.

Where are the Annas—and the Helens—of our generation? Will we also faithfully serve the Lord with fasting and prayer? —A. S.

B. Expressive Witness (v. 38)

38. And she coming in that instant gave thanks likewise unto the Lord, and spake of

him to all them that looked for redemption in Jerusalem.

Anna's words reveal that she had messianic expectations for Jesus (compare Luke 2:30-32). Recognizing redemption to be at hand was a fulfillment of prophecy (Isaiah 52:9). However, what is meant precisely by *redemption in Jerusalem* is not clear. To redeem means to "buy back," or "deliver from danger" (Leviticus 25:29, 48; Hebrews 9:12). Anna could, like many others, have national politics in mind: redemption would mean that Judea, like Israel of old, would be its own sovereign nation again.

That would have had special appeal because Anna was old enough to remember when Rome became the official power in Judea. Memories of life before Rome were enticing, even if those times were less than peaceful. Or she could have the more spiritual redemption from sins in mind.

The Spirit did not fill in any incomplete understanding Anna may have had regarding Jesus' role. This should be a comfort to us all, as we each know only "in part" (1 Corinthians 13:9). God sees fit to use whatever faithful understanding we have to witness to others, just as Anna witnessed to Mary and Joseph that day in the temple.

What Do You Think?

If you are a "senior citizen," what methods of witness and service can you focus on that those of a younger generation might not do as well at?

Digging Deeper

If you are not a senior citizen, what can you do to support their witness and service?

II. In Jerusalem

(Acts 2:16-21)

Acts 2 continues the story of Jesus' followers after His resurrection and ascension. A group of about 120 remained in Jerusalem, including the apostles (minus Judas); Jesus' brothers; and a group of women that included Mary, Jesus' mother (Acts 1:14-15).

On Pentecost, 50 days after the Passover, the Holy Spirit descended on this group in spectacular fashion (Acts 2:1-4). This dramatic event drew a diverse crowd as an audience for Peter (2:5-11). It was an ideal setting to explain the significance of the death and resurrection of Jesus.

Visual for Lessons 3 & 9. *Have this visual on display as a backdrop as you distribute copies of the "Calling Intersections" exercise from the activity page.*

A. Unbiased Spirit (vv. 16-18)

16. But this is that which was spoken by the prophet Joel.

The word *this* refers to the speaking and hearing in the native languages of those gathered (Acts 2:11). By way of explanation, Peter's quotation *spoken by the prophet Joel* that follows comes from Joel 2:28-32.

17-18. And it shall come to pass in the last days, saith God, I will pour out of my Spirit upon all flesh: and your sons and your daughters shall prophesy, and your young men shall see visions, and your old men shall dream dreams: and on my servants and on my handmaidens I will pour out in those days of my Spirit; and they shall prophesy.

The prophet Joel, about whom we know virtually nothing, had foreseen the day of the Lord centuries earlier. That day would be a time when God would intervene dramatically in the history of Israel (see Joel 2:1). *The last days* refers to the beginning of the final era in God's plan for humanity. We have been in these last days for some 2,000 years now (Hebrews 1:1-2; 1 Peter 1:20; 1 John 2:18). A widespread distribution of God's *Spirit* would be a sign that the new era had dawned.

The inclusion of Gentiles was anticipated by the phrase *all flesh* (compare Galatians 3:26-29). Then, lest he be misunderstood, Joel inclusively specified both genders and the spectrum of age groups as conduits for God's communication. Those whom society or culture previously viewed as being ineligible to speak on behalf of God would be empowered to do just that!

Joel's prophecy reveals that God's eligibility criteria are not necessarily what people expect. Peter spoke as if this prophecy was fulfilled, implying that some of the female followers of Jesus already had received this gift.

What Do You Think?

How should you react if someone comes to you claiming to have received a message from God in a dream or a vision?

Digging Deeper

Which texts help best in framing your decision: Acts 9:10-12; 10:3-19; 16:9-10; 18:9-10; 26:19; 2 Corinthians 11:12-15; Colossians 2:18; 2 Peter 2:1; 1 John 4:1-3; 2 John 9; Jude 8; Revelation 22:18? Others?

B. Wonders and Signs (vv. 19-21)

19-20. And I will shew wonders in heaven above, and signs in the earth beneath; blood, and fire, and vapour of smoke: the sun shall be turned into darkness, and the moon into blood, before that great and notable day of the Lord come.

The specific *wonders* and *signs* noted here did not occur on the Day of Pentecost. Even so, there were supernatural sounds and visual phenomena that accompanied the coming of the Holy Spirit (Acts 2:2-3). This part of the prophecy may point ahead to the second coming of Christ (compare Luke 21:25-28).

21. And it shall come to pass, that whosoever shall call on the name of the Lord shall be saved.

The events on the Day of Pentecost were not primarily about the miraculous gifting of the Holy Spirit or about the inclusion of both genders in prophetic ministry. The scope of salvation is more than welcoming men and women equally, and much more than the ability to prophesy. Rather, the primary issue is the announcement of salvation to all who *call on the name of the Lord* (see Romans 10:9-13). Peter himself did not at this point fully understand the sweeping nature of the word *whosoever,* given his growing understanding in Acts 10:1–11:18.

Not included in today's printed text is the crowd's reaction of asking what they must do and Peter's calling them to repent and be baptized (Acts 2:38).

III. In Caesarea

(Acts 21:8-9)

The following brief account occurred near the end of Paul's third missionary journey, in AD 58. Thus more than two decades had passed since the Day of Pentecost. At the point where we join the narrative, Paul and companions were nearing the end of their multi-stop sea voyage.

A. Evangelist Father (v. 8)

8. And the next day we that were of Paul's company departed, and came unto Caesarea: and we entered into the house of Philip the evangelist, which was one of the seven; and abode with him.

Luke, the author of this narrative, was a traveling companion of Paul (see Colossians 4:14) and was with him at the time of this incident. This is indicated by use of the word *we.*

In reading of the arrival *of Paul's company . . . unto Caesarea,* we take care to observe that this is the coastal city of Caesarea Maritima, not the inland town of Caesarea Philippi (Matthew 16:13; etc.). Caesarea Maritima served as a Roman administrative center and military headquarters. About 60 miles northwest of Jerusalem, this city figures prominently in the book of Acts (see Acts 9:30; 10:1, 24; 11:11; 12:19; 18:22; 23:33; etc.).

Philip the evangelist (who is not to be confused with the apostle Philip) lived in Caesarea. He is one of the "seven men of honest report, full of the Holy Ghost and wisdom" chosen for the ministry described in Acts 6:1-6. He later crossed cultural boundaries to preach the gospel to Samaritans (8:4-25), and then to an Ethiopian eunuch (8:26-40). Philip's home became a way station for Paul as he journeyed to Jerusalem for the final time.

What Do You Think?

What do the changing roles of Philip the evangelist (Acts 6:1-6; 8:4-7, 26-40; and 21:8) teach you about how to react to God's changing calls on your life?

Digging Deeper

In what ways does the further consideration of Stephen's changing roles (Acts 6–7) cause you to modify your answer, if at all?

B. Prophetesses (v. 9)

9. And the same man had four daughters, virgins, which did prophesy.

The description of Philip's *four daughters* as *virgins* indicates their status as being unmarried (compare 1 Corinthians 7:34). As such, they lived in their father's house (see Lesson Context: Judaism), where Paul was staying.

The four daughters *which did prophesy* and their evangelist father were likely well-known to Luke's readers and were celebrated as servants among fellow Christians in the area. Although this is a reasonable conclusion by inference, nothing further is recorded of Philip and his daughters.

What Do You Think?

In what ways can you better encourage fellow believers to use their spiritual gifts?

Digging Deeper

Are the best ways to encourage women to do so the same best ways to encourage men? Why, or why not?

Prayerful Impressions

Several years ago, Leonie joined our church staff as missions minister. She often has occasion to share a Scripture that addresses a situation; along with that may come a perception or challenge. When I asked her how this process works, she shared that as she enters into a time of prayer, she asks, "Lord, what do You want to say?" As she waits, Leonie is often impressed by everyday images or word pictures—along the lines of Jesus' parables—that may provide insight and hope for people and their circumstances.

If those individuals are present, Leonie strives to present her impressions in such a manner that it may be God's way of speaking to them. And she checks that her words are based on and consistent with Scripture, which is God's primary way of communicating with us, of course.

When you pray, do you expect God to listen and answer? —A. S.

Conclusion

A. Gifted Women

An aged widow. A group of women who had followed Jesus and remained in Jerusalem after His ascension. A band of four unmarried sisters. The New Testament offers these as examples of first-century women who were endowed with the gift of prophecy. Important questions exist regarding whether the spiritual gift of prophecy continues yet today (compare Zechariah 13:1-6; 1 Corinthians 13:8-12; Hebrews 1:1-2). But those questions, as important as they are, are not the focus of this lesson.

The focus, rather, is on using one's giftedness in answering God's call to ministry. As one observer put it, "When the church is working properly, every woman as well as every man will be using at least one spiritual gift in ministry to others in the body of Christ" (see also 1 Corinthians 12:1-11 and 1 Peter 4:10).

B. Prayer

Father, we thank You for the prophetic voices You have given to Your people. We thank You for the examples of Anna, the Pentecost women, and the daughters of Philip as faithful people who served You. May we be as faithful! We pray in the name of Jesus, in whom we are one. Amen.

C. Thought to Remember

God gifts people for ministry according to His will and plans, not ours.

Involvement Learning

Enhance your lesson with KJV Bible Student *(from your curriculum supplier) and the reproducible activity page (at www.standardlesson.com or in the back of the* KJV Standard Lesson Commentary Deluxe Edition*).*

Into the Lesson

Write these six nouns on the board, on two separate lines as shown here:

Summons / Bidding / Invitation

Bequest / Endowment / Grant

Inform the class that you are looking for two synonyms or near synonyms, one for the first line of words and another for the second line of words. As learners call out responses, write them on the board. Do not, however, indicate whether the answers are right or wrong.

After there are no more responses, work back through the synonyms your learners proposed and have them vote on which are best fits—two words, one for each line. (Final expected responses are *call* for the first line and *gift* for the second line.) If learners seem stumped at any point, give the hint that each word you're looking for has only four letters.

Option. Before class begins, place on chairs copies of the "His Plan, Not Ours" exercise from the activity page, which you can download. Learners can begin considering it as they arrive.

Begin a transition to Bible study by asking, "Speaking in a secular, nonbiblical sense, what's the relationship between the concepts of *gift* and *call*?" (Expect to hear words such as *talent, aptitude,* and *ability* explored.) Complete the transition to Bible study by asking, "Speaking in a biblical sense, what's the relationship between the concepts of *gift* and *call*?" Do not react with either approval or disapproval to the responses; instead, merely summarize those responses on the board for further use as the lesson progresses.

Into the Word

Make arrangements in advance to have someone play and dress the part of an elderly Luke, who arrives at this point to read aloud the lesson text. As your Luke finishes and turns his back to depart, implore him to stay a bit longer and consent to an interview. Use the following list of questions (and/or others of your own devising) in your interview; be sure to give your Luke the same list in advance for his preparation.

1–As you think back on these three episodes, what common elements do you see?

2–Why are those common elements important?

3–In what ways do those three episodes diverge from one another?

4–What is the significance of those divergences?

5–Given your expert knowledge of the Old Testament, what surprised you, and why?

6–What didn't surprise you, and why?

Option. Have the man portraying Luke stay a few more minutes to take questions from your class, by prior agreement.

Return to the listing of the relationships between the concepts of *gift* and *call,* which you left on the board; work back through the list for corrections or improvements that you or your learners see to be biblically necessary.

Into Life

Have students pair off and discuss (1) ways that Christians sometimes value the Spirit's influence in some of their fellow believers more than in others and (2) how to correct this. Reconvene after eight minutes for whole-class discussion.

Divide into groups of no more than five each and call for volunteers to (1) thank God that He chooses all believers to do His will in diverse ways to reflect the unity of the church, (2) confess tendencies to value the Spirit's influence in some people more than in others, and (3) ask for forgiveness for undervaluing contributions of fellow Christians.

Option. Distribute copies of the "Calling Intersections" exercise from the activity page for learners to complete in pairs as indicated.

Called to Testify

Devotional Reading: John 1:37-51
Background Scripture: John 1:37-51; 4:25-42

John 4:25-42

25 The woman saith unto him, I know that Messias cometh, which is called Christ: when he is come, he will tell us all things.

26 Jesus saith unto her, I that speak unto thee am he.

27 And upon this came his disciples, and marvelled that he talked with the woman: yet no man said, What seekest thou? or, Why talkest thou with her?

28 The woman then left her waterpot, and went her way into the city, and saith to the men,

29 Come, see a man, which told me all things that ever I did: is not this the Christ?

30 Then they went out of the city, and came unto him.

31 In the mean while his disciples prayed him, saying, Master, eat.

32 But he said unto them, I have meat to eat that ye know not of.

33 Therefore said the disciples one to another, Hath any man brought him ought to eat?

34 Jesus saith unto them, My meat is to do the will of him that sent me, and to finish his work.

35 Say not ye, There are yet four months, and then cometh harvest? behold, I say unto you, Lift up your eyes, and look on the fields; for they are white already to harvest.

36 And he that reapeth receiveth wages, and gathereth fruit unto life eternal: that both he that soweth and he that reapeth may rejoice together.

37 And herein is that saying true, One soweth, and another reapeth.

38 I sent you to reap that whereon ye bestowed no labour: other men laboured, and ye are entered into their labours.

39 And many of the Samaritans of that city believed on him for the saying of the woman, which testified, He told me all that ever I did.

40 So when the Samaritans were come unto him, they besought him that he would tarry with them: and he abode there two days.

41 And many more believed because of his own word;

42 And said unto the woman, Now we believe, not because of thy saying: for we have heard him ourselves, and know that this is indeed the Christ, the Saviour of the world.

Key Verse

Many of the Samaritans of that city believed on him for the saying of the woman, which testified, He told me all that ever I did. **—John 4:39**

CALL IN THE NEW TESTAMENT

Unit 3: The Call of Women

LESSONS 9–13

LESSON AIMS

After participating in this lesson, each learner will be able to:

1. Summarize the impact of the Samaritan woman's witness.

2. Explain the sense and reference of Jesus' illustration in John 4:35.

3. Identify elements of Jesus' approach to evangelism that he or she will use.

LESSON OUTLINE

Introduction
- A. Unnamed but Not Unimportant
- B. Lesson Context

I. A Woman's Declaration (John 4:25-30)
- A. Messiah Revealed (vv. 25-26)
- B. Disciples Startled (v. 27)
- C. City Challenged (vv. 28-30)

II. A Crop Prepared (John 4:31-38)
- A. Spiritual Food (vv. 31-33)
- B. Spiritual Harvest (vv. 34-35)
- C. Spiritual Reward (vv. 36-38)
  Speaking to be Understood

III. A Community Transformed (John 4:39-42)
- A. The Woman's Testimony (v. 39)
- B. The Samaritans' Request (v. 40)
- C. The People's Belief (vv. 41-42)
  Drawn by a Friend's Words

Conclusion
- A. Women of Faith
- B. Prayer
- C. Thought to Remember

Introduction

A. Unnamed but Not Unimportant

The American Midwest is one of the most productive agricultural regions in the world. Large acreage produces tremendous yields as farmers use state-of-the-art seeds, fertilizers, insecticides, and specialized equipment. Farming has grown to be so productive that only 2 percent of the American population needs to live and work on farms to feed the other 98 percent.

But those figures were reversed for most of history: before mechanization as a result of the industrial revolution, 98 percent of people lived on farms due to the labor-intensive nature of the work. It's no wonder, then, that agricultural contexts, references, parables, illustrations, etc., are encountered so often in the pages of the Bible. That was their world—a world foreign to the large majority of people living in industrialized countries today.

To grasp the truths of the Bible most fully, we need to step into that world. Why did Jesus decline a suggestion for lunch by speaking of sowing, reaping, and harvest? What connection did He see between fruit and eternal life? And what did all that have to do with an unnamed foreign woman with whom He had just spoken? Today's lesson answers those very questions.

B. Lesson Context

Fullest understanding of today's text requires some insight into the relationship between Jews and Samaritans in Jesus' day. When King Solomon died in about 930 BC, the nation of Israel split into two parts: the northern 10 tribes were then often referred to collectively as Israel, while the remaining tribes to the south were called Judah (example: Jeremiah 50:4).

King Omri of Israel built the city of Samaria to be his capital in about 875 BC (1 Kings 16:23-24). He ruled from Samaria as did his infamous son Ahab (16:29), establishing the city as a lasting site. Both kings aroused God's ire because of their idolatrous religious practices (16:25, 33).

Ignoring warnings of the prophets led to judgment (2 Kings 17:13). The ultimate form of that judgment came when the Assyrians destroyed the northern kingdom of Israel about 722 BC (17:5-18). Many Israelites were exiled, and outsiders were brought in to resettle the land (17:24). Israelites who were not taken into exile were left impoverished and without clear identity for many years .

Eventually, the resulting mixture of people came to be known as Samaritans. They developed a religion that accepted the five books of Moses but did not recognize the other books that make up the Old Testament. When Samaritans offered to help rebuild the Jerusalem temple destroyed in 586 BC, the Jews refused (Ezra 4:1-5). This angered the Samaritans, and we see some of this anger come out when Nehemiah began to rebuild the city walls (Nehemiah 4:1, 2).

About a century before Christ, a ruler of Judea destroyed the Samaritans' rival temple on Mount Gerizim. This and other things caused deep animosity between Samaritans and Jews. For the Jews of Jesus' time, Samaritans were not quite Gentiles but were definitely not Jews either (see Matthew 10:5; note the attempt to discredit Jesus in John 8:48).

Our lesson begins after Jesus and a Samaritan woman discussed her marriage situation (John 4:16-18). Jesus' knowledge of her personal life astounded her. For this reason, she addressed Him as a prophet (4:19). She changed the subject to the less personal but quite controversial topic of the proper site for worship. Jesus' answer cut through this temple-location controversy to get to the heart of worship: spiritual surrender to the Lord (4:23-24). Such truth telling had opened the woman to discuss matters of the heart as today's text opens.

I. A Woman's Declaration

(John 4:25-30)

A. Messiah Revealed (vv. 25-26)

25. The woman saith unto him, I know that Messias cometh, which is called Christ: when he is come, he will tell us all things.

Both Jews and Samaritans looked for the *Messias*, or *Christ*; these Hebrew and Greek words both mean "anointed one." The Jews believed He would be a national leader who would free them from foreign oppression, based on expectations tied to King David (2 Samuel 7:12-16). Because Samaritans held only the books of Genesis through Deuteronomy as Scripture, they did not share any such expectation. Instead, they emphasized the Messiah's role as a teaching prophet who would *tell . . . all things* and bring the people back to true faith, reminiscent of Moses (see Deuteronomy 18:15-18).

26. Jesus saith unto her, I that speak unto thee am he.

Jesus did not seek to set the woman straight regarding whether the Jewish or the Samaritan understanding of the Christ was correct. Instead of laying out every Scripture regarding himself (something He would do after the resurrection; see Luke 24:25-27), Jesus simply claimed to be the one she was waiting to meet.

The woman had already affirmed Jesus to be a prophet. Her reaction to His escalating claim to be *the* longed-for Messiah is delayed until John 4:28-29, below.

B. Disciples Startled (v. 27)

27. And upon this came his disciples, and marvelled that he talked with the woman: yet no man said, What seekest thou? or, Why talkest thou with her?

The *disciples* returned just then, having come from the village with food (John 4:8). The author, John, was one of these men, so he had firsthand knowledge of the group's reactions. They *marvelled,* but were not bold enough to ask Him *What* or *Why.* Their timidity contrasts with the woman's own insistence on asking Jesus questions (4:9, 11-12).

HOW TO SAY IT

Ahab	*Ay*-hab.
Assyrians	Uh-*sear*-e-unz.
Gerizim	*Gair*-ih-zeem or Guh-*rye*-zim.
Messiah	Meh-*sigh*-uh.
messianic	mess-ee-*an*-ick.
Omri	*Ahm*-rye.
Palestine	Pal-uh-staihn.
Samaritans	Suh-*mare*-uh-tunz.
Sychar	*Sigh*-kar.

C. City Challenged (vv. 28-30)

28. The woman then left her waterpot, and went her way into the city, and saith to the men.

The woman's abandonment of *her waterpot*—representing the errand that brought her in contact with Jesus in the first place—to return to *the city* suggests a hurried, excited departure. In initiating conversation with *the men* there, she cast aside any cultural restraints from doing so. Any shame at being an adulteress was overcome. She had to spread the news.

> *What Do You Think?*
> What "baggage" do you need to leave behind so that your witness for Christ is not impeded?
> *Digging Deeper*
> In what ways do the things of Matthew 4:20-22; Mark 1:20; 10:28; Hebrews 12:1; etc., differ from one another in terms of how, when, and what to leave them behind?

29. Come, see a man, which told me all things that ever I did: is not this the Christ?

Her straightforward message has two parts. First, she gave evidence that Jesus was something more than an ordinary man. Second, she proposed, in the form of a question, a tentative conclusion to that evidence. In wondering whether Jesus might be *the Christ,* the woman challenged others to *come* and investigate for themselves.

30. Then they went out of the city, and came unto him.

The woman's testimony intrigued the people enough so that they wanted to investigate her claims. She was a disreputable person in this community, but they could not ignore her earnest and fascinating testimony. If this man truly was the Messiah, they wouldn't want to miss a chance to meet Him and hear His teaching.

II. A Crop Prepared

(John 4:31-38)

A. Spiritual Food (vv. 31-33)

31. In the mean while his disciples prayed him, saying, Master, eat.

The *disciples* either mentally dismissed the woman as being unimportant or simply moved on to what they thought was a more pressing task: lunch. Perhaps they themselves were hungry and wanted Jesus to begin the meal.

32. But he said unto them, I have meat to eat that ye know not of.

The word *meat* refers to food in general, and Jesus' cryptic statement forms something of a parallel to the "living water" He offered to the woman earlier (John 4:10). It also foreshadows Jesus' coming self-description as "the bread of life" and "living bread" (6:48-51).

33. Therefore said the disciples one to another, Hath any man brought him ought to eat?

The confused *disciples* did not detect His reference to spiritual rather than physical food. And once again, they did not ask Jesus the question that was on their minds. Instead, they spoke *one to another* (compare Matthew 16:5-12).

B. Spiritual Harvest (vv. 34-35)

34. Jesus saith unto them, My meat is to do the will of him that sent me, and to finish his work.

A theme of the book of John is that Jesus had been sent by the Father with a mission *to finish* (also John 5:36; 17:4). At the heart of this work was bringing people to faith in Jesus (6:29). Knowing of the disciples' confusion, *Jesus* began explaining: His *meat* was spiritual in nature. Doing the work of *him that sent* Jesus (5:19) was the great sustenance for His soul. While the disciples had been away in pursuit of food for the body (4:8), Jesus had been busy ministering to an open-minded woman. Doing so was what energized Him.

35a. Say not ye, There are yet four months, and then cometh harvest?

Jesus began to apply an illustration or metaphor by describing a typical agricultural timeframe. His disciples are well aware that crops are ready to *harvest* following the sowing of *four months* earlier.

35b. Behold, I say unto you, Lift up your eyes, and look on the fields; for they are white already to harvest.

This verse is one of the great missionary mandates in all of Scripture. The time for *harvest* is not future! The time for evangelism, the harvest of souls, is now! The *fields* Jesus wanted the disciples to see were not plots of wheat or barley, but of people. We might imagine that as Jesus spoke He pointed to the people coming toward Him from the city (John 4:30, above).

For a field to be *white* means the heads of grain have turned from green to a light-brown color. This indicates the grain is fully mature. When it comes to sharing the gospel, there is no time to waste. As on that auspicious day in Samaria, so too are fields ripe and awaiting harvest today. Some of the disciples had been told previously that they were to become "fishers of men" (Matthew 4:19; Mark 1:17); now they hear, in effect, that they will be farmers of men as well!

C. Spiritual Reward (vv. 36-38)

36. And he that reapeth receiveth wages, and gathereth fruit unto life eternal: that both he that soweth and he that reapeth may rejoice together.

In the Palestine of Jesus' day and before, farming involved intensive labor from people and animals. Field laborers prepared the soil, sowed seed, watered, and weeded. When harvest (reaping) time came, different persons might cut the grain stalks, bundle the sheaves, thresh the grain, and winnow the chaff in larger operations.

In evangelism as in farming, there is sowing and reaping (compare Matthew 13:1-9, 18-30). The gospel must be shared (sowed) for faith to bear *fruit* (be ready to reap). The result is a crop of believing persons (see 1 Corinthians 3:6). The goal is not a full granary, but a full Heaven—full of saved souls, those who have *life eternal.*

The workers are rewarded with satisfaction for productive work. They will *rejoice together,* both now and in the hereafter (see Luke 15:3-32; compare Galatians 6:7-9).

37. And herein is that saying true, One soweth, and another reapeth.

Jesus quoted a traditional *saying.* Reaping requires previous work: sowing. If no seeds are planted, there will be nothing to harvest. Though the disciples didn't realize it quite yet, the moment to reap was swiftly approaching (see John 4:39-42, below).

> *What Do You Think?*
> Which skill do you need most to work on: sowing or reaping? How will you do that?
> *Digging Deeper*
> How does 1 Corinthians 3:6-9 influence your thoughts in this regard?

38. I sent you to reap that whereon ye bestowed no labour: other men laboured, and ye are entered into their labours.

This verse has a sense of climax for God's plan to fashion a people according to His will. Prophets had been sent to call people to repentance, the most recent being John the Baptist (see Mark 1:4; Acts 13:24). Moses' testimony recorded in the law had sown seeds among the Samaritans. Jesus himself further prepared the heart of the Samaritan woman. Little did Jesus' followers know at the time that they were being trained to fulfill the coming Great Commission (Matthew 28:19-20).

Speaking to Be Understood

I grew up in the city. But my first ministry was to a small town in Iowa. Because I wanted to minister effectively, I had to gain a basic understanding of farming life. This involved learning a new vocabulary, almost a new language.

I knew what corn and beans looked like when they came out of a can. But it was a different matter to see what they looked like in a vast field and to be able to talk about that competently. When preaching and teaching, it was helpful to translate my theological language into terms more relevant to the people.

When Jesus spoke of a ripe spiritual crop, His audience understood Him easily. He spoke their language. As we bring the gospel to the unbelieving world, we may sometimes unwittingly speak in "Christian-ese," a language that has no meaning outside of our own "city . . . on an hill" (Matthew 5:14). How can you change your "city" language to enhance your witness to a "farming" world?

—C. R. B.

III. A Community Transformed

(John 4:39-42)

A. The Woman's Testimony (v. 39)

39. And many of the Samaritans of that city believed on him for the saying of the woman, which testified, He told me all that ever I did.

The idea of testimony leading to faith is a central pattern in the Gospel of John (see John 1:7). Its author desires to testify about Jesus and bring readers to faith (21:24). Jesus' inspired words and miraculous works are testifiers themselves—that He is the one sent by the Father, the Messiah both the Jews and the Samaritans have been looking for (see 5:36). All this is ultimately reflected in the book's purpose statement, found in John 20:30-31.

The episode at hand is an integral part of this intent. The Samaritan woman's acceptance that Jesus had supernatural knowledge of details of her life brought her to trust Him and share her testimony with others. The result was that many *believed on him*, accepting that He was God's promised Messiah.

The triggers that lead to faith are different for each person. We want to expect that people will believe when they hear a clear, simple presentation of the gospel—and this does indeed happen. But other approaches may be used too. A dramatic life experience may drive people to find God. The story of a friend whose heart was changed can be a powerful motivation to believe.

> *What Do You Think?*
> How might you discern situations that call for personal testimony over a logic- or evidence-based presentation of the gospel (John 14:11; Acts 17:2; etc.), and vice versa?
> *Digging Deeper*
> What other Scripture passages are helpful in making this distinction?

B. The Samaritans' Request (v. 40)

40. So when the Samaritans were come unto him, they besought him that he would tarry with them: and he abode there two days.

Given the cultural context, it is surprising that *Samaritans* would ask a Jew to visit with them (see Lesson Context; compare John 4:9b; Luke 9:51-53). This speaks to the powerful impact Jesus has already had in this brief encounter.

> *What Do You Think?*
> What, from your personal experience, can you teach a fellow believer about crossing boundaries with the gospel?
> *Digging Deeper*
> From best to worst, how would you rank-order your skills at reaching across the boundaries of gender, ethnicity, socioeconomic status, and nationality?

C. The People's Belief (vv. 41-42)

41-42. And many more believed because of his own word; and said unto the woman, Now we believe, not because of thy saying: for we have heard him ourselves, and know that this is indeed the Christ, the Saviour of the world.

For some of the Samaritans, the woman's testimony was enough for them to believe (John 4:39, above). Now we read of belief also having come to *many more . . . because of his own word.* These particular villagers did not discount the woman's testimony, but they needed more—they needed their own experience (compare and contrast 20:25). Beyond the small group of the disciples (2:11), these Samaritans stand as the first community in the Gospel of John who accept Jesus as *the Christ.* (John 2:23 speaks of many who "believed in his name" in Jerusalem, but that was not a close-knit community like this one.)

The concept of Christ was discussed earlier (see John 4:25, above). That marked an escalation in the woman's faith, and now the phrase *Saviour of the world* marks an escalation for the entire community. Whereas their messianic expectations had focused thus far on what the Christ would do for Samaritans, they had come to grasp that Jesus had come for much more than just Samaritans. He came not merely to teach about right worship or to restore Samaria; He came to save the world (John 3:16-17).

> *What Do You Think?*
> Which aspects of Jesus' encounter with the Samaritan can and should you use in your interactions with unbelievers? Explain.
> *Digging Deeper*
> Which aspects should you *not* use? Why?

Drawn by a Friend's Words

In his early adulthood, one of my grandfathers was a functioning alcoholic. He worked all week, but when Saturday came, he got drunk. Grandpa was a mean drunk, willing to fight anyone. One day a friend came by and said, "You ought to go down to the church. The preacher can quote more Scripture than you can imagine."

His friend's challenge struck a chord in Grandpa's heart. He went to the meeting, and he turned to Christ. Life changed for Grandpa and his family. Alcohol was no longer a part of their home. The ripples of this faithful decision are still seen throughout our family.

The Samaritan woman's testimony caused waves in her community. She aroused their curiosity sufficiently that they went to hear Jesus. His words caused them to believe in Him. When the story of your life is told, how many people will be able to say that they sought Jesus because of your testimony?
—C. R. B.

Conclusion

A. Women of Faith

The story of Jesus' encounter with the woman at the well serves several purposes in the book of John. It teaches the spiritual nature of true worship (John 4:23-24). It clarifies the identity of Jesus as the chosen Messiah, or Christ, from God (4:25-26). It portrays Jesus as fearlessly moving beyond the boundaries of orthodox Judaism to an awkward encounter with a Samaritan (4:9). And it demonstrates the influence a person of conviction and urgency can have when talking to others about Jesus (4:28-30, 39). She was both a part of the harvest and a farmer-sower. Her work contributed to a fruitful harvest, indeed!

Visual for Lesson 10. *Have this visual on display as a backdrop to one, two, or all three of the exercises on the activity page as learners work on them.*

Many who read the Gospel of John can identify with her: a forlorn, rejected person, ostracized by her community. A woman who came to get water at a time of day when she knew others wouldn't be there—only to encounter Jesus and be transformed. The village's object of derision became the mouthpiece of the Lord to bring others to faith.

It would be nice to know the name of the Samaritan woman. It makes us wonder about other women of faith whose names are lost to history. Many of them have spoken out to bring others to faith. Many taught their sons and daughters to pray. Many read Scripture to their children to plant seeds of faith. Some even have lived with unbelieving husbands who finally submitted to Christ as Lord after years of patient prayer by their wives.

Their names may be unknown to us, but they are not unknown to God. He has written their names "in the Lamb's book of life" (Revelation 21:27). Someday in Heaven, we may be able to look into that book and learn the Samaritan woman's name, the name of one whose testimony changed her community forever. Will yours?

B. Prayer

Father, give us the boldness of the Samaritan woman in sharing the good news about Jesus! It is in His name we pray. Amen.

C. Thought to Remember

Help reap the fields that are ripe for harvest!

Involvement Learning

Enhance your lesson with KJV Bible Student *(from your curriculum supplier) and the reproducible activity page (at www.standardlesson.com or in the back of the* KJV Standard Lesson Commentary Deluxe Edition*).*

Into the Lesson

Distribute handouts (you prepare) on which are printed the following:

I know a person who. . .

- ❑ *is a social outcast*
- ❑ *has mixed up religious beliefs*
- ❑ *avoids followers of Jesus*
- ❑ *interrupts plans*

Begin by asking participants to check the boxes as indicated. Stress that learners not write names, initials, or anything else identifying. After one minute, call for shows of hands regarding how many had four boxes checked, how many had three, etc. (For a bit of humor, ask who had boxes checked because they themselves fit the description.) Make a transition by saying, "Today we're going to see what we can learn from Jesus' interaction with someone for whom we would have checked all four boxes."

Into the Word

Ask a volunteer (notified in advance) to give a two-minute summary of the Lesson Context. Then call for four volunteers to read today's text, one each to read the words of the narrator, Jesus, the Samaritan woman, and the people of the town. Before the reading, ask class members to use their handouts to identify how the Samaritan woman could be described with each of the labels used in the introductory activity above. After the reading, put learners into study pairs for further consideration of how the Samaritan woman fit those categories.

After reconvening for a few minutes of whole-class discussion, distribute copies (you prepare) of the following true/false quiz. Before doing so, stress that this is a one-minute, closed-Bible quiz; the Scripture references with each statement are for learners to score their own quizzes after the time limit of one minute expires.

1–Jesus had to convince the Samaritan woman that a Messiah was promised to her people too (John 4:25). 2–The disciples readily saw the conversation of Jesus with the woman as normal (4:27). 3–The woman told the townspeople about Jesus' request for water (4:28-29). 4–Jesus said they'd be required to plant spiritual seeds for many years before they could expect a harvest of souls (4:36-38). 5–Jesus used the analogy of farming to encourage the disciples to move slowly, be patient, and wait for results (4:35). 6–The woman's neighbors in town rejected what she had to say, because someone of her reputation couldn't be believed (4:39). 7–The townspeople rushed out to tell Jesus to leave the area (4:40). 8–Ultimately, the townspeople were far more convinced by the woman's testimony than by anything Jesus could add to it (4:42). (Expected responses: all are false.)

Option. Distribute copies of the "Interacting with Nonbelievers" exercise on the activity page, which you can download. Have pairs or triads complete as indicated. Compare and contrast results in ensuing whole-class discussion.

Into Life

Refer back to the designations on the handout from the beginning of the lesson. Work down through them as you ask this question for each one individually: "How does today's lesson give you confidence to initiate spiritual conversations with the person you had in mind?" Encourage free discussion.

Option 1. Distribute copies of the "Sow or Reap?" exercise from the activity page, allowing learners one minute to complete individually as indicated; then share names with a prayer partner to close the class.

Option 2. Distribute copies of the "An Urgent Task" exercise from the activity page for learners to complete individually as indicated. This can be a take-home if time is short.

Called to Support

DEVOTIONAL READING: Romans 4:13-25
BACKGROUND SCRIPTURE: Mark 15:40; 16:1-9; Luke 8:1-3; John 20:10-18

Luke 8:1-3

1 And it came to pass afterward, that he went throughout every city and village, preaching and shewing the glad tidings of the kingdom of God: and the twelve were with him,

2 And certain women, which had been healed of evil spirits and infirmities, Mary called Magdalene, out of whom went seven devils,

3 And Joanna the wife of Chuza Herod's steward, and Susanna, and many others, which ministered unto him of their substance.

Mark 15:40

40 There were also women looking on afar off: among whom was Mary Magdalene, and Mary the mother of James the less and of Joses, and Salome.

John 20:10-18

10 Then the disciples went away again unto their own home.

11 But Mary stood without at the sepulchre weeping: and as she wept, she stooped down, and looked into the sepulchre,

12 And seeth two angels in white sitting, the one at the head, and the other at the feet, where the body of Jesus had lain.

13 And they say unto her, Woman, why weepest thou? She saith unto them, Because they have taken away my Lord, and I know not where they have laid him.

14 And when she had thus said, she turned herself back, and saw Jesus standing, and knew not that it was Jesus.

15 Jesus saith unto her, Woman, why weepest thou? whom seekest thou? She, supposing him to be the gardener, saith unto him, Sir, if thou have borne him hence, tell me where thou hast laid him, and I will take him away.

16 Jesus saith unto her, Mary. She turned herself, and saith unto him, Rabboni; which is to say, Master.

17 Jesus saith unto her, Touch me not; for I am not yet ascended to my Father: but go to my brethren, and say unto them, I ascend unto my Father, and your Father; and to my God, and your God.

18 Mary Magdalene came and told the disciples that she had seen the Lord, and that he had spoken these things unto her.

Key Verses

It came to pass afterward, that he went throughout every city and village, preaching and shewing the glad tidings of the kingdom of God: and the twelve were with him, and certain women, which had been healed of evil spirits and infirmities, Mary called Magdalene, out of whom went seven devils. —**Luke 8:1-2**

Call in the New Testament

Unit 3: The Call of Women

Lessons 9–13

Lesson Aims

After participating in this lesson, each learner will be able to:

1. List the acts of devotion by the women who followed Jesus.
2. Explain the importance of women being the first eyewitnesses to testify about Jesus' resurrection.
3. Describe some ways to demonstrate his or her loyalty to Jesus.

Lesson Outline

Introduction
- A. Celebrity
- B. Lesson Context

I. Women in Jesus' Ministry (Luke 8:1-3; Mark 15:40)
- A. Day by Day (Luke 8:1-3)
- B. In Crisis (Mark 15:40)

II. Mary, Jesus' Witness (John 20:10-18)
- A. Sad Scene (vv. 10-11)
  - *The Great Disappointer*
- B. Angels Appear (vv. 12-13)
- C. Rabboni Revealed (vv. 14-18)
  - *A Familiar Voice*

Conclusion
- A. He Found Her
- B. Prayer
- C. Thought to Remember

Introduction

A. Celebrity

Oscar Wilde (1854–1900) declared, "There is only one thing in the world worse than being talked about, and that is not being talked about." The idea is that bad publicity at least keeps the public aware of the celebrity's existence. Not getting any publicity can be the death knell to a person's "well-knownness."

There is no doubt that Jesus was a celebrity, although the term doesn't do justice to Him. He was celebrated for the value of His teachings and for the miracles that He performed. His teachings and His miracles both brought joy to those who followed Him. As we consider some of the women who experienced that joy, theirs can be ours as well.

B. Lesson Context

Jesus became well known in the Jewish villages and towns of Galilee by traveling among the people. Peter described this by saying Jesus "went about doing good" (Acts 10:38), a ministry that included teaching, healing, and casting out demons (see Mark 1:14-15, 34). Jesus traveled with a large group that included the core 12 disciples and others. The opportunity for women to play a prominent role in Jesus' ministry made it unusual. Jerusalem had no famous women rabbis. The Jewish high council, the Sanhedrin, had no female members. The prominent sects, the Sadducees and Pharisees, were made up of men only.

The inclusion of women who were not the wives or other family of the disciples was even more unusual (compare 1 Corinthians 9:5). Many charges were made against Jesus during His ministry, including drunkenness, Sabbath breaking, blasphemy, and using the power of Satan (see Mark 3:22-23; Luke 7:34; John 5:18; etc.). Because women traveled with them regularly, we might expect similar charges regarding sexual sins. But no record claims that either Jesus or any of His disciples (male or female) were accused of sexual immorality while they ministered together.

Mary Magdalene was one of these women. She has been especially misunderstood throughout history. Some factions have tried to uncover a romantic entanglement between Mary Magdalene and Jesus. These stories are found only in sources written long after the first century.

For example, a second- or third-century nonbiblical collection of sayings called *The Gospel of Philip* presents Mary Magdalene as Jesus' "companion." *The Gospel of Mary*, another heretical document, claims that Jesus revealed special, secret knowledge to Mary alone.

Other fanciful legends claim that Mary traveled from Jerusalem after the crucifixion to the south of France. Medieval accounts sometimes included Mary in the legends concerning the Holy Grail —the cup Jesus supposedly used at the last supper and that supposedly was used to collect some of His blood at the cross. Yet the actual biblical accounts about Mary Magdalene are sparse on details and have none of these legendary elements. Her real witness is even greater than those!

I. Women in Jesus' Ministry

(Luke 8:1-3; Mark 15:40)

Luke 4:14-15 introduced Jesus' first preaching tour of Galilee. Now Luke 8:1 takes us to the beginning of Jesus' second preaching tour there.

A. Day by Day (Luke 8:1-3)

1a. And it came to pass afterward, that he went throughout every city and village, preaching and shewing the glad tidings of the kingdom of God.

Luke summarizes Jesus' strategy for the near future: He continued to tour Galilee, visiting *every city and village.* Cities were larger population centers that had markets and government officials. Villages were small clusters of homes where people who worked the farms lived, perhaps alongside a few merchants and craftsmen. Both villages and cities would have one or more synagogues, which were community centers for Jewish worship.

Jesus' *preaching and shewing the glad tidings of the kingdom of God* took three forms. First, He taught on this by use of parables (example: Luke 8:4-15). Second, He demonstrated the nearness of the kingdom through power over demonic forces (8:26-39). Third, He performed miraculous healings, even raising the dead (examples: 8:43-48, 53-56).

1b. And the twelve were with him.

The twelve refers to those disciples whom Jesus also called apostles (see Luke 6:13-16).

2a. And certain women, which had been healed of evil spirits and infirmities.

Certain women also followed Jesus from village to village. Perhaps because "the twelve" of the previous verse were all men, sometimes we forget that women also travelled with Jesus. They played important roles in His ministry, though often in the background (see Luke 8:3c, below).

The Greek word translated *healed* suggests a total restoration, not just the absence of disease. Physical health is restored when *infirmities* are overcome; spiritual health is restored when *evil spirits* are driven out.

2b. Mary called Magdalene, out of whom went seven devils.

The name *Mary* is a form of the name of Moses' sister, Miriam; she was a prophetess and musician-leader of women during the exodus from Egypt (Exodus 15:20). Mary's nickname, *Magdalene*, comes from her home, the village of Magdala located near Tiberias on the western coast of the Sea of Galilee. This would be like calling someone from the city of Dallas "Tex," a nod to his home state.

HOW TO SAY IT

Alphaeus	Al-*fee*-us.
Arimathaea	*Air*-uh-muh-***thee***-uh (*th* as in *thin*).
Chuza	*Koo*-za.
Galilee	*Gal*-uh-lee.
Herod Antipas	*Hair*-ud *An*-tih-pus.
Magdala	*Mag*-duh-luh.
Magdalene	*Mag*-duh-leen or Mag-duh-*lee*-nee.
rabboni	rab-*o*-nye.
Salome	Suh-*lo*-me.
synagogue	*sin*-uh-gog.
Tiberias	Tie-*beer*-ee-us.
Zebedee	*Zeb*-eh-dee.

Visual for
Lesson 11

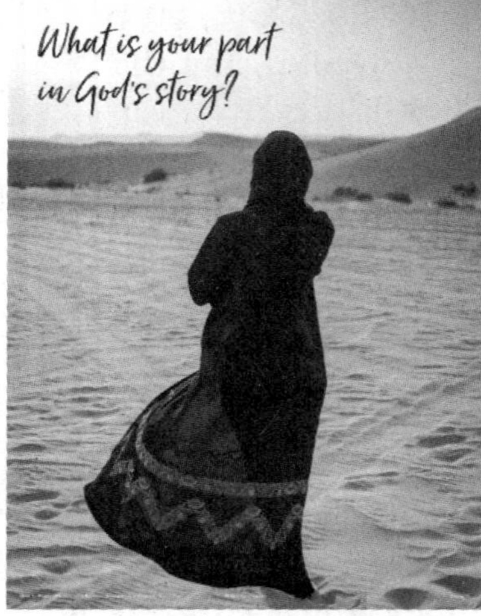

Point to this visual as you ask, "How will you know when you have the right answer to this question?"

Mary Magdalene is mentioned at least twice in each Gospel, making her one of the most frequently mentioned women in the New Testament. Hers is the most dramatic story among these women, for Jesus drove *seven devils* from her. Those were malevolent nonhuman spiritual beings that could enter and influence a person. We can assume that the situation was fully beyond Mary's ability to control. No details exist in the Gospels about this exorcism, but Mary's story seems to have been known among Jesus' followers.

Many mistakenly identify Mary Magdalene with the sinful woman who washed Jesus' feet in Luke 7:36-50. That proposal seems to be strengthened by the similar account of a woman named Mary who anointed Jesus' feet in John 12:1-3. But the sinful woman of Luke 7 is not named there, and Mary Magdalene is named not long after (today's text). We might conclude therefore that Luke surely (1) would have known whether the two women were one and the same and (2) would have made the identification if it were the case. But that is an argument from silence.

The claim that the Mary of John 12 was Mary Magdalene ignores the fact that there are five other women by the name of Mary in the Gospels, so we should take care not to misidentify them (example: Matthew 27:56, 61). The Mary of John 12 is Mary of Bethany, the sister of Martha and Lazarus.

3a. And Joanna the wife of Chuza 's steward.

Joanna likely had resources to contribute to the costs of sustaining the traveling group. Her husband, *Chuza*, served the Galilean governor Herod Antipas. Chuza's position as *steward* was a trusted one, and likely came with an excellent salary.

3b. And Susanna.

Susanna is otherwise unknown in the New Testament. She shares a name with a Jewish heroine whose story occurs in an apocryphal (spurious) addition to the book of Daniel.

3c. And many others, which ministered unto him of their substance.

At least some of the *many others* were undoubtedly motivated to be near Jesus because of being healed by Him. They followed Jesus out of selfless gratitude and provided money, time, and other support for His ministry. Such women were the unsung heroes of the group, just as many noble women in churches are today.

What Do You Think?

In what ways can you improve your behind-the-scenes support of your church's ministries?

Digging Deeper

What was an occasion that surprised you when your behind-the-scenes support suddenly thrust you into the limelight, such as in Acts 6? How did you handle it?

B. In Crisis (Mark 15:40)

40a. There were also women looking on afar off.

Our text skips ahead to the crucifixion, where several *women* refused to abandon Jesus (compare and contrast Mark 14:27, 50-52, 66-71; John 19:26, 38-39). While some women watched from *afar off,* others stood much closer—close enough to hear Jesus speak from the cross (John 19:25-26). One or more women may be in both groups, moving back and forth as Jesus suffered. The listing in John 19:25 differs from what follows here, suggesting that none of the Gospel writers intended to give an exhaustive listing of the women present.

40b. Among whom was Mary Magdalene, and Mary the mother of James the less and of Joses, and Salome.

Mary Magdalene is perhaps the leader of this group, being named first. The second *Mary* is further identified by the naming of her sons. *James the less* is likely the son of Alphaeus mentioned in the list of apostles (Mark 3:18); the phrase *the less* may distinguish him from the more prominent apostle James, the son of Zebedee. This Mary may also have been the mother of Levi/Matthew (Mark 2:14). The third woman, *Salome*, is probably "the mother of Zebedee's children" (Matthew 27:56).

The time for following Jesus was not over for these loyal women. They remained with Him in those dreadful hours, watching and waiting for an opportunity to minister to the Savior once more. That opportunity came a few hours later when they observed where Jesus' body was laid (Mark 15:47) and resolved to remedy His hasty burial with customary spices (16:1).

II. Mary, Jesus' Witness

(John 20:10-18)

We meet Mary Magdalene for the third time, this occasion being resurrection morning. Arriving at the tomb, she had found it opened (John 20:1). She ran to tell Peter and John, who then ran to the tomb to see for themselves (20:2-9).

A. Sad Scene (vv. 10-11)

10-11. Then the disciples went away again unto their own home. But Mary stood without at the sepulchre weeping: and as she wept, she stooped down, and looked into the sepulchre.

Once again, the reaction of *the disciples* can be compared and contrasted with that of *Mary* Magdalene (see on Mark 15:40, above). Whereas the men went *home* to think about what the empty tomb could mean, Mary stayed.

> *What Do You Think?*
> In what ways can you help encourage the members of your church to adopt and develop the "staying power" of Mary?
> *Digging Deeper*
> In what ways is Mary's "staying power" like and unlike your own? Why?

The sepulchre was a cave-like room carved into the limestone hillside. Although Mary already knew it was empty, she probably hoped to notice something missed earlier, some hint of what had happened. Mary's heart was broken at this apparent insult to her Lord.

The Great Disappointer

My wife and I thought our family was complete with a son and daughter when we learned that another child was coming. Several months later, we welcomed Mary Elizabeth into our home. Five weeks after that, our delight turned to grief with Mary's sudden death.

I retreated into work and studies, an expression of denial and deep disappointment in the dashing of our hopes and dreams for Mary. My wife poured herself into caring for our other two children. In doing so, she nurtured them through their grief, in contrast to my emotional absence.

The disciples' reaction of heading home suggests that they reacted to Jesus' death as I did to Mary's: back to "business as usual" to occupy their minds. Mary Magdalene responded more as my wife did: seeking to find whatever meaning and solace she could in the middle of her pain. By doing so, Mary Magdalene met the risen Lord. What does this suggest about proper Christian reactions to death, the great disappointer? —C. R. B.

B. Angels Appear (vv. 12-13)

12. And seeth two angels in white sitting, the one at the head, and the other at the feet, where the body of Jesus had lain.

Jesus' *body* had been laid on a carved ledge inside the tomb. But instead of holding that body, it had become witness to the presence of *two angels*. Though their *white* clothes could have clued Mary regarding their identity (compare Matthew 28:2-3; Luke 24:4), the angels also could have looked rather ordinary (Mark 16:5; see John 20:13, below). Their sitting *at the head* and *the feet* emphasized the absence of the expected occupant.

13. And they say unto her, Woman, why weepest thou? She saith unto them, Because they have taken away my Lord, and I know not where they have laid him.

Despite their unexpected presence, Mary did not seem to recognize the two angels as supernatural beings. Their question was not a rebuke but an act of kindness, inquiring as to the nature of her pain. Though addressing her as *Woman* may seem abrupt or rude to modern ears, the term here should be taken as a respectful address.

Regardless of who these two were or why they were there, Mary blurted out the cause of the great burden on her heart. The mystery of Jesus' absence could be solved if someone would just tell her *where they have laid him*, presumably in another tomb for reasons unknown to Mary. She did not consider that Jesus may not be dead (compare Luke 24:5-8).

C. Rabboni Revealed (vv. 14-18)

14. And when she had thus said, she turned herself back, and saw Jesus standing, and knew not that it was Jesus.

Apparently not expecting an answer from the white-clad visitors, Mary *turned* from the tomb and saw another person in the garden. We are told this is *Jesus* before Mary knew, much like we knew the other two were actually angels. How could she have failed to recognize this person she loved so much? Perhaps her tears obscured her vision.

This is not the only time after the resurrection that disciples fail to recognize Jesus (see Luke 24:13-16; John 21:4). His post-resurrection body was different in some way (Luke 24:30-32; John 20:19, 26). But that body also bore the marks of the crucifixion (John 20:20, 27). The changes in His appearance plus the utter impossibility of His being alive probably contributed mightily to her lack of recognition.

> *What Do You Think?*
>
> What improvements can you make in staying on guard against things that cloud your full awareness of Christ in your life?
>
> *Digging Deeper*
>
> In what ways do the blindnesses in Matthew 15:13-14; 23:16-26; John 9:39-41; 2 Peter 1:5-9; and Revelation 3:17 warn you to action in this regard?

15. Jesus saith unto her, Woman, why weepest thou? whom seekest thou? She, supposing him to be the gardener, saith unto him, Sir, if thou have borne him hence, tell me where thou hast laid him, and I will take him away.

Jesus repeated the angels' question (John 20:13, above), thus pushing to the heart of Mary's suffering. He already knew she was weeping because of His death and was seeking His body.

Mary, still not recognizing Jesus, repeated her response (John 20:13). She assumed this man was *the gardener* and therefore someone who would know what had happened (see 19:41). The tomb where Jesus' body had been placed, that of Joseph of Arimathaea (19:38-42), was apparently located within a well-maintained garden.

> *What Do You Think?*
>
> Since Jesus already knew the answer to the question He was asking, what does His technique teach you about how to counsel grief-stricken people?
>
> *Digging Deeper*
>
> How does 1 Kings 19:9b-10 further help frame your answer?

16. Jesus saith unto her, Mary. She turned herself, and saith unto him, Rabboni; which is to say, Master.

Jesus did not explain. In one of the most dramatic moments found in the Gospel accounts, He simply spoke her name.

And she knew His voice. She had heard Jesus say her name many times before. All her plans unraveled, for there was no corpse to minister to.

Mary addressed Jesus with the title of respect she had used many times. *Rabboni* is a variation on the title rabbi, which means "my teacher." The form used by Mary may imply heightened respect, something like "my honored teacher."

A Familiar Voice

"Grampa, this is your granddaughter. I'm in trouble in [a foreign country]. I've been arrested on a phony charge, and I need $500 so I can be released and come home."

In my surprise, I thought that the call might be

genuine. However, some things didn't ring true: no name, wrong number, vague about details, *almost* but *not quite* my granddaughter's voice.

I told the caller I would call back, hung up, and called my granddaughter's phone number. She, in her familiar voice, assured me that she was in no trouble. Such scam calls can purport to come from many sources: the IRS, the Social Security Administration, your bank, a computer company, even a "kidnapper"!

When Mary met Jesus, she didn't recognize Him at first. She was still in shock from the events of the last few days. But when Jesus spoke, there was no longer a question about His identity. She knew the sound of her rabbi's voice.

We should stay in the Word of God so much that we are familiar with His voice there. That way, if we should get a "scam call" of false teaching, we'll know it's not the Lord. —C. R. B.

17. Jesus saith unto her, Touch me not; for I am not yet ascended to my Father: but go to my brethren, and say unto them, I ascend unto my Father, and your Father; and to my God, and your God.

Jesus' command *Touch me not* has a dimension beyond merely rejecting a hug. Apparently, Mary's desire was to somehow detain Jesus, to cause Him to stay with her and the other disciples. However, Jesus would ascend to His *Father*. There would be no negotiating His departure.

Instead of clinging to Him, Mary was to go back to the men who had been there earlier (John 20:10, above) and update them on what had actually happened and been said at the tomb.

18. Mary Magdalene came and told the disciples that she had seen the Lord, and that he had spoken these things unto her.

Mary Magdalene did not prepare an elaborate presentation for *the disciples*. Her testimony was basic and beautiful.

Sometimes the most effective witnessing is in telling of our experience with Jesus and the changes He brings to our lives. Mary had plenty to say that day—explaining how a heartbroken, sobbing woman became a joyous, confident eyewitness for the disciples.

Jesus knew her name, and He called her to serve Him by being His witness.

Conclusion

A. He Found Her

We often portray nonbelievers who come to church as "seekers"; we say that those who seek Jesus will find Him. In today's story, Mary Magdalene, a firm disciple and believer, was a seeker in a different sense: she sought Jesus' body and was not easily dissuaded from her quest. But that quest was mistaken, for there was no longer a dead body.

Try as she might, Mary did not find Jesus. He found her. Jesus had first found Mary to deliver her from demonization. He then found her weeping in a tomb, a woman for whom the recent days had been a dark nightmare.

Isaiah promised, "[God] will come and save you" (Isaiah 35:4). As it was with Mary, so it is with us: If we seek Jesus but don't find Him, it may be because our search is based on a mistaken idea. We clear up any mistakes by reading the facts of Jesus' life, death, resurrection, and ascension in the Bible. That's where hearing His call starts.

What Do You Think?

In what ways does Jesus' resurrection encourage you most today? Why?

Digging Deeper

When was an occasion that a time of discouragement was overcome by refocusing on His resurrection? How did you grow from this experience?

B. Prayer

Father, we thank You for the hope we have through Your Son Jesus, a hope that overcomes our fears. May we—like Mary and the other women who followed Jesus throughout His ministry, crucifixion, and resurrection—never lose our desire to serve You. In Jesus' name we pray. Amen.

C. Thought to Remember

Jesus knows where and how to find those who seek Him.

Involvement Learning

Enhance your lesson with KJV Bible Student *(from your curriculum supplier) and the reproducible activity page (at www.standardlesson.com or in the back of the* KJV Standard Lesson Commentary Deluxe Edition*).*

Into the Lesson

Begin class by asking participants to pull out all their customer loyalty cards. Announce that you have a prize for the one who has the most such cards; these include grocery cards that give discounts, coffee shop cards earning free coffee, etc. To the winner, give a humorous "Least Loyal Customer" certificate (you prepare) having so many cards indicates a *lack* of loyalty!

Ask, "What is your loyalty to these vendors based upon?"

Alternative. Place on chairs copies of the "Favorite Brands" exercise from the activity page, which you can download. After students complete this individually, there is no need to discuss results.

After either activity, lead into the Bible study saying, "The depth of our devotion to certain stores or products can vary greatly. However, our devotion to God should be constant. Today we have something to learn from a person whose devotion was just that."

Into the Word

Have three volunteers read the three passages of today's Scripture, one each. Then divide the class into three groups (or multiples of three for larger class). Distribute handouts (you prepare) on which are printed the following tasks.

Motivation Group—Read Luke 8:1-2 and write an explanation as to why Mary Magdalene was so loyal to Jesus.

Support Group—Read Luke 8:3 and Mark 15:37-47, looking for specific ways that Mary tangibly supported Jesus during His ministry and even at His crucifixion.

Resurrection Group—Read John 20:10-18, looking for ways that Mary demonstrated her loyalty after the resurrection of Jesus.

After about five minutes, reconvene the class and have a spokesperson from each group share discoveries. Refer to relevant portions of the lesson commentary to support discussion and correct wrong conclusions as necessary.

Some possible and/or expected responses: **Motivation Group**—Jesus delivered Mary Magdalene from seven devils. **Support Group**—Mary Magdalene supported Jesus out of her own means; she didn't desert Him during the crucifixion and burial. **Resurrection Group**—Trying to prepare Jesus' body for burial properly, Mary was entrusted with instructions from the risen Jesus himself.

Option. Distribute copies of the "Mary Magdalene's Loyalty" exercise from the activity page for students to complete the middle column in study pairs or triads. Save the final column for the Into Life section, below.

Into Life

Distribute index cards on which you have printed the following phrases, one phrase per card:

financial support / hospitality / emotional support / defending the helpless / grief support / communication support

Say, "On these cards I've written ways that Mary expressed her devotion to Jesus. What are some possibilities for showing our own loyalty to Jesus in a way described on your card?" Also encourage students to identify specific people in the church who demonstrate their loyalty to Jesus in one or more of the ways on the cards. Ask, "What is it about these people that inspires us? How can we be more like them?"

Alternative. If you used the "Mary Magdalene's Loyalty" activity above, have the students complete the third column. After a few minutes, have volunteers share their answers in whole-class discussion. Say, "Let's choose one of these suggestions to put into practice in the coming days." After doing so, promise to begin next week's class with a discussion of how things went.

Called to Explain

Devotional Reading: Colossians 4:7-15
Background Scripture: Acts 18:1-26; Romans 16:3-4; 1 Corinthians 16:19; 2 Timothy 4:19

Acts 18:1-3, 18-21, 24-26

1 After these things Paul departed from Athens, and came to Corinth;

2 And found a certain Jew named Aquila, born in Pontus, lately come from Italy, with his wife Priscilla; (because that Claudius had commanded all Jews to depart from Rome:) and came unto them.

3 And because he was of the same craft, he abode with them, and wrought: for by their occupation they were tentmakers.

. . . .

18 And Paul after this tarried there yet a good while, and then took his leave of the brethren, and sailed thence into Syria, and with him Priscilla and Aquila; having shorn his head in Cenchrea: for he had a vow.

19 And he came to Ephesus, and left them there: but he himself entered into the synagogue, and reasoned with the Jews.

20 When they desired him to tarry longer time with them, he consented not;

21 But bade them farewell, saying, I must by all means keep this feast that cometh in Jerusalem: but I will return again unto you, if God will. And he sailed from Ephesus.

. . . .

24 And a certain Jew named Apollos, born at Alexandria, an eloquent man, and mighty in the scriptures, came to Ephesus.

25 This man was instructed in the way of the Lord; and being fervent in the spirit, he spake and taught diligently the things of the Lord, knowing only the baptism of John.

26 And he began to speak boldly in the synagogue: whom when Aquila and Priscilla had heard, they took him unto them, and expounded unto him the way of God more perfectly.

Romans 16:3-4

3 Greet Priscilla and Aquila my helpers in Christ Jesus:

4 Who have for my life laid down their own necks: unto whom not only I give thanks, but also all the churches of the Gentiles.

Key Verses

Greet Priscilla and Aquila my helpers in Christ Jesus: who have for my life laid down their own necks: unto whom not only I give thanks, but also all the churches of the Gentiles. —**Romans 16:3-4**

Call in the New Testament

Unit 3: The Call of Women

Lessons 9–13

Lesson Aims

After participating in this lesson, each learner will be able to:

1. List several facts about Priscilla and Aquila.
2. Explain the importance of the ministry of Priscilla and Aquila in relation to Paul's.
3. Write a note of appreciation to a ministry partner.

Lesson Outline

Introduction
- A. Power Couples
- B. Lesson Context

I. Partners with Paul (Acts 18:1-3, 18-21, 24-26)
- A. Making Tents (vv. 1-3)
- B. Making Disciples (vv. 18-21)
- C. Making a Preacher (vv. 24-26)
  - *Chaos or Cooperation*

II. Leaders with Legacy (Romans 16:3-4)
- A. Assisting an Apostle (v. 3)
- B. Rewarding Risk (v. 4)
  - *Personal Correspondence*

Conclusion
- A. By Ones and Twos
- B. Prayer
- C. Thought to Remember

Introduction

A. Power Couples

When you hear the phrase *power couple*, who comes to mind? Some might think of historical matches, like Cleopatra and Marc Antony. Others may consider more recent examples, such as Beyoncé and Jay-Z.

It's not hard to understand that the phrase refers to those who wield great influence. It's almost too basic to point out that the phrase requires exactly *two* people, usually who are married or otherwise romantically involved. Although conflict can arise in such unions, part of their power is found in common purpose. They often work together toward artistic growth, social change, or economic gain, etc. Their shared goal is not a compromise; they both believe whole-heartedly in the worthiness of their prize and work cooperatively to attain it. When that shared vision is lost, the power of the couple falters, and often the bond between the two dissolves.

Lasting and happy power couples complement each other. The strengths of one fill in the weakness of the other, and vice versa. Although they may have differing roles, neither partner is considered superior or more valuable than the other. The sum of their parts is greater than what each would be individually. And so it is with the power couple we meet in today's lesson.

B. Lesson Context

The book of Acts begins in Jerusalem and ends in Rome. The military and political center of the first century, Rome had a significant Jewish population. Christianity came to Rome early, likely within a few months after the resurrection of Christ. On the Day of Pentecost, visitors from Rome heard the gospel preached, and undoubtedly some of them were baptized (Acts 2:10, 41). Then they returned home to spread Christianity in the imperial city.

That spread seems to have been confined to Jews for many years. As a result, Christians of Jewish background coexisted with unbelieving Jews in tight urban spaces, jockeying for control of various synagogues. Tensions grew; violence resulted.

Rather than sort out the instigators, Emperor Claudius expelled all Jews from the city, whether Christian or non-Christian, in AD 49. Jews were not readmitted to the city until the death of Claudius in AD 54.

These events form the backdrop of Paul's meeting two Jews from Rome, Priscilla and Aquila, in Corinth in about AD 51. In the meantime, Christians of Gentile background in Rome established house churches (Romans 16:5, 10-11, 14-15), a development that caused some tension when Jewish Christians returned to the city.

I. Partners with Paul

(Acts 18:1-3, 18-21, 24-26)

A. Making Tents (vv. 1-3)

1a. After these things Paul departed from Athens.

Paul had left his primary companions, Silas and Timothy, behind in Berea (Acts 17:13-14) while he himself traveled south. His time in *Athens,* while dramatic, did not result in planting a church. He was ridiculed by the philosophers for his belief in the resurrection (17:32); even so, he left behind a few new believers (17:34).

1b. And came to Corinth.

Paul proceeded about 50 miles west to *Corinth.* This city was the seat of Roman government for the area, the residence of the deputy Gallio (Acts 18:12). Corinth, Greece, was a commercial hub, a crossroads for trade because of the business of transporting ships across the Isthmus of Corinth (less than four miles wide) using an ancient kind of railway. This saved ships hundreds of miles of perilous sea journey around the Peloponnesian Peninsula, making it worth the expense. This positioned Corinth as a primary way station for goods and people coming to and from Rome and the eastern parts of the empire.

Corinth was also a religious city, with people of pagan beliefs and Jewish faith living there. Unsurprisingly, then, it had a synagogue (Acts 18:4). Paul's habit on visiting a city was to find the synagogue in order to teach fellow Jews the gospel of Jesus Christ (example: 17:1-4).

2a. And found a certain Jew named Aquila, born in Pontus, lately come from Italy, with his wife Priscilla.

Despite *Aquila* being a Latin name ("eagle"), the man was Jewish. He hailed from the Greek region on the south shores of the Black Sea known as *Pontus,* an area where many Jewish merchants lived (see Acts 2:9). Aquila had made his way to *Italy* at some point.

Priscilla is an affectionate nickname for a woman named Prisca (see 2 Timothy 4:19). We do not know if she came from a Jewish family, although that is likely. Nor do we know if she was from Rome or moved there at another time.

2b. (Because that Claudius had commanded all Jews to depart from Rome:) and came unto them.

See the Lesson Context.

3. And because he was of the same craft, he abode with them, and wrought: for by their occupation they were tentmakers.

Paul joined this couple in a way we have not seen of him to this point in Acts: working at a trade for a living. (First Thessalonians 2:9 and 2 Thessalonians 3:7-10, portions of two letters Paul wrote while in Corinth, indicate that he had worked to support himself previously while in Thessalonica.) All three were *tentmakers,* a new piece of personal information about Paul. He was trained to be a rabbi by the famous Gamaliel (Acts 22:3), and all rabbis of this period had a professional skill—carpentry, baking, etc.

A tentmaker of this era worked with heavy material such as leather or woven goat hair. The

HOW TO SAY IT

Aquila	*Ack*-wih-luh.
Cenchrea	*Sen*-kree-uh.
Claudius	*Claw*-dee-us.
Ephesus	*Ef*-uh-sus.
Gamaliel	Guh-*may*-lih-ul or Guh-*may*-lee-al.
Hellenistic	*Heh*-leh-nihs-tic.
Peloponnesian	*Peh*-luh-puh-***nee***-shun.
Prisca	*Pris*-kuh.
Septuagint	Sep-*too*-ih-jent.
Thessalonica	*Thess*-uh-lo-***nye***-kuh.

tents being sold in Corinth were durable products used in semi-permanent situations. Construction of such tents required arduous handwork, using palm guards and hefty needles as pieces were stitched together with leather straps. It was a skilled profession with a ready market, thus allowing Paul to earn a living.

The importance of Paul's willingness to support himself in this manner is seen when he wrote to the church in Corinth several years later (see 1 Corinthians 4:12; 9:1-18; compare Acts 20:34). The accommodations that Paul shared with Aquila and Priscilla may have served as personal lodging, tent factory, and sales shop concurrently. Skilled craftsmen were in demand in a commercial center like Corinth, and Paul probably was able to make these arrangements quickly.

In the language of the church, this verse is the origin of the tradition of "tentmaking"—bivocational ministry in which church workers receive all or part of their income from employment outside the ministry. In the case of Priscilla, Aquila, and Paul, having an income-producing skill allowed them to be self-supporting as necessary. This gave them the freedom to relocate quickly as circumstances required. In the case of the tentmaking couple, they followed Paul to Ephesus (see Acts 18:19, below) and eventually returned to Rome (see Romans 16:3, below), doing ministry at both places in addition to Corinth.

B. Making Disciples (vv. 18-21)

18a. And Paul after this tarried there yet a good while, and then took his leave of the brethren, and sailed thence into Syria, and with him Priscilla and Aquila.

Paul stayed in Corinth for about 18 months (Acts 18:11), but eventually decided to return to *Syria*. Initially, *Priscilla and Aquila* accompanied him, leaving their business in Corinth. No other married couple in the New Testament is like Priscilla and Aquila. They worked together as a team par excellence. It is hard for us to think of one without the other, as it must have been in the first-century church. Luke presents this couple as companions in business and in ministry. Although Luke does not say they were already Christians when Paul met them, this seems to have been the case.

> *What Do You Think?*
>
> What action can you take to identify and better support ministries that are especially suited to a teamwork of married couples?
>
> *Digging Deeper*
>
> What do the further mentions of this husband and wife team in Romans 16:3 (below); 1 Corinthians 16:19; and 2 Timothy 4:19 indicate to you in this regard?

18b. Having shorn his head in Cenchrea: for he had a vow.

Cenchrea, as Corinth's port town on the eastern side of the Isthmus of Corinth, was the natural place for the trio's departure. The *vow* Paul made was likely some form of the Nazarite vow, outlined in Numbers 6:1-21. The vow would have included letting his hair grow. Cutting his hair now suggests that the vow was at an end, though it is possible he would shave *his head* to initiate a vow too. Taking this sort of vow was not compulsory but was a physical sign of a time of spiritual reflection and renewal. Though he was willing to accommodate his lifestyle to relate to people he encountered in ministry (1 Corinthians 9:19-23), Paul continued His Jewish practices (Acts 21:26; etc.).

> *What Do You Think?*
>
> What things are important enough for you to take a vow for? Why?
>
> *Digging Deeper*
>
> Should texts such as Numbers 30:2; Matthew 5:33-37; 23:16-22; and James 5:12 apply? Why, or why not?

19. And he came to Ephesus, and left them there: but he himself entered into the synagogue, and reasoned with the Jews.

Ephesus (which means "desirable") was located on the southwest coast of present-day Turkey. This city served as the capital of the Roman province Asia Minor and was the third-largest city in the Roman Empire. At the time of Paul's arrival,

Ephesus had a large Jewish population with a well-established *synagogue.*

Paul set off a riot in Ephesus in the process of establishing one of the most noteworthy churches in biblical times (Acts 19). On his third missionary journey, Paul would spend the better part of three years in the city (20:31). The church in Ephesus was one of seven to receive a special message from Christ (Revelation 2:1-7).

20-21. When they desired him to tarry longer time with them, he consented not; but bade them farewell, saying, I must by all means keep this feast that cometh in Jerusalem: but I will return again unto you, if God will. And he sailed from Ephesus.

Although Paul received a favorable reception in *Ephesus,* he was in a hurry to get to *Jerusalem* and fulfill his vow. *This feast* likely refers to Passover, the most important annual observance for Jewish people. This would put Paul on a specific timeline, adding urgency in returning to Jerusalem on time. Passover took on new significance for Christian Jews because of its association with the death and resurrection of Jesus (Mark 14:1–16:8). Apparently *God* did *will* Paul to return to Ephesus (see Acts 19:1).

What Do You Think?

How will you respond when you hear others refer to "God's will" in improper ways?

Digging Deeper

What are examples of passages that refer to the will of God as (1) His desire and His decision, (2) His desire and human decision, and (3) human decision and His permission?

C. Making a Preacher (vv. 24-26)

24. And a certain Jew named Apollos, born at Alexandria, an eloquent man, and mighty in the scriptures, came to Ephesus.

While *Ephesus* had a large Jewish population, *Alexandria,* Egypt, was arguably the world center of Greek-thinking (Hellenistic) Judaism. The Septuagint, the Greek Old Testament, was translated in Alexandria—appropriate, given the city's reputation as a center of knowledge.

Apollos was probably educated in systematic interpretation of Scriptures, using methods drawn from Greek philosophers. Apollos's being *eloquent* is evidence of this education, which would include learning to speak clearly and reasonably. He had far more than a casual acquaintance with *the scriptures.*

25. This man was instructed in the way of the Lord; and being fervent in the spirit, he spake and taught diligently the things of the Lord, knowing only the baptism of John.

Apollos's knowledge of *the way of the Lord* indicates that the Christian message had spread to the great city of Alexandria. It had made inroads into its famous Jewish schools, producing students like Apollos. The result was to be passionate and *fervent* when he taught *the things of the Lord.* This reminds us of Paul's synagogue discussions and foreshadows what Apollos did after relocating to Corinth (Acts 18:28).

Though Apollos's teaching was done *diligently,* he did not yet know the full gospel. *The baptism of John* was a ritual cleansing on the basis of repentance (Acts 13:24). It did not include the gift or baptism of the Holy Spirit, something that began at Pentecost (1:5; 2:38; compare 19:1-7). It is one thing to argue academically and know that Jesus is the fulfillment of the Scriptures' prophesying a coming Messiah. It is a much deeper, transformative experience to receive His gift of the Holy Spirit and live in His power.

26. And he began to speak boldly in the synagogue: whom when Aquila and Priscilla had heard, they took him unto them, and expounded unto him the way of God more perfectly.

The Ephesian *synagogue* had not yet divided on the basis of belief or nonbelief in Jesus (see Acts 19:9). *Aquila and Priscilla* likely were active in that synagogue when they *heard* Apollos's teaching. Realizing that his understanding of the Christian message was missing an important component, they met with Apollos privately to bring him to a better understanding of the whole gospel message.

We should note the gravity of this misunderstanding. A message that does not include the Holy Spirit is hardly a full measure of the good news, the gospel of Jesus Christ. The first-century church recognized important connections among preaching about Jesus, baptizing, and the Holy Spirit (see Matthew 28:19; Ephesians 4:4-6; etc.).

To his credit, Apollos accepted this instruction readily and became one of the most influential preachers of the first century. The prominence of Apollos in the writings of Luke and Paul (examples: 1 Corinthians 1:12; 3:5-6; 4:6) speaks also of the importance of Apollos's instruction by Aquila and Priscilla.

> *What Do You Think?*
>
> Under what circumstances would you correct someone's inadequate knowledge of Scripture versus "just letting it go"? Why?
>
> *Digging Deeper*
>
> What texts in addition to Romans 14:5-6 and 1 Corinthians 8 help you decide?

Chaos or Cooperation

A couple lived quietly on their farm. Day in, day out they repeated the same chores. He fed pigs and cows, raked hay, cut wood, repaired worn-out tools, and spruced up weathered farm buildings. She cooked, cleaned, fed chickens and collected eggs, washed clothes, and weeded the garden.

One evening the husband became convinced that his wife's work was preferable to his. So he persuaded her to switch chores. When they did, one mishap followed another—wandering cows and pigs, burned bread, broken eggs, an overturned washtub, etc. Without knowing how to do the other's job, the day became chaos.

Luke never mentioned how Priscilla and Aquila divvied up their work, either with regard to tentmaking or to ministry. We can confidently say, though, that Priscilla and Aquila, unlike the farm couple, valued their own tasks and how each partner helped the other meet their shared goals. God used their cooperation in great ways, not just to keep their own house running but to expand the Lord's kingdom throughout the Roman Empire! How does cooperation in your partnerships expand His kingdom today? How *should* it?

—C. M. W.

II. Leaders with Legacy

(Romans 16:3-4)

A. Assisting an Apostle (v. 3)

3. Greet Priscilla and Aquila my helpers in Christ Jesus.

We finish this lesson with the "greetings section" of Romans 16. Paul returned to Corinth during his third missionary journey and wrote to the church in Rome about AD 57 (see Acts 20:2-3). Although he had never been to Rome (Romans 1:11-13), he knew many people there (see 16:5-15, not in our printed text). To refer to *Priscilla and Aquila* as *helpers* accorded them both a high level of respect among Paul's associates (compare Romans 16:21; 2 Corinthians 8:23; Philemon 24). Incidentally, the Greek word underneath the translation "helpers" is the source of our word *synergy*.

> *What Do You Think?*
>
> When should you acknowledge others by name for their help, knowing that you run the risk of irritating those whom you do not mention?
>
> *Digging Deeper*
>
> What insights do you gain here as you consider the entirety of the list in Romans 16 as well as Philippians 2:25; 4:2-3, and 21-22?

B. Rewarding Risk (v. 4)

4a. Who have for my life laid down their own necks.

In both Corinth and Ephesus, Paul had been in danger. In Corinth, his Jewish opponents hauled him before the proconsul's judgment seat. While Paul himself avoided punishment, the synagogue leader was beaten by the crowd (Acts 18:17).

In Ephesus, Paul encountered a deadly threat in the form of a riot instigated by the silversmiths. Paul was prevented from trying to calm the Ephesian crowd by his "disciples" (Acts 19:23-30). Perhaps these included Priscilla and Aquila. They might have been involved in Paul's escape from Corinth, at risk to themselves as well.

Also possible is some other dangerous situation that occurred during Paul's three years in Ephesus about which no record remains.

4b. Unto whom not only I give thanks, but also all the churches of the Gentiles.

From Paul's letters, we know that *the churches* in both Corinth and Ephesus had Gentile members (1 Corinthians 12:12-14; Ephesians 2:1-14). These churches had reason to be thankful for Priscilla and Aquila not only because they protected Paul but also because they continued to minister to *Gentiles.* As Paul's life was preserved by the couple, so were Gentiles whose eternal lives were secured through their unbiased ministry.

Personal Correspondence

My mother loved to encourage friends and family. She handwrote letters, cards, and notes. She talked about things she was puzzled about in the Bible, or something she heard in a sermon, or a funny thing about her pets.

At my mother's funeral, the preacher of our home congregation read two letters from the many he had received from her. He told us those letters had a knack for arriving just when he needed encouragement the most. In times of need, he could reread a letter and be encouraged by my mother's love.

My mother would have shrugged it off as nothing extraordinary. She considered the preacher like one of us children. Writing to him was just a way to show she cared.

Just as my mother's preacher would reread the notes she sent, so we can reread Paul's letters. How do his greetings to his coworkers encourage you? And how can you encourage a coworker of yours today? —C. M. W.

Conclusion

A. By Ones and Twos

We learn many things from studying the ministry of Priscilla and Aquila. We see a married couple who worked and ministered as a team. There was no competition between them, whether they were building tents or building up the people of God. We see a family willing to relocate whenever God called them, supporting themselves in the original bivocational ministry. Their obedience to God's will made them cherished compan-

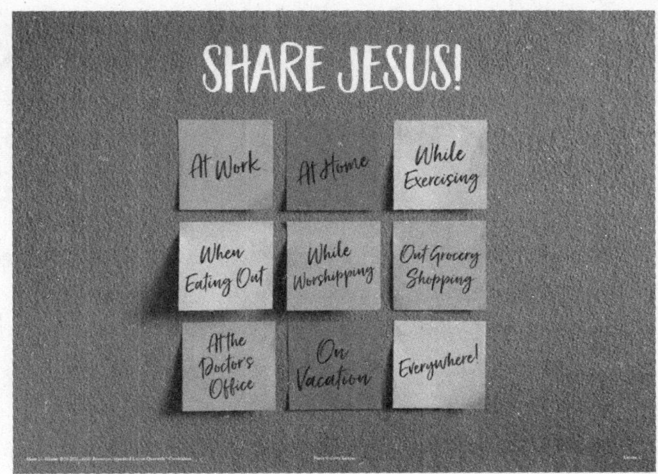

Visual for Lesson 12. *Use these nine notes as starters for discussing what contexts call for ministering in teams rather that as individuals (and vice versa).*

ions to Paul. We see a woman and her husband whom Paul considered to be his "helpers," a designation of high praise.

And we have an example of a sincere and talented preacher receiving private corrective teaching from wiser believers. Apollos's teaching had omitted a crucial Christian doctrine. The discreet yet powerful witness of this godly and faithful married couple was the right remedy at the right time. Their investment in Apollos yielded benefits when he moved to Corinth to minister among their friends in that church (see 1 Corinthians 3:6).

Whether single like Paul or part of a couple like Priscilla and Aquila, *all* God's people have responsibilities to one another. We must "hold fast the profession of our faith without wavering . . . [and] consider one another to provoke unto love and to good works" (Hebrews 10:23-24).

B. Prayer

Father, our churches need believers who are committed to ministries of upreach, outreach, and inreach! Grant that we may be wise and knowledgeable to encourage and correct—and to be encouraged and corrected. In Jesus' name we pray. Amen.

C. Thought to Remember

Women and men, singles and couples
—all are called to minister.

Involvement Learning

Enhance your lesson with KJV Bible Student *(from your curriculum supplier) and the reproducible activity page (at www.standardlesson.com or in the back of the* KJV Standard Lesson Commentary Deluxe Edition*).*

Into the Lesson

As participants arrive, have the following question on the board:

What are some of the best performing teams?

Jot responses on the board as they are voiced. Once you have several listed, ask, "Why are they so good?" Give the class several minutes to share their reasons.

Alternative. Distribute copies of the "Famous Partners on TV" exercise from the activity page, which you can download. Allow one minute for learners to complete as indicated. After that minute, ask why these partners worked well together.

After either activity say, "Some teams work well together to achieve evil purposes (example: Acts 5:1-10), while others work well together for godly purposes. Today we are going to be looking at one such incredible team in the latter category."

Into the Word

Divide the class into four teams. Give each team a slip of paper on which you have written the following:

Corinthian Team: Acts 18:1-3
Ephesian Team: Acts 18:18-21
Alexandrian Team: Acts 18:24-26
Roman Team: Romans 16:3-4

Challenge teams to improve on their given team names based on information they read in their assigned texts. After groups have had a few minutes to deliberate, call for groups to read their assigned texts aloud and announce their teams' improved names. *Option:* Extend the discussion by having teams suggest improvements on other teams' names.

Option or Alternative. Distribute copies of the "Find the Opposite" exercise on the activity page, assigning its completion to research teams. You can assign work to teams either by the exercise's horizontal rows or by its vertical columns. If assigning by row, you will need five teams, one for each trait; if assigning by column, you will need four teams, one for each name.

If you use the five-team approach, say, "Take the negative trait you've been assigned and see if your team can find one instance of its opposite for each of the four people listed." If you use the four-team approach, say, "Research your assigned person and see if you can find an example of an opposite to each of the five negative traits."

Allow time for whole-class discussion of discoveries. If learners could benefit from considering other texts in order to fill out their charts, have these ready to suggest: 1 Corinthians 1:12-13; 3:3-9; 4:1-7; 16:19.

Into Life

Say, "As we wrap up today, let's focus on how we might have the same type of relationship that we see among Paul, Priscilla, and Aquila." Then pose the following questions for discussion. *Teacher Tip:* Ask only one question at a time, allowing discussion to run its course before posing the next.

1–What would a "tentmaking relationship" look like in your situation?
2–Who needs to be discipled by your walking alongside that person as you witness for Jesus?
3–In what ways could you better support the leadership of our church to accomplish its mission?

Distribute note cards and envelopes. Offer learners the chance to write a thank-you note to someone who has had an impact on his or her life much like Priscilla and Aquila did on the lives of Paul and/or Apollos. (Completion rate will be much higher if this is kept as an in-class activity rather than a take-home.) Encourage mailing them!

Called to Serve

Devotional Reading: Psalm 33:1-12
Background Scripture: Acts 16:11-15, 40; 1 Corinthians 1:26-30

Acts 16:11-15, 40

11 Therefore loosing from Troas, we came with a straight course to Samothracia, and the next day to Neapolis;

12 And from thence to Philippi, which is the chief city of that part of Macedonia, and a colony: and we were in that city abiding certain days.

13 And on the sabbath we went out of the city by a river side, where prayer was wont to be made; and we sat down, and spake unto the women which resorted thither.

14 And a certain woman named Lydia, a seller of purple, of the city of Thyatira, which worshipped God, heard us: whose heart the Lord opened, that she attended unto the things which were spoken of Paul.

15 And when she was baptized, and her household, she besought us, saying, If ye have judged me to be faithful to the Lord, come into my house, and abide there. And she constrained us.

. . . .

40 And they went out of the prison, and entered into the house of Lydia: and when they had seen the brethren, they comforted them, and departed.

1 Corinthians 1:26-30

26 For ye see your calling, brethren, how that not many wise men after the flesh, not many mighty, not many noble, are called:

27 But God hath chosen the foolish things of the world to confound the wise; and God hath chosen the weak things of the world to confound the things which are mighty;

28 And base things of the world, and things which are despised, hath God chosen, yea, and things which are not, to bring to nought things that are:

29 That no flesh should glory in his presence.

30 But of him are ye in Christ Jesus, who of God is made unto us wisdom, and righteousness, and sanctification, and redemption.

Key Verse

When she was baptized, and her household, she besought us, saying, If ye have judged me to be faithful to the Lord, come into my house, and abide there. And she constrained us. —**Acts 16:15**

Call in the New Testament

Unit 3: The Call of Women

Lessons 9–13

Lesson Aims

After participating in this lesson, each learner will be able to:

1. Identify on a map the locations mentioned.
2. Compare and contrast the roles of Paul and Lydia in planting the church in Philippi.
3. Improve in his or her best area of service in categories of inreach, outreach, and upreach.

Lesson Outline

Introduction
- A. Career and Hospitality
- B. Lesson Context

I. Entry to Europe (Acts 16:11-15, 40)
- A. Philippi (vv. 11-12)
- B. The Prayer Meeting (v. 13)
- C. Lydia's House (vv. 14-15, 40)
  - *Humble Hospitality Builds Churches*

II. Correction to Corinth (1 Corinthians 1:26-30)
- A. Calling the Ordinary (v. 26)
- B. Confounding the Wise (vv. 27-29)
  - *All Things Are Possible*
- C. Inclusion in Christ (v. 30)

Conclusion
- A. Serving as God Desires
- B. Glorying in the Cross
- C. Prayer
- D. Thought to Remember

Introduction

A. Career and Hospitality

Hospitality can make careers. Dolley Madison (1768–1849), wife of US president James Madison, was a great political asset in her husband's career. James certainly had merit as a great writer and political mind, being called today the Father of the Constitution. But he was a shy man, not given to promoting his own interests.

After they wed, Dolley's parties made people feel welcome and turned guests into political supporters. As the First Lady, Dolley largely shaped what it meant to hold that position in terms of hospitality and volunteerism.

Deidre Mathis's hospitality career began when she was a world traveler on a tight budget. She would stay in hostels to save money. Deidre's experiences of bonding with other women travelers inspired her to open her own hostel in downtown Houston. Her hostel combines her love of connecting with people with her passion for business. Hospitality made her welcome around the world; now she welcomes the world to Houston.

Going the other direction, we might say that careers can fund hospitality as well. This direction is the focus of an individual in today's lesson.

B. Lesson Context

Paul and his companions began their second missionary journey around AD 52. It began with revisits to some of the cities Paul had visited on the first journey. These included Derbe, Lystra, and (perhaps) Iconium (Acts 16:1-2).

From there they headed west to Troas. While in Troas, Paul had a vision of a "man of Macedonia" who entreated him to come over to Macedonia and help (Acts 16:9). The vision served as a warrant for Paul to cross the Aegean Sea and enter Europe with the gospel—his first time to do so. Paul's initial visits to the cities of Philippi and Corinth both occurred during this trip.

The city of Philippi sat in a commanding position on the fertile plain of the Gangites River, surrounded by mountains on three sides. Its site is in the northeast quadrant of modern Greece. About 400 years old when visited by Paul, Philippi was a major Macedonian city. Philippi's name comes from King Philip II of Macedon, who conquered the city in 356 BC and renamed it for himself.

That was one of the first steps in Philip's domination of the entire Greek peninsula. It set the stage for his successor and son, Alexander the Great, to march east and conquer territories all the way to India. The gold mines for which the city of Philippi was known provided great wealth for both leaders to fund their military campaigns. But the apostle Paul was in search of gold of a different kind, and he found it.

I. Entry to Europe

(Acts 16:11-15, 40)

A. Philippi (vv. 11-12)

11. Therefore loosing from Troas, we came with a straight course to Samothracia, and the next day to Neapolis.

Troas was a major seaport on the eastern shore of the Aegean Sea. There Paul, Silas, and others were joined by Luke, for the "they" of Acts 16:8 changes to "we" in 16:10. These missionaries boarded a ship for Macedonia, going by way of the small island-city of *Samothracia* to the western Aegean port city *Neapolis*. From Troas to Neapolis was about 150 miles, which they sailed in two days.

12. And from thence to Philippi, which is the chief city of that part of Macedonia, and a colony: and we were in that city abiding certain days.

Neapolis served as a seaport to the important city of *Philippi* (see Lesson Context). The journey between the two cities was about nine miles. In 168 BC, the city became a Roman *colony*, a place where veteran soldiers could retire and receive a tract of land to farm. Philippi was the easternmost point on the Via Egnatia, the great Roman highway of about 535 miles in length, that crossed the Greek peninsula. Philippi appeared to be a good city for the missionaries' task, for they decided to stay *certain days*.

B. The Prayer Meeting (v. 13)

13. And on the sabbath we went out of the city by a river side, where prayer was wont to be made; and we sat down, and spake unto the women which resorted thither.

Paul's usual strategy was to visit the city's synagogue *on the sabbath* to teach fellow Jews about Jesus (example: Acts 13:14b-15, 26-42). Tradition required that a community have 10 married Jewish men to have a synagogue, but that number seems to have been unavailable in this overwhelmingly Gentile city.

Instead, a group met outside the city gates *by a river side*. This place could have been by the Gangites River, about a mile west of town, but this is uncertain. A place *where prayer was wont to be made* is a way of describing any synagogue. Since there was no synagogue there, the phrase suggests that those who gathered intended their meetings to be similar to those that occurred in synagogues.

> *What Do You Think?*
> How would you characterize your ideal place to pray?
> *Digging Deeper*
> For you personally, how does the issue of *where* to pray interact with the issue of *how* to pray?

This prayer group seems to have consisted solely of *women*. In addition to that demographic, Paul would have encountered them in terms of one of three religious persuasions: as Jews, as proselytes (converts to Judaism; see Acts 13:43), or as God-fearing Gentiles who had not converted to Judaism (10:2, 22).

The third category is most likely, given the nature of the city of Philippi. Paul's willingness to minister to a group of Gentile women echoed Jesus' own ministry at Jacob's well (John 4:1-42; see lesson 10).

C. Lydia's House (vv. 14-15, 40)

14. And a certain woman named Lydia, a seller of purple, of the city of Thyatira, which worshipped God, heard us: whose heart the Lord opened, that she attended unto the things which were spoken of Paul.

Interestingly, the *certain woman named Lydia* bears the ancient name of the Kingdom of Lydia, which existed 1200–546 BC. It encompassed roughly the western half of the modern country of Turkey. So the woman Lydia was named after the area within which her town of *Thyatira* was located —an area from which Paul had just come, after having received a vision in which a "man of Macedonia" had invited him to come over (Acts 16:9)! There is a certain irony in all this.

In Paul's day, Thyatira was the chief source of dyed fabric. The woman Lydia specialized in *purple* fabric. This particular work was difficult but profitable for those with skill. To sell purple cloth was to deal in luxury items, so it is likely that Lydia had prosperous business connections in her hometown and sold products in far-flung cities like Philippi.

Like the Gentile Cornelius (Acts 10), Lydia *worshipped God* and may have been drawn to the Jewish faith without converting to it (contrast 13:43). Many barriers existed against full inclusion with the Jewish people. But Luke regularly recognized the faithfulness of those people who, like Lydia, worshipped and feared God (13:16, 26) or were otherwise "devout" (10:2). As Paul encountered such a one here, so he would again (17:4, 17).

Surely Lydia's prior worship of God had prepared her heart to hear Paul's message. *The Lord*, not Paul or his rhetoric, then *opened* her *heart* to Paul's presentation of the gospel. God had gone before His missionary, and God will continue after His missionary finishes. As Paul will later write to the Corinthians, one person might plant a seed and another might water, "but God [gives] the increase" (1 Corinthians 3:6).

15. And when she was baptized, and her household, she besought us, saying, If ye have judged me to be faithful to the Lord, come into my house, and abide there. And she constrained us.

Lydia responded to Paul's message with faith. We can imagine that Lydia *and her household* were *baptized* right there at the river without delay. (The importance of baptism is seen in Acts 2:38; 22:16; Romans 6:3-5; Galatians 3:27; Colossians 2:12-13; Titus 3:5; etc.).

As an outflowing of gratitude to God for accepting her into His family, Lydia invited Paul and his companions to her *house* to stay for a while. Asking the men to judge whether she was *faithful to the Lord* reveals that this was also a test. Would the Jewish men visit the home of a Gentile woman? How included in God's kingdom was she *really*? By insisting that the missionaries join her, Lydia revealed her own conviction that she and all her household were now entirely acceptable to the Lord. Nothing was lacking in her salvation.

Given Lydia's vocation, we receive the impression that hers was a generous home, both in physical size and in hospitality.

What Do You Think?

What are some ways you can help provide and promote a ministry of hospitality?

Digging Deeper

What imperatives and boundaries do Acts 28:7; Romans 12:13; 16:23; 1 Timothy 5:10; Titus 1:8; Hebrews 13:2; 1 Peter 4:9; 2 John 9-11; and 3 John 8 establish in this regard?

40. And they went out of the prison, and entered into the house of Lydia: and when they had seen the brethren, they comforted them, and departed.

While in Philippi, Paul and Silas were arrested for casting a spirit of divination out of a fortune-telling slave girl (Acts 16:16-24). Following the

HOW TO SAY IT

Aegean	A-*jee*-un.
Corinth	*Kor*-inth.
Corinthians	Ko-*rin*-thee-unz (*th* as in *thin*).
Derbe	*Der*-be.
Galatians	Guh-*lay*-shunz.
Gentile	*Jen*-tile.
Iconium	Eye-*ko*-nee-um.
Macedonia	Mass-eh-*doe*-nee-uh.
Neapolis	Nee-*ap*-o-lis.
omnipotent	ahm-*nih*-poh-tent.
omniscient	ahm-*nish*-unt.
Philippi	Fih-*lip*-pie or *Fil*-ih-pie.
Samothracia	Sam-o-*thray*-shuh.
Silas	*Sigh*-luss.
Thyatira	*Thy*-uh-***tie***-ruh (*th* as in *thin*).
Troas	*Tro*-az.

conversion of their guard and release from *prison* (16:25-39), Paul and Silas returned to *the house of Lydia*. The unjust treatment of the missionaries was traumatic for them and the new congregation. This became a time for all to be *comforted.*

Lydia's home in Philippi surely became the initial meeting place for this group of believers. However, the book of Philippians, written a decade or so later, contains no reference to Lydia. We can only surmise that she was no longer in Philippi, perhaps having moved to Thyatira or elsewhere—maybe even having passed away. Her legacy of hospitality, service, and faithfulness endured in this church, however, as Paul celebrated the partnership those of the church had maintained "from the first day until now" (Philippians 1:5).

Humble Hospitality Builds Churches

Elijah A. Frost organized a church in Cassville, Missouri, in 1885. The church met on Elijah's front porch. Frost wasn't a preacher, but he knew how to pray. He loved Jesus, the Word of God, and his neighbors.

His great hospitality invited others to learn and grow with him. These few dedicated Christians—praying in Christ's name, praising God though spiritual songs, and trusting in God's holy Word—turned a humble porch into a sanctuary.

Similarly, Lydia met with a few women at the river. Out of her humble prayer group would spring the greatest church in all of Asia Minor. The fledgling church began with women. The church grew in large part thanks to Lydia's hospitality.

Our churches are going to grow in the same way. How can your humble home and godly hospitality bless the church as Brother Frost and Lydia did?

—C. T.

What Do You Think?

In our era of ready access to restaurants and hotels, what emphasis should you and your church place on in-home hospitality? Why?

Digging Deeper

In what ways does a need for short-term versus long-term hospitality change your answer, if at all? Why?

II. Correction to Corinth

(1 Corinthians 1:26-30)

A. Calling the Ordinary (v. 26)

26. For ye see your calling, brethren, how that not many wise men after the flesh, not many mighty, not many noble, are called.

Paul had planted the church in Corinth in about AD 52. Now, in about AD 56, he writes a letter to that church while ministering in Ephesus. The letter is in response to troubling reports of factions and disunity (1 Corinthians 1:11).

Paul reminded the Corinthian Christians of what they had been before coming to Christ. Their church did not begin with leaders who had great educations, widespread social influence, or distinguished families. Doubly, Paul may have wanted to remind the Corinthians that their (mostly) Gentile backgrounds had prevented them from attaining any standing among God's people before.

Regarding being *wise . . . after the flesh,* Paul was well acquainted with the dangers there. He himself was able to quote Greek philosophers and scholars (see 1 Corinthians 15:33; Titus 1:12; Acts 17:24-29) while recognizing the overall defects in philosophies not grounded in Scripture (1 Corinthians 1:20; 2:1-5; Colossians 2:8).

What Do You Think?

Without giving directive advice, how would you counsel an unbeliever who was prideful of his or her status in life?

Digging Deeper

Under what circumstances would you and would you not use Scripture as part of your discussion (contrast Acts 17:10-12 with 17:16-34)?

B. Confounding the Wise (vv. 27-29)

27. But God hath chosen the foolish things of the world to confound the wise; and God hath chosen the weak things of the world to confound the things which are mighty.

Paul sees the great irony in all of this. All human wisdom and power are finite things and miniscule when compared to the power and

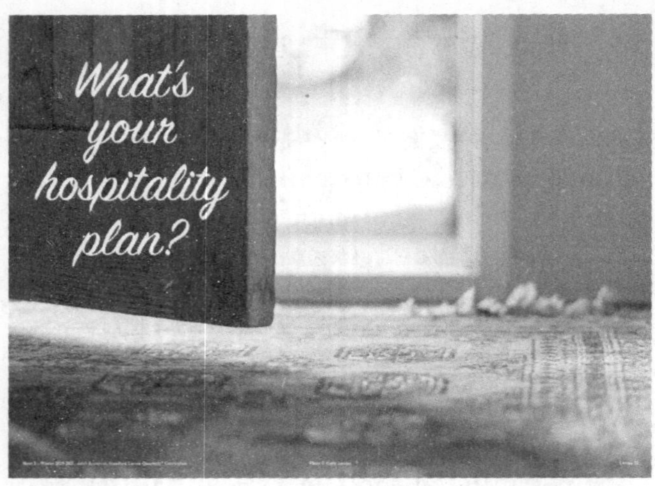
What's your hospitality plan?

Visual for Lesson 13. *Point to this visual as a way to introduce the discussion question in the bottom of the left column of page 221.*

wisdom of God. God is omnipotent (all-powerful) and omniscient (all-knowing) in ways humans barely begin to understand.

But God does not often choose to dazzle people into belief by displays of might and intelligence. God prefers to use *the foolish* and *the weak things of the world* to communicate His loving concern and His plan for humankind (see 1 Corinthians 1:28, below). In so doing, God is able *to confound* the world's expectations. In 1 Corinthians 1:23, Paul referred to the crucifixion of Christ as a "stumblingblock." Christ's atoning death on the cross was scandalous, not what the Jews expected from their Messiah (compare Galatians 3:13-14).

We are reminded of Peter, who, when told that Jesus would accomplish the Father's will by Jesus' humiliation, suffering, death, and resurrection in Jerusalem, exclaimed, "Be it far from thee, Lord" (Matthew 16:22). Peter did not expect the Messiah to bring victory through death.

28. And base things of the world, and things which are despised, hath God chosen, yea, and things which are not, to bring to nought things that are.

The word translated *base* is the antonym of the word for "noble" in 1 Corinthians 1:26—literally, "ignoble." In the Roman world, there was nothing more ignoble than a cross, the torture-execution for the worst criminals. It was especially problematic to Jews because of the curse of hanging on a tree (Deuteronomy 21:23).

Christians today see the cross as a comforting and victorious symbol. Churches display it. We wear it on necklaces and other jewelry. We even tattoo it on our bodies. Not so in Paul's day. The cross was shameful; nothing could be more despised among polite society. But God does not play by society's rules or expectations. A Christian seeing a cross in the first century would be struck by the completely unexpected and humbling circumstances of Jesus' sacrifice. What is scandalous for us may be glorious for God.

All Things Are Possible

My 7-year-old grandson Alex: "I'm hungry!"

My daughter, Sarah: "That's impossible! You just ate lunch!"

Alex: "Mom, all things are possible with God. You might want to jot that down!"

My grandson is absorbing some important truths in his Sunday school class! While a silly example, his words are a great reminder that all things really *are* possible with God.

Lydia's story seems impossible. A man invited Paul to come to Macedonia (Acts 16:9), but Paul didn't find a man. He found Lydia, an independent, apparently single, wealthy woman. She was already the leader of a women's prayer group. She became a charter member of what would become one of the most influential churches in the area. Again, we think, "Impossible!"

Indeed, "with God, all things are possible" (Mark 10:27). What impossible task is God calling you to undertake for Him? —C. T.

29. That no flesh should glory in his presence.

God's upside-down plan ensures that no one can claim credit for their own salvation. *No flesh* would think of the plan God enacted as the solution to human sinfulness. The paradoxical nature of the gospel does not allow for anyone to receive self-created *glory* in God's *presence.*

Paul's example is instructive. His miracles did not speak to his own power, but to God's (1 Corinthians 2:4-5). And his preaching of the gospel was persuasive not because of his own eloquence. The Corinthians prided themselves as discerning, intelligent people—they could be impressed by a well-reasoned speech of no substance. But Paul had instead presented a message of the utmost importance. The truth of the gospel, not human skill, had convinced the Corinthian Christians.

C. Inclusion in Christ (v. 30)

30. But of him are ye in Christ Jesus, who of God is made unto us wisdom, and righteousness, and sanctification, and redemption.

God's *wisdom,* unlike the world's, finds fulfillment *in Christ Jesus. Righteousness* invokes a legal term that means even though we are guilty of our sins, "no penalty" is the sentence. The prophets often took this word further, defining it not in terms of a lack of wrong actions but as the presence of right actions (examples: Isaiah 33:15; Ezekiel 3:20-21; Hosea 10:12).

The Holy Spirit works *sanctification* in us, teaching us to identify sin and empowering us to overcome it (Galatians 5:13-21) and produce the fruit of the Spirit (5:22-26). This allows us to live holy lives that would be impossible without God's power (Romans 8:1-16).

Redemption is a term associated with being freed from slavery. In the Roman Empire, a slave could purchase his or her own freedom. But sinners have no way to pay for our own freedom. We have not only been bought by the blood of Jesus—we have been set free from our slavery to sin (Romans 6:17). Instead we serve righteousness (6:18).

Put together, righteousness, sanctification, and redemption describe the reality of being in Christ (Ephesians 1:11). Through the cross God has made a way for us to be restored to fellowship with Him. This is our salvation in Jesus Christ.

> *What Do You Think?*
> What are some practical ways for you to live more fully as a witness that you have righteousness, sanctification (holiness), and redemption in Christ?
>
> *Digging Deeper*
> What specific, personal weakness in this regard does 1 Corinthians 1:31 challenge you on? What other passages apply?

Conclusion

A. Serving as God Desires

Our last four weeks have explored the examples of Anna, the prophetess daughters of Philip, the Samaritan woman, Mary Magdalene, and Priscilla. In Lydia's case, she made use of her status and wealth to serve God. Her influence brought her household to Christ and had a ripple effect in Philippi. Her prosperous business allowed her to host Paul and his companions in her house, as well as the church that would grow from their efforts. These efforts were not accomplished for the glory of Lydia or Paul. Both sought only to follow Christ and lead others to Him.

We might summarize the accounts from this unit and say that each woman served where God gave her opportunity and gifting. The same holds true today. When a woman senses God's calling on her to use her job, her social connections, and/or the spiritual gifts He gave her for His glory, she can and will find a way to serve. While the same is true for men, the nature of women's ministries has often been less visible and sometimes considered less critical in spreading the gospel.

B. Glorying in the Cross

As Paul wrote in 1 Corinthians, God chose the cross to show His wisdom instead of using what was already honored and revered in *any* human society. And the foolishness of the world became the wisdom of God. God still uses people following the way of the cross to show His wisdom to the world. Let us all continue to seek His wisdom and remain open to other "foolish" things God may choose in place of the "wise." In this way, we seek only God's glory.

C. Prayer

Lord God, all Christians need places to serve! May we answer You as You call us to the right place at the right time and gift us in the right way to do Your will. We pray in Jesus' name. Amen.

D. Thought to Remember

Seek the wisdom of the cross.
Serve in its shadow.

Involvement Learning

Enhance your lesson with KJV Bible Student *(from your curriculum supplier) and the reproducible activity page (at www.standardlesson.com or in the back of the* KJV Standard Lesson Commentary Deluxe Edition*).*

Into the Lesson

Option. Before class begins, place on chairs copies of the "Places of Transition" word-search puzzle. Learners can begin working on this as they arrive.

Begin with a one-minute individual exercise as you distribute slips of paper (you prepare) on which you have printed the following question:

> By yourself, estimate how many total 'person hours' it took to edit and fit the copy of the lesson we're now studying. Make your estimate for the teacher guide only, not for the student book. Don't include time for proofreading, contract management, visuals, etc.

After the minute is up, call for responses and jot them on the board. After each response, ask, "What is your basis for that estimate?" (Expect that most will be in the category of wild guesses.)

Then inform learners that you are going to work together to prepare a more precise estimate. Ask each learner to give an estimate for each lesson's elements individually: (1) the discussion questions in the five boxes, (2) the two verbal illustrations together (segments headed with ☙), (3) the verse by verse commentary itself, and (4) this Involvement Learning page. After getting a tally for a section, compute the average. Then add all tallies together for the overall average. (*Actual averages* for the four sections in a single lesson are 2.9, 1.5, 12.4, and 1.9 hours respectively—a total of 18.7 hours.)

Regardless of the final tally, ask your learners about their levels of confidence during the two tries: Was it better to work as a team or individually? Why? Use responses to lead into today's lesson on partnerships in teamwork.

Into the Word

Summarize the Lesson Context. Then ask a volunteer to read Acts 16:11-15, 40. Distribute handouts (you prepare) with the following task (same task for all groups): *Compare and contrast the roles of Paul and Lydia in planting the church in Philippi. [**Compare** means how they were similar; **contrast** means how they were different.]*

Call time after a few minutes for whole-class discussion of discoveries.

Read 1 Corinthians 1:26-30 to the class. Share with students a hand-drawn picture of yourself that depicts who you were before Jesus. Give a perspective on how your relationship with Jesus has changed you. Allow a minute for learners to sketch their own "before" and "after" self-portraits. Discuss results. Reread 1 Corinthians 1:26-30 without commenting; just let the text speak for itself.

Into Life

Divide the class in half. Have one of the halves brainstorm all the types of gatherings that happen at the church building. Instruct the other half to brainstorm all types of gatherings that could occur in homes.

After five minutes, have each group share its list. Then create a table on the board with three columns intersected by three rows. Label the columns *Inreach Events / Upreach Events / Outreach Events* (one label per column). Label the three intersecting rows as follows: *Better in Homes / Better at the Church Building / OK at Either* (one label per row).

Using the lists from both groups, as well as further discussion, have the class help you fill out the chart. *Teacher Tip:* If the anyone asks what *inreach, upreach*, and *outreach events* are, don't answer. Instead, turn the question over to the class to answer—force them to think. Provide these responses as a last resort: *inreach* deals with teaching fellow Christians for greater spiritual maturity, bearing one another's burdens, etc.; *upreach* deals with worship and prayer; *outreach* concerns evangelism and benevolence. *Option.* Distribute copies of the "Church Planting" exercise on the activity page as a take-home for private reflection.

PROPHETS FAITHFUL TO GOD'S COVENANT

Special Features

Lessons

Unit 1: Faithful Prophets

Unit 2: Prophets of Restoration

Unit 3: Courageous Prophets of Change

Quarterly Quiz

Use these questions as a pretest or as a review. The answers are on page iv of This Quarter in the Word.

Lesson 1

1. The Lord said he would raise up a(n) ______ like Moses from the Israelites. *Deuteronomy 18:18*

2. The penalty for prophesying in the name of other gods was death. T/F. *Deuteronomy 18:20*

Lesson 2

1. What was Joshua told to remove because where he stood was holy? (sword, shoe, helmet) *Joshua 5:15*

2. On the seventh day, the priests sounded the ________ and Jericho's walls fell. *Joshua 6:16, 20*

Lesson 3

1. The sin that incited the Lord's anger against Judah was idolatry. T/F. *2 Kings 22:17*

2. Josiah, king of Judah, was promised to be spared the coming disaster. T/F. *2 Kings 22:19-20*

Lesson 4

1. Obadiah feared being killed if he announced Ahab's presence to Elijah. T/F. *1 Kings 18:8-9*

2. Ahab referred to Elijah as "he that ________ Israel." *1 Kings 18:17*

Lesson 5

1. Jesus suffered for our what? (pick two: ignorance, iniquities, transgressions, tendencies, indiscretions) *Isaiah 53:5*

2. "We like _____ have gone astray." *Isaiah 53:6*

Lesson 6

1. Priests and Levites were the only ones not guilty of intermarriage. T/F. *Ezra 10:5*

2. The taking of strange wives increased the trespass of______. T/F. *Ezra 10:10*

Lesson 7

1. The names of Nehemiah's opponents were what? (pick three: Artaxerxes, Ezra, Geshem, Jezebel, Sanballat, Tobiah) *Nehemiah 2:19*

2. Nehemiah acknowledged that his opponents had a small but historic right in Jerusalem. T/F. *Nehemiah 2:20*

Lesson 8

1. To get bread, the Judeans had submitted to what peoples? (pick two: Assyrians, Greeks, Egyptians, Persians) *Lamentations 5:6*

2. Because of the punishment, dancing had turned into ________. *Lamentations 5:15*

Lesson 9

1. Micaiah saw "all Israel . . . as ________ that have not a ________." *1 Kings 22:17*

2. A spirit promised to protect King Ahab. T/F. *1 Kings 22:22*

Lesson 10

1. The people were near the Lord in their hearts but far away in mouth and lips. T/F. *Isaiah 29:13*

2. Isaiah prophesied that the blind would see out of what? (darkness, light, glass) *Isaiah 29:18*

Lesson 11

1. Jeremiah told a king to surrender to the Egyptians to be spared. T/F. *Jeremiah 38:17*

2. If the king didn't surrender to the enemy, Jerusalem would be burned. T/F. *Jeremiah 38:21, 23*

Lesson 12

1. The people blamed their ancestors by quoting a proverb involving sour ________. *Ezekiel 18:2*

2. The people needed a new what? (pick two: attitude, command, heart, spirit) *Ezekiel 18:31*

Lesson 13

1. Jonah was called to preach in what great city? (Babylon, Nineveh, Jerusalem) *Jonah 3:2*

2. The great city in which Jonah preached was prophesied to be destroyed in how many days? (666, 40, 3) *Jonah 3:4*

Quarter at a Glance

by Mark Hahlen

They were a combination of preacher, whistleblower, and counselor—they were the prophets of the Old Testament era. They warned people who had turned away from the Lord; and they encouraged the faithful to remain faithful. From time to time, they fortified their calls by foretelling the future intent and plans of the sovereign God.

Words of Faithfulness

The lessons of **Unit 1** highlight the faithfulness of God, who reveals to His people their need to be faithful to Him. Lesson 1 recounts Moses' foretelling of a prophet whom God would raise up within Israel to speak the Lord's words to them. Israel's necessary response would be to obey the prophet. These words anticipate the line of prophets God would send, culminating in the ultimate prophet, Jesus Christ (see Acts 3:17-26).

The faithfulness of Israel in response to the Lord's faithfulness was on display in the conquest of Jericho, lesson 2. In lesson 3, God shows His faithfulness to Josiah, the king of Judah, who had wisely and humbly consulted a true prophet. The unit's final study, lesson 4, focuses on the faithful prophet Elijah, who courageously confronted Ahab, the king of Israel, for forsaking the Lord in favor of the Baals.

Words of Restoration

Lessons of **Unit 2** focus on restoration and hope. These begin with the Easter Sunday lesson that focuses on the connection between Isaiah's fourth Servant Song and the account of Jesus' resurrection in Luke 24.

The sacrifice of Christ on the cross makes possible forgiveness of sins and removes our estrangement from the Father. That estrangement is powerfully illustrated by the prophet Jeremiah in Lamentations 5 (lesson 8). Backsliders, then as now, often must take difficult and decisive action to remove obstacles to a restored relationship with God. But that must be done in order to experience God's blessings. The texts studied in lessons 6 and 7 narrate such decisive action on the part of the post-exilic figures Ezra and Nehemiah.

Words of Change

At the center of the prophetic message is a call to repentance and change, and **Unit 3** focuses on the necessity and possibility of these. In lessons 9 and 11, the prophets Micaiah and Jeremiah courageously spoke truth to powerful individuals who were unwilling to acknowledge and act on that truth. On the other hand, lesson 13 narrates a positive response to a prophetic message on the part of a most unlikely audience: the wicked non-Israelite city of Nineveh. The forgiving response from the Lord in the light of that repentance puts the lie to the old contention that the God of the Old Testament was solely a God of wrath.

> ***The sacrifice of Christ . . . removes our estrangement from the Father.***

In lesson 10, the Lord, through the prophet Isaiah, denounced Judah as a people who "draw near me with their mouth, and with their lips do honour me, but have removed their heart far from me" (Isaiah 29:13). Nevertheless, the prophet anticipates a transformation that will come when the Lord acts to change the people, a change likened to the deaf hearing and the blind seeing.

Ezekiel declares in lesson 12 that the path to such a transformation begins in repentance. Each person stands individually responsible before the loving and holy God, who calls out, "Repent, and turn yourselves from all your transgressions; so iniquity shall not be your ruin. . . . For I have no pleasure in the death of him that dieth. . . . Wherefore turn yourselves, and live" (Ezekiel 18:30-32).

Get the Setting

by Lloyd M. Pelfrey

God and Israel entered into a covenantal relationship at Mt. Sinai. Israel, however, was not faithful in keeping the covenant. God therefore used prophets to remind, review, rebuke, and/or renew the covenant.

The time frame to be considered this quarter ranges from Moses to Nehemiah, a span of one thousand years (about 1445 to 445 BC). The prophets in the Old Testament spoke for God, thus fulfilling the definition of a prophet as illustrated in Exodus 7:1-2. Some prophets became authors of the books of the Old Testament.

The concept of a *prophet* was well known in the biblical era. Nations from Egypt to Babylon had this concept in their cultures. Clay tablets from Nineveh and Mari (in northern Syria) witness to this fact. Differences and similarities existed in the ways that prophets functioned in Israel and in other nations.

Through Dreams (etc.)

Prophetic dreams are mentioned frequently in Genesis, starting in chapter 20. A key verse in this regard is Numbers 12:6: "If there be a prophet among you, I the Lord will make myself known unto him in a vision, and will speak unto him in a dream."

But Moses warned that false prophets may also have dreams (see Deuteronomy 13:1-5). Idolatrous prophets considered dreams a primary method of communication from their supposed deities. A prophecy was deemed more valid if the prophet had the same dream on consecutive nights. The prophets of the court and lay persons alike were supposed recipients for such "divine" communications.

Usually the so-called prophets did not do anything to cause the dreams. On occasion, however, some went through rituals that were thought to aid dreaming. King Gilgamesh in *The Epic of Gilgamesh* is an example of someone trying to cause a dream.

For Royalty

Kings were often the ultimate recipients for the dreams, and it was the task of the prophets to interpret them for the kings (compare Genesis 41:1-8; Daniel 2). The messages might include promises about becoming a king, announcements of military victories, or assurances that the deities were supporting the king. One example is an Assyrian king who was told that 60 gods were watching over him. (This was Esarhaddon; see 2 Kings 19:37.)

Warnings concerning future events were part of some prophecies. When a pagan god was reported to say that the land would soon have another ruler, there was cause to be concerned! Most scholars are of the opinion that such "predictive" prophecies were written after the events had already occurred.

For the People

In Israel, however, many prophets lived and served when the nation did not have kings—it was the people who needed to hear the messages. This was the case for prophets such as Moses, Joshua (to whom the Lord spoke about 14 recorded times), the unnamed prophet in Judges 6:7-10, and Samuel. Ezekiel's prophecies were primarily for the captives in Babylon, not for any kings back in Judah. The Jews who returned from the Babylonian captivity were under Persian rule, so there was no king in Israel in the days when Haggai, Zechariah, and Malachi spoke and wrote prophetic messages.

Because of Covenant

A major contrast between the prophets of Israel and their pagan counterparts was the concept of *covenant*. A critical concern for the Lord's prophets was that Israel was not faithful in keeping the covenant. We too live under covenant—the new covenant in Christ. The lesson is the same today: it is vital not only to enter into the covenant with Christ, but also to keep faith with that covenant.

Mon, May 17	**Treat Each Other Fairly**	Deuteronomy 24:14-18
Tue, May 18	**Take Personal Responsibility**	Jeremiah 31:27-30
Wed, May 19	**The Sinning Child Is Punished**	Ezekiel 18:10-13
Thu, May 20	**The Righteous Child Is Rewarded**	Ezekiel 18:14-18
Fri, May 21	**Personal Accountability for Sin**	Ezekiel 18:19-24
Sat, May 22	**God Is Compassionate and Fair**	Ezekiel 18:25-29
Sun, May 23	**Repent and Live Rightly**	Ezekiel 18:1-9, 30-32
Mon, May 24	**Jonah's Experience Foreshadows Christ's**	Matthew 12:38-42
Tue, May 25	**A Lasting Message of Repentance**	Luke 11:29-32
Wed, May 26	**Jonah Resists God's Call**	Jonah 1:1-12
Thu, May 27	**Sailors Make Vows**	Jonah 1:13-16
Fri, May 28	**Jonah Resents God's Grace for Others**	Jonah 4:1-5
Sat, May 29	**God's Compassion Overrides Jonah's Comfort**	Jonah 4:6-11
Sun, May 30	**God's Mercy Prevails**	Jonah 3

Answers to the Quarterly Quiz on page 226

Lesson 1—1. prophet. 2. true. **Lesson 2**—1. shoe. 2. trumpets. **Lesson 3**—1. true. 2. true. **Lesson 4**—1. false. 2. troubleth. **Lesson 5**—1. sheep. 2. iniquities, transgressions. **Lesson 6**—1. false. 2. Israel. **Lesson 7**—1. Geshem, Sanballat, Tobiah 2. false. **Lesson 8**—1. Assyrians, Egyptians. 2. mourning. **Lesson 9**—1. sheep, shepherd. 2. false. **Lesson 10**—1. false. 2. darkness. **Lesson 11**—1. false. 2. true. **Lesson 12**—1. grapes. 2. heart, spirit. **Lesson 13**—1. Nineveh. 2. 40.

This Quarter in the Word

Mon, Mar. 1	**Remember God's Acts of Deliverance**	Psalm 77:11-20
Tue, Mar. 2	**Listen to Moses**	Luke 16:24-31
Wed, Mar. 3	**Instructions for Passover, Part 1**	Exodus 12:43-50
Thu, Mar. 4	**Instructions for Passover, Part 2**	Numbers 9:9-14
Fri, Mar. 5	**Consecrate All Firstborn to God**	Exodus 13:1-2; Deuteronomy 15:19-20
Sat, Mar. 6	**Feast of Unleavened Bread**	Exodus 13:3-10
Sun, Mar. 7	**God Leads Through Prophets**	Deuteronomy 18:15-22
Mon, Mar. 8	**Rahab's Faithfulness**	Hebrews 11:23-31
Tue, Mar. 9	**Jesus Heals a Blind Man**	Luke 18:35-42
Wed, Mar. 10	**Manna and Local Produce**	Joshua 5:8-12
Thu, Mar. 11	**Marching Around Jericho**	Joshua 6:6-14
Fri, Mar. 12	**Rahab and the Spies Plan**	Joshua 2:15-24
Sat, Mar. 13	**Rahab Saved; Jericho Destroyed**	Joshua 6:22-25
Sun, Mar. 14	**Joshua Conquers Jericho**	Joshua 5:13–6:5, 15-16, 20
Mon, Mar. 15	**God Loves Covenant Keepers**	Psalm 25:1-10
Tue, Mar. 16	**Entering God's Promised Rest**	Hebrews 4:1-11
Wed, Mar. 17	**Covenant with Israelites**	Deuteronomy 29:1-6
Thu, Mar. 18	**Josiah Prepares to Repair the Temple**	2 Kings 22:1-7
Fri, Mar. 19	**Josiah Seeks Guidance**	2 Kings 22:8-13
Sat, Mar. 20	**Josiah Leads in Covenant Renewal**	2 Kings 23:1-3
Sun, Mar. 21	**Josiah Spared from Judgment**	2 Kings 22:14-20

Mon, Mar. 22	**Elijah with Moses and Jesus**	Mark 9:2-8
Tue, Mar. 23	**John the Baptist as "Elijah"**	Mark 9:9-13
Wed, Mar. 24	**Elijah Sent to King Ahab**	1 Kings 18:1-4
Thu, Mar. 25	**Elijah Challenges Idolaters**	1 Kings 18:20-26, 30-33, 36-39
Fri, Mar. 26	**Elijah in the Wilderness**	1 Kings 19:1-8
Sat, Mar. 27	**God Commissions Elijah**	1 Kings 19:9b-15
Sun, Mar. 28	**King Ahab Meets Elijah**	1 Kings 18:5-18
Mon, Mar. 29	**Isaiah Foretells Suffering Servant**	Isaiah 52:13–53:3
Tue, Mar. 30	**Jesus, The Suffering Servant**	Acts 8:26-35
Wed, Mar. 31	**Jesus Foretells His Death**	Luke 18:31-34
Thu, Apr. 1	**Jesus Raised from Death**	Luke 24:1-12
Fri, Apr. 2	**Risen Christ Appears to Disciples**	Luke 24:13-27
Sat, Apr. 3	**Christ Revealed in Breaking of Bread**	Luke 24:28-35
Sun, Apr. 4	**Christ Interceded for Sinners**	Isaiah 53:4-11a
Mon, Apr. 5	**A Light to Jews and Gentiles**	Acts 26:19-23
Tue, Apr. 6	**Live the New Life in Christ**	Ephesians 4:17-24
Wed, Apr. 7	**Do Not Defile the Land**	Leviticus 18:24-30
Thu, Apr. 8	**Ignoring God Leads to Judgment**	Zechariah 7:8-14
Fri, Apr. 9	**Hearing the Law**	Nehemiah 7:73b–8:6
Sat, Apr. 10	**Responding to the Law**	Nehemiah 8:9-12
Sun, Apr. 11	**Committed to Obedience**	Ezra 10:1-12
Mon, Apr. 12	**Daniel Intercedes for Jerusalem**	Daniel 9:4-6, 15-19
Tue, Apr. 13	**Nehemiah and Temple Reforms**	Nehemiah 13:4-9
Wed, Apr. 14	**Nehemiah and Levitical Reforms**	Nehemiah 13:10-14
Thu, Apr. 15	**Nehemiah and Sabbath Reforms**	Nehemiah 13:15-22
Fri, Apr. 16	**Nehemiah and Marriages Reforms**	Nehemiah 13:23-27
Sat, Apr. 17	**Nehemiah Comes to Rebuild**	Nehemiah 2:1-10
Sun, Apr. 18	**Nehemiah Inspires Rebuilding**	Nehemiah 2:11-20

Mon, Apr. 19	**Praise for God's Wonderful Works**	Psalm 111
Tue, Apr. 20	**God's Blessings Intended for All**	Zechariah 8:18-23
Wed, Apr. 21	**The Lord, Our Sovereign**	Psalm 102:12-22
Thu, Apr. 22	**Plea for Mercy for Jerusalem**	Psalm 79
Fri, Apr. 23	**Mourn the Destruction of Zion**	Jeremiah 9:17-22
Sat, Apr. 24	**God's Love Never Ends**	Lamentations 3:22-33
Sun, Apr. 25	**Remember and Restore Us**	Lamentations 5
Mon, Apr. 26	**Elisha Prophesies to Jehoshaphat**	2 Kings 3:9-17
Tue, Apr. 27	**Kings Propose Battle Against Syria**	1 Kings 22:1-6
Wed, Apr. 28	**Micaiah Resists False Prophecy**	1 Kings 22:7-14
Thu, Apr. 29	**A Spirit Will Entice**	2 Chronicles 18:18-22
Fri, Apr. 30	**King Ahab Fatally Wounded**	1 Kings 22:29-40
Sat, May 1	**Jehoshaphat Promotes Peace**	1 Kings 22:41-46
Sun, May 2	**Micaiah Speaks Truth**	1 Kings 22:15-23, 26-28
Mon, May 3	**Discipline Immorality**	1 Corinthians 5:1-5
Tue, May 4	**Uphold Justice**	Exodus 23:1-9
Wed, May 5	**Seek and Find**	Jeremiah 29:10-14
Thu, May 6	**Lip Service Is Not Enough**	Mark 7:1-8
Fri, May 7	**Jerusalem Punished and Rescued**	Isaiah 29:1-8
Sat, May 8	**Judah, Blind to God's Ways**	Isaiah 29:9-12
Sun, May 9	**Bright Future to Come**	Isaiah 29:13-24
Mon, May 10	**Apostles Speak Truth to Council**	Acts 4:13-22
Tue, May 11	**Jeremiah Arrested and Imprisoned**	Jeremiah 37:11-16
Wed, May 12	**Ebedmelech's Trust Honored**	Jeremiah 38:7-13; 39:15-18
Thu, May 13	**Jeremiah Reaffirms a Prophecy**	Jeremiah 37:17-21
Fri, May 14	**Jeremiah's Last Days in Jerusalem**	Jeremiah 38:24-28
Sat, May 15	**Jerusalem Destroyed; People Exiled**	2 Kings 25:1-12
Sun, May 16	**Zedekiah Must Submit to Babylon**	Jeremiah 38:14-23

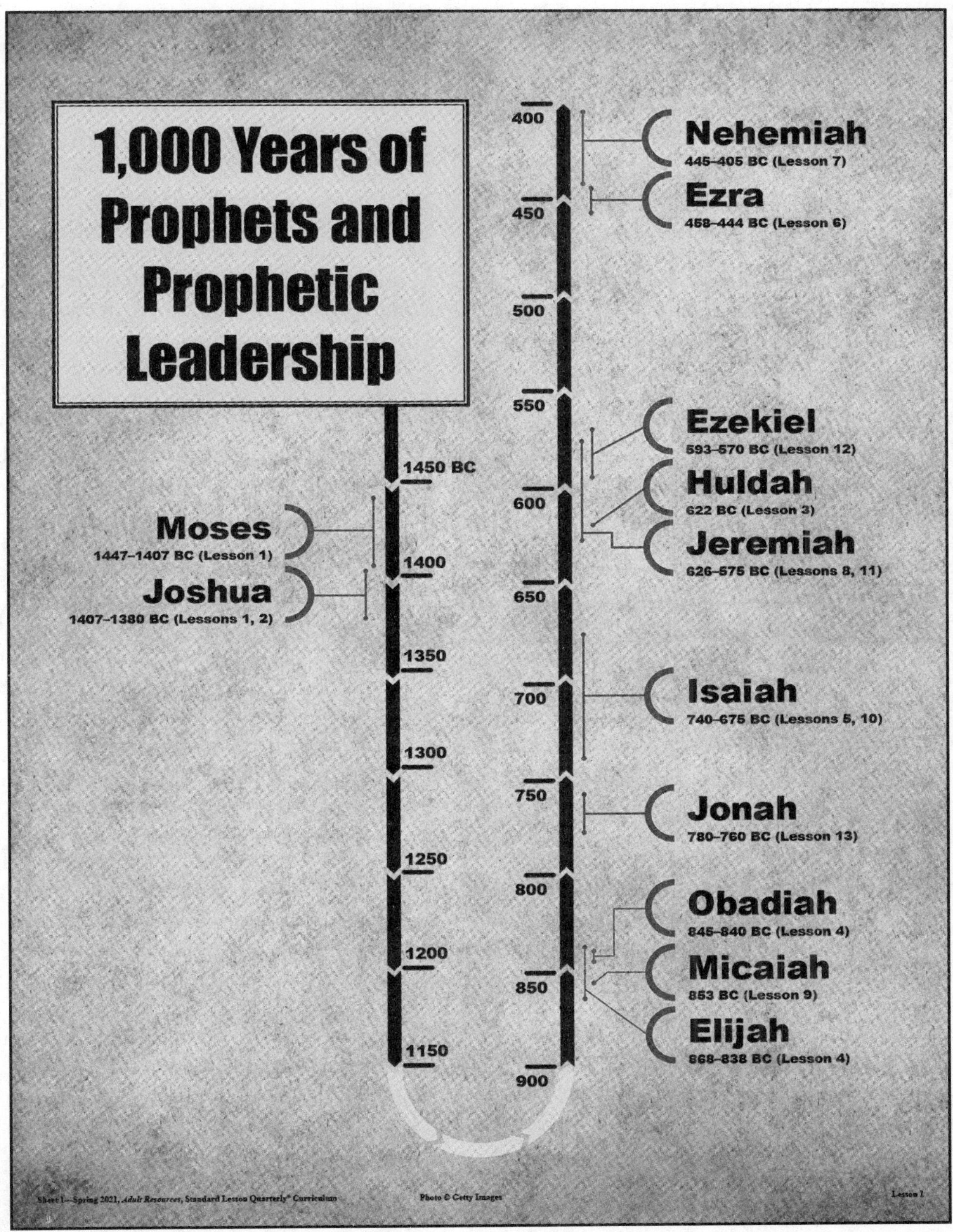

1,000 Years of Prophets and Prophetic Leadership
1450 BC
1400
1350
1300
1250
1200
1150
900
850
800
750
700
650
600
550
500
450
400
Moses
1447–1407 BC (Lesson 1)
Joshua
1407–1380 BC (Lessons 1, 2)
Elijah
868–838 BC (Lesson 4)
Micaiah
853 BC (Lesson 9)
Obadiah
845–840 BC (Lesson 4)
Jonah
780–760 BC (Lesson 13)
Isaiah
740–675 BC (Lessons 5, 10)
Jeremiah
626–575 BC (Lessons 8, 11)
Huldah
622 BC (Lesson 3)
Ezekiel
593–570 BC (Lesson 12)
Ezra
458–444 BC (Lesson 6)
Nehemiah
445–405 BC (Lesson 7)
Sheet 1—Spring 2021, Adult Resources, Standard Lesson Quarterly® Curriculum
Photo © Getty Images
Lesson 1

Discussion Tools That Work

Teacher Tips by Jerry Bowling

Questions lie at the heart of discussion-based teaching. Questions serve a vital role for sustaining learning beyond the classroom. But *how* a teacher constructs and poses questions requires skill and practice that can make a difference between a sustained, engaging conversation and a session that goes nowhere.

Some Types of Questions

Beginning teachers can benefit from using a mix of questions and preparing them in advance. The starting point here is in recognizing certain categories or types of questions:

- *Relational* questions call for comparisons. Example: "How does this concept relate to what we studied about Paul's Jewish heritage that we discussed last week?"
- *Clarifying* questions probe deeper for evidence. Example: "What do you find in this text that supports your viewpoint?"
- *Big-idea* questions search for what's most important. Example: "What insight is most valuable from today's lesson?"
- *Experiential* questions seek personal relevance. Example: "What are some ways to apply Jeremiah's admonition to return to the Lord?"

Some Discussion Methods

No matter what mix of question types you use, you should use them in such a way that all voices in your class are heard and valued. The teacher who simply stands up front and poses questions runs the risk of having one or two assertive students dominate the discussion. Here are some techniques to encourage broad participation:

- *Double Wheel.* Prepare in advance several open-ended questions such as in one or more of the four types above. During class, group students into two concentric circles of equal numbers. Have those in the inside circle face outward and those in the outside circle face inward. Then give each learner one or more slips of paper on which you have reproduced questions, one question per slip. Have each learner pose his or her question(s) to the other learner of the facing pair for response. (*Alternative:* Instead of open-ended questions, use incomplete statements such as "I think Peter's greatest challenge was . . .") After one minute of discussion, signal students in the outside circle to move one person to the right and use a different question. Repeat the process as appropriate for the size of your class.
- *Conversation Circles.* Arrange student seating in circles of four or five. Pose (or write on the board) a question for discussion within the circles. Any student can begin the responses within the respective circles. Announce that (1) the response is limited to one-minute's duration and (2) no interruptions are allowed. When you call time after the minute, the person on the first respondent's right responds to the same question, same rules. Repeat until all four or five in the circles have responded. Debrief as a whole class.

Some Best Practices

As you can see from the types and methods above, it's important to construct your questions in advance—don't just use whatever comes to mind in the middle of teaching! A good starting point is the five questions that come with each lesson in this commentary; these are almost always of the "experiential" (application) type.

As you either construct your own and/or modify the ones that come with each lesson, follow these best practices:

- Make each question ask about one thing only.
- Order questions in a logical sequence.
- Make questions answerable (not too broad).
- Focus questions on transformation more than mere information.

Prophet of Deliverance

Devotional Reading: Psalm 77:11-20
Background Scripture: Exodus 12:28-50; Deuteronomy 18:15-22

Deuteronomy 18:15-22

15 The LORD thy God will raise up unto thee a Prophet from the midst of thee, of thy brethren, like unto me; unto him ye shall hearken;

16 According to all that thou desiredst of the LORD thy God in Horeb in the day of the assembly, saying, Let me not hear again the voice of the LORD my God, neither let me see this great fire any more, that I die not.

17 And the LORD said unto me, They have well spoken that which they have spoken.

18 I will raise them up a Prophet from among their brethren, like unto thee, and will put my words in his mouth; and he shall speak unto them all that I shall command him.

19 And it shall come to pass, that whosoever will not hearken unto my words which he shall speak in my name, I will require it of him.

20 But the prophet, which shall presume to speak a word in my name, which I have not commanded him to speak, or that shall speak in the name of other gods, even that prophet shall die.

21 And if thou say in thine heart, How shall we know the word which the LORD hath not spoken?

22 When a prophet speaketh in the name of the LORD, if the thing follow not, nor come to pass, that is the thing which the LORD hath not spoken, but the prophet hath spoken it presumptuously: thou shalt not be afraid of him.

Key Verse

The LORD thy God will raise up unto thee a Prophet from the midst of thee, of thy brethren, like unto me; unto him ye shall hearken. —**Deuteronomy 18:15**

Photo: Getty Images

Prophets Faithful to God's Covenant

Unit 1: Faithful Prophets

Lessons 1–4

Lesson Aims

After participating in this lesson, each learner will be able to:

1. Summarize what God said about the prophet and message to come.
2. Explain how Moses' words were intended to guide Israel as God's covenant people.
3. Prepare a set of guidelines for distinguishing true from false teaching today.

Lesson Outline

Introduction
- A. Time to Step Aside
- B. Lesson Context

I. Authority (Deuteronomy 18:15-18)
- A. Raised Up by the Lord (v. 15)
  - *What Can and Can't Change*
- B. Requested by the People (vv. 16-18)

II. Accountability (Deuteronomy 18:19-22)
- A. To Listen and Obey (v. 19)
- B. To Punish False Prophets (v. 20)
  - *Deadly Prophets*
- C. To Test Any Claim (vv. 21-22)

Conclusion
- A. Plan for the Future
- B. Prayer
- C. Thought to Remember

Introduction

A. Time to Step Aside

In January 2019, fans of the Cincinnati Reds baseball team received a shock: Marty Brennaman, the popular radio voice of the Reds, announced that he was retiring from broadcasting following the 2019 season. That season marked the 46th year that Brennaman brought the play-by-play action of the Reds to countless fans.

Brennaman became somewhat emotional as he announced his retirement. And who wouldn't understand that? To be at *any* job for 46 years is an admirable accomplishment. Brennaman had seen the Reds at their best (watching "the Big Red Machine" in the 1970s) and at their weaker moments (the 1980s, when the team did not make it to the post season).

He expressed his gratitude to the fans for their support through the years, acknowledging that he could never have achieved what he had without their backing. At the time of Brennaman's announcement, it was not yet clear who would succeed him as the primary radio voice of the Reds. But there was no doubt that the individual would have some extremely large shoes to fill.

Moses had led the children of Israel for 40 years, guiding them through such triumphant moments as the parting of the Red Sea. But he also led as he wandered with them in the wilderness as he shared their consequence (but not their guilt, except for the incident described in Deuteronomy 32:51) of unbelief and failure to trust God. Then it was time for a transition in leadership. What respective roles would God and the people have in this transition?

B. Lesson Context

Today's lesson begins a new quarter of studies titled "Prophets Faithful to God's Covenant." Often when people think of the prophets, they think of prophetic books of the Old Testament. These are frequently divided into Major Prophets (5 books) and Minor Prophets (12 books), based on the length of these books (except Lamentations, which is "major" by association with the prophet Jeremiah).

There were, however, many other prophets besides those who wrote books that are part of the Bible. Today's study comes from the book of Deuteronomy, the fifth and final book of what is often called the Pentateuch, the Torah, or the five books of Law. (See the Lesson Context of lesson 2 for a discussion of the 5-12-5-5-12 arrangement of the Old Testament books. Moses spoke the contents of the book (Deuteronomy 1:1) and recorded it (31:9, 22, 24). This same book concludes with the declaration that since the book's writing, "there arose not a prophet . . . in Israel like unto Moses, whom the Lord knew face to face" (34:10). Thus Moses was a prophet of the Lord as well as the lawgiver to God's covenant people.

The title "Deuteronomy" comes from the Septuagint, which is the Greek translation of the Old Testament. It means "second [giving of the] law." This is fitting because the book witnesses to Moses' farewell speech to the second generation of Israelites. He was preparing them to cross the Jordan River and enter the promised land, and they needed to hear the law for the context of their generation (Deuteronomy 1:1-8).

In its function as "second [giving of the] law," Deuteronomy repeats contents from previous instruction to the people (compare Exodus 20:1-17; Deuteronomy 5:1-21). At the same time, some of the material had special relevance to those who were to enter the promised land and drive out its inhabitants (see chapter 20).

Deuteronomy 18, from which today's lesson is drawn, is the climax of a series of instructions concerning various leadership positions that would offer guidance to God's people. Reading the directives for a king gives a sense of how different a king in Israel was to act compared to those who ruled other nations (17:14-20).

HOW TO SAY IT

Asherah	Uh-*she*-ruh.
Baal	*Bay*-ul.
Balaam	*Bay*-lum.
Balak	*Bay*-lack.
Deuteronomy	Due-ter-*ahn*-uh-me.
Horeb	*Ho*-reb.
Moabites	*Mo*-ub-ites.
Pentateuch	*Pen*-ta-teuk.
Septuagint	Sep-*too*-ih-jent.
Sinai	*Sigh*-nye or *Sigh*-nay-eye.
Torah	*Tor*-uh.

I. Authority

(Deuteronomy 18:15-18)

A. Raised Up by the Lord (v. 15)

15. The Lord thy God will raise up unto thee a Prophet from the midst of thee, of thy brethren, like unto me; unto him ye shall hearken.

While Moses did not specifically identify this *Prophet*, he did offer some distinguishing characteristics. First, the prophet would be *from the midst of* the Israelites, a member of the covenant people. For this reason, the one to come could be expected to be faithful to God's law and not attempt to lead the people into idolatry (see Deuteronomy 18:20, below).

Second, the prophet would be *like* Moses in certain respects; this characterization is clarified later (see Deuteronomy 18:18, below). The command *ye shall hearken* implies the third characteristic: that the prophet would be someone who had authority (compare Mark 1:22), someone to whom the people needed to listen to and obey.

What Do You Think?

In what ways can you improve guardrails in terms of whom you will listen to and whom you won't?

Digging Deeper

How do passages such as Jeremiah 27:9-15 and 2 Timothy 4:3-4 help you answer this?

The capitalization of the word *Prophet* is not reflected in the Hebrew text, which does not have separate upper- and lower-case letters. But capitalizing the designation reflects the fact that Moses' words had not lost their significance by the time of Jesus. For instance, a question directed at John the Baptist was, "Art thou that prophet?" (John 1:21), which John promptly denied before pointing to Christ (1:26-27; compare 1:24). Peter and Stephen quoted Deuteronomy 18:15 in Acts 3:22

and 7:37, respectively, in declaring its ultimate fulfillment in Jesus.

An earlier fulfillment, closer at hand for Moses' audience, was found in the man Joshua. He was the one who became the leader of Israel after Moses' death (Deuteronomy 3:28; 31:1-8). When the people listened to him, things went well (example: Joshua 6; see lesson 2). But when they trusted their own human nature, unpleasant consequences followed (example: Joshua 7). The names *Joshua* and *Jesus* both mean "the Lord is salvation" (see Lesson Context for lesson 2).

What Can and Can't Change

When I was a child, refrigerators and stoves were white. In the 1960s when my wife and I purchased appliances for our new house, avocado green and harvest gold were the favored colors. We chose harvest gold, then replaced them in the 1990s with a lighter shade called bisque.

In the current century, black and stainless steel are popular, along with a nostalgic resurgence of white. For the last few years, "slate"—gray, in other words—has been *the* color in home decorating, from floors to walls, cabinets, and now appliances. Regarding matters of cultural taste, change seems to be the only constant.

Cultural change affects the church. Changing leadership styles, worship formats, and architectural preferences are evidence of this. But what never changes is the word of God. To put it succinctly, methods change but the message doesn't. Moses' successor was to be like him in the sense that their messages from God would be 100 percent in unison. But the successor may or may not have a personal style like that of Moses. How can we do better in the church at distinguishing changeable methods from the unchangeable message? Perhaps 1 Corinthians 9:20-22; 2 Peter 2:1; and 1 John 4:1 are good places to start.—C. R. B.

B. Requested by the People (vv. 16-18)

16. According to all that thou desiredst of the Lord thy God in Horeb in the day of the assembly, saying, Let me not hear again the voice of the Lord my God, neither let me see this great fire any more, that I die not.

This promise of a coming prophet was rooted in a request made by the Israelites when *God* spoke to them at *Horeb* (another name for Mount Sinai; compare Exodus 19:11; Malachi 4:4). After God spoke, the people expressed extreme fear and trepidation at hearing *the voice of* God in that terrifying setting. They pleaded with Moses to speak to them instead of having the Lord do so, lest they die (Exodus 20:19-21).

They had good reasons to be afraid. God had commanded the people to gather at the foot of that mountain and had given strict commandments regarding how close they could get to it—with dire consequences for disobedience (Exodus 19:12-13, 20-24). The scene had been marked by a mighty display of thunder, lightning, *fire*, smoke, the deafening sound of a trumpet, and the shaking of the mountain itself (19:16-18). God then spoke to the people what we call the Ten Commandments (20:1-17).

17. And the Lord said unto me, They have well spoken that which they have spoken.

This further summarizes what the Lord said to Moses at Mount Sinai (Deuteronomy 5:27-28). Because of the people's legitimate fear of the Lord, Moses continued to serve as the mediator between God and the people.

18. I will raise them up a Prophet from among their brethren, like unto thee, and will put my words in his mouth; and he shall speak unto them all that I shall command him.

While this verse clearly anticipates Joshua's role in Israel (see Deuteronomy 18:15, above), the Lord also pointed to spiritual leadership beyond both Moses and Joshua. God would ensure that the people did not have an excuse to imitate the nations as those nations sought to divine God's desires by forbidden means (see 18:9-14). Prophets chosen by God would provide access to the *words* of the Lord.

All legitimate prophets spoke only what the Lord told them (example: 1 Kings 22:14; see lesson 9). They proclaimed the words of God boldly, often at the risk of their own lives. The Old Testament prophets foreshadowed the ultimate prophet, Jesus—the one who became "God with us" (Matthew 1:22-23). Jesus conveyed God's words as none of Jesus' predecessors ever could. And since John the Baptist was "more than a prophet" (Luke 7:26), how much greater in that sense was Jesus himself (Matthew 21:11; 16:13-16). Moses' words foreshadowed the many prophets God would send, leading ultimately to Jesus' own ministry.

What Do You Think?

What strategies can you implement to ensure that you speak words that have God's approval?

Digging Deeper

Which of Job 42:7; Luke 6:45; Acts 19:13-17; and Ephesians 4:29 motivates you most to do so?

II. Accountability

(Deuteronomy 18:19-22)

A. To Listen and Obey (v. 19)

19. And it shall come to pass, that whosoever will not hearken unto my words which he shall speak in my name, I will require it of him.

To *hearken* to the *words* God speaks through His appointed messengers implies obedience to those words. If obedience does not follow, then one has not truly listened. The price for rejecting the Lord's words is great: He will call the disobedient person to account. The most extreme example of God's judgment for failing to hear and obey came in the form of the Assyrian and Babylonian exiles (see lessons 8, 11).

B. To Punish False Prophets (v. 20)

20a. But the prophet, which shall presume to speak a word in my name, which I have not commanded him to speak.

Those who *presume to speak* for God without being *commanded* to do so are false prophets (compare Matthew 7:15). Moses gave God's people two tests to use in determining whether a person's claim to be a prophet of the Lord was legitimate.

The first criterion was to verify the content of the alleged prophet's message. Was it consistent with the previously revealed word of the Lord? If it did not square with that divine standard, then the prophet's teaching had to be rejected and the man himself judged as a false prophet. The prophet Isaiah later urged his audience to conduct this test (Isaiah 8:19-20).

Closely related to this criterion was the nature of a person's character. For example, the prophet who is "like unto" Moses (Deuteronomy 18:15, above) will be characterized by humility (Numbers 12:3). Those who were arrogant and self-serving did not exhibit this trait (compare Matthew 7:15-19). The character of a prophet had to align with what God has revealed as good for His people (contrast Jonah 1). Thus we have two sides of the same coin: content of character had to match content of message.

20b. Or that shall speak in the name of other gods, even that prophet shall die.

The second criterion is seen in the phrase *speak in the name of other gods.* To do so constituted a clear violation of the first commandment (Exodus 20:3). This same test was outlined by Moses in Deuteronomy 13:1-5. The test included the additional caution regarding an alleged prophet's ability to perform impressive signs or wonders. Such a person was to be rejected if those wonders were accompanied by encouragement to worship other gods. Idolatry proved the person to be a false prophet, no matter how spectacular his sign or wonder may be. The direction of his leadership always trumped any kind of miraculous sign (compare Exodus 7:11; Matthew 24:24).

This is not to say that only Israelite prophets were empowered to speak the truth. Balaam is an example of a foreign prophet who was also a true prophet (see Numbers 22–24). He was called by the Moabite king Balak to curse the people of Israel. However, Balaam insisted that he would only speak what the Lord revealed to him. Because of this, Balaam blessed Israel repeatedly instead of cursing them even once.

What Do You Think?

How do the cautions of Matthew 24:4-5; Ephesians 5:6; and/or 2 Timothy 3:13-16. help you heed the warning of Deuteronomy 18:20?

Digging Deeper

What other passages convict you in this regard?

Visual for Lesson 1

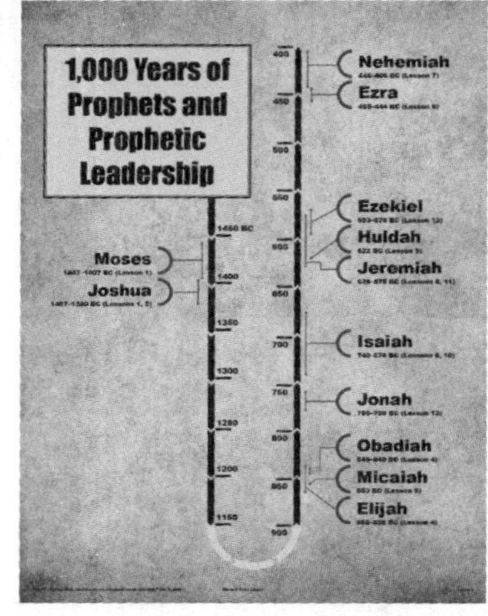

Keep this time line posted all quarter to orient your students to Old Testament chronology.

How faithfully did Israel carry out the command to put false prophets to death? Apparently not very well since false prophets seem to have become more prevalent after the nation divided in 930 BC. Their number increased during the reign of wicked King Ahab of northern Israel (reigned 874–853 BC), who promoted the worship of the false god Baal and his consort Asherah. The king encouraged prophets who claimed to speak for these deities, and so those prophets and their idolatry flourished. Elijah ordered those prophets put to death after the Lord's triumph over the prophets of Baal at Mount Carmel (1 Kings 18:19, 40).

False prophets tried to counter the message of Micaiah (1 Kings 22:5-28; see lesson 9) and stood in the way of prophets like Jeremiah (Jeremiah 28) and Micah (Micah 3:5-8). False prophets were allowed not only to live but were encouraged to advise! Their messages resulted in great damage to the spiritual welfare of God's covenant people (compare Matthew 24:11).

Deadly Prophets

The Bible witnesses to many who spoke at the genuine direction of God. These prophets spoke the truth and offered a clarion call to repentance. On the other hand, many self-anointed prophets throughout history have been little more than cult leaders who led unwitting admirers astray.

An extreme example is Jim Jones of the so-called People's Temple. He led 918 of his followers to commit suicide in Guyana in 1978. Another example is David Koresh. He confused his followers with his grandiose messianic claims, telling them that only he could interpret the Bible correctly. He died with 75 followers in the fiery destruction of the Branch Davidian compound in 1993.

The followers of Jones and Koresh suffered greatly for having believed the instructions of their leaders. Neither of these false prophets had the best interests of their followers at heart.

Moses warned the people of Israel that they had to pay careful attention to what others would tell them. They were to discern whether what those purported prophets said was true. How do you guard yourself against falling prey to false teachers? —C. R. B.

C. To Test Any Claim (vv. 21-22)

21. And if thou say in thine heart, How shall we know the word which the LORD hath not spoken?

The question posed here and the accompanying answer (see Deuteronomy 18:22, below) addressed predictive prophecies by an alleged prophet. Of course, God could have openly, visibly identified a false prophet when such a charlatan came among the people. God could then have put the deceiver to death himself as God's law required. But God has always desired that His people become spiritually mature and discerning. He wanted His people Israel to be able to "give the test" when necessary.

22. When a prophet speaketh in the name of the LORD, if the thing follow not, nor come to pass, that is the thing which the LORD hath not spoken, but the prophet hath spoken it presumptuously: thou shalt not be afraid of him.

Although it would take some time and patience, the people could *always* recognize a false *prophet* if *the thing* spoken *in the name of the Lord* did not come *to pass*. It is important to add that just because an individual's prediction does come true does not in and of itself validate that person as a true prophet of the Lord. This issue was addressed earlier by Moses, in Deuteronomy 13:1-5 (also see 18:20b, above).

In the matter of predictive prophecy, the problem of course is when a prediction will not come to pass for many years. If the prophecy fails to come true at the appointed time, the so-called prophet may have already died before his word could be judged. Thus he may have been able to gather a large following during life and to avoid judgment as a deceiver.

In that case, we can look at the alleged prophets' motives. Micah 3:5, which notes such prophets declaring "peace" in one situation, then turning around and predicting "war"—whatever suits their agenda at the time. False prophets tend also to "go along with the crowds" in predicting what people want to hear (2 Kings 22:12-13; Jeremiah 6:14; 8:11; etc.).

The verb *be afraid* occurs 10 times in the Old Testament. In 6 of those instances, it refers to fear of another human being (Numbers 22:3; Deuteronomy 1:17; 18:22; 32:27; 1 Samuel 18:15; Job 19:29); 1 time for fear shown by fictitious gods (Job 41:25); 1 time for fear on behalf of a calf-idol (Hosea 10:5); and 2 times as the reverence to be shown to the true God (Psalms 22:23; 33:8). It is somewhat paradoxical, but it is our fear (reverence) for the Lord that causes us not to fear (be terrified of) anything else—especially false prophets.

> *What Do You Think?*
>
> In what kinds of cases, if any, should you intercede on behalf of someone who has spoken for God presumptuously? Why?
>
> *Digging Deeper*
>
> Does 1 Samuel 25:23-27 help you answer that question? Why, or why not?

Conclusion

A. Plan for the Future

The retirement of a trusted leader can be a time of great stress. If succession plans are not put into place or are not carried out with wisdom and integrity, the organization experiences undue stresses that can spell its demise. God did not want this for His people, and so Moses was given a word by which to reassure them that they would still be led by the Lord and His chosen prophets even after the 40-year tenure of Moses.

That leadership had spanned two generations. Moses had taught the Israelites what they needed to know in living as God's covenant people. Moses wanted to make certain that the people would not engage in practices that would enslave them to the gods of the peoples around them. He wanted the people to be delivered from those influences and fully committed to the Lord as their only God.

This is no less true for Christians. The apostle John gave this warning in Revelation 22:18-19:

> Every man that heareth the words of the prophecy of this book, If any man shall add unto these things, God shall add unto him the plagues that are written in this book: And if any man shall take away from the words of the book of this prophecy, God shall take away his part out of the book of life, and out of the holy city, and from the things which are written in this book.

Although "this book" signifies Revelation, it's easy to imagine that the warning applies to the Bible's 65 other books as well. The Scriptures provide the standard by which we are to evaluate any teaching we hear or read.

> *What Do You Think?*
>
> What boundaries do Matthew 7:1-5, 15-20, and 1 John 4:1-6 establish for you in applying today's lesson?
>
> *Digging Deeper*
>
> Where are you weakest in that regard?

B. Prayer

Father, may we ever be grateful for Jesus, the ultimate fulfillment of the prophet to follow Moses—and more! Empower us to remain faithful to Him. In Jesus' name we pray. Amen.

C. Thought to Remember

God provides guidance for His people.

VISUALS FOR THESE LESSONS

The visual pictured in each lesson (example: page 238) is a small reproduction of a large, full-color poster included in the *Adult Resources* packet for the Spring 2021 Quarter. That packet also contains the very useful *Presentation Tools* CD for teacher use. Order No. 3629121 from your supplier.

Involvement Learning

Enhance your lesson with KJV Bible Student *(from your curriculum supplier) and the reproducible activity page (at www.standardlesson.com or in the back of the* KJV Standard Lesson Commentary Deluxe Edition*).*

Into the Lesson

Announce a 30-second silent brainstorming exercise: learners are individually to jot on paper some qualities of a good leader. After time is up, call for similar brainstorming regarding the qualities of an untrustworthy leader, again taking no more than 30 seconds. Compare and contrast results in whole-class discussion. Analyze whether certain attributes apply to leaders in a secular context but not in a church context and, vice versa.

Option or *alternative.* Before learners arrive, place at chairs copies of the "Significant Events, Surprising Leader" exercise from the activity page, which you can download. Participants can begin working on this as they arrive.

After discussing either or both of these activities, make a transition by saying, "It is important to follow good leaders who guide us through possible and impossible situations."

Into the Word

Distribute copies of the following closed-Bible pretest, one per participant. You may wish to reformat it or add to it. Say that you will collect the tests after learners score it themselves, but they are not to put their names on them.

Choices, Choices!

___ 1. Another name for Sinai is (a) Horeb; (b) Mizpah; (c) Egypt; (d) Goshen.

___ 2. The Lord promised to raise up a prophet like unto (a) Moses; (b) Isaiah; (c) Ezra; (d) Joel.

___ 3. The fate of a false prophet was to be (a) imprisoned; (b) beaten; (c) executed; (d) excommunicated.

___ 4. When encountering a false prophet, the people were *not* to react with (a) revenge; (b) fear; (c) cursing; (d) laughter.

___ 5. The voice of the Lord at Horeb had been associated with (a) wind; (b) rain; (c) fire; (d) an eclipse of the sun.

___ 6. At Horeb, the people had feared that, were they to hear the voice of the Lord again, they would (a) laugh; (b) die; (c) repent; (d) return to Egypt.

Have learners score their tests as you read today's lesson text aloud. (*Answers:* 1–a; 2–a; 3–c; 4–b; 5–c; 6–b.) After collecting the anonymous tests, write the numerals 1 through 6 on the board vertically. Tally the number of right and wrong responses for each; use this as an indicator of where to emphasize Bible study.

Option. Following study of the Bible text, erase the board and administer the same test again with the same instructions and procedures. Tally the results to determine improvements in Bible knowledge.

Into Life

Form small groups and give to each a handout (you prepare) printed with this question: *What are some ways to spot false teachers or false prophets in the church?* Include on the handout the following Scripture and other resources you deem relevant: Zechariah 13:1-6; Matthew 7:15; 24:24; 1 Corinthians 12:28-29; 1 Timothy 1:3-7; 2 Timothy 4:3; 1 John 4:1; Jude 17-19; Revelation 2:20; 22:14-15.

Have groups present conclusions in ensuing whole-class discussion. Do so by rotating in a one-text-per-group fashion until all passages are addressed. (*Option.* If time is short, give each group at the outset only three or four texts, making sure that all texts are covered.)

Wrap up by re-forming groups and challenging each to propose one or two guidelines for distinguishing true from false teaching today. Use the groups' suggestions to create a comprehensive list in ensuing whole-class discussion.

Option. Distribute copies of the "Prophet to Come, Prophet Who Came" exercise from the activity page for learners to complete as indicated. Close with prayer.

Prophet of Conquest

Devotional Reading: Hebrews 11:23-31
Background Scripture: Joshua 5:13–6:27

Joshua 5:13-15

13 And it came to pass, when Joshua was by Jericho, that he lifted up his eyes and looked, and, behold, there stood a man over against him with his sword drawn in his hand: and Joshua went unto him, and said unto him, Art thou for us, or for our adversaries?

14 And he said, Nay; but as captain of the host of the Lord am I now come. And Joshua fell on his face to the earth, and did worship, and said unto him, What saith my lord unto his servant?

15 And the captain of the Lord's host said unto Joshua, Loose thy shoe from off thy foot; for the place whereon thou standest is holy. And Joshua did so.

Joshua 6:1-5, 15-16, 20

1 Now Jericho was straitly shut up because of the children of Israel: none went out, and none came in.

2 And the Lord said unto Joshua, See, I have given into thine hand Jericho, and the king thereof, and the mighty men of valour.

3 And ye shall compass the city, all ye men of war, and go round about the city once. Thus shalt thou do six days.

4 And seven priests shall bear before the ark seven trumpets of rams' horns: and the seventh day ye shall compass the city seven times, and the priests shall blow with the trumpets.

5 And it shall come to pass, that when they make a long blast with the ram's horn, and when ye hear the sound of the trumpet, all the people shall shout with a great shout; and the wall of the city shall fall down flat, and the people shall ascend up every man straight before him.

. . . .

15 And it came to pass on the seventh day, that they rose early about the dawning of the day, and compassed the city after the same manner seven times: only on that day they compassed the city seven times.

16 And it came to pass at the seventh time, when the priests blew with the trumpets, Joshua said unto the people, Shout; for the Lord hath given you the city.

. . . .

20 So the people shouted when the priests blew with the trumpets: and it came to pass, when the people heard the sound of the trumpet, and the people shouted with a great shout, that the wall fell down flat, so that the people went up into the city, every man straight before him, and they took the city.

Key Verse

The Lord said unto Joshua, See, I have given into thine hand Jericho, and the king thereof, and the mighty men of valour. **—Joshua 6:2**

Prophets Faithful to God's Covenant

Unit 1: Faithful Prophets

Lessons 1–4

Lesson Aims

After participating in this lesson, each learner will be able to:

1. Describe how God prepared Joshua for his role in conquering the city of Jericho.
2. Explain why the Lord used such an unconventional strategy for conquering a city.
3. Develop a plan to take personal obedience to the Lord seriously.

Lesson Outline

Introduction
- A. Preparing the Troops
- B. Lesson Context

I. Special Message (Joshua 5:13-15)
- A. Joshua's Caution (v. 13)
- B. Messenger's Command (vv. 14-15)
  - *Take Off Your Shoes*

II. Sovereign Plan (Joshua 6:1-5)
- A. Jericho's Status (v. 1)
- B. The Lord's Strategy (vv. 2-5)

III. Simple Obedience (Joshua 6:15-16, 20)
- A. Surrounding the City (vv. 15-16)
- B. Seizing the City (v. 20)
  - *Tearing Down Walls*

Conclusion
- A. Follow Directions
- B. Prayer
- C. Thought to Remember

Introduction

A. Preparing the Troops

On June 5, 1944, General Dwight D. Eisenhower addressed the Allied troops who were preparing to take part in the D-Day invasion that would occur the following day. As Eisenhower walked among those troops, he knew that many of them would not survive the attack. He felt great responsibility for the deaths that would occur. But Eisenhower masked his own fears in order to alleviate that of the soldiers. "It's very hard to look a soldier in the eye when you fear that you are sending him to his death," Eisenhower said later. But it was important both to Eisenhower and to the men he addressed that he express his care and regard for them.

In today's text the leader of the Israelites received a message from his "commander in chief," the Lord, regarding the conquest of the promised land. As instructive as the example of Eisenhower was and is, that of the Lord to Joshua is immeasurably greater.

B. Lesson Context

We think of Joshua's role as a military commander before that of being a prophet—if we think of him at all as a prophet. He is remembered much more for his actions with the sword than for his proclamations of God's messages to the Israelites.

But was Joshua a prophet? For one thing, he was Moses' successor, and Moses was called "a Prophet" (Deuteronomy 18:15; see lesson 1). Further, God spoke through Joshua to give directions to Israel, and that is one characteristic of a prophet (Hebrews 1:1). Joshua challenged the people to put away their idols and commit themselves fully to the Lord (Joshua 23:1–24:28), a common task of prophets. And Joshua may be considered a prophetic forerunner of Christ. The names *Joshua* and *Jesus* both mean "the Lord is salvation." As Joshua led ancient Israel into the promised land of Canaan, Jesus leads generations of God's faithful people into the promised land of Heaven.

The first mention of Joshua in Scripture is in Exodus 17:8-16, a context not long after the exodus and the parting of the Red Sea. So by the time of the events of today's lesson text, Joshua had witnessed many mighty works of God.

The book of Joshua begins with the Lord's exhortations to Joshua following Moses' death—repeating several times the directive for Joshua to be strong and have courage in fulfilling his sacred duties (Joshua 1:6, 7, 9, 18). Joshua had been assured of the Lord's presence, just as the Lord had guided Moses (3:7). God's presence with Joshua also points to Joshua's calling from God, an event that precedes a true prophet's ministry. The book of Joshua goes on to trace the Israelite's entry into the promised land (Joshua 1–5), conquests and settlements in it (chapters 6–21), and covenant renewal (chapters 22–24).

Christians have come to consider the book of Joshua to fit the category of "history" in the Old Testament's 5-12-5-5-12 arrangement of its 39 books (5 books of law, 12 of history, 5 of poetry, 5 by major prophets, 12 by minor prophets). But to Jewish readers the book of Joshua was part of the Former Prophets (along with Judges, 1 & 2 Samuel, and 1 & 2 Kings). Though the Former Prophets are very different from Latter Prophets (like Isaiah or Hosea), these books are concerned with God's guiding the people through His chosen leaders. The first such leader in this section being Joshua, followed by the judges, etc. The writer of the book is unknown, though it is likely he was a prophet or a priest himself.

Joshua 3–4 records how the Israelites crossed the Jordan River on dry land, much as the previous generation had crossed the Red Sea on dry land under Moses' leadership. Following further spiritual preparation of the people—including circumcision of those men who had not been circumcised during the wandering in the wilderness (Joshua 5:2-9) and through the observance of the Passover (5:10)—the Israelites were almost ready for the task of conquering the promised land.

HOW TO SAY IT

Canaan	*Kay*-nun.
Horeb	*Ho*-reb.
Jericho	*Jair*-ih-co.
Rahab	*Ray*-hab.
Sinai	*Sigh*-nye or *Sigh*-nay-eye.

I. Special Message

(Joshua 5:13-15)

A. Joshua's Caution (v. 13)

13a. And it came to pass, when Joshua was by Jericho.

The city of *Jericho* was located about 10 miles northwest of the Dead Sea and 5 miles west of the Jordan River. Cities of antiquity were sited with three concerns in mind: access to water, access to trade routes, and defensibility. Jericho had all three. Because of nearby springs of water, the city was an oasis in the dry Jordan landscape. Jericho was also a strategic place to begin conquest of Canaan because of its proximity to trade routes. Jericho depended on its walls for defense, a focus of this lesson.

We should be careful not to confuse the Jericho of the Old Testament with the Jericho of the New Testament. Though called by the same name, the Jericho of Jesus' day was located above the site of Old Testament city, the latter having been about 800 feet below sea level.

13b. That he lifted up his eyes and looked, and, behold, there stood a man over against him with his sword drawn in his hand: and Joshua went unto him, and said unto him, Art thou for us, or for our adversaries?

Based on Joshua's initial reaction to the appearance of this armed *man*, there is no reason to think he looked extraordinary in any way. But putting two facts side by side yields an amazing scene: (1) Joshua's question indicates his uncertainty regarding whose side the man is on, yet (2) Joshua *went unto* this armed man anyway! The scene is therefore one of confidence in the protective presence of the Lord (see Lesson Context). As to the answer to Joshua's question, he was about to find out that the answer wasn't a simple "us" or "them"!

B. Messenger's Command (vv. 14-15)

14a. And he said, Nay; but as captain of the host of the Lord am I now come.

This individual was likely an angel of the Lord, perhaps the same one whom God had promised would go before His people to lead them into the promised land (Exodus 23:20-23). The phrase "Lord of hosts" is familiar, appearing more than 200 times in the Old Testament. But the normal order of the underlying Hebrew words is reversed here and in the verse that follows. Thus we have *host of the Lord*. The word *host* is used as a reference to an armed force (Judges 4:15; etc.). The man's identifying himself as *captain* reinforces the military overtones of his unsheathed sword and the armed force at his command (compare 1 Samuel 12:9).

The man does not give Joshua a straightforward endorsement of allegiance. Whether the man was for or against the Israelites depended upon their faithfulness and obedience to *the Lord*.

14b. And Joshua fell on his face to the earth, and did worship, and said unto him, What saith my lord unto his servant?

Angels, as created beings, do not accept worship (Revelation 19:10; 22:8). Therefore the posture of *worship* Joshua adopted may have been intended only in a sense of indicating great respect, as very similar language is translated in Ruth 2:10; 1 Samuel 25:23; and 2 Samuel 14:22.

Realizing that such a man would not show up just to chit-chat, Joshua's question sought to get to the heart of the man's errand immediately. Joshua's referring to himself as *servant* and to the man as *my lord* are two more indications of Joshua's great respect for this messenger sent by God.

> *What Do You Think?*
> What's the single most important thing your church needs to do better in order to hear and heed the Lord's messages properly?
> *Digging Deeper*
> What will be your part in making that happen?

15. And the captain of the LORD's host said unto Joshua, Loose thy shoe from off thy foot; for the place whereon thou standest is holy. And Joshua did so.

The captain of the Lord's host did not immediately reveal the nature of his visit. His directive echoes the scene of the burning bush episode involving Moses at Mount Horeb (Sinai) in Exodus 3:4-5. This incident provides another link between Moses as God's prophet and Joshua as his legitimate successor (Deuteronomy 18:15; Joshua 1:1-9; see lesson 1).

Take Off Your Shoes

When I decided it was time to visit the Holy Land, as it is referred to, I went as a skeptic. My initial frame of mind was that of criticism. I questioned the traditional designations of places identified with Jesus' life and ministry. I also reacted against the building of shrines over some of those locations.

I was caught by surprise, however, when my trip turned into a spiritual pilgrimage! At some point, I found myself appreciating the land that gave birth to our faith. I was able to recognize it as holy because of what was done there by Jesus and others, like Joshua. One might say that I mentally removed my shoes in amazement at what God had done in that land.

When was the last time you figuratively took off your shoes in reverence for what God has done in the place where you stand? —C. R. B.

> *What Do You Think?*
> Under what circumstances, if any, should you consider certain places to be holier than others? Why?
> *Digging Deeper*
> What role should Deuteronomy 12:1-4; Acts 7:30-33; Romans 14:5; and/or Colossians 2:16 have in your answer?

II. Sovereign Plan
(Joshua 6:1-5)

A. Jericho's Status (v. 1)

1. Now Jericho was straitly shut up because of the children of Israel: none went out, and none came in.

This note interrupts the captain's conversation with Joshua briefly (see Joshua 5:15, above). In so doing, it reveals part the "defensibility" aspect of *Jericho* (see Lesson Context). The fact that *none went out, and none went in* speaks not only to the city's ability to control access but also to the reason for the heightened security measures: the threat posed by *the children of Israel.*

Joshua had previously sent two spies into the city to assess the situation there. And although they had gained entrance, one or more alert members of the populace had informed authorities not only of the intrusion itself but also where the spies were located. Under protection from Rahab, the spies had learned that the city was in a state of panic because of reports of what the Lord had done to the kings east of the Jordan River (Joshua 2).

B. The Lord's Strategy (vv. 2-5)

2. And the LORD said unto Joshua, See, I have given into thine hand Jericho, and the king thereof, and the mighty men of valour.

Surprisingly, *the Lord* himself, not the captain of the Lord's host, addressed Joshua. This could indicate either (1) that the captain prepared Joshua for the Lord to arrive on the scene or (2) that the Lord had chosen first to introduce himself as captain of the host before identifying himself more fully. Either would be in keeping with ways that God had interacted with great men in the past (compare Genesis 18:1-2; Exodus 3:1-4).

The description of the forthcoming conquest of *Jericho* in terms of its *king* and *mighty men of valour* reassured Joshua that the victory would be complete; it was to be a decisive win for Israel. Neither king nor soldiers would escape. We should not that the Lord did not say "I will give," but *I have given.* The victory is so assured that He spoke of it as already having happened (compare Joshua 8:1; 10:8).

The promised land was a gift from God to Israel (Numbers 13:1, 2; Deuteronomy 4:21; 6:23; 8:10). They had done nothing to earn or deserve such a gift; it was a demonstration of God's gracious treatment of them as His covenant people (7:7-9). Because of this fact, their life in the land was to be different from that of the nations they dispossessed. That could happen only with a "clean sweep" (see Deuteronomy 7:1-6). God's assured victory in Jericho was to be indicative of the sort of military campaigns the people should plan on.

Walking in circles can get you exactly where God wants you.

Visual for Lesson 2. *Point to this visual while asking learners of times when they felt they were "walking in circles" but ended up seeing God at work.*

3. And ye shall compass the city, all ye men of war, and go round about the city once. Thus shalt thou do six days.

Because God was the giver of the land, His instructions for taking the land had to be followed. Here He began to outline His strategy for conquering Jericho. Merely circling a *city* was not an efficient military tactic, especially without being part of a larger plan to lay siege or attack outright. It could however heighten the fear the people inside were already feeling. But it could also lose the element of surprise, as Joshua effectively used later (Joshua 8:10-29; 10:6-11). Perhaps the latter was the Lord's intent so that the Israelites would realize that the victory was solely by His might, not theirs.

One estimate of the circumference of Jericho was approximately 2,000 feet, or just over one third of a mile. The marching would not take place right next to the wall, of course, lest the Israelites be in danger of arrows. A safe distance might therefore require a walk of a mile or more.

According to the military census in Numbers 26:1-2, 51, there were 601,730 Israelite men able to bear arms. The amount of time the march would take depended on the width of the marching formation and the speed of the pace.

4. And seven priests shall bear before the ark seven trumpets of rams' horns: and the seventh day ye shall compass the city seven times, and the priests shall blow with the trumpets.

Unlike other nations, military success in Israel didn't depend on numbers, technology, or skill. Rather, it depended on the Lord's presence. *The ark* would symbolize that presence. But to trust in the symbolism without actually being led by the Lord was a recipe for disaster (example: 1 Samuel 4). Obeying God was the key to victory.

Other verses make clear that the priests marched on the first six days as well (Joshua 6:13-14, not in our printed text). The deviation from the pattern of the six days marked the fact that *the seventh day* would bring a different result.

Armies need ways to communicate, and the *trumpets* of curved *rams' horns* served that purpose here. Use of trumpets for other communication purposes are seen in Leviticus 25:9; 1 Kings 1:34; 2 Kings 9:13; and Psalm 81:3. Trumpets made from different material are seen in Numbers 10:1-10.

5. And it shall come to pass, that when they make a long blast with the ram's horn, and when ye hear the sound of the trumpet, all the people shall shout with a great shout; and the wall of the city shall fall down flat, and the people shall ascend up every man straight before him.

After days of hearing only shorter blasts of horns, the *long blast* on the seventh day would probably feel like a grand celebration for Israel. The shouts of *all the people* in combination with that blast would precede the Lord's bringing down *the wall of the city.* No other military action would be necessary for God to raze Jericho's defenses. For *every man* to go in *straight before him* would ensure they did not get in each other's way.

> *What Do You Think?*
> What's the single most important thing you can do today to hold yourself accountable to acting as the Lord desires?
> *Digging Deeper*
> Which single Scripture passage convicts you most in this regard? Why?

Joshua 6:6-14 (not in our printed text) records the obedience of the people, the priests, and the armed men to Joshua's orders. Emphasized within these verses is his command for the people to remain completely silent until the time to shout. Only the priests' horns were to be heard.

III. Simple Obedience

(Joshua 6:15-16, 20)

A. Surrounding the City (vv. 15-16)

15-16. And it came to pass on the seventh day, that they rose early about the dawning of the day, and compassed the city after the same manner seven times: only on that day they compassed the city seven times. And it came to pass at the seventh time, when the priests blew with the trumpets, Joshua said unto the people, Shout; for the Lord hath given you the city.

The people obeyed everything that Joshua told them from the Lord, with no deviations (see Joshua 6:12-14). At this time they continued to obey as the procedure changed as noted.

Joshua spoke again as though *the Lord* had already given them Jericho. This city was being conquered through God's power, not through Israel's greatness or might. Though it had not yet happened, it was as good as accomplished.

> *What Do You Think?*
> Under what circumstances, if any, should Christians accept credit for something? Why?
> *Digging Deeper*
> How do texts such as Daniel 4:19-37; John 5:44; 8:54; Acts 12:20-23; 1 Corinthians 3:6; 11:1; and 15:9-11 help frame your answer?

Joshua 6:17 (not in our printed text) contains a reminder to spare Rahab and her family because of her protecting the spies previously (see Joshua 2). Everything else in the city was dedicated to destruction. No treasure or possession was to be spared for any reason (6:18-21).

The importance of following directions applied not only to the conquest of Canaan but was to be a central feature of Israelite faith henceforth. It was to be the key not only to conquering the land but also keeping it. The key to remaining in the land would never be found in military might, economic strength, or by mastering the tactics of international diplomacy. It would be found only in continuing to recognize the land as a gift from God and honoring Him as the giver in every phase of life. To fail in this regard was a guarantee that no matter how powerful the army or how strong the economy, the Israelites would surely forfeit the gift God had given them.

B. Seizing the City (v. 20)

20. So the people shouted when the priests blew with the trumpets: and it came to pass, when the people heard the sound of the trumpet, and the people shouted with a great shout, that the wall fell down flat, so that the people went up into the city, every man straight before him, and they took the city.

The people once again followed every command the Lord had given to Joshua (compare Joshua 6:2-5, above). Although we wonder how many *people went up into the city* after *the wall fell down flat,* no record was made. While arguing from silence is often unconvincing, we may guess that numbers are not given because they were not the key to victory. God's power was.

> *What Do You Think?*
> What mental and spiritual guardrails should we have in place before concluding that the misfortunes of unbelievers are God's doing?
> *Digging Deeper*
> How does distinguishing between what God *causes* and what He *permits* aid your answer?

Tearing Down Walls

A wall can have a powerful significance beyond its mere physical presence. The Berlin Wall is a prime example, since it represented the tense relationship between the United States and the Soviet Union during the Cold War. In 1987, amidst political upheaval in the Eastern Bloc and in the Soviet Union, U.S. President Reagan challenged the Soviet leader: "Mr. Gorbachev, tear down this wall!" Two years later, the Berlin Wall came down, and a powerful symbol of fear and division disappeared.

Ancient Jericho relied on a wall surrounding the city to protect its inhabitants from invaders. As individuals, many of us have built walls in our hearts and minds for a similar purpose: to protect our self-esteem, to guard against challenges to our prejudices, etc.

Often such walls end up destroying our relationships with family members and friends. Sometimes those walls are so strong that only the power of God can break them down. What walls have you built in your heart that need to be torn down?

—C. R. B.

Conclusion

A. Follow Directions

Consider the faith required to trust and obey God's directions for conquering the city of Jericho (Hebrews 11:30). When first hearing the plan, many Israelites may have thought *What kind of strategy is this? Who conquers a city with such a battle plan?* The answer: God does, and His people do so by faith in Him.

God's bizarre (to human thinking) plan had an important spiritual lesson to teach the Israelites: Receiving the promised land could only be accomplished on God's terms. The people were not to compromise, ignore, or tweak the terms in any way. Even though the commands of God were unconventional, those commands were to be obeyed.

Christians do well to remember that God's commands are still meant to be obeyed without equivocating. Though Christians may disagree about some particulars, we know from Jesus that our first command is to love the Lord (Mark 12:30), and loving Him involves obedience (John 14:15). May we obey everything the Lord has revealed to us that we may receive His blessings!

B. Prayer

Father, thank You for leading us with Your Word and Your Spirit. May they strengthen our obedience to You! In Jesus' name we pray. Amen.

C. Thought to Remember

Victory follows obedience
to the Lord.

Involvement Learning

Enhance your lesson with KJV Bible Student *(from your curriculum supplier) and the reproducible activity page (at www.standardlesson.com or in the back of the* KJV Standard Lesson Commentary Deluxe Edition*).*

Into the Lesson

Ask learners to name TV shows they like that feature a main character who always comes out on top by using unusual, improvised methods and/or devices. If learners are slow in responding, don't be hasty in filling the silence with an example—let them think for a while. If learners need an example after 15 seconds of silence, you can mention *MacGyver* and/or similar shows.

Discuss why such shows are attractive. After discussion, lead into the Bible study by saying, "The book of Joshua offers multiple accounts that are as dramatic as such TV shows, and more so! Let's see what just one of its episodes can teach us in the twenty-first century."

Into the Word

Option. As a preface to the activity in the paragraph below, distribute to study pairs copies of the "Strategies and Tactics" exercise from the activity page, which you can download. Assign one text per pair to complete as indicated. Use discoveries to compare and contrast with the conquest of Jericho as the Bible study proceeds.

If you have exactly 11 class members, assign one verse of today's text to each. If you have more than 11 class member, assign the 11 verses and duplicate some assignments. If you have fewer than 11 class members, assign the 11 verses by giving some participants two or three verses.

Announce that the class will be drawing today's true story in a sequence of panels. Assure your learners that artistic talent (or lack thereof) doesn't matter. Distribute supplies appropriate to the task and ask learners to take only one minute per panel to draw their assigned text(s). For learners who are overly self-conscious about their lack of artistic ability, say that they can use words to describe their assigned verse, without using words of the verse itself (a text-only example for Joshua 6:20 might be "Hooray, we won!").

Once all the panels are finished, collect them and shuffle. Then affix them randomly to the board in a horizontal line and ask learners to make suggestions for putting them in the proper order. (Rule: No one is allowed to comment on the placement of the picture he or she drew.)

If you used the optional activity to begin this section of the lesson, do a final compare and contrast between the account of the conquest of Jericho and those of the four entries on the activity page handout.

Into Life

Ask the group to state spiritual preparations they see in today's text and related texts regarding spiritual preparations to the victory at Jericho. Within the lesson text itself, expect learners to mention the worship of Joshua 5:14 and the honoring of holy ground in 5:15.

Option. To see the lesson in its wider context, ask learners to note how and why victory at Jericho was followed by the defeat described in Joshua 7. Expect responses certainly to include the secret sin of Achan. But learners also may note that there is no record of Joshua's having prayed to seek the Lord's blessing before that battle; instead, he relied on the advice of humans (Joshua 7:1-5).

Next, give each participant a blank index card and challenge them to write on it one area in which they intend to take personal obedience to the Lord more seriously in the week ahead—and indicate how they will do so. Allow one minute for private thought on this task. Suggest that learners post their cards where they will see them daily in the week ahead.

Option. If you wish to weave into this task the subject of spiritual disciplines, distribute copies of the "Discipline Deficiency" exercise from the activity page. Use of this exercise in study pairs may result in accountability partnerships being formed.

Prophet of Wisdom

Devotional Reading: Psalm 25:1-10
Background Scripture: 2 Kings 22

2 Kings 22:14-20

14 So Hilkiah the priest, and Ahikam, and Achbor, and Shaphan, and Asahiah, went unto Huldah the prophetess, the wife of Shallum the son of Tikvah, the son of Harhas, keeper of the wardrobe; (now she dwelt in Jerusalem in the college;) and they communed with her.

15 And she said unto them, Thus saith the LORD God of Israel, Tell the man that sent you to me,

16 Thus saith the LORD, Behold, I will bring evil upon this place, and upon the inhabitants thereof, even all the words of the book which the king of Judah hath read:

17 Because they have forsaken me, and have burned incense unto other gods, that they might provoke me to anger with all the works of their hands; therefore my wrath shall be kindled against this place, and shall not be quenched.

18 But to the king of Judah which sent you to enquire of the LORD, thus shall ye say to him, Thus saith the LORD God of Israel, As touching the words which thou hast heard;

19 Because thine heart was tender, and thou hast humbled thyself before the LORD, when thou heardest what I spake against this place, and against the inhabitants thereof, that they should become a desolation and a curse, and hast rent thy clothes, and wept before me; I also have heard thee, saith the LORD.

20 Behold therefore, I will gather thee unto thy fathers, and thou shalt be gathered into thy grave in peace; and thine eyes shall not see all the evil which I will bring upon this place. And they brought the king word again.

Key Verse

Because thine heart was tender, and thou hast humbled thyself before the LORD, when thou heardest what I spake against this place, and against the inhabitants thereof, that they should become a desolation and a curse, and hast rent thy clothes, and wept before me; I also have heard thee, saith the LORD. **—2 Kings 22:19**

Photo: Getty Images

Prophets Faithful to God's Covenant

Unit 1: Faithful Prophets

Lessons 1–4

Lesson Aims

After participating in this lesson, each learner will be able to:

1. Identify the two major parts of Huldah's prophetic message.

2. Explain the key verse (2 Kings 22:19) in light of the text's spiritual principles.

3. Pray for seven national leaders by name in the week ahead, one each day.

Lesson Outline

Introduction
- A. The Source Matters
- B. Lesson Context

I. A Word Sought (2 Kings 22:14)
- A. The Delegation (v. 14a)
- B. The Prophetess (v. 14b)
  - *Where Do You Go for Wisdom?*

II. A Word for Jerusalem (2 Kings 22:15-17)
- A. Judgment Is Coming (vv. 15-16)
- B. Judgment Is Deserved (v. 17)

III. A Word for the King (2 Kings 22:18-20)
- A. God Heard (vv. 18-19)
  - *A Humble Leader*
- B. God Will Act (v. 20)

Conclusion
- A. Responding in Faith
- B. Prayer
- C. Thought to Remember

Introduction

A. The Source Matters

The Information Age in which we live is a double-edge sword: the massive amount of useful information is accompanied by massive amounts of factual errors and bias. Which customer review is the reliable guide to booking a hotel room or trying a new restaurant? Which news network should you count on as being the most trustworthy? To what commentators and analysts do you turn to make unbiased sense of current events? What source of information can be trusted above all others?

In the lesson text for this week, we encounter a young king who was faced with similar questions. His decision is still instructive after many centuries.

B. Lesson Context

The events recorded in this week's text took place in the days of Josiah, king of Judah (reigned 640–609 BC). He was a godly king known for his tireless attempts to purify Judah's worship and the temple (2 Kings 22:1–23:25; 2 Chronicles 34:1–35:19).

In the years preceding Josiah's rise to the throne, the kings of Judah had vacillated between devotion to the Lord and to idols. Josiah's great-grandfather Hezekiah (reigned 724–695 BC) had instituted a set of religious reforms in Judah that were intended to restore proper worship of the Lord (2 Chronicles 29–31). But gross unfaithfulness to the God of Israel characterized the reign of Hezekiah's son Manasseh (694–642 BC). He rebuilt pagan worship shrines his father had destroyed. Manasseh encouraged worship of the Baals as well as that of the sun, moon, and stars (example: 2 Kings 23:11). Manasseh went so far as to offer his son in child sacrifice and built pagan altars within the Lord's temple itself (2 Kings 21:1-18). Late in his reign, Manasseh repented of his sin (2 Chronicles 33:10-17). But his former evil contributed directly in Judah's ultimate destruction and exile (2 Kings 21:10-16; 23:26; 24:3-4).

Josiah's father, Amon (reigned 642–640 BC), returned to the idolatry that characterized the earlier years of Manasseh. King Amon was assassinated in a palace coup after a two-year reign, and the "people of the land" made his 8-year-old son Josiah king in his place (2 Kings 21:19-26; 2 Chronicles 33:20-25).

Godly advisers among Judah's aristocracy apparently influenced Josiah. Some are named in today's text. Other godly contemporaries included well-known prophets. Zephaniah, a descendant of King Hezekiah, prophesied during the reign of Josiah (Zephaniah 1:1). Jeremiah's prophetic ministry began in the thirteenth year of Josiah (Jeremiah 1:1-2), five years before this event. No doubt their ministries were an impetus in Josiah's reforms leading up to these events. The result was that when Josiah was 16 years old, "he began to seek after the God of David his father" (2 Chronicles 34:3). In the twelfth year of Josiah's reign, he began to purge the land of pagan idols and shrines (34:3-7).

About six years later, King Josiah ordered a renovation of the temple (2 Kings 22:3). The Book of the Law was found within the temple in the process (22:8). Scholars disagree regarding the exact identity of the book that was found. Some believe it was a copy of the entire Law of Moses (the first five books of the Old Testament, otherwise known as the Pentateuch). Others believe it was only the book of Deuteronomy or some portion of it. Sometime in the previous decades during the reigns of wicked Manasseh and Amon, the Book of the Law had been lost and forgotten. Or perhaps idolatrous priests intentionally "misplaced" it in order to hide the guilt of their own apostasy.

When Shaphan reported to Josiah on the process of the repair project, Shaphan also alerted the king to the discovery of the book. Given Josiah's reaction of distress to what he heard read from that book (see 2 Kings 22:11), Deuteronomy may well have been the book's identity; it detailed the punishments Israel would suffer if the people failed to keep the covenant.

These curses would culminate in exile from the land (Deuteronomy 29:25-28). Realizing the guilt of Judah, Josiah commissioned a delegation to inquire of the Lord concerning the wrath that the king feared would soon be visited on him and his kingdom (2 Kings 22:12-13). A description of the nature of that delegation is how today's lesson text opens.

I. A Word Sought

(2 Kings 22:14)

A. The Delegation (v. 14a)

14a. So Hilkiah the priest, and Ahikam, and Achbor, and Shaphan, and Asahiah.

The word *so* introduces the first action taken as a result of King Josiah's order in 2 Kings 22:12-13. That first action is the forming of the delegation. Seven men bear the name *Hilkiah* in the Old Testament. The one here was not only a *priest,* but was "the high priest" (22:4, 8).

Ahikam was a son of the scribe *Shaphan* (2 Kings 22:12). Members of this family seem to have been devout followers of the Lord, as borne out later (see Jeremiah 26:24; 29:1-3; 36:10-12; 39:14). *Achbor,* another official in Josiah's court, was the father of Elnathan, who became an official in the court of King Jehoiakim, Josiah's son (Jeremiah 26:22; 36:11-12, 24-25). *Asahiah* was earlier designated as a "servant of the king's" (2 Kings 22:12).

> *What Do You Think?*
> Under what circumstances in the church should you act as a messenger between two parties? When should you not?
> *Digging Deeper*
> What circumstances call for face to face conversation rather than text messages?

B. The Prophetess (v. 14b)

14b. Went unto Huldah the prophetess, the wife of Shallum the son of Tikvah, the son of Harhas, keeper of the wardrobe; (now she dwelt in Jerusalem in the college;) and they communed with her.

Huldah the prophetess appears elsewhere only in the parallel account to this event in 2 Chronicles 34:22-28 (although name spellings differ there). Nothing more is known about her except what is given in these two accounts. Jewish tradition holds that she and Jehoiada the priest were both buried in Jerusalem (2 Chronicles 24:15-16), an honor reserved for those of King David's family. This bolsters the impression that the delegation felt no hesitation in consulting Huldah. *Communed with* refers simply to a conversation, not to a meal or to a religious ceremony.

Although female prophets in Israel were rarer than male ones, Huldah's role is not without precedent in the Old Testament. Miriam (Exodus 15:20), Deborah (Judges 4:4), and the unnamed wife of Isaiah (Isaiah 8:3) precede her in being designated *prophetess* (contrast Nehemiah 6:14).

Huldah's husband, *Shallum,* may have been Jeremiah's uncle (Jeremiah 32:7). The dwelling of this husband and wife *in the college* is uncertain in location, but it likely indicates a particular quarter of Jerusalem. Elsewhere in this book, the underlying Hebrew word for "college" is translated "second" (2 Kings 23:4; 25:18).

Where Do You Go for Wisdom?

In my early 20s, I enjoyed going to my small town's only grocery store and listening to the older men's conversation. I expected wisdom, but often I heard only complaints about the changing world. I would laugh to myself about this ongoing theme. Now I'm the age that some of those fellows were, and I sometimes find myself thinking as they did. As we age, we are tempted to idealize "the good old days" and become negative about the present.

The delegation in today's text could have gone to the ancient equivalent of the small-town grocery store to bemoan their times. Instead, they sought counsel with Huldah, who could give them a word from the Lord. When you face change, do you reinforce your negative thinking by consulting with cynics of like mind, or do you find wisdom by seeking guidance from the Lord? —C. R. B.

II. A Word for Jerusalem

(2 Kings 22:15-17)

A. Judgment Is Coming (vv. 15-16)

15. And she said unto them, Thus saith the Lord God of Israel, Tell the man that sent you to me.

Huldah begins her response with the prophetic formula *thus saith the Lord.* Her use of this phrase, which occurs more than 400 times in the Old Testament, marks her as a true prophet (see 2 Kings 22:16, 18-19, below). Adding *God of Israel* emphasized the Lord's sovereignty over the nation and His relationship to it. God chose to associate himself with Israel specifically. Though this fact should have had implications for how the people behaved, this did not often play out in reality.

Huldah's referring to King Josiah as *the man that sent you to me* created space between the king and herself. Though he was powerful, she was the one who had heard a true word from God to share. Her words reminded the delegation that Josiah was merely a man who, like all people, was subject to God's reign.

16. Thus saith the Lord, Behold, I will bring evil upon this place, and upon the inhabitants thereof, even all the words of the book which the king of Judah hath read.

By using the prophetic formula *thus saith the Lord* a second time, Huldah emphasized that her words came from the Lord, not from her own convictions. The word *behold* marks the beginning of the words God spoke through Huldah. Its use in Old Testament prophecy typically introduces God's dramatic intervention in threat or promise (example: 1 Kings 11:31).

HOW TO SAY IT

Achbor	*Ak*-bor.
Ahikam	Uh-*high*-kum.
Asahiah	As-uh-*hye*-uh.
Elnathan	El-*nay*-thun.
Harhas	*Har*-haz.
Hezekiah	Hez-ih-*kye*-uh.
Hilkiah	Hill-*kye*-uh.
Huldah	*Hul*-duh.
Jehoiada	Jee-*hoy*-uh-duh.
Jehoiakim	Jeh-*hoy*-uh-kim.
Jeroboam	Jair-uh-*boe*-um.
Josiah	Jo-*sigh*-uh.
Shallum	*Shall*-um.
Shaphan	*Shay*-fan.
Tikvah	*Tick*-vuh.

The first part of Huldah's oracle (continued in 2 Kings 22:17, next) concerned *Judah* in general plus Jerusalem and/or its temple (*this place*) in particular (compare 1 Kings 8:29-30, 35; 2 Kings 22:17-20; Jeremiah 7:20). In the context at hand, it most likely indicates Jerusalem in general since the destruction of the temple without concurrent destruction of the city wouldn't make sense.

As great as King Josiah's desire was to spare his nation, he could not save Judah from coming judgment. Thus, Huldah indicated that Josiah's worst fears were justified (see 2 Kings 22:13). Moses had warned that destruction would come if the Israelites were disobedient to the Lord (example: Deuteronomy 28:15-68). Later prophets based their judgment oracles on warnings found in the Law of Moses (examples: Jeremiah 6:16-19; Amos 2:4-5). Josiah may have heard these calamities read straight out of Deuteronomy 28:15-68 (see 2 Kings 22:10-11). Even if he heard some other text, the curses would be very similar to those of Deuteronomy 28.

The Hebrew word indicating that the Lord was about to *bring evil* does not refer to moral evil. Instead, it should be understood as physical harm or affliction (Genesis 31:52; Psalm 34:19) or similar. This announcement of coming judgment through calamity echoes earlier announcements against the dynasties of the wicked kings Jeroboam (1 Kings 14:10-11) and Ahab (21:20-22). It also parallels the indictment in 2 Kings 21:10-15 that was delivered by prophets in the days of Josiah's grandfather Manasseh.

What Do You Think?

How would you respond to someone who proposes that a certain modern disaster was due to the sin of those affected by it?

Digging Deeper

Under what circumstances should you work Luke 13:1-5 into the discussion?

B. Judgment Is Deserved (v. 17)

17. Because they have forsaken me, and have burned incense unto other gods, that they might provoke me to anger with all the works of their hands; therefore my wrath shall be kindled against this place, and shall not be quenched.

Judah's having *forsaken* God for idols would result in punishment. What Moses had warned about (Deuteronomy 28:20; 29:25; 31:16-17), Huldah recognized as forthcoming reality in Judah. Jeremiah also cited Judah's having *burned incense unto other gods* as evidence of their idolatry; that was the means by which the nation provoked the Lord's *anger* (Jeremiah 1:16; 19:4; 44:3, 8). Both the idols and the sacrifices offered to the idols were *works of their hands*. Tragically humorous is Isaiah 44:19:

> None considereth in his heart, neither is there knowledge nor understanding to say, I have burned part of it in the fire; yea, also I have baked bread upon the coals thereof; I have roasted flesh, and eaten it: and shall I make the residue thereof an abomination? shall I fall down to the stock of a tree?

God's anger was abundantly justified since it had been provoked by intentional human rebellion; this had happened so often that the limits of the Lord's patience were exceeded. Zephaniah indicated that Judah was rotten to the core (Zephaniah 3:6-8). The fire of God's judgment was *kindled*, and it would *not be quenched*.

What Do You Think?

What can you do to ensure that a hobby or favorite activity doesn't become an idol?

Digging Deeper

What Scripture texts help you most in doing so? Why?

III. A Word for the King

(2 Kings 22:18-20)

A. God Heard (vv. 18-19)

18a. But to the king of Judah which sent you to enquire of the Lord, thus shall ye say to him,

Huldah's message of judgment against Judah was not the final word. Whereas she had previously identified Josiah simply as "the man that sent you to me" (2 Kings 22:15, above), she here identified him specifically as *the king of Judah*. This description highlighted Josiah's leadership

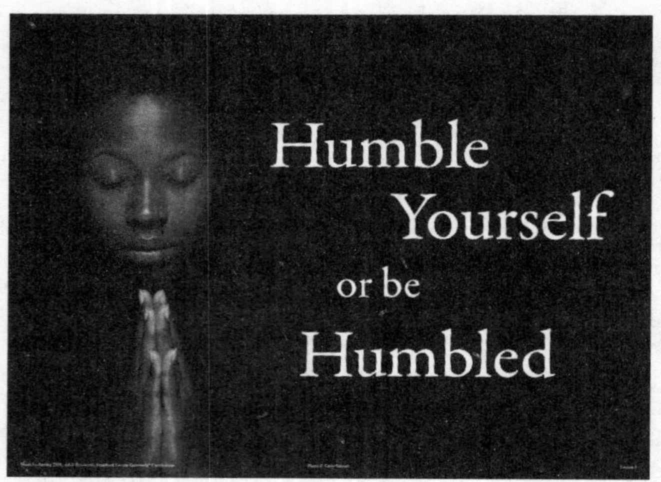
Humble
Yourself
or be
Humbled

Visual for Lesson 3. *Point to this visual as you ask learners to name modern actions that are equivalent to Josiah's tearing of his clothing (verse 19).*

role. The Hebrew behind the phrase *enquire of the Lord* occurs only six times in the Old Testament, always in context of great seriousness (here and Genesis 25:22; 1 Kings 22:8; Ezekiel 20:1; 2 Chronicles 16:12; 22:9).

18b. Thus saith the Lord God of Israel, As touching the words which thou hast heard.

The prophetess once again used the prophetic formula *thus saith the Lord God* (see 2 Kings 22:16, above) to reinforce that her words came from God. This repetition emphasized the Lord's special relationship with all *of Israel*.

19. Because thine heart was tender, and thou hast humbled thyself before the Lord, when thou heardest what I spake against this place, and against the inhabitants thereof, that they should become a desolation and a curse, and hast rent thy clothes, and wept before me; I also have heard thee, saith the Lord.

When Shaphan read the law to Josiah, the king was shaken to his core. He had torn his *clothes* to signify his grief (2 Kings 22:11). That was an appropriate response to the words of the scroll that announced that Jerusalem would *become a desolation and a curse*. God had heard Josiah and had seen his weeping and the state of his *heart*. So God had decided to honor the king's humble and contrite response (compare Zephaniah 2:3; 3:12).

Moses had described such repentance as a prerequisite for the Lord's restoring Israel after it fell under His judgment (Leviticus 26:40-42). Such humble repentance had led God to delay the demise of Ahab's dynasty (1 Kings 21:29), to postpone judgment in the days of Hezekiah (2 Chronicles 32:26), and to restore Josiah's grandfather Manasseh (2 Chronicles 33:10-13). The New Testament highlights the centrality of humility and repentance before God (examples: Matthew 18:4; James 4:6, 10; 1 Peter 5:5).

What Do You Think?

What characteristics of humility should be most evident in your daily walk with Christ?

Digging Deeper

Is humility best understood in light of opposites such as pride or arrogance as described in Romans 1:28-32; James 4:16; 2 Peter 2:10, 18? Why, or why not?

The prophetic formula *saith the Lord* underscores that God has honored the king's contrition. Its repetition throughout Huldah's prophecy does more than just legitimize her as a spokesperson for God. It also gave the king's delegation confidence to repeat to the king what they had learned, knowing that the prophecy was reliable.

A Humble Leader

A colleague and I once moderated a church's congregational meeting concerning whether the minister should resign or be fired. We arrived to see a congregation self-destructing. Tempers were flaring; voices were raised in anger. In the heat of the meeting, the minister declared that if he received 50.1 percent of the vote, he would stay.

My colleague and I concluded that the minister's pride had become a key factor in the church's troubles. We asked for a recess and talked privately with him. He acknowledged that his staying would split the church and mar its witness in the community. Reluctantly, he decided to resign.

Many kings of Israel and Judah paid little heed to God's Word because they were so impressed with themselves. By contrast, Josiah was a model of humble leadership. He placed God and the welfare of his nation before himself, and God blessed him as a result. What steps can you take to humble yourself for the good of God's people? —C. R. B.

B. God Will Act (v. 20)

20a. Behold therefore, I will gather thee unto thy fathers, and thou shalt be gathered into thy grave in peace; and thine eyes shall not see all the evil which I will bring upon this place.

The final use of *behold* emphasized Huldah's climactic statement to the king and invited contrast with its previous use in 2 Kings 22:16, above. The Lord would honor the king by protecting him from the punishment coming against Judah. The phrase *I will gather thee unto thy fathers* is a variation on the formula "[name] slept with his fathers" as used throughout 1 and 2 Kings (examples: 1 Kings 2:10; 11:43; 15:24; 2 Kings 16:20; 20:21). The king would not experience *the evil* (see on 2 Kings 22:16, above) that God would bring on the temple, Jerusalem, and Judah.

The phrase *thou shalt be gathered into thy grave in peace* may seem to contradict what we know about Josiah's death in battle (2 Kings 23:29-30). But the idea is that Josiah would die at peace with God. He would not personally witness what the words of the book anticipated and what Huldah confirmed: the devastating destruction of Jerusalem and of the temple at the hands of the Babylonians in 586 BC (2 Kings 25).

The message of God through Huldah confirmed anew His righteousness, faithfulness, and mercy. God would be faithful to the word He had uttered centuries before when He warned Israel of the penalties that would result from unfaithfulness to the covenant.

> *What Do You Think?*
> What would you say to a fellow Christian who fully expects to escape all consequences God may visit on the idolatrous culture around us?
> *Digging Deeper*
> Which biblical precedents back you up?

20b. And they brought the king word again.

The message of the prophetess and the words of the book resulted in Josiah's convening the nation for a covenant renewal ceremony. He also enacted further measures to cleanse the temple and the land from elements of idolatry (2 Kings 23:1-25; 2 Chronicles 34:29-33).

Judah was spared while Josiah was alive. But after his death, Judah returned to evil ways and experienced the promised curses: the destruction of Jerusalem and the temple at the hands of Nebuchadnezzar as well as the exile in Babylon (2 Kings 23:31–25:21).

Conclusion

A. Responding in Faith

The events recorded in 2 Kings 22 highlight both the importance of engaging with God's words and responding to them. It seems absurd that the Book of the Law was neglected and lost to the people of Judah! Yet is that any more ridiculous than the Bible's loss to myriads of Christians who rarely read it? We must guard against losing Scripture in our churches, our homes, and our lives.

We honor God when we do His will as recorded in Scripture (John 14:15; etc.). Josiah sought to do just that through his reforms after the Book of the Law was found. He *acted* on the words he had heard from that book. He showed remorse over the sin of his people, and he sought godly insight into what he had heard read to him.

Scripture study must always lead us to repentance and action based on what we encounter in its pages. This is the faithful response to learning God's will. That process involves consulting competent interpreters of Scripture (Romans 12:4-8; 2 Timothy 2:2) and studying it alongside other believers who are willing to hold us accountable to its words (Acts 2:42; Hebrews 10:24-25). May we, like Josiah, surround ourselves with faithful companions as we seek God's guidance.

B. Prayer

Father, we praise You as the God of mercy and grace whose love for us has been demonstrated in mercy to Josiah and ultimately through Your Son, Jesus Christ. We ask that You forgive us when we fail to heed Your Word. In Jesus' name we pray. Amen.

C. Thought to Remember

God hears those who humbly seek Him.

Involvement Learning

Enhance your lesson with KJV Bible Student *(from your curriculum supplier) and the reproducible activity page (at www.standardlesson.com or in the back of the* KJV Standard Lesson Commentary Deluxe Edition*).*

Into the Lesson

Option. Before learners arrive, place at chairs copies of the "Five Milestones of 1 and 2 Kings" exercise from the activity page, which you can download, for individuals to complete as indicated. This brief exercise will sketch the broader context in which today's lesson occurs.

Begin class by writing the following "quote" on the board:

> *The problem with quotes on the internet is that it is hard to verify their authenticity.*
> —Abraham Lincoln

Ask learners what is suspicious about this attribution. After the obvious answer and some chuckles, ask what news sources and information outlets your learners trust. Jot responses on the board as they are voiced. (The follow-up question "Why?" is best not asked, lest the discussion become political.) Make a transition by noting that everyone realizes that some sources are more reliable than others in accuracy, which today's lesson brings home to the twenty-first century Christian.

Into the Word

Give each participant a handout (you prepare) featuring the following title and questions:

2 Kings 22:14-20 . . . and a Bit More

1. Who were the direct participants?
2. What action occurred?
3. Where did it take place?
4. When did the action of the text occur?‡
5. Why did the action of the text occur?‡

As you distribute handouts to pairs or triads of learners, announce a prize to the team that scores the most points. Say that 15 points are possible, but do not be more specific than that. Inform teams that the last 2 questions (marked with ‡) will take them outside today's lesson text for answers.

Expected responses and scoring: 1–Hilkiah the priest, Ahikam, Achbor, Shaphan, Asahiah, Huldah the prophetess, and the Lord (1 point each, total of 7 points possible; penalize 1 point for answering King Josiah—he wasn't there personally); 2–those whom the king sent to the prophetess received a message from God (1 point); 3–in a specific area of Jerusalem (2 points possible; award only 1 point for the bare answer "Jerusalem"); 4–622 BC (award 3 points for this answer, which must be deduced by consulting 2 Kings 22:3 and using a conversion timeline; award only 2 points for the answer "eighteenth year of Josiah's reign"; award only 1 point for the answer "during Josiah's reign"); 5–Book of the Law was found, per 2 Kings 22:8 (award 2 points for this reference; award only 1 point for less specific responses).

Award a humorous Due Diligence certificate (or other appropriate prize), which you have prepared in advance, to the team scoring the most points.

Into Life

Give everyone an index card. Ask them to write the name of a disaster that could befall them in the week ahead, but not to write their own names. Collect the (anonymous) cards, shuffle them, then read them. After each card is read, pause to ask where the person with the designated fear should go for reliable help and information.

Alternative. Distribute copies of the "Many Sources" exercise from the activity page for learners in study pairs to complete as indicated. Compare and contrast entries in ensuing whole-class discussion.

As learners depart (not sooner), distribute handouts that feature the names of seven church leaders (mixture of your church's leaders and national luminaries) and seven political leaders (mixture of national, state, and local). Challenge learners to post it in a place where they will pray for one named person in each category in the seven days until class meets again. Include on the handouts the text of 1 Timothy 2:1-2.

March 28
Lesson 4 (KJV)

Prophet of Courage

Devotional Reading: Luke 19:28-39
Background Scripture: 1 Kings 18–19; Matthew 17:1-13

1 Kings 18:5-18

5 And Ahab said unto Obadiah, Go into the land, unto all fountains of water, and unto all brooks: peradventure we may find grass to save the horses and mules alive, that we lose not all the beasts.

6 So they divided the land between them to pass throughout it: Ahab went one way by himself, and Obadiah went another way by himself.

7 And as Obadiah was in the way, behold, Elijah met him: and he knew him, and fell on his face, and said, Art thou that my lord Elijah?

8 And he answered him, I am: go, tell thy lord, Behold, Elijah is here.

9 And he said, What have I sinned, that thou wouldest deliver thy servant into the hand of Ahab, to slay me?

10 As the Lord thy God liveth, there is no nation or kingdom, whither my lord hath not sent to seek thee: and when they said, He is not there; he took an oath of the kingdom and nation, that they found thee not.

11 And now thou sayest, Go, tell thy lord, Behold, Elijah is here.

12 And it shall come to pass, as soon as I am gone from thee, that the Spirit of the Lord shall carry thee whither I know not; and so when I come and tell Ahab, and he cannot find thee, he shall slay me: but I thy servant fear the Lord from my youth.

13 Was it not told my lord what I did when Jezebel slew the prophets of the Lord, how I hid an hundred men of the Lord's prophets by fifty in a cave, and fed them with bread and water?

14 And now thou sayest, Go, tell thy lord, Behold, Elijah is here: and he shall slay me.

15 And Elijah said, As the Lord of hosts liveth, before whom I stand, I will surely shew myself unto him to day.

16 So Obadiah went to meet Ahab, and told him: and Ahab went to meet Elijah.

17 And it came to pass, when Ahab saw Elijah, that Ahab said unto him, Art thou he that troubleth Israel?

18 And he answered, I have not troubled Israel; but thou, and thy father's house, in that ye have forsaken the commandments of the Lord, and thou hast followed Baalim.

Key Verse

He answered, I have not troubled Israel; but thou, and thy father's house, in that ye have forsaken the commandments of the Lord, and thou hast followed Baalim. **—1 Kings 18:18**

Prophets Faithful to God's Covenant

Unit 1: Faithful Prophets

Lessons 1–4

Lesson Aims

After participating in this lesson, each learner will be able to:

1. Tell what happened during the meetings between Elijah and Obadiah, then between Elijah and Ahab.
2. Explain a purpose of a prophet's ministry as it confronted the righteous and the wicked.
3. Write a message of encouragement to someone whose ministry requires a special measure of courage.

Lesson Outline

Introduction

A. The Source of Courage

During my ministry with a church in Cincinnati, I visited almost weekly an older lady in the congregation. She resided in a nursing care facility. On entering the driveway of the building, one noticed a sign that usually featured some kind of clever saying. For about a month, the sign read "Inhale courage, exhale fear." Every time I saw that sign, I thought, "If only it were that easy—to receive courage by simply breathing in and lose one's fears by breathing out."

In the classic movie *The Wizard of Oz*, all the cowardly lion had to do to find the courage he wanted was to receive a medal from the wizard. It was inscribed with the word *Courage*. Again, if only it were that easy.

Some of the most courageous individuals anyone could ever encounter are the prophets of the Old Testament. One of these is highlighted in today's lesson. He is Elijah, a man who was used by God to confront one of Israel's most wicked kings, Ahab, and his ruthless wife, Jezebel. The times demanded someone who would not back down in the face of brazen defiance of the true God of Israel, and Elijah was that man. He did not receive his courage from a medal; his "mettle" came from the Lord himself.

B. Lesson Context

Today's Scripture covers the early portion of the ministry of the prophet Elijah (who prophesied about 869 to 838 BC). He proclaimed the word of the Lord during one of the most critical periods of Old Testament history. His ministry began after the split of the nation into two kingdoms (931 BC): Israel (the northern kingdom) and Judah (the southern kingdom).

The first king of the north, Jeroboam I (931–910 BC), began his reign by violating the first two of the Ten Commandments (Exodus 20:3-4). He set up two golden calves for the people to worship: one in the northern part of the northern kingdom, in Dan, and one in the southern part, in Bethel (1 Kings 12:28-29). This made it easier for those in the north to embrace pagan worship.

The reign of King Ahab in northern Israel (874–853 BC) was characterized by economic prosperity, at least at the outset (1 Kings 22:39; compare 2 Chronicles 18:1). It was also a time of spiritual poverty (1 Kings 18:17-40). Idol worship became more prevalent when Ahab married Jezebel. She was the daughter of the king of Zidon and a devout worshipper of the god Baal (1 Kings 16:31; 18:3, 19). Baal was a fertility god, believed to be in control of anything to do with giving life, whether to animals, plants, or human beings.

First Kings 17 begins with the sudden appearance of Elijah. He boldly proclaimed that "there shall not be dew nor rain these years, but according to my word" (17:1). Moses had warned God's people of the abomination that idolatry constituted in the sight of God (Deuteronomy 4:15-24). Famine was listed among the curses that would result from disobeying God's law (28:23-24; compare Leviticus 26:19-20). A declaration of famine amounted to a grave insult to Baal (and to Ahab and Jezebel) and constituted a direct challenge to the authority of that fictitious god.

Following this announcement of a famine, Elijah went into hiding for a time. The prophet hid by the brook Cherith (until the brook dried up), then traveled northward to Zarephath of Zidon (Jezebel's homeland!). There he stayed with a widow, for whom he offered two unforgettable demonstrations of God's power. First, her supply of oil and meal to prepare bread for her household did not run out during the famine; and second, her son was raised from the dead (1 Kings 17:8-24). Both miracles revealed the Lord's authority in matters of fertility, where Baal was believed to be in control.

Following this time away from the northern kingdom, Elijah was spiritually prepared to speak and demonstrate the Lord's authoritative word. He could return to Ahab's realm and confront the defiant, disobedient king.

I. Ahab and Obadiah

(1 Kings 18:5-6)

A. Surviving a Famine (v. 5)

5. And Ahab said unto Obadiah, Go into the land, unto all fountains of water, and unto all brooks: peradventure we may find grass to save the horses and mules alive, that we lose not all the beasts.

The name *Obadiah* is used of some 12 different men in the Old Testament, in addition to the book of the same name. This particular man is first mentioned in the biblical record in 1 Kings 18:3, where he is described as the "governor of [King Ahab's] house." This likely means that Obadiah was in charge of Ahab's palace in Samaria (capital of the northern kingdom of Israel) and assisted in the administration of official matters.

Obadiah was a man of remarkable courage, given the position he held and the faith he embraced. He is described as someone who "feared the Lord greatly" (1 Kings 18:3). His faith was not a private matter. But he must have been careful in how he exercised it, given the devotion of Ahab and Jezebel to Baal (see 18:13, below).

Horses and mules were necessary for transportation and carrying loads. It is worth noting that *Ahab* did not express concern for people who were suffering or dying during the famine. Perhaps he was preoccupied with keeping his army supplied with animals necessary for military preparedness. The situation in the kingdom had become so desperate that the king and one of his chief officials, not the usual workers, were tasked with finding sustenance for the animals.

B. Surveying the Land (v. 6)

6. So they divided the land between them to pass throughout it: Ahab went one way by

HOW TO SAY IT

Ahab	*Ay*-hab.
Baal	*Bay*-ul.
Baalim	Bay-uh-*leem*.
Bethel	*Beth*-ul.
Cherith	*Key*-rith.
Elijah	Ee-*lye*-juh.
Jeroboam	Jair-uh-*boe*-um.
Jezebel	*Jez*-uh-bel.
Obadiah	O-buh-*dye*-uh.
Zarephath	*Zair*-uh-fath.
Zidon	*Zye*-dun.

himself, and Obadiah went another way by himself.

Ahab realized how difficult it would be for one man to cover that extent of territory. He proceeded to divide the northern kingdom *between* the two of them. The hope was that they would find enough grazing area to keep their livestock alive.

II. Elijah and Obadiah

(1 Kings 18:7-15)

A. Unexpected Meeting (v. 7)

7. And as Obadiah was in the way, behold, Elijah met him: and he knew him, and fell on his face, and said, Art thou that my lord Elijah?

Elijah probably would have been traveling south from Zidon, where the prophet had been helping the widow at Zarephath (1 Kings 17:8-24). It is likely that *Obadiah* was traveling through the northern part of Israel when the two men *met*.

Obadiah's question reflects some measure of doubt that this was *really* Elijah, or disbelief that he was seeing Elijah at all. Addressing Elijah as *my lord* reflected the reverence with which Obadiah held the prophet as God's messenger. The title did not imply deity.

B. Unwelcome Order (vv. 8-14)

8. And he answered him, I am: go, tell thy lord, Behold, Elijah is here.

Elijah confirmed that he himself was speaking to Obadiah as part of a command to return to Ahab. Although Obadiah had called Elijah *lord*, Elijah implied that Obadiah had actually been honoring and serving Ahab. This may have been a subtle dig or an outright test of Obadiah.

9. And he said, What have I sinned, that thou wouldest deliver thy servant into the hand of Ahab, to slay me?

Obadiah assumed that if Elijah were asking him to put his life in such jeopardy, it must be to punish him for a particular sin he had committed (compare 1 Kings 18:12, below). Obadiah's thinking was similar to that of the widow in Zarephath, who accused Elijah of punishing her sin by taking her son from her (17:18). Calling himself Elijah's *servant* rejects the idea that *Ahab* had Obadiah's true allegiance. Thus Obadiah distanced himself from any implied sin, especially of idolatry, that could result from serving Ahab in any capacity.

Obadiah anticipated Ahab's reaction to Elijah's message. For Obadiah to leave Elijah alone in order to travel to Ahab (we do not know how far apart the two men were at this point) would anger the king, who had already stood by as his wife killed God's prophets (see 1 Kings 18:13). Would Ahab suspect that Obadiah was a supporter of Elijah and a worshipper of Elijah's God?

> *What Do You Think?*
> How can you improve your reputation of being a tactful person in your spheres of influence?
> *Digging Deeper*
> How does Daniel 2:14 in its context help frame your response?

10. As the Lord thy God liveth, there is no nation or kingdom, whither my lord hath not sent to seek thee: and when they said, He is not there; he took an oath of the kingdom and nation, that they found thee not.

In contrast to the prophet who feared this task would leave him dead, *the Lord . . . liveth* (see 1 Kings 18:15, below). The promises of Obadiah and Elijah were made before God. This marks both men as true prophets. They served the living God, not idols or fictitious, powerless gods (see 18:26-29, not in our printed text).

We need not assume that there was literally *no nation or kingdom* that Ahab hadn't questioned about Elijah's whereabouts. Rather, Obadiah described (using hyperbole) how intensely Ahab had searched for the prophet. The rulers in Zidon probably had not realized that Elijah had been among them (1 Kings 17:9). Had they been, they would have risked Ahab's wrath by lying under *oath* that they had not seen the prophet.

Wanted!

"East Area Rapist" and "Golden State Killer" are names for the criminal who killed at least 13 people, raped more than 50, and brought fear to many others in California between 1974 and

1986. For years, law enforcement followed every lead available, but the case grew cold.

The manhunt came back to life in 2018, when a distant relative uploaded his own DNA profile onto an open-source genealogy website. This eventually led the police to a man in his 70s who had resided in the areas where the crimes had been committed. His DNA was a match to DNA found at various crime scenes, and the suspect was arrested.

Obadiah may have been exaggerating when he told Elijah that Ahab had sent out searchers to *every* nation. But it tells us that Ahab's search for Elijah was just as tenacious as the search for the Golden State Killer. What does the intensity of your search for Jesus say about you? —C. R. B.

11-12a. And now thou sayest, Go, tell thy lord, Behold, Elijah is here. And it shall come to pass, as soon as I am gone from thee, that the Spirit of the LORD shall carry thee whither I know not; and so when I come and tell Ahab, and he cannot find thee, he shall slay me.

If Ahab heard from Obadiah that he had met *Elijah* without arresting him, the king would be infuriated. The implication of not immediately bringing Elijah to Ahab would be that Obadiah was lying to the king—something that one just did not do!

The phrase *and it shall come to pass* indicates that Obadiah considerd what he had to say next to have been a foregone conclusion. In his own estimation, Obadiah would pay with his life when *the Spirit* whisked Elijah away. We often think of the Spirit's work in the prophets' lives in terms of their speech and writing (example: 2 Peter 1:20-21). However, Obadiah was more concerned with the Spirit's ability to move or hide a person supernaturally, as He had done with Enoch (Genesis 5:24; compare 2 Kings 2:16b; Ezekiel 8:3; Acts 8:39).

Obadiah knew something of how prophets *of the Lord* operated in obedience to Him (Deuteronomy 18:15-22; see lesson 1). Though Elijah intended to appear before Ahab, it would only happen if God allowed it. In fact, God had commanded it (1 Kings 18:1-2, not in our printed text).

What Do You Think?

How do a person put the brakes on his or her imagination to keep it from running wild and paralyzing action?

Digging Deeper

When was a time that fear of a hypothetical outcome stopped you in your tracks?

12b-13. But I thy servant fear the LORD from my youth. Was it not told my lord what I did when Jezebel slew the prophets of the LORD, how I hid an hundred men of the LORD's prophets by fifty in a cave, and fed them with bread and water?

Obadiah began a defense of his personal character and devotion to *the Lord* as a reason why his life should not be put in danger. He had lived up to the meaning of his name, "*servant* of the Lord." In fact, he'd grown up from his *youth* fearing God, a sign of wisdom (Psalm 111:10; Proverbs 1:7).

Obadiah's actions on behalf of *the Lord's prophets* were evidence that he feared the Lord. Some prophets already had been put to death under Jezebel's direction, but we have no idea of how many. Obadiah's hiding *an hundred* in two caves and smuggling in supplies for them was indeed a dangerous task (see 1 Kings 18:4). Not only did he have to be very sneaky with large amounts of *bread and water*, but chances of discovery were heightened during that time of drought and the famine it produced.

14. And now thou sayest, Go, tell thy lord, Behold, Elijah is here: and he shall slay me.

Obadiah repeated 1 Kings 18:12a to emphasize the danger that *Elijah* was putting him in.

What Do You Think?

Considering anew the question "Under what circumstances in the church should you act as a messenger between two parties?" on p. 251, how does today's text modify your thought?

Digging Deeper

What did you learn from a time you made a wrong choice in this regard?

C. Unwavering Promise (v. 15)

15. And Elijah said, As the Lord of hosts liveth, before whom I stand, I will surely shew myself unto him to day.

Elijah's first recorded prophecy that neither dew nor rain would fall on Israel opened with a similar oath (1 Kings 17:1). The oath at hand was as trustworthy as any promise could ever be. In it, Elijah expanded on Obadiah's oath (18:10, above): not only does God live, but He is *the Lord of hosts*. This is a warrior image of God, leading the heavenly angels in battle against evil. The title called Obadiah's attention to God's power, not just His presence.

The additional words *before whom I stand* indicated the close relationship between the Lord and Elijah (compare Jeremiah 15:1). As the Lord's spokesman, Elijah stood ready to go, speak, and do whatever his commander desired.

> *What Do You Think?*
> What are some ways Christians can reassure one another in times of fear or doubt?
> *Digging Deeper*
> In what ways, if ever, is 2 Kings 6:13-17 a precedent for offering such reassurance?

III. Elijah and Ahab
(1 Kings 18:16-18)

A. Antagonistic Reception (vv. 16-17)

16. So Obadiah went to meet Ahab, and told him: and Ahab went to meet Elijah.

Elijah's word and oath satisfied *Obadiah* and settled any doubts he may have had about returning without *Elijah*. This was the first time King *Ahab* and Elijah would meet face-to-face following the three-and-a-half-year famine that had devastated the entire northern kingdom of Israel.

17. And it came to pass, when Ahab saw Elijah, that Ahab said unto him, Art thou he that troubleth Israel?

The phrase *and it came to pass* echoes Obadiah's previous fears and shows them to have been unfounded in this case (see 1 Kings 18:12, above). Ahab's greeting on seeing *Elijah* was the very opposite of Obadiah's (see 18:7, above). Ahab's words reflect the utter contempt in which he held prophets like Elijah. This disdain was based on the bad reports prophets frequently brought him (example: 22:8).

But in a sense, Ahab was right. Any true prophet of the Lord will trouble people when he or she confronts them with the truth about their sinfulness and their need to repent. Ahab was justified in accusing Elijah of being the cause of the famine of the past three and a half years (James 5:17). However, his larger point is way off the mark. God's judgment would not have occurred had *Israel* remained faithful to the Lord alone (see 1 Kings 18:18, below).

Projection

I had used my father's old Kodak a number of times when one day I suddenly realized that I wanted to be a photographer. I was "seeing pictures" as I looked at the world. Soon, I bought a 35mm camera that served me well as I learned my new craft. I liked taking color slides that could be projected onto a screen many times the size of that small piece of film.

My current camera is essentially a computer with a lens attached. Nevertheless, I still view my pictures by projection: captured on the camera's tiny electronic sensor, they are projected onto my computer screen. A video projector can make the picture big enough for a large auditorium.

In criticizing others, we may "project" onto them our own faults, making them appear larger in that other person. When Ahab condemned Elijah as bringing trouble to Israel, the king was projecting his own spiritual failings onto the prophet. How can you ensure that you do not project your own sins and shortcomings on others?

—C. R. B.

B. Honest Answer (v. 18)

18. And he answered, I have not troubled Israel; but thou, and thy father's house, in that ye have forsaken the commandments of the Lord, and thou hast followed Baalim.

Elijah did not back down in the face of the king's anger. He threw Ahab's accusation back at him, letting him know that the king and the idolatry of his *father's house* were the real troublemakers in Israel.

The famine had come upon the land because of the idolatrous practices that had first been encouraged by Ahab's father, Omri (1 Kings 16:25-26; see Lesson Context). These practices were furthered through Ahab's efforts in promoting the worship of Baal (16:30-33), with the enthusiastic support of Jezebel (21:25-26).

English usually forms the plural by adding an "s" on the end of a noun; Hebrew forms the plural by adding "im." Hence, *Baalim* is the plural form of Baal, occurring about 18 times in the Old Testament. The word means "lord" or "possessor," and the plural may refer to different manifestations of this so-called god.

> *What Do You Think?*
> When condemned or mocked for following God's Word, how should you respond?
> *Digging Deeper*
> Should your response be the same in all situations? Why, or why not?

Not long after Ahab and Elijah's meeting, both the king and the people saw a clear demonstration of the impotence of idolatry and the power of Elijah's God—at the contest on Mount Carmel. Even that, however, did not convince Ahab to change his evil practices and renounce his idolatry (1 Kings 18:20-40, not in our printed text). Though he repented late in life (21:27), Ahab is still remembered primarily for all the trouble he caused Israel.

Conclusion

A. Who's the Troublemaker?

Courage has always been the trademark of God's spokespeople (examples: Joshua 1:6-7, 9, 18; Amos 7:10-17). Like Elijah, these prophets continued to proclaim courageously and lead faithfully according to the Lord's words. And like Elijah, these prophets were considered troublemakers.

In many parts of the world today, an increased measure of courage is required to preach and teach

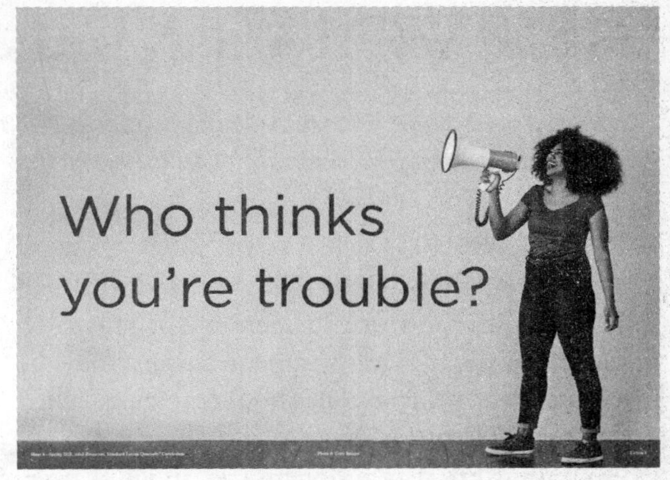

Visual for Lesson 4. *While discussing verse 17, have the class brainstorm situations in which they could be called trouble for speaking for God.*

the gospel. Defiant authorities in countries like China or Sudan consider followers of Jesus to be modern troublemakers. Such leaders work hard to silence missionary voices. In India, Christian ministers have been beaten by Hindu radicals. The country of Turkey has displaced Christians searching for a place of worship. And all over the world, Christian refugees seek new homes in nations that will welcome them in peace. (Do an internet search for "the 10 most dangerous places to be a Christian.")

Let us pray for these faithful servants of the Lord, that they may be established, strengthened, settled (1 Peter 5:10), and empowered with the courage that has always characterized God's people in an often hostile world. May we learn from the examples of courage of our ancient prophets and our fellow Christians in the world today.

B. Prayer

Father, empower us with courage to live out our faith and speak Your word on Your behalf. We pray for our fellow believers in other lands where living for You means putting their lives on the line daily. May they respond with Holy Spirit–empowered courage to the challenges they face. In Jesus' name we pray. Amen.

C. Thought to Remember

Be a courageous, Spirit-led troublemaker!

INVOLVEMENT LEARNING

Enhance your lesson with KJV Bible Student *(from your curriculum supplier) and the reproducible activity page (at www.standardlesson.com or in the back of the* KJV Standard Lesson Commentary Deluxe Edition*).*

Into the Lesson

Option. Place at chairs copies of the "Profiles in Courage" exercise from the activity page, which you can download. Do not say anything about the exercise; merely shrug your shoulders when asked any question about it.

After mysteriously ignoring the previous exercise (if you used it), write the word *courage* on the board vertically as the start of a whole-class acrostic exercise. Invite learners to call out single-word qualities they associate with courage. Mention three rules at the outset: (1) the word called out must have a letter in common with the word *courage,* (2) the letter in common must not have been taken by a previous call-out, and (3) no one is allowed to voice a second word until everyone has had a chance to voice one.

Write called-out words horizontally on the board, ensuring that they intersect with *courage* at the letter in common. The exercise ends when seven intersecting words are written. The finished product should look something like this, but with words your learners have voiced:

de**C**isive
Optimistic
Unflappable
motivato**R**
articul**A**te
or**G**anized
focus**E**d

After you've written the seven words, take a vote as to which word of the seven best describes courage. Then make a transition by saying, "It will be interesting to see how well your chosen word and the other six fit with the two examples of courage in today's lesson."

Into the Word

Set the stage for Bible study by asking a learner in advance to prepare a three-minute summary of the Lesson Context to be delivered at this time. Then give each learner a handout (you prepare) that features two columns intersected by four rows. The two column headings are *Obadiah* and *Elijah*; label the four rows down the left as follows:

1–What God called him to do
2–How he responded to God's call
3–Why God's call required courage
4–I personally identify with him because . . .

Ask learners, in groups of three to six, to complete the top six of the eight intersections, using today's text. The bottom two intersections are then completed individually in a minute of private reflection. Discuss results in ensuing whole-class discussion. Allow volunteers to voice their "I personally identify" entries, but don't put anyone on the spot to do so. (*Option:* To extend this study, distribute copies of the "A Tale of Three Men" exercise from the activity page for groups to complete as indicated; follow with whole-class discussion.)

Into Life

Make prior arrangements for one of these three presentations to occur at this point:

- a learner reports on persecuted Christians
- you share examples from the work of a missionary supported by your congregation
- a member of your church staff or missions committee brings that report

Ask class members to consider taking time this week to write notes of encouragement to persecuted Christians to gain courage from the Lord. Distribute names and addresses of possibilities for this, which you've researched in advance.

Option. Distribute copies of the "My Prayer for Courage" exercise from the activity page. Give individuals one minute to jot down ideas, and then ask volunteers to share what they've written.

Return to the words learners chose in the opening acrostic. Pose these questions: Which word best fits Obadiah? Elijah? Which word is most necessary for persecuted Christians? Why?

The Suffering Servant

Devotional Reading: Philippians 2:1-11
Background Scripture: Isaiah 52:13–53:12; Luke 24:1-35

Isaiah 53:4-11a

4 Surely he hath borne our griefs, and carried our sorrows: yet we did esteem him stricken, smitten of God, and afflicted.

5 But he was wounded for our transgressions, he was bruised for our iniquities: the chastisement of our peace was upon him; and with his stripes we are healed.

6 All we like sheep have gone astray; we have turned every one to his own way; and the Lord hath laid on him the iniquity of us all.

7 He was oppressed, and he was afflicted, yet he opened not his mouth: he is brought as a lamb to the slaughter, and as a sheep before her shearers is dumb, so he openeth not his mouth.

8 He was taken from prison and from judgment: and who shall declare his generation? for he was cut off out of the land of the living: for the transgression of my people was he stricken.

9 And he made his grave with the wicked, and with the rich in his death; because he had done no violence, neither was any deceit in his mouth.

10 Yet it pleased the Lord to bruise him; he hath put him to grief: when thou shalt make his soul an offering for sin, he shall see his seed, he shall prolong his days, and the pleasure of the Lord shall prosper in his hand.

11a He shall see of the travail of his soul.

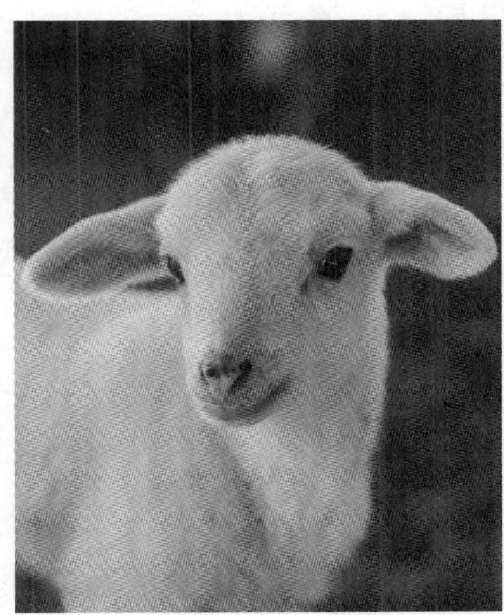

Key Verse

He was wounded for our transgressions, he was bruised for our iniquities: the chastisement of our peace was upon him; and with his stripes we are healed. **—Isaiah 53:5**

Photo: Getty Images

Prophets Faithful To God's Covenant

Unit 2: Prophets of Restoration

Lessons 5–8

Lesson Aims

After participating in this lesson, each learner will be able to:

1. Restate what the servant of the Lord would accomplish through suffering.
2. Explain how Jesus fulfilled Isaiah's prophecy.
3. Write a prayer of thanksgiving to the Lord, using language from today's passage, and use it as a source of family or personal devotions each day this week.

Lesson Outline

Introduction
- A. Climbing to the Summit
- B. Lesson Context: The Prophecies of Isaiah
- C. Lesson Context: The Servant

I. The Servant's Death (Isaiah 53:4-9)
- A. Grief, Sorrow, Affliction (vv. 4-6)
  - *Why Do We Suffer?*
- B. Oppression, Slaughter, Burial (vv. 7-9)

II. The Servant's Delight (Isaiah 53:10-11a)
- A. Sovereign Purpose (v. 10)
  - *Aging Gracefully*
- B. Sacred Success (v. 11a)

Conclusion
- A. Relishing the View
- B. Prayer
- C. Thought to Remember

Introduction

A. Climbing to the Summit

Kyle Yates, an Old Testament scholar who taught seminary for many years, once referred to Isaiah 53 as the "Mount Everest" of Old Testament prophecy. That analogy brings to mind the reality that mountain summits are not reached without first doing a lot of hiking up difficult terrain. Sometimes during our "hike" through the Bible, we may question the value or relevance of what we are reading. And so we struggle through the laws and regulations in Leviticus and rush quickly through the genealogies that fill the first nine chapters of 1 Chronicles. As we do, we may wonder why we even began the climb in the first place!

But reaching a summit-passage like Isaiah 53 makes us realize that the climb is worthwhile. This is all the more so when we consider that the existence of the New Testament ensures that Old Testament summit-passages are clearer to us than they were even to the original readers. Specialized "guides" such as Acts 8:32-34 and Romans 10:16 assist us in our journey to understand Isaiah 53 specifically while the general guides of Romans 15:4 and 2 Timothy 3:16 establish the importance of doing so for the Old Testament as a whole.

B. Lesson Context: The Prophecies of Isaiah

The importance of the book of Isaiah is seen in the fact that it is quoted over five dozen times in the New Testament. Isaiah prophesied in Jerusalem during dismal times for God's people. His prophetic call came "in the year that king Uzziah died" (Isaiah 6:1), which would have been 740 BC. The latest historical event recorded (not prophesied) by the prophet is the death of the Assyrian ruler Sennacherib (37:37-38), which occurred in 681 BC. That makes for a lengthy period of ministry, so it is not out of the question to assume that Isaiah's call came when he was a teenager or a bit older.

The span of Isaiah's prophetic ministry included the fall of the northern kingdom of Israel to Assyria in 722 BC. The southern kingdom of Judah was in danger of going the same route in 701 BC. However, the presence and the prayers of a godly king,

Hezekiah (Isaiah 37:14-20), resulted in an outcome far different from what the north experienced. Isaiah assured the king that the capital city of Jerusalem would be spared (37:33-35), and it was—in a miraculous act of deliverance (37:36).

With Spirit-empowered insight, Isaiah spoke of a future day when Jerusalem would *not* be delivered; it would come under the control of the Babylonians (Isaiah 39:5-7). But Isaiah also promised that the Lord was not finished with Jerusalem or with His people. The Lord would rebuild the city through the efforts of a ruler whom Isaiah named: Cyrus (44:24–45:1). But Isaiah looked beyond even this restoration to someone far greater than Cyrus.

C. Lesson Context: The Servant

The Lord's "servant" is one of the most striking figures in the book of Isaiah. The term *servant* is sometimes a reference to the entire nation of Israel, describing the special relationship the covenant people have with the Lord (example: Isaiah 41:8). In other places, *servant* appears to describe a remnant of God's people, referring specifically to those who remained following captivity in Babylon (example: 48:20).

There are still other passages where the word *servant* points to one individual who was assigned a very special role to fulfill. Four passages in Isaiah—often called Servant Songs—function in this way to point to the Messiah: Isaiah 42:1-9; 49:1-6; 50:4-9; and 52:13–53:12. (Isaiah 61:1-4 can also be included since Jesus applied it to himself [Luke 4:16-21].) This servant would carry out his tasks in a way that neither the nation of Israel nor the remnant could ever do.

The servant passage studied today is the fourth in the list, beginning, "Behold, my servant shall deal prudently, he shall be exalted and extolled, and be very high" (Isaiah 52:13). The passage then describes the astonishment and rejection that many would experience at the servant's lowly and repulsive appearance (52:14–53:3). It seems so inappropriate for someone "exalted and extolled" not to also have a striking physical presence! But nothing in the servant's background speaks of greatness at first glance. Our printed text begins with an explanation of the servant's sorrows and griefs that are introduced in Isaiah 53:3.

Christians have long and rightly interpreted the prophetic Servant Songs as fulfilled in Jesus alone. For instance, Isaiah 53:7-8 (see below) makes up the passage that the Ethiopian eunuch was reading when Philip approached his chariot. The Ethiopian asked whether the prophet was speaking of himself or someone else. And Philip "began at the same scripture, and preached unto him Jesus" (Acts 8:35). No other figure appears in Scripture who claims to be the servant, and only Christ fulfills all that was written about that servant in these passages. The importance of today's text is seen in the fact that the New Testament quotes from the song in which it occurs seven times.

I. The Servant's Death

(Isaiah 53:4-9)

A. Grief, Sorrow, Affliction (vv. 4-6)

4. Surely he hath borne our griefs, and carried our sorrows: yet we did esteem him stricken, smitten of God, and afflicted.

In keeping with how suffering was often viewed in biblical times (both Old and New Testaments; examples: Job 4:7-8; John 9:2), those who witnessed the servant's suffering saw it as a punishment from *God*. The servant was deemed to be bearing the *griefs* and *sorrows* associated with his own sinful actions. No one would assume that he was suffering on account of the wrongdoings of others.

Followers of Jesus can readily see these words as a compelling description of Jesus' suffering on the cross. Those who mocked Him there voiced their belief that God had abandoned Him—that He was *stricken, smitten*, and *afflicted* (see Matthew 27:43-44). There was a sense in which the servant was stricken by God, in that Jesus fulfilled God's "determinate counsel and foreknowledge" (Acts 2:23). But why He suffered matters tremendously. Being only partially right about Jesus' suffering means being terribly wrong about what it could accomplish.

Jesus' death was the ultimate example of substitutionary atonement. In the Law of Moses, atonement for sins was fulfilled through God's accepting the sacrifice of animals (Leviticus 1:4-5; Numbers 6:16; etc.). They were substitutes for the people who had sinned and so deserved to die (Romans 6:23). Jesus became the perfect sacrifice for others' sins (Romans 3:25; 1 Peter 2:24). For this reason, we no longer offer sacrifices of grain or oil or animals; Jesus is the last and perfect sacrifice (Hebrews 10:10-14).

While we usually focus on the impact of Jesus' death as an atoning sacrifice for our sins, we must keep in mind that this impact affects every aspect of our humanity, both spiritual and physical. Jesus died so that a complete reversal of the curse of sin could be accomplished (see Genesis 3:14-19; Isaiah 65:17; Revelation 21:5). The wholeness of body accomplished by Jesus' servanthood is illustrated in Matthew 8:14-17. Immediately following a description of Jesus' healing ministry and His power to cast out unclean spirits, Matthew wrote that all this happened "that it might be fulfilled which was spoken by Esaias the prophet" (Matthew 8:17).

During Jesus' earthly ministry, miracles and signs demonstrated that He possessed power to heal all brokenness, sinful or otherwise (example: Mark 2:1-12). His return will usher in new heavens and a new earth from which sin and its consequences will be banished (Revelation 21:1-4). Until that day, Jesus takes our infirmities and sicknesses, not by healing them immediately in every instance but by providing grace in those circumstances. His grace empowers us and enhances our testimony to others (see 2 Corinthians 12:7-10).

5. But he was wounded for our transgressions, he was bruised for our iniquities: the chastisement of our peace was upon him; and with his stripes we are healed.

The emphasis on how the servant suffered for humanity continues. We are guilty, but Jesus was treated as though *He* were. *Chastisement* signals the consequence for sin, the consequence *we* deserved. *Peace* with God is the result (Romans 5:1); indeed Christ is our peace (Ephesians 2:14-17).

Why Do We Suffer?

Patricia was my wife for 58 years before succumbing to cancer. She also had endured decades of chronic, severe pain. She had contracted polio as a child. As the years added up, she experienced the effects of degenerative disc disease, then post-polio regression syndrome.

At one point during those years, a well-meaning Christian woman approached Pat. "I can't understand why God is doing this to you," she said. "There must be something terribly wrong with your spiritual life to make God give you all this pain."

Pat's response was twofold: "God isn't doing this to me; it's the effect of disease. And why this is happening is far less important than how I respond to it."

The woman's misguided concern was based on an ancient misunderstanding of how God works: that when someone suffers, it is because of one's sin (example: John 9:2). In this mistaken light, Jesus—given His degree of suffering—must have been the most terrible sinner ever! However, Jesus' suffering came to Him because *we* have sinned. How does Jesus' suffering help you overcome the stigma of your own wounds? —C. R. B.

6. All we like sheep have gone astray; we have turned every one to his own way; and the LORD hath laid on him the iniquity of us all.

Here human beings are compared to *sheep*, which are known for easily wandering *astray* into what is harmful to them. While we were all born inclined to sin (Psalm 51:5), we also choose sin (compare Romans 6:1-2). Humanity's descent into sin is not something we have no part in; we make choices to turn from God. Yet the one against whom we sin, whose law and standards we treat with contempt, placed our wrongdoings and their punishment on the servant. *All* is repeated to emphasize that every one of us has sinned, and the servant has given His life for each of us.

What Do You Think?

Without beginning with Scripture, how would you respond to an unbeliever who claims to have no sin?

Digging Deeper

Consider Paul's technique in Acts 17:16-31.

If we are sheep, who will shepherd us? At the risk of mixing metaphors (see Isaiah 53:7, below), we note that Jesus declared himself as our shepherd (John 10:1-18; 1 Peter 2:25). Like a shepherd, Jesus takes responsibility for our lives. If we are enticed by sin and so die, Jesus the shepherd takes the loss to heart and grieves over the consequences of our sinfully misguided actions (compare Luke 13:34).

B. Oppression, Slaughter, Burial (vv. 7-9)

7a. He was oppressed, and he was afflicted, yet he opened not his mouth.

The servant would respond to his cruel treatment with silence. This may not seem very significant. But when we ponder who Jesus was and the power in His spoken word, such silence should produce a reverent silence within us. Jesus used His words to heal the sick (Matthew 8:5-13), raise the dead (John 11:43), calm storms (Mark 4:39), and work other miracles (example: Luke 4:31-36). Yet when it came to defending himself, He said nothing (Matthew 26:63a; 27:12-14).

Notably, however, Jesus did not remain silent when others were being harmed, especially by leaders who should have cared for them. He called out the enemies who would kill Him—the scribes and the Pharisees—for the ways their hypocrisy damaged the people of Israel (example: Matthew 23:13-36). His speech on behalf of others contributed to the hatred those powerful leaders felt for Jesus (26:3-5). Yet He did not argue on His own behalf to proclaim His innocence.

7b. He is brought as a lamb to the slaughter, and as a sheep before her shearers is dumb, so he openeth not his mouth.

Sheep imagery links this concept to Isaiah 53:6. The comparison to *a lamb* being led *to the slaughter* emphasizes humility and (apparent) powerlessness. A lamb could not overpower the priest who would slaughter it for a sacrifice.

Such language did not become triumphal until the early believers began to understand Jesus as the Lamb of God. In that role, He fulfilled His Father's plan to be the perfect sacrifice for the sins of the world (John 1:29). This same sacrificial Lamb is worshipped in Heaven and by every creature that exists: "Blessing, and honour, and glory, and power, be unto him that sitteth upon the throne, and unto the Lamb for ever and ever" (Revelation 5:13).

What Do You Think?

Under what circumstances would you take Isaiah 53:7 as a precedent for not responding to an oppressive situation?

Digging Deeper

How do texts such as Amos 5:13; Matthew 26:62-64; Acts 16:37; 22:25; 24:10-16; and 1 Peter 2:20-23 influence your answer?

8a. He was taken from prison and from judgment.

This verse prophesied the travesty of a trial that Jesus experienced at the hands of His enemies. In their bitter hatred of Jesus, they denied Him any semblance of a fair proceeding. For example, a person could not be put to death except on the testimony of two or three witnesses according to Deuteronomy 17:6. The witnesses called to testify against Jesus did not agree in their testimony (Mark 14:55-59), but He was still found guilty and crucified.

8b. And who shall declare his generation?

This seems to be a indictment against Jesus' fellow Jews. They not only failed to protest His condemnation, they demanded it (Luke 23:21).

8c. For he was cut off out of the land of the living: for the transgression of my people was he stricken.

Jesus' life was *cut off out of the land of the living* at about age 33 (compare Luke 3:23). Even so, the injustice that He, the servant, experienced and the shameful circumstances surrounding His execution fulfilled a high and holy purpose. Yes, He was *stricken*, but only so that His death could serve as a substitutionary atonement for us (again, Isaiah 53:5, above).

9. And he made his grave with the wicked, and with the rich in his death; because he had done no violence, neither was any deceit in his mouth.

Jesus fulfilled this passage in two ways. First, Jesus was an innocent man who was convicted as if He were a notorious criminal; when a crowd was offered a choice between releasing Him or a man guilty of murder and insurrection, it chose the latter (Mark 15:6-15). As a result, Jesus was hung between two criminals as if He were one of them. Jesus had engaged in violence to clear the temple (John 2:14), but He never committed a violent act that would call for Roman crucifixion.

Second, Jesus was buried in the grave of a rich man. Normally criminals at the time of Jesus who were executed were left unburied. Eventually, the beasts and the birds consumed their flesh. Jesus, however, was treated differently as two factors came together: a request by Jewish leaders to get the bodies off the crosses, which was followed by Jesus' interment in the tomb of Joseph of Arimathaea, a wealthy man (Matthew 27:57; John 19:31-42).

> *What Do You Think?*
> What would you say is the single-most important practice Christians could adopt or improve on to eliminate deceitful speech patterns?
>
> *Digging Deeper*
> Do you see this as a big problem or a minor one? Why do you say that?

II. The Servant's Delight

(Isaiah 53:10-11a)

A. Sovereign Purpose (v. 10)

10a. Yet it pleased the Lord to bruise him; he hath put him to grief: when thou shalt make his soul an offering for sin.

The Lord was at work in and through the servant's suffering, though not in the sense that God was punishing the servant for his own sins (see Isaiah 53:4, above). In truth, the servant's suffering and death constituted *an offering for sin.* The Hebrew term used here refers to the trespass offering (see Leviticus 5:1–6:7).

What made this offering distinct from others was the connection between the sin committed and the remedy stipulated in the law. Jesus' atoning death on the cross was exactly what humanity needed. And it was a sacrifice that needed to be offered only once (Hebrews 7:26-27; 9:24-28). By Jesus' death He destroyed "him that had the power of death, that is, the devil" (Hebrews 2:14).

10b. He shall see his seed, he shall prolong his days, and the pleasure of the Lord shall prosper in his hand.

The number of Jesus' disciples—*his seed*—has continued to grow since the first century AD, when His church was established. That the servant *shall prolong his days* likely points to Jesus' resurrection. That was by no means obvious to any Jewish interpreter before Jesus had actually been raised from the dead. Only then did His disciples begin to grasp how He fulfilled many prophecies, including this one. The Hebrew word translated *pleasure* is also translated "desire" in the Old Testament (2 Samuel 23:5; etc.), and that is the sense here.

> *What Do You Think?*
> How would you answer a person who questions the fairness of Jesus being punished for sins committed by others?
>
> *Digging Deeper*
> If you are unsure how to answer, study the nature of the grace system, beginning with 2 Corinthians 5:21.

Aging Gracefully

Our culture is fixated on staying young. We use cosmetic surgery and hairpieces. We shun words that suggest we are growing old, and we use euphemisms such as "passed on" instead of speaking plainly about death. The hopeful phrase "She's gone to be with the Lord" can be employed to soften the blunt fact that death has robbed us of the presence of a loved one.

However, many of us have found that there are advantages to getting old—advantages such as seniors' discounts! But even better, wisdom can come with age. If we've been paying attention to what life's experiences have taught us, we can bless younger generations with the benefit of knowledge we gained over the years.

Isaiah foretold Jesus' suffering, but he also revealed that Jesus would see His spiritual children prosper. Jesus lives and sees countless generations of His followers living out their days in spiritual blessedness. For the Christian, aging gracefully means more than becoming a kindly grandparent or uncle or aunt. It is the grace of God at work, making us more like Jesus. —C. R. B.

B. Sacred Success (v. 11a)

11a. He shall see of the travail of his soul.

Jesus was able to look at the *travail,* or suffering, He went through and know that He did indeed accomplish the work given to Him. Hebrews 12:2 says that Jesus "for the joy that was set before him endured the cross, despising the shame, and is set down at the right hand of the throne of God." Just as we cannot begin to understand the depth of Jesus' suffering at the cross, we cannot imagine the joy that He felt after He uttered the words "It is finished" (John 19:30).

Conclusion

A. Relishing the View

As with many mountaintop experiences, it can be difficult to return to life below after leaving the magnificent scenery of Isaiah 53 behind. That is perhaps the most powerful of the Servant Songs in its prophetic depiction of the suffering experienced by Jesus at the cross as He died for the sins of others.

Jesus' death was not an accident or random tragedy as we use those terms. Rather, His death was the fulfillment of a divine plan to rescue lost humanity. The study of a passage such as Isaiah 53 should not end with the lesson. We can return to it and scale its heights again and again, as often as we like—and we should.

Prophets like Isaiah yearned to know more about how their prophecies would come to pass (1 Peter 1:10-12). But it was not granted to those men to live in the era of fulfillment (Hebrews 11:39-40). That is our privilege as Christians, who possess the sacred Scriptures of both Old and New Testament. It is we who are able to see from the mountain's summit what Isaiah could see only partially, from somewhere farther down.

May we never take such a sacred privilege for granted.

HOW TO SAY IT

Arimathaea	*Air*-uh-muh-***thee***-uh (*th* as in *thin*).
Cyrus	*Sigh*-russ.
Esaias	E-*zay*-us.
Hezekiah	Hez-ih-*kye*-uh.
Isaiah	Eye-*zay*-uh.
Messiah	Meh-*sigh*-uh.
Sennacherib	Sen-*nack*-er-ib.

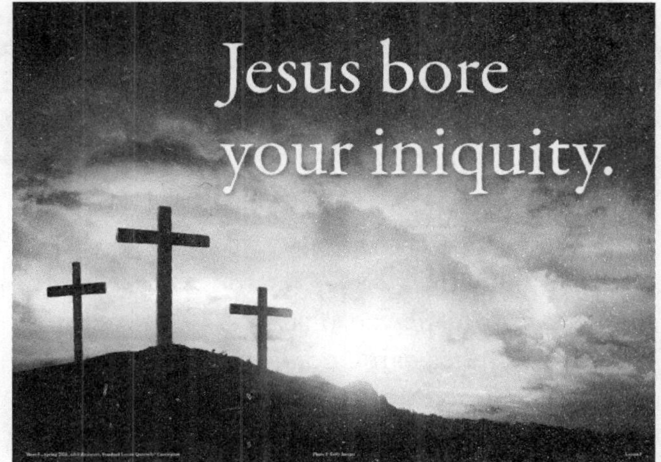

Visual for Lesson 5. *Point to the statement on this visual as you introduce the question associated with verse 10.*

What Do You Think?

How will study of today's text result in changes to your thoughts, words, and actions?

Digging Deeper

Consider also use of today's text in the New Testament: Matthew 8:16-17; Acts 8:32-35; 1 Peter 2:22-25.

B. Prayer

Father, thank You that Jesus came in the fullness of time to fulfill prophecies such as Your wonderful words recorded by Isaiah. Thank You for the amazing love demonstrated by Jesus in His undeserved suffering for undeserving sinners such as us. In Jesus' name we praise You. Amen.

C. Thought to Remember

Jesus makes both the prophecies of Scripture and our lives complete.

INVOLVEMENT LEARNING

Enhance your lesson with KJV Bible Student *(from your curriculum supplier) and the reproducible activity page (at www.standardlesson.com or in the back of the* KJV Standard Lesson Commentary Deluxe Edition*).*

Into the Lesson

Write the words *Suffering* and *Service* on the board, or on displayed placards. Give each person a blank index card and announce that participants have one minute to write a sentence that includes both words on the board. Stress that you will collect the cards and that students should not sign them.

After calling time, collect the cards. Note similarities or unusual combinations as you read them aloud. Then pose these questions for discussion: 1–In what contexts, if any, does service always include suffering? 2–What are some notable examples of service that include suffering?

Make a transition by saying, "Today's lesson includes some of the most beautiful and oft-quoted passages in Scripture. But these also describe a harsh reality of a certain suffering. Let's investigate."

Into the Word

Briefly present the setting for today's passage, using material from the Lesson Context. Then group students into triads. Give to half the groups an assignment to read today's text and to make a bullet-point list of what Isaiah said about the servant. Assign the other groups the task of listing specific actions of Jesus that fulfilled the prophecy. (*Option:* Put the assignments on handouts so you don't have to repeat verbal instructions.) Allow at least six minutes to make the lists.

Call the groups together. Read Isaiah 53:4 and ask volunteers from the **Isaiah said** groups to share what they listed from this verse. Then ask volunteers from the **Jesus fulfilled** groups to share what they discovered in that regard.

Continue in this back-and-forth pattern as you work through each verse of the lesson. (*Option:* Write participants' responses on the board as they are voiced, under appropriate headings.)

Alternative. Distribute copies of the "Servant Songs" exercise from the activity page, which you can download. This exercise will allow learners to see today's text in a broader context of the other four Servant Songs in Isaiah. There are a total of 40 verses to consider, and the five songs vary widely in length. Therefore, you will need to think carefully in advance regarding how many groups there will be, how many participants will be in each group, how much time to allow, and how to keep things moving briskly when groups report conclusions in the ensuing all-class discussion.

Into Life

Send students back to their initial groups to make a third list regarding what the servant's suffering did for them (all groups working on the same activity). As they do, write *What the Servant's Suffering Did for Me* on the board. After several minutes, call for reflections as you pause between reading individual verses of the lesson. Jot responses on the board.

Send class members back to their triads one more time and ask each group to write exactly one sentence (no more than a dozen words) of thanksgiving or praise to God for something specific the Suffering Servant has done for them. Groups should arrive at their sentence by consensus, which will require more thinking than mere majority vote.

Option 1. Play a recording of the sections in Handel's *Messiah* that have put Isaiah 53:4-6 to music. (If your classroom is equipped, you could project an appropriate video that includes these verses.) Encourage class members to jot down phrases that particularly strike them or emotions they feel as they hear the Scripture set to music.

Option 2. Distribute copies of the "Servant Thanks" exercise from the activity page. This devotional prayer-writing activity is designed for students to begin in class but finish at home.

The Faith-in-Action Preacher

Devotional Reading: Ezekiel 18:25-32
Background Scripture: Ezra 9–10

Ezra 10:1-12

1 Now when Ezra had prayed, and when he had confessed, weeping and casting himself down before the house of God, there assembled unto him out of Israel a very great congregation of men and women and children: for the people wept very sore.

2 And Shechaniah the son of Jehiel, one of the sons of Elam, answered and said unto Ezra, We have trespassed against our God, and have taken strange wives of the people of the land: yet now there is hope in Israel concerning this thing.

3 Now therefore let us make a covenant with our God to put away all the wives, and such as are born of them, according to the counsel of my lord, and of those that tremble at the commandment of our God; and let it be done according to the law.

4 Arise; for this matter belongeth unto thee: we also will be with thee: be of good courage, and do it.

5 Then arose Ezra, and made the chief priests, the Levites, and all Israel, to swear that they should do according to this word. And they sware.

6 Then Ezra rose up from before the house of God, and went into the chamber of Johanan the son of Eliashib: and when he came thither, he did eat no bread, nor drink water: for he mourned because of the transgression of them that had been carried away.

7 And they made proclamation throughout Judah and Jerusalem unto all the children of the captivity, that they should gather themselves together unto Jerusalem;

8 And that whosoever would not come within three days, according to the counsel of the princes and the elders, all his substance should be forfeited, and himself separated from the congregation of those that had been carried away.

9 Then all the men of Judah and Benjamin gathered themselves together unto Jerusalem within three days. It was the ninth month, on the twentieth day of the month; and all the people sat in the street of the house of God, trembling because of this matter, and for the great rain.

10 And Ezra the priest stood up, and said unto them, Ye have transgressed, and have taken strange wives, to increase the trespass of Israel.

11 Now therefore make confession unto the Lord God of your fathers, and do his pleasure: and separate yourselves from the people of the land, and from the strange wives.

12 Then all the congregation answered and said with a loud voice, As thou hast said, so must we do.

Key Verse

Ezra rose up from before the house of God, and went into the chamber of Johanan the son of Eliashib: and when he came thither, he did eat no bread, nor drink water: for he mourned because of the transgression of them that had been carried away. —**Ezra 10:6**

PROPHETS FAITHFUL TO GOD'S COVENANT

Unit 2: Prophets of Restoration

LESSONS 5–8

LESSON AIMS

After participating in this lesson, each learner will be able to:

1. Summarize Ezra's reaction to the people's sin.
2. Explain why intermarriage with foreigners caused Ezra grief.
3. Write a confession to God for a specific sin and a corresponding course of repentant action.

LESSON OUTLINE

Introduction

A. The Way of Escape

Escape rooms are becoming a fun-time phenomenon for a variety of ages. The premise is simple. A group of people pay to be locked in a room and left with a series of clues and hints to utilize in solving a creative puzzle in order to escape. This is all done with a given time limit that is certain to get the blood pumping as the clock ticks down and pressure mounts.

Now, imagine that a lone figure in the corner actually has the answers to provide the way out. In fact, the group was told upon entering that someone had the answers they needed. Who in their right mind would hear that kind of information and not use it to ensure the success of the group? Victory is on the line!

There are times in relationship with God when people essentially lock themselves up and put their lives on the line. Yet, when solutions are offered for real problems, people have a choice: to listen to their guide or to go it alone. Will the solution be applied or not?

B. Lesson Context

Under the leadership of Nebuchadnezzar, the Babylonian Empire overtook Jerusalem and exiled the people of Israel in 586 BC (see lesson 8 Lesson Context). Eventually, the Persian King Cyrus defeated Babylon. He released Jewish exiles to return home to Jerusalem in 538 BC for the express purpose of rebuilding the temple (see Ezra 10:1a, below). Following that first wave of returning exiles in 538 BC was a second led by Ezra in 458 BC (7:7, 13). He desired to restore the people to a state of faithful adherence to God's law (7:25-27). The third and final wave of exiles returned to Jerusalem in 444 BC, led by Nehemiah (Nehemiah 2:1-9; see lesson 7).

Ezra was a scribe of the Law of Moses, commissioned by God (Ezra 7:6). Ezra was made aware that the people of Israel had committed grave sins (chapter 9). The most glaring infraction was that they had intermarried with people groups outside of Israel (Deuteronomy 7:3). This prohibition was not based on any racial or ethnic enmity.

Rather, God warned in Deuteronomy 7:4 that foreign faiths "will turn away thy son from following me" (compare 2 Corinthians 6:14-18). Yet even as they returned from exile for sin, men of Judah were marrying pagan women! If these men were divorcing Jewish wives as well, the result was abuse of divorce laws and resulting hardship for the former wives (compare Malachi 2:13-16; Matthew 19:1-9). Ezra's reaction to the people's disobedience serves as the subject of today's lesson.

I. Conviction of Sin

(Ezra 10:1-4)

A. Confession and Weeping (v. 1)

1a. Now when Ezra had prayed, and when he had confessed, weeping and casting himself down before the house of God.

After the initial shock of the report *Ezra* received (see Lesson Context), he immediately took it to heart. Ezra led by example. The sincerity of his distress over Judah's sins is emphasized by the intensifying verbs used to describe his actions (compare Nehemiah 1:3-6). Ezra's physical posture matched his spiritual posture before the Lord. Both body and spirit were marked by brokenness and sorrow.

The house of God refers to the temple that had been rebuilt after Solomon's temple was destroyed in the Babylonian conquest (2 Chronicles 36:19; Ezra 3:7-13; 6:13-18). Construction was completed in 515 BC, and this second temple stood until the Romans destroyed it in AD 70.

1b. There assembled unto him out of Israel a very great congregation of men and women and children: for the people wept very sore.

People of all ages need good leaders. This is as true in the area of repentance as anything else. When charting revivals in the Old Testament, movements toward God often started with one leader feeling a burden (examples: 1 Samuel 7; 2 Kings 22:1–23:30; 2 Chronicles 29–31). Though the circumstances varied, the initiating factor for revival was someone acting on behalf of the people. The leaders may have had a private revelation or realization, followed by the gathering of an assembly, as here in verse 1. Here, Ezra's own conviction and contrition became an example for others to gather before the Lord and weep over their sins.

> *What Do You Think?*
> What factors must be present for you to truly regret your sins and repent of them?
> *Digging Deeper*
> Are those factors the same for all Christians? Why, or why not?

The Power of Confession

When Jim and Cammy (names changed) got married, neither was a Christian. During Cammy's second pregnancy, Jim left. They divorced. After Cammy's second daughter was born, a friend led Cammy to the Lord. She remarried, this time to a Christian who loves her daughters as his own.

Jim spiraled into alcoholism, destroying two more marriages. One day, gun in hand, he cried out to God, "If you're real, help me!" Through a friend's witness, Jim found Christ. He wrote to his daughters and to Cammy, expressing repentance and asking for forgiveness. Later he spoke face-to-face with them all, reaffirming his repentance and how Christ had changed him.

Twenty-five years later, Jim, Cammy and her husband, and their daughters are all friends, having found forgiveness in Christ. As Ezra led Israel in confessing their sins, he was bringing the nation to a restored relationship with God. How can your own confession of sin repair your relationship with God and those you hurt? —C. R. B.

B. Covenant and Courage (vv. 2-4)

2a. And Shechaniah the son of Jehiel, one of the sons of Elam, answered and said unto Ezra, We have trespassed against our God, and have taken strange wives of the people of the land.

In the Old Testament, there are at least nine men named *Shechaniah,* nine named *Jehiel,* and eight named *Elam*. Sorting them out is difficult! The Shechaniah who speaks here is a descendant of David according to 1 Chronicles 3:1, 21-22. His father, Jehiel, was likely also the father of

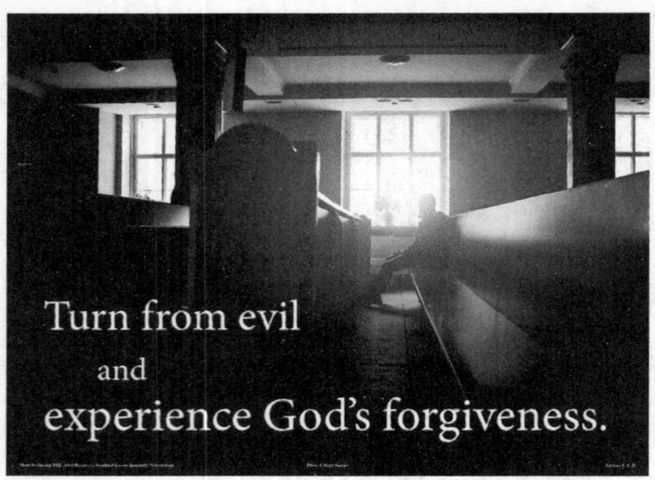
Turn from evil
and
experience God's forgiveness.

Visual for Lessons 6 & 13. *While discussing verse 11, point to this visual as you ask what situations need to be turned from to experience forgiveness.*

Obadiah, one of the returning exiles (Ezra 8:9). Jehiel is included in a grouping of those guilty of intermarriage (Ezra 10:17-18, 26, not in our printed text). It is plausible that Shechaniah overcame personal and familial shame to speak up and not attempt to cover up his family's sin.

The Hebrew word translated *trespassed* regularly denotes the violation of a covenant relationship or other expected behavior in the Old Testament (example: 1 Chronicles 5:25). Marital unfaithfulness is a frequent analogy regarding Israel's relationship with God, with Israel being the adulterous wife (see Isaiah 62:5; Jeremiah 3:8; Ezekiel 16:22-38).

The *strange wives* were women not part of the covenant people. Israel had been repeatedly warned that *the people of the land* of Canaan would lead them into apostasy (Deuteronomy 7:1-4; Joshua 23:12-13). Whether these particular wives were guilty of such a thing is unknown. However, the sad example of Solomon—the wise king whose foreign wives "turned away his heart after other gods" (1 Kings 11:4)—should have stood as a grave warning in the time after the exile. Ezra's contemporary Nehemiah reminded the people of Solomon's failure, exhorting them not to suffer the same fate (Nehemiah 13:26-27).

2b. Yet now there is hope in Israel concerning this thing.

A repentant heart is what makes *hope* possible for right relations with God to be restored. God's patience with His people is demonstrated time and again throughout the Old Testament. The prophets often invoked past episodes of God's gracious deliverance in order to motivate the people toward obedience. Ezra reminded the remnant in Jerusalem that "God hast punished us less than our iniquities deserve" (Ezra 9:13).

Hope is always grounded in the possibility of God's mercy. After a moral failure or personal tragedy, hope exists because, as King David learned firsthand, God is "good, and doest good" (Psalm 119:68). Hope grounded in God's goodness led others to write of God's being gracious, slow to anger, and full of mercy (see Psalms 103:8; 145:8; Joel 2:13; Jonah 4:2).

3a. Now therefore let us make a covenant with our God to put away all the wives, and such as are born of them, according to the counsel of my lord, and of those that tremble at the commandment of our God.

Now therefore signals a step forward from the sins of the past and present, as defined in Ezra 10:2. This suggestion from Shechaniah is drastic and may appear cruel to modern readers. Some might wonder if God really wanted the men to send *away* their *wives* and children, considering Deuteronomy 21:10-14. But in the days following the return from Babylon, the people were very aware of how unfaithfulness had led to their removal from the promised land. Foreign women could very well lead their husbands back into idolatry, as had happened to King Solomon. Thus the threat the foreign wives posed was too great to ignore. The people had to be intent on being holy in order to please God.

We should note that God's covenant people were not to mistreat non-Israelites who lived among them—quite the opposite (see Leviticus 19:33-34; 23:22)! But treating non-Israelites with kindness isn't in the same category as intermarriage. The extraordinary circumstances the people faced called for extraordinary action.

Shechaniah referred to Ezra deferentially as *my lord*. This acknowledged Ezra's authority to decide and lead the people based on what he believed was right. Ezra, after all, was both student and teacher of the Law of Moses. His conclusions on this matter were well-informed.

Reverence and awe were given to God's words as if God himself were present. God helps those "poor and of a contrite spirit, [who] trembleth at [God's] word" (Isaiah 66:2).

3b. And let it be done according to the law.

In view is *the law* that forbade certain marital unions (see Lesson Context). Notable lawbreakers in this regard included Salmon (who married Rahab, a Canaanite) and Boaz (who married Ruth, a Moabite). These two women are honored as ancestors of Jesus himself (Joshua 2:1; Ruth 4:10; Matthew 1:5). But the captivity from which the Jews had returned was a vivid reminder of the dangers of idolatry. Maybe some non-Jewish wives were exceptions to the rule, like Rahab and Ruth. But the law existed because such cases *were* exceptions, not the rule. And we also note that Rahab and Ruth professed allegiance to God in both word and action (Joshua 2:11; Ruth 1:16).

What Do You Think?

When considering Ezra 10:3 alongside Exodus 34:16; 1 Kings 11:4; Matthew 5:32; Romans 7:1-3; 1 Corinthians 7:12-14, 39; 2 Corinthians 6:14; and 1 Timothy 5:8, how should Christians react to similar situations today?

Digging Deeper

What other texts and contexts are relevant?

4. Arise; for this matter belongeth unto thee: we also will be with thee: be of good courage, and do it.

We can only imagine the overwhelmingly emotional toll of separating from one's wife and children. The difficulty of the demand is what brought forth the strong imperative *Arise*! This marks the beginning of the shift from conviction to action on the part of the leaders.

II. Call to Appear

(Ezra 10:5-8)

A. Everyone Promises (v. 5)

5. Then arose Ezra, and made the chief priests, the Levites, and all Israel, to swear that they should do according to this word. And they sware.

Ezra made sure that *the chief priests, the Levites, and all Israel* were on the same page. Opposition to the task ahead had to be absolutely minimized (see Ezra 10:15)! So the leaders and lay people made a covenant with God to "put away all the wives, and such as are born of them" (10:3).

What Do You Think?

In what ways can you better support a fellow Christian in taking action to repent of sins?

Digging Deeper

How would that action differ, if at all, when dealing with sin of a group?

B. Ezra Mourns (v. 6)

6. Then Ezra rose up from before the house of God, and went into the chamber of Johanan the son of Eliashib: and when he came thither, he did eat no bread, nor drink water: for he mourned because of the transgression of them that had been carried away.

During this emotional day, *Ezra* withdrew to be alone in the dwelling of *Johanan*. That man and his father, *Eliashib,* were Levites (Nehemiah 12:23). We recall that all priests were Levites, but not all Levites were priests.

While the people were grieved and motivated to action, Ezra was overcome with his own grief regarding *the transgression*. His fast from *bread* and *drink* seems to have been spontaneous, a result of the pain in his spirit. When we think of mourning, it is usually in relation to death—the loss of a loved one or someone special. Ezra carried a sense of loss as he reflected on years his people wasted as they chased false gods and denied the Lord.

C. Proclamation Issued (vv. 7-8)

7-8. And they made proclamation throughout Judah and Jerusalem unto all the children of the captivity, that they should gather themselves together unto Jerusalem; and that whosoever would not come within three days, according to the counsel of the princes and the elders, all his substance should be forfeited, and himself separated from the congregation of those that had been carried away.

The word *they* likely refers to the chief priests and Levites to whom Ezra gave special charge to spread news of the covenant. But it could mean that each person bore the responsibility to herald the agreed upon terms of their resolution.

Three days was a quick turnaround for a message to be proclaimed and journeys to be undertaken through all *Judah* and back to *Jerusalem*. But the speed with which repentance and action would happen throughout would indicate the importance the people put on rectifying their wrongs.

The severe consequences for not coming to Jerusalem also reveals the seriousness of the people's resolution. Forfeiting one's land and possessions and being cut off from *the congregation* would be the same treatment the foreign wives experienced. Those so penalized would have to find their homes elsewhere, away from God's people.

III. Call to Action

(Ezra 10:9-12)

A. Fearful People (v. 9)

9. Then all the men of Judah and Benjamin gathered themselves together unto Jerusalem within three days. It was the ninth month, on the twentieth day of the month; and all the people sat in the street of the house of God, trembling because of this matter, and for the great rain.

Ten of the 12 tribes of Israel had been removed to Assyrian exile more than 180 years previous (2 Kings 17:6). So only the two tribes of *Judah and Benjamin,* having returned from Babylonian exile, remained to answer the call to come to *Jerusalem*.

The twentieth day of the [ninth] month corresponds to early December. *Rain* is normal at that point in the year. So in addition to the spiritual *trembling,* there was also physical shivering in the cold, heavy rain. How often the spiritual and physical overlap! Distress to one's body, whether in the form of illness, injury, or mere discomfort, often goes hand in hand with spiritual distress. Sometimes one results in the other; at other times they seem to have independent causes, but the presence of both multiplies the misery. In such conditions *all the people sat* outside and waited.

B. Fearless Preacher (vv. 10-11)

10. And Ezra the priest stood up, and said unto them, Ye have transgressed, and have taken strange wives, to increase the trespass of Israel.

Sometimes *Ezra* is referred to as *the priest* (here and in Ezra 10:16), sometimes he is referred to as "the scribe" (Nehemiah 8:1, 4, 13; 12:36), and sometimes by both of those terms together (Ezra 7:11, 21; Nehemiah 8:9; 12:26). His statement *increase the trespass of Israel* implies that the people hadn't learned the lesson of the exile. Instead of working to decrease sin, they were working for the opposite (compare 2 Chronicles 28:13). So Ezra restated the charge (compare Ezra 10:2a, above).

> *What Do You Think?*
> What leadership role are you gifted to exercise when dealing with communal, collective sin?
> *Digging Deeper*
> What leadership actions in this regard should be personal and private rather than public?

11. Now therefore make confession unto the Lord God of your fathers, and do his pleasure: and separate yourselves from the people of the land, and from the strange wives.

Confession is the first response to conviction and a necessary step toward reconciliation with God (compare 1 John 1:9). The next step is to follow through *and do [God's] pleasure,* that is, what He commanded in the first place, what He has desired all along.

To be required to separate *from the strange wives* was not necessarily a judgment on any specific conduct on the wives' part since no such conduct is listed. Instead, those wives were assumed to retain the priorities and religious practices of *the people of the land* among whom they had grown up. Only by severing their influence could the men of Judah and Benjamin be certain that the wives wouldn't tempt them to idolatry.

C. Faithful Practice (v. 12)

12. Then all the congregation answered and said with a loud voice, As thou hast said, so must we do.

Concluding this part of the text is the *loud voice* of a unified people who experienced conviction of sin. Ezra's leadership helped foster that commitment. Any spiritual leader worth following will always direct people to God and His glory only.

> *What Do You Think?*
> In what kinds of situations would collective, communal reactions be more appropriate than private, individual reactions?
> *Digging Deeper*
> How do 1 Corinthians 5:1-2, 9-13 and 2 Corinthians 2:5-11 help frame your answer?

"Good Sermon Today, Preacher!"

I suspect it's the same in most homes: parents frequently tell their children to clean up their rooms, but the kids keep dragging their feet. The parents' approach may vary from gentle reminders to exasperated verbal assault such as "Your room looks like a pigpen!" Parents have been known to bribe with an increase in monetary allowance and/or punish by withholding privileges or imposing time-outs and groundings.

Without thinking about it, Dad and Mom might be guilty of the same behavior they dislike in their offspring. The parents hear the minister speaking of God's standards and think, *Yes, that's something I should pay attention to someday.* They may compliment the minister, saying, "Good sermon today, preacher!" That's like their child responding to "Clean up your room" with, "Good idea, Mom. I'll get around to it."

Even after Judah's "time-out" in Babylon, it took a while for God to get the people to "clean their room." Finally, under Ezra's dedicated leadership, they responded with a positive yes to God's instructions. In what situation are you putting off doing what God wants? —C. R. B.

Conclusion

A. Content with Mere Conviction?

One of the great gifts for Christian instruction in the Old Testament is seeing episode after episode of Israel's rebellion against God and God's subsequent restoration of His covenant people. In today's text, we have been party to yet another instance of this. The people of God were again in danger of sliding back into idolatry because of their disobedience to God's law. This is a reminder that God's laws are put in place for our good and His glory. Like the ancient Jews, we too are tempted by the culture that surrounds us—including the temptation to marry unbelievers (see 2 Corinthians 6:14-18).

God's mercy provided hope for Israel to be restored to a right relationship with Him. But that required someone who would take the lead! Not everyone is gifted in the same way in this regard, and different leaders may respond differently to the same problem. (It's rather humorous to contrast Ezra's leadership style in Ezra 9:3 with that of Nehemiah in Nehemiah 13:25.) But it all begins with having a burden of the heart and soul.

God's forgiving grace is available to us because of the person and work of Jesus Christ. The church is His bride (2 Corinthians 11:2; Revelation 19:7-9; 21:2, 9; 22:17). May we be faithful to our bridegroom!

B. Prayer

Dear Father, guard our hearts against rationalizing our sins! Convict us so that repentant action may follow! May Your Word ever guide us to be faithful. In Jesus' name we pray. Amen.

C. Thought to Remember

Action is the hallmark of true conviction.

HOW TO SAY IT

Assyrian	Uh-*sear*-ee-un.
Babylonian	Bab-ih-*low*-nee-un.
Cyrus	*Sigh*-russ.
Eliashib	E-*lye*-uh-shib.
Hezekiah	Hez-ih-*kye*-uh.
Jehiel	Jay-hi-*eel*.
Johanan	Jo-*hay*-nan.
Josiah	Jo-*sigh*-uh.
Nebuchadnezzar	*Neb*-yuh-kud-***nez***-er.
Nehemiah	*Nee*-huh-***my***-uh.
Shechaniah	She-*kawn*-yay.

Involvement Learning

Enhance your lesson with KJV Bible Student *(from your curriculum supplier) and the reproducible activity page (at www.standardlesson.com or in the back of the* KJV Standard Lesson Commentary Deluxe Edition*).*

Into the Lesson

Put class members into pairs to complete this sentence:

The toughest decision I ever made was ______.

After a few minutes, ask volunteers to share results of their discussions with the whole class. Make a transition by saying, "As we explore the thoughts and actions of a man in today's lesson, think about whether his decisions were harder than any you've ever had to make."

Into the Word

Create the setting by summarizing the Lesson Context as well as key elements of Ezra's mourning and prayer that is recorded in Ezra 9.

Distribute handouts (you prepare) with the following, or simply write them on the board:

What Ezra felt: ______________

Advice Ezra received: ______________

What Ezra demanded: ______________

How people responded: ______________

Ask a volunteer to read today's text while class members listen for entries for these four. Then summarize the facts of the story by commenting on each as appropriate.

Have class members regroup with partners they chose earlier. Give some pairs the following on handouts (you prepare) to complete:

How does today's passage illustrate the following?

- Sin cannot be excused.
- God will restore those who repent.
- Sin results in suffering.
- Recognizing sin for what it is is vital for restoring relationship with God.
- Sin among God's people must be addressed, even by those not personally guilty of the sin at issue.
- One person who mourns sin can lead a whole nation to repent.
- God does not take sin lightly.

Give the other study pairs the following set of questions on handouts (you prepare):

What might have happened . . .

- if Ezra had condemned the people without naming himself among the nation that had failed?
- if Shechaniah had tried to minimize the seriousness of the people's sin?
- if Ezra had chosen a less severe remedy for the sinful intermarriages?
- if the leading priests and Levites had failed to take the oath Ezra demanded?
- if Ezra had experienced only disappointment or disgust instead of agony at the unfaithfulness?

Reconvene for whole-class discussion of discoveries, insights, and conclusions.

Option. After the discussion, distribute copies of the "What Would You Say?" exercise from the activity page, which you can download for learners to complete in pairs as indicated. Be prepared to offer your own conclusions.

Into Life

Distribute slips of paper and ask participants to write down (in code, if they wish) one personal sin they have avoided confronting, adding a course of action to correct this problem and remove the sin. Stress that you will not collect the slips; rather, learners are to put them where they will serve as a reminder to bring their sin and their repentance before God in prayers this week.

Option. Distribute to study pairs copies of one or two sentences of the "Stinkin' Thinkin'" exercise from the activity page along with instructions. Allow three minutes for discussion before having the whole class consider the entire list.

Close with a time of guided prayer as you challenge learners to pray silently in response to this prompt: "God, help me know that my sin matters. Thank You for forgiveness through the sacrifice of Your Son! As I remember that sacrifice, I will take the following actions to reject this sin."

The Restoring Builder

Devotional Reading: Daniel 9:4-6, 15-19
Background Scripture: Nehemiah 2:11-20; 13:1-22

Nehemiah 2:11-20

11 So I came to Jerusalem, and was there three days.

12 And I arose in the night, I and some few men with me; neither told I any man what my God had put in my heart to do at Jerusalem: neither was there any beast with me, save the beast that I rode upon.

13 And I went out by night by the gate of the valley, even before the dragon well, and to the dung port, and viewed the walls of Jerusalem, which were broken down, and the gates thereof were consumed with fire.

14 Then I went on to the gate of the fountain, and to the king's pool: but there was no place for the beast that was under me to pass.

15 Then went I up in the night by the brook, and viewed the wall, and turned back, and entered by the gate of the valley, and so returned.

16 And the rulers knew not whither I went, or what I did; neither had I as yet told it to the Jews, nor to the priests, nor to the nobles, nor to the rulers, nor to the rest that did the work.

17 Then said I unto them, Ye see the distress that we are in, how Jerusalem lieth waste, and the gates thereof are burned with fire: come, and let us build up the wall of Jerusalem, that we be no more a reproach.

18 Then I told them of the hand of my God which was good upon me; as also the king's words that he had spoken unto me. And they said, Let us rise up and build. So they strengthened their hands for this good work.

19 But when Sanballat the Horonite, and Tobiah the servant, the Ammonite, and Geshem the Arabian, heard it, they laughed us to scorn, and despised us, and said, What is this thing that ye do? will ye rebel against the king?

20 Then answered I them, and said unto them, The God of heaven, he will prosper us; therefore we his servants will arise and build: but ye have no portion, nor right, nor memorial, in Jerusalem.

Key Verse

Said I unto them, Ye see the distress that we are in, how Jerusalem lieth waste, and the gates thereof are burned with fire: come, and let us build up the wall of Jerusalem, that we be no more a reproach.

—Nehemiah 2:17

Photo: Getty Images

Prophets Faithful To God's Covenant

Unit 2: Prophets of Restoration

Lessons 5–8

Lesson Aims

After participating in this lesson, each learner will be able to:

1. Summarize the results of Nehemiah's nighttime excursion around Jerusalem.
2. Explain why faith in the Lord and careful planning are not necessarily contradictory.
3. Prepare a testimony of how God's hand has been at work in his or her life.

Lesson Outline

Introduction
- A. Upgrading the Ugly
- B. Lesson Context

I. Surveying the City (Nehemiah 2:11-16)
- A. Arriving and Waiting (v. 11)
- B. Diagnosing the Damage (v. 12-16)
  - *Assessing the Situation*

II. Summoning the Leaders (Nehemiah 2:17-18)
- A. Encouragement to Build (v. 17)
- B. Evidence of God's Hand (v. 18)
  - *The Importance of Buy-In*

III. Scorning the Critics (Nehemiah 2:19-20)
- A. Words of Contempt (v. 19)
- B. Words of Conviction (v. 20)

Conclusion
- A. Good Hands
- B. Prayer
- C. Thought to Remember

Introduction

A. Upgrading the Ugly

In my city, I occasionally see signs that read, "We Buy Ugly Houses." Apparently the persons or companies who post these signs are interested in renovating "ugly houses" in order to sell them for a profit. The original home was undervalued because of its various flaws; the refinished product is intended to have good return on investment. The proliferation of television shows, magazine articles, and websites devoted to "flipping" houses demonstrates the wide appeal of this business.

Long ago, Nehemiah was interested in renovating an "ugly city," the once great city of Jerusalem. He wanted to address a condition of disrepair and confusion in Jerusalem, but his deeper motives and his leadership skill in so doing still have much to teach us today.

B. Lesson Context

Jerusalem had been a distinguished city, the political and spiritual capital of the nation of Israel under David's leadership (1 Chronicles 11:4-9; 15). Solomon added to its greatness by the magnificent temple that he built there (2 Chronicles 3). But following the division of the nation and the rise of ungodly kings who allowed idolatry and accompanying abhorrent practices to flourish in the land, Jerusalem became filled with such wickedness and evil that the judgment of God fell on it. In 586 BC the Babylonians finally breached the city walls, following a siege of 18 months (see lesson 8). The city's state of massive disrepair still existed in the time of Nehemiah, some 140 years later.

Nehemiah was cupbearer to Artaxerxes (Nehemiah 1:11), king of the Persians, who ruled from 465 to 425 BC. The Persians had conquered the Babylonians in 539 BC. Cyrus, ruler of the Persians at the time, had permitted any of the Jews who desired to do so to return to their home. Approximately 50,000 did (Ezra 2:64-65), but there were those, such as members of Nehemiah's family, who chose to remain in Persia.

Nehemiah 1 describes what happened in the twentieth year of Artaxerxes, which would have been 445 BC. Nehemiah received news from his brother, Hanani, of the sad state of affairs back home in Jerusalem:

> The remnant that are left of the captivity there in the province are in great affliction and reproach: the wall of Jerusalem also is broken down, and the gates thereof are burned with fire (Nehemiah 1:3).

Deeply troubled over such disheartening conditions, Nehemiah responded with tears, fasting, and fervent prayer (1:4). He confessed his own sins and the sins of his fellow Jews and begged the Lord to honor His promise to bless His people if they turned from their sinful ways (1:5-10).

Nehemiah then asked the Lord that he might receive mercy from the king (Nehemiah 1:11). That involved Artaxerxes's granting permission to Nehemiah to travel to his homeland of Judah and lead an effort to repair the wall and the gates of his beloved city of Jerusalem (2:1-9).

Nehemiah's request included protection for the journey (contrast Ezra 8:22) and also provision of supplies needed for the projects that were planned. While the king did indeed grant Nehemiah's request, Nehemiah knew that any favor he had been shown had come from the Lord to whom he had prayed (2:4) and whose "good hand" (2:8) would be seen time and again in the upcoming endeavors.

When Nehemiah arrived, he gave the territory administrators the letters provided by King Artaxerxes that verified the king's support for Nehemiah's undertaking. The letters also confirmed the king's allocation of the resources needed for the rebuilding efforts (Nehemiah 2:7-9).

I. Surveying the City

(Nehemiah 2:11-16)

A. Arriving and Waiting (v. 11)

11. So I came to Jerusalem, and was there three days.

The journey from Susa, the capital city of the Persian Empire, *to Jerusalem* was nearly 1,100 miles. A daylight walking pace of two miles per hour for six days per week (resting on the Sabbath) means a trip of about three months' duration. The *three days* therefore provided some needed rest for Nehemiah after such a long journey. The break also gave him the opportunity to plan his strategy, an approach he would use again before confronting another problem (Nehemiah 5:6-7).

What Do You Think?

What factors should cause you to determine that a strategic, multi-day delay on a project is not merely procrastination?

Digging Deeper

Was Paul admitting to procrastination in Acts 22:16? Why, or why not?

B. Diagnosing the Damage (vv. 12-16)

12. And I arose in the night, I and some few men with me; neither told I any man what my God had put in my heart to do at Jerusalem: neither was there any beast with me, save the beast that I rode upon.

Nehemiah was aware of the fact that not everyone in the territory was on board with what he was planning to do (Nehemiah 2:10). Thus an excursion by *night* under cover of darkness was most likely the best way to examine the city and assess what needed to be done. Only a *few men* needed to accompany Nehemiah on such a mission; perhaps they were residents of Jerusalem who knew the layout of the city and could serve as guides. Or they might have been trusted advisers who had also traveled from Persia and could offer wise counsel. There was also no need for a large number of animals, whose sound might attract attention to the group (see 2:14, below).

Nehemiah was secretive about his intention to rebuild Jerusalem's walls and gates. Disclosing his plans too early could put the entire enterprise in jeopardy, so Nehemiah bided his time to gather information. His sense of appropriate timing was a quality that made Nehemiah a capable leader.

13. And I went out by night by the gate of the valley, even before the dragon well, and to the dung port, and viewed the walls of Jerusalem, which were broken down, and the gates thereof were consumed with fire.

It appears that Nehemiah did not make a complete circuit of Jerusalem but only of the southern

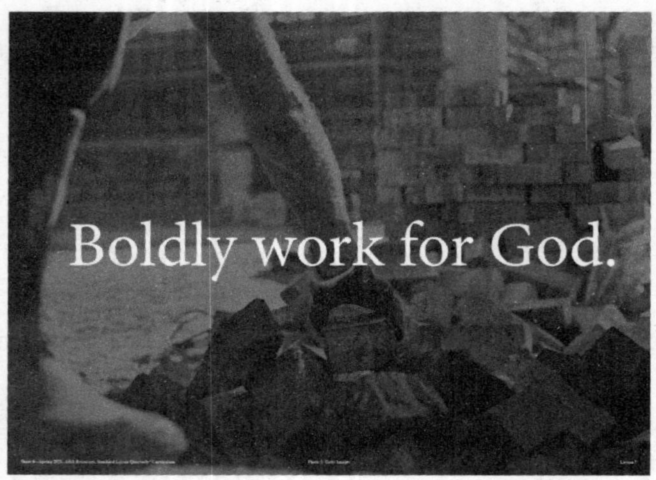

Visual for Lesson 7. *While discussing verse 20, ask the class for examples from their lives when working for God yielded both opposition and blessing.*

area (see Nehemiah 2:14-15, below). At the same time, locating precisely some of the places cited is difficult. *The gate of the valley* appears to have been at the southwestern side of Jerusalem. Second Chronicles 26:9 records that King Uzziah of Judah built a tower there. Nehemiah 3:13 notes the repairs done to the gate itself and this section of the wall and includes the detail that it covered "a thousand cubits" (or 1,500 feet).

The location of *the dragon well* is disputed, though it is often identified with the pool of Siloam on Jerusalem's southern side. *The dung port* may describe the gate leading to the trash dump in the Hinnom Valley, to the south of Jerusalem. This also required repair (Nehemiah 3:14).

The scene before Nehemiah was very much in keeping with what his brother Hanani had described to him (Nehemiah 1:3). Nehemiah's survey of the walls and gates must have disturbed him. It's one thing to hear a report of destruction (see Lesson Context) and quite another to see it firsthand.

14. Then I went on to the gate of the fountain, and to the king's pool: but there was no place for the beast that was under me to pass.

The gate of the fountain was possibly situated in the southeastern wall of Jerusalem. *The king's pool* may have been a part of King Hezekiah's project to bring water into the city to improve its odds of survival in a prolonged siege (2 Kings 20:20). The rubble at the pool was so excessive that *the beast* Nehemiah was riding could not get through. This detail emphasizes the enormity of the devastation he found in Jerusalem.

15. Then went I up in the night by the brook, and viewed the wall, and turned back, and entered by the gate of the valley, and so returned.

The brook mentioned here is probably the Kidron, a name also attached to the accompanying valley east of Jerusalem. Nehemiah thus retraced his path, going *back* to *the gate of the valley* where he started (Nehemiah 2:13).

16. And the rulers knew not whither I went, or what I did; neither had I as yet told it to the Jews, nor to the priests, nor to the nobles, nor to the rulers, nor to the rest that did the work.

This verse again highlights the secrecy of Nehemiah's journey by night (compare Nehemiah 2:12). In these initial planning stages, there was wisdom in gathering information and considering his plans carefully without questioning a large group of people about the strategy needed to address the required repairs. To have done the latter may have resulted in immediate negativity —a "we can't do that" attitude. See the better approach, next.

What Do You Think?

What kinds of ministries may need to be conducted with a level of secrecy at first?

Digging Deeper

How do texts such as Matthew 6:3-6; Mark 7:24; and John 7:10; 18:20 inform your answer? Are you comfortable working in secret when that mode is called for? Why, or why not?

Assessing the Situation

I served for many years as an administrator and professor in Christian colleges. In each one, we assessed our work. Peer review of teachers' classroom work was done regularly. At the end of the semester, students were asked for input about their classes. Financial operations were scrutinized by both internal and external auditors. Since these were Christian colleges, we also sought to determine if the totality of institutional programs encouraged the spiritual growth of our students. We asked individual and church supporters whether we were fulfilling our mission. All of these assessment tools helped us to carry out our mission of providing excellence in education.

Nehemiah's first step toward rebuilding Jerusalem's wall was assessing the damage caused by the Babylonian siege many decades earlier. The Bible encourages us—by example and command—to regularly assess our personal spiritual condition (Psalm 119:33-36; Romans 12:1-3). How does doing so prepare you to serve Christ? —C. R. B.

II. Summoning the Leaders

(Nehemiah 2:17-18)

A. Encouragement to Build (v. 17)

17. Then said I unto them, Ye see the distress that we are in, how Jerusalem lieth waste, and the gates thereof are burned with fire: come, and let us build up the wall of Jerusalem, that we be no more a reproach.

Nothing is said about the span of time between Nehemiah's excursion and his meeting with the groups named in the previous verse. Most likely he convened them as soon as he could, given that the condition of *the wall* left *Jerusalem* vulnerable to attack.

There was an important emotional reason to have strong walls in a city, too. The city was an object of derision and mockery (*a reproach*) in its current state (compare 2 Chronicles 7:19-22; Psalm 44:13-14). Jerusalem was the holy city, the site of God's temple. It needed to be maintained in a way appropriate to this distinction. Thus Nehemiah described the decrepit state of Jerusalem as something that was not only troubling to the residents of the city but also disdainful to outsiders.

Nehemiah used the first-person plural pronouns *we* and *us.* He identified with those who were concerned about the dismal condition of Jerusalem. The solution as he saw it was of practical value. Rebuilding *the wall* offered protection as well as going a long way toward rehabilitating the feeling that Jerusalem itself was in ruins. Three considerations determined where ancient cities were built: (1) access to water, (2) access to trade routes, and (3) defensibility. A great city needed all three! A city without walls was vulnerable to enemy armies. Nehemiah 13:15-22 reveals a way that the completed walls would help the residents of the city obey God.

> *What Do You Think?*
> Do you respond more readily to an appeal to help fix an obvious deficiency, or to an appeal to improve an existing "good enough" situation? Why is that?
> *Digging Deeper*
> Considering Luke 12:16-21, what helps you keep pure motives in the second situation?

B. Evidence of God's Hand (v. 18)

18a. Then I told them of the hand of my God which was good upon me; as also the king's words that he had spoken unto me.

Nehemiah was speaking to people who perhaps had become rather skeptical concerning God's plan and purpose for them and for the city of Jerusalem. Over the years since the return of the exiles from captivity in Babylon, various attempts to rebuild Jerusalem had been thwarted (see Ezra 4).

At first Nehemiah's proposal may have sounded like just another plan that would meet with failure and simply add to the people's disillusionment. But when he spoke of *the hand of my God which was good upon me*, he offered reason for new hope of success. Throughout the Old Testament, the mention of God's hand represents the work that God does in the world (examples: Exodus 6:1; Joshua 4:24; Isaiah 41:17-20).

When Nehemiah came to the Lord in prayer after hearing of the sad condition of Jerusalem, he noted how the Lord had redeemed the covenant people, of whom Nehemiah was a part, with a "strong hand" (Nehemiah 1:10). Nehemiah was able to provide evidence that God's hand was at work on His people's behalf. Previous rebuilding had been stymied by opposition (Ezra 4). But at this time Artaxerxes had given his approval and full support to the work in Jerusalem. Even so, the true king, the King of kings, was the one in ultimate control of His people's welfare.

18b. And they said, Let us rise up and build. So they strengthened their hands for this good work.

The people's response must have emboldened Nehemiah and lifted his spirits. The fact that the people then *strengthened their hands* fits nicely with the image of God's hand on the project. The fact of God's powerful hand leading and blessing does not eliminate the need for human hands to do their part. He prefers to work through people instead of just accomplishing His purposes all on His own (compare and contrast Isaiah 6:8; Ezekiel 22:30).

What Do You Think?

At what stage of a ministry project should you, as a leader or follower, pause for a private evaluation of motives for participating?

Digging Deeper

How can the record of the differing motives behind the "let us build" lines of Genesis 11:4; Nehemiah 2:18; 2 Chronicles 14:7; and Ezra 4:1-5 help frame your conclusion?

The Importance of Buy-In

On the television show *Shark Tank*, entrepreneurs demonstrate their products to a group of wealthy investors—the "sharks"—who then question the entrepreneurs before they decide whether to "buy in." They ask about the entrepreneurs' personal investment in the company, how long their product has been on the market, how much profit has been made, and any personal information that might bear on the sharks' interest in financing the project. Buy-in offers involve money on loan, a percentage of ownership in the company, and/or control over running the company in exchange for the investment, manufacturing, or marketing expertise the shark can offer.

Nehemiah realized he needed buy-in from Jerusalem's leadership to have success rebuilding the city's walls. Church leaders who ignore this principle do so at their own risk. A program will succeed only with the congregation's support. What does the health of your church's ministries say about the congregation's record on buy-ins? And what does that reveal, in turn, about prayer practices to get God's buy-in?

—C. R. B.

III. Scorning the Critics
(Nehemiah 2:19-20)

A. Words of Contempt (v. 19)

19. But when Sanballat the Horonite, and Tobiah the servant, the Ammonite, and Geshem the Arabian, heard it, they laughed us to scorn, and despised us, and said, What is this thing that ye do? will ye rebel against the king?

Sanballat the Horonite, and Tobiah the servant, the Ammonite have already been introduced as villains (see Nehemiah 2:10). Any worthwhile undertaking for the Lord is bound to encounter opposition of some kind; consensus is desirable but is not always achieved (compare Ezra 10:15).

The word *Horonite* may indicate that Sanballat is from Bethhoron, a town about 12 miles from Jerusalem (1 Chronicles 6:68). Though likely part of a northern Israelite tribe, he always opposed Nehemiah's work on behalf of Judah and Jerusalem (example: Nehemiah 6). *The Ammonite* people, located east of the Jordan River, had long been enemies of Israel (example: Deuteronomy 23:3-4), and *Tobiah* was not an exception. He was related by marriage to some of Nehemiah's companions and had many supporters among the Jews (Nehemiah 6:17-19; see lesson 6).

Arabians were also a Transjordan people. During the Persian period (539–331 BC), they engaged in much trade and commerce. *Geshem* may have been opposed to any program promoting the welfare of the Jews if he saw it as a threat to his business dealings (vested interests).

An accusation of rebelling *against the king* had succeeded in halting an earlier rebuilding effort (Ezra 4). But Nehemiah had the full backing of the king. He knew the claims of his critics were baseless.

B. Words of Conviction (v. 20)

20a. Then answered I them, and said unto them, The God of heaven, he will prosper us; therefore we his servants will arise and build.

There is no record of Nehemiah's mentioning King Artaxerxes in his reply to the scoffing of his enemies. Instead, he appealed to a higher court: *the God of heaven.* Since God had guided Nehemiah to this point, Nehemiah knew that God was not going to abandon him or the people who had committed themselves to *arise and build.*

20b. But ye have no portion, nor right, nor memorial, in Jerusalem.

The Hebrew word translated *portion* is used to refer to God's division of the promised land among the tribes of Israel (examples: Joshua 14:4; 18:5; 19:9). Any portion Sanballat had had as an Israelite was revoked when God sent the 10 northern tribes into exile for their faithlessness (2 Kings 17:6-23; compare Ezra 4:3; Acts 8:21).

Regarding the idea of *memorial,* see Exodus 28:12. The opponents did not have the historical ties to the city that Nehemiah and his coworkers did. They had no legal *right* (compare 2 Samuel 19:28) to interfere with what Nehemiah was doing. With the king's complete support, Nehemiah boldly drew a clear line that would remain intact despite any continued resistance that his enemies directed his way (Nehemiah 4, 6, etc.).

What Do You Think?

Under what circumstances would you refuse the help of someone else on a ministry project?

Digging Deeper

How do Mark 9:38-40; 1 Corinthians 5:11; and Ephesians 5:11 influence your answer, if at all?

Conclusion

A. Good Hands

Often when asking for help, we say, "Give me a hand with this." An often told tale illustrates the wisdom of asking for help when a task is too big for us.

As the story goes, a father watched through the kitchen window as his small son tried to move a large rock in the yard. The boy couldn't get quite enough leverage to tip the rock over.

At one point the father came outside and asked the boy, "Can't you lift the rock?"

"No, Dad, I just can't do it."

"Are you using all the strength you have?"

The boy responded, "Yes, but I just can't move it."

The father replied, "No, you're not using *all* the strength you have because you haven't asked me to help."

Nehemiah was going to have, not just one rock, but a whole pile of rocks and rubble to move in order to rebuild the wall of Jerusalem. But heavenly and earthly hands would give him more than enough help.

Nehemiah could have sung, as a precursor to the old hymn, "He's got the whole wall in His hands." Like the little boy, our efforts matter, but they will not succeed all on their own. If we ask our Father for help, He has us and every task He gives us in His hands as well. Fervent prayer on the part of Nehemiah played a vital part (Nehemiah 1:4-6, 11; 2:4; 4:9; 6:14).

B. Prayer

God, give us Your powerful hand! Without it we are weak; with it we have strength to overcome any obstacle. Let us rise up and build Your church, confident in Your promise to be with us. May our hands be strengthened for the work to which You have called us. In Jesus' name we pray. Amen.

C. Thought to Remember

Pray for God's powerful hand to be at work in your life daily.

HOW TO SAY IT

Ammonite	*Am*-un-ite.
Artaxerxes	Are-tuh-*zerk*-seez.
Babylonian	Bab-ih-*low*-nee-un.
Cyrus	*Sigh*-russ.
Geshem	*Gee*-shem (*G* as in *get*).
Hanani	Huh-*nay*-nye.
Horonite	*Hor*-oh-night.
Nehemiah	*Nee*-huh-***my***-uh.
Persia	*Per*-zhuh.
Sanballat	San-*bal*-ut.
Susa	*Soo*-suh.
Tobiah	Toe-*bye*-uh.
Uzziah	Uh-*zye*-uh.

INVOLVEMENT LEARNING

Enhance your lesson with KJV Bible Student *(from your curriculum supplier) and the reproducible activity page (at www.standardlesson.com or in the back of the* KJV Standard Lesson Commentary Deluxe Edition*).*

Into the Lesson

Have the following sentences on your board as class members arrive:

Someone opposed my decision when . . .

I objected to someone's decision when . . .

I supported someone's decision when . . .

Ask participants to turn to someone next to them (preferably not a spouse) and swap stories that begin with one of these phrases. After a few minutes, call for volunteers to share with the class the story they heard (that is, not one of their own stories). Ensure that the one who "owns" the story doesn't mind it being shared with the class.

Transition by saying, "Today, we'll (1) consider the application of the old saying 'timing is everything' when doing God's work and (2) reactions people have when they see that work being done."

Into the Word

Establish the historical setting for today's lesson by summarizing material from the Lesson Context. As you read today's text aloud, have participants imagine what Nehemiah was thinking or feeling at each juncture of the story.

Divide the class into pairs or triads and give each group a slip of paper on which you have printed one of the following regarding Nehemiah 2, today's text: **Secrecy Group**: verses 11-12; **Inspection Group**: verses 13-16; **Announcement Group**: verses 17-18; **Opposition Group**: verses 19-20. (For larger classes, make duplicate assignments; for smaller classes, give more than on assignment to groups.)

Ask participants to imagine they are writing an entry in Nehemiah's diary after the event(s) on their slip(s) happened, picturing themselves in that time and place. After about five minutes, have volunteers read aloud, in Scripture text order, their diary entries. Spend time discussing how the four segments interact and are interdependent.

Option 1. Distribute copies of the "It's a Secret!" exercise from the activity page, which you can download. Discuss the top half of this particular exercise as a class; then have participants form study pairs (or triads) to answer the two questions in its bottom half. Discuss conclusions as a class.

Option 2. To expand consideration of opposition to Nehemiah, distribute copies of the "A Tale of Three Enemies" exercise from the activity page. Have participants work in study pairs to complete it as indicated. Discuss conclusions as appropriate.

Into Life

To remind your learners of Nehemiah's testimony of God's hand on his life and his leadership (verse 18), distribute handouts (you prepare) on 8½″x 11″paper with the following instructions:

Taking no more than one minute . . .

1–Trace an outline of your hand.

2–Label the fingers with up to four life incidents, one per finger (leave thumb blank), in which you have seen God's leading.

3–Put a star beside the most significant incident.

After the one-minute time limit, have participants share in their groups the most important life crossroads where God's guidance made the difference.

Finally, challenge students to label the thumb with a situation where they're still seeking God's guidance (you could use the analogy of a thumb used for hitchhiking). After a time limit of one minute, ask volunteers to share situations.

In closing whole-class discussion, pose the following questions regarding the thumb labels:

1–How have your experiences been like Nehemiah's?

2–How does your review of God's past guidance encourage you about the guidance you now seek?

For each situation shared, ask a volunteer to pray about it. Close with these prayers for God's guidance in the lives of your class members.

The Nation's Plea

Devotional Reading: Lamentations 3:22-33
Background Scripture: Lamentations 5

Lamentations 5

**1 Remember, O Lord, what is come upon us:
consider, and behold our reproach.
2 Our inheritance is turned to strangers, our
houses to aliens.
3 We are orphans and fatherless, our mothers are as widows.
4 We have drunken our water for money;
our wood is sold unto us.
5 Our necks are under persecution:
we labour, and have no rest.
6 We have given the hand to the
Egyptians, and to the Assyrians, to be
satisfied with bread.
7 Our fathers have sinned, and are
not; and we have borne their iniquities.
8 Servants have ruled over us: there
is none that doth deliver us out of their
hand.
9 We gat our bread with the peril of
our lives because of the sword of the wilderness.
10 Our skin was black like an oven because
of the terrible famine.
11 They ravished the women in Zion, and
the maids in the cities of Judah.
12 Princes are hanged up by their hand: the
faces of elders were not honoured.
13 They took the young men to grind, and
the children fell under the wood.
14 The elders have ceased from the gate, the
young men from their musick.
15 The joy of our heart is ceased; our dance
is turned into mourning.
16 The crown is fallen from
our head: woe unto us, that we
have sinned!
17 For this our heart is faint;
for these things our eyes are dim.
18 Because of the mountain of
Zion, which is desolate, the foxes
walk upon it.
19 Thou, O Lord, remainest
for ever; thy throne from generation to generation.
20 Wherefore dost thou forget
us for ever, and forsake us so long time?
21 Turn thou us unto thee, O Lord, and we
shall be turned; renew our days as of old.
22 But thou hast utterly rejected us; thou art
very wroth against us.**

Key Verse

Turn thou us unto thee, O Lord, and we shall be turned; renew our days as of old. **—Lamentations 5:21**

Photo: Getty Images

Prophets Faithful To God's Covenant

Unit 2: Prophets of Restoration

Lessons 5–8

Lesson Aims

After participating in this lesson, each learner will be able to:

1. Describe the historical context of the book of Lamentations.
2. Summarize the reasons for the people's mourning.
3. Lament having sinned against God.

Lesson Outline

Introduction
- A. In Memory Of
- B. Lesson Context

I. Confrontation (Lamentations 5:1-15)
- A. Remember! (v. 1)
- B. Results of "Their" Sins (vv. 2-14)
- C. Reversal (v. 15)
  - *Words for Mourning*

II. Confession (Lamentations 5:16-22)
- A. Of "Our" Sins (vv. 16-18)
- B. Of the Lord's Reign (v. 19)
- C. Of Hope and Fear (vv. 20-22)
  - *Has God Forgotten You?*

Conclusion
- A. Called to Lament
- B. Prayer
- C. Thought to Remember

Introduction

A. In Memory Of

When is the last time you heard a sermon or lesson from the book of Lamentations? Christians in the Western world have a difficult time with this question. Lamentations has been largely neglected in favor of texts that call us to joyful worship. Even in personal devotional time, Lamentations is often bypassed in favor of almost anything else. We don't like to dwell on pain, which is what Lamentations does. Think about it: Would you rather watch a cheery movie about the birth of Christ or a solemn movie about His crucifixion?

But remembering tragedy, as important as that is, isn't the only purpose of Lamentations. The book can also teach us much about our relationship with God—if we let it.

B. Lesson Context

The book of Lamentations reflects the period of about 586–538 BC, the period of Babylonian captivity. Assyria had taken the northern tribes of Israel into exile earlier, in 722 BC (2 Kings 17:1-6). "There was none left but the tribe of Judah only" (17:18). But despite the warnings of many prophets, Judah continued in sin (21:10-15). The writer of Lamentations, commonly taken to be Jeremiah (see the Lesson Context of lesson 9), had warned Judah for many years that God's judgment was coming (Jeremiah 25:2-11).

As instruments of God's wrath, the Babylonians destroyed Jerusalem in 586 BC (2 Chronicles 36:15-20). Many who were left alive were carried into exile; the weak and the poor were left behind to contend with foreign settlers (2 Kings 25:1-21).

The five chapters of Lamentations do not shy away from describing that devastation and its aftermath. Lack of food resulted in starvation (Lamentations 2:12; 4:4-5) and cannibalism (2:20; 4:10). Those who did not die by the sword were weak with hunger and disease (4:9).

For all the chaos of the setting, Jeremiah was very intentional in the literary forms he used when writing this book. The first four chapters are all acrostics. This means that each verse begins with a different letter of the Hebrew alphabet, in consecutive order. In English this would mean beginning the first verse with A, the second with B, etc. There are 22 letters in the Hebrew alphabet, thus there are 22 verses in each of chapters 1, 2, and 4. Chapter 3 is a bit different with 66 verses because the acrostic format appears there three times.

This tight orderliness was perhaps a way for Jeremiah to organize what he saw. If so, it is a subtle hint that, though on the surface all seems lost, order still exists—or at least *could* exist again.

Lamentations 5 does not have an acrostic pattern. That is not accidental, since it is the same length as chapters 1, 2, and 4. The discontinuance of the careful pattern seems to mimic the ebbing fortunes of the people. For all their cries to God, no help seemed to be forthcoming (compare 3:44).

I. Confrontation

(Lamentations 5:1-15)

A. Remember! (v. 1)

1. Remember, O Lord, what is come upon us: consider, and behold our reproach.

Though the acrostic pattern disappears in this chapter (see Lesson Context), Jeremiah continued to use characteristic Hebrew repetition. Piling on synonyms was a way Hebrew poetry emphasized a point. This characteristic is evident throughout the lesson text. The effect is to give a full account of the pain of the people, who speak as one here.

Asking God to *remember* is not primarily a plea for Him to recall information, but for Him to act. *Consider* and *behold* both echo *remember.* Putting these three verbs together conveys a sense of urgency for God to see what is happening to His people and to act without delay.

The phrase *What is come upon us* suggests that the people saw themselves as passive recipients of the tragedy that had befallen them; the phrase *our reproach* is parallel (compare Psalm 44:13-16). But the people's circumstances were because of their sins, not mere twists of fate. Lamentations 1:5; 2:14; and 3:42 reveal the whole story.

B. Results of "Their" Sins (vv. 2-14)

2. Our inheritance is turned to strangers, our houses to aliens.

The *inheritance* (and its poetic parallel, *our houses*) in the promised land was of great importance to Israel. It was a sign of God's faithful promise to Abraham (Genesis 15:18; 17:8) and continuing faithfulness to Abraham's descendants. Laws governed inheritance to ensure that no one in Israel would lose the family's land permanently (see Leviticus 25:13-16, 23-34; Numbers 36:7-9). Imagine, then, how devastating it was for that inheritance—with all its God-ordained safeguards—to be lost *to strangers* and *aliens* (compare Job 19:15, where the underlying Hebrew words also are parallel to one another). The land's falling into the hands of people who were outside of God's covenant jeopardized Judah's ever receiving it back.

3. We are orphans and fatherless, our mothers are as widows.

Orphans (*fatherless* children, not necessarily motherless) and *widows* were protected people under God's covenant (example: Deuteronomy 10:18). They were to be taken under the wing of the community so that they could thrive in less than ideal conditions (24:19-21). In a horrible reversal of fortunes, God's judgment has created widows and orphans in Judah, just as He warned (Exodus 22:24; Jeremiah 15:8; 18:21).

What Do You Think?

With James 1:27 in mind, how can you be more proactive in seeking out those in need?

Digging Deeper

What parts of such a ministry, if any, should be reserved for those especially gifted in it?

4. We have drunken our water for money; our wood is sold unto us.

Both the *water* and the *wood* (along with all other resources) in the promised land had been given to the Israelites for their use. Paying *money* to the invaders from Babylon emphasizes that the land was no longer controlled by Judah; this suggested to the mourners that God had abandoned the covenant (see Deuteronomy 28:15-68).

5. Our necks are under persecution: we labour, and have no rest.

This verse recalls the *persecution* and endless

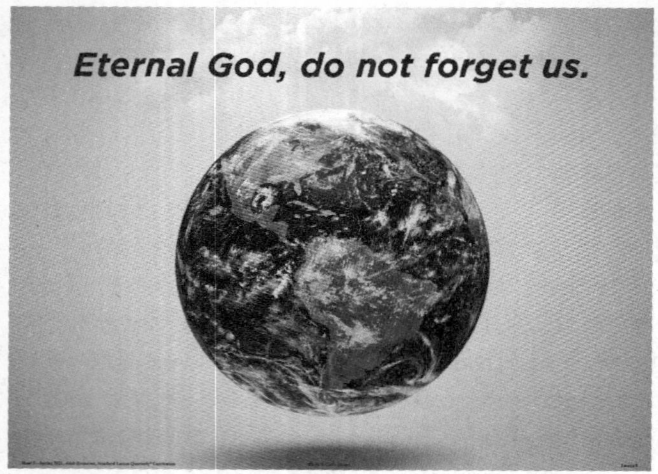
Eternal God, do not forget us.

Visual for Lesson 8. *Have this visual on display as pairs of students pray together for situations in which God seems to have forgotten their needs.*

labour that Israel had experienced in Egypt (example: Exodus 5:1-18). After the Lord had delivered Israel from that slavery, He had revealed His laws to them, laws that included the command to *rest* on the Sabbath (20:8-11). Being forced to break that command by those chosen to carry out God's judgment was seemingly more evidence of God's distance and abandonment.

6. We have given the hand to the Egyptians, and to the Assyrians, to be satisfied with bread.

The Assyrians were foes more recent than *the Egyptians* (see 2 Kings 18:17-37). The fact that the Judeans asked these two antagonistic nations for help further indicates the desperate consequences of the Babylonian conquest (compare Jeremiah 2:36; Hosea 7:11; 9:3).

> *What Do You Think?*
> What is the best course of action to take in light of whatever or whomever is now oppressing you or a loved one?
>
> *Digging Deeper*
> How can you know whether such oppression is a natural consequence or God's own reaction?

Bread was a basic food staple. It was something that the people had been able to make for themselves when their fields were their own to sow and harvest. Reference to bread can also imply food in general (see Lamentations 5:9, below). The need to appeal to Assyria and Egypt for aid could have resulted from the fields having been devastated by the invading Babylonian army.

7. Our fathers have sinned, and are not; and we have borne their iniquities.

In many places, the Bible affirms that each person suffers for his or her own wrongdoing (examples: Genesis 18:16-33; Ezekiel 18:2-4; John 9:1-3). However, biblical precedent exists for a generation to suffer for the *iniquities* of its *fathers.* The curses that God included in the covenant as potential discipline clearly expressed that people who were not the original guilty parties would suffer (example: Deuteronomy 5:9). Part of the reason for this generational suffering was the ripple-effect inheriting of sinful behaviors and habits, which required God's attention (compare Jeremiah 14:20; 16:12).

Those who lifted their voices in this lament certainly felt the shock waves of the sins of previous generations. But throughout those generations, God had warned about judgment (see Lesson Context). Even more, God had promised to relent from punishment when the people repented (example: Jeremiah 18:7-8; compare Jonah 3:4-10).

The Babylonian exile, shocking in its scope, marked the end of God's patience. The book of Lamentations is witness to how horrifying that judgment was. Jeremiah did not refrain from asking whether this punishment fit the crime (Lamentations 2:20-22). Indeed, God acknowledged that the Babylonians had overstepped their role in carrying out His decreed judgment; they would be punished for that (Isaiah 47; Habakkuk 2:2-20).

8. Servants have ruled over us: there is none that doth deliver us out of their hand.

Judah lost its kings when one surrendered to the besiegers (2 Kings 24:10-16) and his replacement rebelled (24:17–25:21). The people taken to Babylon were ruled by Babylonian *servants* there, while those left in Judah had to obey similar servants (24:22). Those who remained behind suffered the shame of being governed by foreigners within the borders of the promised land.

9. We gat our bread with the peril of our lives because of the sword of the wilderness.

There may not have been much more to eat

than *bread* in the land (contrast Lamentations 5:6, above). *The sword* represents all the violence the people still feared and experienced. Its appearance in *the wilderness* probably refers to the special dangers of trying to harvest any food.

10. Our skin was black like an oven because of the terrible famine.

The reference to *an oven* may be a way of referring to a raging fever; the literal translation *our skin was black* calls to mind food that has been burned to a crisp (compare Job 30:30). The great hunger that the *famine* created has opened the door to all kinds of ailments (compare Lamentations 4:8-9).

11. They ravished the women in Zion, and the maids in the cities of Judah.

Women and *maids* are parallel terms that refer to adult females. Whether they were married or not, they suffered sexual violation throughout *Zion* and *the cities of Judah*—also parallel terms. God's laws established punishment for sexual violence (examples: Deuteronomy 22:25-29). But to the invaders, this means nothing.

12a. Princes are hanged up by their hand.

The *princes,* representing the monarchy and advisers, perhaps had expected treatment in accordance with their positions. Being executed in a public way such as implied here was a grave indignity. The spectacle of their deaths was meant to remind the people of their powerlessness.

12b. The faces of elders were not honoured.

The *elders* were due reverence based on their wisdom gained with age. Given the parallelism of the two lines of this verse, it seems likely that the dishonor afforded them was also public execution. The fate of King Zedekiah comes to mind: the last thing he saw before his eyes were gouged out was the slaughter of his sons and all his officials. Then the king was bound and taken to a Babylonian prison where he died (Jeremiah 52:10-11).

13. They took the young men to grind, and the children fell under the wood.

Typically it was female slaves who were the ones to *grind* grain. But this task has fallen to *young men* who would be better suited to different tasks. In contrast, *the children* are given work much too difficult for them. The image is that of falling under their burden of sin—the weight of its punishment.

14. The elders have ceased from the gate, the young men from their musick.

In gated cities like Jerusalem, *elders* congregated at a main *gate* to decide legal cases, to reach business agreements, etc. (see Ruth 4:1-12). The absence of the elders from their usual place speaks to the complete upheaval of the government. The lack of *musick* further reveals the cultural upheaval that is evident throughout this book. The *young men* are grinding grain (Lamentations 5:13, above) rather than engaging in the expected artistic pursuits.

C. Reversal (v. 15)

15. The joy of our heart is ceased; our dance is turned into mourning.

In Psalm 30:1-3, the psalmist rejoiced in God's deliverance from enemies and sickness. The opposite is seen here: the conquered people suffered from both, with *joy* turning to *mourning* (contrast Psalm 30:11). How utterly hopeless their current situation seemed!

Words for Mourning

It was one of the darkest days I experienced as president of a Christian university: a precious little girl lost her life in a tragic accident on our campus. The next day, hundreds of mourners gathered in the college chapel. We were almost too brokenhearted to pray.

Yet in those dark days, prayer was our greatest resource. Amid intense grief, it was heartfelt prayers and laments that knit our campus together and helped us care for the family who had lost their child.

HOW TO SAY IT

Assyria	Uh-*sear*-ee-uh.
Babylon	*Bab*-uh-lun.
Jebusites	*Jeb*-yuh-sites.
Judah	*Joo*-duh.
Nebuchadnezzar	*Neb*-yuh-kud-***nez***-er.
Zedekiah	Zed-uh-*kye*-uh.
Zion	*Zi*-un.

Faith comes easily when the music of your life is joyful. But what will you say and how will you pray when your joy turns to mourning? —D. F.

II. Confession

(Lamentations 5:16-22)

A. Of "Our" Sins (vv. 16-18)

16a. The crown is fallen from our head.

This verse summarizes the societal and governmental upheaval that the people have experienced. Though *the crown* represented the monarchy, the monarchy itself represented Judah.

16b. Woe unto us, that we have sinned!

These mourners had claimed that they suffered for previous generations' sins (Lamentations 5:7, above). Here they take responsibility for their own sin. The word *woe* expresses their grief.

> *What Do You Think?*
> How bad would the consequences for your sin have to be for you to grieve openly?
> *Digging Deeper*
> What was a time in the past when you should have done so? Why did you not?

17-18. For this our heart is faint; for these things our eyes are dim. Because of the mountain of Zion, which is desolate, the foxes walk upon it.

Weakness of *heart* and *eyes* resulted from the fate of *the mountain of Zion*. This place had great significance, first as the stronghold of the Jebusites that David defeated (Joshua 15:63; 2 Samuel 5:6-7). David's palace had been built there (2 Samuel 5:9-11) as had the temple (1 Kings 6:1; 7:51).

We need not assume Jeremiah had only one of these specific ideas in mind. After all, the people mourned for the fate of the city, the monarchy, and the temple. The presence of *foxes* in the heart of the capital city marks the profound desolation of Jerusalem.

B. Of the Lord's Reign (v. 19)

19. Thou, O Lord, remainest for ever; thy throne from generation to generation.

Although the *Lord* has been addressed throughout the chapter, He has not been called out since verse 1. This absence emphasizes the feelings of distance that the people felt. The call on Him now is a brief moment of praise.

To speak of God's eternal *throne* emphasizes His role as King. It is He who has the power and authority to decide and impose punishment. Having existed *from generation to generation,* He knows how unfaithful those generations have been (see Lamentations 5:7, 16, above). Yet knowing that God's presence can be counted on can be a source of comfort, even if in the current moment He seems far off.

C. Of Hope and Fear (vv. 20-22)

20. Wherefore dost thou forget us for ever, and forsake us so long time?

The Lord does not *forget* as people do, as though His memory were faulty. Yet knowing that God is indeed "from generation to generation" (previous verse) makes the question of His forgetting or forsaking all the more painful. Though Jeremiah had offered words of encouragement previously (see Lamentations 3:22-33), those seem to be a drop in the bucket in light of the overwhelming pain that continued.

Has God Forgotten You?

When James Hurley was 5 years old, his parents and 13-year-old brother lost their lives in an accident involving a private airplane. After the tragedy, a cousin and her family adopted James, along with his two other brothers and his sister. Together they started a new life.

James admits that for many years he asked himself why God had allowed this tragedy. But as he grew older, he learned of his parents' faith, and he saw his cousin's faith in action. Eventually, he realized how blessed he and his siblings were to grow up in a family that practiced their faith openly.

Now in his 60s, James has found peace and gratitude for God's love. The people in Jerusalem were desperate to find this peace, but feared that God had forgotten them. What makes the difference in your life when it feels like God has forgotten you? —D. F.

What Do You Think?

How would you comfort and guide someone who feels forgotten by God?

Digging Deeper

How do passages such as Job 2:11–3:26; 13:4-5; 16:2-5; 23:1-4; 29:1-3 frame your answer?

21a. Turn thou us unto thee, O Lord, and we shall be turned.

Language of turning speaks of repentance. The people did not trust themselves to *turn* to the *Lord* as they should (compare Jeremiah 31:18-19). Certainly their history proved that they struggled to turn to God on their own. For this reason, they asked that God would give His grace to them by turning them himself.

God would honor this prayer by giving hearts of flesh in place of stone (Ezekiel 11:19; 36:26). The ultimate answer to the plea of the half-verse before us is found in the church, where we are "transformed by the renewing of [our] mind" (Romans 12:2; compare Hebrews 8:10).

21b. Renew our days as of old.

Though the *days as of old* were full of disobedience, they were days when God showered His people with blessings in the land He had given them (Deuteronomy 28:1-13). The desire was not simply to *renew* those days, but for transformation by the repentance of the people.

22. But thou hast utterly rejected us; thou art very wroth against us.

After fleeting expressions of hope, the people turned once again to what they feared was true. Could God be so *very wroth* with them that He would *utterly* reject them forever (compare Malachi 4:6)?

What Do You Think?

How do we keep the genuine sorrow of repentance from becoming merely a pity party?

Digging Deeper

Without giving directive advice, how would you counsel someone who has failed to do so?

The book ends here on this issue. God does not answer. Jeremiah offered no further words of hope (contrast Psalm 22). The people were not consoled; the wound was not healed (Jeremiah 30:12-15). This reality emphasized the depth and breadth of God's anger.

Conclusion

A. Called to Lament

In the midst of our suffering, we know that God is still trustworthy and faithful. However, there are times when we do not *feel* that He is still trustworthy or faithful. We do not know where God is when we confess and repent of our sins but do not experience mercy in the consequences. We find that worship and praise lag behind the mourning and lament. Like those left in a destroyed Jerusalem, all we can see is devastation; the only thing we want is to make sure God sees and knows what we are experiencing.

Lamentations helps us find language to tell God the very deep, very real pain that we remember or still experience. The book serves as an invitation to take those things to God. As Paul wrote, "Neither death, nor life, nor angels, nor principalities, nor powers, nor things present, nor things to come, nor height, nor depth, nor any other creature, shall be able to separate us from the love of God, which is in Christ Jesus our Lord" (Romans 8:38-39). Though the inclusion of Lamentations in the Bible may seem odd, it gives evidence of the truth of Paul's assertion. No siege, no famine, no cannibalism, no destruction, no forced labor, no exile could separate God's people from His love.

God demonstrated this love in Jesus Christ, making a way for all people to turn to the Lord and experience His blessings. Through Jesus' great suffering, we have been added to those people who will be freed from all suffering (Revelation 21:4).

B. Prayer

Father, strengthen us to be willing to turn our hearts to You! Help us to be honest with You as Jeremiah and Jesus were honest with You in their suffering. In Jesus' name we pray. Amen.

C. Thought to Remember

Let sorrow draw you closer to God.

Involvement Learning

Enhance your lesson with KJV Bible Student *(from your curriculum supplier) and the reproducible activity page (at www.standardlesson.com or in the back of the* KJV Standard Lesson Commentary Deluxe Edition*).*

Into the Lesson

Give each participant an index card. Say, "Take no more than one minute to write the title of a song that resonated with you during a time of hardship. Once everyone is done, we will guess who chose which song." Collect completed cards, shuffle them, and begin reading the song titles, pausing between each to allow guesses as to which class member wrote the name of the song. (*Option.* Ask the writer to share the reason for choosing it.)

Option. Before class members arrive, place at their chairs copies of the "The Js Have It!" exercise from the activity page, which you can download. Learners can begin working on this as they arrive.

Lead into the Bible study by asking, "Should we keep our pain to ourselves, or should we express it? Let's see how the writer of Lamentations handled that question."

Into the Word

Group learners into study triads. Then introduce a two-part "deep dive" into Lamentations 5 as you distribute handouts (you prepare) as follows:

Part 1: *Background Research*

1–Who was Jeremiah, the suggested author?

2–What was the name of the city once "full of people" that is mourned in Lamentations 1:1?

3–When was the time frame of Lamentations?

[*Where answers can be found:* 1–Jeremiah 1:1-3; 2–Lamentations 1:7-8, 17; 2:10, 13, 15; 4:12; 3–see Lesson Context]

Part 2: *Digging into Lamentations 5*

1–Does "remember" in verse 1 imply that it's possible for the Lord to "forget" (see verse 20)? Why, or why not?

2–What was the "inheritance" that was lost in verse 2, and why was it called that?

3–What historical event might be recalled in verse 5?

4–How does verse 7 relate to Jeremiah 31:29-30 and/or Ezekiel 18:1-4?

5–What do verses 8-18 reveal regarding the conditions of the covenant people at the time?

6–In what way does the chapter change at verse 19?

Inform learners of websites for research via smartphones (www.biblegateway.com, etc.). Allow time to present findings in whole-class discussion. After findings are presented, encourage participants to express how this information enhances their appreciation for this passage. Use this discussion as a transition to the Into Life segment.

Into Life

Divide the class into teams to conduct a mock debate on this proposition:

Resolved:
It's usually best to keep one's grief private.

The **Affirmative Team** will offer arguments in favor of the proposition; the **Negative Team** will counter with the opposite. Research in advance Scriptures that support (or seem to support) one side over the other; provide these to the teams. Possible texts to provide:

- For the **Affirmative Team:** the book of Job; Ezekiel 27:1, 31-32; Matthew 5:4; Romans 12:15
- For the **Negative Team:** Ezekiel 24:16-17, 22-23; 1 Corinthians 7:29-30a; 1 Thessalonians 4:13

These are just starters for your own research, however. Also research various debate formats for the one that's best for your class.

Option 1. Distribute copies of the (public domain) first stanza and the refrain of the hymn "It Is Well" on the activity page. After singing these, have a preselected participant tell the tragic story of the writer, Horatio G. Spafford (1828–1888). Coordinate this in advance so your participant has time to research the story.

Option 2. Follow Option 1 by playing a recording of the song "Oh, Danny Boy." Then lead a discussion of how the Christian lyrics of "It Is Well" are like and unlike the secular lyrics of "Oh, Danny Boy." Challenge learners to ponder which of the two compositions is most like their own expressions of sadness and disappointment.

Speaking Truth to Power

Devotional Reading: 1 John 3:23–4:3a; Deuteronomy 18:19-22
Background Scripture: 1 Kings 22:1-40

1 Kings 22:15-23, 26-28

15 So he came to the king. And the king said unto him, Micaiah, shall we go against Ramothgilead to battle, or shall we forbear? And he answered him, Go, and prosper: for the Lord shall deliver it into the hand of the king.

16 And the king said unto him, How many times shall I adjure thee that thou tell me nothing but that which is true in the name of the Lord?

17 And he said, I saw all Israel scattered upon the hills, as sheep that have not a shepherd: and the Lord said, These have no master: let them return every man to his house in peace.

18 And the king of Israel said unto Jehoshaphat, Did I not tell thee that he would prophesy no good concerning me, but evil?

19 And he said, Hear thou therefore the word of the Lord: I saw the Lord sitting on his throne, and all the host of heaven standing by him on his right hand and on his left.

20 And the Lord said, Who shall persuade Ahab, that he may go up and fall at Ramothgilead? And one said on this manner, and another said on that manner.

21 And there came forth a spirit, and stood before the Lord, and said, I will persuade him.

22 And the Lord said unto him, Wherewith? And he said, I will go forth, and I will be a lying spirit in the mouth of all his prophets. And he said, Thou shalt persuade him, and prevail also: go forth, and do so.

23 Now therefore, behold, the Lord hath put a lying spirit in the mouth of all these thy prophets, and the Lord hath spoken evil concerning thee.

. . . .

26 And the king of Israel said, Take Micaiah, and carry him back unto Amon the governor of the city, and to Joash the king's son;

27 And say, Thus saith the king, Put this fellow in the prison, and feed him with bread of affliction and with water of affliction, until I come in peace.

28 And Micaiah said, If thou return at all in peace, the Lord hath not spoken by me. And he said, Hearken, O people, every one of you.

Key Verse

Micaiah said, As the Lord liveth, what the Lord saith unto me, that will I speak. —**1 Kings 22:14**

PROPHETS FAITHFUL TO GOD'S COVENANT

Unit 3: Courageous Prophets of Change

LESSONS 9–13

LESSON AIMS

After participating in this lesson, each learner will be able to:

1. Identify the roles of Ahab, Jehoshaphat, and Micaiah.

2. Compare and contrast how each of those three related to God's truth.

3. Create a plan to pursue and apply God's knowledge in the week ahead.

LESSON OUTLINE

Introduction

A. Truth Distorted

Have you ever sought out counsel that would tell you what you want to hear, rather than truth, so that you could press forward with your own agenda? Herein is an important lesson we can learn from George Washington.

As the first president of the United States, Washington had no precedent to follow when choosing the men who would shape his thinking and the new government. Wisely, Washington chose an eclectic group of people to fill cabinet positions and be his closest advisers. They were from different parts of the country, and they had different views on how the government should operate. Instead of choosing advisers exclusively from his state of Virginia, Washington chose to surround himself with people who had the same ultimate goals in mind. The varied opinions about how to achieve common goals helped President Washington make choices that were more informed and wiser.

Unfortunately, Ahab did not make similar decisions. He surrounded himself with false prophets who told him whatever he wanted to hear. But this lesson focuses on the one prophet who refused to compromise the truth.

B. Lesson Context

The role of the books 1 & 2 Kings is often misunderstood by the modern reader. Because they cover much of the same times and events as 1 & 2 Chronicles, we often read them as retelling the same story, slightly differently. (In fact, today's text has a parallel in 2 Chronicles 18.) While there is truth to this, the original readers of 1 & 2 Kings actually associated them with 1 & 2 Samuel; in the Greek version translated before Christ, these four books are known as 1, 2, 3, and 4 Kingdoms. And although it's natural to categorize these as books of history, we do well to remember that no book of the Bible seeks merely to give us a history lesson. Every book in the Bible intends to tell us something about God.

The Old Testament narratives, 1 & 2 Kings included, were passed down with the intention of revealing truth about the relationship between God and His people. These books were read by the Babylonian exiles, who had many deep and painful questions regarding the benefits of being chosen by God. Jerusalem's destruction and the exile of its people raised questions about God's sovereignty and love.

The books we think of as history address these issues by telling the story of God's people, picking up with the conquest of the promised land in Joshua and ending with the exile in 2 Kings. Collectively, the books tell the story of Israel's persistent rebellions against the terms of the covenant, divine judgment in the form of the curses prescribed in Deuteronomy 27–28, Israel's returns to God, and God's resulting mercy.

First Kings 22 opens by describing a conversation between two kings: Ahab of northern Israel (reigned 874–853 BC) and Jehoshaphat of southern Judah (reigned 873–849 BC). Before launching a joint military initiative, Ahab decided to consult his prophets to learn whether God would give him victory (1 Kings 22:10). Consulting God (or false gods) before battle was customary (examples: Judges 20:18; 1 Samuel 23:2; Ezekiel 21:21).

Ahab followed this practice, but he sought divine guidance from about 400 false prophets. These men were charged with discerning God's will while having no access to Him! Their counsel was united: God would grant victory in the expected battle (1 Kings 22:1-6). A favorable report, delivered from a unified front, would certainly convince the two kings of the veracity of their message!

But King Jehoshaphat was unimpressed by the verdict of the false prophets. Jehoshaphat's reign was characterized by religious reform and the suppression of idolatry (2 Chronicles 17:3-6). But he found himself in a compromised position because he had entered into a political alliance with the spiritually lapsed northern kingdom. In an attempt to do right, Jehoshaphat asked Ahab if he didn't have a prophet of the true God who could be consulted. Ahab admitted that Micaiah was such a prophet.

HOW TO SAY IT

Ahab	*Ay*-hab.
Ai	*Ay*-eye.
Amon	*Ay*-mun.
Arameans	*Ar*-uh-***me***-uns.
Athaliah	Ath-uh-*lye*-uh.
Israel	*Iz*-ray-el.
Jehoram	Jeh-*ho*-rum.
Jehoshaphat	Jeh-*hosh*-uh-fat.
Joash	*Jo*-ash.
Josephus	Jo-*see*-fus.
Micaiah	My-*kay*-uh.
Naboth	*Nay*-bawth.
Ramothgilead	*Ray*-muth-***gil***-ee-ud.

I. A Sarcastic Prophecy
(1 Kings 22:15-16)

A. Leading Question (v. 15)

15. So he came to the king. And the king said unto him, Micaiah, shall we go against Ramothgilead to battle, or shall we forbear? And he answered him, Go, and prosper: for the LORD shall deliver it into the hand of the king.

Ahab despised *Micaiah* because of the series of negative reports that the prophet had made against the king. The unnamed prophet in 1 Kings 20:35-43 was suggested by both the Talmud and the first-century Jewish historian Josephus to have been Micaiah. Little else is known about this prophet.

Ramothgilead was a city of refuge within the tribe of Gad (Deuteronomy 4:43). It was located on a large plain, making chariot warfare possible (see 1 Kings 22:31-38, not in our printed text). In Ahab's day, the Arameans held the city (22:3, not in our printed text). In the days of Rome, this people group came to be known as Syrians. Israel had some ethnic relationship to Arameans (see Deuteronomy 26:5), including Bethuel who was Rebekah's father (Genesis 22:20-23). Despite these ancestral links, the Arameans were often opposed to Israel, either instigating or experiencing warfare with the nation (examples: Judges 3:8, 10; 2 Samuel 8:5-6).

Micaiah surprised *the king,* Ahab, by telling him exactly what he wanted to hear and what the other prophets had already told him. Based on Ahab's prior characterization of Micaiah (1 Kings 22:8, not in our printed text), we might also be surprised that Micaiah has immediately agreed with the majority of prophets affirming Ahab's future success (22:13-15).

What Do You Think?

What guardrails can we erect to avoid giving to others counsel that is actually in our own best interests?

Digging Deeper

What should you do if you see this problem in another person?

"What Do You Want to Hear?"

I like to ask my mom for her opinion. Generally, I ask her about something small, like which shoes look better. I hear my mom's opinion and her reasons, but I am very quick to choose the other option. I do this because I already know what I want to hear; I just want someone else to agree with me.

At this point, Mom essentially refuses to give me a real answer. She knows that I will disregard it and do what I want. Can you blame her? After my asking year after year what shoes look best and almost always choosing the other ones, why would she bother giving me her real opinion?

It's hard to blame Micaiah for his response to Ahab. Much like my mom, Micaiah was exhausted from telling Ahab God's sovereign truth just to have it ignored in the face of what Ahab wanted to do all along. How often do we ask God for His truth, find it, and promptly choose what we wanted to hear instead of what He said? It's time to start following God's truth instead of merely asking for it. —L. G.

B. Frustrated Retort (v. 16)

16. And the king said unto him, How many times shall I adjure thee that thou tell me nothing but that which is true in the name of the LORD?

King Ahab interpreted Micaiah's affirming response as a bald-faced lie, not even meant to be believed. Ahab's asking *how many times* implies that Micaiah had fallen into the pattern of sardonically telling the king whatever it was he wanted to hear.

The king ironically demanded that Micaiah fulfill his prophetic duty and only relay God's word (Deuteronomy 18:18). But Ahab wasn't interested in hearing God's actual will. He only used his prophets to legitimize the plans that were already in his heart (see 1 Kings 22:22, below).

II. A Sincere Prophecy

(1 Kings 22:17-23)

A. God's Truth, Part 1 (v. 17)

17. And he said, I saw all Israel scattered upon the hills, as sheep that have not a shepherd: and the LORD said, These have no master: let them return every man to his house in peace.

Micaiah dropped his act, causing the atmosphere in the room to immediately darken. *Israel* would be thrown into as much disarray *as sheep* without *a shepherd* (see 1 Kings 22:28, below). When they realized they had *no master,* the army would scatter—not haphazardly but *every man to his house.* Returning *in peace* might mean that, though leaderless, the army would be better off without their previous master. Or it might simply mean that the fighting would be over for a time.

B. King's Irritation (v. 18)

18. And the king of Israel said unto Jehoshaphat, Did I not tell thee that he would prophesy no good concerning me, but evil?

Ahab's response to Micaiah's prophecy suggests that the prophet was brought to court more as a jester or curiosity than as a legitimate adviser. Ahab's heart was so hardened against God that he was able to dismiss Micaiah's warning as just one more *evil* thing the prophet said about *the king of Israel.*

King Jehoshaphat's nonreaction is equally disturbing. Jehoshaphat worshipped the God of Israel and took measures to suppress idolatry in his nation (see Lesson Context). But here he failed to advise the other king to heed the word of the Lord.

The northern kingdom enjoyed military prowess during this period of their combined histories. With their allies, Israel held off the encroaching Assyrian Empire. The alliance between Israel and Judah was secured by the marriage of Ahab's daughter Athaliah to Jehoshaphat's son Jehoram (2 Kings 8:16-18). So we see two kings, one idolatrous and one godly, who witnessed the testimony of God's true prophet and for their own reasons refused to alter their foolhardy plans.

What Do You Think?

What are some proper ways to react to those who expect us to tell them what they *want* to hear rather than what they *need* to hear?

Digging Deeper

How would your response differ, if at all, to someone who is in authority over you rather than the other way around? Why?

C. God's Truth, Part 2 (vv. 19-23)

19. And he said, Hear thou therefore the word of the LORD: I saw the LORD sitting on his throne, and all the host of heaven standing by him on his right hand and on his left.

Unlike verse 15, here Micaiah uses the *word of the Lord* formula to reveal that what followed came from God, not the prophet's own mind. *All the host of heaven* may refer to angels (see Psalms 103:20-21; 148:2; Luke 2:13); another possibility is that the phrase refers to the heavenly bodies worshipped as gods by pagan nations (see Deuteronomy 4:19; 2 Kings 17:16; 21:3; Jeremiah 19:13). Whether real angels or fictitious deities, the image is that God is the only one *sitting on* a *throne.* This is a visual image of God's sovereignty over everything, real or imagined.

20. And the LORD said, Who shall persuade Ahab, that he may go up and fall at Ramoth-gilead? And one said on this manner, and another said on that manner.

This verse makes explicit what was implied in 1 Kings 22:17, above: *Ahab* would die on the battlefield. Such a sentence was just since Ahab had followed the ways of his evil queen, Jezebel, and led the northern kingdom into the idolatrous worship of Baal (1 Kings 16:31-33). Unlike Ahab's prophets, who all answered the king in unison, God's court was filled with lots of ideas, giving various plans for how to lure Ahab to his death.

21. And there came forth a spirit, and stood before the LORD, and said, I will persuade him.

From among the council, a volunteer stepped forward and expressed willingness to take up the task of luring King Ahab into battle, and, by extension, to his death. Keeping in mind that court members might be composed of fictitious deities, the exact identity of the *spirit* is less significant than is his depicted role in the unfolding spiritual drama (compare and contrast Job 1:6-12; 2:1-7).

22. And the LORD said unto him, Wherewith? And he said, I will go forth, and I will be a lying spirit in the mouth of all his prophets. And he said, Thou shalt persuade him, and prevail also: go forth, and do so.

Psychologists today might say that the spirit enticed Ahab with the king's own confirmation bias. This false belief arises from choosing only to consider evidence that confirms what a person already wanted to believe. In this case, the *lying spirit* unified *all* the king's *prophets* in order to strengthen the evidence that favored Ahab's false hope: that he would have victory over his enemies.

The Lord giving approval to this plan is one example of God's sovereign right to judge evildoers. Although Ahab had humbled himself following the theft of Naboth's vineyard (see 1 Kings 21), old habits apparently die hard. Ahab did not want to listen to the prophet of the Lord, preferring the pleasant prophecies of his old prophets. Ironically, if Ahab chose to listen to Micaiah now, the prophecy would not have come true! But the man's character was known not only to the prophet but also to God (see 22:29-38).

23. Now therefore, behold, the LORD hath put a lying spirit in the mouth of all these thy prophets, and the LORD hath spoken evil concerning thee.

Micaiah presented Ahab with a message of judgment. But implicit in that message was the opportunity for repentance (compare Jonah 3). Mercifully, Ahab was given the opportunity to

Visual for Lesson 9. *Point to this visual as you ask how its imperative informs your learners' responses to the question associated with verse 18.*

admit his sinful state, repent, and break off his doomed campaign.

The Lord used Ahab's character and the deference of the king's prophets to deceive the man. God never lies, but He does work through humans to accomplish His purposes, whether they do good or ill. God also never does moral *evil*, but He can put events into motion that from a human perspective are catastrophic. In this case, the *lying spirit* intensified human dynamics already in play to ensure that Ahab would be fooled.

III. A Sure Prophecy

(1 Kings 22:26-28)

A. King's Fury (vv. 26-27)

26. And the king of Israel said, Take Micaiah, and carry him back unto Amon the governor of the city, and to Joash the king's son.

Ahab's response was anything but one of repentance. Referencing *the governor of the city* and *the king's son* lets the reader know that Ahab was so determined to silence Micaiah that he evoked both local and national authorities to ensure the prophet's secure incarceration.

27. And say, Thus saith the king, Put this fellow in the prison, and feed him with bread of affliction and with water of affliction, until I come in peace.

Micaiah was to remain in his cell and be given grim rations until Ahab returned safely from battle. Ahab's sentence assumed that his triumphant return would expose the jailed prophet as a charlatan. Though Ahab expected to return *in peace*, the prophecy had revealed that only his men would do so (1 Kings 22:17, 28).

Ahab's command had the effect of silencing the prophet. The king knew that if word got out that he himself was under divine judgment, it could lead to poor troop morale on the eve of battle or even embolden a rival to attempt a coup. Plus, the king just didn't like the prophet.

> *What Do You Think?*
> What can you do, if anything, to prepare in advance for times of affliction?
> *Digging Deeper*
> Which part of Matthew 24:9-13 is most helpful in answering this?

Quantity over Quality

When I was younger, I stayed with my grandparents for a week. My grandma was not feeling very well, and a confidante convinced her that I was a very disrespectful child. My grandma reported this to my parents. I was in a lot of trouble, but I continued to defend what I knew to be true. I was innocent of these charges!

Due largely to my grandparents' position of authority, they were initially believed. However, my aunt had also spent time with me that week. She advocated for me and presented the truth to my parents. I was released from my punishment.

Micaiah was the small, lone voice of truth. Since that truth did not align with the majority of authoritative voices, he was placed in prison. In the world today, voices tell us lies every day. But truth is still truth, and we can heed its voice if we desire. What crowds are preventing you from heeding God's truth? —L. G.

B. Prophet's Promise (v. 28)

28. And Micaiah said, If thou return at all in peace, the Lord hath not spoken by me. And he said, Hearken, O people, every one of you.

The question of whether *Micaiah* spoke the truth would be determined on the battlefield. If

Micaiah truly spoke for God, then Ahab would die, never returning home *in peace* as the king assumed. Micaiah was so confident in what he'd heard from God that he challenged those present to be witnesses. Ahab's death would not only vindicate Micaiah, but God as well.

Ahab died, just as Micaiah said (1 Kings 22:29-38). Micaiah's fate in prison is unknown.

> *What Do You Think?*
>
> How should you go about testing the statements of one who claims to speak for the Lord?
>
> *Digging Deeper*
>
> What texts in addition to Deuteronomy 13:1-3; 18:21-22; Matthew 7:15-20; Mark 13:21-23; 2 Peter 1:19–2:3; and 1 John 4:1-3 help you frame your answer?

Conclusion

A. Truth Displayed

Today's passage illustrates the timeless struggle to relate to the truth properly. The individuals in today's lesson provide us with three stances that people exposed to God's truth can take.

King Ahab is easily vilified due to his idolatry, miscarriages of justice, and antipathy toward God's prophets. However, whenever we find ourselves willfully in rebellion to the truth, we see shades of Ahab within our own spirits. When we find ourselves in this precarious state and are then admonished by concerned friends, we should realize that this is a form of God's mercy, even when their words challenge and inconvenience us (Proverbs 27:5-6). Yet we need to be alert to possible Ahab-like tendencies in others and be prepared to admonish those who clearly ignore God in their choosing of unholy paths.

In Jehoshaphat, we have a case study of a person who desired to please God but lacked consistent, faithful follow-through. All believers, from senior ministers to occasional pew-fillers, can find themselves walking in this king's shoes. That happens when we are hesitant, for whatever reason, to execute a God-given plan. Any of us can find ourselves tempted as Jehoshaphat was. So when we encounter a fellow believer in a similar situation, the correct response is to offer encouragement and wise counsel.

As a prophet, Micaiah was bound by the simple adage that he was only to preach the word that God gave him and not add or subtract from that word (compare Deuteronomy 4:2). We see Micaiah's ability to think and speak independently in the face of a hostile crowd of 400 false prophets, two powerful leaders, and a prevailing climate of wickedness. The prophet's outspokenness reminds us that speaking truth can result in very negative consequences. Micaiah was aware of this, but was still obedient to God. We can build a life centered on truth through the regular study of God's Word. That's how we discipline ourselves to hear the voice of the Lord and to obey that voice—one opportunity at a time.

Many people today, as in Micaiah's day, prefer to question God's truth rather than their own sinful patterns. This isn't to say that doubt and confusion are never legitimate. But we must be aware of the possibility that sometimes our "confusion" over truth has the function of legitimizing ungodly behavior. We must echo apostle Paul's words, "Let God be true, but every man a liar" (Romans 3:4).

> *What Do You Think?*
>
> Which thought in today's text do you have the hardest time coming to grips with? Why?
>
> *Digging Deeper*
>
> Considering Romans 15:4; 1 Corinthians 10:1-4; and 2 Timothy 3:16-17, what extra effort will you expend to resolve this uncertainty?

B. Prayer

God, we thank You for revealing Your truth. Now we ask that Your truth be revealed in our words and actions. Help us not only to be people knowledgeable of Your Word, but also be people who make decisions that are consistent with Your Word. In Jesus' name we pray. Amen.

C. Thought to Remember

Our commitment to truth is measured in our actions.

Involvement Learning

Enhance your lesson with KJV Bible Student *(from your curriculum supplier) and the reproducible activity page (at www.standardlesson.com or in the back of the* KJV Standard Lesson Commentary Deluxe Edition*).*

Into the Lesson

As class members arrive, jot the following mixed sentence on the board:

have along along to to go get you

Begin by asking class members to arrange the words into a sentence silently and to raise hands when they know the answer. After a volunteer shares the correct sentence, "You have to go along to get along," encourage discussion regarding contexts where class members have heard or used this expression. (*Option.* If you prefer a shorter version of the saying, reduce it from eight words to five to end up with "go along to get along.")

Tell the class, "Today's text will help us see the outlook of this saying in a biblical light."

Into the Word

To set the context for the lesson, give each of six learners one of the tasks below, which you have written on six slips of paper (one task per slip, numbered as shown):

1–Summarize 1 Kings 16:29-33
2–Summarize 2 Chronicles 17:1-6
3–Summarize 2 Chronicles 18:1
4–Summarize 1 Kings 21:25-29
5–Summarize 1 Kings 22:1-5
6–Summarize 1 Kings 22:6-14

Ask those holding the slips to each read the assigned passage to the class, in order, adding any summary observations they deem appropriate. Use the Lesson Context and personal research to fill in gaps. (*Option.* Have a Bible time line on display that you can point to as the summaries proceed.)

Next, give each participant a handout (you prepare) on which is printed the following brief matching exercise:

? Ahab . . . . .in rebellion against the truth?
? Jehoshaphat . . . . aligned with the truth?
? Micaiah . . . . uncommitted to the truth?

Learners should quickly recognize these to be the *answers*:

✓Ahab . . . . in rebellion against the truth.
✓Jehoshaphat . . . . uncommitted to the truth.
✓Micaiah. . . . . aligned with the truth.

Group learners into study pairs or triads to look for further evidence of three truths (thus far they have been looking only at context passages). After several minutes, ask pairs or triads to report findings. Discuss and resolve differences as a class. (*Option.* Depending on time available, assign only one of the three names to each pair or triad instead of all three to each.)

Into Life

Remind class members of the scrambled sentence from the beginning of the class period. Send students back to their pairs or triads with this question and task:

1–How does that sentence relate to today's lesson?
2–Make a list of how people in general today might be like the character they studied—that is, how and why people rebel against truth, compromise truth, or stand up for truth in spite of pressure to do otherwise.

After a few minutes, allow class members to report items from their list. Follow by asking which character in today's story challenges them most, and why. (*Option.* If your class can tolerate a more personal inquiry, ask them to rate themselves from *1–totally uncommitted* to *10–totally committed* in regard to truth in daily life.) Ask volunteers to share steps Christians could take to move themselves higher on this scale.

Options. Distribute copies of one or both of the exercises on the activity page, which you can download, for learners to complete. Give careful thought to the sizes and constituencies of the groups you use for discussion, given the nature of each scenario—you want the discussion to shed "light," not "heat"!

May 9
Lesson 10 (KJV)

Offering Hope for the Future

Devotional Reading: Jeremiah 29:10-14
Background Scripture: Isaiah 29

Isaiah 29:13-24

13 Wherefore the Lord said, Forasmuch as this people draw near me with their mouth, and with their lips do honour me, but have removed their heart far from me, and their fear toward me is taught by the precept of men:

14 Therefore, behold, I will proceed to do a marvellous work among this people, even a marvellous work and a wonder: for the wisdom of their wise men shall perish, and the understanding of their prudent men shall be hid.

15 Woe unto them that seek deep to hide their counsel from the Lord, and their works are in the dark, and they say, Who seeth us? and who knoweth us?

16 Surely your turning of things upside down shall be esteemed as the potter's clay: for shall the work say of him that made it, He made me not? or shall the thing framed say of him that framed it, He had no understanding?

17 Is it not yet a very little while, and Lebanon shall be turned into a fruitful field, and the fruitful field shall be esteemed as a forest?

18 And in that day shall the deaf hear the words of the book, and the eyes of the blind shall see out of obscurity, and out of darkness.

19 The meek also shall increase their joy in the Lord, and the poor among men shall rejoice in the Holy One of Israel.

20 For the terrible one is brought to nought, and the scorner is consumed, and all that watch for iniquity are cut off:

21 That make a man an offender for a word, and lay a snare for him that reproveth in the gate, and turn aside the just for a thing of nought.

22 Therefore thus saith the Lord, who redeemed Abraham, concerning the house of Jacob, Jacob shall not now be ashamed, neither shall his face now wax pale.

23 But when he seeth his children, the work of mine hands, in the midst of him, they shall sanctify my name, and sanctify the Holy One of Jacob, and shall fear the God of Israel.

24 They also that erred in spirit shall come to understanding, and they that murmured shall learn doctrine.

Key Verse

They also that erred in spirit shall come to understanding, and they that murmured shall learn doctrine.

—Isaiah 29:24

Photo: Getty Images

PROPHETS FAITHFUL TO GOD'S COVENANT

Unit 3: Courageous Prophets of Change

LESSONS 9–13

LESSON AIMS

After participating in this lesson, each learner will be able to:

1. Describe God's intentions regarding the spiritual condition of Israel.

2. Give an example of a similar spiritual condition today.

3. Create a personal plan to guard against ritualism in worship.

LESSON OUTLINE

Introduction
- A. Stone(walling) Hearts
- B. Lesson Context

I. Unfaithful Worship (Isaiah 29:13-14)
- A. Present Indifference to God (v. 13)
- B. Future Awe of God (v. 14)
  - *Wonderful?*

II. Unfaithful Plans (Isaiah 29:15-22)
- A. Hidden Plans Are Judged (vv. 15-16)
  - *Appearances Can Be Deceiving*
- B. Followed by Flourishing (vv. 17-19)
- C. Judgment for the Unjust (vv. 20-21)
- D. Followed by Restoration (v. 22)

III. Faithful Worship (Isaiah 29:23-24)
- A. Based on God's Character (v. 23)
- B. Expressed Through God's Word (v. 24)

Conclusion
- A. Intimate Hearts
- B. Prayer
- C. Thought to Remember

Introduction

A. Stone(walling) Hearts

Dr. John Gottman studies marriage and the forces likely to break a union apart. After years of research, he identified four relational traits that reliably predict divorce: contempt, defensiveness, stonewalling, and criticism. He refers to these metaphorically as the Four Horsemen of the Apocalypse.

Criticism becomes destructive when a spouse's value and worth are questioned instead of specific behaviors. Generalizations are made, and the spouse on the receiving end begins to feel resentful and overwhelmed. Contempt manifests itself through eye rolls and insults, which telegraph that one partner believes that he or she possesses exclusive moral high ground within the relationship.

Signs of defensiveness become legion. A defensive spouse might respond to perceived criticism with verbal argumentativeness. A pattern of assuming the role of victim in the face of criticism is another form of excessive self-protection. When these three habits are practiced over time, stonewalling results. A spouse begins to withdraw emotionally from the relationship for self-protection or out of a sense of not knowing how to respond in a productive manner.

Gottman's Four Horsemen are intended to identify marital decay. This model can also be useful when measuring the quality of a person's relationship with God. But this is not a new insight, as today's text reveals.

B. Lesson Context

A predominant theme of the book of Isaiah is God's sovereignty over history. The fictitious pagan fertility gods were imagined to be caught in never-ending cycles of birth, life, and death. For pagans, history endlessly turned on itself. Their gods were doomed to the same repetitive beats as were mere mortals.

By contrast, the God of Israel stood outside of history. Since He brought all things into being (Isaiah 40:21-31), how could it be otherwise? He demonstrated mastery over history by giving Isaiah visions of what would occur before, during, and after the Babylonian exile. That tragedy extended from the destruction of the temple in 586 BC until release from captivity in 538 BC.

The most immediate new thing that God would do was to use a foreign power, Assyria, to accomplish His will by disciplining Israel for their sin and corruption. During Isaiah's tenure as a prophet (740–681 BC), Assyria was the region's sole superpower. Founded in Mesopotamia in about 1750 BC, that nation's period of most militant expansion began in about 1100 BC.

Assyria's most coveted prize, Egypt, lay to the west. However, several smaller nations on the eastern coast of the Mediterranean Sea, including the divided northern and southern kingdoms of Israel and Judah, stood in its path. The risk of invasion was constant.

Two centuries before Isaiah's time, King Solomon had accumulated immense wealth through his initiative of international commerce. That fact, along with prosperity in the interim, made the covenant people an attractive target for the aggressive Assyrian Empire. Both Israel and Judah experienced years of prosperity after they divided into two kingdoms (Isaiah 2:7; etc.). Assyria menaced both for years.

The threat diminished during the reigns of less bellicose Assyrian monarchs. However, Tiglath-pileser III (reigned 745–727 BC) renewed Assyrian designs against both Israel and Judah (2 Kings 15:29). The prophets Hosea and Amos had issued the earliest warnings, in the eighth century BC (examples: Hosea 10:6; Amos 3:11). At the time, their prophecies must have been seen as outlandish to a nation enjoying peace. But during Isaiah's ministry as a prophet, predicted doom became reality.

Ahaz, king of Judah from 735 to 715 BC, allied with Assyria to foil aggression by Aram and northern Israel, paying steep tribute in the process (2 Kings 16:7-8). Eventually, however, he felt pressure to rebel against Assyria and shift allegiance to Egypt. The prophets warned both northern Israel and southern Judah against such entanglements, but they were ignored (Hosea 7:11, 16; etc.). God instructed both nations to place their trust in Him, not pagan empires and their fictitious gods.

Beginning in the period of Hezekiah's reign (about 724–695 BC), Isaiah preached five "Woe Sermons" that included further warning against such alliances. These five sermons are found in Isaiah 28:1–33:24, each opening with the word *Woe* (28:1; 29:1; 30:1; 31:1; 33:1). The sermons establish the rationale behind God's judgment, yet also offer hope that God would someday restore the nation predicted to fall. Today's study concerns both.

Leading into today's text is a sad observation regarding ignorance of the Word of the Lord as delivered through the prophet (Isaiah 29:11-12).

I. Unfaithful Worship

(Isaiah 29:13-14)

A. Present Indifference to God (v. 13)

13. Wherefore the Lord said, Forasmuch as this people draw near me with their mouth, and with their lips do honour me, but have removed their heart far from me, and their fear toward me is taught by the precept of men.

The failure to heed the contents of the scroll in Isaiah 29:11-12 (not in our lesson text) results in (or results from) the characterization we see here: insincere piety. The people's worship was little more than "going through the motions"; it was empty and meaningless. *With their mouth, and with their lips* the people professed loyalty and devotion to God, but their hearts weren't in it.

Isaiah had confessed his own and his people's unclean lips when he was called by God (Isaiah 6:5). Here the lips appeared to speak what was right. But whatever pious words they uttered were nullified by hearts that had little passion or desire for a genuine relationship with God. Centuries later, Jesus would apply these very words to the scribes and Pharisees in His day (Matthew 15:1-

HOW TO SAY IT

Assyria	Uh-*sear*-ee-uh.
Babylon	*Bab*-uh-lun.
Mediterranean	*Med*-uh-tuh-***ray***-nee-un.
Mesopotamia	*Mes*-uh-puh-***tay***-me-uh.
Tiglathpileser	*Tig*-lath-pih-*lee*-zer.

9; Mark 7:5-8). There, Jesus adds His own characterization: *hypocrites.*

> *What Do You Think?*
> What self-tests can you conduct to ensure that your heart matches what you say about God?
> *Digging Deeper*
> Considering Mark 7:6, what level of importance will you attach to this task?

B. Future Awe of God (v. 14)

14. Therefore, behold, I will proceed to do a marvellous work among this people, even a marvellous work and a wonder: for the wisdom of their wise men shall perish, and the understanding of their prudent men shall be hid.

The Lord's response is to shatter the apathy with *a marvellous work among this people, even a marvellous work and a wonder*. Literally the promise is, "I will treat this people wonderfully, wonderfully and with wonder." This is something wonderful beyond description! But what is this wonderfully wonderful wonder? The second half of the verse before us is cited by Paul in 1 Corinthians 1:19 as justification for his statement "the preaching of the cross is to them that perish foolishness; but unto us which are saved it is the power of God" (1:18). Paul goes on to comment on how God has "made foolish the wisdom of this world" and brought it down to nothing by means of the cross (1:19-25).

The cross of Christ should move us to humble worship—the kind that was sadly lacking in Isaiah's day. No "precept of men" (Isaiah 29:13), no matter what it may be, can produce the degree of worship that the wonder of the cross can. May we who have accepted the crucified and risen Christ as Savior never lose our sense of wonder at that which so-called intellectual people of the world ridicule!

Wonderful?

A passenger on a large jet was acting strangely. He looked at the magazine in the seat-back pouch and whispered, "Wonderful!" He stroked the fabric of his seat cushion and repeated the word, "Wonderful!" He looked out the window and said, "Wonderful!" He looked at the flight attendant and murmured, "Wonderful!"

The eccentric man's seatmate was uneasy. "What's this 'Wonderful, wonderful!' all about?" he demanded.

"Up until two days ago, I had been blind since birth. I visited a gifted surgeon, and now I can see! Everything looks wonderful!"

God's wonderful work doesn't always look that way to us. It can look mundane or even foolish. It can look like a mere seat back pouch, or it can be seen in a hard worker doing her job as though she were employed by God (Colossians 3:23). What wonderful, godly, redeemed pieces of God's world can you celebrate today? —C. T.

> *What Do You Think?*
> What additional guardrails can you erect to protect yourself from worldly "wisdom" as this verse is used in 1 Corinthians 1:18-19?
> *Digging Deeper*
> What other texts speak to you on this issue?

II. Unfaithful Plans
(Isaiah 29:15-22)

A. Hidden Plans Are Judged (vv. 15-16)

15. Woe unto them that seek deep to hide their counsel from the Lord, and their works are in the dark, and they say, Who seeth us? and who knoweth us?

Those who fancy themselves to be wise and intelligent are frequently those who *seek deep to hide their counsel from the Lord*. This means that they stop at nothing to conceal their sinful plans from God. If only they would exert similar efforts to discover the truth that God has gone to great depths to reveal to humanity!

The wayward seem to believe that God is subject to the same limitations that restrict humans. Supposedly, He cannot know or see what is planned or done *in the dark*. But as David rightly observes, "Yea, the darkness hideth not from thee; but the night shineth as the day: the darkness and the light are both alike to thee" (Psalm 139:12;

compare Daniel 2:22; Jonah 2; and 1 Corinthians 4:5).

16. Surely your turning of things upside down shall be esteemed as the potter's clay: for shall the work say of him that made it, He made me not? or shall the thing framed say of him that framed it, He had no understanding?

The reason that the plotters and schemers of Isaiah 29:15 think and act as they do is that they have a faulty view of God. They have turned His authority structure *upside down*. Such is the inevitable outcome when humans refuse to acknowledge that they are created in the image of God (Genesis 1:26). They think of themselves as the potter, as if they were in charge.

But *the potter's clay* has no right to command the potter, and it is utter foolishness for the clay to deny that the potter made him or her (see Romans 9:21). The Hebrew word translated *framed* in this verse is a variation of the word used to describe how "the Lord God *formed* man of the dust of the ground" in Genesis 2:7.

True worship can never come from a mind-set that considers human beings to be the potter. This displays the utmost contempt for the true potter, who is God alone. Ignoring the prophet's insistence to trust God instead of pagan nations was absurd. Isaiah has painted the scene of a piece of fine art attempting to correct and guide the hand of the creating artist, even while the artist was immersed in the creative act!

> *What Do You Think?*
> What can and should you include in your prayers that will correctly acknowledge God's position relative to yours?
> *Digging Deeper*
> What Scriptures speak to you on this issue?

Appearances Can Be Deceiving

Wearing old work clothes, I was on my back underneath the church water fountain when I heard the entry door open. Because I didn't want to snake my arm out of the water fountain, I simply said, "Hello."

A man's voice said, "Hi."

Visual for Lesson 10. *Point to this visual and allow up to one minute of reflection before opening discussion on the questions associated with verse 13.*

When I turned a little, I could see his shoes and his salesman's display case in his hand. He asked, "You the only one here?" He was looking into the empty office.

"Yep," I said.

"I guess I'll come back another time when someone is here."

He was looking for someone in particular: the minister. I am he, but the visitor assumed I was the maintenance man. Because I didn't look like a preacher, he missed an opportunity to make a sale. Concurrently, I neglected the opportunity to share the gospel with a fellow human being. Neither of us was true to our calling. Isaiah would remind both the salesman and me to be who God created us to be. Do you do that? —C. T.

B. Followed by Flourishing (vv. 17-19)

17. Is it not yet a very little while, and Lebanon shall be turned into a fruitful field, and the fruitful field shall be esteemed as a forest?

Lebanon was known for its forests, which supplied lumber for building projects (see 2 Chronicles 2:8-9; 1 Kings 5:6). To take a majestic forest and create *a fruitful field* from it isn't a comment on the quality of the forest or the field as much as it is that of massive reversal. Likewise, fields that had already proven themselves fertile would become instead *forest*. Isaiah used these upheaval images as metaphors for the massive changes Israel would undergo when God renewed them in ways they never expected. This theme continues through the end of our printed text.

18. And in that day shall the deaf hear the words of the book, and the eyes of the blind shall see out of obscurity, and out of darkness.

Isaiah 29:11-12 (not in today's lesson text) described *the words of the book* as being incomprehensible and/or inaccessible. These go hand in hand with spiritual deafness and blindness (compare 42:19-25). But in the future, God's *words* will be so accessible to the people that even *the deaf* and *blind* would hear and read the words of the book (compare Psalms 146:8; Isaiah 32:1-4).

> *What Do You Think?*
> What can you do to protect yourself from spiritual blindness and deafness?
> *Digging Deeper*
> Are you more in danger of spiritual blindness resulting in spiritual deafness or vice versa?

19. The meek also shall increase their joy in the LORD, and the poor among men shall rejoice in the Holy One of Israel.

Those who normally find themselves oppressed by the mighty and wealthy will find themselves rejoicing over how God acts on their behalf. A key phrase here is *the Holy One of Israel.* It occurs in 31 verses in the Old Testament, and 25 of those are in Isaiah. The *joy* of which this verse speaks is to be found in Him (Isaiah 12:6), not in pagan nations (10:20; 31:1). He is the Maker (17:7; 45:11), the Lord God (30:15), the Redeemer (41:14; 43:14; 47:4; 48:17; 49:7; 54:5), the Lord of hosts (47:4).

The unholy spirits of the demonic realm correctly recognized the Holy One in the person of Jesus (Mark 1:24; Luke 4:34). Some humans correctly came to recognize Him that way as well (Acts 3:14; 1 John 2:20). In the Beatitudes, Jesus echoed the promises in the verse before us (Matthew 5:5; Luke 6:20).

C. Judgment for the Unjust (vv. 20-21)

20-21. For the terrible one is brought to nought, and the scorner is consumed, and all that watch for iniquity are cut off: that make a man an offender for a word, and lay a snare for him that reproveth in the gate, and turn aside the just for a thing of nought.

The purveyors of injustice will receive exactly the opposite of what is promised in Isaiah 29:19. God intended judges to uphold the concerns of the poor, and He reserves fierce anger for those who use their position to harm them (see Proverbs 28:27; Amos 5:10; Matthew 23:14).

D. Followed by Restoration (v. 22)

22. Therefore thus saith the LORD, who redeemed Abraham, concerning the house of Jacob, Jacob shall not now be ashamed, neither shall his face now wax pale.

God assured the nation by invoking the names of two patriarchs with whom God had established His covenant centuries before (Exodus 2:24; etc.). But the record of Scripture is that God's people proved themselves incapable and unwilling to maintain a holy status before God. Moses had introduced God's perfect law to the people (Exodus 20; etc.), but they did not obey it. Their restoration was not precipitated by renewed effort on their part, but in God's unilateral act of mercy.

III. Faithful Worship

(ISAIAH 29:23-24)

A. Based on God's Character (v. 23)

23. But when he seeth his children, the work of mine hands, in the midst of him, they shall sanctify my name, and sanctify the Holy One of Jacob, and shall fear the God of Israel.

If at the time of restoration, Jacob were to observe *Israel,* the nation bearing his name as changed by God (Genesis 32:28), he would see renewed devotion to God. In spite of the Israelites' unfaithfulness, they will remain as God's creative *work.* As such, God has remained committed to them until He finishes what He started in them. Human unfaithfulness does not deter God (see 2 Timothy 2:13).

To *sanctify* God's *name* is to acknowledge God's inherent holiness. We cannot add to God's holiness. But we can add to the number of those who know His holiness and also worship Him. Israel would come to worship and obey God with a sense of awe and reverence when He turns everything upside down (see Isaiah 29:17, above).

To *fear the God of Israel* is a parallel statement to *sanctify my name*. To do one is to do the other. The result is to be appropriate reverence for the Lord as He allows people the opportunity to marvel at His holiness. Since Jacob's name was changed to Israel, *the Holy One of Jacob* and *the God of Israel* are parallels. Calling God by either or both titles is to acknowledge that He chose Jacob/Israel, loved him from before he wrestled with God (Genesis 32:22-30), and proved that love by settling Jacob's descendants in the land of promise that would belong to his descendants (Psalm 136:21; compare Jeremiah 33:11; Hosea 2:23).

But that settlement and resettlement were only shadows of God's act of mercy ultimately accomplished through the work of Christ on the cross. Paul wrote, "If any man be in Christ, he is a new creature: old things are passed away; behold, all things are become new" (2 Corinthians 5:17). We come to Christ admitting that we depend on His generous gift of salvation (Ephesians 2:8-9) and the rest in our eternal home that is to follow (Hebrews 4).

B. Expressed Through God's Word (v. 24)

24. They also that erred in spirit shall come to understanding, and they that murmured shall learn doctrine.

This future time of renewal is to be marked by increased sensitivity to God's Word. The Hebrew word translated *murmured* occurs in only six other places in the Old Testament; in two of those, it is used of the wilderness wanderings who griped about their situation (Deuteronomy 1:27; Psalm 106:25). When the time of revival came to pass, the people would do the opposite as they value *doctrine* (compare Deuteronomy 32:2; Psalm 119).

Conclusion

A. Intimate Hearts

Today's passage offers hope for all who find themselves far from God despite any robust religious heritage. In every generation churches are filled with those who have devoted themselves fully to God. But there are also those who attend out of habit or a sense of duty. Outside observers might consider this group to be highly religious. However, their true spiritual state is not hidden from God. He feels the coldness of their worship. He sees the plans they make without consulting Him in prayer or study of Scripture. The unjust ways with which these congregants treat their neighbor are not hidden from God.

The way back now is the same as it was in Isaiah's day: regardless of our current level of spiritual fervency, we need to live mindful of the reality that God judges each person justly. We have to discard the illusions that our thoughts are private before God. He sees our true spiritual condition, even when we don't allow ourselves that same insight.

God the Father, through the completed work of Christ and the present indwelling of His Holy Spirit, is able and willing to free us so we can love Him with the entireties of our hearts, souls, and abilities (compare Deuteronomy 6:5; Matthew 22:37). There is no question regarding His ability and our inability in that regard. Neither is there any question about His willingness to do so. The only question on the table is our willingness to allow Him to renew us.

Are we?

What Do You Think?

Which thought in today's text do you have the hardest time coming to grips with? Why?

Digging Deeper

Considering Psalm 51:10; Luke 10:27; Ephesians 5:11; and 1 John 1:5-6, how will you resolve this difficulty?

B. Prayer

Father, we are ever capable of straying from You! May our worship and service to You never find us lacking in devotion. Renew our hearts today so that the unbelieving world can see Christ in us. In Jesus' name we pray. Amen.

C. Thought to Remember

God is able and willing to renew our hearts.

Involvement Learning

Enhance your lesson with KJV Bible Student *(from your curriculum supplier) and the reproducible activity page (at www.standardlesson.com or in the back of the* KJV Standard Lesson Commentary Deluxe Edition*).*

Into the Lesson

Write these two thoughts on the board as competing proposals:

1. Rituals are good and necessary

2. Rituals are damaging and dangerous

Ask half the class to make a list of reasons in favor of Proposal 1 while the other half makes a list supporting Proposal 2. (If the halves of the class total more than six learners each, have participants form smaller groups with duplicate assignments.) Contrast lists in the ensuing whole-class discussion. Record responses on the board as they are voiced.

Make a transition by saying, "We may be wondering if the Bible can help us sort through these opposing viewpoints. Let's find out as we turn to the prophet Isaiah."

Into the Word

Use the Lesson Context to locate today's text in a section of warning, or "Woe Sermons." (*Option.* To expand and deepen the study of the context, distribute copies of the "God's 'Woe to' Warnings" exercise from the activity page, to be completed by the same groups, above.)

After discussion of context reassign students into groups of four. Ask half the groups to create a list titled "Sins of God's People" as they work through the text. The other groups are to create a list titled "How God Will Respond" as they see promised in the lesson text. Allow five minutes and then reconvene for whole-class discussion of the lists. Challenge groups to examine the thoroughness of groups who had the other task.

Into Life

Display this definition:

***Ritual:** a series of actions performed according to a prescribed order.*

Below or beside it, display this definition:

***Ritualism:** the regular observance or practice of ritual, especially when excessive or without regard to its function.*

Contrast these to ensure that learners do not see the word *ritual* as an inherently negative word. When that is established, distribute handouts (you prepare) featuring three columns that are headed this way:

Rituals / Meaningless / Meaningful

Ask students to re-form their groups of four to complete the handout. Include instructions to list in the first column as many rituals of Christian worship as they can. In the middle column, they should jot down one or more ways that each of the rituals can become meaningless. In the third, they are to suggest what must happen in the Christian's heart for each of these rituals to become or remain meaningful to self and to God.

After several minutes, reconvene for whole-class discussion of suggestions. Spend most of the time discussing specific steps a Christian can take to make sure his or her heart is right with God so that worship rituals are not merely an exercise in going through the motions.

Option. Write this proposition on the board:

It is better to participate in Christian worship with little thought than to ignore it altogether.

Form the class into two debate teams: one to advocate the proposition, the other to deny it. Research debate formats ahead of time to decide which one best fits the nature and size of your class.

Option. Distribute copies of the "Searching for Meaning" exercise from the activity page, which you can download, as learners depart. To encourage after-class completion, stress that you will discuss results as a first order of business when the class meets again next week.

Preaching Doom

Devotional Reading: Jeremiah 38:7-13; 39:15-18
Background Scripture: Jeremiah 37–38

Jeremiah 38:14-23

14 Then Zedekiah the king sent, and took Jeremiah the prophet unto him into the third entry that is in the house of the Lord: and the king said unto Jeremiah, I will ask thee a thing; hide nothing from me.

15 Then Jeremiah said unto Zedekiah, If I declare it unto thee, wilt thou not surely put me to death? and if I give thee counsel, wilt thou not hearken unto me?

16 So Zedekiah the king sware secretly unto Jeremiah, saying, As the Lord liveth, that made us this soul, I will not put thee to death, neither will I give thee into the hand of these men that seek thy life.

17 Then said Jeremiah unto Zedekiah, Thus saith the Lord, the God of hosts, the God of Israel; If thou wilt assuredly go forth unto the king of Babylon's princes, then thy soul shall live, and this city shall not be burned with fire; and thou shalt live, and thine house:

18 But if thou wilt not go forth to the king of Babylon's princes, then shall this city be given into the hand of the Chaldeans, and they shall burn it with fire, and thou shalt not escape out of their hand.

19 And Zedekiah the king said unto Jeremiah, I am afraid of the Jews that are fallen to the Chaldeans, lest they deliver me into their hand, and they mock me.

20 But Jeremiah said, They shall not deliver thee. Obey, I beseech thee, the voice of the Lord, which I speak unto thee: so it shall be well unto thee, and thy soul shall live.

21 But if thou refuse to go forth, this is the word that the Lord hath shewed me:

22 And, behold, all the women that are left in the king of Judah's house shall be brought forth to the king of Babylon's princes, and those women shall say, Thy friends have set thee on, and have prevailed against thee: thy feet are sunk in the mire, and they are turned away back.

23 So they shall bring out all thy wives and thy children to the Chaldeans: and thou shalt not escape out of their hand, but shalt be taken by the hand of the king of Babylon: and thou shalt cause this city to be burned with fire.

Key Verse

Jeremiah said unto Zedekiah, If I declare it unto thee, wilt thou not surely put me to death? and if I give thee counsel, wilt thou not hearken unto me? **—Jeremiah 38:15**

Prophets Faithful to God's Covenant

Unit 3: Courageous Prophets of Change

Lessons 9–13

Lesson Aims

After participating in this lesson, each learner will be able to:

1. Explain the context of Jeremiah's ministry in the days of King Zedekiah.
2. Contrast Zedekiah's indecisiveness with Jeremiah's resolve.
3. Write one action to take in the week ahead to counteract an unholy trait that characterizes him or her in a weak moment.

Lesson Outline

Introduction
- A. Unheeded Warnings
- B. Lesson Context

I. A Secret Meeting (Jeremiah 38:14-16)
- A. Information Request (v. 14)
- B. Setting Terms (vv. 15-16)
  - *Listen Carefully*

II. A Private Prophecy (Jeremiah 38:17-23)
- A. Results of Obedience (vv. 17-20)
  - *Beware the Bypass*
- B. Consequences of Rebellion (vv. 21-23)

Conclusion
- A. A Successful Ministry
- B. Prayer
- C. Thought to Remember

Introduction

A. Unheeded Warnings

Katsuhiko Ishibashi, a seismologist and university professor in Japan, for years warned that many of Japan's nuclear power plants were at risk for significant damage from earthquakes. Though he and his colleagues warned about possible catastrophe, they were largely ignored. When a magnitude 9.0 earthquake occurred off the northeastern coast of Japan's main island in March 2011, the resulting tsunami caused massive damage to the nuclear power station in Fukushima.

The ensuing radioactive fallout forced some 160,000 people to evacuate their homes across an area of approximately 300 square miles. Studies and reports since published vindicate Ishibashi's warnings about possible disaster at the site.

When the nation of Judah faced God's wrath for their many violations of the covenant with God, the Lord commissioned Jeremiah to sound the warnings and call them to repentance. Perhaps it was not too late for this faltering nation and their king to avert the disaster and desolation that awaited them.

B. Lesson Context

The prophet Jeremiah delivered God's message to the nation of Judah from 627 until the mid-580s BC. That was roughly a century after the prophet Isaiah. Five kings reigned over Judah during Jeremiah's ministry. Josiah, the first of these five, was righteous (2 Kings 23:25). The four following him, however, were all wicked. These included Jehoiachin, who was removed from the throne and taken into captivity when the Babylonians invaded in 597 BC (24:12). King Nebuchadnezzar of Babylon replaced Jehoiachin with that man's uncle, Mattaniah, renaming him Zedekiah in the process (24:17).

Zedekiah wavered between service to the Babylonian king and rebellion against that overlord. Zedekiah ruled for Judah's final decade as a nation before it fell in 586 BC.

The destruction of Judah at the hands of Babylon that Isaiah had foreseen decades earlier (see 2 Kings 20:16-18) drew near during Jeremiah's day. Like the northern kingdom of Israel before, Judah's unfaithfulness to the covenant had exhausted the Lord's great patience. Jeremiah proclaimed that the Lord would use the Babylonians as instruments of judgment against Judah (Jeremiah 20:4-6).

Throughout his prophetic ministry, Jeremiah warned Jerusalem in word and in deed of the coming destruction. He illustrated this message in symbolic actions (examples: Jeremiah 13:1-11; 19:1-15; 27:1-11). Yet rarely did anyone take this prophet seriously (37:2). His oracles were misunderstood and dismissed as the rhetoric of a traitorous, pro-Babylonian sympathizer (37:11-13). Jerusalem's more "loyal" prophets proclaimed peace, safety, and deliverance. Their fabricated, uninspired message was believed among the populace.

Twice in Judah's closing months, while Jerusalem was under siege, Jeremiah endured punishments for his message of doom. First, he was beaten and held in a dungeon cell for many days (Jeremiah 37:15-16). Zedekiah, however, summoned him from the dungeon and released him into the courtyard of the guard (37:21). There he continued to reveal the unpleasant things God told him (38:1-3).

Zedekiah's officials took exception to Jeremiah's preaching because his warnings were deemed treasonous and demoralizing (Jeremiah 38:4). With Zedekiah unwilling to oppose them, the officials had Jeremiah put down into a muddy dungeon (38:6). But a high official named Ebed-melech gathered 30 men (also with Zedekiah's concession) to lift Jeremiah out of the mud and rescue him from certain death (38:8-13).

I. A Secret Meeting

(Jeremiah 38:14-16)

A. Information Request (v. 14)

14. Then Zedekiah the king sent, and took Jeremiah the prophet unto him into the third entry that is in the house of the Lord: and the king said unto Jeremiah, I will ask thee a thing; hide nothing from me.

When the Babylonians returned and besieged Jerusalem and defeat seemed near, *Zedekiah* began to summon *Jeremiah* for conversations. *The third entry that is in the house of the Lord* probably indicates a back entrance from the palace to the temple. The king apparently wanted a private setting where he could talk with Jeremiah outside of his officials' hearing (see Lesson Context). Perhaps Zedekiah thought that Jeremiah might reverse his oracles of judgment and the Lord would grant Jerusalem a reprieve after all.

This was not the first such conversation (see Jeremiah 34:6-7; 37:17). Zedekiah's repeated summoning of Jeremiah shows that at least part of him respected Jeremiah's advice, if not his standing as an inspired prophet of God. Yet his terse command that Jeremiah *hide nothing from* him shows that Zedekiah did not yet understand that Jeremiah always told the king everything God told the prophet.

B. Setting Terms (vv. 15-16)

15. Then Jeremiah said unto Zedekiah, If I declare it unto thee, wilt thou not surely put me to death? and if I give thee counsel, wilt thou not hearken unto me?

Jeremiah certainly feared for his life and may have considered whether repeating earlier warnings was worth the risk. God had given him assurances of protection at the time of his calling, even from kings and officials (Jeremiah 1:18-19; 15:20-21). Yet Jeremiah still feared, for he too was human with doubts (1:6; 15: 18; 20:7). Given recent events, he had every reason to believe that a harsh word against Zedekiah could spell his own demise (26:20-23).

Jeremiah surmised that Zedekiah was hoping for a more favorable word from the Lord this time. But the prophet also knew that no favorable word would be forthcoming.

HOW TO SAY IT

Ebed-melech	Ee-bed-*mee*-lek.
Jehoiachin	Jeh-*hoy*-uh-kin.
Josiah	Jo-*sigh*-uh.
Mattaniah	Mat-uh-*nye*-uh.
Nebuchadnezzar	*Neb*-yuh-kud-***nez***-er.
Zedekiah	Zed-uh-*kye*-uh.

> *What Do You Think?*
> Under what circumstances is it wise for you to question someone's motives, if ever? Why?
> *Digging Deeper*
> In what ways do 1 Corinthians 4:5; Philippians 1:15-18; and James 4:3 guide your answer?

Listen Carefully

I was in my truck listening to a new CD when I noticed a strange percussion instrument. The beat was out of place. The *doink* sound was annoying and didn't work well with the hymn "Whisper a Prayer." The song ended, but when "Morning Had Broken" started playing, there was that percussion beat again!

I turned up the music, and the misplaced beat faded. I drove home with the radio at full volume, no *doink* to be heard. But when I pulled into my driveway and turned the radio down, the sound returned! Then I saw the seat belt warning light flashing.

If I had fastened my seat belt, the percussive warning would have ended. I had ignored a warning that I was in danger. Like Zedekiah, I looked for solutions to the problem I *thought* I had instead of perceiving the real danger. What discord in your life is warning you about danger? —C. T.

16. So Zedekiah the king sware secretly unto Jeremiah, saying, As the Lord liveth, that made us this soul, I will not put thee to death, neither will I give thee into the hand of these men that seek thy life.

The king continued the secret conversation by giving *Jeremiah* the purported assurance of safety that he sought. Whether or not *Zedekiah* was sincere was one question; the more important question was whether he would follow through. His word meant little because, unlike his father, Josiah (2 Kings 23:24-25), or his brother Jehoiakim (Jeremiah 36:1-2, 4, 20-26), his character was not dependably good or evil.

Zedekiah believed he held Jeremiah's life in his hands. He ironically swore this oath by *the Lord . . . that made us this soul,* a poetic way of acknowledging that God gives life. The king inadvertently acknowledged that God is actually the one who decides between *life* and *death.*

II. A Private Prophecy

(Jeremiah 38:17-23)

A. Results of Obedience (vv. 17-20)

17a. Then said Jeremiah unto Zedekiah, Thus saith the Lord, the God of hosts, the God of Israel.

Jeremiah knew that this king would likely waffle, given past behavior (example: Jeremiah 34:8-22). Even so, the prophet still proclaimed the word from the Lord, come what may. This is the mark of true commitment. Jeremiah did not ask what Zedekiah wanted to learn or tell the king what he hoped to hear. Even if Jeremiah had wanted to withhold the message, he would have failed anyway. The word of God was like a fire in Jeremiah's bones (20:9), impossible to hold back whether anyone listened or not (6:10-11).

Piling up designations for *the Lord* emphasized that *the God of hosts* was the true king in Israel. God had allowed the Israelites to have a human king because they desired to be like the other nations (1 Samuel 8:5-9). He knew this was a result of faithlessness and would also lead to more faithlessness.

Referring to the Lord as *the God of Israel* has implications for how the people were called to conduct themselves (compare Leviticus 26). But idolatry and injustice had landed them in a position to face God's punishment. They did not act as people who belonged to the Lord.

17b. If thou wilt assuredly go forth unto the king of Babylon's princes, then thy soul shall live, and this city shall not be burned with fire; and thou shalt live, and thine house.

The Lord's offer to spare Zedekiah's life upon surrender to the Babylonians accords with terms previously stated (Jeremiah 21:8-9). God's offer to spare the *city* from fiery destruction might seem like an astonishing, last-minute reversal (compare 21:10; 34:2, 22; 37:9-10). But the Lord has the freedom to change His mind about either blessing or punishment for a nation that alters its course

(Jeremiah 18:5-10). He did so for Nineveh at the preaching of Jonah (Jonah 3:10). The Lord did not offer a solution in which Zedekiah was allowed to remain king in Jerusalem. But the Lord did offer a solution that would avoid Jerusalem's being burned to the ground or Zedekiah's experiencing great personal violence.

The nation of Judah apparently had chances early on to avert disaster entirely (Jeremiah 4:1-4). Yet God eventually was determined unreservedly to punish Judah (4:27-28). Although judgment in Babylon was by this time assured, God still offered mercy to His people and their king (compare 1 Kings 21:20-29). Nonetheless, Jeremiah offered a glimpse of what would occur if Zedekiah made other choices. Accepting God's mercy in judgment would mitigate some of the horrible consequences that otherwise would follow.

Christians still experience God's discipline tempered by His mercy, even though we don't always recognize it as such (1 Corinthians 11:31-32; Hebrews 12:4-11). This is part of the process of God's using all things for our good (Romans 8:28). This isn't to say we will enjoy all things or that all things will seem good at some point. Instead, *all* things that happen to us and around us are meant to make us into the image of Jesus (8:29).

18. But if thou wilt not go forth to the king of Babylon's princes, then shall this city be given into the hand of the Chaldeans, and they shall burn it with fire, and thou shalt not escape out of their hand.

Jeremiah's words implicitly called for Zedekiah to ignore the officials who were urging him not to surrender (Jeremiah 27:12-15). But beyond Zedekiah's lack of character and the grave sins of Judah, there was another reason Jeremiah could be resigned to Jerusalem's being burned by *the Chaldeans.* The prophets had been warning of Judah's destruction for many years (2 Kings 21:10-15; Isaiah 39:6; Micah 3:12; compare Jeremiah 7:25-26; 25:4; 26:17-18). Though God can change His mind (see commentary on Jeremiah 38:17b, above), He also clearly stated that blessing resulted from obedience and curses came from faithlessness (Deuteronomy 30:15-18). Without repentance and obedience, Jerusalem had no hope of experiencing God's great mercy.

19. And Zedekiah the king said unto Jeremiah, I am afraid of the Jews that are fallen to the Chaldeans, lest they deliver me into their hand, and they mock me.

Had *Zedekiah* feared the Babylonians themselves, it would be hard to blame him. Even fearing his own officials is understandable to an extent, since his predecessor, Jehoiakim, was probably murdered by his own officials the last time the Babylonians invaded (Jeremiah 22:18-19; 36:29-31).

The fear he expressed at this point, however, seems comparatively insignificant. Some of Jerusalem's citizenry already had surrendered to the Babylonians (here called *Chaldeans*). Zedekiah did not want to expose himself to their scorn or potential murderous mistreatment.

What Do You Think?

Which speaks to you most deeply: the moral courage of Jeremiah or the moral cowardice of Zedekiah? Why?

Digging Deeper

What does that motivate you to do?

Beware the Bypass

When driving, we want to get to our destination as quickly as possible. Faster is better, and we dislike any kind of inconvenience. To wait at a stoplight can be a major annoyance. For some, driving slowly in a queue of traffic can quickly turn annoyance into infuriation. In the name of convenience, freeways bypass town after town. We love to jump on the interstate, put the car on cruise control, and just go!

Living life in the fast lane is appealing. But where are we going so quickly? Zedekiah was hoping for a quick way to avoid the troubles that Jeremiah said were coming. But by looking for a bypass, Zedekiah actually set himself and the people on the fast track to destruction. If you're taking spiritual shortcuts, are you actually bypassing the *true* way as revealed by God? —C. T.

20. But Jeremiah said, They shall not deliver thee. Obey, I beseech thee, the voice of the Lord, which I speak unto thee: so it shall be well unto thee, and thy soul shall live.

Zedekiah had tried to make the issue into a purely political matter, but he was oblivious to the real issue. *Jeremiah* thus directed the king back to the core spiritual realities.

Obedience to *the Lord* was Zedekiah's only viable course of action. The promise *thy soul shall live* probably referred more to quality of life than mere survival, for Zedekiah was already guaranteed to survive (Jeremiah 34:4-5). Indeed, the quality of Zedekiah's life after remaining rebellious to both God and Nebuchadnezzar ended up being quite poor (52:8-11).

B. Consequences of Rebellion (vv. 21-23)

21. But if thou refuse to go forth, this is the word that the Lord hath shewed me.

Jeremiah made clear that this preview of the future comes from God. Contrary to what Zedekiah might have thought, the prophet himself could not set the course. He had no more control over what happened than a weather forecaster has control over the weather.

> *What Do You Think?*
> How can we overcome the fear of "negative talk" when such talk is clearly called for?
> *Digging Deeper*
> If a context required negative talk on your part, how would you prepare for the likelihood of being called judgmental?

22. And, behold, all the women that are left in the king of Judah's house shall be brought forth to the king of Babylon's princes, and those women shall say, Thy friends have set thee on, and have prevailed against thee: thy feet are sunk in the mire, and they are turned away back.

Zedekiah's *house* would fall if he didn't do as the Lord had revealed (see Jeremiah 38:17, above). This could refer to his family in general, his descendants, or (less likely) the Davidic line entirely.

Jeremiah painted a picture of Zedekiah's *women* (referring to wives and concubines) ridiculing him as they became captives to the Babylonians. Women in war suffer immensely at the hands of oppositional forces. If Zedekiah cared for the women of his household, he would follow Jeremiah's counsel. That would spare the women's being taken into the houses of *Babylon's princes* for whatever purpose those men desired.

Maybe to curry favor and maybe just out of heartbreak, the women would mock Zedekiah because of his officials' treachery. Many of those advisers already had deserted him (Jeremiah 37:19), and the rest would soon follow. Jeremiah knew what betrayal felt like (20:10) as well as having his *feet . . . sunk in the mire* (38:6). Zedekiah would have no Ebedmelech to rescue him from the metaphorical pit (38:7-13). Jeremiah hoped this grim vision would appeal to the king's fear and self-interest and result in obedience.

23. So they shall bring out all thy wives and thy children to the Chaldeans: and thou shalt not escape out of their hand, but shalt be taken by the hand of the king of Babylon: and thou shalt cause this city to be burned with fire.

Jeremiah built on his dire prophecies by emphasizing that not only Zedekiah's *wives* but also his *children* would go into Babylonian exile. Like their mothers, children suffer horribly in wartimes. This is a clear escalation of Jeremiah's appeal not to Zedekiah's logical side but to his emotional center. What father would willingly subject his children to seeing their mothers *taken* captive and their *city . . . burned with fire*?

> *What Do You Think?*
> Should consequences for others be the primary factor in your moral choices? Why, or why not?
> *Digging Deeper*
> What biblical passages support your answer?

Yet even hearing the sad fate that awaited his family failed to move Zedekiah. He was more concerned about keeping the secret from his officials, maybe even protecting Jeremiah, than about obedience to God or the consequences that awaited him (see Jeremiah 38:24-26, not in our printed text).

The dates given in Jeremiah 39:1-2 compute to a siege of 18 months, ending on July 18, 586 BC. The king and some of his soldiers fled Jerusalem at night (Jeremiah 39:4; 2 Kings 25:4; compare Ezekiel 12:12). The Babylonians hunted him down, however, and captured him.

Zedekiah's sentence was to see his sons put to death before his own eyes, be blinded afterward, then taken in shackles to Babylon (2 Kings 25:7). His officials, what few remained at that point, were executed (Jeremiah 39:6). The city of Jerusalem was burned to the ground (2 Kings 25:9).

Zedekiah's demise came by God's hand (Jeremiah 34:22; Ezekiel 12:13-14). That was something even the Babylonians themselves realized (Jeremiah 40:1-3). Such was the fate of one who trusted in human wisdom rather than believing that God would do what He said (Proverbs 3:5-8).

Visual for Lesson 11. *While pointing to this visual, ask learners for examples of times when they faced consequences for not properly heeding warnings.*

Conclusion

A. A Successful Ministry

What other ministry of doom would we hold in such high esteem as Jeremiah's? He was a failure by human standards: accused falsely instead of believed, persecuted by officials, betrayed by family. No one obeyed Jeremiah's words. Even after his predictions about Zedekiah and Jerusalem were fulfilled, Jeremiah continued to be disbelieved and dismissed (Jeremiah 43:1-3).

Yet from the standpoint of faith, the life of Jeremiah was successful by God's standards. The contrast between him and Zedekiah could hardly be starker. Zedekiah was one whose mind wavered moment by moment as he tried to save his own skin in his own way. He had no meaningful faith, no courage, no enduring principles. All the while Jeremiah remained true to his calling, willing to deliver the word of God, even though he knew it could cost him dearly. He was open to God's leading even through doubts, tears, and fears. Those are the marks of real success.

Jeremiah is a book for today's times. Christians too can expect the world to ignore our message and ridicule our convictions. We can expect hostility to arise in areas where the gospel is proclaimed boldly.

In some nations, this results in loss of relevancy and influence. In others, it results in torture, rape, or beheading. Though Christ is with us always (Matthew 28:20), Christian discipleship carries no guarantee of personal comfort or applause. But like Jeremiah, we must learn to see the world as God sees it and remain true to our calling. We must continually pray that we will speak the truth boldly (Ephesians 6:19-20).

What Do You Think?

Which thought in today's text do you have the hardest time coming to grips with? Why?

Digging Deeper

Considering how your decisions can affect others, what extra effort will you expend to resolve this uncertainty?

B. Prayer

Father, teach us what it means to live successfully in Your sight. Give us the strength to proclaim Your message to the world boldly, come what may. In Jesus' name we pray. Amen.

C. Thought to Remember

Proclaiming God's message is risky,
but to ignore that message is fatal.

Involvement Learning

Enhance your lesson with KJV Bible Student *(from your curriculum supplier) and the reproducible activity page (at www.standardlesson.com or in the back of the* KJV Standard Lesson Commentary Deluxe Edition*).*

Into the Lesson

Introduce a game of opposites by stating that you are going to write a word on the board and class members are to voice opposite meanings. State that responses cannot include any part of the word you write (examples: *untruthful* and *fearless* are disallowed as responses for opposites of *truthful* and *fearful*).

Start by writing the word *courageous*. After jotting learner responses next to it, proceed likewise with the words *petty, resolute, truthful,* and *fearful*. Keep the process moving briskly. Depending on the nature and size of your class, one or more of these options may be appropriate:

Option 1: Put the words on handouts for use by small groups or study pairs. *Option 2:* Announce that no one can answer twice until everyone has answered once. *Option 3:* Use brainstorming, in which no evaluation of the responses is allowed.

Make a transition by gesturing to the board as you say, "People are complex creatures who can be curious mixtures of these at various times. Let's see how today's text helps us sort through these with two examples from history." (Leave everything on the board throughout the lesson.)

Into the Word

Before a volunteer reads today's printed text aloud, ask half the class to be alert for King Zedekiah's motives and thoughts among the words and their opposites you have left on the board. Ask the other half to do the same regarding the prophet Jeremiah. After the reading, allow class members to tell what they heard; put a *Z* on the board next to words that apply to Zedekiah; use the letter *J* to do the same regarding Jeremiah.

Option. Reinforce the lesson by giving each learner one of the six false statements from the "Fixing Falsehoods" exercise on the activity page, which you can download. Read the instructions aloud. Allow one minute for learners to fix their statements and find the passage in today's text that validates the fix. Compare results among those who have the same statement.

Option. To place today's study in the larger context of the relationship between Zedekiah and Jeremiah, distribute copies of the "Three Confrontations" exercise from the activity page. Have each learner consult with one or two others to complete it as indicated. Compare results in ensuing whole-class discussion.

Into Life

Distribute handouts (you prepare) that list the following proposals:

- Faithfulness to God doesn't always result in an easy life.
- God's mercy will stretch far, but eventually He may exert punishment.
- Self-interest can blind us to God's will.
- God will not ignore unfaithfulness.

Ask students in groups of four to six to decide how today's lesson illustrates each proposal. After six or eight minutes, allow class members to compare and contrast their responses with those of other groups in whole-class discussion.

Return to the words listed on the board from the opening activity and ask learners to select silently one of the negative words that most characterizes them in a weak moment. Follow by then asking to write one step they can take in the week ahead to move themselves closer to the opposite of that negative word.

Call for volunteers to share what they've written in both regards, but don't put anyone on the spot to do so. Be prepared to reveal your own negative inclination and needed step away from it.

End with a time of guided prayer. Mention each positive attribute of Jeremiah and pause after each to allow class members time to pray silently about how it can be a stronger attribute of their own relationship with God.

Preaching to the Exiles

Devotional Reading: Psalm 147
Background Scripture: Ezekiel 18

Ezekiel 18:1-9, 30-32

1 The word of the LORD came unto me again, saying,

2 What mean ye, that ye use this proverb concerning the land of Israel, saying, The fathers have eaten sour grapes, and the children's teeth are set on edge?

3 As I live, saith the Lord GOD, ye shall not have occasion any more to use this proverb in Israel.

4 Behold, all souls are mine; as the soul of the father, so also the soul of the son is mine: the soul that sinneth, it shall die.

5 But if a man be just, and do that which is lawful and right,

6 And hath not eaten upon the mountains, neither hath lifted up his eyes to the idols of the house of Israel, neither hath defiled his neighbour's wife, neither hath come near to a menstruous woman,

7 And hath not oppressed any, but hath restored to the debtor his pledge, hath spoiled none by violence, hath given his bread to the hungry, and hath covered the naked with a garment;

8 He that hath not given forth upon usury, neither hath taken any increase, that hath withdrawn his hand from iniquity, hath executed true judgment between man and man,

9 Hath walked in my statutes, and hath kept my judgments, to deal truly; he is just, he shall surely live, saith the Lord GOD.

. . . .

30 Therefore I will judge you, O house of Israel, every one according to his ways, saith the Lord GOD. Repent, and turn yourselves from all your transgressions; so iniquity shall not be your ruin.

31 Cast away from you all your transgressions, whereby ye have transgressed; and make you a new heart and a new spirit: for why will ye die, O house of Israel?

32 For I have no pleasure in the death of him that dieth, saith the Lord GOD: wherefore turn yourselves, and live ye.

Key Verse

All souls are mine; as the soul of the father, so also the soul of the son is mine: the soul that sinneth, it shall die. —**Ezekiel 18:4**

Photo: Getty Images

Prophets Faithful to God's Covenant

Unit 3: Courageous Prophets of Change

Lessons 9–13

Lesson Aims

After participating in this lesson, each learner will be able to:

1. Quote the mistaken proverb the exiles believed.
2. Explain the reasons for the exiles' misconception regarding how God judges people.
3. Evaluate his or her preparedness to identify, avoid, and correct blame-shifting.

Lesson Outline

Introduction

A. Imagined Righteousness

The phrase *vicarious nostalgia* refers to a feeling of yearning for a past that one never actually lived. This term could describe a person born in the 1980s who loves a 1950s aesthetic and thinks of those years as simpler and better in many ways. It can describe a desire to return to "the good old days" that didn't actually happen the way one imagines or even remembers.

For years, Garrison Keillor hosted a popular radio show in which he told touching and humorous stories about the citizens of a small fictional town in Minnesota. Each week he closed his program with the familiar sign-off, "Well, that's the news from Lake Wobegon, where all the women are strong, all the men are good-looking, and all the children are above average." These descriptions are obviously caricatures, meant to capture a feeling of community pride more than an attainable reality. Yet, a place like Lake Wobegon can inspire vicarious nostalgia for all of us who live more complicated lives than the strong women, good-looking men, and brilliant children of that town.

An overstated self-assessment is dangerous enough in nostalgia. However, lacking a correct view of oneself is a devastating flaw. In this week's lesson, the exiles didn't understand their own role in the difficult situation the nation was facing. They assigned fault to their parents while claiming their own moral innocence.

B. Lesson Context

Ezekiel, a contemporary of Jeremiah, prophesied during and after the final chaotic years of the kingdom of Judah. He was called by God "in the fifth day of the [fourth] month . . . which was the fifth year of king Jehoiachin's captivity" (Ezekiel 1:1-2). Jehoiachin reigned only three months in 597 BC before the Babylonians conquered Jerusalem and took him, along with thousands of the most prominent and skilled people of Judah, to Babylon (2 Kings 24:14). This detail dates the beginning of Ezekiel's book in 592 BC.

The group of deportees included the prophet Ezekiel (Ezekiel 1:1-3). The ruin of Jerusalem was devastating for the exiles. Jeremiah's book of Lamentations captures the anguish that the destruction of the city and loss of human life caused (see lesson 8). Though some were left in Jerusalem and wider Judah, the survivors to whom Ezekiel spoke were those taken away to Babylon (see lesson 8 Lesson Context). They lived together by the river Chebar.

The Babylonian exile created great uncertainty about the people's relationship with God. Could God, who had allowed His holy city to be ravaged and His people carried into exile, still care for the people? And if He still cared, could He actually *take* care of them in a foreign nation?

I. A Proverb

(Ezekiel 18:1-4)

A. Repeated by the People (vv. 1-2)

1. The word of the Lord came unto me again, saying.

The word of the Lord is a common phrase used in Ezekiel to emphasize that the Lord spoke to His prophet. This phrase occurs dozens of time in this book—far more often than in any other Bible book. Its frequent use in Ezekiel emphasizes that God communicated with His people even in exile. His continuing to speak to Ezekiel was meant in part to reassure the people that God was still with them in a foreign land.

Selective Hearing

My son was playing a video game. At the door of his room, I shouted, "Turn that noise down!"

No response. That's when it dawned on me: he couldn't hear. *That's why he doesn't always do what I ask him!* I thought.

I went into the kitchen to look up the number of an audiologist as I popped the tab of a cold soda. I didn't get the cola to my lips before I heard my son shout, "Would you bring me one too?" He couldn't hear me ask to turn down the noise, but he heard a soda-can tab from two rooms away! He didn't have an auditory problem; he had selective hearing.

But don't we all? We only hear fully what we want to hear. Like teenagers with parents, we can selectively ignore the word of the Lord. Are you *really* listening to God? —C. T.

2. What mean ye, that ye use this proverb concerning the land of Israel, saying, The fathers have eaten sour grapes, and the children's teeth are set on edge?

As the exiles wallowed in the misery of their situation, now in its sixth or seventh year (Ezekiel 8:1; 20:1), they naturally tried to come to grips with the reason for it. In so doing, they landed on a *proverb* that became popular. A proverb is a short, pithy statement used to express a general truth in a memorable way. The prophet Jeremiah was also confronted with this same proverb in his situation back in Judea (Jeremiah 31:29-30).

The Targum, a first-century AD Aramaic paraphrase of the Hebrew Bible, gives the meaning of the proverb: "The fathers sin, the children suffer." Therefore, *The fathers have eaten sour grapes, and the children's teeth are set on edge* expresses the belief that those in exile (the children) are unjustly bearing the punishment for the sins of earlier generations (the parents). Claiming that their problem is inherited, the exiles deny responsibility or guilt on their part.

> *What Do You Think?*
> What old sayings do you need to let go of? Who will hold you accountable for progress?
> *Digging Deeper*
> How does Lamentations 5:7 (lesson 8); Matthew 5:27-28; etc., illustrate a need to do so?

The proverb has some truth to it in that the sins of one generation can have lasting effects on the next. We may think of how children suffer today when a breadwinning parent is sent to jail for a crime. Ezekiel himself pointed out that the exile was the result of covenant unfaithfulness by many generations of Israelites (Ezekiel 16). God had revealed himself as the one "visiting the iniquity of the fathers upon the children unto the third and fourth generation" (Exodus 20:5). The exiles' ancestors were indeed guilty (example: 2 Kings 21:1-16). But this generation had been expelled from the promised land because of their own sin.

B. Refuted by God (vv. 3-4)

3. As I live, saith the Lord God, ye shall not have occasion any more to use this proverb in Israel.

The fact that the sins of one generation have consequences for another is not the same as saying that God punishes an innocent group for the sins of a guilty group. Although there are times when the all-knowing and sovereign God deems this to be fitting, it is rare and certainly not the norm. The problem in today's text is that the exiles specifically apply their *proverb* to disavow any culpability for their situation. In so doing, they can claim that God is unjust in his dealings with them (Ezekiel 18:25-29; 33:17-20).

> *What Do You Think?*
> In what ways will the truism in Proverbs 26:9 guide your use and non-use of maxims?
> *Digging Deeper*
> What foundational problem do you see when you compare these two old sayings: "Too many cooks spoil the broth" and "Many hands make light work"?

4. Behold, all souls are mine; as the soul of the father, so also the soul of the son is mine: the soul that sinneth, it shall die.

Everyone belongs to God since He is the sovereign Creator. This included His chosen people as well as their Babylonian oppressors. His justice was not and is not limited by national borders (see Ezekiel 25–32). Therefore He has the right to declare that *the soul that sinneth, it shall die.* Each person is responsible to God for his or her own sin, and God will deal with each person individually. In giving the Israelites His law, God commanded that "fathers shall not be put to death for the children, neither shall the children be put to death for the fathers: every man shall be put to death for his own sin" (Deuteronomy 24:16).

This principle applied to how God dealt with His exiled people. His judgments are fair and true. It was pointless for the exiles to insist on their innocence (Romans 3:23). The apostle Paul echoed Ezekiel's words by stating that "the wages of sin is death" (6:23).

II. A Case Study
(Ezekiel 18:5-9)

A. A Man's Actions (vv. 5-9a)

5. But if a man be just, and do that which is lawful and right.

This verse sets up the first of three case studies. The second and third, in Ezekiel 18:10-17, are not part of today's lesson text. For the hypothetical *man* introduced here to be *just* is another, parallel way of saying that he does *that which is lawful and right.* It's interesting to note how rare it is for the Hebrew words translated "just," "lawful," and "right" to occur in the same verse; the only other place is Jeremiah 23:5. Specifics follow.

6a. And hath not eaten upon the mountains, neither hath lifted up his eyes to the idols of the house of Israel.

Eating *upon the mountains* refers to participation in idolatrous cult practices that were common in the mountain regions (compare 2 Kings 23:1-8; contrast 21:1-3). These high places featured altars, often dedicated to the worship of Canaanite deities such as Baal. To look *to the idols of Israel* was to worship and seek help from false gods or to make an image of the true God for worship.

Proper love for God begins with worshipping no other gods (compare Exodus 20:3-6). The righteous person didn't turn to false gods for assistance. He or she remained dependent on God alone for health and protection.

The exiles were hundreds of miles away from the high places of their fathers' idols. But the exiles were surrounded by the countless deities of the Babylonians. The temptation of straying to other gods remained real, especially when the exiles considered their uncertainty regarding God's continuing care.

6b. Neither hath defiled his neighbour's wife, neither hath come near to a menstruous woman.

The just man also was careful to stay morally pure. The Law of Moses prohibited not only adultery (Exodus 20:14) but also intercourse during a woman's menstrual period (Leviticus 15:19-33; 18:19). The penalty for violation of the latter was that "both of them shall be cut off from among their people" (20:18). Some suggest that the reason for this restriction was because of the special role of blood in atoning for sins, respecting certain rights of women, or to maintain ceremonial purity. Whatever the reason, the righteous man observed this statute as well.

7. And hath not oppressed any, but hath restored to the debtor his pledge, hath spoiled none by violence, hath given his bread to the hungry, and hath covered the naked with a garment.

The righteous man also exhibits godly love toward others. Righteousness consists of more than merely doing no harm. A just person uses his or her resources to provide for the material needs of others (James 2:15-16). These examples are all forms of economic righteousness shown to *the debtor* and *the hungry* and *the naked*. These are representative of other needy neighbors as well.

We note that all the positive and negative actions addressed here are covered in the Law of Moses (see Exodus 20:15; 21:2; 22:21, 26-27; Deuteronomy 15:7-11; 23:19-20). The righteous man never lies about or wrongs a neighbor for any reason, in careful obedience to Deuteronomy 5:20-21. Rather, he keeps his distance from evil and all forms of judicial corruption (16:19). In short, such a man puts God's law above any opportunity to gain at the expense of another.

8. He that hath not given forth upon usury, neither hath taken any increase, that hath withdrawn his hand from iniquity, hath executed true judgment between man and man.

The economically vulnerable often found themselves (and still do today) in positions where they had no choice but to accept the terms of predatory lenders. God viewed the practice as evidence that His people had forgotten Him (Ezekiel 22:12). He is the protector of the downtrodden, and He expected His people to be the same (Psalm 82:3; Proverbs 14:31).

While the wicked people took advantage of the poor in various ways, the righteous person in Israel did not charge interest on loans *(usury)* to fellow Israelites. And while interest could be charged to a foreigner, it still had to be restrained (Deuteronomy 23:19-20).

What Do You Think?

If your locality had a ballot initiative to limit interest rates charged on so-called payday loans, should this text be used to influence how Christians vote on it? Why, or why not?

Digging Deeper

How do Matthew 25:27 and Luke 19:23 influence your response, if at all? Why?

9a. Hath walked in my statutes, and hath kept my judgments, to deal truly.

Here we have a sparkling example of the parallelism that is a hallmark of Hebrew poetry: *hath walked* is another way of saying *hath kept*. Likewise, God's *statutes* are the same as His *judgments*. These same two sets of parallels of the underlying Hebrew terms are also found in Ezekiel 11:20; 18:9; 20:19, 21; 37:24. Comprehensively, the righteous person does not follow the selfish, sinful ways of others in any respect.

B. God's Verdict (v. 9b)

9b. He is just, he shall surely live, saith the Lord GOD.

God will not judge or punish the *just* person for the sins of others—period. We may note in passing that the capitalization of the phrase *the Lord GOD* indicates different Hebrew words than does the capitalization of the phrase "the LORD . . . God" as the latter occurs in, for example, Ezekiel 20:5b. There are three single-word Hebrew names for God in the Old Testament: Yahweh, Adonai, and Elohim. The phrases "the Lord GOD" and "the LORD . . . God" indicate different combinations of these names.

III. A Call

(EZEKIEL 18:30-32)

A. To Repent (vv. 30-31)

30-31a. Therefore I will judge you, O house of Israel, every one according to his ways, saith the Lord GOD. Repent, and turn yourselves from all your transgressions; so iniquity shall not be your ruin. Cast away from you all your transgressions, whereby ye have transgressed.

What follows recalls Solomon's prayer that God would forgive the people of their sins and heal their land when they repented (2 Chronicles 6:36-39). Israel's sense of national connectedness had diminished following the division into two kingdoms after Solomon's death in 930 BC. A sense of moral responsibility for the sins of the community followed. However, the Scriptures insist that both guilt and salvation have a corporate aspect (example: 1 Corinthians 5:6-11). Sinful characteristics are transmitted from generation to generation. But God affirmed that He would also judge each person individually, according to his or her walk before God.

This is important enough to restate in a slightly different way. God said that He would judge the *house of Israel* [collective singular, corporate aspect], *every one of you according to his ways* [personal singular]. Although each person was responsible for his or her own guilt before the Lord, individual decisions affected the community as a whole. The collective singular *house of* shows that the covenant God had with Israel was corporate; it included the whole of Israel. The singular *every one of you* shows that the overall moral tone of the community was formed on the collective choices of individuals. The Israelites were to look not at the conduct of their ancestors but to their own. The people were to rid themselves of any and all personal sin. To repent is to avoid the judgment of death that sin brings. God would be gracious and forgive all who turned to Him in repentance.

What Do You Think?

What are some practical ways for Christians to be accountable to one another in keeping sin in the rearview mirror?

Digging Deeper

Which kinds of biblical texts most help you in letting go of sin: texts that stress the positive results of doing so, or texts that stress the negative result for not doing so?

31b. And make you a new heart and a new spirit: for why will ye die, O house of Israel?

Those in the generation experiencing exile were worthy of the judgment that also could have fallen on the prior generation. However, God was equally clear that condemnation wasn't inevitable. He defined repentance as the rejection of one's past sinful ways, and He appealed to the *house of Israel* to accept *a new heart and a new spirit.* God had already promised to do this (Ezekiel 11:19).

God's rhetorical question *Why will ye die?* meant that the sentence of death was not inevitable since God extended an offer of forgiveness through repentance. Each individual had the freedom to choose life or death. If the people did not have free will, then they would not have been responsible. People are capable of knowing right from wrong, and God deals with us on that basis. The blame for one's sin and judgment cannot be shifted to God, Satan, nature, nurture, parents, or circumstances.

B. To Live (v. 32)

32. For I have no pleasure in the death of him that dieth, saith the Lord God: wherefore turn yourselves, and live ye.

God takes *no pleasure* in the destruction of His creation (Ezekiel 33:11). He wants to deliver people from their unfaithfulness and *the death* that it brings. He judges, but He also provides all people with the means of salvation, so they can avoid that judgment. God issues an invitation to repent and live, as He has done so many times before. He demonstrates love by his willingness to set people free from their sinful past and the punishment they deserve (John 3:16; 2 Peter 3:9). Yet He demonstrates His holiness by not allowing sin to continue indefinitely.

Autonomy

I find the reality of autonomous vehicles terrifying. Thinking about it causes me to remember a joke from the days when aviation was young.

A passenger airplane had reached its cruising altitude. A recorded message came over the speakers, reminding the passengers to keep their seat belts on. That was followed by an announcement: "The captain will soon come back to greet you. Don't worry, the plane is on automatic pilot, and nothing can go wrong, nothing can go wrong, nothing can go wrong . . ."

Autonomous cars. Autonomous planes. Autonomous people. We are constantly in the presence of men and women who have wrested their lives from God and are moving forward on autopilot. How often are we numbered among them as we fight for control that is rightly only God's? Only by repenting and turning back to God with our whole lives can we expect to be forgiven our sins and live fully. —C. T.

Conclusion

A. Actual Righteousness

The exiles imagined themselves to be the victims of a cosmic injustice. They viewed themselves as serving a sentence intended for the prior generation. The history of God's people reveals that they had always been incapable of keeping the covenant. Before Moses brought the Ten Commandments down from Mount Sinai, Aaron had already constructed the gold calf and led the people into idolatry. The book of Judges outlines the nation's checkered history of obeying God.

The exiles were not unique in their ability to view themselves as morally superior to the prior generation. Jesus called out similar duplicity in the Pharisees, who insisted that if they had been alive at the time of the prophets, they would not have murdered them (Matthew 23:30). Indeed, they had already plotted to kill Jesus (12:14). The apostle Paul's words "Let God be true, but every man a liar" (Romans 3:4) fit well in Ezekiel's defense of God's justice.

The hearts of the people were always incapable of obeying God fully. So God promised a new creative act: He would give the people new hearts, ones capable of being sensitive and obedient to God's Word.

HOW TO SAY IT

Adonai (Hebrew)	Ad-owe-*nye*.
Canaanite	*Kay*-nun-ite.
Chebar	*Kee*-bar.
Elohim (Hebrew)	El-o-*heem*.
Jehoiachin	Jeh-*hoy*-uh-kin.
Yahweh (Hebrew)	*Yaw*-way.

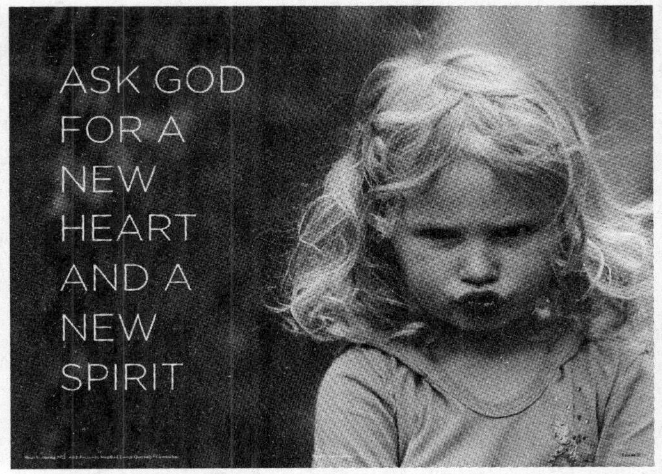

ASK GOD
FOR A
NEW
HEART
AND A
NEW
SPIRIT

Visual for Lesson 12. *Point to this visual to introduce a contrast between maturity levels of God's intent (v. 31) and people's proverb (v. 2).*

This truth was intended to prevent Ezekiel's audience from slipping into the despair or apathy that came with believing they were the victims of their parents' decisions. Each person was charged with the responsibility of turning from his or her sinful ways and returning to God, in order that they would avoid being destroyed by the consequences of their own sins. This is ultimately fulfilled through following Jesus in the plan of salvation. Those who do so receive the Holy Spirit, who daily recreates our hearts and minds to be like Christ.

> *What Do You Think?*
> Which thought in today's text do you have the hardest time coming to grips with? Why?
> *Digging Deeper*
> What extra effort will you expend to resolve this uncertainty?

B. Prayer

God, we see moral goodness in ourselves, but You see Your image marred with sin. We confess that Your assessment of our situation is correct. We thank You for providing mercy and renewal. In Jesus' name we pray. Amen.

C. Thought to Remember

If we cannot acknowledge God's judgment, we will see no need to receive His forgiveness.

Involvement Learning

Enhance your lesson with KJV Bible Student *(from your curriculum supplier) and the reproducible activity page (at www.standardlesson.com or in the back of the* KJV Standard Lesson Commentary Deluxe Edition*).*

Into the Lesson

Divide the class in half; for larger classes, subdivide the halves into fours. Ask groups in one half to discuss problems they had to overcome because of how they were brought up. Ask the other half to discuss problems children today will need to overcome because of how they are being reared now.

Reconvene after five minutes and pose these questions: 1–Was this easy or difficult to discuss? 2–How common is it to blame parents for the inadequacies of their children? 3–How legitimate is it to do that? 4–What are instances when children flourished in spite of their parents?

Use responses to the last question as a transition to Bible study.

Into the Word

Write on the board these three words as headers of three columns, one each:

Relational / Psychological / Sinful

After a class member reads aloud Ezekiel 18:2 and Jeremiah 31:29, say, "Realizing that God condemns this saying, how does it support and how is it different from the experiences we shared in our opening discussion?" After each response, ask which heading it goes under and write it there.

Have learners go back into the groups above to read Ezekiel 18:1-9. Instruct groups to make a list of possibilities implied by this starter: *How to know if a person is just and right.* After five minutes, have groups report; write their conclusions on the board. For clarification, note how this list of behaviors is repeated in verses 10-13 and 15-17. Ask learners to read verses 30-32 and summarize in one sentence the truth expressed there. Compare and contrast those summaries as a class.

Option: Distribute copies of the "Sins of the Fathers" exercise from the activity page, which you can download. Use the "jot three steps" instruction as a transition to Into Life.

Into Life

Return class members to their groups and ask each group to discuss one of the following scenarios, which you have reproduced on handouts:

1–I was ashamed to go to church my whole life because everyone there knew about my father's problems. They knew about the bills he didn't pay. They knew about the money he'd embezzled from his company before he was fired and spent years in jail because of this crime. They'd heard the rumors about his secret girlfriends. They'd suspected that his "business trips" to Nevada and New York were really just covers for drinking, gambling, and womanizing. My father never told me he was sorry for any of that; I was deeply humiliated. His reputation splashed onto me, and I felt sure that people were talking about my family behind my back whenever I showed up at youth group or worship.

2–I was in church several times a week when I was growing up at home. My dad was an elder. My mom was a member of the missions committee. We had visiting guest speakers in our home all the time, and we spent summer vacations at a Christian camp where my parents were workers. As soon as I could get away from all this churchiness, I did. Now that I'm older, I can see why religion was important to my folks, but that doesn't mean I have time for it. I want something different than what my parents had. And besides, I was baptized when I was 10. I figure that that and all those hours I spent in church activities pretty well seals my future with God.

How does today's Scripture help us decide how to respond to either?

After a few minutes, ask groups to share their conclusions with the whole class. Possible questions to pose:

1–When are you most susceptible to blaming your upbringing for your current behavior?

2–When are you most tempted to believe that your "family faith" is good enough in God's eyes?

3–How do you solve these two problems?

Preaching to Enemies

Devotional Reading: Jonah 2
Background Scripture: Jonah 3

Jonah 3

**1 And the word of the Lord came unto Jonah
the second time, saying,
2 Arise, go unto Nineveh, that great city, and
preach unto it the preaching that I bid thee.
3 So Jonah arose, and went unto Nineveh,
according to the word of the Lord. Now
Nineveh was an exceeding great city of three
days' journey.
4 And Jonah began to enter into the city a
day's journey, and he cried, and said, Yet forty
days, and Nineveh shall be overthrown.
5 So the people of Nineveh believed God,
and proclaimed a fast, and put on sackcloth,
from the greatest of them even to the least of
them.
6 For word came unto the king of Nineveh,
and he arose from his throne, and he laid
his robe from him, and covered him with
sackcloth, and sat in ashes.
7 And he caused it to be proclaimed and
published through Nineveh by the decree of
the king and his nobles, saying, Let neither
man nor beast, herd nor flock, taste any thing:
let them not feed, nor drink water:
8 But let man and beast be covered with
sackcloth, and cry mightily unto God: yea,
let them turn every one from his evil way, and
from the violence that is in their hands.
9 Who can tell if God will turn and repent,
and turn away from his fierce anger, that we
perish not?
10 And God saw their works, that they
turned from their evil way; and God repented
of the evil, that he had said that he would do
unto them; and he did it not.**

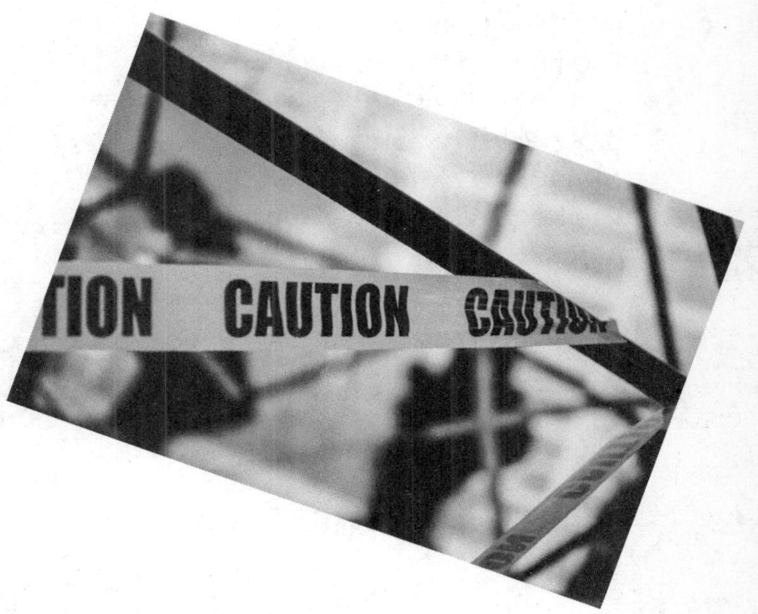

Key Verse

God saw their works, that they turned from their evil way; and God repented of the evil, that he had said that he would do unto them; and he did it not. —**Jonah 3:10**

Photo: Getty Images

Prophets Faithful to God's Covenant

Unit 3: Courageous Prophets of Change

Lessons 9–13

Lesson Aims

After participating in this lesson, each learner will be able to:

1. Define "repentance."

2. List reasons why the Ninevites' reaction to Jonah's proclamation was unexpected.

3. Commit to one needed change to obey God more fully.

Lesson Outline

Introduction

- A. A Satisfying End
- B. Lesson Context

I. The Word of the Lord (Jonah 3:1-4)

- A. Repeated (vv. 1-2)
- B. Revealed (vv. 3-4)
  - *Whom to Exclude?*

II. The People of Nineveh (Jonah 3:5-10)

- A. Repenting (vv. 5-8)
  - *Covering the Hate*
- B. Hoping (v. 9)
- C. Spared (v. 10)

Conclusion

- A. Grace Without Borders
- B. Prayer
- C. Thought to Remember

Introduction

A. A Satisfying End

Imagine that you are nearing the end of a book you just can't put down. You anticipate a satisfying ending. But the book actually ends by telling you that the whole thing had been a dream. *What? Why was I so invested in this? That's unfair!* Few things are more frustrating to a reader than an unsatisfying ending to an otherwise excellent book.

Or what if the book ended in the middle of a sentence and offered no resolution to any of the conflicts contained within it? What makes a really atrocious ending to a book is when that ending has nothing to do with the book itself, or it explains away the drama of the book in a ridiculous manner, or it fails to actually end up somewhere. Such endings make an entire read feel like a waste of time because nothing that happened actually mattered.

All Jonah wanted was an ending that made sense to him regarding the story of the Ninevites. They deserved to be destroyed. They had done *nothing* to merit a happy ending. Everyone for miles around could see that they should be destroyed. But how would God write the ending of this drama?

B. Lesson Context

Though the book of Jonah is only four chapters long, it has much to teach us about the character of God. But the book reveals Jonah's character as well. He reacted to his call like no other prophet in the Old Testament. Those prophets consented to speak for God even when they would rather not (Exodus 4:10-12; Jeremiah 1:6-9; etc.). Jonah chose not only to keep his mouth closed but also to try to run away from God (Jonah 1:1-3).

Jonah appeared to have been willing to live in self-imposed exile rather than deliver a message of repentance to wicked Nineveh, an important city of the aggressive Assyrian Empire. In this way, Jonah held a mirror up to Israel, a nation that would prefer to believe that God's choosing them meant He cared about them *exclusively*. Perhaps Jonah and his fellow Israelites needed to read the "all the nations of the earth" part of Genesis 18:18; 22:18; and 26:4 again!

Even so, Israel had good reason to desire God's sole protection. Assyria was a powerful, expansive nation when Jonah received his call from God in about 780 BC. (See the Lesson Context of lesson 10.) The city of Nineveh, to which Jonah was called, was a royal residence for the king of Assyria. The city was massive (see Jonah 3:3, below) and had a reputation for violence and cruelty (see 3:8, below). Jonah was not someone who had fallen into provincial small-mindedness. His nation—in fact the known world—would be safer if the barbarous Assyrians were destroyed.

Ultimately, Israel's fear of Assyria was justified. Assyria invaded the northern kingdom of Israel in 722 BC, plundered it, carried people into captivity, and resettled the territory (2 Kings 17). While history doesn't provide detailed accounts of the Assyrian invasion, we have no reason to believe that the aggressors didn't commit atrocities on the northern kingdom of Israel as done elsewhere.

That was after Jonah's time. Even so, he certainly preferred to avoid his assigned task entirely. In addition to his escape attempt (Jonah 1:3), Jonah later revealed his deep disappointment in God (4:1-3). However, God insisted that Jonah fulfill his prophetic tasks. Even Jonah didn't dare try to escape God's calling a second time.

I. The Word of the Lord

(Jonah 3:1-4)

A. Repeated (vv. 1-2)

1. And the word of the Lord came unto Jonah the second time, saying.

Jonah would not be relying on his own counsel when on his mission (see Lesson Context). He was the chosen messenger of, for, and by *the Lord*. Jonah is designated as a prophet in 2 Kings 14:25, and the formula in the verse before us is associated with other prophets (examples: Jeremiah 1:1-2; Hosea 1:1). Jonah's prior disobedience had not disqualified or exempted him from being God's chosen vessel (see Jonah 1:3).

2. Arise, go unto Nineveh, that great city, and preach unto it the preaching that I bid thee.

This command repeats what God originally told Jonah. Noticeably missing is the previous emphasis on the city's evil, seen in the phrase "their wickedness is come up before me" (Jonah 1:2). The prophet was already aware of that fact, but didn't see the remedy as God saw it. Jonah's desired remedy was fiery judgment; God's remedy was repentance (see 4:1-2, not in our lesson text). *Preach unto it the preaching* is another way to command Jonah to speak only what God would tell him. Jonah's marching orders had not changed.

We wonder why would God send an Israelite prophet to a nation that threatened His chosen people. The answer is found in the last verse in the book:

> Should not I spare Nineveh, that great city, wherein are more than sixscore thousand persons that cannot discern between their right hand and their left hand? (Jonah 4:11)

In other words, God's love is not determined or constrained by national boundaries. We live in a world in which nationalism is on the rise—and so it has always been. Exceptionalism, a cousin of nationalism, is the belief that a certain society is superior to all others. Ancient Israel had nationalistic and exceptionalistic pride due to the fact that they were chosen by God uniquely (compare Deuteronomy 9:4; Matthew 3:9). It's not hard to see that trait in Jonah himself when we read the entirety of the book.

> *What Do You Think?*
> How should the designation of Nineveh as a "great city" inform our missionary endeavors today, if at all? Why?
> *Digging Deeper*
> What conclusions should we *not* draw? Why?

B. Revealed (vv. 3-4)

3. So Jonah arose, and went unto Nineveh, according to the word of the Lord. Now Nineveh was an exceeding great city of three days' journey.

His time inside the great fish had taught Jonah the price of disobedience (Jonah 1:17–2:10). Here we see the evidence of having learned that lesson. The *three days' journey* ironically matches Jonah's three days in the fish (Jonah 1:17).

One suggestion regarding the meaning of *an exceeding great city of three days' journey* is that it includes the time necessary for Jonah to stop and preach neighborhood by neighborhood. Archaeology has determined the size of Nineveh to have encompassed some 1,730 acres. Combining this with the population figure we see in Jonah 4:11 gives us a hint of the strength of the Assyrian Empire.

4. And Jonah began to enter into the city a day's journey, and he cried, and said, Yet forty days, and Nineveh shall be overthrown.

Jonah walked one-third of the way into the city before delivering God's message. Given his lack of enthusiasm to this point, the prophet likely was giving God bare minimum obedience. We do much the same when we obey the letter of God's law but do not allow our hearts to be changed by His commands.

The recorded sermon is simple but powerful, just five words in the Hebrew. This could be all that Jonah said, or it could be a summary of a longer sermon. Lacking from the recorded text here is a call to repentance. This seems to be in keeping with Jonah's mind-set to this point: he seems not to have wanted to mention the possibility that God would forgive. After all, the Ninevites were an evil people who deserved judgment!

The number *forty* has symbolic meaning in the Bible. Rain fell for that number of days in judgment on wicked humanity (Genesis 7:17). Forty was the number of years the Israelites wandered in the desert because of their faithlessness (Numbers 14:33-35). It was the number of days Jesus fasted before facing the tempter (Matthew 4:2-10). In each case, God considered the completion of this number of days or years to be sufficient to excise evil or prove its absence. Nineveh's having that amount of time before being *overthrown* was nothing more than fair in God's reckoning.

Whom to Exclude?

John grew up in church, where he learned to love his neighbors and extend grace. But he also learned to stay away from people who drank, smoked, gambled, and, well, sinned (per his definition). He grew to believe that people who had not repented should feel the full impact of those sins. That would be the best way for them to learn the errors of their ways.

John shared Jonah's mind-set. When we are challenged because of whom God shows grace, we must follow His leading rather than relying on our perception of what is "fair." We have all sinned (Romans 3:23).

Having received God's grace—and remembering that grace by its nature isn't "fair"—who are we to decide those to be excluded from experiencing it as well? —L. M-W.

HOW TO SAY IT

Assyria	Uh-*sear*-ee-uh.
Elohim (Hebrew)	El-o-*heem*.
Jonah	*Jo*-nuh.
Nineveh	*Nin*-uh-vuh.
Ninevites	*Nin*-uh-vites.
Yahweh (Hebrew)	*Yaw*-way.

II. The People of Nineveh

(Jonah 3:5-10)

A. Repenting (vv. 5-8)

5a. So the people of Nineveh believed God.

Several startling events are recorded in the book of Jonah, but one of the greatest is the tremendous response to Jonah's pointed message. The faith of *the people* depended not on Jonah's rhetoric or enthusiasm for the subject (see Jonah 3:4, above). Instead their reaction speaks to the work of the Spirit of God in their midst, although not specifically stated as such.

The Ninevites, of course, had their own gods. Nineveh was home to the temple of Ishtar, goddess of love and war. Ashur, from which Assyria got its name, was both a city and a god. Other gods of Assyrian or Babylonian invention were also worshipped in Nineveh. But at this point the people *believed God,* the underlying Hebrew of that designation being Elohim, not Yahweh (see notes on these names in lesson 12, page 325). When the word *Elohim* is used without the word *Yahweh* being adjacent, the implication is that of the Creator of the universe (Genesis 1).

Of course, the Lord is both Creator of everything in the earth and Ruler over Israel specifically. Old Testament texts, especially the Psalms, often use the names interchangeably. But the Ninevites' belief seems to have been tied only to God as He makes himself known through creation (see Romans 1:18-20), rather than to God as He reveals himself more fully in the Law of Moses.

5b. And proclaimed a fast, and put on sackcloth, from the greatest of them even to the least of them.

Fasting from food or drink was a common religious practice in many nations during biblical times. It could be practiced privately or corporately. The practice indicated self-denial, repentance, and/or humility. In the case of the Ninevites' fasting, all of these applied. *Sackcloth* was a rough material that was generally made from goat hair; wearing sackcloth signified submission (example: 1 Kings 20:31-32) or intense distress (example: 2 Kings 19:1). Fasting combined with wearing sackcloth added intensity to the picture (compare Psalm 35:13). A spiritual change was happening throughout that city!

What Do You Think?

On what occasions should fasting be promoted today, if any? Why do you say that?

Digging Deeper

Should Acts 13:2-3; 14:23 be foundational for your answer? Why, or why not?

6. For word came unto the king of Nineveh, and he arose from his throne, and he laid his robe from him, and covered him with sackcloth, and sat in ashes.

The phrase *for word came* is similar to that used to describe God's revelation to Jonah (Jonah 1:1; 3:1). This implies that a true word from God made it to *the king of Nineveh*. But unlike Jonah, the king didn't attempt to flee from God. Instead, he humbled himself and exchanged his royal robes for the coarse clothing of the penitent masses. His sitting *in ashes* may have been a sign that the king took additional responsibility for the cities he had destroyed by fire (compare Jeremiah 31:40).

Critics have questioned the accuracy of this

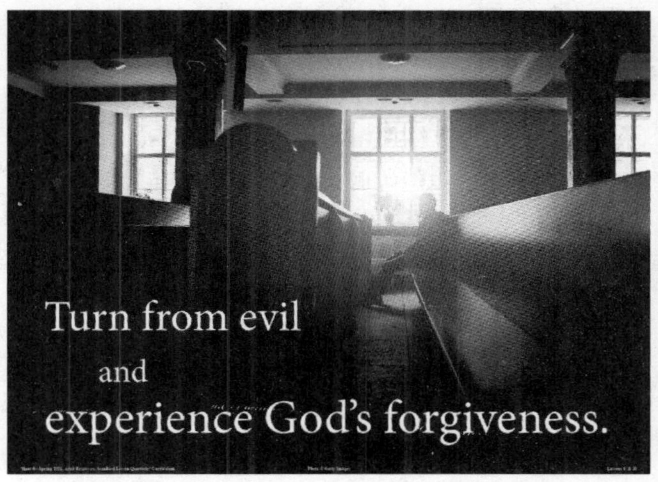
Turn from evil
and
experience God's forgiveness.

Visual for Lessons 6 & 13. *While discussing the questions associated with verse 5b, ask the class how fasting can be evidence of turning from evil.*

account by charging that a king would not have lived in *Nineveh* during Jonah's day because the city did not become Assyria's capital until later. But Nineveh was a major city in the nation, and kings did reside there occasionally. Further, the hectic conditions in Assyria at the time may have caused some provincial leaders to assume titles of royalty (compare the various "king of . . ." designations in Joshua 10:3).

Here we see a pagan monarch responding to God in a more obedient fashion than God's own prophet! This upended expectations about who responds to God appropriately. The Assyrians in Nineveh responded in submissive humility while the prophet from Israel had done the opposite. Righteous reactions from outsiders are seen in such important later events as the Magi's intent to worship the young Jesus (Matthew 2).

7-8a. And he caused it to be proclaimed and published through Nineveh by the decree of the king and his nobles, saying, Let neither man nor beast, herd nor flock, taste any thing: let them not feed, nor drink water: but let man and beast be covered with sackcloth, and cry mightily unto God.

The king showed his support for the fasting initiative not only by participating in it, but by intensifying its terms. The fast was originally limited to the citizens of *Nineveh*, but livestock were also to be denied food and *water*. To cover these animals in *sackcloth* was a symbol of the city's repentance.

Though we often think of the consequences of sin being confined to humans, this verse underscores that the natural world also suffers because of sin (Romans 8:19-22). God's last recorded response to Jonah also reinforced the fact that God cares for *all* of His creation, not just the human parts (Jonah 4:10-11).

For the king to risk the health of the city's livestock by causing them to fast indicates that he believed that destruction was imminent. If *God* didn't see genuine repentance, the well-being of the livestock wouldn't matter anyway.

Covering the Hate

What do you feel strongly enough about to "wear" on your skin forever? Some people use tattoos to commemorate a beloved spouse, a dearly departed friend, or even Mom. Others have hobbies, symbols of their faith, or pictures of their BFF inked into their skin. Sadly, some choose symbols of hatred.

Not all who choose a tattoo that proclaims racial or ethnic hatred find those biases permanent, however. They repent of those attitudes and want the symbols of their former beliefs to disappear. For some, this may involve tattoo removal. For others, cover-ups are a popular option. For either, repentance can be an expensive process.

Either a cover-up or a removal is like wearing sackcloth—permanently. The message is the same: there is an inward change, seen now on the outside. Repentance requires a forever-removal. How is the Holy Spirit convicting you in that regard?

—J. A. K.

8b. Yea, let them turn every one from his evil way, and from the violence that is in their hands.

The king seems to have recognized that empty ritual would yield no benefit (compare Isaiah 58:3-7). True repentance begins with the heart and is verified through righteous behavior. For that reason, the king commanded his people to reject their *evil* lifestyle. The word *way* refers to well-established patterns of sin, which must be forsaken (compare Jeremiah 25:5).

The violence of Assyria is seen in archaeological discoveries. Assyrian reliefs and written descriptions record atrocities committed against prisoners of war. These artifacts depict scenes of gruesome torture. Those not tortured to death were deported to Assyrian cities to work as slaves on building projects. The Assyrians indulged in these monstrous tactics to strike fear in the hearts of any nation who dared to oppose them. The city of Nineveh was called on to repent of a way of life built on such violence.

> *What Do You Think?*
> What are some godly ways to respond after suffering violence at the hands of another?
> *Digging Deeper*
> Categorize your answer in terms of thoughts, words, and actions.

B. Hoping (v. 9)

9. Who can tell if God will turn and repent, and turn away from his fierce anger, that we perish not?

God did not need to *repent* as though He had done something wrong—He hadn't done anything to Nineveh yet! Rather, the idea here is more of God's changing His mind about something and then acting in accordance with that change of mind. *Turn* is a great image for this (compare Jeremiah 18:8; 26:3). A change of God's mind would result in a change of His action. The king's hope in this regard was not unfounded, but it also wasn't assured. The people had been told they would *perish.* For God to follow through on His word to them would be just.

C. Spared (v. 10)

10. And God saw their works, that they turned from their evil way; and God repented of the evil, that he had said that he would do unto them; and he did it not.

As the king and the people hoped, *God saw* their repentance as demonstrated in *their works.* As in the previous verse, we see language of God's repentance, and the explanation is the same. Of course, God does not do *evil* in a moral sense. The idea is to be understood in a physical sense of punishment. God does indeed visit judgment, sometimes in the form of destruction, on people in keeping with His just nature (example: Genesis 18:20–19:29).

This verse is one of the key passages in Jonah. It captures God's forgiving nature (compare Jonah 4:2-3, 8-9). Here we see seeds of the gospel. Salvation is offered to all peoples—regardless of nation, language, or culture. The apostle Peter wrote that God was "not willing that any should perish, but that all should come to repentance" (2 Peter 3:9). For God has *always* so loved the world (John 3:16).

The historical record tells us, however, that Nineveh's repentance didn't last. The prophet Nahum, who came along about 150 years after Jonah, catalogued specific sins of which Nineveh was guilty. These included violence, corruption, and idolatry (Nahum 3).

Nineveh suffered destruction in 612 BC. Before that, God used the Assyrian Empire as an instrument of His wrath against His rebellious and idolatrous covenant people. But Assyria went too far in this role and ended up on the receiving end of what they had inflicted on others (Isaiah 10:5-19).

> *What Do You Think?*
> What's your main takeaway from today's lesson regarding modern missionary endeavors?
> *Digging Deeper*
> How will you act on that takeaway for your church?

Conclusion

A. Grace Without Borders

Throughout Scripture, we witness time and time again that God loves mercy (Exodus 33:19). The story of Nineveh illustrates this in extreme fashion: the enemies of God's own people were spared when they turned their hearts toward Him.

God's intention for *all* humanity is to encounter His love and remain in it. The apostle Paul catalogued all of the forces incapable of separating God's people from God's love (Romans 8:38-39). No outside force can cause that separation. But we can voluntarily cause it ourselves by rejecting His will as we become as the Ninevites had been. When we do so, repentance is the cure, as the Ninevites discovered.

Today, we also should accept the reality that God's work will not be limited by geopolitical lines. We see Jonah's attitudes in both individuals and faith communities who fixate over which groups of sinners are too far beyond the reach of God's love. Meanwhile, we are reminded that we have a Savior who dined with sinners (Luke 7:34) and reserved His fiercest anger for the self-congratulating Pharisees (11:39-52).

Our Lord intends to establish a new people, from every tribe and tongue (Revelation 7:9). God's love will go everywhere. We can experience joy at the prospect, or we can resist this reality. Our attitude does not change what God will do for our enemies, but it will change how we react to His blessing those we would curse.

Think about it: if God was concerned for a petulant prophet and a morally bankrupt city, then His loving commitment to us will remain unshaken. We can celebrate that God is "a gracious God, and merciful, slow to anger, and of great kindness" (Jonah 4:2). And in the face of divine kindness, we, like the citizens and rulers of ancient Nineveh, can repent.

> *What Do You Think?*
> Which thought in today's text do you have the hardest time coming to grips with? Why is that?
> *Digging Deeper*
> What extra effort will you expend to resolve this uncertainty?

B. Prayer

God, You disregard our borders and share Your love wherever You please. We praise You for this because we are dependent on Your mercy. In Jesus' name we pray. Amen.

C. Thought to Remember

No human boundaries limit God's grace.

Involvement Learning

Enhance your lesson with KJV Bible Student *(from your curriculum supplier) and the reproducible activity page (at www.standardlesson.com or in the back of the* KJV Standard Lesson Commentary Deluxe Edition*).*

Into the Lesson

Have the following phrase on the board as students arrive:

The most significant change I ever made was . . .

Group learners into pairs to share completions of this phrase. After about five minutes, ask volunteers to share with the whole class. Possible questions to pose as they do: 1–Why were you willing to change? 2–Why is change difficult? 3–What's a change you've resisted? 4–What does that experience tell you about leading others to change?

Make a transition by saying, "As you think about your experiences with change, you'll be able to reflect on why today's Bible story is so remarkable."

Alternative. Distribute copies of the "What Does It Say?" exercise from the activity page, which you can download, for learners to complete in pairs as indicated.

Into the Word

Read the lesson text aloud. Then distribute handouts (you prepare) of two charts. Have the following four headings on the first chart: *What Jonah Did / What the Ninevites Did / What the King of Nineveh Did / What God Did.* Have the following three headings on the second chart: *How Jonah Changed / How the Ninevites Changed / How God Changed.*

Ask students to complete these charts by working together in groups of four to eight as they study today's text together. (*Option.* You may allow all the groups to work on both charts or you may ask half the groups to complete the first while the other half completes the second.) Regarding the *How God Changed* category, be ready to challenge learners to justify their response there in light of Malachi 3:6 and James 1:17.

Option. Distribute copies of the "Read All About It!" exercise from the activity page. Have learners work in groups to complete it as indicated. (Or divide your class into thirds to have two of the groups complete, one each, the two charts above while the third group completes the "Read All About It" exercise.)

After several minutes, allow groups to report back to the class. At an appropriate point, ask, "Which change in this story surprises you most, and why?":

A–Jonah's change of heart and willingness to preach?
B–The Ninevites' repentance and turn to God?
C–God's change of decision on destroying the Ninevites?

Into Life

Give two blank slips of paper to each class member. Ask them to write on one slip their completion of this statement, which you write on the board:

The world situation I most wish would change is . . .

Inform students they should leave their slips anonymous because you will be reading them to the class. Collect slips after no more than one minute and do so. As you read them aloud, make special note of responses that are repeated or express similar thoughts. Discuss what will be required for the desired changes to happen. Remind participants that the only changes we can control are those we make in ourselves. Follow that by asking whether the situation in Nineveh would have changed if Jonah had not changed first. Challenge learners to think of the self-change they can make in anticipation of the change they want to see happen.

On the second slip, ask learners to write the name of someone who needs to turn to Christ. You will not collect these slips; instead, learners can keep them as prayer reminders in the coming week. Again challenge class members to consider changes they can and should make in themselves before expecting change in the people named.

CONFIDENT HOPE

Special Features

Lessons

Unit 1: Jesus Teaches About Faith

Unit 2: Faith and Salvation

Unit 3: Faith Gives Us Hope

Quarterly Quiz

Use these questions as a pretest or as a review. The answers are on page iv of This Quarter in the Word.

Lesson 1

1. Jesus said that not even the Queen of Sheba could match a flower's glory. T/F. *Matthew 6:28-29*

2. Jesus said to seek first God's kingdom and His _______. *Matthew 6:33*

Lesson 2

1. When a storm struck their boat, what was Jesus doing? (sleeping, preaching, fishing) *Matthew 8:24*

2. What kind of faith did Jesus say that the disciples had? (little, average, great) *Matthew 8:26*

Lesson 3

1. A woman with a bleeding problem touched Jesus' clothing to be healed. T/F. *Matthew 9:20*

2. Jesus said that the woman was made whole because of her what? (love, boldness, faith) *Matthew 9:22*

Lesson 4

1. When Jesus walked on the water, the disciples shouted in delight. T/F. *Matthew 14:26*

2. When Peter began to sink, he cried out for the Lord to save him. T/F. *Matthew 14:30-31*

Lesson 5

1. Those with leprosy were required to cry out "_______!" *Leviticus 13:45*

2. How many men with leprosy did Jesus heal? (10, 40, a legion) T/F. *Luke 17:12-14*

Lesson 6

1. Paul was anxious to visit the Romans so that he could impart some _______ gift. *Romans 1:11*

2. Paul affirmed that the righteous were to live by _______. *Romans 1:17*

Lesson 7

1. Paul affirmed that Abraham's belief was counted as righteousness. T/F. *Romans 4:3*

2. What two words did Paul use to describe Abraham's circumcision? (seal, pain, regret, sign, mark) *Romans 4:11*

Lesson 8

1. God "shed abroad in our hearts" His _______ "by the Holy Ghost." *Romans 5:5*

2. "While we were yet _______, Christ died for us." *Romans 5:8*

Lesson 9

1. Paul emphasized the need to believe with one's what? (mouth, heart, hand) *Romans 10:10*

2. The prophet Paul quoted as saying "Lord, who hath believed our report" was who? (Jeremiah, Esaias [Isaiah], Amos) *Romans 10:16*

Lesson 10

1. Without faith it is impossible to _______ God. *Hebrews 11:6*

2. People of faith desire a heavenly what? (calling, life on earth, country) *Hebrews 11:16*

Lesson 11

1. Sinning willfully results in no more sacrifice for sin. T/F. *Hebrews 10:26*

2. It is a fearful thing to fall into the hands of the _______ God. *Hebrews 10:31*

Lesson 12

1. The spirit of antichrist is already in the world. T/F. *1 John 4:3*

2. Those "born of God overcometh the _____." *1 John 5:4*

Lesson 13

1. Paul says we are to live by _______, not by sight. *2 Corinthians 5:7*

2. Paul states that all must appear before whose judgment seat? (Christ's, the Holy Spirit's, the angels') *2 Corinthians 5:10*

QUARTER AT A GLANCE

by Patrick L. Mitchell

OFTEN IT TAKES a tragedy or other setback to force us to switch off the autopilot of everyday life. When that happens, the result can be an exposure of the cracks in our beliefs and the asking of the deeper questions of life. That was one result of the tragedy of 9/11, the 20th anniversary of which will be observed in a few months. That event seemed to dash hopes in life's stability, and it led otherwise unchurched people to pack out worship services over the weeks that followed.

Even though church attendance soon began to drop back to "normal" levels, the tenacity of hope made itself felt in, among other things, the form of a $3 million hope sculpture in New York City in 2014. But the question remains: What or who is the proper object of a confident hope?

Unit 1—Jesus Teaches About Faith

History is witness to humanity's preference to found hope on what is seen rather than on what is unseen. The Lord's words in Jeremiah 2:13 ring true in all eras:

> My people have committed two evils; they have forsaken me the fountain of living waters, and hewed them out cisterns, broken cisterns, that can hold no water.

Notice that the cisterns at issue represent things that humans construct in order to meet perceived needs. The five lessons of unit 1 show us human self-focus in this regard. People hope to have enough food and clothing, and they use worry in an attempt to remedy a lack of those things (lesson 1). When no human remedy comes to mind, the results are fear and doubt (lessons 2 and 4). The proper reaction in all cases is to look to Jesus first (lessons 3 and 5).

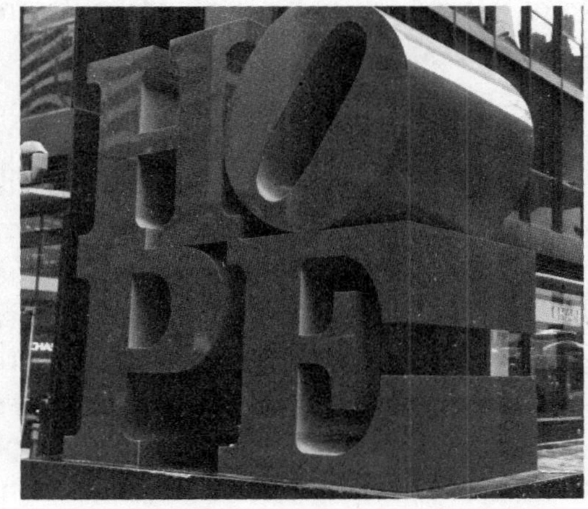

Unit 2—Faith and Salvation

Unit 2 makes the transition from hope regarding earthly, physical needs in unit 1 to our hope for eternal salvation. Abraham is a double-sided example in this regard. On the one hand, he is the preemient example of faith (lesson 7); on the other hand, he is an example of someone who tried to take personal control when doubts arose regarding lack of an heir (Genesis 16). We follow Abraham's good example and avoid repeating his attempt to take control from God as we lift our eyes above earthly circumstances to focus on the power of the gospel (lesson 6), how we have peace with God (lesson 8), and the scope of salvation (lesson 9).

History is witness to humanity's preference to found hope on what is seen.

Unit 3—Faith Gives Us Hope

This unit explores the connections between faith and hope. Some form of the Greek originals behind those two words occur together in the same verse over a dozen times in the New Testament. Two such verses are part of lessons 7 and 8 in unit 2; two more are part of lessons 10 and 11 of unit 3.

As you study the inseparable connection between faith and hope, your appreciation of God's character and power will grow. His character and power are our confidence in troubling times. His sovereignty is our stability when the waves of life ebb and flow. His faithfulness is our fortress when tempted to despair. His righteousness is our refuge when the enemy attacks. To have conquering faith in God (lesson 12) is to have a faith that focuses on eternity (lesson 13).

Get the Setting

by Patrick L. Mitchell

When reading the New Testament, it is easy to overlook the context of Jesus' ministry while focusing on its content. But therein lies something of a dilemma: the fullness of that content can be grasped only with a firm understanding of its context. That context is best framed in the concept of confident hope.

Pillars of Messianic Hope

The Old Testament texts seen to witness most clearly to the coming of Messiah are Genesis 49:10; Numbers 24:17; and Isaiah 11:1-6. From these and other texts emerged at least four pillars that undergirded hope in such a deliverer:

- ***Monotheism***: there is only one God—Israel's God (compare Deuteronomy 6:4; Mark 12:29)
- ***Election***: God's choosing of Israel to reign in the promised land (compare Isaiah 9:7; John 11:48)
- ***Covenant***: God's promises to Israel in the first five books of the Bible (compare Genesis 17:1-8; John 8:39)
- ***Temple***: God's decision that the center of Israel's life would be a restored temple in Jerusalem (compare 1 Kings 9:1-3; John 4:20)

In some cases, mistaken beliefs of some people as recorded in the New Testament reflect nonbiblical speculations written in the centuries between the Old and New Testaments. A few examples of these are the book of Jubilees, the Psalms of Solomon, and various works by Philo of Alexandria. When we place those alongside tunnel-vision interpretations of certain Old Testament texts, we can see why Jesus was rejected by many Jews: He just didn't fit their expectations.

Challenges of Unmet Expectations

Consider, for example, Ezekiel 37:21-28. There God promised that He would gather scattered Israel to dwell in their own land; that He would be their God; that a king from David's line would sit on the throne; that an everlasting covenant of peace would exist with God; and that everyone would "know that I the Lord do sanctify Israel, when my sanctuary shall be in the midst of them for evermore." From that passage and others such as Isaiah 9:6 and 42:1, it is not hard to see why Jews of Jesus' day had specific hopes regarding Messiah. After hearing these promises told and retold century after century, it seems natural (at least in 20/20 hindsight) that certain expectations would become ingrained in religious thought (compare Matthew 17:10-13; Luke 7:18-20; John 3:1-10; 4:25; 7:12, 25-27, 52; 10:33; Acts 1:6).

Yet there seemed to be no end to foreign oppression. After centuries of domination by Babylon, Persia, Greece, and Rome, the Israelites were still, in effect, exiles in their own land! Anna of Luke 2:36-38 was old enough to have remembered the Roman conquest of Jerusalem in 63 BC. Yet it was this very context—the era of the so-called Roman Peace—when "the fulness of the time was come" and "God sent forth his Son" (Galatians 4:4).

The misplaced Jewish hope in the Messiah was that of deliverance from physical, national bondage—"another exodus" as some have called it. We see this in Jesus' rebuke of Peter in Matthew 16:23; Peter's concept of the Messiah he had just confessed did not allow for the possibility that the Messiah could be killed, which implied mission failure. Even as late as Jesus' ascension, the disciples still clung to a wrong notion of deliverance (Acts 1:6).

Hope of Eternal Life

Bible history is recorded so "that we . . . might have hope" (Romans 15:4). An important part of that history lesson is that we should not repeat the errors of others (1 Corinthians 10:1-13). A recurring problem in the pages of the New Testament is that people saw Jesus only through the lens of their preconceived expectations. Do we do the same, or do we allow Him to correct those expectations?

Mon, Aug. 16	**Testing Our Love for God**	Deuteronomy 13:1-4
Tue, Aug. 17	**Keeping His Commandments**	John 14:15-24
Wed, Aug. 18	**Discerning Truth and Error**	1 John 4:1, 4-6
Thu, Aug. 19	**Knowing God, We Can Love Others**	1 John 4:7-12
Fri, Aug. 20	**Faith Is the Victory**	1 John 5:1-3
Sat, Aug. 21	**Believers in Jesus Have Life**	1 John 5:6-12
Sun, Aug. 22	**Faith Overcomes Obstacles**	1 John 4:2-3, 13-17; 5:4-5
Mon, Aug. 23	**From Death to Life**	1 Corinthians 15:16-23
Tue, Aug. 24	**Strengthening the Inner Being**	Ephesians 3:14-21
Wed, Aug. 25	**God Judges Every Deed**	Ecclesiastes 12:9-14
Thu, Aug. 26	**God's Judgment Is Impartial**	Romans 2:4b-11
Fri, Aug. 27	**Paul, Confident in Ministry**	2 Corinthians 4:1-6
Sat, Aug. 28	**Entering the Presence of Jesus**	2 Corinthians 4:7-15
Sun, Aug. 29	**Live the Faith Confidently**	2 Corinthians 4:16–5:10

Answers to the Quarterly Quiz on page 338

Lesson 1—1. false. 2. righteousness. **Lesson 2**—1. sleeping. 2. little. **Lesson 3**—1. true. 2. faith. **Lesson 4**—1. false. 2. true. **Lesson 5**—1. Unclean. 2. 10. **Lesson 6**—1. spiritual. 2. faith. **Lesson 7**—1. true. 2. sign, seal. **Lesson 8**—1. love. 2. sinners. **Lesson 9**—1. heart. 2. Esaias (Isaiah). **Lesson 10**—1. please. 2. country. **Lesson 11**—1. true. 2. living. **Lesson 12**—1. true. 2. world. **Lesson 13**—1. faith. 2. Christ's.

THIS QUARTER IN THE WORD

Mon, May 31	**Worried? Seek God's Counsel**	1 Samuel 9:5-10
Tue, Jun. 1	**God Cares for His People**	Ezekiel 34:11-16
Wed, Jun. 2	**Rich? Set Your Hope on God**	1 Timothy 6:17-19
Thu, Jun. 3	**Enlarge Your Faith Practices**	Matthew 17:14-20
Fri, Jun. 4	**Overcome Worry through Faith**	Luke 12:22-34
Sat, Jun. 5	**Serve God with Your Whole Heart**	Matthew 6:19-24
Sun, Jun. 6	**Live Worry Free Every Day**	Matthew 6:25-34
Mon, Jun. 7	**Do Not Fear the Storm**	Mark 4:35-41
Tue, Jun. 8	**Do Not Fear Persecution**	Matthew 24:9-14
Wed, Jun. 9	**No Separation from God's Love**	Romans 8:31-39
Thu, Jun. 10	**I Have Overcome the World**	John 16:25-33
Fri, Jun. 11	**Choose to Follow Me Now!**	Matthew 8:18-22
Sat, Jun. 12	**Jesus Delivers the Demonized**	Matthew 8:28-34
Sun, Jun. 13	**Jesus Stills the Storm**	Matthew 8:23-27
Mon, Jun. 14	**Reminders of God's Commandments**	Numbers 15:37-41
Tue, Jun. 15	**Witnesses to Girl's Healing**	Luke 8:40-42a, 49-56
Wed, Jun. 16	**Faith to Touch Jesus**	Luke 8:42b-48
Thu, Jun. 17	**Jesus Opens Eyes**	Matthew 9:27-31
Fri, Jun. 18	**Jesus Restores Speech**	Matthew 9:32-34
Sat, Jun. 19	**Join the Lord's Harvest**	Matthew 9:35–10:1
Sun, Jun. 20	**Faith in God Heals Many Ills**	Matthew 9:18-26

Mon, Jun. 21	**Sing of the Lord's Faithfulness**	Isaiah 38:16-20
Tue, Jun. 22	**Dying for the Faith**	Matthew 14:1-12
Wed, Jun. 23	**The Crowd's Hunger Satisfied**	Matthew 14:13-21
Thu, Jun. 24	**Believe the One Sent to You**	John 6:22-29
Fri, Jun. 25	**The Sick Are Healed**	Matthew 14:34-36
Sat, Jun. 26	**Speak Confidently to the Powerful**	Mark 13:9-12
Sun, Jun. 27	**Savior of the Fearful**	Matthew 14:22-33
Mon, Jun. 28	**God Welcomes Foreigners**	Isaiah 56:1-8
Tue, Jun. 29	**Naomi's Sorrow Turns to Joy**	Ruth 4:3-6, 13-15
Wed, Jun. 30	**Treatment of Leprosy**	Leviticus 13:1-8
Thu, Jul. 1	**Healed Men Share Their Good News**	2 Kings 7:3-11
Fri, Jul. 2	**Many Samaritans Believe in the Savior**	John 4:39-42
Sat, Jul. 3	**Doing What Needs to Be Done**	Luke 17:1-10
Sun, Jul. 4	**Cultivate Gratefulness**	Leviticus 13:45-56; Luke 17:11-19
Mon, Jul. 5	**Apollos and Paul, Builders**	1 Corinthians 3:1-11
Tue, Jul. 6	**Entrusted with the Gospel**	Galatians 2:1-10
Wed, Jul. 7	**Grace and Peace to All**	Romans 1:1-7
Thu, Jul. 8	**God's Righteous Wrath**	Romans 1:18-23
Fri, Jul. 9	**God's Just Actions**	Romans 1:24-32
Sat, Jul. 10	**God's Righteous Actions**	2 Peter 2:4-9
Sun, Jul. 11	**Effect of the Gospel**	Romans 1:8-17
Mon, Jul. 12	**God's Covenant with Abraham**	Genesis 15:1-8
Tue, Jul. 13	**Blessed Through Abraham**	Genesis 12:1-9
Wed, Jul. 14	**Promise Realized by Faith**	Romans 4:13-15
Thu, Jul. 15	**For All Who Share Abraham's Faith**	Romans 4:16-18
Fri, Jul. 16	**Belief Despite Impossible Odds**	Romans 4:19-21
Sat, Jul. 17	**Christians Share Abraham's Faith**	Romans 4:22-25
Sun, Jul. 18	**Abraham, Father of the Faithful**	Romans 4:1-12

Mon, Jul. 19	**Jesus, Not Suffering, Matters**	Matthew 5:9-12
Tue, Jul. 20	**Jesus Matters, Not Suffering**	Philippians 1:12-20
Wed, Jul. 21	**Suffering for Christ**	2 Corinthians 11:21b-30
Thu, Jul. 22	**In Hope Our Salvation Is Secure**	Romans 8:18-25
Fri, Jul. 23	**Free Gift of Jesus Brings Justification**	Romans 5:12-17
Sat, Jul. 24	**Grace Leads to Eternal Life**	Romans 5:18-21
Sun, Jul. 25	**Justified Through Faith**	Romans 5:1-11
Mon, Jul. 26	**Obey God with Heart and Voice**	Deuteronomy 30:6-14
Tue, Jul. 27	**God's Salvation Announced**	Isaiah 52:1-10
Wed, Jul. 28	**Call on the Name of the Lord**	Joel 2:28-32
Thu, Jul. 29	**Gentiles Justified by Faith**	Galatians 3:6-14
Fri, Jul. 30	**For the Salvation of the Gentiles**	Romans 10:1-4
Sat, Jul. 31	**A Foolish Kind of Deafness**	Romans 10:18-21
Sun, Aug. 1	**Salvation Is for Everyone**	Romans 10:5-17
Mon, Aug. 2	**Love of Money, Root of Evil**	1 Timothy 6:6-10
Tue, Aug. 3	**Control Yourself**	1 Thessalonians 4:1-7
Wed, Aug. 4	**Abraham, Father of the Faithful**	Acts 7:2-7
Thu, Aug. 5	**Examples of the Faithful**	Hebrews 11:4-7, 17-27
Fri, Aug. 6	**Faith in Daily Life**	Hebrews 13:1-9, 17-19
Sat, Aug. 7	**Offer Sacrifices to God**	Hebrews 13:10-16
Sun, Aug. 8	**Living Actions of Faith**	Hebrews 11:1-3, 8-16
Mon, Aug. 9	**Save Your Life by Losing It**	Mark 8:31-37
Tue, Aug. 10	**Respond to Abusers with Blessings**	1 Peter 3:9-19
Wed, Aug. 11	**Be Faithful Until Death**	Revelation 2:8-11
Thu, Aug. 12	**Sanctified by Christ's Sacrifice**	Hebrews 10:1-10
Fri, Aug. 13	**The Inner Life of New Believers**	Hebrews 10:11-18
Sat, Aug. 14	**Approach God with a Pure Heart**	Hebrews 10:19-22
Sun, Aug. 15	**Act to Preserve the Faith**	Hebrews 10:23-36

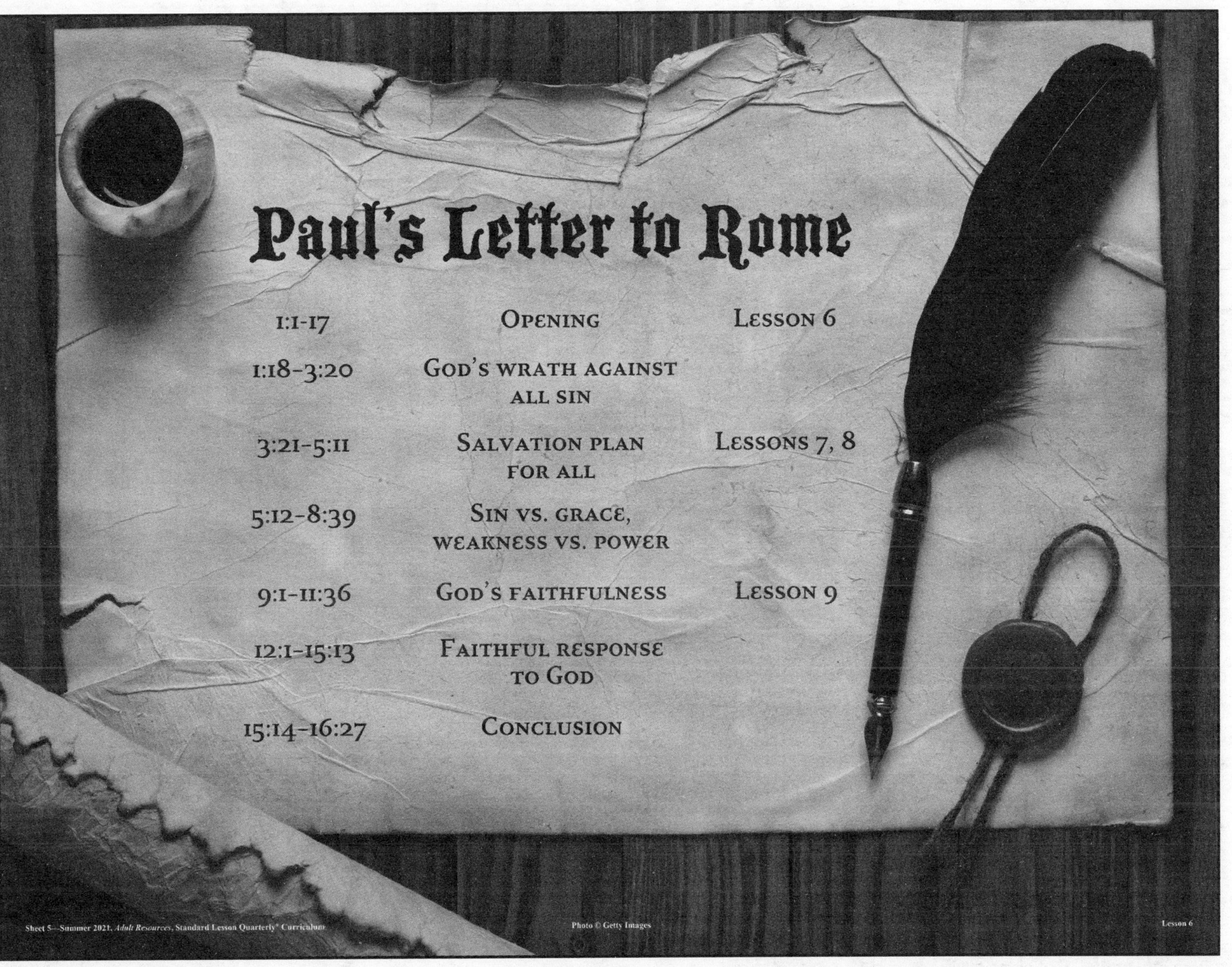

Paul's Letter to Rome
1:1-17 Opening Lesson 6
1:18–3:20 God's wrath against all sin
3:21–5:11 Salvation plan for all Lessons 7, 8
5:12–8:39 Sin vs. grace, weakness vs. power
9:1–11:36 God's faithfulness Lesson 9
12:1–15:13 Faithful response to God
15:14–16:27 Conclusion
Sheet 5—Summer 2021, Adult Resources, Standard Lesson Quarterly® Curriculum
Photo © Getty Images
Lesson 6

Icebreakers: How and Why

Teacher Tips by Jerry Bowling

An icebreaker is a tool you can use to enhance discussion by involving students at the outset of the lesson. An icebreaker is a short (2–6 minutes) nonthreatening activity that can be lighthearted or reflective.

Learning is best served when the teacher plans icebreakers with a connection to the lesson at hand. Use of icebreakers recognizes the students' need to talk. That, in turn, recognizes a desire to learn.

Lighthearted Icebreakers

These are used at the beginning of a lesson to foster interaction. They also help classmates get to know one another better. Examples:

- Form pairs standing back-to-back. At the word "Go," participants turn and face each other. Without speaking, one does the following: (1) makes the other person smile or (2) stays solemn for as long as possible.
- Form pairs and choose one of the following questions to discuss: What is the weirdest food you've ever eaten? What is your favorite dessert? What is one thing still on your bucket list? What is your favorite travel destination?

Reflective Icebreakers

These explore key biblical concepts. They point toward discipleship by exploring learner experiences connected with the heart of the discussion. They focus on some part of a lesson or suggest some form of service beyond the classroom. Examples:

- A lingering question I have about today's Bible lesson is . . .
- The part of this text that made the most sense to me is . . .
- If Amos's preaching were a sandwich, what type would it be?
- Using the Bible lesson text, each person in a group is to add a word on the board until the team constructs a complete sentence focused on the lesson.
- Post four large signs on the walls featuring these four statements, one each: Strongly Agree, Agree, Disagree, Strongly Disagree. Have students move to a sign of their choice as you read one or more agree/disagree statements to the class.

Some Dos and Don'ts

By now it should be apparent that the best icebreakers enhance the learning experience by creating an atmosphere of safe openness. Icebreakers also grant permission to have a bit of fun in the process. Here are some guidelines in this regard:

- Never force participation. Let students know they are free to opt out.
- Ensure the appropriateness of the activity in terms of class size. What works with a class of 11 might not work as well with a class of 23.
- Ensure the appropriateness of the activity in terms of class demographics. What a 32-year-old student finds engaging might be off-putting to a 62-year-old participant.
- Ensure the appropriateness of the activity in terms of classroom layout. Certain seating arrangements might not foster move-around interactions as other layouts would.

Fight for Feedback

Within a day or two after the class, ask for forthright feedback from one of your students. Here are some questions you could ask:

- What seemed to be the goal of the icebreaker? Was that goal achieved? Why, or why not?
- What reactions did you notice or hear from other class members?
- Why should I or should I not use this icebreaker again?
- What icebreaker ideas for a lesson on [next week's text] come to mind?

June 6
Lesson 1 (KJV)

FREED FROM WORRY

DEVOTIONAL READING: Ezekiel 34:11-16
BACKGROUND SCRIPTURE: Matthew 6:19-34

MATTHEW 6:25-34

**25 Therefore I say unto you, Take no thought
for your life, what ye shall eat, or what ye shall
drink; nor yet for your body, what ye shall put
on. Is not the life more than meat, and the body
than raiment?**
**26 Behold the fowls of the air: for they sow
not, neither do they reap, nor gather into barns;
yet your heavenly Father feedeth them. Are ye
not much better than they?**
**27 Which of you by taking thought can add
one cubit unto his stature?**
**28 And why take ye thought for raiment?
Consider the lilies of the field, how they grow;
they toil not, neither
do they spin:**
**29 And yet I say
unto you, That even
Solomon in all his
glory was not arrayed
like one of these.**
**30 Wherefore, if God so clothe the grass of
the field, which to day is, and to morrow is cast
into the oven, shall he not much more clothe
you, O ye of little faith?**
**31 Therefore take no thought, saying, What
shall we eat? or, What shall we drink? or,
Wherewithal shall we be clothed?**
**32 (For after all these things do the Gentiles
seek:) for your heavenly Father knoweth that
ye have need of all these things.**
**33 But seek ye first the kingdom of God, and
his righteousness; and all these things shall be
added unto you.**
**34 Take therefore
no thought for the
morrow: for the mor-
row shall take thought
for the things of itself.
Sufficient unto the
day is the evil thereof.**

KEY VERSES

Your heavenly Father knoweth that ye have need of all these things. But seek ye first the kingdom of God, and his righteousness; and all these things shall be added unto you. —**Matthew 6:32b-33**

Confident Hope

Unit 1: Jesus Teaches About Faith

Lessons 1–5

Lesson Aims

After participating in this lesson, each learner will be able to:

1. Identify the nature of God's faithful care.
2. Compare and contrast the concepts of "being worried" and "being concerned."
3. Write a prayer that hands over worries to God.

Lesson Outline

Introduction

A. What, Me Worry?

From its appearance in 1952 until it stopped monthly publication in 2019, *Mad* magazine poked fun at politics, television, movies, and everyday American life. Its irreverent theme was that the powerful and influential were continually phony and corrupt. In the pages of *Mad,* everything was falling apart.

On the cover of nearly every *Mad* magazine from 1954 until 2019 was a cartoon image of a gap-toothed, grinning boy who looked like he cared for nothing except making mischief. Christened Alfred E. Neuman, his motto was "What, me worry?" *Mad* was saying that the world might be unraveling, but those who read *Mad*'s cheeky parodies could adopt the cover boy's devil-may-care indifference.

Worry is a universal human experience. Our brains constantly provoke us to evaluate our circumstances and identify threats to our well-being. Threats are many, but even when they are minor, we exaggerate them or imagine threats that do not exist. We leave ourselves with restlessness, sleeplessness, loss of appetite, short tempers, and feelings of hopelessness. We would like to have Alfred E. Neuman's carefree outlook, but we cannot pull it off.

Jesus addresses our deep capacity to worry in today's text. He tells us not to worry, but He does so differently from others. And His conclusions are cause for great faith in God.

B. Lesson Context

Today's text is near the middle of Jesus' discourse known as the Sermon on the Mount (Matthew 5–7). Containing some of the best known of Jesus' teachings, the sermon answers the question raised by Jesus' announcement of the coming of God's kingdom (4:17): What is life like under God's rule?

Jesus' answers touch on the most sensitive areas of human experience. God will bless the weak and lowly (Matthew 5:3-6), those who reflect God's character (5:7-9), and those who suffer in the name of Jesus (5:10-12). God's people will be ambassadors of His redeeming truth (5:13-16), fulfilling God's will with lives that are righteous inside and out (5:17-30). Their integrity and love will reflect God's own, extending even to those who wish them ill (5:31-48). They will be godly not simply on the outside, where others can see, but also inside, where God alone sees (6:1-8, 14-24). God's people will let Him judge others, as they pursue His righteousness and give help to others in that pursuit (7:1-6).

Repeatedly in the sermon, Jesus addressed the problem of worry. Subjects under God's rule are to pray for God's will to be done in all the earth, dependent on Him to supply the resources, grace, and strength that they need daily (Matthew 6:9-13). They live in confidence that God is a kind, generous Father who gladly gives His children what they need to thrive (7:7-12).

Our text is preceded by statements that contrast the trust of a citizen in God's kingdom with the life of someone who lacks that trust. If God cannot be trusted to provide for us, we must provide for ourselves by accumulating and hoarding possessions. But we know those will fail us in the end. Only storing "treasures in heaven" works in the long run. This happens as we put our confidence in God's reliable promise to provide (Matthew 6:19-21).

I. More Than Birds

(Matthew 6:25-27)

A. Freedom from Worry (v. 25)

25. Therefore I say unto you, Take no thought for your life, what ye shall eat, or what ye shall drink; nor yet for your body, what ye shall put on. Is not the life more than meat, and the body than raiment?

The focus of worry is first on survival. For the vast majority of people in Jesus' day, food was grown on one's own land, water drawn from wells daily, and clothing (*raiment*) sewn by hand. Those tasks required an enormous share of one's time, energy, and resources. Most people did not have disposable income. They used all they had to meet their most basic needs.

Jesus was reorienting their focus away from worry and toward trust. For the person who knows the true God and believes that He now rules the world, the perspective is different. There is *more* to *life* than food and clothing.

B. Provision for the Weak (v. 26)

26. Behold the fowls of the air: for they sow not, neither do they reap, nor gather into barns; yet your heavenly Father feedeth them. Are ye not much better than they?

In Jesus' day as now, *the fowls of the air* (birds) are of little value and very vulnerable. But in God's design, they are fed not by their industry but by the *Father.* They *gather* whatever food God provides for them in the natural ecosystem. Jesus used this imagery to argue from the lesser to the greater: if God provides for birds, how much more will He care for people created in His image?

Jesus was not encouraging people to stop growing food. He assumed, rather, that sowing, harvesting, and storing are what people ought to do. After all, God created humans to work in the garden (Genesis 2:15), and He commanded Israel to work (Exodus 20:9; compare 2 Thessalonians 3:10). The idea, rather, is one of trust as a hallmark of faith: because God feeds the birds, how much more are we to trust Him!

Bird Watching

What would our world be without birds? How silent the earth would be without the tweets, chirps, honks, quacks, hoots, and whistles that fill the air with musical serenades!

Think of the wonder of a bird's nest. Birds use whatever materials are available—sticks, grass, moss, mud, and their own saliva—to build places of protection from bad weather and dangerous predators. And what would our lives be if birds had not inspired us to develop the power of flight? Tiny hummingbirds can hover or fly forward,

HOW TO SAY IT

Galilee	*Gal*-uh-lee.
Gentiles	*Jen*-tiles.
omniscientent	ahm-*nish*-unt.
Solomon	*Sol*-o-mun.

backward, upward, sideways, and upside down—all with their wings averaging 53 flaps per second. Eagles soar by catching thermals like sailplanes. Feathers adorn wings that are strong but lightweight, flexible but sturdy.

The heavenly Father endowed birds with amazing abilities, and He provides for them daily. As you ponder how much He cares for them, do you trust the Father to care for you? —D. F.

C. The Futility of Worry (v. 27)

27. Which of you by taking thought can add one cubit unto his stature?

To the comparison with birds, Jesus adds the observation that worry *can add* nothing to life. *Taking thought*, the stressful anticipation of terrible things that might happen in the future, accomplishes nothing lasting. The word translated *stature* can refer either to height or length of life. The expression *one cubit* normally is a measure of physical length, about 18 inches, the distance from an adult's elbow to fingertip. However, the context is not about height but survival. If we understand the reference to be to length of life instead of physical stature, then the "cubit" probably represents a span of time.

What Do You Think?

How would you respond to a real worrywart who says, "I'm not worried—I'm concerned"?

Digging Deeper

If you were to ask the worrywart to rephrase "can add one ____" in verse 27 with a word that personalizes the verse to him or her, what might that word reveal?

II. More Than Flowers

(Matthew 6:28-30)

A. Provision for the Helpless (vv. 28-29)

28. And why take ye thought for raiment? Consider the lilies of the field, how they grow; they toil not, neither do they spin.

Raiment (clothing) is a necessity for humans. For Jesus' audience, clothing was difficult to come by (compare Matthew 6:25, above). Nothing was automated; there were no textile mills. Rather, sheep had to be raised and shorn personally. Flax had to be grown and harvested. Fibers had to be spun into thread. Threads had to be woven into cloth on manual looms. Cloth had to be cut and sewn into garments.

All these processes were done by hand, requiring much time and energy. In the end, only the wealthy owned much more than a single garment per person (compare Judges 14:12). Being without adequate clothing left a person without protection from natural phenomena and signaled a low status as society saw things (compare 1 Corinthians 4:11).

Jesus contrasted this situation with that of common wildflowers. These plants did no work, and certainly did nothing that compared with the tedious handcraft by which Jesus' audience clothed themselves. Flowers were quite ordinary in Galilee, as they are today. Even so, God made them beautiful.

29. And yet I say unto you, That even Solomon in all his glory was not arrayed like one of these.

Solomon was the wealthiest king on earth when he ruled over Israel (1 Kings 10:14-29). When people the world over came to Solomon to hear his wise teaching, they regularly brought rich gifts for him, including "garments, and armour" (10:25). Surely the king with the most splendid palace also had the most beautiful clothing!

But the sight of the wealthiest king's clothing could not rival the sight of a meadow in full bloom. God's care for common flowers surpasses how any person can dress himself or herself.

B. Provision for Small Faith (v. 30)

30. Wherefore, if God so clothe the grass of the field, which to day is, and to morrow is cast into the oven, shall he not much more clothe you, O ye of little faith?

Again Jesus argued from the lesser to the greater. The *grass of the field* lasts only for a season. Then, even the most beautiful blooms dry up and are used in fires for cooking. If God gave splendid clothing to the common plants, how *much more* would He do so for His people? Jesus' audience could see that God cared for the plants. They should see the same for themselves.

In Matthew Jesus used the phrase *ye of little faith* to rebuke His disciples when they failed to trust Him while in danger or need (compare Matthew 8:26 [see lesson 2]; 14:31 [see lesson 4]; 16:8). In every instance, Jesus provided what His "little faith" followers needed.

Jesus commended great faith on occasion (Matthew 8:10; 15:28). But faith as small as a mustard seed can accomplish great things (17:20). Even so, faith that doesn't grow is a stagnant faith (compare 2 Thessalonians 1:3).

III. Trusting God
(Matthew 6:31-34)

A. Questions Worry Asks (v. 31)

31. Therefore take no thought, saying, What shall we eat? or, What shall we drink? or, Wherewithal shall we be clothed?

With the word *therefore,* Jesus began to shift from what not to do to what to do. Another context in which Jesus instructs to *take no thought* is Matthew 10:19 and its parallels in Mark 13:11 and Luke 12:11. The idea is not one of ignoring common-sense planning (see Luke 14:28-32; Romans 15:24; etc.). Rather, what Jesus condemned was undue anxiety (compare Matthew 13:22; Luke 8:14; 21:34; Philippians 4:6).

> *What Do You Think?*
> How do you keep from using Jesus' imperative as an excuse not to do sound planning?
> *Digging Deeper*
> How does Luke 14:28-33 help you frame your answer to this question?

B. Worry and Ignorance (v. 32)

32. (For after all these things do the Gentiles seek:) for your heavenly Father knoweth that ye have need of all these things.

Gentiles refers to those not of the Jewish faith. A common trait among Gentiles was their worship of false gods (example: Deuteronomy 7:1-6). The Gentiles had God's general revelation through nature (Romans 1:18-20), but had not received God's special revelation of His inspired Word (compare Acts 17:22-23). Those who fret over life's necessities are behaving as if they had not received God's Word—like Gentiles do.

The *heavenly Father* is all-knowing (omniscient). He recognizes every human need (compare Matthew 5:45). He is ready and able to meet human needs. To fret is to indicate lack of faith regarding God's character and power.

> *What Do You Think?*
> What are some right and wrong ways to counsel someone who seems overcome with worry?
> *Digging Deeper*
> What could be consequences of quoting today's text and/or Romans 8:28 in this process?

C. Replacing Worry with Faith (vv. 33-34)

33. But seek ye first the kingdom of God, and his righteousness; and all these things shall be added unto you.

In contrast to the one who worries unduly is the person who seeks *first the kingdom of God.* Jesus' followers want above all for God's will to be done everywhere as He reigns (Matthew 6:10). We are to be focused not on providing for ourselves as did Demas (2 Timothy 4:9), but on serving, obeying, and sharing God. The parable in Luke 12:15-21 stands as an additional warning in this regard.

To seek God's kingdom goes hand in hand with seeking *his righteousness.* The two cannot be separated (compare Matthew 5:6, 10, 20; Romans 14:17; Hebrews 1:8). What Jesus expresses here is the active pursuit of righteousness, which complements His earlier statements. For those in the kingdom of God, nothing matters as much as having God's righteousness—His right way—prevailing in the world.

To seek God's kingdom and righteousness before our basic needs appears to make us more vulnerable. But in fact, the opposite is true. Because God reigns in His kingdom, He is able to grant His people exactly what they need, when they need it.

Visual for Lesson 1. *While discussing the question associated with verse 34b, ask how following this imperative could upend the learners' lives.*

No less than Jesus himself promises that those who seek first the kingdom will receive *all these things*—namely the basic needs of life. God's provision is more reliable than anything we could plan and accumulate for ourselves. By yielding first attention to matters of God's kingdom, we as Christians acknowledge that we do not hold ultimate power over our survival. God does! And God promises that He provides for His people under His rule.

We cannot stress enough that this promise has to do with God's meeting our needs, not our wants. Many have distorted this text and others like it to suggest that if people pursue God's kingdom vigorously enough, then God will grant material abundance, whatever we ask for. That obviously ignores the emphasis of this passage (compare James 4:3).

Jesus speaks entirely of foundational needs. The whole emphasis of His teaching in this section is on trust in God and submission to His will. Those who do so realize that they are not in a position to specify the precise amount of material goods that they require. Rather, they trust God to give them what they need in the right amount. They express faith not by demanding more, but by believing that what God supplies is sufficient.

It is also important to note that Jesus' teaching does not imply that people do nothing for their own support. We seek the kingdom first, but we continue to obey God's purpose for humanity as expressed in creation: to do useful work in the world (example: 2 Thessalonians 3:12).

The issue is not whether or not to work, but in how we approach our work (compare 2 Thessalonians 3:8; 1 Timothy 1:8; 2 Timothy 2:21; 4:5). Pursuing God's kingdom frees us from anxiety as we work because we trust God, not to test Him. We see our work not as the means of providing for ourselves, but as God's provision for our needs. Further, we are to see our work as a way of serving God and pursuing God's right way.

Jesus demonstrated personally what it means to seek God's kingdom first. The kingdom came through Jesus' willing death for the sake of those who deserved only death. Though like anyone He did not want to die, Jesus committed himself to the kingdom plan (Matthew 26:42). At first, His death appeared to be the most terrible end to His story. But just as Jesus had promised, He rose to life again (16:21; 28:5-7). Jesus now lives a triumphant, never-ending life for God's triumphant, never-ending kingdom.

The Priority Principle

If you want to make your own soup from scratch, be careful when you add ingredients. As a novice soup-maker, I dumped all the ingredients into the pot at the same time. After an hour of simmering, some items remained undercooked, while others were limp and overdone.

Eventually I learned to start with the firmer items (potatoes, dried beans) and add the softer items (onions, celery, and seasoning) later in the process. A rule we could call "the priority principle" helped improve my soups: Decide what takes priority and add that before anything else.

This principle applies in the spiritual realm as well: God's kingdom and His righteousness come first. If we try to get every little thing in our lives

VISUALS FOR THESE LESSONS

The visual pictured in each lesson (see example above) is a small reproduction of a large, full-color poster included in the *Adult Resources* packet for the Summer Quarter. That packet also contains the very useful *Presentation Tools* CD for teacher use. Order No. 4629121 from your supplier.

in order before pursuing God's kingdom and righteousness, we will end up with a life that resembles my early soup. Are your priorities in order?

—D. F.

34a. Take therefore no thought for the morrow: for the morrow shall take thought for the things of itself.

Jesus' closing remarks remind us again that God is in control of the future over which we have much less, if any, power. To *take . . . no thought* means to have no worry, to not fret. Jesus does not exclude prudent planning or saving (see again Luke 14:28-32 and Romans 15:24). Rather, His words remind us that our planning and saving ought not be motivated by fear. Instead, it is directed by trust in God and for His will.

The expression *the morrow shall take thought for the things of itself* is ironic but clear: "The future," an inanimate entity, obviously does not worry. People, however, are more than capable of worrying! We worry not only about tomorrow, but also about months and years into the future! The God who is sovereign over the future promises to care for His people. Even if the worst happens, God's people can be confident that He will provide for us, both in this life and in the life to come.

What Do You Think?

Considering Luke 11:24-26, what are some thoughts to you can use to help you push worry away permanently?

Digging Deeper

Get specific! Don't answer the above with a vague generality such as "prayer" or "more faith."

34b. Sufficient unto the day is the evil thereof.

Why worry about tomorrow when there are *sufficient* problems today? For the follower of Jesus, the focus is not to be on the uncertain future, but on the concrete present. To worry about tomorrow could be classified as poor stewardship if it results in today's problems going unaddressed. Jesus calls His people to be obedient in "the now," not anxious about "the later."

Conclusion

A. With Us to the End

Few passages of the Bible challenge us relentlessly throughout life as much as does this one. Do you see all the ways it makes us think about our lives? Trusting God for the future, seeking His kingdom constantly as the first priority, makes us ponder how we use our time, where we place our efforts, how we relate to the people around us, and how we feel inside.

Jesus gives His followers a great responsibility in this passage. But we are missing the point if we feel burdened by that responsibility. When we listen carefully, we realize that Jesus is not making our lives harder with these words. Rather, He is making our lives easier. We are free from the burden of worry when we submit to God.

Clearly, worry does not keep us alive and well. Only God's provision can sustain us through the trials of life. And certainly only God can give us a life that triumphs over death. God's provision is powerful. He provides exactly what His people need. Trusting in God's provision is the antidote to worry. Do you worry but rename it something like "concern" to pretend you are not violating Jesus' command?

What Do You Think?

Which part of today's lesson will you have the most problem applying to your life?

Digging Deeper

Who can and will you confide in to help you through this struggle?

B. Prayer

God our Father, give us confidence in Your provision so that our worries are silenced! As You do, may we respond with trust so that our hearts will pursue Your rule. Grant us strength in the Holy Spirit to pursue Your righteousness as subjects in Your kingdom. In Jesus' name we pray. Amen!

C. Thought to Remember

"Worry . . . empties today of its strength."

—Corrie ten Boom (1892–1983)

INVOLVEMENT LEARNING

Enhance your lesson with KJV Bible Student *(from your curriculum supplier) and the reproducible activity page (at www.standardlesson.com or in the back of the* KJV Standard Lesson Commentary Deluxe Edition*).*

Into the Lesson

Write the following on the board for one minute of silent reflection:

The time I was most worried was . . .

After calling time, ask learners to form pairs and to share responses and how worrying helped solve the problems. After two minutes reconvene for whole-class sharing of insights.

Alternative. Before learners arrive, place in chairs copies of the "Corrie on Worry" exercise from the activity page, which you can download. Allow students in pairs to unscramble the sentence. (It is also found, in a shorter version, as the lesson's Thought to Remember.)

Tell the class, "Today as we study some familiar advice from Jesus about worry, let's contrast His teaching with our tendencies."

Into the Word

Write this question on the board:

Why should we not worry?

Then ask a volunteer to read today's text aloud while class members listen for answers to that question. Form pairs or triads to make lists of all reasons that Jesus gives in the lesson text for not worrying. After about five minutes, have each group share an item from its list that another group has not already mentioned. Write those discoveries on the board as the groups report. Expect the resulting list to look something like this:

- Life is more important than "stuff."
- Since God takes care of the less valuable, then He will take care of the more valuable—us.
- Worry doesn't add anything to life.
- Pagans pursue material things as their priority.
- God knows what we need.
- We'll have everything we need if we seek first His kingdom and righteousness.

Before class, recruit several learners to bring pictures or objects that illustrate God's care of animals, trees, flowers, etc. (*Alternative.* Bring these yourself.) Pass them among class members so that everyone can see them up close. Ask how these serve to underscore what Jesus says in His sermon. Encourage open discussion.

Next, have a class member recruited ahead of time deliver a two-minute lecture on the topic, "Materialism Then and Now." (*Alternative.* Prepare and deliver this mini lecture yourself.) Use information from the Lesson Context and commentary that follows it to open a discussion on what we call "disposable income." Ask who had it and didn't back in Bible times; follow by asking who has it and who doesn't today. (*Option.* Turn the latter discussion into an in-class research activity using smartphones; challenge learners to find a calculator that computes where they stand with regard to wealth among the world's population.)

Into Life

Form teams to debate the following resolution, one side affirming it, the other side denying it.

Resolved: *Today, Jesus' teaching applies differently to those who worry about necessities to survive vs. those who worry about non-necessities.*

Research and use the best debate format, given the nature of your class. (*Option.* Recruit team leaders days ahead of time for advance preparation.)

Alternative. Distribute copies of the "Worry and Health" exercise from the activity page to research groups of three to five learners. After teams reach conclusions, reconvene for whole-class discussion.

After either alternative, wrap up by brainstorming outcomes of taking Matthew 6:33 seriously. Conclude with a minute of silence for learners to write a prayer that hands worries over to God.

Option. As learners depart, distribute copies of the "My Seeking Week" exercise from the activity page to be completed as a take-home. Promise to discuss results during next week's class.

June 13
Lesson 2 (KJV)

Delivered from Fear

Devotional Reading: Psalm 107:23-32
Background Scripture: Matthew 8:23-27; Mark 4:35-41; Luke 8:22-25

Matthew 8:23-27

23 And when he was entered into a ship, his disciples followed him.

24 And, behold, there arose a great tempest in the sea, insomuch that the ship was covered with the waves: but he was asleep.

25 And his disciples came to him, and awoke him, saying, Lord, save us: we perish.

26 And he saith unto them, Why are ye fearful, O ye of little faith? Then he arose, and rebuked the winds and the sea; and there was a great calm.

27 But the men marvelled, saying, What manner of man is this, that even the winds and the sea obey him!

Key Verse

He saith unto them, Why are ye fearful, O ye of little faith? Then he arose, and rebuked the winds and the sea; and there was a great calm. —**Matthew 8:26**

CONFIDENT
HOPE

Unit 1: Jesus Teaches About Faith

LESSONS 1–5

LESSON AIMS

After participating in this lesson, each learner will be able to:

1. Recall key elements of Jesus' stilling of the storm.

2. Compare and contrast the text with the other "little faith" passages of Matthew 6:30; 14:31; 16:8; and Luke 12:28 in their contexts.

3. Repent of an instance of a lack of faith.

LESSON OUTLINE

Introduction

A. What Are You Afraid Of?

Context can cause the question above to be answered in different ways. It all depends on when, where, why, how, and by whom it is asked.

As an honest inquiry into what causes fear, we know that people experience fears of various kinds. Some common fears are fears of open spaces (agoraphobia) and closed spaces (claustrophobia). Much rarer is a fear of dogs (cynophobia) and of cats (ailurophobia). Between these two is a list that is virtually endless. And fears are very individualized. Sometimes they seem to make little sense—such as fear of mice on the part of a strong, smart person. Fears may be connected with traumas that have left an indelible mark on a person.

There is another way we can use the title question: it can be meant rhetorically—as a statement rather than an inquiry. The sense is something like, "You know that you have no reason to be afraid." We all wish that we could say this to ourselves and our fears would disappear. Unfortunately, fear tends to persist even when we try to reason ourselves out of it.

Fear, as a God-given self-defense mechanism, can trigger a reaction of *fight, flight,* or *freeze.* The problem is that the particular reaction that results may be irrationally inappropriate or even harmful in a given context. At lower levels, chronic fear can ruin appetite, raise blood pressure, and cause ulcers. Fear itself can kill.

Our text today is about a situation that provoked fear: the fear of death in a deadly situation. How Jesus spoke and acted in the face of that fear can teach us much about the Lord we serve.

B. Lesson Context: Sea of Galilee

Jesus' ministry in Matthew's Gospel takes place mostly in Galilee, the northern portion of ancient Israel. The region was named for the body of water at its center, known in the New Testament as the Sea of Galilee or the Sea of Tiberias (John 6:1). It is about 41,000 acres in size, about 12 miles north to south and 7.5 miles east to west. Its size makes it more of a "lake" than a "sea"; by contrast, Lake Erie is about 150 times as large as the Sea of Galilee. Indeed, the latter is referred to as "the lake of Gennesaret" in Luke 5:1. Nestled between steep hills on the east and west, one could stand on the hills and see to the other side. The distance would require much effort to row from one side to the other. The Sea of Galilee was a center of fishing during the time of Jesus. Some of His 12 disciples had been fishermen there (Matthew 4:18-22). These men had much experience with this lake and its dangers.

In addition to fishing, the inhabitants of the area used the lake as a medium of transportation from one village to another. Rowing across the sea was faster than the alternative of walking around on shore. We can imagine that on a typical day the sea was dotted with small boats—some fishing, some carrying travelers. On most days, those boats carried their passengers safely.

C. Lesson Context: Miracles

Following the Sermon on the Mount in Matthew 5–7 (see Lesson Context of lesson 1), which sets forth Jesus' authority in teaching, chapters 8–9 focuses largely on Jesus' miracles. These demonstrate His authority in actions as they consistently pointed to a power that could belong to God alone. With a word, Jesus was able to heal the sick (Matthew 8:5-13), cleanse leprosy (Luke 17:12-19; see lesson 5), cast out evil spirits (Mark 7:24-30), and command the forces of nature (Mark 11:12-14, 19-21). His miracles established that Jesus was either the most wonderful prophet ever sent by God or that He was something more than a prophet.

Jesus did not use His divine power for His own benefit (compare Matthew 4:1-11; 26:53). His miracles were for the sake of others, especially those whose situation seemed hopeless. As such, the miracles were signs that God's kingdom— His promised reign over all creation that restores His righteous purpose—was breaking into the world. God's reign would vanquish the sin-threat and its consequences. God's people would then live in His presence, safe and secure, for eternity.

Jesus' miracles demonstrated that promised future. His enemies attributed His ability to satanic powers (Matthew 12:24) and mocked Him (27:42). Still, Jesus made salvation possible by giving of His life. His resulting resurrection was His greatest act of power. But as we begin today's text, that is yet a year or so in the future. (The events of today's text are also recorded in Mark 4:35-41 and Luke 8:22-25.)

I. The Perilous Situation

(Matthew 8:23-24)

A. Following Jesus (v. 23)

23a. And when he was entered into a ship.

This phrase invites the reader to connect this story to the ones just before it (Matthew 8:18-22). There, Jesus encountered two men as He was about to cross the lake in *a ship*. Both wanted to follow Jesus, so Jesus pointed out the cost of doing so. God's kingdom brings His promised blessings to His people, but it costs those people everything they have (Matthew 13:44-46). It's unclear from that text if either man ended up following Jesus (compare Luke 9:57-62).

23b. His disciples followed him.

Matthew does not specify Jesus' intended destination at this point (contrast Mark 4:35; Luke 8:22). In this Gospel, we have to wait until Matthew 8:28 to discover that He and *His disciples* were headed to "the country of the Gergesenes," on the other side of the lake.

We should note that any follower of Jesus may be referred to in the Gospels as a disciple (example: Matthew 27:57). The term refers to a learner who accepts and assists in spreading the teaching of another. But since the ship obviously had some size limitations, the disciples mentioned were

HOW TO SAY IT

agoraphobia	uh-*gore*-uh-***foe***-be-uh.
ailurophobia	eye-*lur*-uh-***foe***-be-uh.
claustrophobia	*klaw*-struh-***foe***-be-uh.
cynophobia	*sigh*-nuh-***foe***-be-uh.
Galilee	*Gal*-uh-lee.
Gennesaret	Geh-*ness*-uh-ret (G as in get).
Gergesenes	*Gur*-guh-seenz.
Mediterranean	*Med*-uh-tuh-***ray***-nee-un.
Pax Romana *(Latin)*	*Pahks* Ro-*mah*-nah.

most likely only the 12 original ones (see Matthew 10:1-4). As they boarded the ship, they did so in obedience, following their teacher. In Matthew's Gospel, this band of disciples is just beginning to emerge as an identifiable unit.

Jesus did not choose these 12 because they were exemplary in every way, however. All four Gospels portray them largely as failing to understand Jesus' mission (examples: Matthew 16:13-27; Mark 10:35-45; Luke 18:15-17; John 4:25-38). They were often fearful and spiritually deaf (examples: Matthew 14:27; Mark 4:40; Luke 9:45). As he went to His death, He predicted that they would all fall away, even as He looked forward to welcoming them back after His resurrection (Matthew 26:31-32; see 28:16-20). They continued to misunderstand His mission at least up until the time of His ascension (Acts 1:6).

B. In a Deadly Storm (v. 24)

24a. And, behold, there arose a great tempest in the sea, insomuch that the ship was covered with the waves.

As sometimes happened on this lake, a storm *arose* that took the experienced boatmen by surprise. Storms in Galilee travel west to east from the Mediterranean Sea. The area to the immediate west of the lake consists of steep, high hills separated by narrow valleys. That means that storms can appear from the west with little warning for those on the lake since their view of approaching weather is blocked by the hills.

The remains of a first-century fishing boat was discovered along the shore in 1986. Its size (about 27 feet in length and 8 feet in width) indicates that *waves* of just a couple of feet could overwhelm such a vessel, especially when accompanied by rain. In deep water far from shore, these men faced death if their ship did not stay afloat.

24b. But he was asleep.

Mark's account specifies that Jesus was "in the hinder part of the ship, asleep on a pillow" (Mark 4:38). This refers to the stern of the vessel.

Somehow Jesus was sleeping through the rain, wind, waves, and noise. Was He so exhausted He could sleep through anything? Was His stamina so drained that He could not respond? The text does not say. Some students take the position that answering yes to either question would contradict what we and the disciples later learn about Jesus in Matthew 26:36-45 and John 13:3. Others think that a yes answer is possible based on Matthew 4:2; 27:32; and John 4:6.

Either way, the fact of Jesus' sleeping during a storm should not be bypassed too quickly. The psalmist presents sleep as the answer of a confident believer to the dangers of this world (see Psalms 3:5; 4:8). Jesus shows no fear because He truly has no reason to fear. We can safely assume that a deadly storm would awaken most, if not all, of us. But Jesus experienced a freedom from fear that is unlike any in our ordinary experience. This surely points to Jesus' confidence in His identity. He knew His mission was leading Him to the cross (John 12:23-36; 19:30); He would not die on the sea.

What Do You Think?

Under what circumstances should you not allow another person's fear to become your own? Why?

Digging Deeper

What Scripture passages back up your position in this regard?

What to Do While God "Sleeps"

I woke to the sound of gunfire. Another conflict had erupted between refugees and the host community. Tens of thousands of refugees had fled their homeland, where planes were bombing their villages. Now they faced daily uncertainty: lack of food, lack of water. And whenever someone stole a goat or got into a fight, violence and retaliation quickly followed. Was God sleeping?

Some refugees and those of the host community had resorted to violence and vengeance in the midst of God's apparent inaction. But others had developed a deep and transformative faith. Hassan (name changed) had chosen faith. Whenever his neighbors ran to get their rifles, Hassan would stop them and ask them to pray instead. Despite the danger, despite God's seeming slumber, Hassan chose to trust God.

When God "sleeps" through your desperate need, will you respond with bitter violence, or will you step out in faith and encourage others to do the same? Remember: "he that keepeth Israel shall neither slumber nor sleep" (Psalm 121:4).

—D. G.

II. The Act of Deliverance

(Matthew 8:25-27)

A. Cry of the Helpless (v. 25)

25a. And his disciples came to him, and awoke him, saying, Lord.

Unlike Jesus, the *disciples* registered their peril. Their skills on the sea were not enough to protect them from this grave danger. They were all going to die! For Jesus to be sleeping through the storm was incomprehensible to them. They did not yet understand Jesus' identity.

The disciples needed someone more powerful than themselves. And to their credit, they at least knew who that someone was. Other boats were also out on the water (Mark 4:36), but the disciples were focused on their own peril as they addressed Jesus as *Lord.* This term ascribed authority to Him, but exactly what kind of authority they meant isn't entirely clear.

While obviously God is often called Lord, the Greek word translated in this way can just mean master or sir (examples: Matthew 6:24; 27:63). It is possible that the disciples acknowledged Jesus as their teacher, but not as equal to God at this time. Perhaps that idea is like a seed in their minds, about to germinate.

Certainly the disciples had much still to learn about who Jesus is. Even when Peter later declared Jesus to be "the Christ, the Son of the living God" (Matthew 16:16), the disciple immediately showed that what he had just confessed he did not yet understand (see 16:21-27). A clearer understanding of what it meant for Jesus to be the Christ would not come to the disciples until after He rose to life from the grave (example: Luke 24:26-34). Still, the disciples already knew enough to call Him Lord—one superior to them in authority in some way.

25b. Save us: we perish.

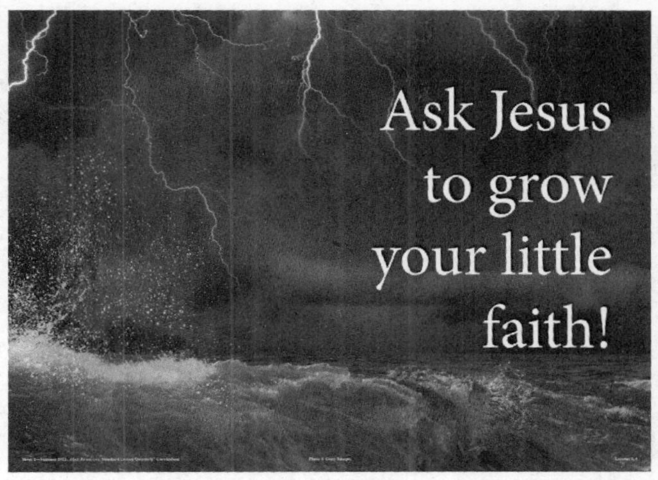
Ask Jesus
to grow
your little
faith!

Visual for Lessons 2 & 4. *While considering verse 26a, have learners pray silently for one minute, asking for growing faith in a specific situation.*

For many believers, the concept of being saved refers primarily (if not exclusively) to God's gift of salvation from sin and death (example: Ephesians 2:4-8). In Jesus' day, however, the Greek word translated *save* and its variants were used for all kinds of rescuing. It was often used by political and military leaders who took credit for benefits they brought to the people they led. This was especially true of the emperors, who "saved" the people in their empire through the Pax Romana (the "Roman Peace").

The Greek word behind the translation could also be used of any act that brought benefit to those in need or protection for those in danger (example: Luke 23:39). Clearly the disciples were asking Jesus to save them from drowning in the stormy sea, not requesting eternal salvation.

We too cry out to Jesus in this way at times. We also fear perishing physically because of events—some of our own making—in this sin-sick world. When we look at the disciples in this account, in many ways we are looking in a mirror.

B. An Authoritative Word (v. 26)

26a. And he saith unto them, Why are ye fearful, O ye of little faith?

The disciples had enough reason to trust Jesus in this terrible storm. The mighty power He had already demonstrated was more than adequate evidence (examples: Matthew 4:23-25; 8:1-13).

Their fear stemmed from their *little faith.* The

word being translated occurs five times in the Gospels (here and Matthew 6:30 [see lesson 1]; 14:31; 16:8; and Luke 12:28). Its use indicates a mild rebuke. If they had much faith, they could trust that Jesus would act for them, even if He did not act immediately. By this point in their experience with Jesus, the disciples should have been able to recognize that such dangers pose no real threat, given the evidence of miracles. This fact should have resulted in showing more courage when facing situations that normally result in fear and anxiety. The five uses of "little faith" reveal sadly that this would not be the last time Jesus would chastise them in this regard.

Jesus' words challenged the disciples to let their faith grow to fit the magnitude of their Lord's power and His gracious goodwill to use it on their behalf. Elsewhere, Jesus taught that "faith as a grain of mustard seed" could move a mountain (Matthew 17:20). Little faith has potential, but in this case fear weakened it.

What Do You Think?

Realizing that fear is a God-given emotion, how will you know when a reaction of fear is natural and when it indicates lack of faith?

Digging Deeper

How do John 7:13; 9:22; 12:42; 1 Peter 3:6, 14; 1 John 4:18; and Revelation 2:10 help frame your answer?

26b. Then he arose, and rebuked the winds and the sea; and there was a great calm.

Jesus' rebuke of *the winds and the sea* is something of a counterpart to His rebuke of the disciples' little faith. Some believe that the Lord will meet their needs only if they have enough faith to satisfy Him. But Jesus saves the small of faith even as He urges them on to greater faith. We should realize, however, that having little faith is perilously close to having no faith (compare Matthew 17:14-20). And, paradoxically, belief and unbelief can exist side by side (Mark 9:24).

For a moment, the act of saving in the lesson text foreshadows saving for eternity. The angel announced to Joseph before Jesus' birth, "He shall save his people from their sins" (Matthew 1:21). Jesus' mighty deeds were visible signs of the greater work He would do to cleanse the guilty and restore them as God's eternal people (Titus 2:11-14).

Jesus' followers went on to face many perilous situations that could easily—and often did—take their lives. They ultimately learned to rely on Jesus to protect them, even to restore life by resurrection (2 Corinthians 4:17). He will always use His almighty, divine power for the long-term benefit of those who love Him. That is true even when (or especially when) the situation seems hopeless and He seems unresponsive to our need (compare Job 30:20; Psalm 22:2; Revelation 6:10).

What Do You Think?

How would you respond to someone who takes today's text to mean we shouldn't bother to wear life jackets when out boating because Jesus is always with us?

Digging Deeper

Going the other way, at what point does a concern for "safety first" become an idol?

Praying from Fear to Faith

At 2:00 a.m. I was still on my knees crying out desperately to the Lord. Foremost on my mind was a stormy conflict that had been brewing between two Christian groups. One group was bent on a course of action that I thought would be disastrous. I begged God to intervene.

As I pleaded with God to prevent this other group's plans, it felt like God spoke silently in a bemused tone, "Would it really be so bad?" The simple rebuke completely changed my outlook. I calmed down, thinking, *Where is my faith? Can't God work through this other group too?*

At that point my prayer shifted from one of desperate pleading to one of trusting that God would accomplish what He desired through whichever group He chose to work through. That would happen even if I didn't understand.

Are your prayers filled with anxious worry or with joyful trust? Can you faithfully follow the one who commands sky and sea—the one who loves us more than we can imagine—regardless of the storm around you? If not, why not? —D. G.

C. A Response of Amazement (v. 27)

27a. But the men marvelled.

As God's words put the waters of the seas in their place (Genesis 1:9-10), so Jesus' words did with the storm. The New Testament makes clear that Jesus is the Creator. That the Creator is able to command His own creation in a miraculous way should not surprise us (see John 11:1-4; Colossians 1:16). But witnessing Jesus' power at work makes the disciples awestruck. This is the frequent reaction when people see Jesus' mighty power at work in the form of miracles and in word (examples: Matthew 9:33; 15:31; 21:20; 22:22; 27:14). Mark emphasizes only the great fear of the disciples (Mark 4:41).

> *What Do You Think?*
> Under what circumstances, if any, is it appropriate to cause fear in another person?
> *Digging Deeper*
> What Scripture passages back you up on that?

27b. Saying, What manner of man is this, that even the winds and the sea obey him!

The disciples recognized that what Jesus did was not the work of an ordinary *man*. The disciples were experiencing what some call "cognitive dissonance" today. What they saw—Jesus commanding *the winds and the sea* and both obeying Him—did not match their normal, day to day experience that storms do not obey human commands.

Psalm 107:23-32 describes a scene very much like the one the disciples had just experienced. Men went out to sea, witnessing the wonders of the waters God created. A storm arose, lifting huge waves, provoking terror in the sailors. They cried out to the Lord, the God of Israel, for protection. God stilled the storm, eliciting joy and thanksgiving from those whose lives had been spared. There was no doubt who had saved them (compare Jonah 2:1-9).

Jesus had just done what the psalmist described God as doing. Only the one who created the wind and the waves in the first place can command them. In Jesus, God had become a man. Because of His mighty power that He graciously exercised on humanity's behalf, they had nothing to fear.

Conclusion

A. Faith Silences Fear

What do you fear? Typically, the things that make us most afraid are those that threaten us in some way because we can't control them. Instead of praying first, we first try our best to gain control. But in the end we recognize that our control is very limited. Disease stalks even those who eat right and exercise. Financial crises strike even the prudent. Accidents happen to the careful. Our protective reach cannot constantly extend as far as those we love.

There is a far superior alternative to trying to maintain control over our circumstances first and, when that fails, turning to the Lord. The alternative is to reverse those priorities. Because Jesus gave His life for us, we can surely trust Him to do for us what He did for 12 men of little faith in a small ship—and more.

The created world is filled with mortal dangers. Our reaction should be that of the psalmist:

> He that dwelleth in the secret place of the most High shall abide under the shadow of the Almighty. I will say of the LORD, He is my refuge and my fortress: my God; in him will I trust. Surely he shall deliver thee from the snare of the fowler, and from the noisome pestilence. (Psalm 91:1-3).

> *What Do You Think?*
> What action will you take to overcome your most troubling fear?
> *Digging Deeper*
> Who can you confide in to help you through this struggle?

B. Prayer

Lord God, we confess that we are a fearful people. Our faith is small. Help us grow in faith as we freely confess our mixture of belief and unbelief as did the man in Mark 9:24 as we entrust ourselves to You. In Jesus' name we pray. Amen.

C. Thought to Remember

Allow the Lord to grow your faith
and silence your fears.

Involvement Learning

Enhance your lesson with KJV Bible Student *(from your curriculum supplier) and the reproducible activity page (at www.standardlesson.com or in the back of the* KJV Standard Lesson Commentary Deluxe Edition*).*

Into the Lesson

Draw a large circle on the board. In the center, write the word *STORM.* Ask class members to mention a time when they experienced a major storm of life; encourage expressions of feelings they had during the storm. Expect responses such as fear, anxiety, worry, pain, uncertainty, loss, calm, and fatalism. Affirm all responses by jotting them inside the circle as they are voiced. (Concentrate on the feelings without pressing for details of the problems.) As this is happening, have a volunteer copy responses onto separate pieces of paper suitable to use flashcards (to be used below).

Make a transition by saying, "Let's see what we can learn by comparing and contrasting these feelings with those of people who were in the very presence of Jesus himself during a storm in the first century AD."

Into the Word

Before having today's text read aloud, distribute the flashcards created above to members of the class as evenly as possible. (*Option.* Depending on how many words you've written and the size of your class, you may find it desirable to ask those holding flashcards to come to the front of the room.)

As the text is read aloud, ask class members to show cards they're holding that reflect what they think the disciples were feeling as each verse is read. Do this slowly, or perhaps do it twice. Then, for every card that was raised, underline the corresponding word inside the circle you created on the board earlier.

Distribute handouts (you prepare) of the following questions to small groups of three or four:

1–What makes us think the disciples felt each of these emotions?
2–Would we add some words to what we've already written to describe what the disciples felt?
3–Was it wrong or sinful for them to be afraid?
4–What did they do that was right?
5–What does their reaction teach us about how to handle our own fears?
6–What differences and similarities do you see in other passages where Jesus voiced concern about "little faith"? (See Matthew 6:30 [last week's lesson]; 14:31; and 16:8.)

Include on the handout the following four column headers for use in discussing question 6. Leave plenty of room for writing underneath:

Where was it	***Who*** was involved	***How*** did it turn out	***What*** can we learn

As groups work through the questions, write the same four column headers on the board. After groups finish working, consolidate groups' input under these headers to compare and contrast discoveries.

Option. For broader comparison with other texts, distribute copies of the "Sailors Afraid" exercise from the activity page, which you can download. Have learners to complete it in groups. Discuss as time allows.

Into Life

Give each learner a slip of paper on which is printed the following:

A time when I gave in to faithless fear was . . .

Ask learners to complete the sentence as you hasten to add that you will not collect them. Allow a time for volunteers to read their completions. (If the nature and mood of the class permits it, you can ask jokingly, "What are the rest of you afraid of?")

Option. Distribute copies of the "Fear Busters" exercise on the activity page. Allow time for learners to work in groups for the Scripture search portion of the activity and then complete the second half of it individually. Encourage placement where learners will see theirs daily, as indicated.

June 20
Lesson 3 (KJV)

HEALED BY FAITH

DEVOTIONAL READING: Proverbs 3:1-8
BACKGROUND SCRIPTURE: Matthew 9:18-26; Mark 5:21-43; Luke 8:40-56

MATTHEW 9:18-26

18 While he spake these things unto them, behold, there came a certain ruler, and worshipped him, saying, My daughter is even now dead: but come and lay thy hand upon her, and she shall live.

19 And Jesus arose, and followed him, and so did his disciples.

20 And, behold, a woman, which was diseased with an issue of blood twelve years, came behind him, and touched the hem of his garment:

21 For she said within herself, If I may but touch his garment, I shall be whole.

22 But Jesus turned him about, and when he saw her, he said, Daughter, be of good comfort; thy faith hath made thee whole. And the woman was made whole from that hour.

23 And when Jesus came into the ruler's house, and saw the minstrels and the people making a noise,

24 He said unto them, Give place: for the mid is not dead, but sleepeth. And they laughed him to scorn.

25 But when the people were put forth, he went in, and took her by the hand, and the maid arose.

26 And the fame hereof went abroad into all that land.

KEY VERSE

Jesus turned him about, and when he saw her, he said, Daughter, be of good comfort; thy faith hath made thee whole. And the woman was made whole from that hour. —**Matthew 9:22**

Photo © Getty Images

Confident Hope

Unit 1: Jesus Teaches About Faith

Lessons 1–5

Lesson Aims

After participating in this lesson, each learner will be able to:

1. Identify common elements of the two miracles of the lesson text.

2. Explain the significance of the two miracles of today's text.

3. Distinguish circumstances when retelling of the two miracles would be appropriate or not in counseling contexts.

Lesson Outline

Introduction

A. Go to the Specialist

Have you ever had to see a specialist? You went to see your regular physician, and, for whatever reason, he or she sent you on to a specialist—someone better trained or with more experience for your situation. When the need is critical, you want the very best help.

Jesus is the ultimate specialist! He specializes in the critical needs of the body and of the soul. As people need to have confidence in a physician's knowledge and skills to treat our needs, so our text challenges us to put our faith in Christ, even in (or especially in) the darkest hours. When others are not specialized enough to help, Jesus is!

B. Lesson Context

Today's lesson takes place late in the second year of Jesus' public ministry. He conducted much of the early part of His ministry around the Sea of Galilee. Specifically, much of the ministry was on the north end, in and around the village of Capernaum. Jesus' popularity was very high (example: Luke 8:4, 19). He taught about life and the kingdom of God in the rural areas and towns along the western side of the sea (example: Matthew 5–7). His teaching was pointed, His spirit magnetic. And having already healed so many people, His reputation had spread far and wide. (See Lesson Context: Sea of Galilee and Lesson Context: Miracles in lesson 2, pages 354–355.)

But public opinion had begun to polarize. People watched and listened to Jesus very closely, but for different reasons. Not everyone adored Him. Today's text occurs in a section of Matthew that contrasts Jesus' authority and power, as demonstrated in miracles, with the objections of religious leaders. Jesus raised their ire by forgiving sins (Matthew 9:2-3), by associating with marginalized people (9:11), and by violating certain traditions (9:14).

Despite the objections of the powerful, Jesus brought God's grace to bear for the blessing of God's people. As Jesus dealt with the crowds, He never lost sight of the individual (example: Matthew 8:1-3). Our text today witnesses to two examples in this regard. Both circumstances involve tragically common instances of human suffering.

The events considered below occurred after Jesus ended His response to a controversy over fasting. He was doing something fundamentally new in God's plan, something that required people to lay aside the old (Matthew 9:16-17). This was no time for mourning and fasting but instead for rejoicing because God's promised redeemer had arrived (9:15). The deeds that followed provided a glimpse of that newness in the kingdom of God. (Mark 5:21-43 and Luke 8:40-56 offer parallel accounts.)

I. A Grieving Family

(Matthew 9:18-19)

A. A Father's Request (v. 18)

18a. While he spake these things unto them, behold, there came a certain ruler, and worshipped him.

The interjection *behold* draws the reader's attention to what happens next (see Matthew 9:20, below). The *ruler* who approached Jesus held a prominent position in the local Jewish community in that he oversaw the day-to-day operations of the synagogue. This man's title suggests that he was respected and mature in his faith in God. Though Matthew did not name the ruler, Luke identified him as Jairus (Luke 8:41).

The ruler *worshipped* Jesus in the posture of a supplicant approaching his king. Though the term can apply to the worship given to God (example: Matthew 4:10), it can also simply indicate great respect for someone of honor or power (example: 2 Samuel 16:4, same word in the Greek version of the Old Testament). Either way, it is a humble posture. The ruler might not have realized Jesus' divine identity. But, like many others, he did recognize Jesus as a man of exceptional authority, and probably at least considered Him to be a great prophet (compare: Luke 7:16; 9:19).

> *What Do You Think?*
>
> What mental posture will you assume the next time you approach God in prayer regarding a need you have? Why?
>
> *Digging Deeper*
>
> What positive and negative elements of the account of Job help you answer this?

18b. Saying, My daughter is even now dead: but come and lay thy hand upon her, and she shall live.

It must have wrenched the ruler's heart to announce that his *daughter* was *dead*. Again, Luke gives more detail: she was 12 years old (Luke 8:42). But the man did not ask Jesus to join him in mourning. Rather, this father made the statement of remarkable faith that we see here. He sought the reversal of his loss, the restoration of his daughter to life.

How did the man come to believe Jesus was capable of miracles, including raising the dead? Certainly he must have heard of Jesus' healing miracles (Matthew 4:23; 8:16; etc.). Perhaps he had witnessed one. But to this point in Matthew's Gospel, Jesus had not raised someone from death. Still, the story of Elijah raising the widow's son (1 Kings 17:17-24) serves as precedent for a prophet's being able to raise the dead. The ruler surely knew the account. The connection is strengthened by the fact that, when the crowds misidentified Christ, they sometimes believed Him to be Elijah (Matthew 16:14). In any case, the father's hope was that Jesus was able to bring the dead back to life.

Prayer for Hope

I entered the hospital room, ready to offer comfort to a mourning family. But I did not want to

HOW TO SAY IT

Capernaum	Kuh-*per*-nay-um.
Elijah	Ee-*lye*-juh.
Galilee	*Gal*-uh-lee.
Israel	*Iz*-ray-el.
Jairus	*Jye*-rus or *Jay*-ih-rus.
Moses	*Mo*-zes or *Mo*-zez.
Sabbath	*Sah*-bawth.
synagogue	*sin*-uh-gog.

interrupt the voices quietly singing hymns in a language I did not know. An immigrant couple stood cradling their baby. The mother sang along with two friends who had come to support them. The father prayed over his infant daughter, who had died. He prayed for strength for his family and for the welcome of his daughter into the arms of God.

The depth of the parents' grief was coupled with a hope and peace I've rarely sensed at the death of a child. Their friends' support, the reassuring sound of the hymns, and, most importantly, the presence of God in the room reminded me that we can find hope in the midst of suffering. Even when God chooses not to provide healing on earth, His presence can bring peace and hope to the family left behind. Will you ask Jesus to journey with you in sorrow? —L. M. W.

B. Jesus' Response (v. 19)

19. And Jesus arose, and followed him, and so did his disciples.

Probably some of the ruler's friends were certain that *Jesus* would not go with *him*. But the great physician, Jesus, makes house calls. And, as usual, *his disciples* followed.

II. A Story Interrupted

(Matthew 9:20-22)

A. A Woman's Need (vv. 20-21)

20. And, behold, a woman, which was diseased with an issue of blood twelve years, came behind him, and touched the hem of his garment.

This transition repeats *behold* (see Matthew 9:18, above), alerting the reader that a new piece of narrative is interrupting. The second account, of an unnamed *woman,* begins here (see Lesson Context). This method of telling the two stories builds tension in the first, as we wait to see what will happen with the ruler and his daughter. It also invites the reader to feel the exasperation that the ruler and the disciples might feel at being stalled on their important errand. Will the girl live or not? We must read on to find out.

The woman's *issue of blood* was what we would call hemorrhaging. This was probably from constant menstruation, a debilitating physical condition. The woman's body would have needed to replace lost blood constantly for *twelve years* (the same amount of time the ruler's daughter had been alive; see Luke 8:42). All her energy would go to that vital need, leaving her weak and vulnerable to other sickness. Furthermore, she "had spent all that she had" going to physicians, who only made her condition worse (Mark 5:26). There had not been any specialist in 12 years who could treat her properly.

This illness also made her life intolerable in being a social outcast. According to the Law of Moses, any flow of blood made a woman ceremonially unclean (Leviticus 15:25). This law was meant to illustrate to the entire nation of Israel the need all people have for God's repeated cleansing. But in application, it meant that the unclean woman could have no social contact with anyone except another woman who was currently menstruating. The clean became unclean by contact with the unclean (examples: Leviticus 15:16-27). So for this woman, the Law of Moses was a curse (compare Galatians 3).

The hem of his garment may refer to one of the tassels that the Law of Moses specified for the garments of the Israelites (Numbers 15:38; Deuteronomy 22:12). Being ritually unclean, the woman could not approach Jesus directly. Thus she attempted to slip in unnoticed. Even so, she risked putting many into unknowing states of being unclean when they brushed against her in the crowd.

21. For she said within herself, If I may but touch his garment, I shall be whole.

The woman did not give in to the despair. Though contact with the unclean normally contaminated the clean person (see commentary above), the woman believed that the reverse would happen. She, like the girl's father, apparently believed that Jesus' power, demonstrated in other miracles, could meet her need as well. Just the slightest *touch* would be enough for a great healing.

The word translated *be whole* is translated "be saved" in other contexts (examples: Matthew 10:22; 19:25). Though we usually think of saving and salvation in spiritual terms, the word could indicate physical healing (as in this text), political release (a typical reason for Roman emperors to refer to themselves as saviors), and other forms of liberation, depending on context.

Understanding the many uses of this word points us to the ways that Jesus intends to save us. Though we will have everlasting life with Him, we can also experience now the kinds of renewal that this woman desired. She wanted an end to her physical suffering; she wanted an end to her years of social ostracism. She needed help that wouldn't cost her money she didn't have.

We too can experience healing and community in Christ. Realizing that she had nowhere else to turn, the woman put her trust in the one whose power could make her well. In her weakness she reached out to Jesus, believing that a mere touch would be enough.

> *What Do You Think?*
> Which actions of the woman and/or the ruler can and should you imitate in approaching Jesus to have your needs met?
> *Digging Deeper*
> How should passages such as Matthew 18:6; Mark 10:13-15; and John 1:44-46 inform your task with regard to others who would approach Jesus?

B. Jesus' Healing Answer (v. 22)

22. But Jesus turned him about, and when he saw her, he said, Daughter, be of good comfort; thy faith hath made thee whole. And the woman was made whole from that hour.

Jesus possessed not only divine power to work miracles but divine knowledge as well. He recognized the touch, even though it was slight and He was in a crowd (compare Mark 5:24, 30; Luke 8:42, 45). He realized that this slight touch signified something of great significance.

This proves that the woman's healing was not some kind of psychosomatic reaction. There was something more here than a woman having believed so strongly that she was going to be well that she actually willed herself to be well. That possibility could not be true because Jesus felt the power go "out of him" (Mark 5:30). Her faith made the healing possible, but the healing power came from outside her.

Seeing the woman, Jesus addressed her with respect and kindness. *Daughter,* a term of endearment, also indicated her need for help and Jesus' acting on her behalf like a good father (another tie to the story of the ruler, which has been paused). Jesus' encouragement *be of good comfort* reassured the woman that she had done nothing wrong and had no reason to fear Jesus' reaction. The other Gospels make clear that the woman was indeed afraid (Mark 5:33; Luke 8:47).

The account comes to its climax as Jesus says *thy faith hath made thee whole.* This is precisely what the woman hoped for (see Matthew 9:21, above). The Law of Moses had separated the woman from society. But the one for whom that law prepared the faithful of Israel to expect had given her new life.

Some conclude from Jesus' words that if a person needs God's miraculous help and does not receive it, then that person does not have enough faith. This is not at all the meaning of Jesus' statement. Jesus commends and celebrates the faithful who seek what He alone can give. When He says words such as "Your faith has made you well," He also acts on their behalf. Effective faith believes that what God supplies will meet the real need regardless of whether or not a miracle is involved. Thus prayers are not necessarily answered on terms we expect. Even Jesus' own prayer to the Father in Luke 22:42 was not answered on the terms Jesus wanted. Yet He committed himself to the Father's will, confident that the Father would be faithful. As important as the greatness of our faith is, the greatness of the Lord's faithfulness is more so.

> *What Do You Think?*
> Without giving directive advice, how would you counsel someone who had been told by a "faith healer" that the person's infirmity was not healed because of a lack of faith?
> *Digging Deeper*
> What Scripture passages will support your counseling?

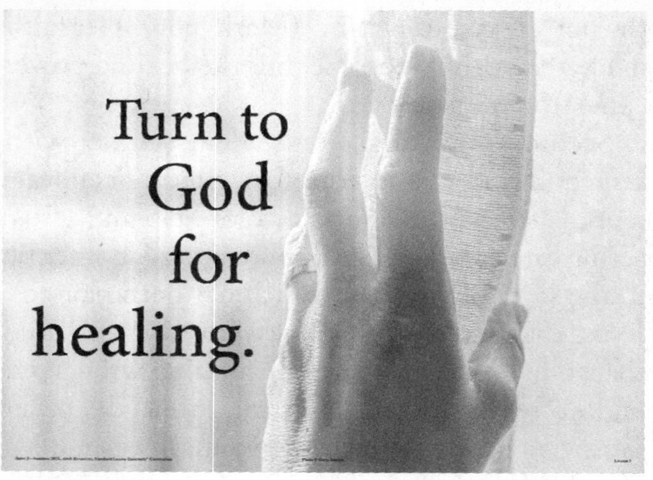

Visual for Lesson 3. *Point to this visual as you pose for class discussion the* What Do You Think? *question associated with verse 21.*

III. A Child Resurrected
(Matthew 9:23-26)

A. A Noisy House (vv. 23-24)

23a. And when Jesus came into the ruler's house.

Having successfully resolved the issue of the woman's bleeding, *Jesus* continued on His way to *the ruler's house* (see Matthew 9:18, above). Jesus had not forgotten the need there.

23b. And saw the minstrels and the people making a noise.

Mourning in ancient Israel was not quiet. *Minstrels*, likely paid to mourn, played their instruments. Family and neighbors would gather to show support by joining in. *The people* expressed sorrow with loud wailing and songs of lament (compare Matthew 11:17; Luke 7:32). The result was much noise in order to demonstrate just how loved the deceased person was.

24a. He said unto them, Give place: for the maid is not dead, but sleepeth.

Jesus' telling the crowd of mourners to *give place* is a command to withdraw, as the word is also translated in Mark 3:7. But here Jesus was not asking merely for quiet in order to concentrate. Rather, the fact that *the maid is not dead, but sleepeth* meant that there was (or shortly would be) no reason to continue mourning. By this statement Jesus was not implying that the girl was in a deep coma that had been mistaken for death. Nor did He mean that she actually was sleeping naturally. He meant that she would not remain dead. Later, Jesus would speak similarly at the death of Lazarus (John 11:1-11), a declaration that the disciples misunderstood (11:12-14; compare and contrast 1 Corinthians 15:51; 1 Thessalonians 4:13).

24b. And they laughed him to scorn.

Jesus' remark seemed absurd to the mourners. They knew death when they saw it. All their own life experiences told them that there was no logical reasoning behind Jesus' statement. Thus their laughter was one of derision (compare Psalm 44:13). Unlike the girl's father, these mourners held out no thought that Jesus could do anything to reverse the state of death.

B. Jesus' Power and Fame (vv. 25-26)

25. But when the people were put forth, he went in, and took her by the hand, and the maid arose.

Matthew described the miracle in terms that match Jesus' declaration that the girl was asleep. Like a parent might take a sleeping child's *hand* to awaken her, so Jesus woke the girl from death. Her resurrection came as a simple touch from Jesus, like the healing of the sick woman. Though most of *the people* were not with Jesus in the room (compare Mark 5:40), they surely saw that the girl was alive again (see Matthew 9:26, below).

> *What Do You Think?*
>
> What should you do, if anything, were you to discover that your class's prayer list was overwhelmingly for physical healing, with few if any requests for spiritual healing?
>
> *Digging Deeper*
>
> In addition to Luke 11:2-4; 22:31-32; 1 Thessalonians 3:10; Philemon 6; and James 5:14-16, what texts would support your actions?

Prayer for Healing

Working as a chaplain, I received a page that a patient was experiencing an emergency. I arrived to find medical personnel scurrying into and out of the room, doing everything possible to save the teenage girl in their care. I stood with her mother, waiting as I listened to her explain her daughter's complicated medical history.

This mother expressed hope that God would heal her daughter, even while knowing that the girl's condition was very poor. I prayed for healing for the girl, who had suffered a great deal because of her illnesses over the years.

A few months later, I learned that the daughter had improved so much that she was able to help other girls in similar situations! Her mother's prayers had been answered. May you also persist in your prayers, even for years, and expect that the Lord hears you. —L. M. W.

26. And the fame hereof went abroad into all that land.

This great miracle, the results of which were seen by many, could not be kept quiet. The spread of this news surely contributed to the crowds that followed Jesus or came out to meet Him when He came near their areas.

Their numbers made it clear that the people needed more attention than Jesus alone could give them. So He sent His disciples out to declare the coming of the kingdom of Heaven (Matthew 9:36–10:8). That initial missionary commission was a prelude to the commission Jesus gave to His followers after His resurrection, a commission that we share today to make disciples of all nations (Matthew 28:18-20).

What Do You Think?

How can you turn your own most serious health problem into a ministry of support for others with the same issue?

Digging Deeper

Think in terms of either your own single-person ministry and a broader church ministry involving others to help you.

Conclusion

A. Abundance in the Midst of Suffering

Matthew introduced the interaction between Jesus and the synagogue but then interrupted it with a second encounter before returning to the first story to wrap it up; the parallel accounts in Mark 5:21-43 and Luke 8:40-56 do so as well. By this arrangement, we note related themes in the two accounts. The themes are that of (1) a 12-year-old girl who had not yet attained womanhood when she died and (2) a woman for whom womanhood has become the source of suffering for as many years as the girl had lived.

Perhaps you see in yourself characteristics of the people in these two accounts. Perhaps you are like a family member of the dead girl, mourning the loss of someone you love. Perhaps you are like the sick woman, suffering with a chronic condition that does not improve. Certainly we all know that grief and suffering will come for us, even if we presently enjoy a moment of calm.

The miraculous power of Jesus does not assure us that we will have no loss or pain. But our text tells us what we can do in the midst of suffering and loss: we can put our trust in the Lord. Our ultimate destiny is a life in which the Lord wipes away our tears (Isaiah 25:8; Revelation 7:17). Even if our pain lasts for years, the Lord will heal it when He raises us with all His people to live with Him forever (21:4). Even when death separates us from those we love, even when we face that separation in our own death, the Lord will reunite His people when He returns (1 Corinthians 15:51-57).

We sometimes refer to Jesus as "the great physician." But He is more than a great medical doctor who knows how to treat and cure diseases. There is power and authority in Jesus, power that eradicates death. There is the power and authority in the resurrected life in Jesus—power and authority for life both now and in eternity.

B. Prayer

Almighty God, we cry out to You in our suffering and our grief. We long for the life that You have in store for us. As we do we recognize the abundance that we now possess through Jesus—even abundance unto eternal life. We thank You for this in Jesus' name. Amen.

C. Thought to Remember

Jesus' power and authority are greater than the worst of our circumstances.

Involvement Learning

Enhance your lesson with KJV Bible Student *(from your curriculum supplier) and the reproducible activity page (at www.standardlesson.com or in the back of the* KJV Standard Lesson Commentary Deluxe Edition*).*

Into the Lesson

Write this phrase on the board:

I remember a time when I was really ill . . .

Ask class members to find partners and to take no more than one minute each to tell a story of a dire sickness—a story that may be shared, without breaking expectations of confidentiality. After two minutes (that is, one minute for each story), allow time for whole-class discussion.

Make a transition by saying, "It's clear that physical illness is an experience common to everyone. But if we see the accounts of Jesus' healings only in terms of 'He can heal me too,' then we miss the bigger picture. Let's see why."

Into the Word

Ask each pair formed for the first activity to join with another pair so that your class is grouped into fours. Distribute handouts (you prepare) that feature three columns like this:

What Do We Learn About . . .

Jesus?	Faith?	Healing?

Challenge groups to answer these questions from Matthew 9:18-26 alone, pretending that they knew nothing about Jesus or faith before reading this passage. After about five minutes, call for group reports to the class as a whole. Use the discussion to explore how Jesus can be misunderstood when His actions are interpreted apart from the context of His ministry as a whole.

Option 1. Explore that context by distributing copies of the "Jesus in Context" exercise from the activity page, which you can download. Depending on the nature of your class, either have learners stay in their groups of four to complete this or return to their original pairs to do so. During whole-class discussion of results, stress that this listing is itself only partial in helping us understand Jesus' mission.

Option 2. Have learners work individually for no more than one minute to complete the "Reactions to Healing" exercise on the activity page as indicated. After calling time, surprise your learners by ignoring what they wrote and instead polling them on which of the four characters they chose to evaluate. Focusing on the reason why, explore what their choices say about them personally.

Write this question on the board for whole-class discussion:

Why did Jesus heal people?

Jot responses on the board as they are voiced. If no one mentions it, be sure to stress that Jesus' healings and other miracles were intended to prove that He was God (John 20:30-31). Explore how we run the danger of committing the error Jesus notes in John 6:26 as we consider our own prayers for healing today.

Into Life

Display the following sentence on the board:

Pray as if everything depends on _____;
take action as if everything depends on _____.

Ask students to guess what words go in the two blanks. After a learner (or you yourself) reveals that the proper words are *God* and *you*, respectively, explore how the main characters in today's story demonstrated this principle.

Wrap up by considering this hypothetical case study: a person with a stage 4 cancer approaches you in despair regarding that diagnosis. What regarding the cancer patient's state of mind and faith would indicate that studying Matthew 9:18-26 together would be helpful? What state of mind or faith would indicate that such a study might be counterproductive? (*Option.* Depending on the nature of your class and being sensitive to the needs of those present, this can be considered either by the class as a whole or in small groups.)

Rescued from Doubt

Devotional Reading: Isaiah 38:16-20
Background Scripture: Matthew 14:22-33

Matthew 14:22-33

22 And straightway Jesus constrained his disciples to get into a ship, and to go before him unto the other side, while he sent the multitudes away.

23 And when he had sent the multitudes away, he went up into a mountain apart to pray: and when the evening was come, he was there alone.

24 But the ship was now in the midst of the sea, tossed with waves: for the wind was contrary.

25 And in the fourth watch of the night Jesus went unto them, walking on the sea.

26 And when the disciples saw him walking on the sea, they were troubled, saying, It is a spirit; and they cried out for fear.

27 But straightway Jesus spake unto them, saying, Be of good cheer; it is I; be not afraid.

28 And Peter answered him and said, Lord, if it be thou, bid me come unto thee on the water.

29 And he said, Come. And when Peter was come down out of the ship, he walked on the water, to go to Jesus.

30 But when he saw the wind boisterous, he was afraid; and beginning to sink, he cried, saying, Lord, save me.

31 And immediately Jesus stretched forth his hand, and caught him, and said unto him, O thou of little faith, wherefore didst thou doubt?

32 And when they were come into the ship, the wind ceased.

33 Then they that were in the ship came and worshipped him, saying, Of a truth thou art the Son of God.

Key Verse

Immediately Jesus stretched forth his hand, and caught him, and said unto him, O thou of little faith, wherefore didst thou doubt? —**Matthew 14:31**

Photo courtesy of Ronald L. Nickelson

Confident Hope

Unit 1: Jesus Teaches About Faith

Lessons 1–5

Lesson Aims

After participating in this lesson, each learner will be able to:

1. Identify common elements between this lesson text and that of lesson 2.
2. Explain the relationship between fear and doubt.
3. Develop a step-by-step plan to replace doubt with trust in one area of spiritual weakness.

Lesson Outline

Introduction
- A. The Challenge of Consistency
- B. Lesson Context

I. Jesus Alone (Matthew 14:22-24)
- A. The Journey Begins (v. 22)
- B. The Lord in Prayer (v. 23)
- C. The Wind Rises (v. 24)

II. Jesus on the Water (Matthew 14:25-31)
- A. A Miraculous Appearance (vv. 25-27)
  Oriented Toward God
- B. A Disciple's Faith (vv. 28-31)
  Grab Jesus' Hand

III. Jesus with the Disciples (Matthew 14:32-33)
- A. The Wind Ceases (v. 32)
- B. The Son of God (v. 33)

Conclusion
- A. Calling Out for Help
- B. Prayer
- C. Thought to Remember

Introduction

A. The Challenge of Consistency

If you enjoy playing a sport, you probably have had a few moments of sports greatness. You sank a long-distance putt, you made a great catch, or you hit a difficult shot. Even if you are not an athletic person, perhaps you can recall some other notable achievement. Things like finishing a crossword puzzle in record time or completing a particularly detailed and time-intensive project flawlessly. In moments like that, someone might say, "That was as good as a professional would do." And we would agree.

At least we would agree for a moment. But if we think about it, we realize that what we manage to do every now and then does not put us on the same level as a professional. A professional performs consistently with excellence. Did you *happen* to perform like a professional? Yes. Can you do it with a professional's consistency? No way!

Our text features a Bible character who reminds us of the challenge of consistency. The text will show us that the power of Jesus, not the consistency of our faith or the frequency of our doubt, is the basis for our security as God's people.

B. Lesson Context

Matthew, Mark, and John place the account of today's text (absent from Luke) after the account of the feeding of the 5,000. (Mark 6:45-52 and John 6:16-21 are the parallel accounts of today's text.) That event had astonished and excited the large crowd of followers, not just because it was a great miracle but because it reminded them of God's miraculous provision of food in the wilderness during the exodus from Egypt in Moses' time (Exodus 16). Knowing that the prophets promised a coming deliverance like the exodus (Isaiah 40:1-5), the crowd's wonder and excitement were on the rise.

Jesus took steps to quiet this enthusiasm. Yes, He was indeed the true king promised by God, the one who would bring freedom to God's people as God did in the exodus. But how He became king, how He freed people, was yet to come in His death and resurrection. Only then would any of His followers, be they members of the 12 or the crowds, be able to understand and respond to Him with greater comprehension of the truth.

Jesus' power was very much on display in that feeding, but so was the disciples' limitation in their thinking (Matthew 14:15-17)—even though it was by then the third year of Jesus' public ministry. The 12 disciples were witnesses to these events, which should have inspired confidence in Jesus. Their challenge was to respond to disappointment, opposition, and danger with faith in Jesus, knowing that His power could overcome every difficulty. But each new threat presented a new occasion to question whether Jesus was worthy of their trust.

Our lesson is set on the Sea of Galilee (see Lesson Context of lesson 2). In 1986, the remains of a boat from the time of Jesus were discovered buried in the mud near the shore of the Sea of Galilee. Excavated and now on display, the boat is probably typical for the time. It measures 27 feet in length and 7.5 feet at its widest point. It could have been propelled with oars, a sail, or both.

Such boats were quite safe when the weather was fine. But storms can arise quickly on this lake. Because its western coastline features steep hills, a storm blowing in from that direction, from the Mediterranean Sea, might be seen by boaters only when it is nearly upon them. A small boat hit by high winds is in a perilous condition, even on such a small lake.

I. Jesus Alone
(Matthew 14:22-24)

A. The Journey Begins (v. 22)

22. And straightway Jesus constrained his disciples to get into a ship, and to go before him unto the other side, while he sent the multitudes away.

There is no record here of Jesus' providing the *disciples* with information about how He would catch up to them later after He traveled alone. Though it's possible that Jesus would walk around the lake, more likely the disciples expected Him to catch a ride in a different *ship.* He also *sent the multitudes away* in order to be alone.

B. The Lord in Prayer (v. 23)

23a. And when he had sent the multitudes away, he went up into a mountain apart to pray.

Though Jesus had previously taught about prayer (Matthew 6:5-15), this is the first instance in which we see Jesus at prayer in Matthew's Gospel. Later Jesus prayed repeatedly the night before His death (26:36-44). Each of the other Gospels also bear witness to Jesus' prayer life (Mark 1:35; Luke 5:16; John 17; etc.).

It is a remarkable part of this story that Jesus, who embodies and exercises the almighty power of God, nevertheless prays earnestly and at length to God the Father. This is critical to our understanding of Jesus. He was the divine Son of God, to whom all authority had been given (Matthew 28:18). He does mighty deeds that demonstrate a power that can belong only to God (9:6-7). Yet Jesus entered the world in submission to the Father. The Father's will must prevail (26:39, 42).

Jesus is the perfect model for humanity's desired submission to and reliance on God. If Jesus, the almighty Son of God, willingly submitted to God the Father, then how much more should we, lacking in Jesus' power and authority, do the same!

23b. And when the evening was come, he was there alone.

The fact that Jesus was *alone* indicates that He was successful in persuading everyone to depart—most by foot homeward, the 12 by boat. *Evening* came as Jesus was left by himself. Any trouble on the boat would be compounded by the darkness now settling over the Sea of Galilee.

> *What Do You Think?*
> In what ways will you use Jesus' practice of prayer in solitude as a model for your own devotional life?
> *Digging Deeper*
> In what ways, if any, should you not do so? Why?

C. The Wind Rises (v. 24)

24. But the ship was now in the midst of the sea, tossed with waves: for the wind was contrary.

The boat was far from land, near the middle of

the lake (compare Mark 6:47). The disciples' progress was hindered by *wind* that pushed against them, making their sails useless. As the wind picked up, the *waves* grew higher, threatening to capsize *the ship*. The vessel may have been taking on water faster than the disciples could bail it out.

The disciples had been in similar danger before, also on the Sea of Galilee (Matthew 8:23-27; see lesson 2). But then Jesus was with them in the ship. Now they were alone, or at least they thought so.

II. Jesus on the Water
(Matthew 14:25-31)

A. A Miraculous Appearance (vv. 25-27)

25. And in the fourth watch of the night Jesus went unto them, walking on the sea.

In the Roman Empire, it was common to divide the night into four roughly equal periods of time, called watches. *The fourth watch* was approximately 3 a.m. to 6 a.m. As this time arrived, the disciples had struggled for hours against the high waves. They were exhausted and probably uncertain of their position *on the sea* after so long in the dark. While they may have hoped for some act of deliverance, we can speculate that at this point their hopes were fading, if not gone altogether.

In this desperate situation, they saw *Jesus* doing the seemingly impossible: *walking on the* water. In the exodus, God had parted the waters of the Red Sea to allow His people to walk on dry land to escape their enemies (Exodus 14:21-22). But here is an action without compare. At the point of the disciples' greatest exhaustion and hopelessness, the Lord came to reassure and rescue. How hard it must have been for them to understand what they were seeing, to believe their own eyes!

26. And when the disciples saw him walking on the sea, they were troubled, saying, It is a spirit; and they cried out for fear.

Added to the disciples' exhaustion and fear was the sight of what they believed to be a disembodied *spirit*. Surely a flesh-and-blood human could not be walking on water, never mind high waves in a storm in the middle of the night! Such a thing had never been done before, so there was no reason to interpret this sight as a physical, natural person. First a storm, now an apparition (compare Luke 24:36-37)! Little wonder that they cried out for fear. They felt assaulted from both the physical and spiritual realms.

27. But straightway Jesus spake unto them, saying, Be of good cheer; it is I; be not afraid.

Jesus did not delay in revealing to the disciples the wholly unexpected truth: they were seeing not a disembodied spirit but their Lord. Therefore they could *be of good cheer* in the midst of the storm. There was no more reason to be fearful of the storm that continued and certainly no reason to fear the one who walked on the water to join them.

The two commands *be of good cheer* and *be not afraid* are two sides of the same coin: the first is a positive command of how to respond, the other is a negative command of how *not* to respond. God was doing extraordinary, unprecedented things—things that caused even the most faithful to fear. But those extraordinary things were intended as blessings, not threats.

After His resurrection, Jesus told the women at the tomb to "be not afraid" (Matthew 28:10). There as here, Jesus' followers didn't understand how He could be present with them. Yet Jesus' promise to all His followers is to be with them always, to the end of this age (28:20), fulfilling the ancient promise of "God with us" (1:23). The disciples might have felt that they were alone, but the Christ who would give His life for them would also remain with them in every circumstance, even when they could not recognize Him.

Oriented Toward God

As a native of the northern hemisphere, I felt a bit disoriented while visiting Australia. During the day, it was strange to watch the sun move across the northern sky instead of the southern sky. At night, I couldn't see the North Star and the Big Dipper. Instead, a constellation known as the Southern Cross is what glimmered in the darkness to help me get my bearings.

Those who live in mountainous areas use the nearby mountains as visual cues to location and direction. But those cues are lost when clouds obscure the view. The people who live in the Pacific Northwest have a saying when Mount Rainier isn't visible: "Even on cloudy days, live like the mountain is out."

Sometimes it's hard to recognize the Lord's presence. Storm clouds obscure His hand of grace. You may be facing a storm right now, but the mountain of God's love is still there. Will you by faith live like the mountain is out? —D. F.

B. A Disciple's Faith (vv. 28-31)

28. And Peter answered him and said, Lord, if it be thou, bid me come unto thee on the water.

The story now shifts to one disciple's reaction to Jesus' self-revelation. *Peter*, with what will come to be characteristic boldness (examples: Matthew 16:16, 22; 17:4; 26:33, 35), spoke up. *If it be* does not express doubt. We might think of it as meaning "*because* it is You."

We might wonder why Peter asked for what he does. This bold request was not about thrill-seeking. Rather, Peter wanted to share what his master was doing. Already Jesus had sent the disciples out to preach, with authority to heal and cast out demons (Matthew 10:1). They were sharing in His ministry, and they desired to reign with Him (20:20-22). So Peter sought to walk with Jesus *on the water* by Jesus' power, following Him as a disciple would.

The word translated *bid* has the force of a command here and as translated elsewhere in various ways (Matthew 8:18; 14:9, 19; etc.). As used here, Peter invited Jesus to command him (Peter) to come. Peter's request was the product of an ambition, but it was a sacred ambition: to stand with his Lord in the Lord's work.

What Do You Think?

Under what circumstances, if any, will it be appropriate for you to respond to a sensed call from God with a request like Peter's?

Digging Deeper

Which test among Judges 6:36-40; Psalm 78:18-20; Malachi 3:10; Matthew 4:1-10; and 27:40 is most like Peter's request? Why?

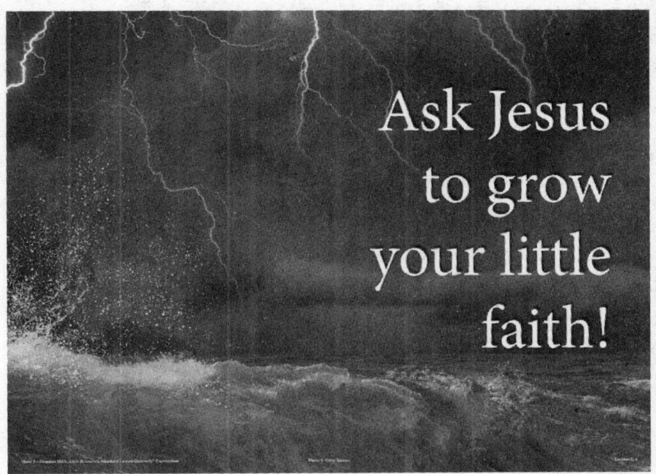
Ask Jesus
to grow
your little
faith!

Visual for Lessons 2 & 4. *Ask the learners for examples of times Jesus used unexpected circumstances to grow their faith.*

29. And he said, Come. And when Peter was come down out of the ship, he walked on the water, to go to Jesus.

Jesus granted Peter's request. And just as had been the case before, when Jesus commanded His followers to do something, He also granted them the power to carry it out. So *Peter* stepped *out of the ship* and indeed *walked on the water* toward Jesus. Peter started faithfully—so far, so good.

30. But when he saw the wind boisterous, he was afraid; and beginning to sink, he cried, saying, Lord, save me.

The same strong *wind* that had buffeted the ship all night continued. As Peter made his way on the water, his situation seemed even more perilous than it was in the ship. The fear he felt before the Lord's appearance rose again. As it did, he could no longer walk on the water.

Peter's doubt in the midst of the storm reveals that his confidence in Jesus could be shaken (see Matthew 26:69-75). Even when the disciples saw Jesus after His resurrection, doubt infected some of them (28:17). Doubt is a powerful, pervasive disposition, especially when faith is challenged in times of trouble (compare James 1:6).

Some would call what Peter was experiencing a failure of faith (see Matthew 14:31, below). But it was not a failure of faith to call out to Jesus to *save* him. Just as the disciples had called out "save us" when they had been in a storm before (Matthew 8:25; see lesson 2), Peter did so again.

This desperate cry, stripped of all self-reliance and pride, can be the essence of faith in Jesus, especially when that faith is troubled by doubt (see Mark 9:24).

To experience doubt or fear is not to have lost faith. When we call out to the Lord for help, we act in faith, confessing our weakness and relying on the Lord's strength. Jesus pronounced blessing on those who were poor in spirit, meek, mourning, and hungry—on those who have great need and who recognize their need (Matthew 5:3-6). When we experience fear and doubt, if our impulse is to pray, our faith is not failing but acting.

> *What Do You Think?*
>
> What practice can you adopt to be on the alert for worldly distractions that tempt you to shift your attention away from Jesus?
>
> *Digging Deeper*
>
> Which passage among Luke 8:14; 21:34; 2 Timothy 4:10; and 1 John 2:15-16 speak to you most pointedly in this regard? Why?

31. And immediately Jesus stretched forth his hand, and caught him, and said unto him, O thou of little faith, wherefore didst thou doubt?

As *Jesus* did on other occasions, He made physical contact with the one whom He delivered (Matthew 8:3, 15; 9:29; 14:36; 17:7; 20:34). Even so, Jesus chided Peter for his *doubt*, as He had previously when the disciples were afraid in a storm (Matthew 8:26; see lesson 2). Peter and the others had had enough experience of Jesus' power and faithfulness to be freed from doubt. But to say there was no good reason for their doubt is not to say that Jesus rejected them because of it. Instead, He delivered them.

When we are guilty of inadequate faith, we can remember what Jesus did in the passage before us. Yes, Peter's faith was weak. Under stress, he was plagued by doubt. But Jesus rescued Peter anyway! Peter's faith was still sufficient to call out to Jesus for help. Our relationship with Jesus depends on how ready we are to recognize our weaknesses and rely on His strength. That extends to trusting that in His strength He can overcome our doubts and worries.

> *What Do You Think?*
>
> What does an examination of the triangular relationship among faith, doubt, and fear reveal that you should do?
>
> *Digging Deeper*
>
> How does a reconsideration of lesson 2 aid you in this regard?

Grab Jesus' Hand

Important things happen when people join hands. A bride and groom hold hands as they recite their marriage vows. Proud graduates shake hands with the college president as they receive their diplomas. Business leaders seal deals by handshake. Friendly hosts extend their hands when they welcome guests into their homes.

Sometimes it's urgent—even life-saving—to join hands. A mother takes the hand of her toddler before they cross the street. A firefighter shouts, "Grab my hand!" to a terrified individual being rescued. A hospice worker extends comfort by holding the dying patient's hand.

Jesus' hands extended love, comfort, security, and welcome to others. With them He blessed children, broke bread, healed the sick, and raised the dead. Jesus reached out His hand and rescued Peter from drowning. Can you picture the Lord extending His hand toward you? Will you take His hand and let Him lift you up? Or will you try to live by the "Pull yourself up by your own bootstraps" philosophy? —D. F.

III. Jesus with the Disciples

(Matthew 14:32-33)

A. The Wind Ceases (v. 32)

32. And when they were come into the ship, the wind ceased.

This storm ended as the earlier one had: as an immediate response from nature to an act from nature's Creator (Matthew 8:26b). We note that Jesus did not rescue Peter by calming the storm, as in Matthew 8:26; rather, Jesus rescued Peter while the storm still raged. The storm disappeared only after *they were come into the ship.*

Jesus does not always calm the storms of life, but He is always there to rescue or calm us in one way or another. Surely we, like Peter and the other disciples in the ship, have enough reason to trust Jesus! What God has revealed to us about the Son is true and trustworthy, ample reason for confidence (Hebrews 1:2-3; 3:6).

B. The Son of God (v. 33)

33. Then they that were in the ship came and worshipped him, saying, Of a truth thou art the Son of God.

The disciples had just witnessed Jesus demonstrate power available only to God. They saw Him empower one of their number to join Him in His sovereign control of the deep. As they were reunited with their master, they *worshipped him,* acknowledging His authority and expressing their submission and dependence. They could conclude nothing less than that Jesus was utterly unlike any other.

For the Jewish people of Jesus' time, the phrase *Son of God* first meant that Jesus was God's promised king, the great Son of David (compare Matthew 1:1 with Mark 1:1). Certainly the disciples were affirming at least that much here. Jesus showed His kingly authority in what He had just done. After Jesus' resurrection, Jesus' followers called Him Son of God with an enhanced understanding (John 20:31). With this phrase they affirmed Him to be both God's king and as God himself.

Conclusion

A. Calling Out for Help

Peter sometimes said and did impressive things. Today's text shows Peter doing something remarkable during a crisis of faith. When he began to doubt, he almost snatched defeat from the jaws of victory! Peter had a problem with consistency.

But Peter is not the most important character in this story. Jesus is. Jesus' power was greater than Peter's doubt, just as it is greater than our doubts. Trusting the Lord, whom we do not see, is hard to maintain when the negative things we do see test our faith. The resulting doubt is the proof that our faith is being tested.

Is doubt, then, a symptom of inconsistent faith? It can be if it is never resolved, if it leads us to abandon our hope and trust in Christ. But if doubt prompts us to call out to the Lord for help, then doubt is a seeking faith—faith that seeks understanding, faith that seeks the divine word of peace in the middle of fear.

When you experienced doubt, did you call out to the Lord? Perhaps you are crying out for help right now. You can know that the Lord hears you and that the certainty of His faithfulness is more important than the size of your faith.

Or maybe your ship is sailing smoothly right now, and you barely think about the Lord's not being in the boat with you. Realize that a time will come when the winds will blow against you all night. And though it may seem that you are alone on the waves, the Lord knows your distress and will come to you if you bid Him do so. Remember: He is with you right now as well. He is always with His people, to the end of the age.

What Do You Think?

Which aspect of this lesson challenges you most in terms of personal application? Why?

Digging Deeper

How will you respond to this challenge?

B. Prayer

Thank You, Father, for Your almighty power at work in Jesus to save and protect us. We affirm His promise not to abandon us, that even when we die, we will live with You. Direct our hearts to You whenever life makes us afraid, we pray. In Jesus' name we pray. Amen.

C. Thought to Remember

Cry out to Jesus, who overcomes our doubt.

HOW TO SAY IT

Galilee	*Gal*-uh-lee.
Mediterranean	*Med*-uh-tuh-***ray***-nee-un.
Rainier	Ruh-*nir*.

Involvement Learning

Enhance your lesson with KJV Bible Student *(from your curriculum supplier) and the reproducible activity page (at www.standardlesson.com or in the back of the* KJV Standard Lesson Commentary Deluxe Edition*).*

Into the Lesson

Write this partial sentence on the board:

Water makes me nervous when . . .

If your class is smaller, ask learners to complete the sentence as you call on each of them in turn. For larger classes, have learners answer the question in triads to ensure that everyone has a chance to respond.

Option or *alternative.* As a closed-Bible pretest, distribute copies of the "True, False, and When?" exercise on the activity page, which you can download. Allow learners only one minute to complete it individually. Assure your class that you will not collect the tests—they will score their own. Have them do so when the minute is up.

After either or both of the above, make a transition by saying, "Water is a tricky thing: it can be life-giving in one context and life-threatening in another. But in either case, the water itself may not be the main issue. Let's see why."

Into the Word

Distribute the following questions on handouts (you prepare):

1–How is Matthew 14:22-33 like 8:23-27 (lesson 2)?
2–How is 14:22-33 different from 8:23-27?
3–What lesson(s) learned from 8:23-27 are reinforced in 14:22-33?
4–What new lesson(s) are learned in 14:22-33?

Have learners form study pairs or triads to respond to the questions. After several minutes, call for reports to the class as a whole; jot conclusions on the board.

Divide the class into two teams to debate the following resolution:

Be it Resolved: *We should think more highly of Peter than the other 11 disciples because he was the only one with enough courage to get out of the boat despite his faith failure as revealed later.*

Research debate formats ahead of time to pick one suitable for the nature of your class. Allow several minutes for the **Affirmative Team** to decide on reasons to support the resolution, while at the same time those on the **Negative Team** come up with reasons to deny the resolution.

After conducting the debate, call for shows of hands regarding how many learners agree with each position. Probe for underlying personal reasons for the choices and use those discoveries as a transition to the next segment.

Option. Distribute again copies of the "True, False, and When?" exercise as a posttest to see how scores have improved. This should be given closed-Bible without access to the pretest.

Into Life

Ask, "When was a time you experienced faith and fear at the same time, as seems to have happened to Peter?" Encourage volunteers to share examples. Ask how this encourages your class members to keep coming to Jesus even when beset with doubts and fears.

Option. Precede the above by having learners discuss in triads their response to the exercise "I Just Don't Get It!" on the activity page. This will cast a wider context for learners to relate their own experiences of faith and doubt.

Distribute note cards to students and ask them to write a better "walking on water" experience with God that they would like to have. Ask them to write on the back side of their card the main obstacle keeping them from having this experience and the first step they can take to overcome it.

Follow that by having learners re-form their triads to share their intentions with classmates. Challenge learners to allow the other members of their triads to propose a second step and a third step for each person. Close with a time of silent prayer. Guide the prayer thoughts with prompts appropriate to the steps they are challenged to take.

Attitude of Gratitude

Devotional Reading: Isaiah 56:1-8
Background Scripture: Leviticus 13–14; Luke 5:12-16; 17:11-19

Leviticus 13:45-46

45 And the leper in whom the plague is, his clothes shall be rent, and his head bare, and he shall put a covering upon his upper lip, and shall cry, Unclean, unclean.

46 All the days wherein the plague shall be in him he shall be defiled; he is unclean: he shall dwell alone; without the camp shall his habitation be.

Luke 17:11-19

11 And it came to pass, as he went to Jerusalem, that he passed through the midst of Samaria and Galilee.

12 And as he entered into a certain village, there met him ten men that were lepers, which stood afar off:

13 And they lifted up their voices, and said, Jesus, Master, have mercy on us.

14 And when he saw them, he said unto them, Go shew yourselves unto the priests. And it came to pass, that, as they went, they were cleansed.

15 And one of them, when he saw that he was healed, turned back, and with a loud voice glorified God,

16 And fell down on his face at his feet, giving him thanks: and he was a Samaritan.

17 And Jesus answering said, Were there not ten cleansed? but where are the nine?

18 There are not found that returned to give glory to God, save this stranger.

19 And he said unto him, Arise, go thy way: thy faith hath made thee whole.

Key Verse

One of them, when he saw that he was healed, turned back, and with a loud voice glorified God.
—Luke 17:15

CONFIDENT HOPE

Unit 1: Jesus Teaches About Faith

LESSONS 1–5

LESSON AIMS

After participating in this lesson, each learner will be able to:

1. Summarize the relationship between the two texts of the lesson.

2. Distinguish between contexts that call for public thanks to God and those where private thanks are more appropriate.

3. State a plan for implementing lesson aim 2 in his or her witness.

LESSON OUTLINE

Introduction
- A. Leprosariums
- B. Lesson Context

I. Unclean (Leviticus 13:45-46)
- A. Physical Indicators (v. 45)
- B. Social Separation (v. 46)

II. Cleansed (Luke 17:11-14)
- A. Lepers' Request (vv. 11-13)
- B. Jesus' Response (v. 14)

III. Affirmed (Luke 17:15-19)
- A. Return of One (vv. 15-16)
- B. Absence of Nine (vv. 17-19)
  - *Neglecting to Say Thank You*
  - *A Complete Healing*

Conclusion
- A. Thanks and Worship
- B. Prayer
- C. Thought to Remember

Introduction

A. Leprosariums

Nancy Brede was taken from her family at age 13 in 1936 after being diagnosed with leprosy. She was isolated with other youth and children at a leprosarium (the modern equivalent of a leper colony) in Hawaii. At best, leprosariums were places where patients could go for medical care; at worst these were places of exile. Nancy and others were quarantined in accordance with Hawaiian law that was in force at the time. Another leprosarium in the United States was located in Carville, Louisiana, from 1894 to 1999.

Due to the infectious nature of leprosy (Hansen's Disease), quarantine was deemed necessary until the advent of antibiotic drug therapies in the twentieth century. Even so, many leprosariums still exist in the world. Leprosy was well known in the ancient world as well. Today's lesson tells of a band of 10 infected, quarantined men who had just one hope: Jesus.

B. Lesson Context

The two Scripture passages in this lesson were written more than 1,000 years apart. But the text from Leviticus gives important context for the account found in Luke. Leviticus 13 is devoted to the identification and regulation of skin diseases as part of the legal code for Israel.

We might be surprised to see such rules, assuming that the Law of Moses covered only religious regulations, prohibitions against crimes such as murder and thievery, etc. However, what we would consider a medical problem was a religious and community issue for God's people. They saw physical afflictions as more than health issues; they understood them as punishment for sin (compare John 9:1-2).

Detection of certain skin conditions identified one as having leprosy; a person with leprosy was unclean. A skin disease was usually treated with washing and quarantine. If the disease did not go away, it was considered ongoing and therefore demanded banishment of the person from the community. This amounted to a sentence of lifelong shame and isolation (example: 2 Chronicles

26:19-21). The appearance of leprosy was a life-altering event that usually ended only with death.

Biblical descriptions of leprosy are not precise enough to narrow it to any single skin condition known today. The term *leprosy* today is identified with Hansen's Disease only—a slowly progressing bacterial infection that causes disfigurement and nerve damage. However, in both the Old and New Testaments, the word *leprosy* seems to describe skin diseases in a more general sense. Leprosy included a scaly skin appearance that could be described as being "white as snow" (Numbers 12:10; compare Exodus 4:6), a condition that might be caused by several diseases.

Tension between Jews and Samaritans is an undercurrent in today's lesson. Jews and Samaritans were religious and ethnic cousins, sharing a common ancestry and both loyal to the Law of Moses (compare John 4:5-26). But events starting with the division of Israel into two kingdoms in about 930 BC, and exacerbated by the northern kingdom's exile in 722 BC, alienated the two groups. After the northern kingdom's exile, those remaining intermarried with the peoples that the conquerors resettled in the land. This mixture of different people and culture resulted in the Samaritans. The Old Testament traces the time line of these events from 2 Kings 17 through Ezra 4 and Nehemiah 4 (compare Luke 9:51-56).

I. Unclean

(Leviticus 13:45-46)

A. Physical Indicators (v. 45)

45. And the leper in whom the plague is, his clothes shall be rent, and his head bare, and he shall put a covering upon his upper lip, and shall cry, Unclean, unclean.

HOW TO SAY IT

Galilee	*Gal*-uh-lee.
Judea	Joo-*dee*-uh.
leprosarium	lep-*ruh*-***sare***-ee-*uhm*.
Leviticus	Leh-*vit*-ih-kus.
Samaria	Suh-*mare*-ee-uh.
Samaritan	Suh-*mare*-uh-tun.

It is hard to overestimate the fear the people of Israel had of leprosy or the sorrow of a family member or friend being diagnosed as a *leper*. Describing this disease as *the plague* suggests that it was considered a divine affliction (see Exodus 11:1, where the same Hebrew word is used). Being dressed in torn *clothes,* a partial face *covering,* and uncovered *head* was associated with mourning (see Genesis 37:34; Ezekiel 24:17). Incurable skin diseases led to a state of perpetual mourning for one's lost life.

Adding to this trauma, the Law of Moses required afflicted persons to announce their presence by shouting *unclean*. This was a warning to steer clear (contrast Luke 17:13, below). This uncleanness prevented persons with leprosy from participating in any of the communal religious activities or feasts (see next).

B. Social Separation (v. 46)

46. All the days wherein the plague shall be in him he shall be defiled; he is unclean: he shall dwell alone; without the camp shall his habitation be.

The *defiled* person had to be quarantined. In Moses' day, the Israelites walked through the wilderness on their way to the promised land (Numbers 14:33-34). So at the time the law was given, those with leprosy had to live outside *the camp*. As the Israelites settled into the promised land, the places of quarantine were outside the villages (compare Luke 17:12, below).

What Do You Think?

Under what circumstances should you keep your distance from those who are spiritually "unclean"? Why?

Digging Deeper

How do you resolve the tensions among Matthew 28:19-20; Romans 16:17; 2 Thessalonians 3:14; and 2 John 10-11 in this regard?

Those afflicted with leprosy suffered not only from the illness itself but also from being ostracized socially. This meant no participation in weddings, funerals, synagogue meetings, and certainly not temple activities. The afflicted persons depended on the kindness and provisions of family members or friends for survival. While medical conditions presenting as skin diseases were not immediately fatal, their resulting exclusions likely caused lives to be shortened by misery.

II. Cleansed

(Luke 17:11-14)

A. Lepers' Request (vv. 11-13)

11. And it came to pass, as he went to Jerusalem, that he passed through the midst of Samaria and Galilee.

The bulk of today's lesson comes from Jesus' final journey *to Jerusalem* (Luke 9:51–19:44). He chose a route that crossed areas where Samaritans might be encountered: through the central part of Palestine. This route began in *Galilee* and moved south through the region of *Samaria* (see Luke 9:52).

On a map, it is easy to see that the shortest route from a town in Galilee to Jerusalem in Judea would take one through Samaria. But Galilean Jews usually made the trip via the Jordan River valley, a longer route, in order to avoid Samaria. As Jesus traveled, He was in a transitional area between Samaritan and Jewish settlements. No geographical features separated the two areas in an obvious way. The distinction was determined by the makeup of the villages, with the Jewish villages of Galilee lying to the north of the Samaritan region (see also Lesson Context).

12. And as he entered into a certain village, there met him ten men that were lepers, which stood afar off.

The social isolation and physical pain of having leprosy probably resulted in more relationships between afflicted Jews and Samaritans than would be the case otherwise. As Jesus reached the edge of *a certain village*, a band of *ten men that were lepers* who lived banished lives was ready to meet Him. We are not told if this village was Jewish or Samaritan, so it may have been either.

The fact that the men *stood afar off* was in compliance with the Law of Moses (see Leviticus 13:46, above; Number 5:2). They probably stayed near the village, where some of them may have had family members who provided food and clothing. But the men did not venture close. Those afflicted with leprosy who ignored the expectation of maintaining proper distance might be driven away by having rocks thrown at them by fearful people.

13. And they lifted up their voices, and said, Jesus, Master, have mercy on us.

The lepers did not presume to approach *Jesus*, choosing instead to shout at Him from a distance. They addressed Jesus as *Master* rather than "rabbi" or "lord." The underlying Greek word being translated in this address is found only in Luke's Gospel in the New Testament (here and in Luke 5:5; 8:24, 45; 9:33, 49). It is a term of respect and deference, primarily found on the lips of Jesus' disciples. Its use by the men with leprosy implies some existing knowledge of Jesus. The author gives the impression that they shouted in unison, indicating a plan formulated before Jesus' visit.

The men are not recorded as having cried out the required, "Unclean!" (see Leviticus 13:45, above). The focus, rather, is on their plea for *mercy*, divine favor (compare Luke 18:38-39). In the case at hand, such mercy would entail God's healing. Requests for God's mercy occur frequently in the psalms (examples: Psalms 30:10; 51:1; 57:1).

> *What Do You Think?*
> Contrasting Luke 17:13 with Matthew 9:21 in lesson 3, under what circumstances should you express your need publicly rather than silently? What about the reverse?
> *Digging Deeper*
> What other examples from Scripture support your conclusions?

The men with leprosy saw Jesus as a conduit of God's grace and mercy. They apparently had heard of Jesus' ministry of healing the sick. Such healing had already included cases of leprosy (Luke 5:12-14; 7:22). Friends or relatives who provided for these men likely had shared stories heard about Jesus as a healer. The preparedness of this band of desperate men indicates that Jesus' arrival at this particular village was expected and eagerly anticipated.

B. Jesus' Response (v. 14)

14a. And when he saw them, he said unto them, Go shew yourselves unto the priests.

Jesus' immediate response was not to heal the men but to command an act that required faith (compare 2 Kings 5:10). To be recognized as cleansed, they needed to be certified by a priest (see Leviticus 13:17; compare Luke 5:14). Jesus instructed them to seek such certification before they were healed, though He spoke as though it had already been accomplished. The nearest *priests* might have been living in the village since priests, who were from the tribe of Levi, had no fixed territory in Israel or Samaria (Numbers 18:20-24).

14b. And it came to pass, that, as they went, they were cleansed.

The text indicates that the 10 men with leprosy were not healed until they began to make their way to the priests as Jesus commanded (contrast Luke 5:12-13). The men were thus rendered clean and free of disease when they obeyed in faith.

We assume that the fact *they were cleansed* means that all visible and invisible manifestations of their affliction disappeared. Hair that had become unnaturally white (Leviticus 13:2-3) returned to its natural color, etc. The men thus realized that their trip to the priests was not a fool's errand, but rather the first step in reclaiming their lives. They would be able to resume their roles in family and village life.

A simple lesson here is that faith that resulted in obedience led to healing (again, compare 2 Kings 5). For the 10 men of our text, this was physical healing. For us, it may be spiritual healing, a cleansing of our "unclean" hearts when we obediently follow Jesus (Acts 2:38-41; etc.).

III. Affirmed

(Luke 17:15-19)

A. Return of One (vv. 15-16)

15-16a. And one of them, when he saw that he was healed, turned back, and with a loud voice glorified God, and fell down on his face at his feet, giving him thanks.

One man's heart drove him to respond in ways that are not attributed to the other nine. First, he

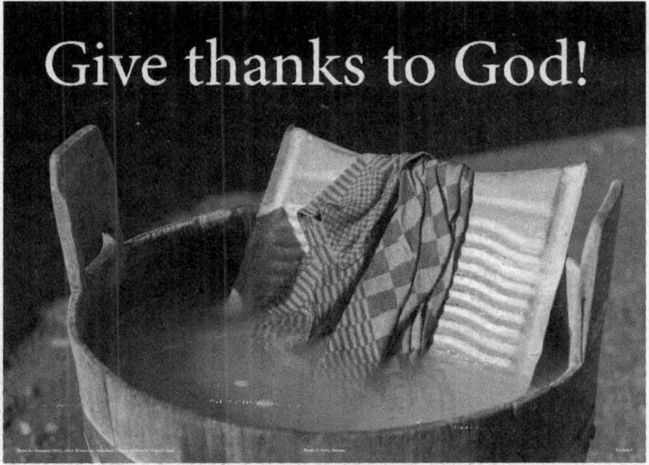

Visual for Lesson 5. *Allow time while discussing verse 16a for each learner to share (as desired) one particular thanksgiving from the past week.*

delayed his trip to a priest as he *turned back* to Jesus; the man's burning desire to be declared clean by a priest was trumped by his desire to show gratitude. Second, in his loudest *voice* he *glorified God* (compare Luke 5:26; 7:16). His words are not recorded, but we can imagine something like our familiar, "To God be the glory, great things He has done!"

Third, the man *fell down . . . at* Jesus' *feet,* which was the extreme posture of submission (compare Luke 8:41). The context indicates a posture appropriate only for worshipping God (see Acts 10:25-26; Revelation 19:10; 22:8-9). The man's mourning for his wretched state (see Leviticus 13:45, above) was transformed into spontaneous praise for the one who brought God's healing to him as he gave *thanks* to Jesus.

All this was the man's instinctive reaction to having been shown mercy. He may not have understood everything that had just happened, but one thing he knew: Jesus had been God's instrument in his healing (compare John 9:25). The man had been shown the mercy requested!

Putting these facts together helps us understand the nature of worship. We glorify God for who He is, extolling His revealed attributes (His transcendent holiness, etc.) We thank God for what He has done in providing the blessings we personally enjoy.

16b. And he was a Samaritan.

The author Luke now reveals the shocking plot twist: the one who thought it more important to return to Jesus before seeing a priest *was a Samaritan*. We assume that the man could be identified this way by some distinctive trait. Perhaps his accent gave him away (compare Matthew 26:73), or maybe it was the precise words he used to glorify God. Distinctive clothing is another possibility. The irony here is similar to that of Jesus' parable of the good Samaritan (Luke 10:30–35), given the hostility between Jews and Samaritans (see Lesson Context).

B. Absence of Nine (vv. 17-19)

17. And Jesus answering said, Were there not ten cleansed? but where are the nine?

Jesus' questions were rhetorical—not expected to be answered literally, but rather meant to grab the attention of those within earshot. The response Jesus sought was one of self-reflection, not one of determining the latitude and longitude location of the absent *nine* who were also healed.

Jesus' questions should serve the same function today as it rings in our ears. Why did only 1 of the 10 pause to first praise God and thank Jesus? When we are blessed, are we more like the 1 or the other 9? Jesus' healing miracles always function to serve a larger purpose than merely "being nice" to someone; miracles serve as teaching opportunities (John 9; etc.).

> *What Do You Think?*
> What can you do to ensure that expressing gratitude for God's blessings is one of your regular practices?
> *Digging Deeper*
> What guardrails can you erect to ensure that such expressions do not become perfunctory?

18. There are not found that returned to give glory to God, save this stranger.

Another curiosity is that the one who did come back was, of all people, a non-Jew—a *stranger*! This was a rebuke to Jews who, of all people, should have accepted Jesus and His mission (compare Matthew 10:5; 15:24; Luke 7:4-9; John 1:11; 4:22; etc.). In the end, relationship with God is demonstrated by one's faith, not by ancestral connections (see Luke 3:8).

Neglecting to Say Thank You

While visiting a science museum, my boys explored. At one point, my oldest was on a stationary bike, testing how fast he could pump his legs, while my 3-year-old stood next to me. When we were ready to move on, I looked down to take the little one's hand only to realize he was not there!

Panic seized me. I paced swiftly through the museum. Yelling out his name, I drew more than a little attention to myself. Almost immediately a museum employee asked how he could help. A two-way radio and several pairs of eyes helped reunite me with my son in short order. With my heart beating wildly, I hugged him tightly, scolded him gently, and moved on.

It wasn't until we were leaving that I realized I had neglected to thank the people who had helped me. My emotional state had resulted in thoughtlessness. Was it the same for the nine? How will you ensure that you do not let an opportunity slip by to thank Jesus for His blessings? —A. B.

19. And he said unto him, Arise, go thy way: thy faith hath made thee whole.

After posing His rhetorical questions for all to hear, Jesus turned to the Samaritan to address him personally. All the men were healed by *faith*, but only this singular Samaritan received the affirmation *thy faith hath made thee whole* (compare Luke 7:50; 18:42). This does not mean that the man had the power to heal himself all along (see Matthew 9:22, lesson 3). It does not mean that the power of his personal faith in and of itself brought about the healing. It means, rather, that the man's trusting expectation in God, as demonstrated by his initial act of obedience to seek out the priests, was pleasing to God, by whose power the leprosy was vanquished.

The word rendered *made . . . whole* is often translated *saved* (see Matthew 8:25b [lesson 2]; 9:21 [lesson 3]). Jesus offered physical healing to some, and it had to be expected by faith. He offered salvation from sins to all, and it too had to be expected by faith.

The good news about Jesus was already moving beyond the confines of Judaism. The good news of Jesus was not limited to a Jewish audience, although there was initially a certain sequence in terms of evangelism priorities (Matthew 10:5; Romans 1:16; etc.).

In the larger picture of Luke–Acts, the Samaritans form a bridge group between Jews and Gentiles. Samaritans were despised by the Jews of Jesus' day, but the Roman world saw Samaritans and Jews as variations of the same religion. Luke's understanding of Jesus' plan for evangelism was for it to begin in Jerusalem and Judea, move to Samaria, and then expand worldwide (Acts 1:8). The incident in today's text is not an exception to that plan since the Samaritan with leprosy sought Jesus out, not the reverse.

What Do You Think?

Returning to a question from lesson 3, how has your view changed, if at all, regarding how to counsel someone who has been told that lack of healing was due to lack of faith?

Digging Deeper

What Scripture passages support your conclusion?

A Complete Healing

Several years ago a close friend of a relative was in a serious car accident. After having spent weeks hospitalized, he was sent home while still in extreme pain. Due to his spinal injuries, he spent months in rigorous physical therapy. It took over a year of exhausting therapies and time off work before he was physically well again.

Even after that, however, he was still injured emotionally and spiritually. He kept himself distant from his spiritual family. He was bitter and angry about his suffering, and he clearly needed a different kind of healing. After two or three years of gentle pushes, he was successfully encouraged to turn back to Christ. Only then was the man truly made well. As happened when the healed Samaritan fell at Jesus' feet, God blessed this friend with a deeper kind of well-being.

The reality of God's blessings is beyond dispute. What is open to question is our reaction when receiving them. What improvements do you need to make in this regard? —A. B.

Conclusion

A. Thanks and Worship

Life doesn't get much worse than the fate of a person with leprosy in Jesus' day: excluded from the community, required to be self-degrading in word and appearance, and destined to live with a slowly fatal and painful disease. It was a living death.

Yet a heart of thankfulness survived in the Samaritan leper. He remains a worthy example of the biblical way to worship. He overcame the urgencies of his life to stop, turn around, and look at Jesus without being distracted. He let praise for God well up from his heart and be expressed in his words. He overcame tunnel vision of "what's next" to adopt a worshipful posture. He gave thanks to the one who has healed him, claiming no credit for himself.

God does not need our thanks. But He created us as beings who need to give thanks (1 Thessalonians 5:18). The unthankful life can become bitter and cold. The thankful heart will find peace and purpose in all circumstances.

May we learn from the man who returned that even in the humblest of circumstances, there is nothing to prevent us from giving praise and thanks to God—nothing except our own selfish and stubborn hearts. May we recognize our spiritual poverty, ask for God's mercy, and give praise and thanks when it arrives.

What Do You Think?

Which part of today's lesson do you have the most trouble with? Why?

Digging Deeper

Other than a church staff member, who can you seek out for help in this regard?

B. Prayer

Lord God, may we worship You without distraction or impatience. We pray in the name of the one who heals and saves, Jesus our Lord. Amen.

C. Thought to Remember

Let us determine to give thanks to God.

Involvement Learning

Enhance your lesson with KJV Bible Student *(from your curriculum supplier) and the reproducible activity page (at www.standardlesson.com or in the back of the* KJV Standard Lesson Commentary Deluxe Edition*).*

Into the Lesson

Divide the class into groups, making sure that at least one person in each group has a smartphone with internet access. Ask groups to search for quotations that express gratitude and choose three they like best. After several minutes, reconvene and ask a group to share one quote with the class. After all groups have shared one, have each group share a second quote. Repeat for each group's third quote. (*Option.* Depending on the size of your class and time available, you may wish to request more or fewer quotes than three.)

Alternative. Research quotes yourself in advance and write them on slips of paper, one each. Distribute the slips to learners, ensuring that everyone has at least one. After each learner reads his or her quote, ask class members to give a thumbs-up for "like it," a thumbs-down for "objectionable," and a thumbs-across for "not sure." Encourage members to share why they reacted as they did, but don't let this drag out.

For a unit review and a transition to today's lesson, distribute copies of this matching quiz:

Problem	Key Verse(s) Solution
1. Fear can vex!	A. Matthew 6:32b-33
2. Doubt can paralyze!	B. Matthew 8:26
3. Worry can distract!	C. Matthew 9:22
4. Faith can heal!	D. Matthew 14:31
5. Gratitude can reveal!	E. Luke 17:15

Have learners work individually to complete the quiz in no more than one minute. Allow use of Bibles to look up key verses; do not allow access to lesson titles. Have learners self-score their quizzes. (*Answers*: 1–B [lesson 2]; 2–D [lesson 4]; 3–A [lesson 1]; 4–C [lesson 3]; 5–E [lesson 5]).

Into the Word

After volunteers read aloud today's lesson texts from Leviticus and Luke, ask, "Without reading something from the notes in your study Bible, what do you know about leprosy in Bible times?" After several responses, fill in missing details from the Lesson Context. Then pose this true/false question for show-of-hands response: "Half the references to leprosy in the Bible occur in the book of Leviticus." (*Answer:* true; 34 of 68 occurrences in the *King James Version* of the word *leprosy* in its various forms) Then pose for discussion, either to the class as a whole or small groups, these questions:

1–Why did nine fail to express gratitude?
2–What can we learn from the Samaritan's response for guiding our own expressions of gratitude to God?
3–How do his expressions of gratitude compare or contrast with our own?

(*Teacher tips.* For whole-class discussions, don't ask all questions at once; instead, ask one and allow discussion to conclude on it before asking the next. For small groups, provide the questions on handouts that you prepare.)

Into Life

Form study pairs and provide each with handouts (you prepare) for the following two tasks:

1–What contexts call for public thanks to God as opposed to contexts where private thanks are more appropriate?
2–Suggest ways to implement that distinction personally.

Allow time for whole-class sharing.

Option. Distribute copies of the "Attitude Adjustment" exercise on the activity page, which you can download. Have learners pick one of the four statements to respond to, time limit of one minute.

Wrap up by asking students to identify which of the five lessons of the unit presents the biggest personal challenge. Ask volunteers to tell which they've chosen and why.

Option. Distribute copies of the "Depicting Gratitude" exercise on the activity page as a take-home.

July 11
Lesson 6 (KJV)

Power of the Gospel

Devotional Reading: Psalm 71:1-6, 17-24
Background Scripture: Romans 1

Romans 1:8-17

8 First, I thank my God through Jesus Christ for you all, that your faith is spoken of throughout the whole world.

9 For God is my witness, whom I serve with my spirit in the gospel of his Son, that without ceasing I make mention of you always in my prayers;

10 Making request, if by any means now at length I might have a prosperous journey by the will of God to come unto you.

11 For I long to see you, that I may impart unto you some spiritual gift, to the end ye may be established;

12 That is, that I may be comforted together with you by the mutual faith both of you and me.

13 Now I would not have you ignorant, brethren, that oftentimes I purposed to come unto you, (but was let hitherto,) that I might have some fruit among you also, even as among other Gentiles.

14 I am debtor both to the Greeks, and to the Barbarians; both to the wise, and to the unwise.

15 So, as much as in me is, I am ready to preach the gospel to you that are at Rome also.

16 For I am not ashamed of the gospel of Christ: for it is the power of God unto salvation to every one that believeth; to the Jew first, and also to the Greek.

17 For therein is the righteousness of God revealed from faith to faith: as it is written, The just shall live by faith.

וְצַדִּיק בֶּאֱמוּנָתוֹ יִחְיֶה׃

ὁ δὲ δίκαιος ἐκ πίστεώς μου ζήσεται.

Key Verse

I am not ashamed of the gospel of Christ: for it is the power of God unto salvation to every one that believeth; to the Jew first, and also to the Greek. —**Romans 1:16**

Confident Hope

Unit 2: Faith and Salvation

Lessons 6–9

Lesson Aims

After participating in this lesson, each learner will be able to:

1. Identify the groups to which Paul acknowledged his debt obligation.
2. Give one example each of being ashamed and being unashamed of the gospel.
3. Create two approaches for sharing the gospel: one for people having some gospel knowledge already and the other for those with much less or no such knowledge.

Lesson Outline

Introduction
- A. "Where the Money Is"
- B. Lesson Context

I. Power of Witness (Romans 1:8-10)
- A. Of a Church (v. 8)
- B. Of an Individual (vv. 9-10)
  Responding to His Call

II. Power of Preaching (Romans 1:11-15)
- A. Spiritual Insight and Fruit (vv. 11-13)
- B. Spiritual Debts and Readiness (vv. 14-15)

III. Power of Faith (Romans 1:16-17)
- A. Overcoming Shame (v. 16)
  The Power of the Gospel
- B. Revealing Righteousness (v. 17)

Conclusion
- A. Come to the Cross
- B. Prayer
- C. Thought to Remember

Introduction

A. "Where the Money Is"

Willie Sutton (1901–1980)—also known as The Actor and Slick Willie—was infamous as a thief. He would arrive at his target, usually a bank or store, just before they opened. On at least one occasion, he had the security guard admit employees as they arrived, then tied them up in an office to prevent any trouble. His disguises included dressing as a telegraph messenger, a policeman, and a maintenance man. Even in the midst of his crimes, Sutton was noted as being quite polite, even gentlemanly.

Sutton was caught several times, and he escaped prison on more than one occasion. After one escape, a tailor's son recognized Sutton. The fugitive had not come to commit robbery but instead to get a suit tailored! When asked why he robbed banks, Sutton replied, "That's where the money is." What other explanation could a person possibly need? Sutton wanted money, banks had money, so logically he went to banks to relieve them of their funds.

Paul was no criminal, but his answer to a certain question might have been similar to Sutton's. Why did Paul go to the cities to preach the gospel? Because that's where the people were!

B. Lesson Context

Cities seemed to hold a special attraction for Paul in a strategic way. Three of his key ministries were in Antioch, Corinth, and Ephesus—all among the 10 largest cities of the empire. But Paul had a burning desire to visit the greatest city of them all, Rome, the capital of the empire and center of the world in those days.

The saying, "All roads lead to Rome" was more than proverbial for Paul. The city was unparalleled in the ancient world. After Rome's decline in late antiquity, Europe would not see anything to rival it until London in the nineteenth century. Paul was convinced that God was calling him to go to Rome.

Paul, formerly Saul the persecutor of Christians, wrote the letter to the Romans in advance of his trip there. A church was growing in Rome, a church made up of individuals who were likely present in Jerusalem on Pentecost (Acts 2:10) and of believers they converted.

Some of those whom Paul had led to Christ seemed to have traveled to Rome ahead of him for one reason or another. That is clear from the list of personal greetings that Paul includes at the end of the letter, in chapter 16. It was important to Paul that they grow in the right direction. They needed a strong doctrinal base, and they needed some practical spiritual counsel. In this letter they received both.

Paul wrote the book of Romans in about AD 58, during his third missionary journey. This timing is supported by Acts 20:2-3, which states that Paul spent three months in Greece. This in turn supports the conclusion that Paul wrote from the Greek city of Corinth, home of a beloved church he had founded and ministered to for 18 months a few years earlier. Staying put in this Greek city among people he knew and loved would have allowed Paul the time to craft such a carefully, masterfully written letter.

The contents of Romans reflect Paul's experience in presenting a gospel that is both doctrinal and relational in matters faced by growing Christians. Paul was in the prime years of his ministry, being able to present the fruit of his personal familiarity with bringing people to Christ and providing an atmosphere for their growth. He was prepared to send a letter that addressed many important issues, countered spiritual errors, and emphasized core truths of the Christian faith.

I. Power of Witness

(Romans 1:8-10)

A. Of a Church (v. 8)

8. First, I thank my God through Jesus Christ for you all, that your faith is spoken of throughout the whole world.

Having introduced himself and laid out the basics of his gospel (Romans 1:1-7), Paul encouraged the Roman Christians by revealing the content of his prayers to God regarding them. Expressing gratitude and thankfulness is characteristic of his letters.

> *What Do You Think?*
> How can you improve the ratio of "thanking for" to "asking for" in your prayer life?
> *Digging Deeper*
> Why is it important to do so?

Paul's observation that *the whole world* had received reports of the faithfulness of this church may partly result from the painful expulsion they had faced. Turmoil in Rome had prompted Emperor Claudius (reigned AD 41–54) to expel from the city all those of Jewish background in about AD 49 (Acts 18:1-2). The turmoil was likely a conflict between Jews who had converted to Christianity and those who had not. The Romans didn't make a distinction between the two at the time, so all those of Jewish background were told to leave town.

When Paul wrote the letter to the Romans, Claudius had died, and Jews had returned to Rome. Within the Christian community, this caused reconsideration of the relationships between Jews, Gentiles, and God.

B. Of an Individual (vv. 9-10)

9-10. For God is my witness, whom I serve with my spirit in the gospel of his Son, that without ceasing I make mention of you always in my prayers; making request, if by any means now at length I might have a prosperous journey by the will of God to come unto you.

Worldwide Christianity would be blessed by a strong, faithful congregation in the great city of Rome. Its location at the transportation hub of the empire would allow the church's witness to spread in all directions. For this and for his anticipated trip, Paul prayed sincerely. He valued the advance of *the gospel of* God's *Son* as his primary objective. His budding relationship with the Christians in Rome was part of his grand vision for bringing the message of salvation to all people of the world.

Although Paul could be bold, even brash, in his claims and plans, we see his humility on display here. His great desire to go to Rome was tempered by his intent to submit to *the will of God*. Our greatest plans, no matter how noble, depend on God's blessing and assistance if they are to be successful.

The route from Corinth to Rome was regularly traveled, taking only a few weeks. But Paul decided to return to Jerusalem before visiting Rome (see Acts 19:21). This delayed his trip to Rome by a year or more. But spiritual guidance couldn't wait, thus the need for this letter to serve that church in the interim.

❧ *Responding to His Call* ❧

I met a minister who planted a church in my city last year. Before then, he had been ministering in his father's church, which was across the country. While there, he had mentored a young man from my city. That young man asked the minister to pray for his family.

The minister did pray and eventually had a phone conversation with the family. During the call, the minister felt a burden for the family and the people of my city. Soon, he told his wife that he sensed a call to move their family across the country to start a church. At the time, he didn't even know the location of my city on a map! Even though it seemed like a big step of faith, the minister heeded God's call.

When God burdens your heart for reaching people, responding to the call is worth the sacrifice. Consider whom God may have been calling you to reach. In what ways have you been resisting? How will you respond this week? —L. H.-P.

II. Power of Preaching

(Romans 1:11-15)

A. Spiritual Insight and Fruit (vv. 11-13)

11. For I long to see you, that I may impart unto you some spiritual gift, to the end ye may be established.

The word *for* introduces the reasons why Paul desired to visit the church in Rome. We should not understand his stated desire to *impart unto* them *some spiritual gift* to refer to something specific since he did not yet know their specific needs. What he probably had in mind was something like "spiritual insight" for guiding the church in providing what the Roman church lacked—something that could be provided only by Paul. Nor should we hear Paul implying that the Roman church was on shaky ground; he was not the one who founded that church, and he had only secondhand knowledge of its situation. More likely what we are seeing here is Paul's understanding of the value of face-to-face fellowship, something that cannot be equaled by letters or messengers.

Paul's writing to these brothers and sisters in Christ was a step toward a long time of teaching and dialogue (see Acts 28:16-31). *The end* or goal of this education was to be the establishment of the Roman church in sound Christian teaching (doctrine) and practice.

12. That is, that I may be comforted together with you by the mutual faith both of you and me.

One of the outstanding aspects of being a Christian, something difficult to explain to nonbelievers, is the comfort and joy we find as we share our "like precious faith" with one another (2 Peter 1:1). We can share the victories we have over sin and death (Romans 8:1-2). We can give honor to God, who promises never to allow us to be separated from His love (8:35-39). We can remind ourselves that all things are working for good according to God's purposes (8:28). We can participate in corporate prayers enlivened by the Holy Spirit we share (8:26-27). We can encourage each other with stories of our life transformations, our resistance to being conformed to the sinful influences of the world (12:1-2).

These themes were a foretaste of the joyous time Paul anticipated when he finally joined the Romans for fellowship.

HOW TO SAY IT

Abraham	*Ay*-bruh-ham.
Antioch	*An*-tee-ock.
Claudius	*Claw*-dee-us.
Corinth	*Kor*-inth.
Ephesus	*Ef*-uh-sus.
Habakkuk	Huh-*back*-kuk.
Pentecost	*Pent*-ih-kost.
Philippi	Fih-*lip*-pie or *Fil*-ih-pie.

13. Now I would not have you ignorant, brethren, that oftentimes I purposed to come unto you, (but was let hitherto,) that I might have some fruit among you also, even as among other Gentiles.

Paul preached and wrote expectantly, anticipating that God would use his words as seed to bear *fruit* (compare 1 Corinthians 3:6-7). Paul's writing suggests that this growth would be seen at least in part in spiritual virtues (see Galatians 5:22-23). He also wanted to preach among the people of Rome because he believed it would result in conversions and changed lives. This was not unfounded fantasy, because Paul had already experienced much fruit during his ministries in Corinth (Acts 18), Philippi (16:12-15, 25-34, 40), and other Gentile cities. As he wrote later, people cannot hear and believe unless there is a preacher (Romans 10:14; see lesson 9).

Paul had a strong sense of God's direction of his ministry. Though Paul had long *purposed* to visit Rome, he had been hindered in each instance. Various circumstances and even spiritual directions changed Paul's plans (see Acts 16:6). And at the time of the writing of Romans, his choice to go to Jerusalem rather than Rome was driven by a deep-seated conviction that no one around him shared (Acts 21:12-14). Paul explained later in the letter that part of what *let* him *hitherto* was his great burden to preach the gospel among unevangelized *Gentiles* (Romans 15:17-22). Paul's travels had been to serve Christ, not simply to find personal fulfillment.

> *What Do You Think?*
> Which problem do you most need to address: being exasperated that God's timing isn't fast enough or that it's moving too fast?
> *Digging Deeper*
> What Bible examples can you offer for each?

B. Spiritual Debts and Readiness (vv. 14-15)

14a. I am debtor both to the Greeks, and to the Barbarians.

Paul described his relationship with unevangelized people he had never met in terms of owing a debt to them. His spiritual duty could only be discharged by preaching the gospel to the unsaved. This concept was central to his passion for the Gentile mission.

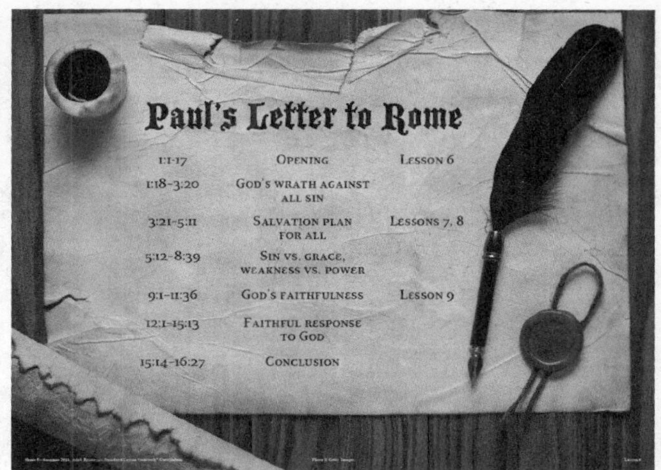

Visual for Lesson 6. *Keep this visual posted during lessons 6–9 so learners can maintain a bird's-eye perspective on the book of Romans.*

Gentiles could be subdivided as two groups of people, based on a Greek understanding of the world. *Greeks* themselves were Gentile unbelievers in the eastern part of the Roman Empire. These were assumed to be the most civilized and most sophisticated citizens in the Roman Empire.

Barbarians were those living beyond the regions of Greek influence, who spoke languages other than Greek (compare and contrast Acts 2:5-11). In Paul's day, Greeks had a strong sense of cultural superiority based on their philosophical traditions and refined language. To them, languages other than Greek sounded like babbling nonsense, "bar-bar-bar," qualifying such speakers as "barbarians." It's been said that after the Romans conquered the Greeks militarily, the Greeks turned around and conquered the Romans culturally. The Romans later adopted the category of barbarian to refer to all people who did not have Greek or Roman heritage.

14b. both to the wise, and to the unwise.

Paul's inclusiveness in preaching indicates that knowledge or education levels are not a criterion for Paul's target audiences (see 1 Corinthians 1:26). Some students propose that Paul used parallelism to mean that the Greeks were *the wise* while the Barbarians were *the unwise.* This would fit the Greek and Roman view of their heritage contrasted with that of other people groups.

15. So, as much as in me is, I am ready to preach the gospel to you that are at Rome also.

At first glance, this verse may seem strange. Why plan to *preach the gospel to* the recipients of this letter, who are already Christians? We should realize that preaching the gospel involves more than initial evangelizing. This is clear in the five dozen or so times Paul used the phrase "the gospel" in his letters.

III. Power of Faith

(Romans 1:16-17)

A. Overcoming Shame (v. 16)

16a. For I am not ashamed of the gospel of Christ.

Elsewhere, Paul noted that the message of the cross was a "stumblingblock" to Jews (1 Corinthians 1:23). The core elements of Paul's preaching would not avoid the historical truth that Jesus had been executed like the worst of criminals (2:2). Jesus' death was easily dismissed by critics as neither heroic nor in obedience to God's will, but as only shameful.

Of course, the shame of the cross was real (Hebrews 12:2). But the gospel reveals that shame was not the full story of Jesus' execution (see Philippians 2:5-11). Therefore Paul was *not ashamed* of the cross. Rather, he gloried in it (Galatians 6:14).

16b. For it is the power of God unto salvation to every one that believeth; to the Jew first, and also to the Greek.

Not only does the gospel possess the power to save *every one that believeth*, it also had the power to break down the walls separating Jews and Gentiles—a point discussed further by Paul in Ephesians. There he explicitly welcomed the uncircumcised who had previously been legally restricted from full participation in the covenant with Israel (see Ephesians 2:11-22).

It is difficult to determine whether the church in Rome consisted mostly of Jewish-Christians or Gentile-Christians. Clearly, both were present (Romans 2:17; 11:13). Some believers of Jewish background in the church in Rome were likely present in Jerusalem on Pentecost and heard the gospel from Peter. Those Jews were among the *first* to hear the good news. But Greeks (Gentiles) also needed to know this *power of God unto salvation*. As we noted in previous lessons of this quarter, the word *salvation* can take a broad range of meanings in the New Testament, depending on context. But not in Paul's writings; he uses that word only in a spiritual sense (examples: Romans 10:1, 10; 11:11; 13:11; 2 Corinthians 1:6; 6:2; 7:10).

> *What Do You Think?*
> In what ways, if at all, does Romans 1:16 help you act according to spiritual priorities?
> *Digging Deeper*
> What do you see those priorities being?

The Power of the Gospel

We had two family members die within the same week: an aunt and uncle who had been married for more than 60 years. It was devastating to lose them, even though the couple had lived long, fulfilling lives. In accordance with her aunt's wishes, my wife was asked to deliver a eulogy at the funeral. She delivered a powerful message of hope from John 14. The family needed to be reminded of the truth that through Christ's death and resurrection Christians have the assurance of eternal union with God.

One family member came to my wife after the service to express how her eulogy had affected him. He had been feeling such a heaviness during the service that it was difficult for him to breathe. But as he had listened, he experienced an easing of his heavy heart. He could breathe normally again as the service concluded.

The gospel has the power to do many things, including breaking the sting of death. How will you allow the gospel's "power unto salvation" help you overcome the next tragedy that comes your way? —L. H.-P.

B. Revealing Righteousness (v. 17)

17. For therein is the righteousness of God revealed from faith to faith: as it is written, The just shall live by faith.

The gospel is the most crucial message ever because *therein is the righteousness of God revealed.* The gospel tells sinful people how to become right with God. That is something that we can never earn or achieve through our own efforts (Isaiah 64:6). Our only hope is to accept by faith the gift of God's righteousness as provided by Him through the death of Jesus. As Paul wrote to the Corinthians, "For [God] hath made him to be sin for us, who knew no sin; that we might be made the righteousness of God in him" (2 Corinthians 5:21).

Paul concluded this summary of his gospel message by quoting a key Old Testament verse for understanding the nature of faith: Habakkuk 2:4. In the original setting of this verse, Habakkuk complained to the Lord about the prosperity of the wicked and the suffering of the righteous, expecting action from God (1:12–2:1). God's final word was that His people must remain faithful, trusting Him for the outcome that vindicates righteousness and justice (2:2-19). Our job is not to try to compel God to act; rather, it is to place our faith in God to do the right thing in His timing.

Christ's death on the cross was the right thing at the right time (Galatians 4:4-5). It's what allows people to become justified, to be treated as faultless before God's throne. The price for our sins has been paid. Paul presents this as a revealing of the nature of God, that He both demands *righteousness* from us and makes this possible despite our sin and weakness. Later Paul will say this allows God to remain completely holy and righteous himself while working to make sinful humanity righteous too. God is both "just, and the justifier" of those who trust Him (Romans 3:26).

The exact meaning of the phrase *from faith to faith* has been debated. But the likely intent of Paul is to show that this whole faith agenda is not a new invention by Christians. God's people have always built a successful relationship with Him on faith. Paul later gave the example of Abraham, whose faith was "counted unto him for righteousness" (Romans 4:3, 22; see lesson 7, Genesis 15:6). Trusting in God is not new, but now we are to include faith in Jesus—that His death has the effect of saving us from our sins. It is faith *then*, faith *now*, and faith *going forward*.

What Do You Think?

How would you explain to someone the difference between a blind faith and the kind of faith Paul talks about?

Digging Deeper

How would that explanation differ to a believer and an unbeliever, if at all? Why?

Conclusion

A. Come to the Cross

The most recognized Christian symbol is the cross. We see it on churches, as jewelry, in logos, in massive monuments, and in cemeteries. For many, the cross is most associated with the latter as it marks a grave of a loved one.

As Christians, we affirm that Jesus' cross is about death. But the cross is also about life, for Jesus' death gives us the possibility of being forgiven of our sins, escaping the penalty of death, and embracing eternal life as a gift. To do this, we must come to the cross in faith. We must not be ashamed. We must come believing that the cross represents the great love of God. We must come convinced that faith in Christ has the power to save us. It is there that our burden of sin was lifted and our spiritual blindness will become the sight of faith.

What Do You Think?

Which concept in today's text requires more "live it out" on your part? Why?

Digging Deeper

How do you plan to make that happen?

B. Prayer

Lord God, may we approach Your throne with faith, unashamed of our love and trust for Your Son, Jesus Christ. May we give all that we have to serve You and to bring the gospel message to those who have not heard. In Jesus' name we pray. Amen.

C. Thought to Remember

The gospel is powerful for all who believe.

Involvement Learning

Enhance your lesson with KJV Bible Student *(from your curriculum supplier) and the reproducible activity page (at www.standardlesson.com or in the back of the* KJV Standard Lesson Commentary Deluxe Edition*).*

Into the Lesson

Ask class members to share a memory of the most important trip they ever took. Note that the question is not about their most enjoyable or most interesting trip, although those descriptions may also apply. Conduct this exercise by either (1) displaying a world map and asking volunteers to walk to it and tell about their trip, (2) giving each learner a handout of a map (you prepare) as they pair off to locate and discuss their trips, or (3) simply posing the question and ask volunteers to share. (*Caution:* Beware of the danger of letting this drag out too long.)

Make a transition to Bible study by saying, "Some trips simply *must* be taken, regardless of (or because of) circumstances. The same was true in Paul's day—let's see why."

Into the Word

Announce a consideration of the context of the book of Romans. Put in a basket the following questions printed on four slips of paper (you prepare in advance), one question per slip:

1–Who was Paul?
2–Why was Rome important?
3–When was the book of Romans written?
4–What problems does Paul address in Romans?

Have four volunteers draw out one slip each to read aloud in sequence as numbered. Allow the volunteer the first chance to answer the question drawn. Follow that by inviting all class members to add to the response. Fill in gaps with information in the Lesson Context of today's lesson.

Have two participants alternate in reading aloud the 10 verses of today's lesson text, Romans 1:8-17. Divide your class into groups of no more than six each. To half the groups, distribute a handout (you prepare) on which is printed these three phrases as headers of three columns:

Reference / Why the Desire / What to Accomplish

Include instructions to complete the chart by examining today's lesson text. Have this printed at the bottom of the handout for completion:

One statement to describe the mission Paul wanted to have among the Romans is ___________

Concurrently, distribute to the other groups handouts (you prepare) featuring these three phrases to be completed:

1–Why the gospel is important:
2–What the gospel achieves:
3–What the gospel reveals:

Option. Modify the above groupings by creating an additional, third grouping of learners. Distribute to this/these group(s) copies of the "Qualifications, Please!" exercise from the activity page to be completed and reported as indicated. Reconvene groups for whole-class sharing.

Into Life

Ask students to gather again in their groups as you distribute the following discussion prompts on handouts (you prepare):

1–The power of the gospel has affected me by . . .
2–Three ways I can better "live by faith" are . . .
3–My biggest challenge in sharing the gospel is . . .

After several minutes, reconvene for whole-class discussion. Use responses to the third discussion prompt to challenge learners to suggest two approaches for sharing the gospel: one for people having some gospel knowledge already and the other for those with much less or no such knowledge. Close with prayers that are suggested by responses to the three discussion prompts: thanks to God for life changes, strength from God for every class member to live by faith this week, help from God to face the challenges shared.

Option. Distribute copies of the "Paul's Mission to Rome" crossword on the activity page as a take-home.

FAITH OF ABRAHAM

DEVOTIONAL READING: Genesis 15:1-6
BACKGROUND SCRIPTURE: Romans 4

ROMANS 4:1-12

1 What shall we say then that Abraham our father, as pertaining to the flesh, hath found?

2 For if Abraham were justified by works, he hath whereof to glory; but not before God.

3 For what saith the scripture? Abraham believed God, and it was counted unto him for righteousness.

4 Now to him that worketh is the reward not reckoned of grace, but of debt.

5 But to him that worketh not, but believeth on him that justifieth the ungodly, his faith is counted for righteousness.

6 Even as David also describeth the blessedness of the man, unto whom God imputeth righteousness without works,

7 Saying, Blessed are they whose iniquities are forgiven, and whose sins are covered.

8 Blessed is the man to whom the Lord will not impute sin.

9 Cometh this blessedness then upon the circumcision only, or upon the uncircumcision also? for we say that faith was reckoned to Abraham for righteousness.

10 How was it then reckoned? when he was in circumcision, or in uncircumcision? Not in circumcision, but in uncircumcision.

11 And he received the sign of circumcision, a seal of the righteousness of the faith which he had yet being uncircumcised: that he might be the father of all them that believe, though they be not circumcised; that righteousness might be imputed unto them also:

12 And the father of circumcision to them who are not of the circumcision only, but who also walk in the steps of that faith of our father Abraham, which he had being yet uncircumcised.

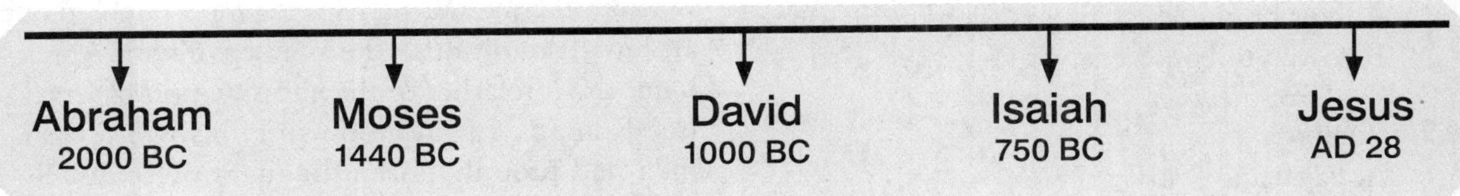

KEY VERSE

Abraham believed God, and it was counted unto him for righteousness. **—Romans 4:3b**

Confident Hope

Unit 2: Faith and Salvation

Lessons 6–9

Lesson Aims

After participating in this lesson, each learner will be able to:

1. Summarize the nature of Abraham's righteousness.

2. Distinguish between "imparted righteousness" and "imputed righteousness."

3. Make a list of ways that imputed (credited) righteousness will direct his or her thoughts and actions in the week ahead.

Lesson Outline

Introduction
- A. The Progenitor of the Printing Press
- B. Lesson Context

I. Ancestor of Israel (Romans 4:1-3)
- A. Not Justified by Works (vv. 1-2)
- B. Justified by Faith (v. 3)
  - *If You Build It, They Will Come*

II. Receiving Righteousness (Romans 4:4-8)
- A. Not an Earned Reward (vv. 4-5)
- B. An Unearned Blessing (vv. 6-8)

III. Father of the Faithful (Romans 4:9-12)
- A. Not Limited by Circumcision (vv. 9-10)
- B. Given to Followers (vv. 11-12)
  - *A Free Reward*

Conclusion
- A. Faith and Work
- B. Prayer
- C. Thought to Remember

Introduction

A. The Progenitor of the Printing Press

In the mid-1400s, a German entrepreneur introduced a process that many identify as the beginning of the modern era. Johannes Gutenberg combined ideas from metallurgy, book production, agricultural methods, and other areas to produce the first European "movable-type" printing press. The crown jewel of his career was the production in 1455 of 180 deluxe copies of the Latin translation of the Bible.

This edition is now known as the Gutenberg Bible, with fewer than 50 known copies surviving. Perhaps the finest example is on display in the Library of Congress in Washington, DC. Gutenberg's printing press allowed for the mass production of books, therefore increasing the desirability of literacy and knowledge. Our digital age is far removed from Gutenberg's press in Mainz, but the precedent he set has earned him the title of Father of Printing, and his influence is still felt today.

The internet has many "Father of the . . ." and "Mother of the . . ." lists. The apostle Paul has one of his own.

B. Lesson Context

During Paul's ministry, a key issue concerned the role of the Jewish law for Christians who were not of Jewish descent. At the time Paul wrote his letter to the Romans, the famous Jerusalem Council had already recognized that Gentiles would be welcomed into the church without being required to keep the Law of Moses (Acts 15:7-11, 19-21, 28-29). This included forgoing circumcision, which symbolized the entire law for Jews (see Romans 4:9, below).

Circumcision was perhaps the most honored of all Jewish traditions. The rite began with Abraham, the forefather of the entire nation of Israel (see Romans 4:1 and following, below). Jewish men had proudly borne the mark of circumcision for hundreds of years, a physical sign of their separation from Gentiles. The traditional adversaries of Israel were called uncircumcised, an epithet spit out in scorn (example: Jeremiah 9:26; see Romans 4:9, below). Any foreigner who wanted to be accepted into Israel had to be circumcised (Exodus 12:48). To be an uncircumcised Jewish man was to be expelled from Israel and thus *not* part of the nation (Genesis 17:14).

Gentiles did not welcome the idea of circumcision as a condition for worshipping God. The physical act of circumcision was culturally repugnant and physically painful. In the Roman world, this hesitation resulted in Gentiles who were attracted to Judaism to be identified as "devout" (Acts 17:4, 17) in contrast with a "proselyte" (Matthew 23:15), who converted fully.

The "devout" chose to honor the Lord. However, they were excluded from full participation in the temple or synagogues because the men in these families had not undergone circumcision. Peter's encounter with Cornelius, during which time the Holy Spirit came to a group of Gentiles (Acts 10:44-48), was the beginning of a new understanding about what would and would not be required in the church (11:15-18).

In part, the discussion of what Jewish customs to retain in the church—and require of Gentiles—was a discussion about the relationship between faith and works. Though these two concepts can be held in tension, most Christians understand that works flow out of faith (James 2:14-26). We are "saved through faith, . . . not of works" (Ephesians 2:8-9). The work that we do for Christ is faith manifesting itself in our lives (2:10); it is not an attempt to save ourselves. Paul's discussion of Abraham considered in our lesson text today is an example of this fact.

Paul ended Romans 3 with a crescendo that emphasized that people can be pronounced righteous only through faith (Romans 3:30). But this raises an important question: What about the ancient and hallowed Jewish law, the law that Moses received from God himself?

I. Ancestor of Israel

(Romans 4:1-3)

A. Not Justified by Works (vv. 1-2)

1. What shall we say then that Abraham our father, as pertaining to the flesh, hath found?

Abraham lived more than 2,000 years before Paul wrote the book of Romans. Abraham's history was preserved by the people of God in oral traditions for several hundred years before it was written down in the book of Genesis.

That man had an incredible relationship with God. He trusted God even when called to journey to a place he had never seen, on the eastern end of the Mediterranean Sea (Genesis 12:1-9; see Romans 4:12, below). Later, Abraham trusted God to provide him with a legitimate heir, his son Isaac, when both he and his wife, Sarah, were advanced in age (Genesis 17:15-22; 18:10-15; 21:1-7). Abraham even trusted God when commanded to sacrifice Isaac on Mount Moriah (22:1-18).

For these and other acts, Abraham is considered to be the *father* of faith (Matthew 3:9; Luke 1:73; etc.). He was one of the first people to model a faithful relationship with God.

Paul focused these facts on his Jewish-Christian readers, identifying Abraham as their father *as pertaining to the flesh.* Paul spoke to those who traced their ancestry to the great patriarch of Genesis. Today we would say Paul spoke to those who would find a DNA match with Abraham. Paul's strategy took his line of argumentation to a time even before Israel was a nation.

2. For if Abraham were justified by works, he hath whereof to glory; but not before God.

Paul set up this verse to establish the source of Abraham's justification. To be *justified* is to be counted or considered righteous. Did *Abraham* earn justification through his acts of obedience, his *works*? No amount of righteous deeds will position a person correctly *before God*, for all men and women have sinned (Romans 3:23).

Paul's original readers knew that Abraham did not always act in a righteous, faithful way. His deceptions concerning the status of Sarah as his sister rather than his wife nearly caused her to be involved in adultery (Genesis 12:10-20; 20:1-18). And though his actions toward Hagar were sadly typical for his day, the way he treated his concubine and son after the birth of Isaac left much to be desired (21:8-21). If Abraham had been *justified by* his good *works*, then he would have had reason to *glory* in himself. But that was not the case.

What Do You Think?

What personal guardrails can you erect to ensure that you keep pride in its proper place and properly expressed?

Digging Deeper

How would you rank-order these passages in terms of relevance to that question: Proverbs 16:18; 2 Corinthians 10:7-18; Ephesians 2:8-9; James 4:16; 1 John 2:16? Why?

B. Justified by Faith (v. 3)

3. For what saith the scripture? Abraham believed God, and it was counted unto him for righteousness.

Paul's statement is a near quote of Genesis 15:6. In that context, Abraham had been lamenting that he had no male heir to carry forward his name and legacy. In a visionary experience, the Lord compelled Abraham to go outside on a clear night to view the uncountable number of stars in the sky. God promised Abraham that the number of his descendants would be like this ocean of stars (Genesis 15:5). So, Abraham had a choice to make: (1) he could trust that God would keep His promise and grant him an heir or (2) he could reject this as impossible.

The evidence in Abraham's life and marriage compelled him to try to help God's plan along. Abraham and Sarah had long since passed the season of producing children (Genesis 17:17). Abraham had resigned himself to the fact that his chief servant would be his heir (15:2) before Abraham took it upon himself to avoid that possibility by having a son with Hagar (16:1-4, 15).

Even so, Abraham's faith did not collapse on the basis of his long wait or the seeming impossibility of the fulfillment of God's promises. Rather than despair or reject the Lord, *Abraham believed God.* He chose to believe that God was capable of keeping His promise and would be faithful to do so. He trusted that God had a plan for him.

So Abraham lived accordingly and expectantly. This stupendous act of faith gave him the status of a righteous person before a holy and utterly righteous God. The word translated *counted* was used in the financial world of Paul's day to describe the act of moving credits into an accounting ledger. An account with a negative balance (an unrighteous or unknown status) now showed a positive balance (*righteousness*).

Putting this analogy into our own context, Abraham's account moved from red ink to black ink. The result for generations to come was that Abraham stood as the father of Israel first, but also of all believers who trust God.

If You Build It, They Will Come

When my best friend felt called to found a Christian school, the task seemed impossible. She had no marketing or administrative training, and she certainly didn't have any money. She was new to town and didn't know anyone. "God will provide," she answered when I asked how she was going to find land. She said the same thing when she had no building on the land, and again when she had no students to fill the building.

Things didn't always go right. But she never doubted it would all come together. She believed, even though it seemed an impossibility. And God provided every person who had the exact skill, material, or financing to create what is now a flourishing, classical Christian school.

Abraham and Sarah were old. Descendants as numerous as the stars? Impossible! Yet Abraham believed. Sometimes he delayed in his obedience or tried his own way. But he never forgot God's word. In life's twists and turns, is your faith still grounded in God's faithfulness? —P. M.

II. Receiving Righteousness

(Romans 4:4-8)

A. Not an Earned Reward (vv. 4-5)

4. Now to him that worketh is the reward not reckoned of grace, but of debt.

Workers are not paid because of *grace* but because they have earned their wages. The *debt* incurred by their employer is thereby discharged.

To be justified by God can never be the result of our works, for we have too many debits in the form of sins. If we really earned what we deserve based on our works, we would all remain dead in sins (Ephesians 2:1-3; Colossians 2:13-14) since "the wages of sin is death" (Romans 6:23). The person who thinks a winning strategy before the throne of final judgment will be to present a list of righteous deeds will be sorely disappointed. No one can be declared righteous through works of the law (Romans 3:20).

5. But to him that worketh not, but believeth on him that justifieth the ungodly, his faith is counted for righteousness.

The phrase *him that worketh not* likely refers to the person who does not depend on personal works to be in a right standing before God. No sinner, whether Gentile or Jew, can ever earn *righteousness*. Were someone able to do so, he or she would not need to be *counted* as righteous by *faith* because such a person would actually *be* righteous.

B. An Unearned Blessing (vv. 6-8)

6. Even as David also describeth the blessedness of the man, unto whom God imputeth righteousness without works.

The line of reasoning moves from one revered Jewish figure (Abraham) to another (*David*), a historical shift of about 1,000 years. Perhaps even more than Abraham's sins, David's sins are remembered to this day. He committed adultery and murder (2 Samuel 11). The fallout from those sins dogged David's personal life (example: 12:14-18).

But David eventually came to know the blessing of forgiven sin (2 Samuel 12:13), the essence of justification. David understood the grace of God as powerful to overcome the guilt of sins. That king's repentance and faithfulness, even when suffering the consequences of his sins, are a great part of why David is called "a man after [God's] own heart" (1 Samuel 13:14; Acts 13:22).

HOW TO SAY IT

Abrahamic	Ay-bruh-*ham*-ik.
Cornelius	Cor-*neel*-yus.
Hagar	*Hay*-gar.
Ishmael	*Ish*-may-el.
Johannes Gutenberg	Yoh-*hahn*-uhs *Goo*-tin-burg.
Moriah	Mo-*rye*-uh.
patriarchs	*pay*-tree-arks.

What Do You Think?

How would you explain to someone the distinction between being credited (or counted) as righteous vs. actually being made righteous?

Digging Deeper

In what circumstances might you explain the difference by using the words imputed and imparted instead? Why?

7-8. Saying, Blessed are they whose iniquities are forgiven, and whose sins are covered. Blessed is the man to whom the Lord will not impute sin.

David wrote of his experience of being forgiven by God, and the quote in the verses before us is that of David's marvelous Psalm 32:1-2. This is a great passage on confession of sin, repentance, and received forgiveness. In it, David exhorted others to realize that happiness is found in God's forgiveness. Only confession can release the disease that wastes the bones of the guilty (32:3-4) and open a person to God's forgiveness (32:5, 11). John wrote about this as well: "If we confess our sins, [God] is faithful and just to forgive us our sins, and to cleanse us from all unrighteousness" (1 John 1:9; compare Psalm 51).

III. Father of the Faithful
(Romans 4:9-12)

A. Not Limited by Circumcision (vv. 9-10)

9. Cometh this blessedness then upon the circumcision only, or upon the uncircumcision also? for we say that faith was reckoned to Abraham for righteousness.

Circumcision was the physical mark given by God to *Abraham* and his male descendants as a sign of the covenant (Genesis 17:11-13). It was given later in Abraham's life by God's command. Abraham and every male in his household were circumcised in obedience to God's requirement (17:10, 23). Abraham chose to obey this command just as he had already obeyed God many times before. The mark itself, though, did not make

Faith is stronger
than works.
Visual for Lesson 7. *Have this visual displayed prominently as you ask learners why the statement on it is true.*

Abraham or the men in his house more righteous. Abraham was already reckoned as righteous because of his *faith* in God.

10. How was it then reckoned? when he was in circumcision, or in uncircumcision? Not in circumcision, but in uncircumcision.

The Jewish people assumed that their blessings were owed at least partly to obedience in circumcision. But Paul argues convincingly otherwise: Abraham's faith was *reckoned* to him as righteousness *before* that sign was implemented, which sign was not commanded until Genesis 17:10. Thus the sign of circumcision was of less importance than the faith behind it.

This fact was important in affirming that circumcision was not necessary for the faith of Gentiles to be valid in following Christ (see Lesson Context). "But he is a Jew, which is one inwardly; and circumcision is that of the heart, in the spirit, and not in the letter" (Romans 2:29; compare Deuteronomy 10:16; 30:6; Jeremiah 4:4).

Outward obedience to God's rules and regulations does not make a person righteous. Only one's faith and God's grace can result in being reckoned as righteous. Following His commands is a sign of our faith; without that faith, the signs are meaningless.

B. Given to Followers (vv. 11-12)

11. And he received the sign of circumcision, a seal of the righteousness of the faith which he had yet being uncircumcised: that he might be the father of all them that believe, though they be not circumcised; that righteousness might be imputed unto them also.

Paul did not disregard *circumcision* as having no value at all, though. This *sign* and *seal of the righteousness of faith* became a key element in the covenant relationship God developed with Abraham's Jewish descendants.

Muslims, who claim lineage to Abraham via Ishmael, still practice circumcision as a religious requirement. They consider it a sign of inclusion in the Muslim community. But in contrast to the Abrahamic faiths of Islam and Judaism, circumcision was and is not imposed as a sign of inclusion in the Christian faith. God's will in this regard was discerned during the first decades of the church's existence (see Galatians 2:1-3 and the Lesson Context).

Because Abraham was counted as righteous before circumcision, Paul argued that that patriarch could therefore be the father of any righteous person, regardless of circumcision. Righteousness is imputed (not imparted) to those who believe. And if this seems repetitious, it's only because Paul himself was repetitious. This is a big deal! And it is worth repeating over and over. Faith is what God wants, not outward signs.

What Do You Think?

When Paul's statement about Abraham's spiritual fatherhood-of-all has its desired impact, what changes should others see in your life?

Digging Deeper

What can you do to accelerate the rate of those changes?

As an aside, we note that some think that Christian baptism is the New Testament parallel to Old Testament circumcision. This viewpoint is based on, among other things, a certain interpretation of Colossians 2:11-12. But the illustration there is to compare baptism with "the circumcision made without hands" (see also Philippians 3:3; compare Ezekiel 44:7). We note that baptism is never referred to as "a sign" or "a seal" in the New Testament (compare 1 Corinthians 1:22;

9:2; 14:22). Baptism, therefore, does not get its meaning from Old Testament circumcision.

12. And the father of circumcision to them who are not of the circumcision only, but who also walk in the steps of that faith of our father Abraham, which he had being yet uncircumcised.

Following Jesus, being a Christian, has nothing to do with physical *circumcision*. Rather, it is about faith and the life that proceeds from a faithful heart. Forgiveness is not earned or owed. It is given by the grace of God to those following the New Testament plan of salvation. Paul describes this as walking *in the steps of that faith of our father Abraham,* who blazed faith-trail centuries before.

> *What Do You Think?*
> What's the single most important thing you can do this week to walk in Abraham's footsteps?
> *Digging Deeper*
> What sense of urgency will you have in doing so, given that Abraham is mentioned more than 70 times in the New Testament?

Paul later presents the law as the means of learning what sin is, and he notes the impossibility of keeping the Old Testament law (see Romans 7). The law does not produce righteousness, but it does yield knowledge of wrongdoing (Galatians 3:21-22). Abraham's work proceeded from his faith, not from keeping the Law of Moses, which was not given until centuries later.

When it came time for Abraham's greatest test of all—the potential sacrifice of Isaac—he chose obedience that was grounded in faith (Genesis 22:1-14). Abraham believed that even if he sacrificed Isaac, his faithful Lord would keep His promise and raise Isaac from the dead (Hebrews 11:17-19). Our hope lies not in righteous deeds but in faith leading to justification by God.

A Free Reward

My son's first job was a paper route. During the week, he would bag each paper and set out to finish delivering before sundown. Though it was hot summer work, all his labors seemed worthwhile when he got his first paycheck. Some weeks later, we visited a coffee drive-through so he could get the two of us beverages. When we reached the window, the barista informed us that the car ahead of us had picked up our tab. This confused our son until we explained what had happened.

There are certain parallels between both cases and today's text. When we work, our time is calculated toward our earned wages. To think salvation comes about the same way is to commit a serious error.

It is the second incident that better illustrates how we have access to salvation: somebody else paid the price, and there was no debt to be paid on our part when we reached the pick-up window. And the grace we receive from God in this regard is so much more refreshing than a beverage! —P. M.

Conclusion

A. Faith and Work

How far do you allow your faith to take you? Do your actions show that your trust in God can overcome doubts and allow you to be obedient to Him? Our faith leads us to entrust our children to God, no matter the circumstances. It guides us to worship God, not money, and to act according to that sole allegiance. Faith requires us to live everyday in trust of God and His plan. So, again, how far do you allow your faith to take you?

> *What Do You Think?*
> Which concept in today's lesson do you see as most important for undergirding how you should change a thought, speech, or action? Why?
> *Digging Deeper*
> What specific, time-bound steps can you take to bring about that change?

B. Prayer

Father, may we live daily as people whose faith results in unconditional trust in You! In Jesus' name we pray. Amen.

C. Thought to Remember

The Lord remains as the Father of the faithful.

Involvement Learning

Enhance your lesson with KJV Bible Student *(from your curriculum supplier) and the reproducible activity page (at www.standardlesson.com or in the back of the* KJV Standard Lesson Commentary Deluxe Edition*).*

Into the Lesson

Write these two column headings on the board:

A Hero from the Past / The Effect on My Present

Invite students to come to the board and write their responses under the two headings. Allow volunteers to elaborate in whole-class discussion.

Transition to Bible study by saying, "Today we will look at a man whose response to God has the power to affect us yet today."

Into the Word

Ask two learners to alternate in reading aloud the verses of today's lesson text, Romans 4:1-12. Then divide the class into study groups of four to six to answer the following questions, which you have prepared for distribution on handouts:

1–Why did Abraham have no basis for boasting to God?

2–On what basis did God impute righteousness to Abraham?

3–What is the significance of Abraham's *first* having believed in God and *then* being circumcised, rather than the other way around?

4–How would you diagram the relationship between faith and works?

5–What's the significance of being *counted* as righteous rather than actually being *made* righteous?

Point students to today's text and allow groups about 10 minutes to answer the questions. Then go through them to fill in gaps by using details from the lesson commentary.

Option. Distribute to one group copies of the "A Story of Faith" exercise from the activity page, which you can download, rather than the five questions above. When you reconvene the class as a whole, let this group report answers first.

Into Life

Ask students to flip their handouts over and write these two column headings at the top:

An Important Component of My Faith

An Important Sign of My Faith

Then ask students to enter under the headers the single elements implied by those respective headers, time limit of one minute to do so. If participants seem to struggle with the difference between a *component* and a *sign,* you can note that a component is a constituent element, while a sign is an indicator. Therefore a sign points to the existence of a constituent element.

When the minute is up, ask class members to find a partner with whom to share what each has written (*Option.* Request that participants not choose their own spouses as partners.) Then ask participants to help their partners with these three tasks, described on handouts (you prepare):

1–Draw an arrow from the entry in the first column to the entry in the second column and write on it how the former results in the latter.

2–Draw an arrow from the entry in the second column to the entry in the first column and write on it how the latter indicates (or should indicate) the presence of the former.

3–Make a list of ways that imputed righteousness will direct their thoughts and actions in the week ahead.

Wrap up by comparing and contrasting today's text with Galatians 2:16; Ephesians 2:8-10; 1 Thessalonians 1:3; James 2:20-26; and this quote from William Booth (1829–1912), founder of the Salvation Army:

> Faith and works should travel side by side, step answering to step, like the legs of men walking. First faith, and then works; and then faith again, and then works again—until they can scarcely distinguish which is the one and which is the other.

Option. Distribute copies of the "A Legacy of Faith" exercise from the activity page, to be completed as indicated in no more than one minute. If distributed as a take-home, encourage completion by promising to begin next week's class with it.

Peace with God

Devotional Reading: Isaiah 53:1-12
Background Scripture: Romans 5:1-11

Romans 5:1-11

1 Therefore being justified by faith, we have peace with God through our Lord Jesus Christ:

2 By whom also we have access by faith into this grace wherein we stand, and rejoice in hope of the glory of God.

3 And not only so, but we glory in tribulations also: knowing that tribulation worketh patience;

4 And patience, experience; and experience, hope:

5 And hope maketh not ashamed; because the love of God is shed abroad in our hearts by the Holy Ghost which is given unto us.

6 For when we were yet without strength, in due time Christ died for the ungodly.

7 For scarcely for a righteous man will one die: yet peradventure for a good man some would even dare to die.

8 But God commendeth his love toward us, in that, while we were yet sinners, Christ died for us.

9 Much more then, being now justified by his blood, we shall be saved from wrath through him.

10 For if, when we were enemies, we were reconciled to God by the death of his Son, much more, being reconciled, we shall be saved by his life.

11 And not only so, but we also joy in God through our Lord Jesus Christ, by whom we have now received the atonement.

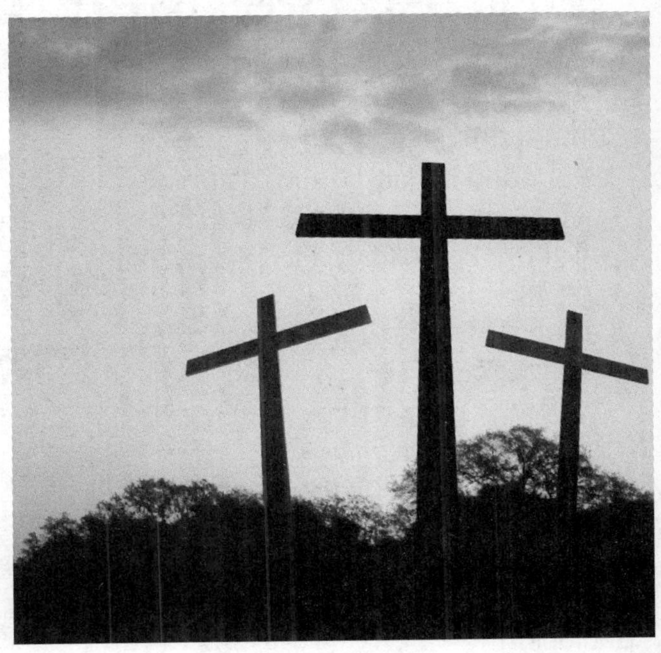

Key Verse

Being justified by faith, we have peace with God through our Lord Jesus Christ. —**Romans 5:1**

Confident Hope

Unit 2: Faith and Salvation

Lessons 6–9

Lesson Aims

After participating in this lesson, each learner will be able to:

1. State the result of being justified by faith.
2. Explain the meaning and significance of Paul's "much more" argument.
3. Recruit an accountability partner to help make progress regarding the growth stages in Romans 5:3-4.

Lesson Outline

Introduction
- A. Sacrifice for Peace
- B. Lesson Context

I. Founded in Faith (Romans 5:1-5)
- A. Peace Made with God (vv. 1-2)
- B. Love Poured into Hearts (vv. 3-5)
  - *Embrace the Struggle*

II. Died for Ungodly (Romans 5:6-8)
- A. The Right Time (vv. 6-7)
- B. The Right Sacrifice (v. 8)
  - *A Risky Investment*

III. Reconciled in Joy (Romans 5:9-11)
- A. Wrath Averted (v. 9)
- B. Salvation Awaiting (v. 10)
- C. Atonement Accepted (v. 11)

Conclusion
- A. Freedom from Fear
- B. Prayer
- C. Thought to Remember

Introduction

A. Sacrifice for Peace

In the 1964 Cold War epic movie *Fail Safe*, a series of mistakes sends a squadron of American planes with nuclear bombs to annihilate Moscow, Russia. Despite every conceivable effort by the American president, he was unable to stop the mission.

Realizing that the Soviet Union's capital city would be destroyed—and desiring to avoid worldwide thermonuclear devastation from retaliatory strikes—the president made a deal with the Soviet premier. They agreed that at the same time the bombs hit Moscow, an equal nuclear strike would lay waste to New York City. Thus an equivalent "eye for an eye" act would even the accounts. The president agreed to this realizing that his beloved wife was in New York City. He knowingly decided to sacrifice her for the sake of world peace.

The great paradox of this film is that the most horrific wartime tactic ever devised by human beings was to be used to forestall hostilities. The saving of hundreds of millions of lives was more important than any single life, even that of the first lady. Parallels between this fictional trade-off and today's lesson text are thought-provoking.

B. Lesson Context

Romans is both the most challenging of Paul's letters to understand and the richest depository of what he calls "my gospel" (Romans 2:16; 16:25). The basis and reality of being justified by faith is the subject of Romans 1–4 in general (see lessons 6 and 7) and 3:24, 28 in particular.

Paul quoted Habakkuk 2:4 in Romans 1:17 to set the tone for the entire book: "the just shall live by faith." Included in the letter are the apostle's understanding of the Old Testament background for the Christian message, the nature of salvation as it is based on the atoning death of Christ, the centrality of faith as the only path for salvation, the changed relationship between Jews and Gentiles in the plan of God, and several other matters.

Only through faith in Christ may eternal life be found. Eternal life cannot be earned by works, although works are important. Eternal life is not inherited by ancestry, although such ancestry is not unimportant (see Romans 3:1-2; 9:4-5). Eternal life, the life of salvation, is found only in a faith that trusts God to save us.

Abraham, the great patriarch of the Jews, was justified by faith (Romans 4:3, quoting Genesis 15:6; see lesson 7). Thus the idea of faith as the core element of one's life is not a Christian innovation. Faith is to be the foundation of our relationship with God. But this was nothing new: faith was to have been central in the pre-Israel period, in the nation of Israel itself, and in the church. Having established these facts in Romans 1–4, Paul moved to implications, today's text.

I. Founded in Faith

(Romans 5:1-5)

A. Peace Made with God (vv. 1-2)

1. Therefore being justified by faith, we have peace with God through our Lord Jesus Christ.

Having established that the life of Abraham is relevant to the Christian, Paul uses the connecting word *therefore* to signal two things. First, the phrase *being justified by faith* summarizes thoughts of Romans 1–4.

Second, the phrase *we have peace with God through our Lord Jesus Christ* introduces a theme that undergoes much expansion and explanation in the verses and chapters that follow. After having sketched the dire condition of humanity in Romans 3:23 ("all have sinned, and come short of the glory of God"), the sun breaks through (or perhaps we should say, "Son"). *Jesus* "was delivered for our offences" and "was raised again for our justification" (Romans 4:25). We are justified by God's actions, not ours. Our sins invite God's wrath; our justification from Him by faith results in peace (compare Luke 2:14).

Perhaps you have heard various definitions of the word *justification*. One such is an appropriate play on the word: being justified means being treated "just as if I'd" never sinned. God himself has provided the means for bridging the rift between Him and humanity, for making peace by satisfying the punishment for sin. That means of peace is Jesus. As Paul has explained and will explain again, since God has forgiven our sins by means of a substitutionary atonement (the death of Jesus), no basis remains for God to impose punishment on those who accept His terms. Christians need not fear future judgment from God.

2a. By whom also we have access by faith into this grace wherein we stand.

The central point is reinforced by use of the word *grace*. There are no "works" that gain our justification. Salvation has been provided by God. It is a gift that we must receive. *Faith* in Jesus gives us *access* to grace. A good way to remember the significance of the word *grace* is to use its five letters to create this phrase:

God's Riches At Christ's Expense

> *What Do You Think?*
> Would you use the letters of the word *grace* to explain that concept to an unbeliever as God's riches at Christ's expense? Why, or why not?
> *Digging Deeper*
> Would you explain to an unbeliever that the word justified means "just-as-if-I'd never sinned"? Why, or why not?

2b. And rejoice in hope of the glory of God.

The word *hope* as frequently used today is often at odds with how the Bible writers use the same word. Often people today use the word *hope* to express a desire that they know has very little chance of becoming reality. They talk about something they would love to have or see happen, but they don't know if it will ever happen. We hear the expression "One can only hope" in contexts of passive resignation where one feels carried along by a series of events that indicate an outcome almost certain to be undesirable. This kind of hope is a forlorn hope; it is not the kind the Bible talks about.

The New Testament uses the word *hope* in the sense of "confident expectation of something

HOW TO SAY IT

Isaiah	Eye-*zay*-uh.
Moses	*Mo*-zes or *Mo*-zez.

good"; the word is never used in a sense of "fearful anticipation." Rather, in Christ we *rejoice in hope*. What He has promised, He will do.

For the one in Christ, there is no doubt. The quality of hope hinges on the character of the one in whom hope is placed. What more needs to be said? We acquire true hope when we abandon the futile practice of trusting in ourselves to shape the future and put our future in the hands of *God*. When we are in Christ we have peace, grace, and hope. And there is more! The concept of hope is so important to Paul that he uses the noun and verb forms of the word *hope* a total of 17 times in Romans alone!

B. Love Poured into Hearts (vv. 3-5)

3. And not only so, but we glory in tribulations also: knowing that tribulation worketh patience.

Here begins a teaching chain of character-building virtues that form the core of the Christian life. We will have *tribulation* (John 16:33), hardship that could drive away all hope. But these troubles build our capacity for *patience*, a virtue close to the heart of our long-suffering Lord (see Romans 9:22; 2 Peter 3:15). This is not a passive resignation, but rather an active continuance (compare Romans 2:7). Difficulties teach us the value of waiting on the Lord (Psalm 37:7).

When faith is our guiding principle, what appears to be a very bad situation can yield good results. (Read Paul's later affirmation in Romans 8:28.) Such results are not always immediately seen (see Genesis 45:4-8).

4a. And patience, experience.

The word translated *experience* is an interesting one, used seven times in the New Testament, and only by Paul. In addition to the two translations "experience" in our text, it is also translated "proof" (2 Corinthians 2:9; 13:3; Philippians 2:22), "trial" (2 Corinthians 8:2), and "experiment" (2 Corinthians 9:13). The overall idea is that of being tested to determine (or improve) one's mettle.

Testing in this regard comes from many directions and at various stages of life. Yet through the patient handling of circumstances, prayerful discovery of solutions, and the discipline of waiting on the Lord, a wealth of experience is gained.

4b. And experience, hope.

That *experience* can provide *hope* not only to the one undergoing tribulations, but also to the one who needs a mentor in that regard, someone who's "been there" (see 2 Corinthians 1:3-4). We live through hardship sustained by the hope that the Lord has the future in His hands. Our confidence in the future can be based only on God's faithfulness in the past.

At this point, Paul may appear to be going in circles. But let us not think of this as a circle but as an advancing spiral. With each round of faith-guided living—which blends trouble and joy and lessons learned—we gain strength.

What Do You Think?

If you're stuck at a particular stage in the sequence Paul mentions, what are some things you can do to get unstuck?

Digging Deeper

What texts in addition to 1 Thessalonians 4:13 help you see the biblical distinction between "hope" and "no hope"?

Embrace the Struggle

Twenty years ago, a neighborhood in my city was overrun with drugs, crime, and poverty. City officials sought out a person who had helped turn things around in a similar neighborhood by means of career-development training. Gail agreed to take on the challenge. Her first step was to buy an old liquor store as her headquarters in the heart of the community.

Gail faced obstacles at first: little interest in training programs, break-ins, and drug paraphernalia left at the front door. Nevertheless, she persisted. As she did, she saw success. People began completing her trainings successfully. The neighborhood began to change as people received better opportunities. The property value of that building soared.

Gail had stepped out with a biblical hope, and she watched God do the impossible. When we adopt a spirit of faithful hope in God in the midst of adversity, He will develop our Christian character through the process. How can you better yield to God in this regard? —L. H.-P.

What Do You Think?

When considering Romans 5:3 alongside James 1:2-4 and 1 Peter 1:5-7, what changes do you need to make in reacting to situations that challenge your faith?

Digging Deeper

What other passages do you find most informative and convicting in this regard?

5. And hope maketh not ashamed; because the love of God is shed abroad in our hearts by the Holy Ghost which is given unto us.

Paul's clarion call in the book of Romans is "I am not ashamed of the gospel" (Romans 1:16). The life of faith exudes confidence and trust. A nuance of the idea of *not ashamed* is to not be dishonored, which is how the same word is translated twice in 1 Corinthians 11:4-5. False fronts and false hopes lead to both. But authentic *hope* in the Lord and His faithfulness is neither. We are not fools to hope in *the love of God*.

This hopeful, faithful approach to life is not self-generated. God changes and empowers us by making His *love* known *in our hearts*. He even provides the means for maintaining what He has given, namely, *the Holy Ghost*. It is He who gives us love and helps us grow in love. When love is clearly visible in the church, it is a sure sign of the Holy Spirit's presence. Elsewhere, the giving of the Holy Spirit is pictured as being poured on people (see Isaiah 44:3; Ezekiel 39:29; Joel 2:29; Acts 10:45). The Holy Spirit is not a reward, but a gift bestowed to empower us to act in love when and where that is not the normal human reaction.

II. Died for Ungodly

(Romans 5:6-8)

A. The Right Time (vv. 6-7)

6. For when we were yet without strength, in due time Christ died for the ungodly.

The fact that *Christ died for the ungodly* is at the center of the Christian faith. That was a monstrous crime, the murder of the innocent Son of God. Paul's insight, though, is that while the enemies of Jesus had nothing but malice in their hearts, God had planned all along for His Son's death to be the means of salvation for humanity.

The high priest spoke better than he knew when he declared that it was better for one man to die than to have an entire nation perish (John 11:49-53). And so it happened *in due time*—God's time! Just as the timing of Jesus' birth was no random chance (Galatians 4:4), neither was His death.

What Do You Think?

What is the single, most important lifestyle or prayer-habit change you need to make to live out your conviction that God's timing is always perfect?

Digging Deeper

How does your response to the question associated with Romans 1:13 in lesson 6 factor in?

The first three chapters of Romans deal with the fact that all sinned and are therefore unrighteous, unjustified, and unholy. Paul was not speaking of careless morality or occasional mistakes. The ungodly turn their backs on God and His expectations knowingly, willingly, and decisively in their preference for sin and its temporary pleasures (compare Titus 3:3). But as Paul says in the beginning of the letter, the ungodly are without excuse for their sins (Romans 1:20). That includes all of us.

7. For scarcely for a righteous man will one die: yet peradventure for a good man some would even dare to die.

What is the difference between *a righteous man* and *a good man?* Some would say that the righteous man describes an especially pious individual who possesses a "holier-than-thou" attitude. He may be highly respected, but he is not the kind of person for whom someone else would be willing *to die*. The good man would be someone whose good deeds make him a much more likable individual, and thus someone for whom others would be more apt to die.

Others believe that there is basically no difference between the righteous man and the good

Through faith in God,
we have peace.
Visual for Lesson 8. *Point to this visual as you ask learners how this picture does or does not illustrate the kind of peace mentioned in Romans 5:1.*

man and that Paul is making the same claim in two ways. Under this proposal, the first part of the verse states Paul's claim in a negative way; the second then restates it, but in a more positive manner. The paradox of Christ's dying for the ungodly contradicts reason as based on human experience. What sort of person would you be willing to die for? Paul knew there were possible examples: a parent dying for a child, a soldier dying for a comrade, etc. Still, the gist of Paul's thought is this: people are not likely to give their lives on behalf of even the best of human beings.

B. The Right Sacrifice (v. 8)

8. But God commendeth his love toward us, in that, while we were yet sinners, Christ died for us.

In spite of our rebellion and ungodliness, God continues to love us. This has nothing to do with our merit and everything to do with God's character (John 3:16-18; 1 John 4:16). God continues to love all sinners and desire their restoration to relationship with Him (2 Peter 3:9). The willing and intentional sacrifice of God's beloved Son is the supreme way that God *commendeth his love toward us*. The death of *Christ* was the final and ultimate sacrifice for sins (see Hebrews 7:27).

Christ did not wait until we were righteous ourselves to die *for us*. When *we were yet sinners,* we could only wait for the harsh justice of God's judgment. But Jesus Christ died for our sins according to God's plan as revealed in Scriptures (1 Corinthians 15:3).

Jesus' sacrifice emphatically illustrates one of His most radical teachings: that His followers should love their enemies (see Luke 6:27, 35; contrast Matthew 5:43). In the context of Jesus' day, this included loving the despised Roman overlords who occupied the land. Love was to be extended also to fellow Jews who collaborated with the Roman occupiers. The good news is that *all* our enemies can become one with us in Christ, part of the family of God.

A Risky Investment

One of my wife's grandmothers immigrated to America from Jamaica. Once she arrived, she worked hard and pursued her education, all the while raising three sons by herself. She invested wisely in buying a home, put money away for retirement, and had multiple streams of income. She did all this to build wealth for her family for generations to come. At her death, she left a sizable fortune that was inherited by her only surviving son and her grandchildren. But she could not know whether they would appreciate it or squander what she had worked so hard for.

Christ's work on the cross was intended to benefit the entire world for generations to come. He knew that some would accept His sacrifice and that others would spurn it. Yet He made the sacrifice anyway.

In what ways do you still do a disservice to Christ's offer by living contrary to His will?

— L. H.-P.

III. Reconciled in Joy

(Romans 5:9-11)

A. Wrath Averted (v. 9)

9. Much more then, being now justified by his blood, we shall be saved from wrath through him.

The substitutionary death of Jesus paid the price for our sins, a price we could never pay on our own. We are now counted as righteous because we are *justified by his blood*. We can be at peace with God. The work of Christ has been done. We are new creatures (2 Corinthians 5:17), we wear a new name, and we have a new destiny. Even so, that destiny will not be realized fully until our time in our present world is finished and our time in Heaven has begun.

Because of Jesus' work, our faith, and God's grace, we no longer need fear the future. We respect the mighty *wrath* of God, but we do not fear it because we have forgiveness *through* faith in Jesus. Thus our past, present, and future are all in God's hands.

B. Salvation Awaiting (v. 10)

10a. For if, when we were enemies, we were reconciled to God by the death of his Son.

The ungodly, the unrepentant sinners, are still *enemies* of *God*. Sin severed the relationship between sinner and Creator. But God has provided the way by which those who are separated from Him can come back. The new relationship is one of *being reconciled*. Salvation involves being returned to an ongoing relationship with God. Reconciliation comes only and always by *the death of his Son*.

10b. Much more, being reconciled, we shall be saved by his life.

Now that Jesus is alive and reigning as Lord, how *much more* will He help those who have accepted His gift of salvation! We can have no doubt that Jesus will return and complete God's plan of redemption. Jesus' resurrected life and reign is the firm basis for the assured hope of our own resurrection. If our hope in Christ goes only as far as this life, then we are to be pitied for having believed a lie (1 Corinthians 15:17-18).

C. Atonement Accepted (v. 11)

11. And not only so, but we also joy in God through our Lord Jesus Christ, by whom we have now received the atonement.

Paul's phrase *and not only so* is an expression meaning "there is more." We have been reconciled (reunited) with *God*. We have been saved from sin and death by means of His grace. As a result, we can have *joy*. Like hope, joy is not a mere fleeting emotion; rather, it is a constant sense of gratitude and praise for all that God has done and will do.

This joyous reaction comes when we focus on God's great gift to us. *We have now received the atonement* that results in being restored children of God. The hostilities have ceased. We are no longer enemies of God or slaves to the fear of death. Through our faith in Jesus Christ, our hope is secure, and our joy is complete. All of what Paul described comes *through our Lord Jesus Christ*.

> *What Do You Think?*
> How would you explain to an unbeliever that having peace with God comes only through Christ?
> *Digging Deeper*
> How will you prepare for a "Surely a loving God would not . . ." kind of reaction?

Conclusion

A. Freedom from Fear

On a grand scale, we understand the truth of Jesus' teaching: the God of all creation chooses to love and save His enemies rather than hate and destroy them (John 3:16-17)—at least for now (Romans 2:5-9). But we must take that grand scale down to the level of the individual person, beginning with ourselves.

Although we live in fearful times, we are not to fear the future. Though people around us fear many things—being laid off, losing loved ones, catastrophic weather, etc.—we are not to let fear of such things control us. The key always is to focus on the future Christ has prepared for us (John 14:2), made possible by the price for peace that Jesus paid on the cross.

B. Prayer

Father, we stand amazed at Your love for us, and we praise You for it. Our hope is in You for having redeemed our past, giving meaning to our present, and delivering us into our future. In Jesus' name we rejoice and pray. Amen.

C. Thought to Remember

Christ's death has brought about
our peace with God.

Involvement Learning

Enhance your lesson with KJV Bible Student *(from your curriculum supplier) and the reproducible activity page (at www.standardlesson.com or in the back of the* KJV Standard Lesson Commentary Deluxe Edition*).*

Into the Lesson

Invite learners in groups of two or three to choose some newspapers and magazines from a stack you bring to class. Request that they search for stories and pictures of situations where peace is desperately needed. State that these can be international conflicts, disagreements between individuals, or private psychological problems. After several minutes, invite each group to describe or show one or two examples to the class as a whole. (*Option.* Include smartphone searches.)

Alternative. Initiate the "conversation circles" technique on page 232 of the spring 2021 quarter (or another technique of your choosing). As you do, distribute on handouts (you prepare) featuring the following two questions for discussion within groups: *In what ways is the world more at peace today than it was when you were a child? In what ways is it less?*

After each member in each group has been allowed one minute to respond to the question, reconvene for whole-class summaries. Lead into Bible study by saying, "The discussions so far have focused on peace between humans. As important as that topic is, there's a peace more vital still."

Into the Word

Write the following thought starter on the board as part one of a multistage study:

I have confidence in my salvation because . . .

Have learners work within their groups to discover the single reason for their salvation. Expect groups to identify the answer in Romans 5:8: "Christ died for us." Those who are more biblically knowledgeable may also mention 5:9, "justified by his blood." Expect that response to this question, which you write on the board as a follow-on:

Why was Christ's death necessary for our salvation?

Use this question as a springboard for groups' diving deeper into what the words *justify, justified, justifier,* and *justification* mean. References to include on handouts (you prepare in the form of a notetaker) are Romans 3:28; 4:2, 5, 25; **5:1, 9,** 16, 18; 8:30, 33; *10:10*; 1 Corinthians 6:11; Galatians 2:16-17; 3:11, 24; 5:4. (Verses in **bold** are part of this week's lesson, verses underlined are part of last week's, and the verse *italicized* is part of next week's.)

For the third and final stage of the study, distribute handouts (you prepare) that feature this listing:

- Verses 1-2: faith, peace, grace, hope
- Verses 3-8: patience, experience, hope, love
- Verses 9-10: blood, reconciled, wrath
- Verse 11: joy, atonement

Include printed instructions to determine how each word relates to the wordgroup *justify, justified, justifier,* and *justification,* just studied. (Since this can be quite time-consuming, consider giving each of four groups just one segment of the listing.) If learners struggle getting started, give a hint by suggesting they pay close attention to the prepositions *by, in, from, through, with,* etc.

Into Life

Challenge learners to identify someone who could help them move along the maturity path of Romans 5:3-5. Ask, in whole-class discussion, how such a mentor is like and unlike an athletic coach. (*Option:* Precede this challenge by distributing copies of the "From Alphabetical to . . ." exercise from the activity page, which you can download; allow one minute for learners to complete it individually, Bibles closed, before whole-class discussion.)

Option. Distribute copies of the "How Do We Know?" exercise on the activity page as a take-home exercise. Encourage its completion by promising to discuss class members' conclusions as class begins next week.

Salvation Available for All

Devotional Reading: Psalm 19:1-14
Background Scripture: Romans 10:5-17

Romans 10:5-17

5 For Moses describeth the righteousness which is of the law, That the man which doeth those things shall live by them.

6 But the righteousness which is of faith speaketh on this wise, Say not in thine heart, Who shall ascend into heaven? (that is, to bring Christ down from above:)

7 Or, Who shall descend into the deep? (that is, to bring up Christ again from the dead.)

8 But what saith it? The word is nigh thee, even in thy mouth, and in thy heart: that is, the word of faith, which we preach;

9 That if thou shalt confess with thy mouth the Lord Jesus, and shalt believe in thine heart that God hath raised him from the dead, thou shalt be saved.

10 For with the heart man believeth unto righteousness; and with the mouth confession is made unto salvation.

11 For the scripture saith, Whosoever believeth on him shall not be ashamed.

12 For there is no difference between the Jew and the Greek: for the same Lord over all is rich unto all that call upon him.

13 For whosoever shall call upon the name of the Lord shall be saved.

14 How then shall they call on him in whom they have not believed? and how shall they believe in him of whom they have not heard? and how shall they hear without a preacher?

15 And how shall they preach, except they be sent? as it is written, How beautiful are the feet of them that preach the gospel of peace, and bring glad tidings of good things!

16 But they have not all obeyed the gospel. For Esaias saith, Lord, who hath believed our report?

17 So then faith cometh by hearing, and hearing by the word of God.

Key Verse

Whosoever shall call upon the name of the Lord shall be saved. —**Romans 10:13**

Confident Hope

Unit 2: Faith and Salvation

Lessons 6–9

Lesson Aims

After participating in this lesson, each learner will be able to:

1. Identify several Old Testament passages Paul uses to make his argument.

2. Explain the danger of isolating the Key Verse from its context.

3. Create a personal plan for better supporting for the spread of the gospel through use of time, talent, and/or treasure.

Lesson Outline

Introduction

A. Rejoice, We Conquer!

B. Lesson Context

I. Preaching the Word (Romans 10:5-13)

A. Ascending and Descending (vv. 5-7)

No Mountain High Enough

B. Confessing and Believing (vv. 8-10)

C. Calling and Saving (vv. 11-13)

Seeing as God Sees

II. Telling the Gospel (Romans 10:14-17)

A. Sending and Preaching (vv. 14-15)

B. Hearing and Obeying (vv. 16-17)

Conclusion

A. Where Does Faith Come From?

B. Prayer

C. Thought to Remember

Introduction

A. Rejoice, We Conquer!

When the Persian fleet and army threatened the Greek peninsula in 490 BC, the leaders in Athens knew that they had to rally their forces to meet this threat. There seemed to be no hope, for the Persians vastly outnumbered the Greeks. Therefore, the elders of Athens decided to send an entreaty to the king of Sparta, a traditional enemy, to ask for help.

They sent a man named Philippides (sometimes spelled Pheidippides) as their emissary. He was a professional herald and long-distance runner. Legend has it that Philippides ran to Sparta and back to Athens in four days, a nearly 300-mile round trip. He returned with the news that the Spartans could not help. The Athenians had no time to wait, so they marched their forces to the plains of Marathon. There they ambushed the invaders and won a great victory over the numerically superior Persian army.

After this triumph at Marathon, Philippides was again called on. This time he ran 26 miles back to Athens to announce the victory to his defenseless and terrified city. Legend has it that he arrived at the city gates with only enough life left to utter "Rejoice, we conquer!" before falling dead. His death was tragic, but his dramatic message was truly good news for the unprotected city. Some good news is worth the sacrificing for!

B. Lesson Context

In Romans 9 Paul introduced a new subject in his letter: the place of the Jews in God's redemptive plan. His discussion sprang from his personal passion for his people (he calls the Jews his "brethren" and his "kinsmen according to the flesh" (9:3) and his desire that they know the Christ who has done so much for him (9:1-5).

That concern continues in Romans 10, which begins with Paul writing, "Brethren, my heart's desire and prayer to God for Israel is, that they might be saved." The apostle described his fellow Jews as zealous, yet lacking knowledge. Their desire to follow the Law of Moses and thereby pursue "their own righteousness" (10:3) was ill-founded, now that "Christ is the end of the law for righteousness to every one that believeth" (10:4). A new way, the way of salvation—by grace through faith—was open for all to accept. But, sadly, many of Paul's "kinsmen according to the flesh" (9:3) rejected it.

Paul then proceeded to contrast righteousness based on keeping the law with righteousness available through faith.

I. Preaching the Word

(Romans 10:5-13)

A. Ascending and Descending (vv. 5-7)

5. For Moses describeth the righteousness which is of the law, That the man which doeth those things shall live by them.

There are only two potential ways to obtain *righteousness,* or a right standing, with God: (1) by keeping *the law* perfectly or (2) by receiving grace through faith. *Moses* is recognized as Israel's lawgiver. So it is fitting to cite him as an authority on lawkeeping.

The *law* is what defines sin and righteousness. The verse that Paul quoted implies that complete obedience to the law will result in life because a person so doing will be righteous (Leviticus 18:5; see also Romans 2:13 and Galatians 3:12). But Paul has already shown that no one obeys the law perfectly (Romans 3:23), so there is no one who can achieve righteousness through keeping the law (Romans 3:20).

The principle of righteousness by lawkeeping places the responsibility squarely on our shoulders. If a person obeyed every aspect of the law perfectly, then he or she would earn a right standing before God. But that *if* is huge—it never happens!

6-7. But the righteousness which is of faith speaketh on this wise, Say not in thine heart, Who shall ascend into heaven? (that is, to bring Christ down from above:) Or, Who shall descend into the deep? (that is, to bring up Christ again from the dead.)

Paul has already drawn a distinction between the "law . . . of works" and the "law of faith" (Romans 3:27). He used this framework again in today's text, but this time the terminology is adjusted slightly to be "righteousness which is of law" (10:5, above) vs. *riotousness which is of faith.* This contrast is also found in Philippians 3:6-9.

To stress the distinction, Paul draws on imagery from Deuteronomy 9:4; 30:12-14 to illustrate the nature of righteousness based on law: it's like trying to *ascend into heaven* in order to *bring Christ down from above* or attempting to *descend into the deep* in order to *bring up Christ . . . from the dead.*

The imagery is not an exact quote from those Old Testament passages. Therefore Paul should be seen as giving an inspired application of those texts for the era of the new covenant. In so doing, he establishes that the righteousness obtained by faith is not based on our deeds or works of law. Even if we could perform supernatural actions such as those described in those passages, that would not be enough to gain right standing with God.

Some Bible commentators have noted the significance of Paul's use of the book of Deuteronomy to make his case for righteousness by faith. Moses spoke the words of Deuteronomy when the Israelites were on the brink of entering the promised land. He wanted to impress on the people the covenant that God had made with them. Here in Romans, Paul desired to impress on his Jewish readers the reality of the new covenant that God has established. Just as God brought His word to Israel through Moses (see Deuteronomy 30:11-14), God has now revealed His living Word in the person of Jesus Christ, whom Paul had already declared to be "the end of the law" (Romans 10:4; compare Colossians 2:14).

Thus it is not by good works or devoted efforts that righteousness with God is obtained. Salvation is not the result of our perfection or hard work. Salvation is the result of Christ's sacrifice as the lamb "without spot" (Hebrews 9:14) in our place. Indeed, we do not have to bring Christ down;

HOW TO SAY IT

cholla	*choy*-ah.
Philippides	Fih-lip-*pea*-deez.
Pheidippides	Feh-dip-*pea*-deez.
Septuagint	Sep-*too*-ih-jent.

He has already come down! Nor do we have to bring Him up from the grave; God has done that (Romans 8:11).

No Mountain High Enough

Yearly pilgrimages are part of certain faith expressions. In Mexico, pilgrims crawl toward the shrine that supposedly marks the place where the mother of Jesus is said to have appeared. In Greece, some travel to a statue that is believed to have miraculous healing powers. And in Tibet pilgrims travel for days, even months, to reach the "holy city" of Lhasa. These trips can result in self-imposed hardships. But they are considered valuable because people believe they will be greatly blessed by completing a pilgrimage.

Paul assured us that we do not have to do any of that. There are no great lengths that Christians need to go to in order to reach God. No level of suffering is required to draw near to Him. Christ has endured all the suffering necessary.

There is indeed suffering in this life, and the Lord asks us to endure it. But faith tells us God is always in reach. Are you spending time and effort to draw near to Him when Christ has already done that for you? —P. M.

B. Confessing and Believing (vv. 8-10)

8. But what saith it? The word is nigh thee, even in thy mouth, and in thy heart: that is, the word of faith, which we preach.

We do not need to travel to Heaven or the deep because *the word* we need is near. It is as close as our mouths and our hearts (Deuteronomy 30:14). Paul always preached justification by faith, not works. These Old Testament references continued here reveal that the law itself testifies to Christ.

> *What Do You Think?*
> Considering Paul's numerous quotations from the Old Testament in this lesson, what lifelong plan can you set in motion to develop your own ever-greater expertise in Scripture?
> *Digging Deeper*
> What emphasis on breadth vs. depth should you adopt? Why?

9. That if thou shalt confess with thy mouth the Lord Jesus, and shalt believe in thine heart that God hath raised him from the dead, thou shalt be saved.

Paul used Moses' comment about the *mouth* to explain a foundational reality of how the way of faith works. Paul expected that those who embraced his message would respond in two ways. First, they would use their mouths to *confess* that Jesus is *Lord* (compare Matthew 10:32-33). Those who do so acknowledge that Jesus is Lord of all creation and our master in all things. This is the core of faith, the open door to the law of righteousness.

Second, Paul's preaching called sinners to have a change in *heart*. When we do, we put aside the faulty reasoning of the world regarding the nature of death (compare 1 Corinthians 15; Colossians 2:20; etc.). Instead, we *believe in* our *heart* that Jesus is risen *from the dead*. The facts of history form the basis for our willingness to acknowledge Jesus as Lord.

Notice the requirement of both an external response (confessing the Lord Jesus) and an internal one (believing in one's heart). These should not be considered works in order to earn righteousness (Ephesians 2:8-10), but as expressions of faith that accept the righteousness God is eager to give.

10. For with the heart man believeth unto righteousness; and with the mouth confession is made unto salvation.

Paul moves to implications or result. We should not be fooled by the simplicity of these expectations. To mouth the words, "Jesus is Lord," appears to be easy, but to say this with a heart of faith will result in a life-changing experience and a new direction. To believe that Jesus is risen from the dead seems straightforward enough, but it requires faith in an event that defies personal experience. This is the pathway of faith (compare John 20:25-29).

Before we move on, we note that just because this verse says nothing about baptism or repentance does not mean that Paul considered those to be insignificant (compare Romans 2:4; 6:3-4). In the context of Romans 10, Paul focused in particular on the *heart* and the *mouth* to emphasize that becoming right with God does not require the kind of efforts described in 10:6-7.

Both believing and confessing are meant to be more than one-time actions associated with becoming a Christian. Faith in Jesus and confession of Him as Lord must become the hallmarks of a Christ-centered life. While living a godly life is crucial, we must also be able to put our faith into words.

What Do You Think?

What mismatches between your heart and your mouth need to be resolved? When will you start the repair job?

Digging Deeper

Should you seek the help of another, or is this strictly a do-it-yourself job? Why?

C. Calling and Saving (vv. 11-13)

11. For the scripture saith, Whosoever believeth on him shall not be ashamed.

Paul quoted the last part of Isaiah 28:16 here and in Romans 9:33. But if we look up this passage in Isaiah we may be confused because in the KJV it says "he that believeth shall not make haste." The solution comes in realizing that Paul quoted from the Greek version of the Old Testament, known as the Septuagint. For the last word in the quote, that version uses a verb that means *ashamed*; this word was a favorite of Paul's—19 of the New Testament's 35 uses of this word and its variants occur in his letters.

In context, Isaiah 28:16 as a whole prophesied the coming Messiah to be "a foundation a stone, a tried stone, a precious corner stone, a sure foundation." Paul used that promise to say that those who correctly understand God's work in sending His Messiah are wise to respond in faith.

12. For there is no difference between the Jew and the Greek: for the same Lord over all is rich unto all that call upon him.

Jews and Gentiles enter into God's promise on the same basis—through faith in Christ. This included everyone, for a person was either a Jew or a non-Jew (Gentile). Jews did not have exclusive rights to God, for He is *the same Lord* to all people (compare Acts 17:24-28). Jews did not have a monopoly on the privilege of having faith in God, even though the promise came through one of their prophets. The one God *is rich* (generous and gracious) to anyone who calls *upon him.*

Seeing as God Sees

A close friend of mine was set to marry a wonderful Christian man a few years after they both experienced devastating divorces. She was ecstatic. But she also feared that she might not treat his seven children like she did her two children.

One day, she was watching his daughters play at the park and turned away for just a moment when she heard a desperate "Mommy, Mommy, Mommy!" Instantly she jumped to her feet, searching the empty park, heart in her throat.

She found them huddled together where the park gave way to desert. The girls had stumbled into a cholla cactus, which were covered in needles. She was indescribably relieved that nothing more serious had happened, and she cried as she tenderly ministered to them.

It was then she knew her fears were unfounded. These were her children, no matter the bloodline. Paul taught the same thing: there is no distinction between Jew and Greek to the heavenly Father. Do you view people as He does? —P. M.

13. For whosoever shall call upon the name of the Lord shall be saved.

Paul quotes Joel 2:32 to reinforce the promise of grace to those who *call upon the name of the Lord* (also see Acts 2:21). This is a common expression in the Old Testament to include active prayer and worship on the part of a believer. The first instance of this, recorded in Genesis 4:26, is usually understood as the first time that men and women sought to worship the Lord in a deliberate manner.

Being *saved* is another way to talk about being declared righteous, being justified, or being forgiven. It includes being reconciled to God (Romans 5:10). Here Paul's inclusion of the idea of calling brings together the act of faith in the heart and confession with the lips, the verbal expression of faith leading to salvation.

Visual for Lesson 9. *Post this visual as you ask learners for examples of how they can preach the gospel even if they never step behind a pulpit.*

What Paul addressed here was central to his agenda, because he, a Jew, was Christ's apostle to the Gentiles (Romans 15:16; 1 Timothy 2:7). All people must come to God through Christ in faith. Gentiles had not been born into Israel, the old-covenant people of God. Even so, for all people there was only "one body, and one Spirit, . . . one hope . . . one Lord, one faith, one baptism, one God and Father" (Ephesians 4:4-6).

II. Telling the Gospel
(Romans 10:14-17)

A. Sending and Preaching (vv. 14-15)

14. How then shall they call on him in whom they have not believed? and how shall they believe in him of whom they have not heard? and how shall they hear without a preacher?

For Paul, preaching the gospel was primary. It was good news, the greatest message in history! But how could "whosoever" *believe* in Christ if His message was unknown to them?

God has chosen to use human instruments to convey His message. This seems to have been His preferred method of operation even back into Old Testament times (examples: Isaiah 6:8; Jeremiah 1:5; Ezekiel 22:30). And so it still is. The good news has to be proclaimed, and that requires *a preacher* to take the message to those who *have not heard*. The Greek word translated *preacher* describes a herald or an announcer who runs ahead of a king and proclaims what the king wishes others to know (compare Daniel 3:4). Certainly, the task of preaching can be done by any Christian who tells the good news to someone else. At the same time, there must be those who will devote their lives to preaching and teaching in the setting of the local church. The church always needs those willing to answer such a calling. And those who are ready to do so need to be supported and sent, as the next verse indicates.

15. And how shall they preach, except they be sent? as it is written, How beautiful are the feet of them that preach the gospel of peace, and bring glad tidings of good things!

Paul quoted from Isaiah again (see Romans 10:11, above), this time from a text that visualizes a herald returning to Jerusalem, running up the mountains in full view of the citizens crowding the wall of the city (Isaiah 52:7). The herald runs up the mountain of Jerusalem to announce a victory over an enemy (compare the lesson's Introduction). In Isaiah, the herald's words are simple: "Thy God reigneth!"

We, the church, have the good news of salvation. We proclaim this through our songs, sermons, confessions of faith, celebrations of the Lord's Supper, and submission to baptism. But ultimately, Jesus wants us to carry His message to the world; we call this charge the "Great Commission" (see Matthew 28:18-20). The church also plays a vital part in sending, as illustrated by Barnabas and Saul (later renamed Paul), who were sent by the church in Antioch on their first missionary journey (Acts 13:1-3).

What Do You Think?

What more can you do in a role of being either one sent to preach or of supporting those sent to preach?

Digging Deeper

What factors should you help your church consider regarding relative emphases on local, national, and international evangelistic efforts?

Those who bear such good news are pictured as having *beautiful . . . feet.* Usually the heralds who traveled many miles to convey a message arrived at their destinations with dusty, dirty feet. The appearance of their feet per se was anything but beautiful; beauty was to be found in the contents of the message delivered. Later Paul described the Christian's armor as including "feet shod with the preparation of the gospel of peace" (Ephesians 6:15).

B. Hearing and Obeying (vv. 16-17)

16. But they have not all obeyed the gospel. For Esaias saith, Lord, who hath believed our report?

Again, the words of Isaiah are cited. This verse, from Isaiah 53:1, comes in the context of one of the most powerful messianic prophecies in the Old Testament. But this particular passage warns us of a harsh reality that can dampen the enthusiasm of preaching and sending: not everyone who hears our message will receive it gladly. In the context of Romans, Paul lamented the fact that so many of his fellow Jews neither *believed* nor *obeyed the gospel.*

The reference to obedience is not used in the sense of works that cause the worker to have earned something. Rather, the thought is along the lines of what might be called "gospel commands"—actions associated with receiving salvation or living it out (example: Acts 2:38).

17. So then faith cometh by hearing, and hearing by the word of God.

Paul's ministry is driven by a simple fact: people who have never heard the gospel have no opportunity to believe the gospel. *The word of God* must be preached for it to be heard! In the process, some will believe and some will not believe (Acts 18:5-8; etc.). But no one will believe the gospel where there is no proclamation of the gospel. An unshared, unpreached gospel is an unreceived gospel—which is no gospel at all.

It is up to the church, the body of Christ, to see that everyone hears about Jesus. That means missionaries, sent and supported. That means teachers, trained and developed. That means preachers, educated and willing.

Many "parachurch" organizations can help accomplish these important tasks, but the local church remains God's primary appointed vehicle for making it possible for men and women to hear the Word of God. The old saying "Preach the gospel at all times. When necessary, use words" is defective because it places the use of words in a secondary position. Words are primary!

What Do You Think?

How would you respond to someone who, quoting Edgar Guest (1881–1959), says, "I'd rather see a sermon than hear one any day"?

Digging Deeper

What role should 1 Timothy 4:15 and 1 Peter 2:12 play in this discussion of Romans 10:17?

Conclusion

A. Where Does Faith Come From?

Faith comes from hearing the gospel, a message proclaimed by preachers. Christ must be preached as having been crucified as the substitutionary atonement sacrifice for sin (1 Corinthians 1:23), and as having risen again for our assured hope (15:4). The church will always need preachers who faithfully proclaim the gospel.

Though many of us are not preachers by vocation, we are still representatives of Christ. If you are praying for opportunities to spread the gospel, God will surely answer your prayers!

What Do You Think?

Which concept in today's lesson most highlights a need for improvement in your level of Bible knowledge? Why?

Digging Deeper

What specific, time-bound steps can you take to bring about that improvement?

B. Prayer

Mighty God, may we be faithful to preach the gospel. May our faith in Jesus never waver in so doing. In Jesus' name we pray. Amen.

C. Thought to Remember

Spread the gospel so others may believe.

Involvement Learning

Enhance your lesson with KJV Bible Student *(from your curriculum supplier) and the reproducible activity page (at www.standardlesson.com or in the back of the* KJV Standard Lesson Commentary Deluxe Edition*).*

Into the Lesson

Write this question on the board:

What is the best news you ever received?

Have learners pair up (with someone other than a family member) to share responses. After two minutes, reconvene for whole-class reporting of results by partners (that is, class members don't share their own responses).

Transition to Bible study by saying, "Today we will consider the best news that was ever experienced by the world. We will also consider how that news must be shared with those who haven't heard it."

Into the Word

To groups of three or four, distribute handouts (you create) that feature a blank chart that looks like this:

	Moses	Isaiah	Joel
Verse(s) in Rom 10:5-17			
Quoted from where			

Have printed at the top this title as a prompt for filling in the chart: *Where and from where Paul used the Old Testament in Romans 10:5-17.*

Encourage learners to use study Bibles, internet resources, etc., to identify the references. (*Expected responses:* **Moses**–verse 5, from Leviticus 18:5; verses 6-8, from Deuteronomy 30:12-14; **Isaiah**–verse 11, from Isaiah 28:16; verse 15, from Isaiah 52:7; verse 16, from Isaiah 53:1; **Joel**–verse 13, from Joel 2:32)

After reaching consensus in the ensuing whole-class discussion, announce that a *what's so* should be followed by a *so what?* Then immediately become personally silent to create an expectation for student responses. Do not be hasty in relieving the silence by offering hints, etc.! Wait at least 15 seconds before doing so. Jot student responses on the board. Follow each suggestion by asking for a reason.

Alternative or Option. Distribute copies of Romans 10:5-17 with these instructions:

1–Underline every verb in the text.
2–Circle every verb that tells how we are to respond to the gospel.
3–Put a star beside each verb that indicates our responsibility to share the gospel.

Ask learners to complete the first task individually. Then, in groups, half the class can complete the second task while the other half completes the third task. Reconvene for a discussion of results.

Into Life

Invite a guest to speak to your class about your congregation's missionary outreach. Ask for a brief report, including challenges, progress, and ongoing needs. Discuss how members of your class can help.

Next, write these three words on the board:

Time. Talent. Treasure.

Ask students, in pairs, to discuss how they individually could use each of these three gifts to spread the gospel more effectively. (Perhaps assign each word to a different third of the class.) After two or three minutes, ask class members to share ideas. Say: "Which of these gifts will you personally commit to use more fully to send or take the good news to those who have not accepted it?"

Option 1. Distribute copies of the "Amazing Stats" exercise from the activity page, which you can download, for study pairs to complete as indicated. *Option 2.* Do the same thing with the "Amazing Quotes" exercise.

After several minutes, ask volunteers to share their discussion with the whole class. Close with prayers for your congregation's efforts to share the gospel across cultures and around the world.

A Necessary Faith

Devotional Reading: Hebrews 11:32-40
Background Scripture: Hebrews 11; 13:1-19

Hebrews 11:1-8, 13-16

1 Now faith is the substance of things hoped for, the evidence of things not seen.

2 For by it the elders obtained a good report.

3 Through faith we understand that the worlds were framed by the word of God, so that things which are seen were not made of things which do appear.

4 By faith Abel offered unto God a more excellent sacrifice than Cain, by which he obtained witness that he was righteous, God testifying of his gifts: and by it he being dead yet speaketh.

5 By faith Enoch was translated that he should not see death; and was not found, because God had translated him: for before his translation he had this testimony, that he pleased God.

6 But without faith it is impossible to please him: for he that cometh to God must believe that he is, and that he is a rewarder of them that diligently seek him.

7 By faith Noah, being warned of God of things not seen as yet, moved with fear, prepared an ark to the saving of his house; by the which he condemned the world, and became heir of the righteousness which is by faith.

8 By faith Abraham, when he was called to go out into a place which he should after receive for an inheritance, obeyed; and he went out, not knowing whither he went.

. . . .

13 These all died in faith, not having received the promises, but having seen them afar off, and were persuaded of them, and embraced them, and confessed that they were strangers and pilgrims on the earth.

14 For they that say such things declare plainly that they seek a country.

15 And truly, if they had been mindful of that country from whence they came out, they might have had opportunity to have returned.

16 But now they desire a better country, that is, an heavenly: wherefore God is not ashamed to be called their God: for he hath prepared for them a city.

Key Verse

Faith is the substance of things hoped for, the evidence of things not seen. —**Hebrews 11:1**

CONFIDENT
HOPE

Unit 3: Faith Gives Us Hope

LESSONS 10–13

LESSON AIMS

After participating in this lesson, each learner will be able to:

1. State the definition of *faith.*
2. Explain the meaning and significance of the key verse.
3. List one change each in the categories of thought, behavior, and speech by which he or she will become more of a stranger to the world.

LESSON OUTLINE

Introduction
- A. The Power of Examples
- B. Lesson Context

I. The Meaning of Faith (Hebrews 11:1-3)
- A. Things Hoped For, Not Seen (vv. 1-2)
- B. Things Created (v. 3)

II. Examples of Faith (Hebrews 11:4-8)
- A. Abel (v. 4)
- B. Enoch (vv. 5-6)
- C. Noah (v. 7)
  - *Hellfire and Brimstone*
- D. Abraham (v. 8)

III. The Goal of Faith (Hebrews 11:13-16)
- A. Promises Far Off (v. 13)
- B. A Country Not Visible (vv. 14-15)
- C. A City God Prepares (v. 16)
  - *Looking for the City*

Conclusion
- A. Imitators of the Faithful
- B. Prayer
- C. Thought to Remember

Introduction

A. The Power of Examples

We live in an age that puts little stock in heroes. This might seem to be a strange assertion on the surface. After all, superhero movies have dominated at the box office for several years now. Consider, though, that the characters at the center of these movies are in categories all their own—amazing to watch but impossible to imitate.

It is much more common in our storytelling to play up the flaws and the personal weaknesses of those heroes who might be realistically presented as worthy of imitation. It is also common to highlight the antihero. This is a central figure who lacks traditional heroic qualities.

This tendency carries over into the world outside of the cinema. Longstanding cultural heroes are regularly brought up for reevaluation and found wanting, etc. Today's text presents challenges: In what ways are the historical figures in our lesson worthy of emulating as faith heroes despite their weaknesses? Should the designation *antihero* be applied to any? Or is there even such a thing as an antihero in a biblical sense? So many questions!

B. Lesson Context

Older commentaries on Hebrews focus on a limited set of questions regarding authorship, recipients, and its worthiness to be considered Scripture. For example, a well-known commentary published in 1876 made an extended argument for authorship by the apostle Paul, a position held by almost no one in our own day.

In keeping with scholarship of the day, the author went on to assert with confidence that the letter was addressed to Jewish converts to Christianity in Palestine. Finally, the writer argued for the book's inclusion in Scripture on four bases: it (1) was written by Paul, (2) was quoted as Scripture, (3) is found in the oldest versions of Scripture, and (4) features internal evidences for such inclusion (namely, its teaching is in harmony with the rest of Scripture).

With the passing of a century and a half since publication of that commentary, we can assert that we know both more and less about the background of Hebrews than we did then. Modern commentaries reflect the wealth of knowledge that we now have about the Jewish and Greek cultural, philosophical, and religious environment in which the letter was written. All of this enriches our understanding of the letter, but gets us no closer to an answer to some of the most basic questions that we still have. Chief among those is the question of who wrote it.

Even though no author is specified, a better understanding of the contexts mentioned above and of the rhetorical skill that lies behind the composition of the letter tells us a lot about the author. The person was educated, based on the quality of the Greek writing. The author also knew Greek culture and philosophy, interacting with both in argument and examples.

Although Hebrews 11 is often treated as a stand-alone unit of Scripture, it is important to note that the writer of the letter has been building toward it by the time it is reached. Although we do not cover them in today's lesson, the themes of faith and patient endurance, touched on in Hebrews 10:35-39, provide the launching point for the discussion of faith in chapter 11. We can see the author building on the idea of faith as pilgrimage as far back as chapters 3 and 4. With that, we turn to the text.

I. The Meaning of Faith

(Hebrews 11:1-3)

A. Things Hoped For, Not Seen (vv. 1-2)

1. Now faith is the substance of things hoped for, the evidence of things not seen.

The phrase *things hoped for* reminds us of the centrality of hope in the overall argument of this letter (example: Hebrews 6:16-20). For that matter, it reminds us of the way in which faith and hope are linked throughout the New Testament (examples: 1 Corinthians 13:13; Galatians 5:5; Colossians 1:5, 23). The phrase *things not seen* calls to mind the Platonic philosophical distinction between the visible and the invisible, the material and the spiritual. In this line of thinking, those things that are invisible are more real and are actually perfected, whereas physical objects are only shadows of the real things. Although Platonic philosophy is not Christian thinking, we can affirm that the spiritual realm is real, has consequences in the lives we live now, and offers greater hope than what we experience in our physical lives today.

But what does it mean that faith is *the substance of things hoped for*, or that it is *the evidence of things not seen*? The meanings are much disputed since there are various possibilities for translating the Greek words behind *substance* and *evidence.* It seems best to understand *substance* as something like "basis for trust or conviction." This can be thought of as a financial metaphor. The substance is like a down payment that serves to give confidence that the full amount will be forthcoming.

The word *evidence*, for its part, seems best understood as "proof" or even "demonstration." We can't go anywhere else in the New Testament to support this conclusion since the Greek word occurs only here. But we can go to the old Greek version of the Old Testament for support. There it occurs several times in contexts of legal argument and proof (Job 6:26; 13:6; 16:21; 23:4, 7).

2. For by it the elders obtained a good report.

The word *for* connects this verse logically with the previous statement. But how does it provide support for the assertion made in Hebrews 11:1, just considered? *Obtained a good report* translates a Greek verb that means "to witness" (translated that way in John 1:8) or "to testify" to the truth of something (as in John 5:39; 7:7; 1 John 4:14). In other words, the faith of *the elders* has been witnessed and attested.

The one who did the attesting was God. That is to say, God is the one who gave a good report as He witnessed the faithfulness of our spiritual ancestors. He is the one who validated their faith in realities that they could not see. We will see shortly why this is important.

What Do You Think?

What's the single most important lifestyle change you will make in order to obtain what is implied in Hebrews 11:2?

Digging Deeper

What positive impact should this have on unbelievers? on fellow believers?

B. Things Created (v. 3)

3. Through faith we understand that the worlds were framed by the word of God, so that things which are seen were not made of things which do appear.

Speaking of the "things not seen" (Hebrews 11:1, above), it is *faith* that shows us the reality of divine creation by the spoken *word of God*. The phrase *things which are seen were not made of things which do appear* is, without question, confusing to our ears. A simpler way to say this might be "so that what we see comes from what we do not see."

What we see is not the sum total of reality! Microscopes and telescopes reveal things not visible to the naked eye. Nevertheless, those realities affect our lives. Even more, there are spiritual realities that are no less important. Even while they remain unseen with physical eyes, by our faith in the evidence recorded in Scripture we know they are there.

Some have suggested that this idea owes its origins to Platonic philosophy (see again commentary on Hebrews 11:1, above). It would be better, though, to acknowledge that this is one place where that ancient line of thought and Christian teaching overlap.

II. Examples of Faith

(Hebrews 11:4-8)

A. Abel (v. 4)

4. By faith Abel offered unto God a more excellent sacrifice than Cain, by which he obtained witness that he was righteous, God testifying of his gifts: and by it he being dead yet speaketh.

The focus now shifts from the creation of the universe to particular individuals who exemplify the truth of Romans 1:17: "The just shall live by faith." *Abel* is the first of 18 biblical figures cited by name in Hebrews 11.

Abel's *more excellent sacrifice* is offered as a *witness that he was righteous,* but we wonder *why* it was more excellent. The account of the murder of Abel in Genesis 4 gives very little insight. It does not say anything about Abel's sacrifice being *more excellent.* It does, however, seem to imply (based on what we later learn about the sacrificial system of the Law of Moses) that offerings of the firstborn animals were superior to offerings of vegetables and fruit.

Some ancient commentators also noted that Genesis 4:5 seems to make a distinction between the person and the offering in such a way as to suggest Cain's attitude was not what it ought to be. Whatever the case may be, *God* testified *of his gifts,* validating them and thereby attesting to Abel's righteousness.

But there is more. Intriguingly, mysteriously, by his faith *he being dead yet speaketh.* This calls to mind the chilling statement of Genesis 4:10: "the voice of thy brother's blood crieth unto me from the ground." There is a sense that the writer of Hebrews understood Abel to still be alive in some sense. Perhaps it is in how Abel's sacrifice demonstrates as a continuing witness that "the just shall live by faith."

> *What Do You Think?*
>
> What habit can you adopt to ensure that your Christian legacy speaks for you after you die?
>
> *Digging Deeper*
>
> What is your reaction to the desire not to leave a legacy as expresed in the gospel song "Only Jesus"?

B. Enoch (vv. 5-6)

5. By faith Enoch was translated that he should not see death; and was not found, because God had translated him: for before his translation he had this testimony, that he pleased God.

The book of Genesis devotes only a few short sentences to *Enoch*. It was enough, though, for the writer of Hebrews (and countless other ancient Jewish writers) to see great significance in what is said there. The word *translated* is used in an older sense that means something like "taken away." The Genesis account notes only that Enoch "walked with God" and "was not; for God took him" (Genesis 5:22, 24). But it does not say why. The writer of Hebrews gives us a glimmer of a reason: *he pleased God* (see Hebrews 11:6, next).

6. But without faith it is impossible to please him: for he that cometh to God must believe that he is, and that he is a rewarder of them that diligently seek him.

The fact that Enoch pleased *God* has brought the writer to this general principle: *without faith it is impossible to please [God].* Faith involves an approach (*he that cometh to God*). There are two requirements of faith: the one who comes must *believe* (1) that God exists (see Hebrews 11:3, above) and (2) that God rewards those who *seek him*.

Belief in God must go further than merely acknowledging His existence. One is called to believe also that He is ready, willing, and able to reward those who search for Him. That, in turn, implies that one must believe in the power and goodness of God.

C. Noah (v. 7)

7. By faith Noah, being warned of God of things not seen as yet, moved with fear, prepared an ark to the saving of his house; by the which he condemned the world, and became heir of the righteousness which is by faith.

The writer has more material to draw from with regard to the next example: *Noah* (see Genesis 6–9). Of significance here is the phrase *things not seen as yet,* which calls to mind the language of Hebrews 11:1. Noah's trust in *God* regarding things Noah could not yet see is indeed the essence of *faith.* That faith *moved* him to act. *Fear* here should be understood as reverence for God (example: 1 Peter 1:17), not as unqualified terror or the guilt that overtakes a sinner (example: 1 John 4:18).

It's easy to imagine Noah's neighbors laughing in condemnation as he built *an ark.* By in the end, it was Noah's active faith that resulted in *the world* being *condemned.* Peter referred to him as a "preacher of righteousness" (2 Peter 2:5). But it would be a mistake to envision Noah pounding a pulpit or standing on a street corner yelling at passersby. It is possible that we are to understand from Peter's declaration that Noah's actions in building the ark (a tangible manifestation of his faith) spoke for themselves. Without his necessarily saying a word, those who saw him were exposed to its message.

On the subject of condemning *the world,* the Bible uses this phrase in three senses:

- As planet Earth in its physical sense (examples: Acts 17:24; Romans 10:18)
- As the world's human inhabitants (examples: Luke 2:1; John 3:16)
- As a system of values opposed to God's (examples: John 14:17; Colossians 2:20)

All three could be in play here since the flood of Noah's day was targeted at each (see also the Lesson Context of lesson 12).

As Noah's decision to act in faith was in and of itself a condemnation of the darkness around him, so it is in our day. The truth of the gospel, faithfully and charitably lived out, is a testimony against sin. It is sufficient on its own to condemn the darkness that is all around us.

What Do You Think?

What step can you take this week to "preach" the positive message of the Gospel that at the same time condemns "the world"?

Digging Deeper

Who are other characters in the Bible that you can look to as examples of condemning the world without speaking hatefully?

Hellfire and Brimstone

"Hellfire and brimstone" was at one time considered by many Christians to be true gospel preaching. One classic example of this emphasis is Jonathan Edwards's sermon, "Sinners in the Hands of an Angry God." Edwards was a New England minister who preached that famous sermon to a church in Enfield, Connecticut, on July 8, 1741.

Today, this kind of sermon is synonymous with all that critics consider to be wrong with Christianity. Within the lifetime of most of us, a shift has taken place in preaching. Without denying the doctrine of eternal punishment, preachers have found that the Christian message gains a more favorable hearing by presenting a positive message.

But the reality is that just as there is a Heaven to gain, there is a Hell to avoid. These are two sides of the same coin. As we witness to friends and neighbors, how do we communicate both realities effectively? —C. R. B.

D. Abraham (v. 8)

8. By faith Abraham, when he was called to go out into a place which he should after receive for an inheritance, obeyed; and he went out, not knowing whither he went.

Abraham acted on his faith (see Hebrews 11:9-12, 17-19, not in our printed text), just like the others we have discussed. This critical point is repeated through these examples and those that follow (11:20-38, not in our printed text).

By nature, human beings want certainty and security. Most of the time, however, we are driven by fear, insecurity, and uncertainty. The fears are so common to human experience that no examples are needed. But chief among them, though, is the fear of the unknown. So many people have been held back from achieving great things for God because of this kind of fear.

When God calls us to a task—as when He *called* Abraham to a higher mission—He calls us to trust in Him and to follow His directions. We may never be called to head out to an open desert as Abraham was, but we will be called to many things that we cannot anticipate or imagine. Are you ready to trust God even when you can't see the finish line or aren't (yet) equipped with the resources to get there?

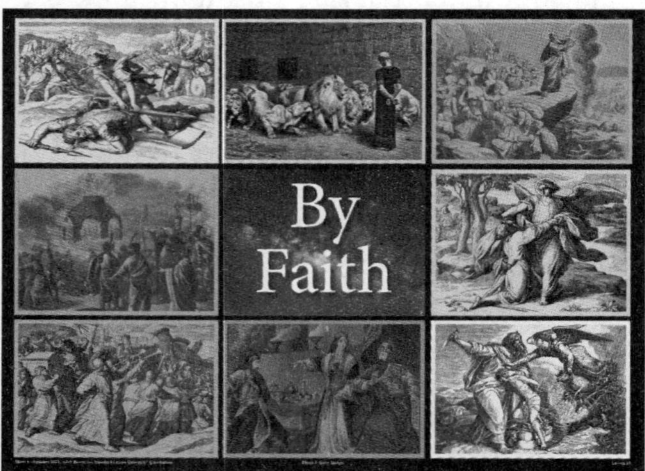

Visual for Lesson 10. *Have this visual posted as a backdrop as your class discusses the application of Hebrews 11:14-16.*

III. The Goal of Faith

(Hebrews 11:13-16)

A. Promises Far Off (v. 13)

13. These all died in faith, not having received the promises, but having seen them afar off, and were persuaded of them, and embraced them, and confessed that they were strangers and pilgrims on the earth.

The discussion of Abraham and Sarah encompasses Hebrews 11:8-12, then the inspired writer offered conclusions. *These all died in faith* does not mean that their faith killed them. Rather, it means they remained faithful to the end of their lives. These faithful people died never having seen the fruits of their labor—the verification of their faith, in other words. All this is difficult to imagine in our impatient world that expects instant gratification and quick results.

But these *strangers and pilgrims on the earth* (see 1 Peter 2:11) still speak in this regard even though they are long deceased. This world was not their final home (compare Genesis 23:4). They did not wander without a goal, though. They were on a pilgrimage to God.

What Do You Think?

Who can you recruit to be an accountability partner to help ensure you both live as "strangers and pilgrims" on earth?

Digging Deeper

How do John 3:16; 1 Peter 2:11-12; and 1 John 2:15 further challenge you in this regard?

B. A Country Not Visible (vv. 14-15)

14-15. For they that say such things declare plainly that they seek a country. And truly, if they had been mindful of that country from whence they came out, they might have had opportunity to have returned.

Faith pointed these heroes forward as they sought *a country* not yet visible to them. Homesickness for *that country from whence they came out* would have become an obstacle to their focus on the better land, should they have yearned to go back (compare Numbers 14:4; Luke 9:62).

It would have been easy for any of the fathers of Israel, given the risks and challenges they faced, to have turned back to the relative comforts of "home." Perhaps some of them briefly entertained the idea. The writer of Hebrews was mindful of this and saw it as relevant for his audience in a spiritual sense. In the first century AD, Jewish-Christians who were on the edge of abandoning their new faith were very mindful of their "old" country, namely the Judaism in which they grew up. They saw there the promise of earthly relief from the various forms of social and economic pressures that they had faced in their decision to follow Christ.

C. A City God Prepares (v. 16)

16. But now they desire a better country, that is, an heavenly: wherefore God is not ashamed to be called their God: for he hath prepared for them a city.

Better is a key word throughout the letter to the Hebrews. Indeed, of the New Testament's 19 occurrences of the Greek word, 13 appear in this book (the other 12 are in Hebrews 1:4; 6:9; 7:7, 19, 22; 8:6 [twice]; 9:23; 10:34; 11:35, 40; 12:24). Even though these heroes of the faith could not yet see it, they acknowledged their destination's superiority by their actions.

All this was a model for the writer's original audience. If they oriented their desires toward *an heavenly* country, they would find there the true and living God—the one who *is not ashamed to be called their God*, who has *prepared for them a city,* a permanent place of rest (see Hebrews 4).

Looking for the City

After dedicating their lives to the ministry of the gospel, my parents moved to a Christian retirement village. When Mom died a few years later, it took a lot of the "spark" out of Dad. His focus began to turn more and more toward Heaven.

One day not long before Dad was called home, my brother Paul was visiting him, as he did regularly. While they were talking, Dad suddenly pointed to the window and said, "Paul, look out there! What do you see?" Paul looked and replied, "Sky and trees." With a sparkle in his eyes that had long been absent, Dad said, "No, it's the city!"

Paul and I are convinced that Dad was catching a glimpse of the better country—the heavenly city—toward which his life's pilgrimage had long been directed. Is that true of your life?—C. R. B.

HOW TO SAY IT

Abel	*Ay*-buhl.
Cain	Cayn.
Enoch	*E*-nock.
Platonic	Pluh-*ton*-ik or Pleh-*ton*-ik.

Conclusion

A. Imitators of the Faithful

The apostle Paul wrote "Be ye followers of me, even as I also am of Christ" (1 Corinthians 11:1). We sometimes undervalue the role of imitation in spiritual maturity. Perhaps you don't feel confident enough to invite others to use your life as a model for their own discipleship. Wouldn't it be arrogant to do so?

Paul didn't see it that way, and neither did the other apostles (compare 1 Peter 5:3). All of us can think of others—ministers, Sunday school teachers, ordinary congregants—who were influential in teaching us and molding us in the life of faith. We too are called to live in such a way that we can add our names to the list of "the just [who] shall live by faith" (Hebrews 10:38).

> *What Do You Think?*
> Which person noted in today's text most inspires you to a lifestyle change? Why?
> *Digging Deeper*
> What role will prayer have in this change?

B. Prayer

Lord God, we come to You acknowledging our struggle to trust Your promises as the distractions of life cause us to lose focus. Strengthen our faith so that we may follow You wherever You lead. In Jesus' name we pray. Amen.

C. Thought to Remember

The faithful look for God's country.

Involvement Learning

Enhance your lesson with KJV Bible Student *(from your curriculum supplier) and the reproducible activity page (at www.standardlesson.com or in the back of the* KJV Standard Lesson Commentary Deluxe Edition*).*

Into the Lesson

Write this challenge on the board:

What is something "instant" that's not as good as the version that takes longer?

Ask participants to discuss this with one or two partners for no more than two minutes before sharing conclusions in whole-class discussion. (Anticipate that most responses will be in the food category; a secondary category is that of cleaning products.)

Make special note of anything mentioned regarding instant aspects of religion(s) or of the complete lack of responses regarding that category. Transition to Bible study by asking, "Many feel lost or abandoned when God doesn't instantly grant their requests. Let's see how the Bible addresses that topic."

Into the Word

Distribute handouts (you create) featuring a blank chart with the following three column headings:

Scripture Reference	How Faith Was Demonstrated	Ways to Imitate That Faith

Out to the left, have printed the names Abel, Enoch, Noah, and Abraham so that the chart has one name for each of four rows that will intersect the three columns.

Divide the class into pairs or triads and ask them to complete the chart. Assign each group one of the four names in the chart and instruct them to start there before moving to the other names on the chart. Instruct students to leave the third column blank as you save it for the Into Life discussion later. (*Option.* Include all the names from Hebrews 11:4-38 on the chart; assign different sections of the list to groups.)

Write the following questions on the board for discussion. (Write only one question at a time; do not write another question until discussion of the one before it is completed.)

1–How did the faith of each of these "heroes" result in something far different from instant gratification?
2–Are you encouraged or discouraged by their examples?
3-How does their experience prod us to keep faith?

Use the third question as your transition to the Into Life section.

Option. Distribute copies of the "Something Better" exercise on the activity page, which you can download. Since this can be very time-consuming, you may wish to assign discrete segments to groups. Discuss results as appropriate.

Into Life

Have participants regroup with their Bible-study partners to complete and discuss the "Ways to Imitate That Faith" column from the Into the Word segment. After several minutes, ask volunteers to share their conclusions with the class as a whole.

Distribute blank slips of paper. Ask students to write down the quality of faith they'd most like to develop personally in thought, behavior, and speech. Below that, suggest that they write a specific action step they can take to begin developing that quality.

Option 1. Time permitting, ask students to name a personal hero and model of faith. Ask volunteers to relate brief stories about them. Press for explanations regarding how their heroes demonstrated faith; write those responses on the board as they are shared. Ask the class to match the qualities in the resulting list with the qualities they have named in the Bible heroes they examined earlier. Discuss how Christians can develop each quality.

Close with prayer for learners to both *have* a hero of the faith and to *be* one.

A Patient, Persevering Faith

Devotional Reading: Psalm 40:1-13
Background Scripture: Hebrews 10:19-39

Hebrews 10:23-36

23 Let us hold fast the profession of our faith without wavering; (for he is faithful that promised;)

24 And let us consider one another to provoke unto love and to good works:

25 Not forsaking the assembling of ourselves together, as the manner of some is; but exhorting one another: and so much the more, as ye see the day approaching.

26 For if we sin wilfully after that we have received the knowledge of the truth, there remaineth no more sacrifice for sins,

27 But a certain fearful looking for of judgment and fiery indignation, which shall devour the adversaries.

28 He that despised Moses' law died without mercy under two or three witnesses:

29 Of how much sorer punishment, suppose ye, shall he be thought worthy, who hath trodden under foot the Son of God, and hath counted the blood of the covenant, wherewith he was sanctified, an unholy thing, and hath done despite unto the Spirit of grace?

30 For we know him that hath said, Vengeance belongeth unto me, I will recompense, saith the Lord. And again, The Lord shall judge his people.

31 It is a fearful thing to fall into the hands of the living God.

32 But call to remembrance the former days, in which, after ye were illuminated, ye endured a great fight of afflictions;

33 Partly, whilst ye were made a gazingstock both by reproaches and afflictions; and partly, whilst ye became companions of them that were so used.

34 For ye had compassion of me in my bonds, and took joyfully the spoiling of your goods, knowing in yourselves that ye have in heaven a better and an enduring substance.

35 Cast not away therefore your confidence, which hath great recompence of reward.

36 For ye have need of patience, that, after ye have done the will of God, ye might receive the promise.

Key Verse

Let us hold fast the profession of our faith without wavering; (for he is faithful that promised).

—Hebrews 10:23

CONFIDENT HOPE

Unit 3: Faith Gives Us Hope

LESSONS 10–13

LESSON AIMS

After participating in this lesson, each learner will be able to:

1. Summarize the nature of the Old Testament passages used to support the writer's argument.
2. Explain why deliberate sin equates to treating Christ's blood as unholy.
3. Make a plan to be an example that encourages fellow believers to be more committed to their service to Christ.

LESSON OUTLINE

Introduction
- A. The Challenge of Faithfulness
- B. Lesson Context

I. Hold Fast (Hebrews 10:23-27)
- A. Profession of Belief (v. 23)
  - *Faith and Honest Doubt*
- B. Provocation to Love (vv. 24-25)
- C. Prospect of Judgment (vv. 26-27)

II. Don't Falter (Hebrews 10:28-31)
- A. Despising Moses' Law (v. 28)
- B. Contempt for the Spirit (vv. 29-31)

III. Remember the Past (Hebrews 10:32-36)
- A. Pain of Persecution (v. 32-34)
  - *Old Mr. Pershing*
- B. Patient Confidence (vv. 35-36)

Conclusion
- A. The Challenge for Every Age
- B. Prayer
- C. Thought to Remember

Introduction

A. The Challenge of Faithfulness

Options. Choice. Variety. These are values that culture embraces. We see this clearly in the options that are presented to us in any grocery store. But this also applies to commitments that are much more meaningful than what kind of breakfast cereal we're going to buy. In the realms of values, spirituality, political ideologies, relationships, career paths, and so forth, we are presented with a bewildering array of choices. The culture in which we live encourages experimentation with all of them as well as a hesitancy to commit to any of them.

In this way of thinking, the only real mistake is to limit one's options or to give up on some options in favor of others. All of this can make the path of Christian discipleship very difficult. In choosing to follow Christ, we turn our back on many other options, many other choices. We may be surprised to learn that the first-century writer of Hebrews has something to say to twenty-first-century Christians in this regard!

B. Lesson Context

What is often called the *letter* to the Hebrews has almost none of the usual characteristics of an ancient letter, apart from a couple of brief greetings at the end (see Hebrews 13:24-25). Instead, the letter relies heavily on action verbs that have to do with speaking and listening; this serves to suggest that we are listening in as a preacher speaks to an audience (examples: 2:5; 6:9; 9:5).

It seems best to understand Hebrews as a first-century *sermon*. The phrase "word of exhortation" (Hebrews 13:22) is the same used in Acts 13:15:

> After the reading of the law and the prophets the rulers of the synagogue sent unto them, saying, Ye men and brethren, if ye have any word of exhortation for the people, say on.

This further bolsters the theory that Hebrews, like the spoken word in Acts, was primarily an oral address. Indeed, 13 of the New Testament's 19 uses of the underlying Greek word for exhortation occur in Hebrews. It is possible that a listener wrote the sermon down so that it could be passed along as a letter to believers.

Arguing for too clean a distinction between written and oral communication would be a mistake, however. There is no reason this document could not have been written as a sermon to be delivered as a letter and then read aloud. In truth, either direction we choose brings us to improved insight into the overall structure of the work.

There is broad agreement that the long central section of the letter is devoted to the main arguments that the preacher is trying to make to his audience. One compelling outline divides the letter this way:

1–Introduction (1:1–2:4)
2–Main Proposition (2:5-9)
3–Arguments (2:10–12:27)
4–Final Exhortation (12:28–13:21)
5–Epistolary Postscript (13:22-25)

Today's text lies at a point of transition from exposition to exhortation. That is the significance of the word *therefore* in Hebrews 10:19. That verse and the two that follow form a crescendo of the doctrinal exposition that then resolves into practical exhortation beginning in 10:22.

Our opening verses (Hebrews 10:23-25) are usually understood to be part of a larger unit inclusive of 10:19-25. In light of that, a brief word about 10:19-22 is in order. This section is part of a larger doctrinal argument about the nature of sacrifice and the superiority of Jesus' sacrifice over the animal sacrifices stipulated under the old covenant (see 7:1–10:25). The doctrinal expositions at the heart of this sermon are each followed by a word of exhortation from the preacher to his audience (example: 7:1–10:25 followed by 10:26-39).

I. Hold Fast

(Hebrews 10:23-27)

A. Profession of Belief (v. 23)

23. Let us hold fast the profession of our faith without wavering; (for he is faithful that promised;).

Our text opens with an exhortation that follows on the first one (see Hebrews 10:22, not in our printed text). What exactly is the preacher encouraging his hearers to do? Given the vivid baptismal imagery of the previous verses, *the profession of faith* seems best understood as a reference to the baptismal confession. Confession was always part of baptism for the first Christians. It was a kind of public vow of commitment to Jesus and the gospel about Him. We cannot, of course, know the exact content of that confession. But both Scripture and early Christian writings suggest that the earliest confessions centered around the person and work of Jesus. Those included His divine status and saving work on behalf of sinful humanity.

Wavering, and thereby falling into apostasy, was exactly the danger that motivated the preacher to deliver this message in the first place. But we should not understand him merely to be pointing an accusing finger at his audience. He understood their circumstances and how strong the temptation to waver, to give up the fight, was for them. So he pointed them to Jesus, reminding them that their faithfulness could not be based on their own meager strength. Rather, it had to be rooted in the prior faithfulness of Jesus himself.

What Do You Think?

What is a wrong way to demonstrate faith when a wave of life crashes your way?

Digging Deeper

Without giving directive advice, how would you counsel a fellow believer who is demonstrating such a wrong approach?

Faith and Honest Doubt

I don't know nearly as much nowadays as I did when I graduated from college! Of course, I jest. But I have learned to be more humble about what I know. Sometimes what "the Bible says" is actually my limited perspective causing me to read into the Bible what I want it to say.

Alfred, Lord Tennyson, in his poem "In Memoriam," put it this way: "There lives more faith in honest doubt, believe me, than in half the creeds." I think I know what Tennyson meant. Merely citing what we know we're "supposed to believe" is not nearly as faithful as actually wrestling with the Scripture when it challenges us.

The question, of course, concerns the difference between "holding fast to faith" and "wavering."

Here's an interesting test to give yourself: When was the last time the Bible changed your mind about . . . anything? —C. R. B.

B. Provocation to Love (vv. 24-25)

24. And let us consider one another to provoke unto love and to good works.

The author's exhortation continues. The *King James Version* translators rendered the underlying Greek text as literally as possible in this instance. *Consider one another* means something like "pay attention to each other" or "focus your minds on helping one another."

This exhortation reminds us that the Christian life is not—cannot be—solely an individual affair. We do not follow the path of discipleship on the basis of our individual determination alone. We have help, support, and encouragement along the way. Indeed, part of being a disciple is offering help and encouragement to each other.

This is not simply a general call for helpfulness. It has specific purpose. Believers are *to provoke unto love and to good works.* The one defines the other: love is not to be understood here as a vague, positive emotion, or merely good feelings toward another person. Love is concrete: it is defined by the doing of good works (see Matthew 25:31-46; James 2:8-13).

25. Not forsaking the assembling of ourselves together, as the manner of some is; but exhorting one another: and so much the more, as ye see the day approaching.

It is important to understand Hebrews 10:24 and 25 together. The stirring up to love and good works primarily takes place in *the assembling of ourselves together.* Love, good works, and the worship assembly are a package deal, so to speak. We cannot isolate one of the three and hold it up as the sole focus of the Christian life. According to the preacher of this sermon, love and good works are synonymous, and they grow out of worship.

This may sound strange, especially to readers who are accustomed to hearing this verse used to elevate church attendance as the pinnacle of the individual Christian's responsibilities. For the preacher of this ancient sermon, participation in the worship assembly was not merely a box to be checked off. Rather, worship is about identity formation.

This was especially true for the people to whom this message was first addressed. Many of them were feeling social pressure to give up on their commitment to Jesus. This manifested itself in a tendency to distance themselves from the community. But the community relied on participation in order to endure in the face of these pressures.

Worship is doubly important in light of *the day* that is *approaching.* The author of these words understood worship in climactic terms. Worship deals with the true nature of reality, most especially the cosmic reality of God's reign over all things. That fact was especially important for a group of people who were beginning to disbelieve in the reality of that claim.

The day approaching is meant to point to Jesus' second coming, or the Day of Judgment. That will be the time when God's kingdom will come in its fullness; His purposes for humanity and all of creation will be fully revealed. The language of *approaching,* or arrival, can be seen in other passages (see Matthew 3:2; 4:17; Mark 1:15; Romans 13:12; James 5:8).

What Do You Think?

How many times per month should you attend church services in order to honor the intent of Hebrews 10:25? Why do you say that?

Digging Deeper

How do you answer that question without becoming legalistic?

C. Prospect of Judgment (vv. 26-27)

26. For if we sin wilfully after that we have received the knowledge of the truth, there remaineth no more sacrifice for sins.

These words hearken back to Hebrews 6:4-8. Many in the preacher's audience seem to have been in danger of turning away from the faith because of the social pressures coming at them from their families. The cost of living the faith, in other words, was becoming too great for them to bear. The idea behind receiving *the knowledge of the truth* is found in the letters of the apostle Paul (see 1 Timothy 2:4; 2 Timothy 2:25; Titus 1:1). It is a way of describing one's entry into the church and its commitments.

To *sin wilfully* after having come to Christ carries the grave consequences of being cut off from the positive benefits of Christ's *sacrifice for sins*. Furthermore, if we assume that the preacher is speaking to wavering believers who wanted to return to Judaism, it also meant that the old rituals were cut off from them. Having been in Christ, they had come to know that animal sacrifices did not purify. So how could any sacrifice for sins remain for them?

27. But a certain fearful looking for of judgment and fiery indignation, which shall devour the adversaries.

Those who continue to sin willfully can anticipate *judgment and fiery indignation* (also Hebrews 9:27; 12:29). The word *fearful* reminds us of that word's two senses: the Christian's fear of God is that of reverent respect; the unbeliever's lack of fear now will become one of terror when judgment arrives. Faithful fear of God drives out fear of everything else (see 2:15; 11:23, 27). But disobeying God should put people in fear because they have become His *adversaries* through their own actions.

II. Don't Falter

(Hebrews 10:28-31)

A. Despising Moses' Law (v. 28)

28. He that despised Moses' law died without mercy under two or three witnesses.

The preacher now took a different tack, appealing to an Old Testament example to support his warning about the danger of apostasy. The word translated *despised* is also translated as some form of the word *reject* in Mark 6:26; 7:9; and Luke 7:30, and that is the sense here. To reject *Moses' law* was to commit apostasy.

Deuteronomy 17 describes the punishment for an Israelite who "wrought wickedness in the sight of the Lord thy God, in transgressing his covenant" by committing idolatry (17:2). Such a person was to be put to death "at the mouth

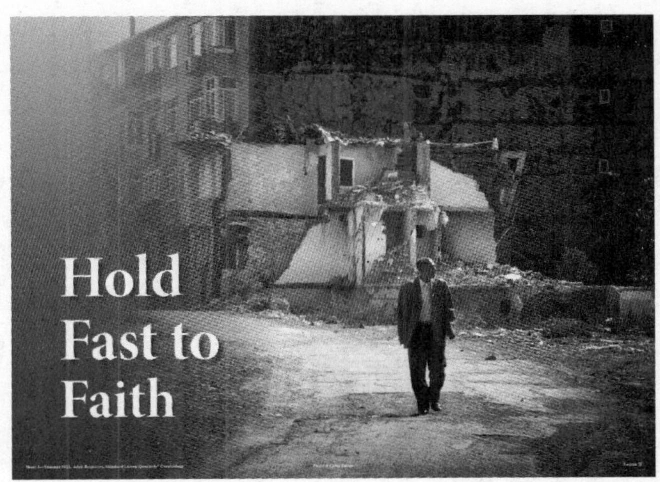

Visual for Lesson 11. *While posing the discussion question associated with verse 25, ask learners how (non-)attendance affects their faith.*

of two witnesses, or three witnesses" (17:6; compare 19:15). The phrasing *without mercy* is not found in this passage. But the idea is found in Deuteronomy 13:6-10. There a similar situation is addressed: the one who tempts others to idolatry is to be stoned: "Thou shalt not consent unto him . . . neither shall thine eye pity him" (13:8; see also Deuteronomy 19:19-21). The reason why the preacher mentions this becomes clear in the next verse, below.

B. Contempt for the Spirit (vv. 29-31)

29. Of how much sorer punishment, suppose ye, shall he be thought worthy, who hath trodden under foot the Son of God, and hath counted the blood of the covenant, wherewith he was sanctified, an unholy thing, and hath done despite unto the Spirit of grace?

The reason for Hebrews 10:28 becomes clear as we recognize the lesser-to-greater form of argument now in view (see also Hebrews 2:1-4). Here it takes the form of "if X was bad, just think how much worse Y will be." That is, if the consequences of apostasy were dire under the old covenant, consider how much worse those consequences are under the new *covenant* of Jesus Christ!

Apostasy is a rejection of the *Spirit of grace*. That is a rare phrase in the Bible, found only here and in Zechariah 12:10). In both instances, the phrase assumes that grace is divine empowerment. Grace is sometimes understood as the free gift of God that comes no-strings-attached. But grace is more than that. Grace empowers us to take up our crosses and follow Christ, giving us the strength to undertake the path of discipleship and service to others in His name. Think of all that is being given up when one rejects the Spirit of grace!

We need the Spirit's empowerment today just as ancient believers did. Like those to whom this letter was originally written, we are weak and frail, prone to wander, and prone to look for an easier way.

What Do You Think?

Beginning with logic rather than quoting Scripture, how would you respond to someone who believes that God's loving nature means we can keep doing whatever we want?

Digging Deeper

What if the person mentioned Samson as an example of someone who did as he pleased yet still enjoyed God's favor?

30. For we know him that hath said, Vengeance belongeth unto me, I will recompense, saith the Lord. And again, The Lord shall judge his people.

The terrible consequences for apostasy, which is the same as having "trodden under foot the Son of God" (Hebrews 10:29). Such consequences are certain for the preacher and his audience because they *know him* who has spoken. Because God spoke the words they will certainly come to pass. The two quotations here are substantially drawn from Deuteronomy 32:35-36, although neither is an exact quotation of the text.

What Do You Think?

What area of life do you most need to give to the Lord in letting Him judge rather than you trying to do so yourself?

Digging Deeper

What passages in addition to 1 Corinthians 6:7 will help you most in this regard? Why?

31. It is a fearful thing to fall into the hands of the living God.

This statement reiterates the point first made in Hebrews 10:26-27 (see above). The phrase *the living God* occurs more often in this book than anywhere else in the Bible (see 3:12; 9:14; 12:22). This God—the only God there is—sweeps away all gods of wood and stone, which are no gods at all (2 Kings 19:18; Isaiah 37:19). He is true to His word, and the consequences of apostasy will come to pass.

III. Remember the Past

(Hebrews 10:32-36)

A. Pain of Persecution (vv. 32-34)

32. But call to remembrance the former days, in which, after ye were illuminated, ye endured a great fight of afflictions.

In challenging his hearers and readers to *call to remembrance the former days,* the preacher is using the strongest exhortation available to him in the Greek language as used in Old and New Testaments. (Less strong versions appear in Mark 11:21; 14:72; 1 Corinthians 4:17; 2 Corinthians 7:15; and 2 Timothy 1:6.)

We should take care to point out that the preacher was not asking them to remember "the good ol' days" with fondness. The challenge to remember is not that of passively recalling information. Rather, it is an act that forms one's identity in order to act in light of "lessons learned" from important events past.

Those *former days . . . after ye were illuminated* are especially important for the preacher's overall argument. Even back then, his hearers had suffered greatly. The sufferings of their present moment, then, were not new. The readers had been through it before, and they had faithfully endured. If they could bear up once, they could bear up twice. The idea of light or *were illuminated* is associated with God's love or salvation in the psalms (Psalms 27:1; 44:3; 78:14).

Old Mr. Pershing

When I was a teenager, my family lived in an old house in Minneapolis. Around the corner lived Mr. Pershing, whom we frequently saw sitting on his front porch. Sometimes we would go over and talk to him. My brothers and I thought of him as incredibly elderly, so we called him "Old Mr. Pershing"—but not to his face.

A few years ago, my brother Dave and I were visiting Minneapolis, and we went by our old home. As we walked around the corner, there sat Old Mr. Pershing on his front porch! We walked up and chatted with him. Once back in our car, my brother and I broke out laughing. We each knew what the other was thinking: *We are both older than Mr. Pershing was when we started calling him "Old Mr. Pershing!"*

Remembering the past gives us perspective. It's as true for us today as it was to the first-century Christians. What has remembering your personal history taught you about walking with God today and tomorrow? What should it? —C. R. B.

33-34. Partly, whilst ye were made a gazingstock both by reproaches and afflictions; and partly, whilst ye became companions of them that were so used. For ye had compassion of me in my bonds, and took joyfully the spoiling of your goods, knowing in yourselves that ye have in heaven a better and an enduring substance.

Here the writer got specific about the former days (Hebrews 10:32, above). Members of his audience had suffered directly, and they had also suffered by being the *companions* of those who suffered persecution. The Greek word behind *gazingstock* only occurs in this verse and means something like "to be made a spectacle" or "to be put on public display." The English word *gazingstock* has fallen out of common use, but it is easily understood if we remember "laughingstock," a similar word that is very much still in use. Someone who is a laughingstock is the target of laughter and ridicule. Likewise, one who is a gazingstock is one who is the target of staring, gazing, and similarly unwanted forms of public attention.

B. Patient Confidence (vv. 35-36)

35-36. Cast not away therefore your confidence, which hath great recompense of reward. For ye have need of patience, that, after ye have done the will of God, ye might receive the promise.

In the final two verses of today's text, the author turned to the importance of *patience.* Those who are tempted to reject the Christ they once accepted should have *confidence* because they know who God is and what He has done for them. That confidence is the basis of a patience that will result in retaining *the promise* of resurrection and eternal life with Jesus (Hebrews 4:1; 9:15).

What Do You Think?

Which part of today's lesson do you struggle with most? Why?

Digging Deeper

What action will you take this week to remedy this problem?

Conclusion

A. The Challenge for Every Age

The story of the audience of the letter to the Hebrews is the story of God's people throughout history. From the days after Pharaoh released the Hebrews from bondage onward, we see the fickleness in God's people in remaining faithful. In many ways, it was no different for the first-century church.

And it is no different for us today. Cultural pressures may vary from place to place and across the centuries, but the challenge of faithfulness remains. By keeping our eyes trained on God's promises in hope, we can remain faithful to the very end and receive everything God desires for us. "Let us lay aside every weight, and the sin which doth so easily best us, and let us run with patience the race that is set before us" (Hebrews 12:1).

B. Prayer

Father, in the midst of strong pressures, grant us strength to remain faithful to Your Son through the Spirit of grace. May we seek each day to live a life worthy of our calling in Him. In Jesus' name we pray. Amen.

C. Thought to Remember

God's promises are certain for
all who walk the difficult
path of faith.

Involvement Learning

Enhance your lesson with KJV Bible Student *(from your curriculum supplier) and the reproducible activity page (at www.standardlesson.com or in the back of the* KJV Standard Lesson Commentary Deluxe Edition*).*

Into the Lesson

Ask for shows of hands regarding students identifying with one of these two statements:

1–Patient perseverance seems to come easier for me than for most others.
2–Patient perseverance seems more difficult for me than for most others.

Form groups of two or three with as equal representation as possible from the showing of hands. Have the resulting pairs or triads discuss this question (distribute on handouts you create or write it on the board):

Does difficulty prod you to try harder, or cause you to give up? Why?

After three minutes, allow volunteers to share their thoughts with the class as a whole.

Make a transition to Bible study by noting that response to difficulties may define who we are, as it did for those to be studied in today's text.

Into the Word

Form groups of four or five; give each group one of the following sets of Bible-study questions on handouts (you prepare).

Worship Group. Find three commands in Hebrews 10:23-25 to answer these questions: 1–How does each of these relate to the other two? 2–How does this picture of the purpose of worship contrast with how some worshippers today feel about formal worship services? 3–Do you obey all three of these commands as a part of your weekly worship? If not, why not? 4–*To Consider Today*: What should happen for worship to help Christians better obey all three of these commands?

Gathering Group. Compare Hebrews 10:25 with 2 Thessalonians 2:1, where the same Greek word behind the translations "assembling" and "gathering" occur—the only two places in the New Testament. 1–How are our gatherings today like what we think that gathering will be? 2–How are they different? 3–What do you look forward to experiencing when you gather with other Christians in Heaven? 4–*To Consider Today:* How does that anticipation affect your feeling about gathering for worship here?

Faithfulness Group. Compare Hebrews 10:26-31 with Hebrews 6:4-6. 1–What spiritual condition do both of these passages consider? 2–How might each of these be interpreted in light of the teaching that surrounds them (see Hebrews 5:11–6:1; 10:28)? 3–Who stands central in the Hebrews 10 passage? What hope do we have if, after naming Christ as Lord, we reject Him? 4–*To Consider Today*: Why is this so difficult to hear in today's culture?

Persecution Group. List all that the believers earlier suffered, according to Hebrews 10:32-34. 1–Which of these sacrifices seems most severe or difficult to you? 2–How would you expect Christians to continue living after enduring such persecution? 3–What encouragement does the author of the text offer in verses 35-36? 4–*To Consider Today:* Does long-term experience with suffering always lead to stronger faith? Why, or why not?

When you call time, allow groups to report to the whole class. *(Option.* Step outside today's lesson text by having learners complete the "A Call to Persevere" exercise on the activity page, which you can download.)

Into Life

Based on those discussions from the fourth questions, have each group outline a devotional talk that challenges them to be examples that encourage fellow believers to be more committed in their service to Christ.

Option. Distribute copies of the "Why Worship?" exercise on the activity page. Have participants work in pairs to complete it as indicated. Have colored pencils or markers available for those who request them. Award a token prize for the most catchy creation.

A Conquering Faith

Devotional Reading: John 14:15-24
Background Scripture: 1 John 4–5

1 John 4:2-3, 13-17

2 Hereby know ye the Spirit of God: Every spirit that confesseth that Jesus Christ is come in the flesh is of God:

3 And every spirit that confesseth not that Jesus Christ is come in the flesh is not of God: and this is that spirit of antichrist, whereof ye have heard that it should come; and even now already is it in the world.

. . . .

13 Hereby know we that we dwell in him, and he in us, because he hath given us of his Spirit.

14 And we have seen and do testify that the Father sent the Son to be the Saviour of the world.

15 Whosoever shall confess that Jesus is the Son of God, God dwelleth in him, and he in God.

16 And we have known and believed the love that God hath to us. God is love; and he that dwelleth in love dwelleth in God, and God in him.

17 Herein is our love made perfect, that we may have boldness in the day of judgment: because as he is, so are we in this world.

1 John 5:4-5

4 For whatsoever is born of God overcometh the world: and this is the victory that overcometh the world, even our faith.

5 Who is he that overcometh the world, but he that believeth that Jesus is the Son of God?

Key Verse

God is love; and he that dwelleth in love dwelleth in God, and God in him. **—1 John 4:16b**

CONFIDENT
HOPE

Unit 3: Faith Gives Us Hope

LESSONS 10–13

LESSON AIMS

After participating in this lesson, each learner will be able to:

1. Tell how to recognize "the Spirit of God."

2. Define the differing senses and references of the words *Spirit* and *spirit.*

3. List three ways he or she can better model God's love.

LESSON OUTLINE

Introduction

A. On Incarnation and Reincarnation

One topic given particular attention during studies at Bible colleges is that of the incarnation. That topic addresses the who, what, when, where, why, and how of the Son of God putting on flesh to become the person Jesus of Nazareth. Today's text is considered in such studies.

A teacher of such a course was surprised one day when a student (who claimed to be a Christian) announced that she was the reincarnation of someone who had lived about 100 years earlier. The teacher's response noted the lack of support for this view in historic Christian thought, the pagan origins of reincarnation theory, and a consideration of Hebrews 9:27: "It is appointed unto men once to die, but after this the judgment." The dialogue further included considerations of reincarnation in terms of what the Bible says about each person's responsibility before God.

In the end, however, the student remained adamant in her belief. Her rejoinder included the exact phrase "regardless of what the Bible says"!

As wrong as the reincarnation theory is, things gets more bizarre still when a cult leader announces himself to be the reincarnation of Christ. For example, the leader of Divine Love Path in Australia claims to be the reincarnated Jesus and says his partner is Mary Magdalene.

Although Scripture refutes reincarnation, it's possible to go too far the other way and deny the incarnation of Christ in the process. This is seen in early Christianity's having its hands full at times dealing with heretics who denied the one real incarnation, which took place in the person of Jesus. How successful we will be in resisting and opposing such heresy may very well depend on how firmly we grasp the truths of today's lesson.

B. Lesson Context

Five of the books of the New Testament are attributed to the apostle John, one of the original 12 disciples (see Matthew 4:21-22; 10:1-4). His five books are the Gospel of John; the letters (also called epistles) that we designate as 1 John, 2 John, and 3 John; and the book of Revelation.

History strongly associates John in his later years with the church in Ephesus. Tradition says he died in the AD 90s. His three letters were probably written in the region of Ephesus for churches in the area, and thus would date from the AD 80s or 90s. John would have been an elderly man at that time. The dignity of his age peeks through in 1 John, where he addressed his readers as his "little children" numerous times.

The idea of overcoming, or being victorious, is a favorite theme of John's. In 1 John 2:13-14 he discussed victory over Satan. In 1 John 4–5, he wrote about overcoming the pressures of the world. As we consider this in today's study, we must be careful to distinguish among three ways the Bible speaks of "the world":

- As planet Earth in its physical sense (examples: Acts 17:24; Romans 10:18)
- As the world's human inhabitants (examples: Luke 2:1; John 3:16)
- As a system of values opposed to God's (examples: John 14:17; Colossians 2:20)

In his first letter John wrote of Satan's system for opposing the work of God on earth (1 John 2:15-17). In this sense, a person of the world lives for the pleasures of the flesh, but a dedicated Christian lives for the joys of the Spirit.

When John wrote his first epistle, Christianity had existed for more than 50 years. His audience faced the pressures of heretical ideas and uncertainty about their salvation. The ideas that would become full-blown gnosticism in the second century AD were already threatening Christianity. One of gnosticism's heretical beliefs was that salvation came through knowledge (Greek: gnosis, from which we have our word *diagnosis*). They also believed that Christ was a spirit who didn't exist in bodily form. The spiritual was viewed as always good, and the physical was viewed as always evil.

I. The Condition

(1 John 4:2-3)

A. Recognition (v. 2)

2. Hereby know ye the Spirit of God: Every spirit that confesseth that Jesus Christ is come in the flesh is of God.

This statement immediately follows John's stress on the need for discernment (1 John 4:1). One vital doctrine of Christianity is that of the divine-human nature of Jesus (John 1:1-18), and the situation in John's day called for the need to emphasize the fact that *Jesus* became *flesh* (see Lesson Context and 2 John 7).

But why was Jesus' having had a real, physical body important? Until the destruction of the temple in AD 70, animals were sacrificed yearly there on the Day of Atonement to remind the Jews that the shedding of blood was necessary to atone for their sins (Leviticus 16; compare Hebrews 9:22). Those sacrifices pointed to the sacrifice that Jesus would one day offer as He gave himself on the cross (Matthew 26:28). If Jesus did not come in the flesh, then He didn't have a body to sacrifice or blood to shed. Thus, it was essential that Jesus be not only fully God but also fully human in order to make salvation possible (1 Timothy 3:16).

Thus John provides a method by which to identify false prophets in this regard: *Every spirit that confesseth that Jesus Christ is come in the flesh is of God.* This test complements Jesus' own words in Matthew 7:15-17 and 24:23-26 regarding the need to identify false prophets.

> *What Do You Think?*
>
> How would you answer someone who claims that 1 John 4:2 contradicts Mathew 7:1, which says we are not to judge?
>
> *Digging Deeper*
>
> What passages in addition to 1 Corinthians 5:9-13 and 2 John 10-11 help frame your answer?

B. Reality (v. 3)

3a. And every spirit that confesseth not that Jesus Christ is come in the flesh is not of God.

As the church was born, the believers continued in "the apostles' doctrine" (Acts 2:42). But several decades later when John wrote his letters, certain people were disseminating false teaching about Christ and departing from the apostolic faith (see Lesson Context).

3b. And this is that spirit of antichrist, whereof ye have heard that it should come.

The word *antichrist* occurs only four times in the New Testament, and only in John's letters (here and 1 John 2:18a, 22; and 2 John 7). Bible students often try to identify this opponent as a singular individual, possibly the "man of sin . . . the son of perdition; who opposeth and exalteth himself above all that is called God, . . . shewing himself that he is God" in 2 Thessalonians 2:3-4 and/or as the (op)poser mentioned in Revelation 20:10.

However, these identifications run into great difficulty, given the fact that John also speaks of antichrist in the plural as he states that "even now are there many antichrists. . . . They went out from us" (1 John 2:18b-19). As we consider how that fact dovetails with the verse before us, we should note that the Greek word behind the translation *spirit* occurs about 380 times in the New Testament. As such, it can refer to different things depending on context. Here, the word *spirit* refers to those who claim to have the inside track on divine communication (see also 2 Thessalonians 2:2).

3c. And even now already is it in the world.

The spirit that was *already* at work in John's time thrives yet today. The Lesson Context explains the differing senses that phrase *the world* can take throughout the New Testament. But we want to zero in on how John uses the term, given that about half the occurrences of the phrase *the world* in the New Testament are in John's inspired books, which themselves constitute only about 14 percent of the New Testament.

The world to John usually refers to sinful humanity. In this sense, the world (that is, humanity) is largely opposed to God (John 3:19). This is the world that has strayed far from its Creator.

II. The Encouragement

(1 John 4:13-17)

A. Holy Spirit (v. 13)

13. Hereby know we that we dwell in him, and he in us, because he hath given us of his Spirit.

A careful reading here might surprise us, because John wrote not only of the *Spirit* dwelling in the heart of the believer (*he in us*) but also *that we dwell in him.* God gives His Spirit not only to dwell in our hearts but also to make it possible that we dwell in the heart of the Father.

This is similar to Jesus' saying, "Abide in me, and I in you" (John 15:4). Our relationship with God is not a one-way street. As God gives us His Spirit, we give God ourselves—we dwell in Him. Paul, in addressing the Athenians, quoted a pagan philosopher as saying correctly that "in him we live, and move, and have our being" (Acts 17:28).

When a person is guided by the Holy Spirit, he or she produces the fruit of the Spirit (Galatians 5:22-26). Thus that becomes a test (contrast Matthew 7:15-20).

B. Confession (vv. 14-15)

14. And we have seen and do testify that the Father sent the Son to be the Saviour of the world.

The *we* refers to the apostles, whom Christ chose as His special messengers (1 John 1:1). Of the original apostolic band, John was likely the only one still living when he wrote in the AD 80s or 90s. He knew that his time was short, so he felt compelled to *testify* yet again before the grave took him as well.

Jesus revealed the Father to sinful humanity as a loving God who has never given up on His lost children, *the world* in rebellion against Him (John 3:17; 1 John 4:3, above). There was nothing accidental or incidental about Jesus' mission; He was *sent* to save. Nothing was more important or central than that for John.

15. Whosoever shall confess that Jesus is the Son of God, God dwelleth in him, and he in God.

HOW TO SAY IT

Augustus	Aw-*gus*-tus.
Ephesus	*Ef*-uh-sus.
epistles	ee-*pis*-uls.
gnosticism	***nahss***-tih-*sizz*-um.
gnostics	*nahss*-ticks.
heresy	*hair*-uh-see.
heretic	*heh*-ruh-tick.
Thessalonians	*Thess*-uh-***low***-nee-unz (*th* as in *thin*).

A purpose running throughout this letter is to answer the implied question, "How do I know I am in a true, saving fellowship with God?" (see 1 John 2:5, 6). John answers this in several ways, and the verse before us provides one of those answers. The confession *Jesus is the Son of God* reflects belief. Even so, we realize that John is not suggesting that confession based on belief is the whole plan of salvation—even demons can make such a confession (see Matthew 8:29; compare James 2:19).

What John is talking about, rather, is embracing Jesus as the authoritative Lord of one's life while rejecting any influence the "spirit of antichrist" (1 John 4:3, above) might have to offer. To confess Jesus in this sense is to follow Him exclusively in a trusting relationship of faith and service. Such a person lives in the presence of God and allows God's Spirit to live in his or her life at the deepest level (compare John 20:31). Other things follow confession in the plan of salvation (see Acts 2:38-39; etc.), but confession is foundational.

A Divine Intervention

In my role as a minister, I've observed a few addiction interventions. One intervention was called because the addict had been driving drunk on several occasions. He denied that he had an addiction. He'd never been arrested or involved in an accident, so his behavior couldn't be too bad—or so he thought.

Members of the man's family told him how his increasingly erratic behavior was affecting them. One by one, they declared their love for him and in vivid terms expressed the emotional pain his behavior was causing. But it was the threat of losing everyone and everything he held dear that finally brought him to acknowledge reluctantly his need for treatment.

Human sin called for an intervention, a vivid demonstration of God's love and holiness. The mission of Jesus was that divine intervention, as it demonstrated both God's love and His holy nature. God warns of the judgment that awaits if we do not respond to His loving and holy Son. Will you remain in denial of your own sin or seek treatment from "the great physician"? —C. R. B.

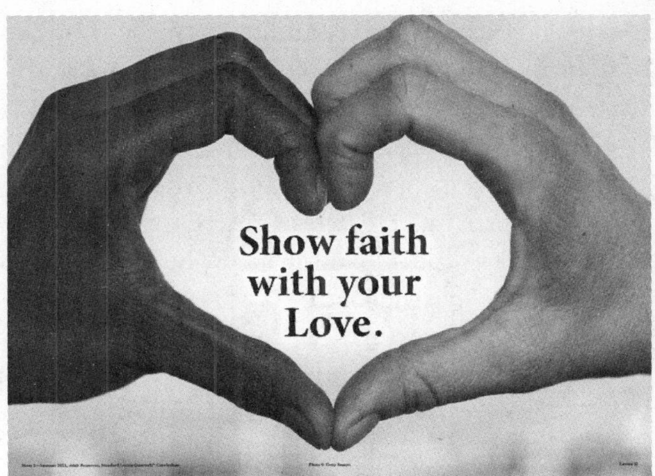

Visual for Lesson 12. *Start a discussion by pointing to this visual and turning its statement into an application question of "How?"*

C. Relationship (v. 16)

16. And we have known and believed the love that God hath to us. God is love; and he that dwelleth in love dwelleth in God, and God in him.

John is often called "the apostle of love," and with good reason: he uses the word *love* by proportion more that any other writer of the New Testament. More than 30 such uses are found in this epistle of 1 John—that's more than once every hundred words! He alone uses the phrase *God is love* (here and in 1 John 4:8). His intent is to assure us of our standing with God as His *love* dwells within us. Here the word *we* includes all who believe in the Son. We become stronger as the love of God is shed abroad in us by the Holy Spirit (Romans 5:5).

In the verse before us, *the love that God hath to us* explains more fully how we dwell in Him. This is a description of relationship. When we understand and accept that love, our relationship is determined. It is a relationship of loving trust, so much so that John can say we live in God and He in us. As we love Jesus, we will keep His commandments (John 14:15; 15:10; 1 John 5:3). Love for Jesus is not based on emotion but on commitment. An indication of this commitment is our love for fellow Christians (1 John 4:19-21). A person can't love Christians without loving God and can't love God without loving the family of God.

This fact cannot be separated from the thought of 1 John 4:15, our previous verse, which conditions our relationship to God with our acknowledgment of Christ as His Son. We cannot accept Jesus as the Son of God without understanding the loving sacrifice His cross represents, a defining expression of God's love for us. When we understand and receive the love of God, it makes us into persons of love as well.

What Do You Think?

In your prayer life, how should you balance the fact of God's love with the fact that He is holy?

Digging Deeper

How do passages such as Hebrews 7:26; 1 Peter 1:15; and Revelation 3:7; 4:8 help frame your response?

D. Judgment (v. 17)

17. Herein is our love made perfect, that we may have boldness in the day of judgment: because as he is, so are we in this world.

Christians have nothing to fear about *the day of judgment* because the judge has already proven His love for us. Those who have reason to fear that day are Satan and anyone—from any era and any nation—who follows the spirit of antichrist (1 John 4:3, above; Revelation 21:7-8).

God will not reverse course and punish those upon whom He has lavished His love. We can have confidence in this fact as we experience the love of God and express that love to others (compare 1 John 2:28; 3:3, 19-21; 4:18, not in our printed text).

III. The Faith

(1 John 5:4-5)

A. Continual (v. 4)

4. For whatsoever is born of God overcometh the world: and this is the victory that overcometh the world, even our faith.

The Christian life begins with *faith* and ends with faith (Romans 1:17). But faith is more than just emotions or intellectual assent (see James 2:14-26). The person having only an emotional or intellectual experience of faith has a dead faith. Such a person knows the right words, but does not back up those words with actions *that overcometh the world*. The faithful mind understands the truth; the faithful heart desires the truth; and the faithful will acts on the truth. John describes this faith as being *born of God* (see 1 John 5:1-2, 18-19).

To overcome is to work actively against the flawed principles by which the world lives (Colossians 2:8, 20-23; see 1 John 4:3, above). The outworking of such principles may be expressed in many categories (see Mark 7:20-23; Romans 1:29-31; Galatians 5:19-21; 1 Peter 2:1). We can sum these up by saying that the world's values are polar opposites to God's command to love one another. When we practice love, we join with Jesus in saying, "I have overcome the world" (John 16:33).

What Do You Think?

What are some ways to encourage a person of dead faith to embrace Christ anew?

Digging Deeper

How do you do so without resorting to a legalistic list of dos and don'ts?

B. Foundational (v. 5)

5. Who is he that overcometh the world, but he that believeth that Jesus is the Son of God?

Jesus is the Greek form of the Hebrew name *Joshua*, both of which mean "savior." In several places in addition to the verse before us, John stresses the fact that the Savior *is the Son of God* (1 John 1:7; 3:8, 23; 4:9, 15). The designation *Son of God* refers to Jesus' "only begotten" status in relation to the heavenly Father (John 1:14, 18; 3:16, 18).

This claim directly opposed those of the first-century Roman world who considered Emperor Augustus and other emperors to be sons of a god. Jewish leaders of the day didn't like Jesus' claim any more than their Roman counterparts did. So they demanded that Jesus should die for blasphemy in that regard (Matthew 26:62-66; compare John 10:31-36).

On what it means to overcome *the world*, see again the Lesson Context and commentary on 1 John 5:4. Both this physical world and its unholy value systems will pass away. But the person who obeys God will live forever (1 John 2:17). John further describes the victory to come in Revelation 3:5, 12, 21. Those who believe the truth about Jesus and act on that truth share in that victory.

> *What Do You Think?*
>
> What is a small way to engage with the world this week instead of retreating from it?
>
> *Digging Deeper*
>
> Would you describe this as being "in the world" but not "of the world" (John 17:11-18)? Why, or why not?

Rekindling the Fire

Newlyweds often want to be together continuously. When issues of everyday life begin to intrude, however, distance can result. For example, if children enter the picture, caring for them can shift the nature of the marital relationship. A couple may decide they no longer love each other because of such shifts.

If they are wise, however, they will seek the guidance of a trusted counselor who will help them to "rekindle the fire." The counseling may result in both parties realizing they should act in loving ways even when (or especially when) they don't feel like it.

This is wise. Since hearts, minds, and bodies work together, then acting in a loving manner (as we know we should) can pull our hearts and minds along the same path.

This applies to the church as well regarding interactions among all Christians. When we find ourselves not "feeling our faith," then acting in the loving ways that we know a faithful Christian should can rekindle the fires of faith. When we focus our attention on living the faith, we will find ourselves overcoming the pull of the world that would draw us away from Christ.

When was the last time you experienced this kind of victory? —C. R. B.

Conclusion

A. Victory

We can have victory and overcome the world only through faith in Jesus Christ, the Son of God. We can overcome as we allow the Holy Spirit, sent after Jesus' ascension, to empower us to do so. God put this plan into action even though those created in His image rejected Him time after time (John 1:10-11; 3:16).

Despite this rejection, God still seeks to save people from a fate of eternal death (2 Peter 3:9). God's plan for this still centers on the life, death, resurrection, and ascension of His beloved Son, Jesus. The plan remains the same today as in the first century AD; it has not changed. In His life, Jesus proved His identity; in His death, Jesus paid the penalty for sin; in His resurrection, Jesus defeated the power of death; in His ascension, He reigns forevermore.

At His second coming, Jesus will rid the world of sin and welcome His children home. Hallelujah! What a Savior we have! Those facts allow us to have confidence as we face the challenges of the world. And as we obey Jesus, we can assist others to do so as well.

> *What Do You Think?*
>
> Which part of today's lesson do you struggle with most? Why?
>
> *Digging Deeper*
>
> What action will you take this week to remedy this problem?

B. Prayer

Heavenly Father, thank You for Your love expressed in sending Your Son to die for the sins of the world! Empower us to overcome the world and model Your love to others. As we do, may we look ever forward to the day of Your Son's return, when we will share in His glory. We pray this in Jesus' name. Amen.

C. Thought to Remember

The only way to overcome the world
is through faith in Jesus.

INVOLVEMENT LEARNING

Enhance your lesson with KJV Bible Student *(from your curriculum supplier) and the reproducible activity page (at www.standardlesson.com or in the back of the* KJV Standard Lesson Commentary Deluxe Edition*).*

Into the Lesson

Write "LOVE" in large letters on the board. Divide the class into pairs or triads. Distribute handouts (you create) on which are printed both of the following tasks. Allow the groups to decide which one of the two they want to complete.

- **The ordinary person who has shown me the most love is ____.** Each group member takes one minute to respond to this prompt with the others in their group. After all have shared, group members may ask each other questions for more information about the persons described.
- **Love is a force today.** Group members use smartphones to look for recent examples of outstanding love. Each group member analyzes motives for the expressions.

After volunteers report results in whole-class discussion, making the following transitional statement: "The greatest motivator for love in our world is the love demonstrated by Jesus Christ. But that love also involves some negative angles. Let's see how and why."

Into the Word

Distribute handouts (you prepare) with the following questions. Have students work in the above groups to answer, using today's Scripture text. Some answers are directly in the text; others require specific application of a general principle or command.

1–What are some ways to test spirits to see whether they are from God?
2–When we do that testing, aren't we violating Jesus' command to "judge not" in Matthew 7:1?
3–How can we know we're dwelling in God?
4–How is it that our love can be made perfect?
5–What should be the Christian's attitude toward the world?
6–What qualities are necessary for us to have the right attitude toward the world around us?

Allow up to eight minutes for this activity, and then ask volunteers to share discoveries. *Responses* should be based on the following references: 1–1 John 4:2; 2–Matthew 7:1 is not a blanket statement against all discerning and evaluating; see also Matthew 7:15-20; 1 Corinthians 5:11-13; etc.; 3–1 John 4:13, 16-17; 4–1 John 4:17; 5–1 John 5:4; 6–1 John 5:4-5.

Option. Ask class members, in the same groups, to create a one-sentence devotional message from this text on the theme "The Christian and the World." After six minutes, ask volunteers to share their sentences with the class as a whole.

Into Life

Give each participant a slip of paper on which you have printed the following issues, one per slip:

serious illness / job loss / parent-child conflict / marital stress / neighborhood issues / financial setback / personal sin

If you desire small-group discussion, give each group one slip; if you desire whole-class discussion, give each learner one slip. Then write this question on the board:

What are three ways you could model God's love to someone who is mired in the situation on your slip of paper?

If you chose small-group consideration, allow several minutes. (*Option.* Extend this consideration by distributing copies of the "Love ≠ Apathy" exercise on the activity page, which you can download. After several minutes of discussion in pairs, or one minute of individual work, call for volunteers to share in whole-class discovery.)

Option. Distribute copies of the "Overcoming the World" exercise on the activity page. Have participants work individually to complete it as indicated in one minute. In the ensuing discussion, also discuss the different senses of what it means to love the world as depicted in John 3:16 and 1 John 2:16.

An Eternal Hope

Devotional Reading: Romans 7:14-26
Background Scripture: 2 Corinthians 4:16–5:10

2 Corinthians 4:16-18

16 For which cause we faint not; but though our outward man perish, yet the inward man is renewed day by day.
17 For our light affliction, which is but for a moment, worketh for us a far more exceeding and eternal weight of glory;
18 While we look not at the things which are seen, but at the things which are not seen: for the things which are seen are temporal; but the things which are not seen are eternal.

2 Corinthians 5:1-10

1 For we know that if our earthly house of this tabernacle were dissolved, we have a building of God, an house not made with hands, eternal in the heavens.
2 For in this we groan, earnestly desiring to be clothed upon with our house which is from heaven:
3 If so be that being clothed we shall not be found naked.
4 For we that are in this tabernacle do groan, being burdened: not for that we would be unclothed, but clothed upon, that mortality might be swallowed up of life.
5 Now he that hath wrought us for the selfsame thing is God, who also hath given unto us the earnest of the Spirit.
6 Therefore we are always confident, knowing that, whilst we are at home in the body, we are absent from the Lord:
7 (For we walk by faith, not by sight:)
8 We are confident, I say, and willing rather to be absent from the body, and to be present with the Lord.

9 Wherefore we labour, that, whether present or absent, we may be accepted of him.
10 For we must all appear before the judgment seat of Christ; that every one may receive the things done in his body, according to that he hath done, whether it be good or bad.

Key Verse

We know that if our earthly house of this tabernacle were dissolved, we have a building of God, an house not made with hands, eternal in the heavens. **—2 Corinthians 5:1**

Confident Hope

Unit 3: Faith Gives Us Hope

Lessons 10–13

Lesson Aims

After participating in this lesson, each learner will be able to:

1. Summarize the basis of Christian confidence.
2. Explain the sense and reference of one or more of Paul's metaphors.
3. Write two brief explanations of the basis of Christian confidence: one to a discouraged believer, and the other to a hard-core unbeliever.

Lesson Outline

Introduction

A. Faith, Not Sight

A science-fiction movie portrays a future world where an evil alien monster can influence people through eyesight. Those infected this way commit destructive acts, even suicide. The solution is to live blindfolded—unable to be infected but also ill-equipped to navigate the currents of life. A climactic scene has the heroine attempting to navigate a dangerous river with two small children, all three blindfolded in a rowboat.

That fictional tale bears resemblance in some ways, but not in others, regarding how a Christian is to live. Christians are not "blind" to the evils of the world. We see them. And the way we can avoid that dark influence is because we also "see" the Lord's way—the way of faith based on evidence. Ours is not a blind(folded) faith. It is a faith based on evidence, a faith grounded in the facts of history. When a crisis looms, will we walk by faith or by something else (see Proverbs 3:5)?

B. Lesson Context

As Paul wrote 2 Corinthians in AD 57, his contemplation of death was more than a spiritual exercise. Paul admitted to his readers that adverse circumstances resulted in being "pressed out of measure, above strength, insomuch that we despaired even of life" (2 Corinthians 1:8; compare 11:24-27).

This expectation of the potential end of his life forms the background for almost everything he writes in the initial chapters of 2 Corinthians. However, he emerges from this contemplation with a triumphant note, proclaiming in 4:8-9: "We are troubled on every side, yet not distressed; we are perplexed, but not in despair; persecuted, but not forsaken; cast down, but not destroyed."

Paul did not allow the prospect of death to deter him from his mission to bring the gospel to Gentiles in cities like Corinth. Some of Paul's anguish may have been caused by false teachers who had come to Corinth to undermine his teachings and his authority. These are the sarcastically designated "very chiefest apostles" referred to in 2 Corinthians 11:5; 12:11. Whether their opposition included death threats is uncertain. But we know that Paul's opponents were not above resorting to such intimidation (example: Acts 18:12-17).

Even so, Paul did not fear dying, for he knew that Jesus had defeated death (1 Corinthians 15:12-32; 2 Corinthians 4:14). Paul also knew that in his day there were many theories of what happened to people after death. The Greeks generally believed in an underworld place, the realm of the dead ruled over by the god Hades. It was a place of residence for souls released from their bodies, resulting in a shadowy spiritual existence. This place, also called Hades, was thought to be filled with gloom and despair, with no hope of ever being released (compare Acts 17:32).

Some Jews and Greeks believed there was no existence after death. The party of the Sadducees was known for teaching there was no resurrection (Matthew 22:23). This was a minority opinion, though, for most Jews believed in a future resurrection of all the dead, who would receive reconstituted bodies in order to stand before God for judgment (examples: John 11:24; Acts 23:8). Being a Pharisee, this had been the general mindset of Paul as well (Acts 23:6). But the resurrection of Jesus from the dead on the third day (rather than at the end, at the general resurrection) brought everything into sharper focus.

I. Weight of Glory

(2 Corinthians 4:16-18)

A. Daily Renewal (v. 16)

16. For which cause we faint not; but though our outward man perish, yet the inward man is renewed day by day.

Having made a strong point about resurrection in the previous verses, Paul moves into the implications. In so doing, he begins by using a Greek word translated *for which cause* that he uses elsewhere seven more times in this book. The translations in these other seven are "wherefore" (2 Corinthians 2:8; 5:9 [see below]; 6:17), "therefore" (4:13 [twice]; 12:10), and "and in" (1:20).

This particular word usually implies that what the writer has just been talking about is self-evident. Paul spoke openly in the previous section concerning the prospect of his death, hinting that his life was in jeopardy (see Lesson Context). This threat, while dire, did not deter him from his mission. He preached Christ, not himself or his fears (2 Corinthians 4:5). This is his point: whether in the short-term or the long-term, Paul knew his life was temporary—and that earthly life was relatively less important than eternal life.

Therefore, Paul said he had found great peace, even in (or especially in) dangerous and discouraging circumstances. Even were his life not to end soon, the effects of aging and stress were only the *outward man* perishing little by little. Paul was growing stronger in his *inward man*—his heart and spirit—as a result of his relationship with the Lord. Daily, constantly, he found inner renewal (compare Ephesians 3:16). That was what kept him going.

What Do You Think?

What is the most important change you would have to make to your daily routine in order to make inner renewal a priority?

Digging Deeper

Predict how Satan might attempt to prevent you from doing so.

B. Momentary Affliction (v. 17)

17a. For our light affliction, which is but for a moment.

Paul put into perspective the dangers regarding his safety and longevity by calling the threats a *light affliction*. Qualifying this as *our* extends his comforting perspective to all of us. No one is exempt from worries caused by our mortality and the eventual death of those we love. But when compared to the eternity that makes up our future, these tribulations are *but for a moment*.

17b. Worketh for us a far more exceeding and eternal weight of glory.

In contrast to these "light afflictions," Paul extols the heaviness of the *weight* of our future *glory*. This is a play on words. Paul writes in Greek, but he is fluent in Hebrew as well. In the latter language, the word for *heavy* (as in "weight") is the same as the word for *honor* (as in "glory"). Thus

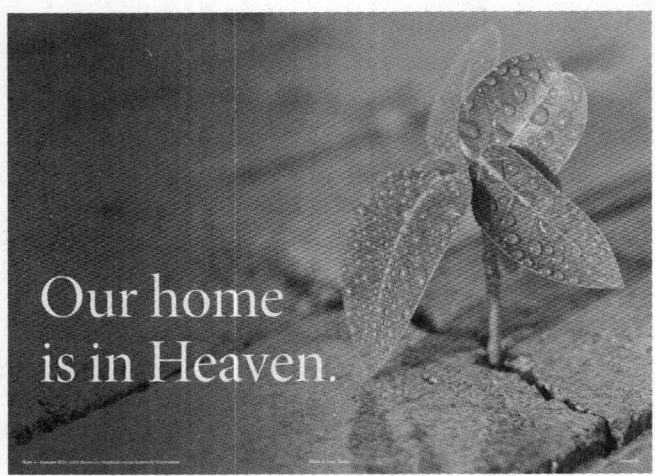

Visual for Lesson 13. *Start a discussion as you point to this visual and ask, "How would your life change if you voiced this from memory daily?"*

he used dramatic phrasing to frame the nature of our future in eternity. As we ponder this, however, we should not understand Paul as saying that the "light afflictions" are ultimately irrelevant. The phrase *worketh for us* carries the sense of "causeth" (as the same word is translated in 2 Corinthians 9:11). Our struggles with life will yield the result of inexpressible and unimaginable glory.

C. Eternity Unseen (v. 18)

18. While we look not at the things which are seen, but at the things which are not seen: for the things which are seen are temporal; but the things which are not seen are eternal.

Paul continues to speak in paradox. We should not focus our sights on troubles in life but instead turn our attention to *things which are not seen*. The things that we can see last for a short time (*are temporal*). Such things may seem significant right now, but this significance fades with time. The things we cannot see have much greater importance because they *are eternal.*

To see the unseen, we must have eyes of faith, trusting the testimony God has provided. We do not want to be "without excuse," the verdict on those who fail to discern the invisible qualities of God even though they should (Romans 1:20). Even more, how do we experience the eternal, our future "weight of glory"? We must do this with hearts of faith, not crushed by the complexities and disappointments of life. We must live out the assurance that comes from believing God raised Jesus from the dead and will raise us too (1 Corinthians 15).

II. Reality of the Spirit

(2 Corinthians 5:1-5)

A. What We Know (vv. 1-3)

1. For we know that if our earthly house of this tabernacle were dissolved, we have a building of God, an house not made with hands, eternal in the heavens.

Paul uses various metaphors to contrast the temporary with the eternal in this letter. In the verse before us, he draws on biblical imagery of a *tabernacle* as a way of understanding our bodily existence (compare 2 Peter 1:13-14). The tabernacle was a movable tent that was eventually replaced by the temple. Thus the metaphor emphasizes the impermanent nature of our bodies. Paul did not fear the destruction of the *earthly house* of his physical body because he had assurance of another *building,* a permanent structure. This *eternal* dwelling place has a prime real-estate location: it is *in the heavens.*

2-3. For in this we groan, earnestly desiring to be clothed upon with our house which is from heaven: if so be that being clothed we shall not be found naked.

This situation of living faithfully while faced with impending death brought Paul to a state of groaning, a word he uses for inward longing (2 Corinthians 5:4, below; Romans 8:23). The challenges of this life sometimes overshadow the magnificence of our future life in glory. A few years later, as Paul endured imprisonment in Rome, he went on to say, "For to me to live is Christ, and to die is gain" (Philippians 1:21).

What Do You Think?

How can you help your church set up a ministry that encourages its members to reach out to one another in times of "groaning"?

Digging Deeper

What problems are likely to occur in churches where members in distress reach out only to a staff member in such times?

Another metaphor for the human body is that of clothing, often conveyed with the phrase "put on." In this world, we "put on the armour of light" (Romans 13:12); we "put on Christ" in baptism (Galatians 3:27); we "put on the new man" and "put on the whole armour of God" (Ephesians 4:24; 6:11); we "put on the new man" as we put on virtues that culminate in charity, or love (Colossians 3:10-14). In the next world, when we are given resurrection bodies, we "put on incorruption, and . . . immortality" (1 Corinthians 15:53). We need not fear some type of spiritual nakedness. Death will not obliterate our identity but, rather, confirm and enhance it if we have "put on Christ."

B. Why It's Important (vv. 4-5)

4. For we that are in this tabernacle do groan, being burdened: not for that we would be unclothed, but clothed upon, that mortality might be swallowed up of life.

Paul further comments on the reality of the "right now" vs. the coming reality of the "not yet." The burdens of life are known so well and experienced so often that we need not even offer any examples—they are in the public domain of common knowledge. The main problem with these burdens is that in directing our attention to the "as is," we take our eyes off of the "to be." Paul's acknowledgement in this regard builds on what Jesus said (see Luke 8:14; 21:34-36).

Paul makes it clear that we should not expect a future existence without a body. Unlike some Greek philosophers of his time, Paul, a Pharisee, would never expect a permanent, eternal existence as some sort of free-floating spirit (compare Acts 17:32; 23:6-8; 24:15; see also Lesson Context). What he longed for was the new body at the time when *mortality*, with all its limitations and frailties, would *be swallowed up of life*. As Paul stressed to the Corinthians in his first letter, in resurrection, "death is swallowed up in victory" (1 Corinthians 15:54; compare Isaiah 25:8; Hosea 13:14).

Camping?

I once heard a stand-up comedian explain in only five words why he never went camping: "Because I have a house."

He then went on to poke fun at an imagined sequence of events. Our ancient ancestors initially slept out in the open. With the passage of time, they eventually saw the advantage of sleeping in caves. As more time passed, they moved on to sleeping in huts. After a few years of that, can it be imagined that anyone would say, "I've got an idea—let's go back to the cave for the weekend!" The comedian then elaborated on how camping appliances were little more than poor imitations of appliances at home.

Being a non-camper myself, all this rang hilariously true to me. I think I understand the appeal of camping (getting close to the creation gets you closer to the Creator, etc.). But the bottom line is that I don't go camping because I have a house.

Yet as much as I like to hang my hat on that fact, I must occasionally remind myself that my earthly houses—my current physical body and my place of physical residence—are both temporary. I should be a good steward of both resources, while not trying to cling too tightly to either. Hmm . . . Could it be that campers have an advantage over us non-campers in that regard? —R. L. N.

5. Now he that hath wrought us for the selfsame thing is God, who also hath given unto us the earnest of the Spirit.

Paul retreats a bit from this future celebration of his own freedom from death to bring a present reality to his readers. We do not just await the glorious gifts of God; we enjoy some of them now. Chief among these blessings is *the Spirit* of God, given as an *earnest of* these future things. We may think of "earnest money" in a real-estate transaction: a potential buyer puts down a deposit

HOW TO SAY IT

Corinthians	Ko-*rin*-thee-unz (*th* as in *thin*).
Hades	*Hay*-deez.
Pharisees	*Fair*-ih-seez.
Sadducees	*Sad*-you-seez.
tabernacle	***tah***-burr-*nah*-kul.
theophanies	the-*ah*-fuh-neez (*th* as in *thin*).
Thessalonians	*Thess*-uh-***lo***-nee-unz (*th* as in *thin*).

to indicate that the offer to purchase is a serious one. The presence/gift of the Holy Spirit in our hearts, given at baptism (Acts 2:38-39), assures us that God fully intends to carry out His side of the covenantal contract (see also Romans 8:16-23; 2 Corinthians 1:22; Ephesians 1:12-14).

III. Walk of Faith

(2 Corinthians 5:6-10)

A. Our Confidence (vv. 6-8)

6. Therefore we are always confident, knowing that, whilst we are at home in the body, we are absent from the Lord.

During the time we exist in our current bodies, we cannot experience the full presence of God. To be *at home* in our present bodies means to be *absent from* the closest presence of *the Lord*. This was the result of the sins of Adam and Eve in the Garden of Eden; the resulting separation and banishment included the loss of direct fellowship with the Lord (Genesis 3:23).

God's holy nature does not tolerate sin in His presence (compare 1 Peter 1:15-16). His holy nature is connected with His glory (Isaiah 6:2-3), and His glory is too great for sinful humans to endure. As the Lord told Moses, "Thou canst not see my face: for there shall no man see me, and live" (Exodus 33:20; compare John 1:18; 1 John 4:12). Places where humans apparently see God directly are what are called *theophanies*—visible manifestations of God, but not God in the fullness of His being (examples: Genesis 32:24-30; Exodus 18:12; 33:11; Isaiah 6:5). Something of a reversal will occur when Jesus returns; at that time, "we shall be like him; for we shall see him as he is" (1 John 3:2).

7. (For we walk by faith, not by sight:).

Our lives must be controlled by the things we know to be true in a sense of faith that is based on evidence. Paul expresses this in one of the greatest statements of the Christian life: we must *walk by faith, not by sight.* Paul's own ministry stands as a testimony to this mind-set, as indicated by his enduring great hardships in obedience to his calling and purpose in ministry (see 2 Corinthians 11:23-29; compare John 20:29).

What Do You Think?

Where is the Lord calling you in your faith walk?

Digging Deeper

What is the single greatest "by sight" challenge that seems to be interfering with this call? How can you overcome it?

Flying as Faith?

Would travel by air be an example of faith? Think about it. We get into a massive machine that is much heavier than air, and we willingly yield control of our lives for a couple of hours to people we don't know. We do so even when visibility is at or near zero. We do so even though we might not understand how the GPS navigation works its wonders. We do so even when we are very well aware of the plane crashes we hear about from time to time.

All the above has to do with a certain type of faith—and there's more than one type. We might call this type "airplane faith"; it is a faith based on historical evidence that chances are much greater than 99 percent that your plane will make it to its destination safely. It is not "blind faith," another type, which is mere belief in something without any objective basis for that belief.

Our faith in the future that God promises is not a blind faith. Rather, it's faith based on the historical fact that God's track record is that of 100 percent reliability, as centuries of historical evidence prove. Is that the kind of faith you have and witness of to others? If not, why not?

—C. R. B.

8. We are confident, I say, and willing rather to be absent from the body, and to be present with the Lord.

Once more Paul affirmed that death did not deter him or cause him to be fearful. He was *confident* in his ministry and life. If God called him *to be absent from the body* (to die), he would accept that willingly. He knew that his death would mean experiencing the full presence of *the Lord*, the full inheritance of his salvation, of which the Holy Spirit was the down payment.

What Do You Think?

What is the single most important change you should make to have more of the kind of confidence of which Paul speaks?

Digging Deeper

What will be your greatest challenge to overcome in doing so?

B. Our Labor (vv. 9-10)

9. Wherefore we labour, that, whether present or absent, we may be accepted of him.

Regarding the opening *wherefore,* see commentary on 2 Corinthians 4:16, above. By this conjunction Paul connects the ideas of our *labour* and being *accepted of him* with being "present with the Lord" of 5:8, just considered. To labor for Christ is not to work for salvation (Ephesians 2:8-9) but to express gratitude as we show that way to others (John 14:15, 23-24; 15:10; 1 Thessalonians 1:3; 1 John 5:3). There are common elements to every Christian's labors (example: 1 Thessalonians 4:9-12). But there are other elements of labor that are unique to the individual (example: Romans 15:20).

10. For we must all appear before the judgment seat of Christ; that every one may receive the things done in his body, according to that he hath done, whether it be good or bad.

The reasoning that follows the *for we* introduction to this verse stands in something of a chain reaction to the "wherefore" result of the previous verse. While we unreservedly look forward to being "accepted of him" (previous verse, above), Paul wanted his readers to remember that actions in this world (*the things done in* [the] *body*) are important and are known to God.

At *the judgment seat of Christ* will occur an evaluation of our lives (see Romans 2:6). This picture of a time of future, heavenly judgment is consistent in Paul's teachings (examples: Acts 17:31; 24:25; Romans 14:10). Christians are already justified (that is, treated as "not guilty") in the eyes of God because the penalty for sin was paid on the cross (see Romans 3:21-26; 5:16). Any misgivings about having to endure judgment are far outweighed by the promise of glory Jesus has purchased for us.

Conclusion

A. Faith, Not Sight Revisited

Paul's world was not a safe place. Cities could be impersonal and nasty. Villages could be hostile and dangerous for outsiders. Roadways always harbored the threat of bandits. Ships could be swamped by storms or attacked by pirates. Even in a case of assault or robbery, justice in court was often unavailable or corrupt. People needed to be ever wary and alert for danger. It seemed prudent to live just day by day in a self-protecting manner.

Even today we hear of incidents that scare us: "Widow bilked out of life savings by online dating." "Ten-year-old girl in a crosswalk struck and killed by texting driver." "Super-infection detected that resists any known treatment." It is easy to despair.

For many, life lurches from one crisis to another. To look beyond one's present sufferings seems impossible. But that is what Paul calls us to do. We are not to fear death. We already enjoy the peace and comfort of the Holy Spirit. Rather than our succumbing to despair, Paul challenges us to walk by faith, not by sight. Yes, we must endure and manage life's crises as they come. But we do so knowing that God is in control and our future is sure. Take a minute to evaluate. Do you walk primarily by faith or by sight?

What Do You Think?

What concept in today's lesson is most difficult for you to see "faith walk" value in? Why?

Digging Deeper

With what spiritually mature person can and will you discuss your misgivings?

B. Prayer

Father, it is tempting to respond to life's challenges using only our own resources. May we instead have faith to trust You, to live as You would have us live. We pray in the name of the one who conquered death, Jesus. Amen.

C. Thought to Remember

Base hope in faith, not sight!

Involvement Learning

Enhance your lesson with KJV Bible Student *(from your curriculum supplier) and the reproducible activity page (at www.standardlesson.com or in the back of the* KJV Standard Lesson Commentary Deluxe Edition*).*

Into the Lesson

Write the phrases "Short-term things" and "Long-term things" on the board as headers of two columns. Ask participants for everyday examples of each; write responses under the appropriate headers. (*Option.* Depending on the nature of your class, change the word *things* to *concerns* or some other descriptor.) Ask students which of the two categories tends to catch their attention most on a daily basis. Follow the expected response of "short-term things" with discussion of why.

Alternative. Before learners arrive, place in chairs copies of the "Walk by What?" exercise from the activity page, which you can download. After learners complete as indicated, award a humorous "Faithful Lexicography" certificate (you prepare) to the learner with the most words that no one else has. Have more than one certificate on hand in case of ties.

After either activity, make a transition by noting that today's lesson has something to say about what the ultimate focus in life should be.

Into the Word

Have two volunteers read aloud today's text from 2 Corinthians, alternating with every verse. Use the Lesson Context to ensure that students grasp the nature of Paul's world in general and the situation of the church in Corinth in particular.

Prior to class, place bits of masking tape on the floor to form a walking course around the room. Call for two volunteers to walk this course. One will walk the course with eyes closed, and the other will act as a guide.

As the two finish, encourage free discussion regarding how the lesson text relates to what class members have just seen. (*Alternative.* Depending on the nature of your class, you may wish to narrate the activity in a hypothetical way instead of having two people actually walk a course.)

Divide the class into discussion pairs or triads. Write this question on the board for group discussion:

What is your greatest desire at the moment?

After a few minutes, reconvene and have a spokesperson from each group share responses for whole-class consideration. After each response, ask, "How does that desire relate to today's text?" Wrap up by asking what happens when people focus on having "Heaven on earth," instead of desiring what today's text says.

Ask someone with a smartphone to look up the Merriam-Webster definition of the noun *purpose* and state that definition for the class; write it on the board. (*Expected response:* "something set up as an object or end to be attained.") Then pose the following question as you write it and the definition on the board: "How does that word relate to today's text?" Encourage free discussion.

Alternative approach to the question. Before any discussion of the question, write on the board three answers of your own. Have learners discuss which of the three is most applicable or defensible; be prepared to do so yourself.

Option. As a posttest, distribute copies of the "Finish the Thoughts" exercise from the activity page. Announce a one-minute time limit, closed Bibles. Allow self-scoring of results.

Into Life

Form groups of three and distribute two blank index cards to each group. Write these instructions on the board:

Write two brief explanations of the basis of Christian confidence: one to a discouraged believer, the other to a hard-core unbeliever.

After groups finish, have them exchange their completed index cards with another group to seek improvements. Reconvene for whole-class consideration of all ideas.

Reproducible Student Activity Pages

Fall Quarter 2020 Love for One Another

YEP—THAT'S FAMILY!

Find the words in the Word List. Then circle the words in the list that are most painful to you personally. Why?

Y G V D Q G G X T P K A F N B F
S Z Q O Y O Y C N V J D O N M A
U E R K H S E Q G E Z I V A A V
O N D P H L F S T Y T A W J U O
L V E Q G Y Q U Z A R H Y E V R
A Y I E S T R A N G E M E N T I
E I N X L K R I U C F Q U V C T
J M E I A O M M O P T D O Y B I
P D L M E I E X T X G I X J K S
W A K J R N D Y P Y Y E O I U M
S J L C T S T R I F E W S N X N
W H S S T N M T C I L F N O C P
M I N F N R P I P B L F X U H S
D N T D C U Z S Z J I S D X E Q
R X V E V C H S U Z Y A L V I R
Z G C K X M X T P H F B S M L K

WORD LIST

ARGUMENTS
BIAS
CONFLICT
DISCRIMINATION
DYSFUNCTION
ENVY
ESTRANGEMENT
FAVORITISM
JEALOUSY
NEGLECT
STRIFE

EXEGESIS, NOT EISEGESIS

Exegesis is the explanation of a Scripture text based on a careful, objective analysis. *Eisegesis*, on the other hand, is the process of interpreting a text in terms of one's own agendas or biases as those are read into the text.

1. How can you guard against reading today's text through the lens of your own family conflicts?

2. How would you gently correct someone who is not being careful in that regard?

3. What other Scripture passages would you say are particularly susceptible to this danger?

Storytelling

From your acquaintances think of a Christian friend or family member who has experienced one of the following. Fill in the chart below with information about how he or she handled the misfortune and how his or her Christian faith was demonstrated during the process.

Problem	Person's Relationship to Me	How He or She Responded	Current Situation
Life-threatening illness			
Serious traffic accident			
Prolonged unemployment			
Sudden death of a family member			

Your Life Tree

Answer these questions:

What fruit do you see in your life?

____

What other fruit would you like to see in your life?

____

What beliefs about God keep you rooted in your faith?

____

How could you make your roots deeper and stronger?

____

Graphic: © rolandtopor

MOVIE PLOT: REVENGE IS MINE

Use the boxes below to describe or depict a series of scenes for a movie about an unbeliever who is contemplating revenge for being mistreated. Base the outcome on one of the following secular quotations; be prepared to discuss how it is unbiblical:

"Revenge is a powerful motivator" (Marcus Luttrell).
"No trait is more justified than revenge in the right time and place" (Meir Kahane).
"The best revenge is massive success" (Frank Sinatra).

Scene 1	Scene 2	Scene 3	Scene 4

Scene 5	Scene 6	Scene 7	Scene 8

"BE IT RESOLVED . . ."

Work as a team to create an argument for one side of a debate as assigned. The ***Affirmation*** side is to create a case that proposes that Joseph would have been justified in taking revenge. The ***Denial*** side is to create a compelling case for the opposite. Each side should anticipate the points the other side will make. Use one or more of these passages to bolster your side's position: Leviticus 19:18; Judges 15:7, 28; Jeremiah 20:10; Romans 12:19.

Points my team needs to stress:

____
____
____
____

What my team should be prepared to refute:

____
____
____
____

Lesson 4, Genesis 45:1-8, 10-15, KJV

JOSEPH'S ACTIONS AND MINE

Review the verses in the column below. Describe Joseph's actions; then speculate on what yours would have been had you been Joseph.

Situations	What did Joseph do?	What would you have done? Why?
v. 1, Joseph is alone with his brothers for the first time in years and . . .		
v. 4, Joseph remembers how his brothers mistreated him and . . .		
v. 5, Joseph reveals his identity and . . .		

GRATEFUL FOR GOD'S BLESSINGS

Romans 8:28 tells us, "all things work together for good to them that love God." That certainly came true for Joseph! Discuss a time when things seemed really bad for you, but God worked it out for good.

Use the lines below to write a prayer of gratitude: ____________________

VALUES MATRIX

Jacob's family members display a broad range of spiritual values—or lack thereof. List the spiritual values that you associate with the following people:

Reuben (Genesis 37:21-22; 49:3-4): ____________________

Judah (Genesis 38, 44:32-34; 49:8-12): ____________________

Joseph (Genesis 39, 49:22-26): ____________________

Jacob (Genesis 27:1-24; 30:25-43; 43:1-14): ____________________

Love that Intercedes

Lesson 5, 1 Samuel 19:1-7, KJV

What Could Go Wrong?

If any of the three main characters in today's lesson (Saul, Jonathan, David) had made different decisions, how might things have turned out? Complete the statements on the right.

What actually happened	What might have happened
1. Saul told Jonathan and his servants to kill David.	Jonathan was afraid to do anything and . . .
2. Jonathan warned David and told him to hide.	Jonathan realized that David might become king instead of him, so Jonathan . . .
3. David believed Jonathan and took his advice.	David mistrusted Jonathan's motives and . . .
4. Jonathan gave Saul compelling reasons for sparing David's life.	Jonathan made a half-hearted, token effort to change his father's mind and . . .
5. Saul heeded Jonathan's wise counsel and promised not to kill David.	Saul's jealousy got the better of him; not only did the death-order stand, but also . . .

Loyalty and Intercession

In what situations can and should you act as an intercessor? Complete any of the following sentences that apply.

Like Jonathan, I can try to work to help ______________________ [name] resolve a current conflict.

Like Jonathan, I can take risks by taking sides and trying to prevent ______________________

____

Like David, I can trust this friend or coworker to stand up for me. ______________________

Like Saul, I can come to my senses and relinquish my anger against ______________________ as I work to resolve our conflict.

Like Saul, I can pay attention to ______________________ [name]'s past and/or current attempts to help resolve a current conflict.

What New Testament passages in addition to Romans 12:18 spurs you to action on these? ______________

____

NATURAL OR GODLY

As the class works through Luke 6:27-36, use the following charts as note-takers. The first one in each chart is done for you as an example.

Enemy's Action	Natural Reaction	Godly Reaction
v. 27 Hates you	*Hate them back; be mean to them.*	*Love them and do good to them.*
v. 28a Curses you		
v. 28b Mistreats you		
v. 29a Slaps your cheek		
v. 29b Takes your cloak		
v. 30 Asks for a favor		

My Action	Natural Action	Godly Action
v. 31 Deciding how to treat others	*Treat them as good or bad as they treat you.*	*Know how you would like to be treated and do that to them.*
v. 32 Deciding whom to love		
v. 33 Deciding whom to do good things for		
v. 34 Deciding whom to lend something to		
v. 36 Deciding to whom you will give mercy		

NOW IT'S PERSONAL

What enemies do you have trouble loving? Post this where you will see it daily in the week ahead.

_____________ hates me, I will respond with love.
_____________ curses me, I will do the opposite in return.
_____________ mistreats me, I will respond with prayer.

I will be merciful as the Father has been to me.

Your Actions: A Case Study

You are driving along an interstate when you notice a car pulled over to the shoulder with its hood up and four-way flashers on. You realize you have at least three options:

- You can stop and offer help
- You can use your cell phone to call for help while you keep driving
- You can ignore the situation

What difference, if any, would these variables make in your decision?

- Time of day: light vs. dark
- Appearance of the driver: scruffy vs. well-dressed
- Location: desolate vs. well-traveled
- Passenger(s) in your car
- State of the weather
- Type of car, its age, condition, and bumper stickers

More Compassion, Less Rationalizing

From Jesus' story—

A surprising insight for me is . . .

____

____

One way I plan to be less like the lawyer, less rationalizing, is by . . .

____

____

One way I plan to be more like the Samaritan, more compassionate, is . . .

____

____

Lesson 8, 1 Corinthians 13:1-13, KJV

HEALTHY OR UNHEALTHY LOVE?

Identify which of the following are healthy (**H**) or unhealthy (**U**) acts of love.

__ 1. Finds pleasure in giving and receiving
__ 2. Rarely shows affection
__ 3. Expects unconditional love
__ 4. Cares but with detachment
__ 5. Looks to others for self-worth
__ 6. Allows individuality
__ 7. Invites growth of others
__ 8. Seeks to change others
__ 9. Does not seek unconditional love
__10. Seeks to get something by giving
__11. Fulfills the law (Romans 13:10)
__12. Believes in equal worth before God

What characteristics do you associate with healthy love? Why?

____
____
____

USING OUR GIFTS IN LOVE

Read through the list of spiritual gifts in Romans 12 and 1 Corinthians 12. Pick the one you believe is your strongest and write it in the box to the left. Then give seven examples of how you can better use it to express love each day this week.

My strongest spiritual gift is . . .

____

How I will better use that strength to express love . . .

Monday: ______________________________
Tuesday: ______________________________
Wednesday: ______________________________
Thursday: ______________________________
Friday: ______________________________
Saturday: ______________________________
Sunday: ______________________________

WHAT DOES THE CONTEXT IMPLY?

People misunderstood Jesus when they took His words literally in contexts where He intended to be understood figuratively (compare Matthew 16:5-12; John 10:1-6; 16:25-30; etc.). In which way is the word ***hour*** used in the passages below? Put a check in the correct box out to the right. Be prepared to explain why you made that choice.

	Literal use for 60 minutes?	Figurative for a time frame?
Matthew 20:12—These last have wrought but one **hour**, and thou hast made them equal unto us, which have borne the burden and heat of the day.		
Matthew 26:40—And he cometh unto the disciples, and findeth them asleep, and saith unto Peter, What, could ye not watch with me one **hour**?		
Luke 22:53—When I was daily with you in the temple, ye stretched forth no hands against me: but this is your **hour**, and the power of darkness.		
Luke 22:59—And about the space of one **hour** after another confidently affirmed, saying, Of a truth this fellow also was with him: for he is a Galilaean.		
John 13:1—Now before the feast of the passover, when Jesus knew that his **hour** was come that he should depart out of this world unto the Father, having loved his own which were in the world, he loved them unto the end.		
John 17:1—These words spake Jesus, and lifted up his eyes to heaven, and said, Father, the **hour** is come; glorify thy Son, that thy Son also may glorify thee.		

What does the above imply regarding interpretation of time references such as "day" (Genesis 1:5; 8:4; Nehemiah 9:3; John 9:4a; 1 Thessalonians 5:5a; etc.), "night" (Genesis 14:15; John 9:4b; 1 Thessalonians 5:5b; etc.); and "year" (Isaiah 61:2; Luke 3:1; 4:19; etc.)?

MY (UN)WILLINGNESS

Rank-order the following tasks from 1 (least unwilling to do) to 6 (most unwilling to do).

__ Clip a disabled person's toenails.
__ Clean up an alcoholic's vomit.
__ Help clean out the house of a hoarder.
__ Watch over a person suffering from Alzheimer's for two hours to give the primary caregiver a break.
__ Use up a vacation day from work to transport a wheelchair-bound person to a medical appointment.
__ Use up several vacation days to take a short-term mission trip to an area that has no running water.

How does today's lesson text convict you on changing unwillingness to willingness? Why?

Abiding Love

Lesson 10, John 15:4-17, KJV

Connecting

Graphic: © elenabs / iStock / Getty Images Plus

Circle the social media applications that you use.

Facebook	*Whatsapp*	*Tumblr*
Instagram	*SnapChat*	*Meetup*
Twitter	*LinkedIn*	*Reddit*
YouTube	*Messenger*	*[other]*
Pinterest	*QQ*	

Which do you find most helpful in connecting with friends and family? Why?____________________

What drawbacks does social media have in comparison with the connecting tools of the pre–social media era? Why? ____________________

Obeying

Compare the passages listed below and determine the common message:
John 15:17 1 Thessalonians 4:9 1 John 3:11

We are to

Do the same with these passages:
John 15:4 1 John 2:24, 27

We are to

Describe one area each where you find it especially difficult to obey these commands.

Confident Love

Lesson 11, 1 John 3:11-24, KJV

Simon Says

Discover the source of confidence we need by following the instructions below!

Source of Confidence

Regarding the phrase above . . .

Delete the last two vowels and every *C* ____________________

Move the fourth and fifth letters to the front ____________________

Change the first *O* to *A* and the final letter to *Y* ____________________

Place letters *TH* between the third and fourth vowels ____________________

Substitute the word *LABEL* for the letter *S* ____________________

Change every *F* to *R* and every *D* to *T* ____________________

Place an *I* after the first *L* ____________________

Reverse the order of the seventh and eighth letters ____________________

Delete the three letters following the second *R* ____________________

God's Outlook vs. World's Outlook

Fill in the blanks with the contrasts you see.

How do I view others?

The world says it's "survival of the fittest." —Herbert Spencer (1820–1903).

God says, "But whoso hath this world's good, and seeth his brother have need, and shutteth up his bowels *of compassion* from him, how dwelleth the love of God in him?" —1 John 3:17

The contrast I see is ____

How do we know what love is?

The world says, "Love is the master key that opens the gates of happiness." —Oliver Wendell Holmes (1841–1935)

God says, "Hereby perceive we the love of God, because he laid down his life for us: and we ought to lay down *our* lives for the brethren." —1 John 3:16

The contrast I see is ____

How should love make us feel?

The world says we feel uncertainty: "When a man is in love, he doubts, very often, what he most firmly believes." —François de La Rochefoucauld (1613–1680)

God says it's confidence: "There is no fear in love; but perfect love casteth out fear." —1 John 4:18

The contrast I see is ____

Lesson 12, Acts 4:32–5:11, KJV

Truth from an Atheist?

How would you evaluate the validity of the "we are born selfish" part of this statement (from an outspoken atheist) in terms of . . .

what the Bible says? ______________________________

your experience with any 2-year-old child? ______________________________

using or not using the old "consider the source" dictum? ______________________________

whether or not it's really all that important to decide if selfishness is something we're born with or is learned? ______________________________

My Response to Need

People in need are all around us! On the following list, rate the likelihood of your responding to each need on a scale of 1 (very unlikely to respond) to 5 (very likely to respond).

The homeless	1 2 3 4 5
Disaster victims	1 2 3 4 5
Cancer research	1 2 3 4 5
Clothing drives	1 2 3 4 5
Disabled veterans	1 2 3 4 5

What one thing will you do to improve in the area of your lowest score?

____

How do you include Matthew 25:40, 45 in improving your response?

____

____

____

HE'LL NEVER AMOUNT TO ANYTHING

Sometimes people are judged unfairly. Match the famous person with his less-than-stellar beginnings.

_____ 1. Flunked out of Yale University—twice!

_____ 2. Didn't speak fluently until age 9.

_____ 3. Screen-test evaluation read "Can't act. Can't sing. Balding. Can dance a little."

_____ 4. After an audition, he was told to go back to driving a truck.

_____ 5. Threw his first book in the trash after it was rejected 30 times.

_____ 6. Dropped out of Harvard to start a computer processing business that failed.

_____ 7. Fired from a newspaper for his lack of creativity and any good ideas.

_____ 8. Told by an editor that he did not know how to use the English language.

a. Stephen King
b. Fred Astaire
c. Rudyard Kipling
d. Albert Einstein
e. Dick Cheney
f. Walt Disney
g. Elvis Presley
h. Bill Gates

A PLACE FOR EVERYONE?

Part 1. Church signs proclaim that everyone is welcome to attend. But consider the following list of visitors who may show up on Sunday morning. Put a check mark beside the one most likely to make it difficult for the church to project the impartial love commanded in Scripture.

__A person obviously lacking in personal hygiene
__A person wearing clothing identifying him or her as a member of a gang
__A person with extensive tattoos and/or other body modifications
__A person wearing revealing clothing
__A person using profanity
__A person reeking of alcohol
__A person who seems to be dressed in contrast to his/her biological sex
__A person with a story of needing help, but who seems to be a con artist

Part 2. Describe an approach that a congregation can take that demonstrates that "mercy rejoiceth against judgment" (James 2:13) without compromising basic Christian values. How do "be wise" passages such as Matthew 10:16; Ephesians 5:15; and Colossians 4:5 contribute to the plan?

____

____

____

____

Lesson 1

Yep—That's Family!

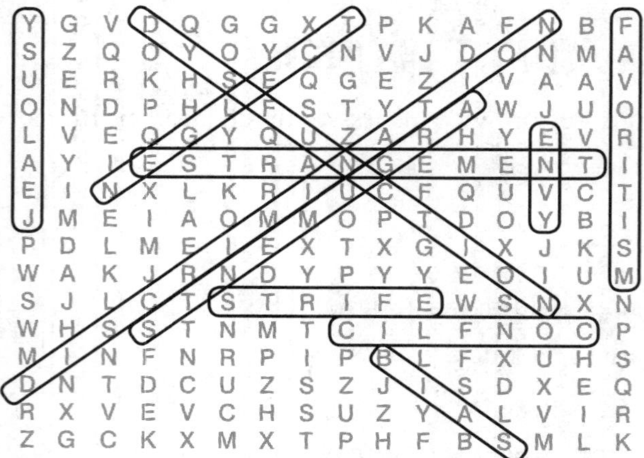

Exegesis—Not Eisegesis: Answers will vary. An obvious passage to mention for number 3 is the parable of the prodigal son (Luke 15:11-32).

Lesson 8

Suggested answers to **Is It Healthy or Unhealthy Love?**: **Healthy**=1, 6, 7, 9, 11, 12. **Unhealthy**=2, 3, 4, 5, 8, 10. Allow students with a different answer to explain their reasons.

Lesson 9

What Does the Context Imply? Matthew 20:12; 26:40; Luke 22:59 refer to a literal time frame of 60 minutes or something close to it. Luke 22:53; John 13:1; 17:1 are figurative for a larger framework of time.

Lesson 11

Simon Says: Reliable Authority

Lesson 12

Truth from an Atheist: Answers will vary.

Lesson 13

He'll Never Amount to Anything: 1=e. 2=d. 3=b. 4=g. 5=a. 6=h. 7=f. 8=c.

Reproducible Student Activity Pages

Winter Quarter 2020–2021 Call in the New Testament

Called to Be Heir

Lesson 1, Matthew 1-6, 16-17; Hebrews 1:1-5 KJV

Jesus' Heritage

The left column mentions a person from Jesus' human heritage. In the right column, tell something about each person or group of people that relates to Jesus.

1. Abraham	
2. Jacob	
3. Judas/Judah	
4. Rachab/Rahab and Ruth	
5. Booz/Boaz	
6. David	
7. Solomon	

Jesus, Our Savior

As you read the words of the following hymn, acknowledge that your spiritual heritage is in Jesus—and thank Him for that.

Jesus, My Savior, Is All Things to Me
by William James Kirkpatrick

Jesus, my Savior, is all things to me;
Oh, what a wonderful Savior is He,
Guiding, protecting, o'er life's rolling sea,
Mighty Deliv'rer—Jesus for me.

Jesus for me, Jesus for me,
All the time everywhere, Jesus for me.

He is my Refuge, my Rock, and my Tower,
He is my Fortress, my Strength and my Pow'r;
Life everlasting, my Daysman is He,
Blessed Redeemer—Jesus for me.

He is my Prophet, my Priest and my King,
He is my Bread of Life, Fountain and Spring;
Bright Sun of Righteousness, Daystar is He,
Horn of Salvation—Jesus for me.

How do you acknowledge that your spiritual heritage is in Jesus?

JOSEPH'S OPTIONS

Matthew 1:18-25 implies some options Joseph faced. Work with a partner or small group to finish the chart.

The Situation	What Joseph Did	What Joseph Could Have Done
Mary was expecting a baby, but Joseph was not the father.	Took Mary as his wife.	
The angel told Joseph to take Mary as his wife.	Believed the angel's message.	

STEP UP YOUR THANKS!

Step 1: Find 14 words applicable to today's lesson in the puzzle grid.
Step 2: In the space below write a prayer of thanksgiving for the gift of Jesus, using all 14 words you discovered.

Word List

GOD
JESUS
GIFT
GAVE
LOVE
BEST
SON
SINS
LIFE
FORGIVEN
ETERNAL
WORLD
SAVE
EMMANUEL

E K A I Z E O L N C S A J M
S V Z H Q E T K I O A Z E K
M L A Q S V G E H F V F S F
Z C S G N O S N R V E M U P
S I N S D L E T T N V P S A
N G H L I V Z W P N A X B T
R Z M N I W U W X S Z L S Q
B F R G F S O Y M V W E W Y
K G R A O R T F I G B G M G
P O A D L B E M M A N U E L
F K Z D X I O T E V J Q D P

WORSHIP AROUND THE WORLD

Worship happens everywhere. Take this true/false quiz about worship around the world.

True	False	1. Durga, a mother goddess, is worshipped in Hinduism.
True	False	2. Mahavira is the supreme god worshipped in Jainism.
True	False	3. The Temple of the True Inner Light believes that psychedelic drugs are god.
True	False	4. Sikhs believe that there is only one deity who is the same for all people of all religions.
True	False	5. Hinduism's Supreme Being manifests as the triad of Brahma, Vishnu, and Shiva.
True	False	6. In Buddhism there is no creator God.
True	False	7. Allah is the supreme deity of Islam.
True	False	8. Shinto gods are considered to be sacred spirits that take the form of things and concepts.
True	False	9. The Dalai Lama is claimed to be the reincarnation of an enlightened being named Chenrezig.
True	False	10. People worship local deities in the folk religion of China.

OLD TESTAMENT PROPHECIES

Match the Scripture with the statement; Scripture may apply to more than one statement. Then dig deeper into these Old Testament prophecies about Jesus' birth and fill in the spaces to the right.

__ 1. Messiah's family lineage	a. Isaiah 11:1-2	What was predicted:
__ 2. Messiah's visitors and their gifts	b. Isaiah 60:1-9	What was stated:
__ 3. Ruler's actions	c. Micah 5:2-4	What was described:
__ 4. God's Spirit on the Messiah		What was stated:
__ 5. Ruler's birthplace		The name of the town:

HOW WOULD YOU PREPARE?

Read the following scenarios and jot responses on the lines.

1. "Which of you, intending to build a tower, sitteth not down first, and counteth the cost, whether he have sufficient to finish it?" (Luke 14:28).
   What preparations, other than getting the cash together, could be made in this situation?

   ____

2. "What king, going to make war against another king, sitteth not down first, and consulteth whether he be able with ten thousand to meet him that cometh against him with twenty thousand?" (Luke 14:31).
   What preparations, other than recruiting more soldiers, could be made in this situation?

   ____

3. Does Matthew 6:25-34 indicate situations where efforts at preparation indicate a lack of faith?
   Why, or why not?

   ____

BAPTISM IN THE NEW TESTAMENT

Fill in this chart for an inductive study of baptism in the New Testament. Not all spaces will be be used for every text. The two blanks at the end of the text column are for passages you think should be added.

Text	Who?	What?	Where?	When?	Why?	How?	By whom?
Matthew 3:13-15							
Matthew 28:19-20							
Acts 2:38							
Acts 22:16							
Romans 6:3-4							
Galatians 3:27							
Colossians 2:12							
Titus 3:5							
1 Peter 3:21							

MINUTE MATCH

Take no more than one minute to match the birthplace or hometown of each person in the lists below. Then put an exclamation mark (!) by the name of every person you think would receive a hearty welcome in that place; put a question mark (?) for the opposite.

___	1. Basking Ridge, New Jersey	a. Johann Sebastian Bach
___	2. Port Huron, Michigan	b. Meryl Streep
___	3. Braunau am Inn, Austria	c. Adolf Hitler
___	4. Eisenach, Germany	d. Rosa Parks
___	5. Munich, Germany	e. Winston Churchill
___	6. Oxfordshire, England	f. Betty Ford
___	7. Grand Rapids, Michigan	g. Thomas Edison
___	8. Tuskegee, Alabama	h. Albert Einstein
___	9. Charlotte, North Carolina	i. Harriet Beecher Stowe
___	10. Litchfield, Connecticut	j. Billy Graham

Compare your answers with at least one other person's in your class. And then decide what reaction you would receive in your own hometown today. In each case, why have you answered as you did?

MY MISSION

Write a prayer asking God for wisdom, strength, and courage to live out the prime responsibility from Luke 4:18-19 that is on your heart. Post this prayer where you will see it daily in the week ahead.

Graphic: © Hulton Archive / Stringer

Lesson 6, Luke 5:1-11, KJV

WHAT WERE THEY THINKING?

Look again at the story recorded in Luke 5:1-11. At each juncture of the story indicated by the verse references below, jot down what the main characters might have been thinking in response to what was happening.

vv. 1-3	What was Jesus thinking? What was Simon thinking?
vv. 4-5	What was Jesus thinking? What was Simon thinking?
vv. 6-10a	What were Simon's companions thinking? What was Simon thinking?
vv. 10b-11	What were Simon and his companions thinking? What was Jesus thinking?

ALL TO JESUS I SURRENDER

You may be familiar with the old hymn whose first stanza goes like this:

All to Jesus I surrender,
All to Him I freely give;
I will ever love and trust Him,
In His presence daily live.

In the space below, write down your typical day's activities. Beside each one write down how you could surrender that part of your day to make yourself a "fisher of men."

	My typical activities during this segment of time	How God could use me then that is in addition to how He's using me now
Early morning		
Late morning		
Afternoon		
Evening		

Be Healed!

Look up the assigned passage(s) and summarize in the space provided.

Scripture	Connection between sin, forgiveness, and physical health
Exodus 15:26	
2 Chronicles 7:13-14	
Psalm 41:1-4	
Psalm 103:1-3	
Isaiah 38:13-20	
John 5:13-17	
John 9:2-3	
James 5:13-16	

Finding Forgiveness

Read the following quotes, and circle those that are logical conclusions after reading today's text. Put a star beside the quotes that bring you the most hope or comfort.

"Forgiveness is the divine miracle of grace; it cost God the Cross of Jesus Christ before He could forgive sin and remain a holy God. . . . When once you realize all that it cost God to forgive you, you will be held as in a vice, constrained by the love of God."

—Oswald Chambers (1874–1917)

"One of the most staggering truths of the Scriptures is to understand that we do not earn our way to heaven. . . . works have a place—but as a demonstration of having received God's forgiveness, not as a badge of merit of having earned it."

—Ravi Zacharias (1946–)

"Christ is the Good Physician. There is no disease He cannot heal; no sin He cannot remove; no trouble He cannot help. He is the Balm of Gilead, the Great Physician who has never yet failed to heal all the spiritual maladies of every soul that has come unto Him in faith and prayer."

—James H. Aughey (1828–1911)

"How sweet the name of Jesus sounds, in a believer's ear! It soothes his sorrows, heals his wounds, and drives away his fear."

—John Newton (1725–1807)

What I Pray for Most

Think about your typical personal prayer times in the last few weeks. In the spaces below, jot down several of the items your prayers most often contain.

1. ______________________________

2. ______________________________

3. ______________________________

4. ______________________________

The Prayer Requests of Jesus

In the spaces below, jot down some of the requests Jesus made in John 17:14-24.

1. ______________________________

2. ______________________________

3. ______________________________

Three Important Themes

Jot down what Jesus says or implies in John 17:14-24 about each of the topics below.

Topic	Witness	Suffering	Unity
What Jesus says about this theme			
How these themes intersect			

His Plan, Not Ours

Discover something important about today's lesson by completing the fallen phrase below. Each letter below the puzzle can be used exactly once in the column directly above it.

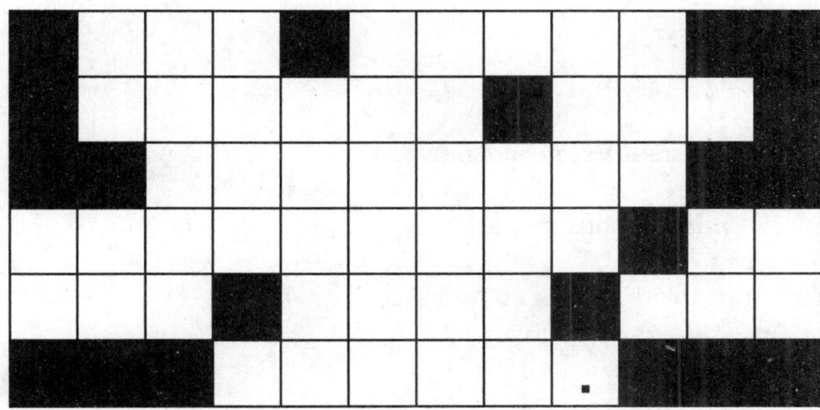

					D	I					
		O	O	L	I	N	L				
	I	C	I	N	I	S	N	G	A		
	G	E	O	W	L	E	F	F	S	N	
A	C	S	P	P	G	I	S	R	O	R	D
H	P	M	D	R	A	L	T	T	Y	T	O

Calling Intersections

While learned skills are not the same as spiritual gifts for ministry callings, there may be some value in the former giving an initial indication of the latter. Fill out the column on the right to explore the possibility. Add entries on the blank lines at the bottom of the left column as they occur to you.

Secular Vocations	Possible Ministry-Calling Overlaps
Automotive technician	
Medical practitioner	
Musician	
Public safety	
Athletic coach	

INTERACTING WITH NONBELIEVERS

Below are some principles found in Jesus' interaction with the Samaritan woman that we can use today. For each one, write a sentence or provide verse references from John 4:25-42 to show how Jesus demonstrates it.

Meet people where they are.

Point people to the truth about Jesus.

Acknowledge the truth, but refrain from condemnation.

Be ready to talk truth when the opportunity arises.

Decide if your audience is ready to make a commitment.

Remember the urgency of the task.

SOW OR REAP?

In the spaces below, write the names of those who seem far from God in the "sowing" column. Write the names of those close to a decision for Jesus in the "reaping" column.

A "Sowing" Situation (Someone I know who is far from God)	**A "Reaping" Opportunity** (Someone I know who seems close to faith)

AN URGENT TASK

The analogy of white harvest fields implies an urgency for evangelism. On the continuum below, choose a spot to indicate how much you feel this urgency.

•______________________________•

Very little *Very strong*

In the space below, write a prayer asking God to move you further to the right on the continuum.

Called to Support

Lesson 11, Luke 8:1-3, Mark 15:40; John 20:10-18, KJV

Favorite Brands

Brand loyalty is defined as "positive feelings towards a brand and dedication to purchase the same product or service repeatedly, regardless of competitor incentives." In each category below, state your favorite brand. Then indicate the depth of your loyalty by completing the chart below.

1. Soda pop ____________________
2. Barbecue sauce ____________________
3. Ice cream ____________________
4. Shampoo ____________________
5. Clothes detergent ____________________
6. Hotel ____________________
7. Automobile ____________________

Write the number of each item in the boxes below to indicate your degree of loyalty to your favorite brand. You may write the number in more than one box.

Always buy	Usually buy	Buy competitor if cheaper	Have recommended it to others

Mary Magdalene's Loyalty

After you complete the middle column, don't fill out the third column until the teacher says to.

Scripture	Mary's expressions of loyalty and support for Jesus	Ways you can express your loyalty for Jesus today
Matthew 27:55-56, 61; 28:1		
Mark 15:40-41, 45-47; 16:1		
Luke 8:1-3; 24:9-10		
John 19:25; 20:1-2, 10-18		

FAMOUS PARTNERS ON TV

Match the column on the left with the correct TV partner by drawing a line from one to the other. Then see if you can name the TV show they appeared in.

Partner A	Partner B	TV Show
1. Jerry Seinfeld	A. Screech Powers	______
2. Will Smith	B. Dwight Schrute	______
3. Zach Morris	C. George Costanza	______
4. Kevin Arnold	D. Shirley Feeney	______
5. Laverne DeFazio	E. Ethel Mertz	______
6. Michael Scott	F. B. J. Hunnicutt	______
7. Lucy Ricardo	G. Paul Pfieffer	______
8. Hawkeye Pierce	H. Carlton Banks	______

FIND THE OPPOSITE

Fill out the row or column as assigned by the teacher. Consult today's texts of Acts 18:1-3, 18-21, 24-26; Romans 16:3-4 as necessary.

	Paul	Priscilla	Aquila	Apollos
Opposite of Inconsiderate				
Opposite of Rude				
Opposite of Apathetic				
Opposite of Domineering				
Opposite of Irresponsible				

Lesson 13, Acts 16:11-15, 40; 1 Corinthians 1:26-30, KJV

Church Planting

When it comes to church planting, every leader has to find a team of people to help get the church off the ground and to serve. If you started a church in your home, what would your key responsibilities be? There are no wrong answers, just use your imagination.

Top 10 Things to Get Done	My Responsibilities
1	
2	
3	
4	
5	
6	
7	
8	
9	
10	

Places of Transition

Find seven places associated with Paul's travels in today's text. The words may be horizontal, vertical, or diagonal.

```
S N B J H V P O U H Q N X L P
Y A Z A H C D W S T E Y U U L
E P M I R S K P I N E S K E J
G O O O A I V K U I A M E J K
F X P O T P T N Y R U A W D T
P D R U P H E A T O Y C S T R
C T M B F A R I Y C Q E K B L
N I W S P G B A E H H D Y S B
G J S O O N N N C Q T O G V N
I J L F I C M V F I P N U Q S
K I P P I L I H P Q A I O S F
S Y R P H A S Q A V X A T U Z
W O J R B K W H C X T O Q R Q
U K D I R I Z G W F J E D L T
B U Z V B E P S F N O K U Y C
```

Word List

- CORINTH
- MACEDONIA
- NEAPOLIS
- PHILIPPI
- SAMOTHRACIA
- THYATIRA
- TROAS

Lesson 1

Jesus' Heritage: Answers will vary.

Jesus, Our Savior: Answers will vary.

Lesson 2

Joseph's Options: Joseph could have divorced Mary privately or divorced her publicly to make an example of her (compare Leviticus 20:10). He also could have disbelieved the angel's message and ignored the angel's instruction.

Step Up Your Thanks:

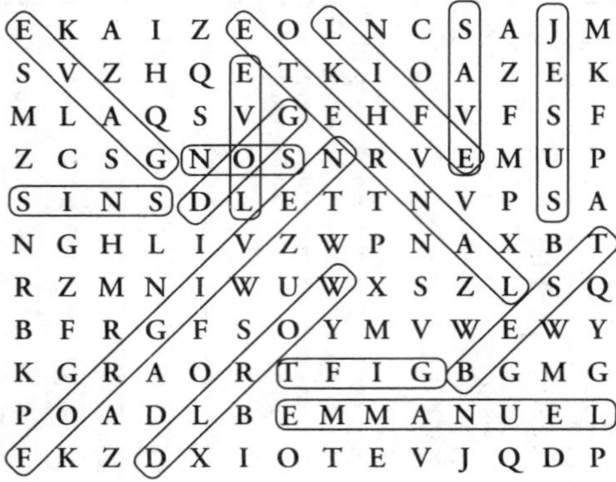

Lesson 3

Worship Around the World: All answers are TRUE.

Old Testament Prophecies: 1=A. 2=B. 3=C. 4=A. 5=C.

Lesson 4

How Would You Prepare? Answers will vary.

Baptism in the New Testament: Answers will vary.

Lesson 5

Minute Match: 1=b. 2=g. 3=c. 4=a. 5=h. 6=e. 7=f. 8=d. 9=j. 10=i.

My Mission: Prayers will vary.

Lesson 6

What Were They Thinking? Answers will vary.

All to Jesus I Surrender: Answers will vary.

Lesson 7

Be Healed! Answers will vary.

Finding Forgiveness: Answers will vary.

Lesson 8

What I Pray for Most: Answers will vary.

The Prayer Requests of Jesus: Answers will vary.

Three Important Things: Answers will vary.

Lesson 9

His Plan, Not Ours: The lesson's Thought to Remember: God gifts people for ministry according to His will and plans.

Calling Intersections: Answers will vary.

Lesson 10

Interacting with Nonbelievers: Answers will vary.

Sow or Reap? Answers will vary.

An Urgent Task: Answers will vary.

Lesson 11

Favorite Brands: Answers will vary.

Mary Magadaline's Loyalty: Answers will vary.

Lesson 12

Famous Partners on TV: 1=C, *Seinfeld.* 2=H, *Fresh Prince of Bel-Air.* 3=A, *Saved by the Bell.* 4=G, *The Wonder Years.* 5=D, *Laverne and Shirley.* 6=B, *The Office.* 7=E *I Love Lucy.* 8=F, *M*A*S*H.*

Find the Opposite: Answers will vary.

Lesson 13

Church Planting: Answers will vary.

Places of Transition:

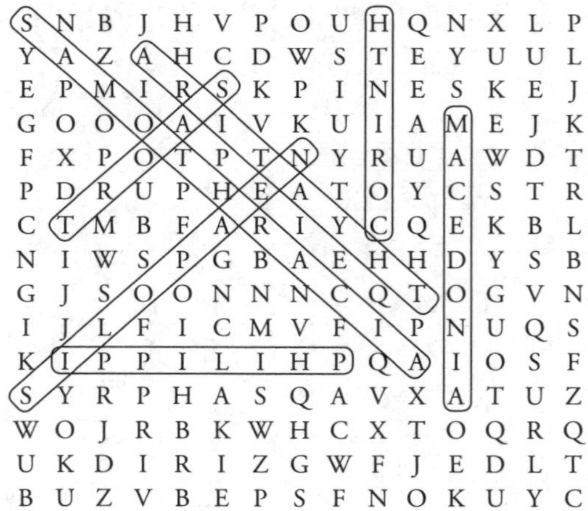

Reproducible Student Activity Pages

Spring Quarter 2021

Prophets Faithful to God's Covenant

SIGNIFICANT EVENTS, SURPRISING LEADER

Background to today's text is the exodus from Egypt. Flip quickly through the three main sections of the book of Exodus and write one surprise to you in each.

I. Redemption
(Exodus 1:1–18:27) ______________________

II. Morality
(Exodus 19:1–24:18) ______________________

III. Worship
(Exodus 25:1–40:38) ______________________

Why do these surprise you?

____

____

____

____

PROPHET TO COME, PROPHET WHO CAME

Look up these passages to determine the identity of the prophet of whom Moses spoke: Acts 3:17-26; John 1:45; 5:46.

1. The name of that prophet is ______________________

2. Considering the Old Testament offices of *Prophet, Priest,* and *King,* give one reason for each title's applying to this person.

Prophet ______________________

Priest ______________________

King ______________________

STRATEGIES AND TACTICS

Work with your study partner to discover the strategies and/or tactics in your assigned text. What was God's role? How important was the size of the attacking force? Jot notes below.

Abram vs. Various Kings (Genesis 14:11-16): ________________________________

Joshua vs. Ai (Joshua 8): ________________________________

Gideon vs. the Midianites (Judges 7:12-24): ________________________________

Jehoshaphat vs. Moab and Ammon (2 Chronicles 20:20-24): ________________________________

DISCIPLINE DEFICIENCY

Take no more than one minute to give quick first impressions:

- In the **Most Christians** column, rank-order the five listed disciplines from 1 (meaning "most deficient, most improvement needed") to 5 (meaning "least deficient, least needing improvement")
- Then do the same for yourself in the **Me** column

	Most Christians	**Me**
Meditating on God's Word Daily (Psalm 119:11)		
Being Thankful (1 Thessalonians 5:18)		
Giving (1 Corinthians 16:2)		
Serving (John 13:14-15)		
Prayer (Romans 12:12)		

How will you work on your most deficient area in the week ahead? What role will this play in your increased obedience to the Lord? ________________________________

FIVE MILESTONES OF 1 AND 2 KINGS

The books of 1 and 2 Kings together can be said to record five major milestones, appearing below in alphabetical order. Without looking in your Bible, number them in chronological order from 1 to 5, with number 1 being the earliest.

_____. Israel split
_____. Judah exiled
_____. Prophets warn
_____. Solomon enthroned
_____. Temple completed

MANY SOURCES

Make entries in the four intersections as the column and row headers suggest. Use general categories (such as "newspapers") rather than specific designations (such as "the Union City Gazette").

	Unreliable Sources of Information	Reliable Sources of Information
In King Josiah's day		
In our day		

In which quadrant do you differ most from the rest of the class? Why?

____
____
____
____
____

Profiles in Courage

Describe the courage of each person listed below.

Courageous person	How he or she demonstrated courage
Jesus (Luke 23:1-4, 26-46)	
Noah (Genesis 6, 7)	
Daniel (Daniel 6)	
Rahab (Joshua 2)	
Peter and John (Acts 4:1-31)	
Paul (Acts 22:30–23:11)	
Other examples (Hebrews 11)	

A Tale of Three Men

Complete the following chart from insights you find in 1 Kings 18:5-18.

	Obadiah	Elijah	Ahab
How he felt about each of the others	about Elijah:	about Obadiah:	about Obadiah:
	about Ahab:	about Ahab:	about Elijah:
How he responded to God's desires			
One word to describe him			

My Prayer for Courage

Think about your life and the challenges to your faith you are experiencing. Jot down at least one way you wish to be more courageous for God. ______________________________

The Suffering Servant

Lesson 5, Isaiah 53:4-11a, KJV

Servant Songs

The text for today's lesson is part of what are called the Servant Songs in the book of Isaiah. Complete the chart below for an overall view of these passages.

Servant Song	Passage in Isaiah	Servant's Tasks	Fulfilled in Jesus
I.	42:1-9		
II.	49:1-6		
III.	50:4-9		
IV.	52:13–53:12		
V.	61:1-4		

Now go back and underline any items that appear more than once among your answers.

Servant Thanks

Use the language of Isaiah 53 to write a prayer of thanksgiving and confession to God. Include not only the ideas but also the actual words of the Scripture in your prayer. Post it where you will see it daily in the week ahead.

Dear God,

THE FAITH-IN-ACTION PREACHER

Lesson 6, Ezra 10:1-12, KJV

WHAT WOULD YOU SAY?

Ezra's bold action requires us to think carefully about why he did what he did. How would you answer someone who said the following?

1. "The remedy for this sin was too harsh!" ____________________

2. "Ezra acted beyond his level of authority!" ____________________

3. "The people were coerced into obeying the will of a dictator!" ____________________

Compare and contrast your answers with another class member.

STINKIN' THINKIN'

Each of the following statements reflects a common attitude among some toward the problem of sin. How do the examples from today's passage refute the thinking behind each one? Jot your reactions in the space provided.

1. "What I did may be wrong, but I'm certainly not the first person to have done it! Cut me some slack!"

2. "Telling the truth about my sin would cause too much hardship and pain for others I love. I lie to protect them."

3. "Habits are habits, and sometimes they're impossible to break. Give me some time while I work on this."

4. "I've prayed about this, and I know God understands."

5. "Sin, sin, sin . . . all you Christians do is fret about sin! Why can't you just live and let live?"

6. "What I do in the privacy of my home is my business, and mine alone. You take care of your own relationship with God and let me worry about myself."

Put a star beside any sentence you may have spoken in the past or any sentence that reflects your thinking today. How does today's study help you change your thinking?

THE RESTORING BUILDER

Lesson 7, Nehemiah 2:11-20, KJV

IT'S A SECRET!

Read today's text, watching for statements of Nehemiah's decision to keep some things secret. In the space below, jot down the verse references or particular phrases that demonstrate that decision.

1. In what circumstances is it appropriate, if ever, for church leaders to keep some things secret from their flock?

2. In what circumstances is it appropriate, if ever, for parents to keep some things secret from their children?

Compare and contrast your conclusions with those of your study partner.

A TALE OF THREE ENEMIES

Read the texts below to discover the tactics of Sanballat, Tobiah, and Geshem—Nehemiah's enemies. Summarize those tactics in the spaces provided.

Nehemiah 4:1-9

Nehemiah 6:1-14

What methods did Nehemiah use to deal with his enemies?

Discuss with another class member how their tactics (1) changed over time and (2) are like and unlike opposition seen against the church today.

THE J'S HAVE IT!

Jeremiah, probable writer of Lamentations, was associated with people and places that begin with the letter J. Circle those below.

<u>Pick two places</u>	<u>Pick two people</u>
Jericho	Jehoiakim
Jerusalem	Jonah
Jezreel	Jonathan
Judah	Josiah

"IT IS WELL"

Sing the hymn below.

When peace, like a river, attendeth my way,
When sorrows like sea billows roll;
Whatever my lot, Thou has taught me to say,
It is well, it is well, with my soul.

[Refrain]
It is well, (it is well),
With my soul, (with my soul);
It is well, it is well, with my soul.

—Horatio G. Spafford (1828–1888)

Do you know the tragic story of the writer, Horatio G. Spafford?

BEING TRUTHFUL TO POWER

Scenario 1

A supervisor asks an employee to pad a bill to a client for services not performed. The supervisor notes that clients never check their invoices carefully. Thus they'll never notice that "we didn't do all this stuff." How should the Christian employee—who at age 59 is desperate to keep his job, health insurance, etc.—react?

Scenario 2

A college freshman who is a Christian is working nights at a restaurant. He is about to throw out uneaten bread that has been on customers' tables, per health department rules. The boss stops him and says, "Just put the pieces that look like they haven't been touched back in the bread drawer; the health department won't catch us on this." How should the employee react?

SPEAKING TRUTH WITH GRACE

Scenario A

A Sunday school teacher is having lunch with a friend, who is a member of his class. The friend secretly believes the teacher should give up the class. For one, the teacher has made several statements that don't square with what the Bible teaches. Furthermore, the lessons seem poorly prepared. How does the friend broach this issue with the teacher, if at all? Should he first speak with a member of church leadership? Why, or why not?

Scenario B

A church elder discovers that the senior minister has been viewing pornography on the church's computer. The elder knows that if this becomes public, several families will quit coming if the minister steps down, but several other families will leave if the minister doesn't resign. What should the elder say, and how and to whom should he say it? In what order should those people be informed—all elders first as a group, the minister first individually, etc.? Why?

Scenario C

Four women who live on the same block are getting together for lunch. One of them, a Christian, is new to the neighborhood and eager to get things off to a good start as she makes friends. At some point, the neighbor who invited her to lunch says, "Well, my husband and I quit going to church years ago. We believe in God, of course, but church just doesn't seem necessary." How does the Christian respond?

GOD'S "WOE TO" WARNINGS

Today's text is part of a section of sermons that warn of judgment. Browse these sermons quickly and list up to five words for each sermon that indicate their contents.

Isaiah 28	________	________	________	________	________
Isaiah 29	________	________	________	________	________
Isaiah 30	________	________	________	________	________
Isaiah 31	________	________	________	________	________
Isaiah 33	________	________	________	________	________

How is the sermon in Isaiah 29 similar to and different from the others?

SEARCHING FOR MEANING

Find the 16 words in the puzzle and then arrange them in a sentence in the space below.

Word List

DISEMPOWER
MEANINGLESS
REPETITIVE
RITUALS
TOWARD
MASSES
LEAD
LIFE
WANT
THEM
YOU
THE
IF
A
OF
TO

T	T	B	H	S	L	A	U	T	I	R	Y	Y	N	U
K	F	H	O	L	O	S	J	D	R	A	W	O	T	R
P	G	D	I	S	E	M	P	O	W	E	R	W	U	U
C	S	Q	L	E	A	D	F	M	X	V	H	C	T	U
G	S	P	J	G	U	K	H	L	X	I	T	V	(A)	N
W	S	D	I	V	U	J	Z	W	U	T	P	L	R	R
S	E	F	I	V	L	M	E	W	F	I	G	G	L	O
M	L	I	C	T	U	G	A	H	N	T	U	C	F	U
J	G	I	P	L	E	N	C	S	T	E	H	J	Q	W
E	N	V	F	F	T	W	H	E	S	P	W	D	K	U
O	I	C	P	E	U	T	B	B	Y	E	E	E	R	E
U	N	O	J	M	B	C	W	P	U	R	S	D	W	S
E	A	L	X	F	W	Z	N	N	F	I	L	G	B	P
Z	E	E	P	P	L	Z	Z	E	B	S	U	F	G	B
U	M	F	M	T	T	H	E	M	V	P	K	T	O	S

PUZZLE ANSWER ____

____

Jot down two or three examples of situtions that support the premise of this sentence.

FIXING FALSEHOODS

Each of the following statements is false in some way. You are to (1) cite the passage from today's text that contradicts the sentence below and (2) reword the sentence to fix the falsehood.

1. Zedekiah was firm in his decision to kill Jeremiah.

2. Zedekiah and Jeremiah had no one-on-one conversations with each other.

3. Jeremiah had complete trust in Zedekiah.

4. Jeremiah encouraged Zedekiah to stand firm in resisting the foreign invaders of Jerusalem.

5. Zedekiah's greatest fear was that the residents of Jerusalem who were not yet taken captive would think less of him.

6. Jeremiah prophesied that Zedekiah would escape the Babylonians.

THREE CONFRONTATIONS

Work with one or two classmates to complete this chart.

Reference	Summary of what Zedekiah said	Summary of Jeremiah's response
Jeremiah 37		
Jeremiah 38:1-13		
Jeremiah 38:14-28		

Lesson 12, Ezekiel 18:1-9, 30-32, KJV

SINS OF THE FATHERS

Make a list of sins Ezekiel told his people to avoid as expressed in Ezekiel 18:5-9. (For comparison, see verses 10-13 and 15-17.) Use the following chart to help you think these through.

Verse	Sins Avoided	Effect of these sins on children of the parents who commit them	Examples of these sins today
5			
6			
7			
8			
9			

Now place a star beside the sin that has had a negative effect on you because of the way you saw it as a child among family members or others who influenced you.

In the space provided, jot three steps you have taken or could take to eliminate from your life the sin you marked above.

1. ____________________ 2. ____________________ 3. ____________________

WHAT DOES IT SAY?

Work with a partner to unscramble the words below.

NGAHEC PPNESHA NEWH ETH ANIP FO HET SUTATS OQU

____

SI TEARGER NHAT EHT NIPA FO A WNE TILAREY.

____

Discuss with your partner how you have seen this sentence true in your life or in history. What does it tell you about why change is sometimes so difficult to achieve?

____

____

____

____

READ ALL ABOUT IT!

Pretend you are writing headlines for an internet news feed in Nineveh as the events recorded in today's text unfold. What headlines would you write for each of the following parts of the story?

Jonah 3:1-3

____

Jonah 3:4

____

Jonah 3:5

____

Jonah 3:6-9

____

Jonah 3:10

____

Lesson 1

Significant Events, Surprising Leader: Answers will vary.

Prophet to Come, Prophet Who Came: Answers will vary.

Lesson 2

Strategies and Tactics: Answers will vary.

Discipline Deficiency: Answers will vary.

Lesson 3

Five Milestones of 1 and 2 Kings: 1=Solomon enthroned. 2=Temple completed. 3=Israel split. 4=Prophets warn. 5=Judah exiled.

Many Sources: Answers will vary.

Lesson 4

Profiles in Courage: Answers will vary.

A Tale of Three Men: Answers will vary.

Lesson 5

Servant Songs: Answers will vary.

Servant Thanks: Answers will vary.

Lesson 6

What Would You Say? Answers will vary.

Stinkin' Thinkin': Answers will vary.

Lesson 7

It's a Secret: Answers will vary.

A Tale of Three Enemies: Answers will vary.

Lesson 8

The J's Have It! Answers are in Jeremiah 1:1-3.

"It Is Well"

Lesson 9

Being Truthful to Power:

Scenario 1—A good strategy is to get the boss to come to the conclusion on his own that his request is unwise. One possible way of achieving this is through use of questions. One might be to ask politely, "Boss, do you realize that if I would lie *for* you, I would also lie *to* you?"

Scenario 2—Asking a question as above, modified to the situation, could be a good approach. Another approach is to suggest an alternative. Example: "Here's an idea, boss: how about we use it for making the bread pudding, which won't violate the health department rules? That way it won't go to waste."

Speaking Truth with Grace:

Scenario A—Gently probing questions can result in the truth coming from the lips of the teacher rather than from those of the inquisitor. One possibility is to ask simply, "How do you think the class is going?" The teacher may jump on that as an opportunity to express inadquacies, etc., which will serve to indicate which way the conversation should be directed.

Scenario B—One possible approach might be to present to a fellow elder or even to the senior minister himself this hypothetical question: "Suppose I discovered that a fellow Christian was using pornography, what should I do?" The tone and content of the reply will guide how the rest of the conversation might proceed.

Scenario C—Since future lunch gatherings are likely, a very low key approach might bring the best solution for the long-term. Rather than quickly pulling out a verbal Hebrews 10:25 and quoting it, an inquiry such as "I'd like to hear more about the journey that led you to that conclusion" may be better at keeping the lines of communication open. Consider how the old saying, "Seek first not to be understood, but to understand" applies.

Lesson 10

God's "Woe to" Warnings: Answers will vary.

Searching for Meaning:

T T B H S L A U T I R Y Y N U
K F H O L O S J D R A W O T R
P G D I S E M P O W E R W U U
C S Q L E A D F M X V H C T U
G S P J G U K H L X I T V A N
W S D I V U J Z W U T P L R R
S E F I V L M E W F I G G L O
M L I C T U G A H N T U C F U
J G I P L E N C S T E H J Q W
E N V F F T W H E S P W D K U
O I C P E U T B B Y E E E R E
U N O J M B C W P U R S D W S
E A L X F W Z N N F I L G B P
Z E E P P L Z Z E B S U F G B
U M F M T T H E M V P K T O S

If you want to disempower the masses, lead them toward a life of meaingless, repetitive rituals."

Lesson 11

Fixing Falsehoods: There are various ways to reword the sentences. The passages used to correct the falsehoods are 1–Jeremiah 38:16; 2–the entire text of the lesson; 3–Jeremiah 38:15; 4–Jeremiah 38:17; 5–Jeremiah 38:19; 6–Jeremiah 38:23.

Three Confrontations: Answers will vary.

Lesson 12

Sins of the Father: Answers will vary.

Lesson 13

What Does It Say? Change happens when the pain of the status quo is greater than the pain of a new reality.

Read All About It! Answers will vary.

Reproducible Student Activity Pages

Summer Quarter 2021 Confident Hope

Freed from Worry

Lesson 1, Matthew 6:25-34, KJV

According to Corrie

Corrie ten Boom (1892–1983), who survived a World War II death camp, made a statement that can help us think about today's text. Find what she said by unscrambling the sentence below. (The capitalization and punctuation are hints.)

empties does empty sorrow; Worry strength. today not tomorrow of its it of

____

Worry and Health

Do an internet search for various combinations of the words *worry, health, stress, illness,* etc. Then list a few pointers on this subject from health professionals. Note the internet addresses (URLs) for your findings so that other class members can find them too.

____

____

My Seeking Week

At the end of each day in the week ahead, review that day in light of Matthew 6:33 by putting one of the following in the space for that day:

- A plus sign (+) on days you acted according to Matthew 6:33
- A zero (0) when you didn't really think about it
- A minus sign (–) on days you did the opposite

Below each symbol jot a few words to indicate why you chose it.

Sunday	Monday	Tuesday	Wednesday	Thursday	Friday	Saturday

Delivered from Fear

Lesson 2, Matthew 8:23-27, KJV

Sailors Afraid

Fill out this chart:

	Psalm 107:23-32	Jonah 1	Acts 27:13-44
1. In what ways are the situations in these texts similar to that of today's text?			
2. In what ways are the situations in these texts unlike that of today's text?			
3. Why did courage disappear?			
4. On a scale from 1 (never) to 10 (very frequent), how often does a similar situation happen today in a literal sense?			
5. On a scale from 1 (never) to 10 (very frequent), how often does a similar situation happen today in a figurative sense?			

Fear Busters

Part 1. Work with a partner or two to find a dozen or so Scriptures to help us with our fears. Use an online resource such as Biblegateway.com or the concordance in the back of your Bibles to search for verses that contain words such as *fear* and *afraid.* Write the passages on the lines below.

____

____

Part 2. Now choose one of these verses for each day of the coming week and jot the reference below. Commit to reading, and perhaps even memorizing, a different "fear buster" each day this week.

Sunday	Monday	Tuesday	Wednesday	Thursday	Friday	Saturday

Healed by Faith

Lesson 3, Matthew 9:18-26, KJV

Jesus in Context

Understand the context for today's study by examining the verses that precede the lesson text.

Reference	What Jesus Did	Why Others Objected	How Jesus Responded
Matthew 9:2-8			
Matthew 9:9-13			
Matthew 9:14-17			

In the space below, summarize your discoveries with one sentence to answer this question:

How did the actions of Jesus clarify His mission more fully?

Reactions to Healing

Write what you imagine **one** person listed below might have recorded in a personal journal after the incident in which they were involved. The journal entry can be bullet points or whole sentences.

The official	The woman	One of the disciples	Someone in the crowd at the house

TRUE, FALSE, AND WHEN?

Draw a line through every false statement about today's text of Matthew 14:22-33. Then put the remaining statements in the correct chronological order as told in the Bible story.

1. Peter, out of love for Jesus, swam to meet Him.
2. Jesus stayed behind while the disciples traveled to the other side of the lake without Him.
3. Jesus watched the disciples from a mountain to see how they'd handle the storm.
4. The minute the storm kicked up, Jesus hurried to save the disciples.
5. Jesus condemned the disciples because of their fear.
6. Jesus appeared to the disciples like a ghost walking on the water.
7. All the disciples asked Jesus if He'd help them walk on the water too.
8. Jesus warned Peter that his faith might not be strong enough to walk on the water.
9. Peter kept his eyes on Jesus, in spite of the storm.
10. Peter walked on the water.
11. The wind died down when Peter and Jesus got back in the boat.
12. Jesus kept Peter, James, and John with him on the shore of the Sea of Galilee.
13. Peter began to sink when he paid attention to the wind and his fear grew.

The correct order for the true statements is: ______________________________

I JUST DON'T GET IT!

Compare and contrast the disciples' faith-strengthening in Matthew 14:33 and the cautious discipleship on the parts of Nicodemus (John 3:1-21) and Joseph of Arimathea (John 19:38). How do we account for the fact that the original disciples became fearful after the crucifixion (John 20:19) while Nicodemus and Joseph became bold (Matthew 27:57; Mark 15:42-43; John 19:38-42)?

____

____

____

Attitude of Gratitude

Lesson 5, Leviticus 13:45-46; Luke 17:11-19, KJV

Attitude Adjustment

Imagine that you overhear people make the following statements. Summarize briefly your thoughts under each one.

1. "I believe God's blessings have come to me because of all I've done for Him."

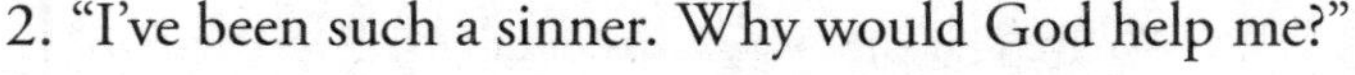

2. "I've been such a sinner. Why would God help me?"

3. "Yes, Sunday worship is important. But the weekends are so full sometimes we just can't make it."

4. "Given my faithful service to God all my life, I frankly don't understand why He seems to be blessing my lukewarm friend more than me."

Depicting Gratitude

Create an illustration of God's work in your life. In the space to the right, draw a picture to represent one or more of the following:

1. "What God did when I cried for mercy."

2. "Here's how I expressed my gratitude for His help."

3. "Here's how I could express gratitude for God's blessings."

PAUL'S MISSION TO ROME

Pull out this crossword puzzle a day or two after class and see how much you remember from the lesson!

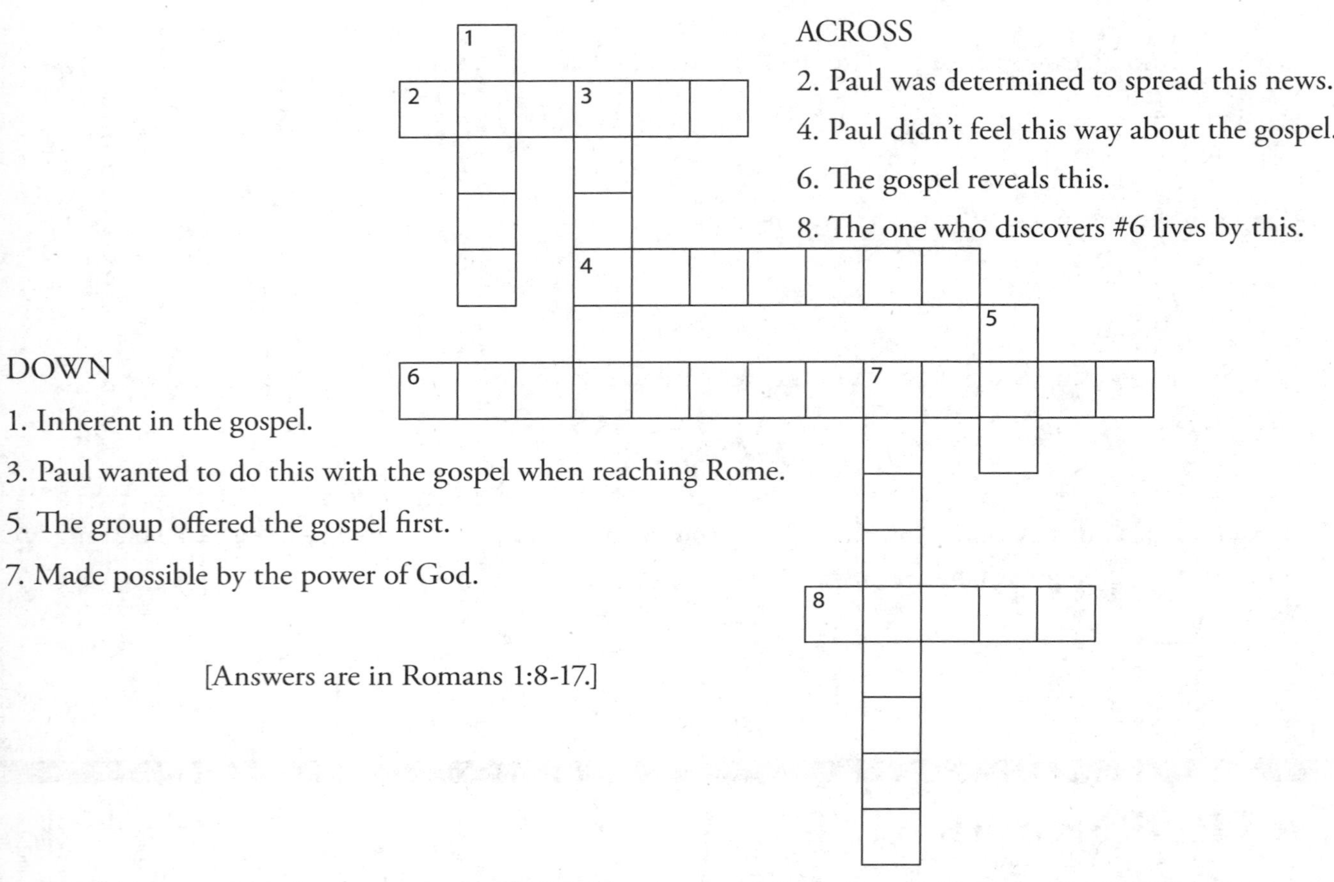

ACROSS

2. Paul was determined to spread this news.
4. Paul didn't feel this way about the gospel.
6. The gospel reveals this.
8. The one who discovers #6 lives by this.

DOWN

1. Inherent in the gospel.
3. Paul wanted to do this with the gospel when reaching Rome.
5. The group offered the gospel first.
7. Made possible by the power of God.

[Answers are in Romans 1:8-17.]

QUALIFICATIONS, PLEASE!

What qualifications were useful for Paul to preach the gospel in Rome, the urban center of the world in the first century AD? Jot a few ideas below ***before*** looking in your Bible.

Then look in Acts 22 and Philippians 3 to discover what you missed.

What do these passages imply regarding preparation to preach the gospel?

Faith of Abraham

Lesson 7, Romans 4:1-12, KJV

A Story of Faith

Remind yourself of the foundation and background for the teaching in today's text by reviewing God's call, His promises, and His covenants with Abraham.

Reference	CALL—What Happened
Genesis 12:1-3	
	PROMISES—What Happened
Genesis 13:14-17	
Genesis 22:15-18	
	COVENANTS—What Happened
Genesis 15:1-21	
Genesis 17:1-27	

A Legacy of Faith

Fill in the blanks below as you think about the impact on you from the faith of someone in an earlier generation and the impact of your faith on the generations to come.

Because ________________ was a model of faithfulness to God, I'm encouraged to be faithful to God today in these ways:

____

I'm praying that my faithfulness will in turn encourage these people to be faithful to Him also:

____

____

FROM ALPHABETICAL TO . . .

The words in the sequence below are in alphabetical order—but that isn't the *correct* order! Fix this by copying them in the proper order in the blanks without looking in your Bible. Then consult Romans 5:3-5 to check yourself.

EXPERIENCE →? *HOPE* →? *NO SHAME* →? *PATIENCE* →? *TRIBULATION*

__________ →! __________ →! __________ →! __________ →! __________

For each characteristic, jot down your experience regarding *how* each leads to the next.

__________ results from __________ because ____________________

__________ results from __________ because ____________________

__________ results from __________ because ____________________

__________ results from __________ because ____________________

HOW DO WE KNOW?

Step 1: Fill in the two blanks.

I struggled to accept God's forgiveness when . . .	I knew I had been forgiven when . . .

Step 2: Why are feelings invalid as a basis of knowing you have been forgiven?

Salvation Available for All

Lesson 9, Romans 10:5-17, KJV

AMAZING STATS

Discuss with your study partner the following conclusions reached by the Barna research organization several years ago.

- Only two out of every five Christ-followers believe they should share with others the importance of reliance on Christ.
- Nearly one-third of evangelicals have not attempted to evangelize others, although they believe they should.
- Apathy toward evangelism is growing among middle-aged and middle-income Christians.

Circle below your top three reactions to these findings and discuss:

Sadness	Indifference	Conviction	Offended	Confusion
Anger	Surprise	Irritation	Frustration	Powerlessness
Disgust	Aching	Trust	Fear	Anticipation
Disbelief	Exasperation	Other (list): ______________________		

AMAZING QUOTES

Rank-order these quotes from 1 to 5, with 1 indicating the quote that most expresses the challenge of today's lesson and most convicts you personally to be more intentional in evangelism.

____ "If he have faith, the believer cannot be restrained. He betrays himself. He breaks out. He confesses and teaches this gospel . . . at the risk of life itself." —Martin Luther (1483–1546)

____ "If you had the cure to cancer, wouldn't you share it? . . . You have the cure to death . . . get out there and share it." —Kirk Cameron (1970–)

____ "The man who mobilizes the Christian church to pray will make the greatest contribution to world evangelization in history." —Andrew Murray (1794–1866)

____ "Any method of evangelism will work if God is in it." —Leonard Ravenhill (1907–1994)

____ "When a man is filled with the Word of God you cannot keep him still. If a man has got the Word, he must speak or die." —Dwight L. Moody (1837–1899)

How does your rank-ordering compare with others?

SOMETHING BETTER

Throughout the book of Hebrews, the author uses the word *better* or *superior* to characterize aspects of the new covenant in Christ. Examine those to discover what should go in the blanks below.

Reference	What's Better	How this speaks to what I should do
Hebrews 1:4		
Hebrews 6:9		
Hebrews 7:4-7		
Hebrews 7:19		
Hebrews 7:22		
Hebrews 8:6		
Hebrews 9:23		
Hebrews 10:34		
Hebrews 11:4		
Hebrews 11:16		
Hebrews 11:35		
Hebrews 11:40		
Hebrews 12:24		

In the space below, write a sentence summarizing the Scripture's teaching about why it's better for Christians of Jewish background to stay with Jesus rather than to return to Judaism:

A Patient, Persevering Faith

Lesson 11, Hebrews 10:23-36, KJV

A Call to Persevere

Read Hebrews 10:19-25 and list below all the reasons to persevere mentioned there.

To Consider Today: List several ways Christians can obey the exhortations of Hebrews 10:22-25. Circle the one that seems the biggest challenge to you, and write in the box one way you could do it.

Why Worship?

Work with a partner or two to create bumper stickers that encourage Christians to worship. Use a catchy phrase to capture the essence of today's teaching.

Lesson 12, 1 John 4:2-3, 13-17; 5:4-5, KJV

LOVE ≠ APATHY

Love includes actively seeking the best interests of others. The challenge for us is to decide how to demonstrate Christian love to others. In the second column, write a specific way you could demonstrate Christian love to those in the category on the left.

People Around Me	How I could model Christ's love to those in this group
The working poor	
The homeless	
First responders	
Those in hospice	
Elected officials	
Other	
Other	

OVERCOMING THE WORLD

Put dots on the globe illustration below to represent places where Christian faith is overcoming the forces for godlessness. In the lines below the map, write a brief explanation for each dot.

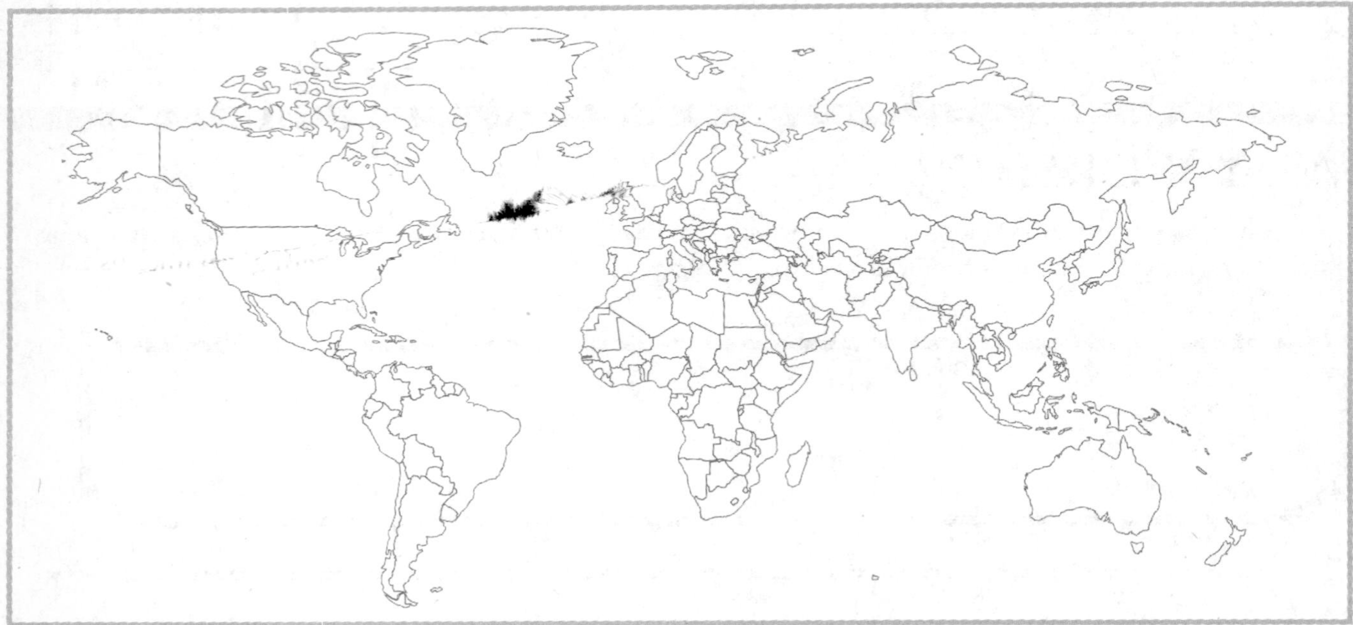

An Eternal Hope

Lesson 13, 2 Corinthians 4:16–5:10, KJV

Walk by What?

Create an acrostic by intersecting the five letters of the word below with five words that relate to walking by faith instead of sight.

F
A
I
T
H

Finish the Thoughts

How much do you remember? Closed Bibles; time limit of one minute!

A. "For we know that if our earthly house of this tabernacle were ____________, we have a building of God, an house not made with hands, ____________ in the heavens."

B. "For we that are in this tabernacle do groan, being ____________: not for that we would be unclothed, but ____________ upon, that mortality might be swallowed up of life."

C. "Now he that hath wrought us for the ____________ thing is God, who also hath given unto us the ____________ of the Spirit."

D. "We are always ____________, knowing that, whilst we are at home in the ____________, we are absent from the Lord."

E. "For we walk by ____________, not by ____________."

When you finish, look up the answers in 2 Corinthians 5:1-10.

Your score: ___ out of 10.

Lesson 1

According to Corrie: Worry does not empty tomorrow of its sorrow; it empties today of its strength.

Responses to the other two activities will be personal to the individual student.

Lesson 2

Sailors Afraid: Responses to questions 1 and 2 should be consistent with the text of Psalm 107:23-32; Jonah 1; and Acts 27:13-44. Responses to questions 3, 4, and 5 can be a matter of subjective impression on the part of the students.

Fear Busters: Many responses are possible.

Lesson 3

Jesus in Context: See Matthew 9:2-7, 9-13, and 14-17 as indicated for expected responses. The final response can be worded in many ways, but it should be consistent with Luke 1:4 and John 20:30-31.

Reactions to Healing: Many responses are possible.

Lesson 4

True, False, and When?: These statements are FALSE: 1, 3, 4, 5, 7, 8, 9, 12. The correct order for the TRUE statements is 2, 6, 10, 13, 11.

I Just Don't Get It: Many responses are possible.

Lesson 5

Many responses are possible for both exercises.

Lesson 6

Paul's Mission to Rome: *Across:* 2–gospel (Romans 1:9, 15); 4–ashamed (1:16); 6–righteousness (1:17); 8–[illegible]h (1:17). *Down*: 1–power (1:16); 3–preach (1:15); 5–Jew (1:16); 7–salvation (1:16).

Qualifications, Please!: Responses to the final question should have a defensible connection with Acts 22 and Philippians 3, as indicated.

Lesson 7

A Story of Faith: Responses will be simple look-ups of the Genesis texts indicated.

A Legacy of Faith: Responses will be personal to the individual student.

Lesson 8

From Alphabetical to . . . : Correct order is tribulation, patience, experience, hope, no shame.

How Do We Know?: Responses will be personal to each student.

Lesson 9

Both activities: Responses will be personal to each student.

Lesson 10

Something Better: Hebrews 1:4–Jesus' status and name; 6:9–things; 7:7–someone's status; 7:19–hope; 7:22–testament; 8:6–ministry and covenant; 9:23– sacrifices; 10:34–substance; 11:4–sacrifice; 11:16–country; 11:35–resurrection; 11:40–plan; 12:24–witness.

Lesson 11

A Call to Persevere: Answers will vary, depending on how students group them.

Why Worship?: The creative aspects of this exercise mean that outcomes will vary widely from student to student.

Lesson 12

Both activities: Responses will be according to students' perspective and spiritual maturity.

Lesson 13

Walk by What?: Many completions are possible.

Finish the Thoughts: A–dissolved, eternal; B–burdened, clothed; C–selfsame, earnest; D–confident, body; E–faith, sight. (All per 2 Corinthians 5:1-10.)